FreeCAD 1.0
A Power Guide for Beginners and Intermediate Users

A premium provider of learning products and solutions
www.cadartifex.com

FreeCAD 1.0: A Power Guide for Beginners and Intermediate Users

Author: Sandeep Dogra
Email: info@cadartifex.com

Published by
CADArtifex
www.cadartifex.com

ISBN: 978-9394074514

NOTICE TO THE READER

The publisher and the author make no representations or warranties concerning the accuracy or completeness of the contents of this work/text and specifically disclaim all warranties, including without limitation warranties of fitness for a particular purpose. The publisher does not guarantee any of the products described in the text nor has performed any independent analysis in connection with any of the product information contained in the text. No warranty may be created or extended by sales or promotional materials. This work is sold with the understanding that the publisher is not engaged in rendering legal, accounting, or other professional services. Neither the publisher nor the author shall be liable for damages arising here from. Further, readers should be aware that Internet websites listed or referenced in this work may have changed or may have been removed in the time between the writing and the publishing of this work.

Examination Copies

Textbooks received as examination copies in any form such as paperback or eBook are for review only and may not be made available for the use of the student. These files may not be transferred to any other party. The resale of examination copies is prohibited.

Electronic Files

The electronic file/eBook in any form of this textbook is licensed to the original user only and may not be transferred to any other party.

Disclaimer

The author has made sincere efforts to ensure the accuracy of the material described herein, however, the author makes no warranty, expressed or implied, concerning the quality, accuracy, or freedom from error of this document or the products it describes.

www.cadartifex.com

Dedication

First and foremost, I would like to thank my parents for being a great support throughout my career and while writing this book.

Heartfelt gratitude goes to my wife and my sisters for their patience and endurance in supporting me to take up and accomplish this challenge.

I would also like to acknowledge the efforts of the employees at CADArtifex for their dedication in editing the contents of this book.

Contents at a Glance

Table of Contents

Preface

FreeCAD is an open-source parametric 3D CAD software, the development of which is completely open-source (LGPL license). FreeCAD was primarily developed for mechanical engineering and product design. However, with its clear and simple user interface, and powerful engineering toolkits, it is now widely used across all engineering disciplines such as mechanical, architecture, finite element analysis (FEA), automobile, 3D printing, and so on. FreeCAD is maintained and developed by a community of passionate developers, users, moderators, and translators, who voluntarily come together to make FreeCAD a free and powerful tool. It is developed by everyone, for everyone.

FreeCAD is a feature-based, fully parametric 3D CAD modeling, Finite Element Analysis (FEA), manufacturing (CAM/CNC), reverse engineering, and documentation software that enables every industry to design real-life products of any size right from the point of conception of an idea to its production. It provides a wide range of powerful tools that lets you create, export, and edit full-precision real-world 3D solid models. It can generate various drawing views of models to create 2D drawings for production, export them for 3D printing or CNC machining, perform Finite Element Analyses (FEA), etc. In addition, FreeCAD allows you to export design data, validate designs, publish 2D drawings, study robot movements, produce machine instructions (G-code) for CNC machines, and so on.

FreeCAD 1.0: A Power Guide for Beginners and Intermediate Users textbook has been designed for instructor-led courses as well as self-paced learning. It is intended to help engineers and designers interested in learning FreeCAD to create 3D mechanical designs. This textbook is an excellent guide for new FreeCAD users and a great teaching aid for classroom training. It consists of 10 chapters and a total of 486 pages covering major workbenches of FreeCAD such as **Sketcher**, **Part Design**, **Assembly**, and **TechDraw**. The textbook teaches you to use FreeCAD mechanical design software for building parametric 3D solid components and assemblies as well as creating 2D drawings.

This textbook not only focuses on the usage of the tools/commands of FreeCAD but also the concept of design. Every chapter in this textbook contains tutorials that provide users with step-by-step instructions for creating mechanical designs and drawings with ease. Moreover, every chapter ends with hands-on test drives that allow users to experience the user-friendly and powerful technical capabilities of FreeCAD.

Who Should Read This Textbook

This textbook is written to benefit a wide range of FreeCAD users, varying from beginners to advanced users as well as FreeCAD instructors. The easy-to-follow chapters of this textbook allow easy comprehension of different design techniques, FreeCAD tools, and design principles.

What Is Covered in This Textbook

FreeCAD 1.0: A Power Guide for Beginners and Intermediate Users textbook is designed to help you learn everything you need to know to start using FreeCAD with straightforward, step-by-step tutorials. This textbook covers the following topics:

Chapter 1, "***Introduction to FreeCAD***," introduces system requirements for installing FreeCAD, different FreeCAD workbenches, user interface components, and methods to invoke shortcut menus. It also explains how to customize the Toolbar Area, change the position of toolbars, edit background color, identify FreeCAD documents, export documents to other CAD formats, save a document, and open an existing document.

Chapter 2, "***Creating and Editing Sketches with FreeCAD***," discusses how to invoke the Sketcher Workbench within the Part Design Workbench. It explains how to specify the units as well as the grids and snap settings. This chapter also introduces methods for drawing lines, arcs, circles, ellipses, elliptical arcs, hyperbolic arcs, parabolic arcs, B-splines, polylines, rectangles, polygons, and slots by using the respective sketching tools. Additionally, this chapter elaborates on creating fillets, trimming sketch entities, extending sketch entities, creating construction sketch entities, applying geometric and dimensional constraints, editing and modifying dimensions, and different states of a sketch.

Chapter 3, "***Creating Base Feature of a 3D Solid Model***," introduces how to create pad and revolution features. It also explains various methods for navigating a model, displaying standard views, and changing the display style of a model, in addition to the application of Navigation Cube.

Chapter 4, "***Creating Datum Geometries***," introduces various methods for creating additional datum planes, axes, and points by using the respective tools.

Chapter 5, "***Creating Pocket and Groove Features***," discusses how to create pocket and groove features by removing the material from the model. The chapter also describes methods for projecting external geometries onto the sketch, displaying a section view and an earlier state of a model, reordering features, deleting and editing features, and defining display properties to the model. Further, it explains how to tag the degrees of freedom of assembly components and move a component along its free and fixed degrees of freedom.

Chapter 6, "***Creating Pipe, Loft, and Helix Features***," explains how to create additive pipe features, multi-section additive pipe features, subtractive pipe features, additive loft features, and subtractive loft features, in addition to additive and subtractive helix features.

Chapter 7, "***Mirroring and Patterning Features***," introduces how to mirror features of a model about a mirroring plane. It also discusses creating a linear pattern, a polar pattern, and a multi-transform pattern.

Chapter 8, "***Creating Holes and Dress-up Features***," discusses how to create standard or customized holes such as counterbore and countersink as per standard specifications. It also discusses the methods for creating different types of dress-up features: fillet, chamfer, thickness (shell), and angular draft for applying treatment to the existing edges and faces of a model.

Chapter 9, "***Creating Assemblies***," introduces methods for creating assemblies by using the Top-down assembly approach and the Bottom-up assembly approach. It also discusses methods for installing the **Assembly** workbench, inserting components, and applying different types of joints for assembling components.

*Chapter 10, "**Creating 2D Drawings**,"* discusses how to invoke the **TechDraw** workbench for creating a 2D drawing of a part or an assembly. It also explains how to insert a drawing sheet, edit the title block text of a sheet, create an independent 2D projection view, modify the scale of a view, create multiple linked 2D projection views of a model, and display hidden lines on the views. This chapter also elaborates on creating a section view and a detail view, in addition to applying dimensions and exporting a drawing as DXF and SVG files.

Icons/Terms used in this Textbook

The following icons and terms are used in this textbook:

Note

Note: Notes highlight information requiring special attention.

Tip

Tip: Tips provide additional advice, which increases the efficiency of the users.

Menu

A menu is a list in which a set of tools are grouped, see Figure 1.

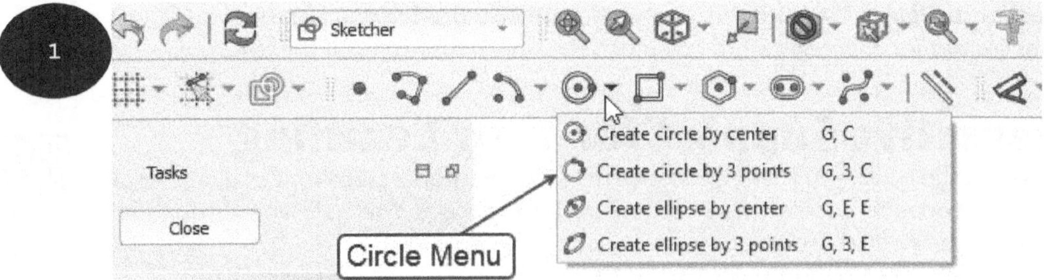

Drop-down List

A drop-down list is a list in which a set of options are grouped, see Figure 2.

Check Box

A check box allows you to turn on or off the uses of a particular option, see Figure 2.

Field

A Field allows you to enter a new value, or modify an existing value, as per your requirement, see Figure 2.

Button

A Button appears as a 3D icon and is used for confirming or discarding an action, see Figure 2.

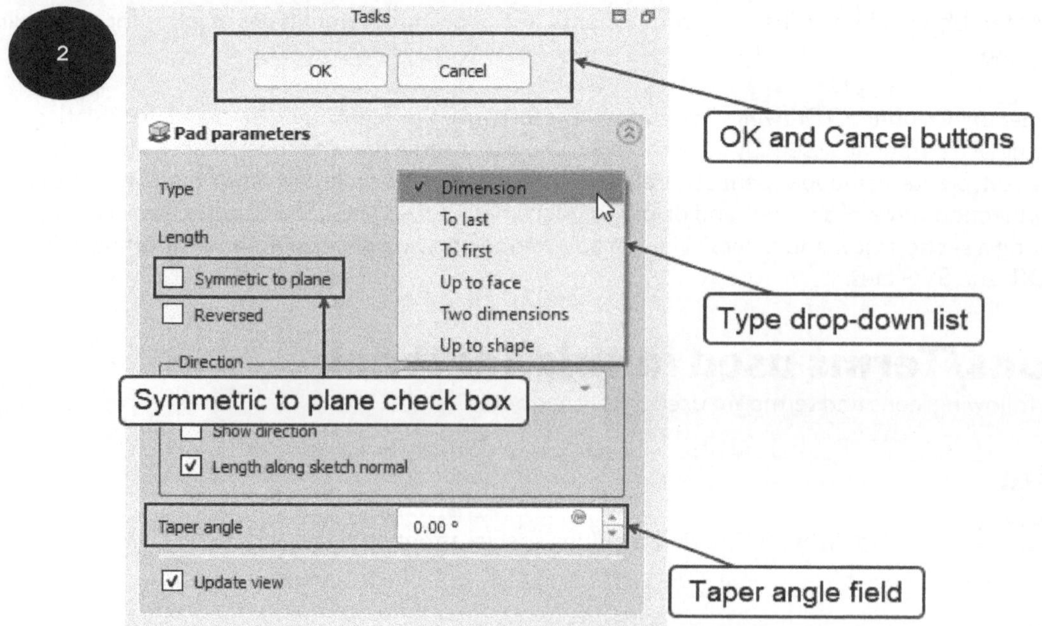

How to Download Online Resources

Students and faculty members can download all parts/models used in the illustrations, Tutorials, and Hands-on Test Drives (exercises) of the textbook. In addition, faculty can also download PowerPoint Presentations (PPTs) of each chapter of the textbook.

To download the free online teaching and learning resources of the textbook, log on to our website (*cadartifex.com/login*) by using your username and password. If you are a new user, you need to first register (*cadartifex.com/register*) to download the online resources of the textbook.

Interactive Support for Your Learning

Throughout the book, you'll find QR codes next to key tutorial steps for certain tutorials. Scan these codes to access video demonstrations, designed to help you through any challenging parts of the process.

How to Contact the Author

We value your feedback and suggestions. You can email us at *info@cadartifex.com*. You can also log on to our website *www.cadartifex.com* to provide your feedback regarding the textbook as well as download the free learning resources.

We would like to express our sincere gratitude to you for purchasing the **FreeCAD 1.0: A Power Guide for Beginners and Intermediate Users** textbook. We hope that the information and concepts introduced in this textbook help you to accomplish your professional goals.

1

Introduction to FreeCAD

This chapter discusses the following topics:

- Installing FreeCAD
- Getting Started with FreeCAD
- Starting a New Document
- Working with Workbenches
- Invoking Different Workbenches
- Exploring the User-Interface Components
- Invoking a Shortcut Menu
- Customizing the Toolbar Area
- Defining the Position of Toolbars
- Changing the Background Color
- Identifying FreeCAD Documents
- Exporting Documents to Other CAD Formats
- Saving a Document
- Opening a Document

Welcome to the world of 3D parametric Computer-Aided Design (CAD) with FreeCAD. FreeCAD is an open-source parametric 3D CAD software, the development of which is completely open-source (LGPL license). FreeCAD was primarily developed for mechanical engineering and product design. However, with its clear and simple user interface, and powerful engineering toolkits, it is now widely used across all engineering disciplines such as mechanical, architecture, finite element analysis (FEA), automobile, 3D printing, and so on. FreeCAD is maintained and developed by a community of passionate developers, users, moderators, and translators, who voluntarily come together to make FreeCAD a free and powerful tool. It is developed by everyone, for everyone.

FreeCAD is a feature-based, fully parametric 3D CAD modeling, Finite Element Analysis (FEA), manufacturing (CAM/CNC), reverse engineering, and documentation software that enables every industry to design real-life products of any size right from the point of conception of an idea to its production. It provides a wide range of powerful tools that let you create, export, and edit full-precision real-world 3D solid models. It can generate various drawing views of models to create 2D drawings for production, export them for 3D printing or CNC machining, perform Finite Element Analyses (FEA), etc. In addition, FreeCAD allows you to export design data, validate designs, publish 2D drawings, study robot movements, produce machine instructions (G-code) for CNC machines, and so on.

Installing FreeCAD

If FreeCAD is not installed on your system, you must install it first. However, before starting the installation of FreeCAD, you must assess the system requirements and ensure that you have a system that can run FreeCAD correctly. The following are the system requirements for the installation of FreeCAD.

1. Operating Systems: Windows 7/8/10/11, MacOS 10.12 or later, or a Linux distribution.
2. Processor: 64-Bit processor (multi-core processor with a clock speed of 2GHz or higher recommended).
3. RAM: 4 GB RAM minimum (8 GB or more recommended).
4. Graphics Card: OpenGL-compatible graphics card (Dedicated graphics card with OpenGL 4.0 support or higher recommended).
5. Hard Drive Space: A minimum of 1GB of free disk space is required after installation (SSD with at least 10GB of free disk space recommended).

Note: FreeCAD is an open-source parametric 3D CAD software available for free download and installation. To download FreeCAD, visit the FreeCAD website at *freecad.org/downloads.php*

Getting Started with FreeCAD

When you have FreeCAD installed on your system, launch it by double-clicking the FreeCAD icon available on your desktop. After loading all the required files, the startup user interface of FreeCAD appears, displaying the **Start** page, see Figure 1.1.

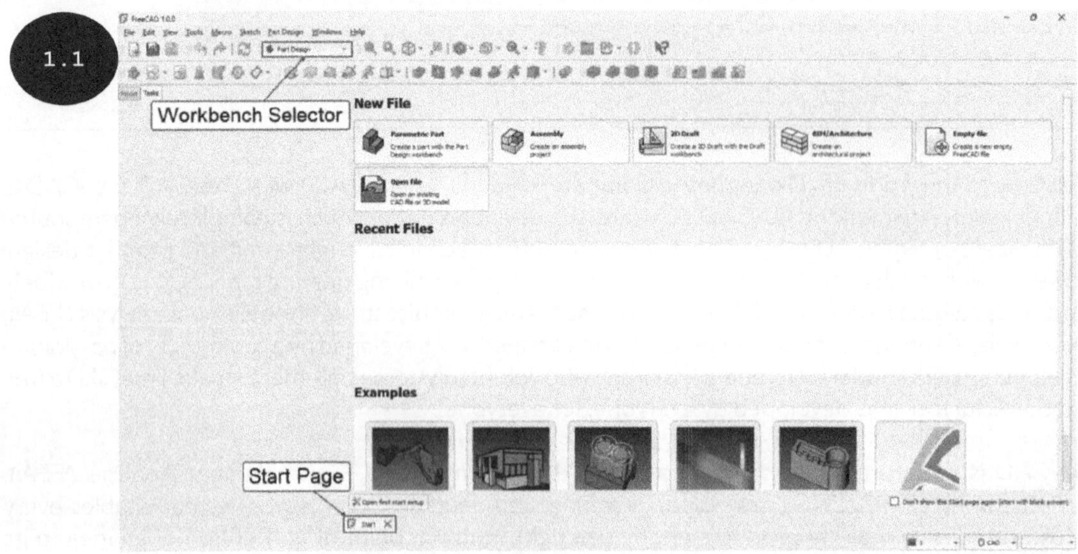

Note: When you launch **FreeCAD** for the first time after installation, the **Welcome to FreeCAD** dialog box will appear, see Figure 1.2. This allows you to set your default preferences such as **Language**, **Unit System**, and **Navigation Style** using the corresponding drop-down lists. You can also access this dialog later by clicking the **Open first start setup** button located at the bottom of the startup interface of the **Start** page, refer to Figure 1.1.

In addition, you can choose a visual theme: **FreeCAD Light** or **FreeCAD Dark**, by clicking the respective button in the **Theme** section of the dialog box. By default, FreeCAD uses the Light theme.

Once you have configured the language, unit system, navigation style, and theme, click the **Done** button to exit the dialog box.

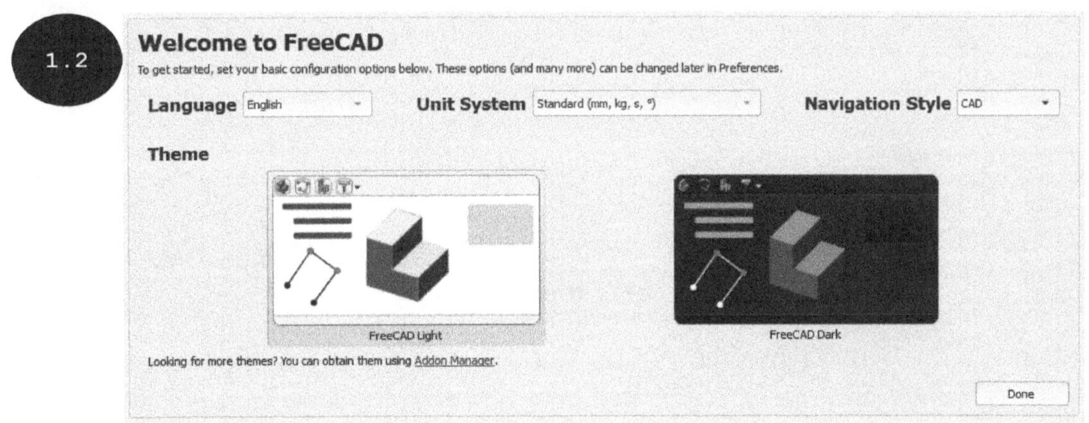

1.2

The **Start** page serves as a welcome screen and is divided into three sections: **New File**, **Recent Files**, and **Examples**.

New File: The **New File** section provides options to start a new parametric part design document, assembly document, 2D draft document, BIM/Architecture document, or an empty document. It also allows you to open an existing CAD file or 3D model using the **Open File** button.

Recent Files: The **Recent Files** section displays a list of recently used documents for quick access.

Examples: The **Examples** section showcases a collection of FreeCAD example files for reference and learning.

Starting a New Design Document

In FreeCAD, you can start a new design document to create a 3D solid part, an assembly, a 2D drawing, and more by using the respective buttons available in the **New File** section of the **Start** page, see Figure 1.3.

1.3

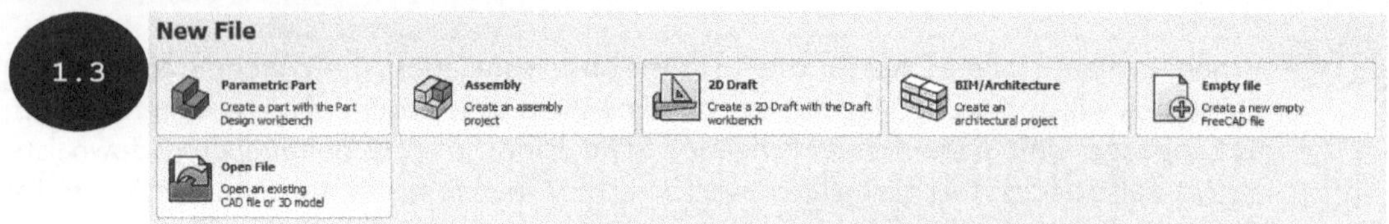

To begin a new design document for creating a 3D solid part, click the **Parametric Part** button in the **New File** section. This action opens a new document with the default name "**Unnamed:1**" in a separate tab, which becomes active by default, see Figure 1.4. The tools in the **Toolbar Area** of the document are enabled, allowing you to begin creating a new parametric part design.

1.4

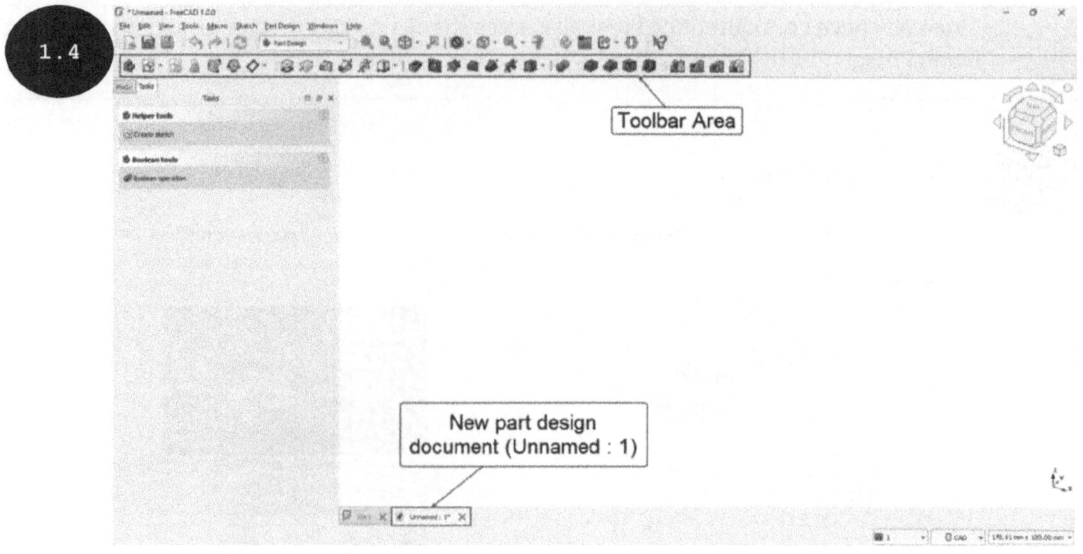

Note: The availability of toolbars in the **Toolbar Area** of a new design document depends on the currently activated workbench. By default, the **Part Design** workbench is activated. You can switch between different workbenches within a design document by selecting the desired one from the **Workbench Selector** located in the **Workbench** toolbar, see Figure 1.5.

1.5

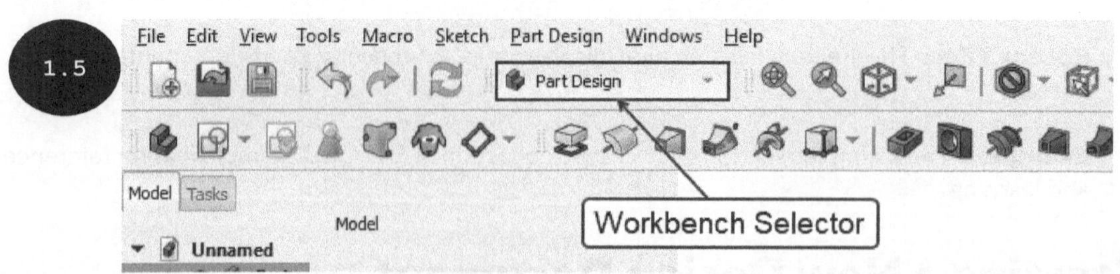

Alternatively, to start a new design document, you can click the **New** tool in the **File** toolbar on the **Start** page (see Figure 1.6), or choose **File > New** from the **Standard Menu**, refer to Figure 1.7. After the new document is opened, you can select the desired workbench using the **Workbench Selector** to access its corresponding tools.

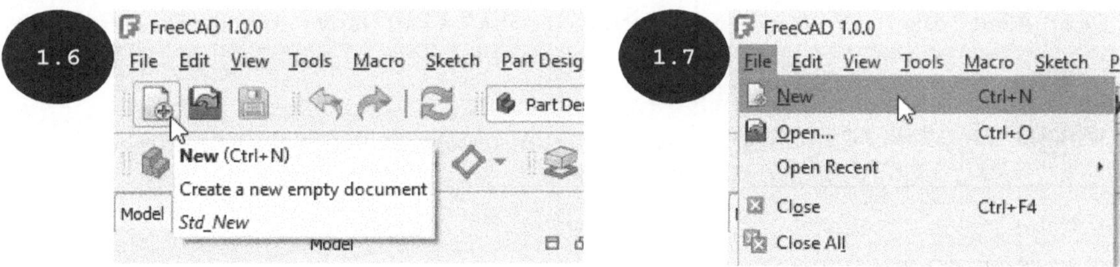

Working with Workbenches

Workbenches are defined as task-oriented environments in which different tools and commands are organized according to design objectives. For example, the **Part Design** workbench contains various tools and commands for creating 3D solid designs, the **Assembly** workbench contains tools for creating assemblies. You will learn about creating 3D solid parts and assemblies in later chapters. Similarly, the **TechDraw** workbench contains tools and commands for creating 2D drawings. You can switch between different workbenches within a document. The method for invoking different workbenches of FreeCAD is discussed next.

In FreeCAD, after starting a new document, you can invoke the desired workbench to create a 3D solid part, an assembly, or a 2D drawing using the **Workbench Selector**, see Figure 1.8.

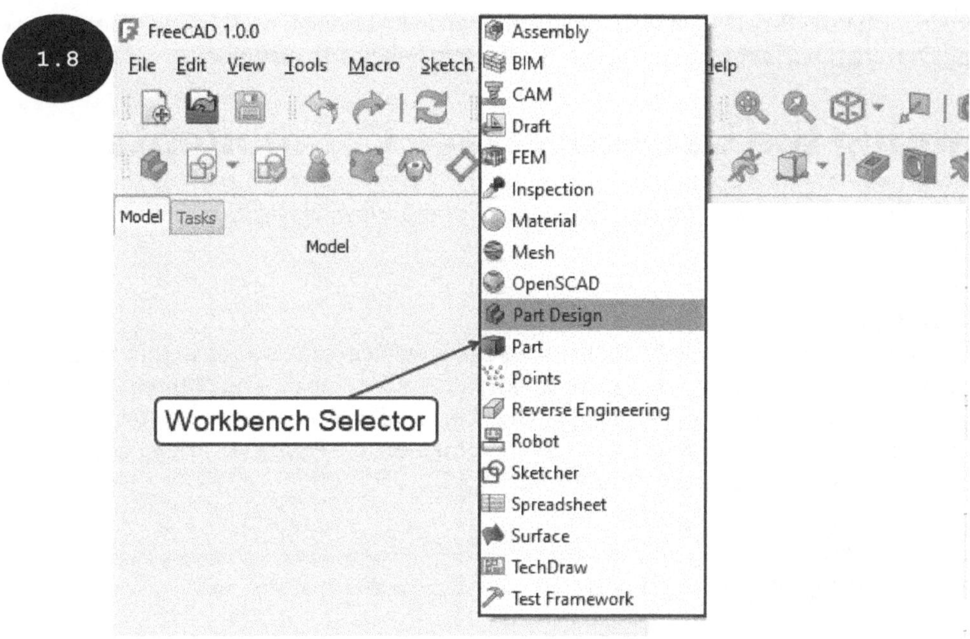

Select the **Part Design** in the **Workbench Selector** to access the **Part Design** workbench, see Figure 1.9.

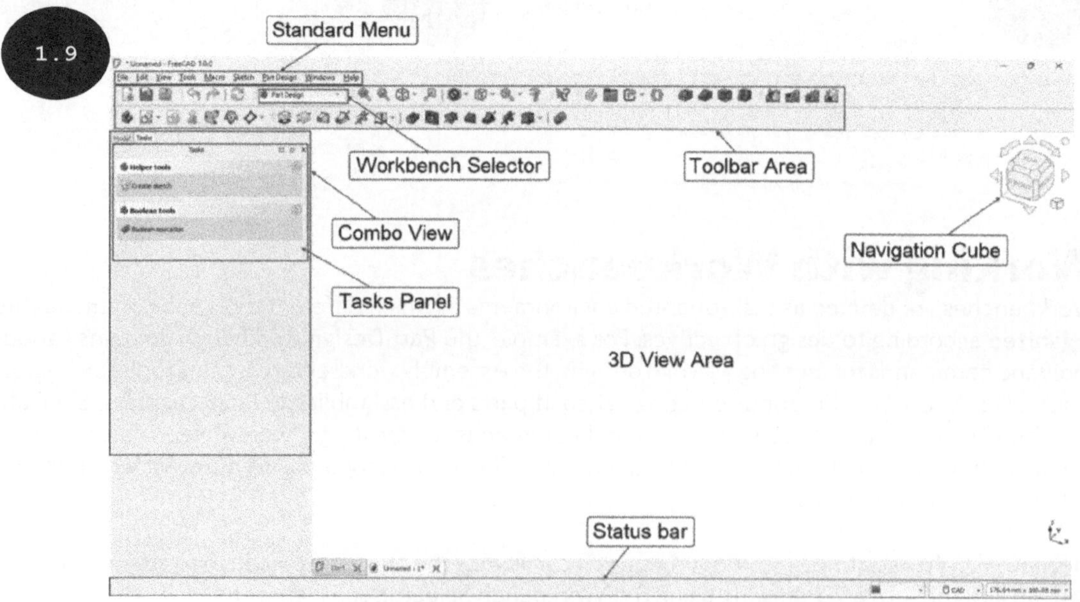

Similar to invoking the **Part Design** workbench, you can invoke other FreeCAD workbenches such as **Sketcher**, **Drawing**, and **TechDraw** using the **Workbench Selector**, as required.

Exploring the User-Interface Components

The various user-interface components of the **Part Design** workbench such as the **Toolbar Area**, **Workbench Selector**, **Standard Menu**, **Status Bar**, **Combo View**, **Navigation Cube**, **Task Panel**, and **3D View** are discussed next.

Toolbar Area

The **Toolbar Area** contains different toolbars that provide access to various tools specific to each workbench. For example, the **Part Design** workbench contains toolbars with different tools specific to creating 3D solid models, see Figure 1.10. Similarly, the **TechDraw** workbench contains toolbars with different tools specific to creating 2D drawings for production, see Figure 1.11. In later chapters, you will learn about creating 3D solid models and 2D drawings.

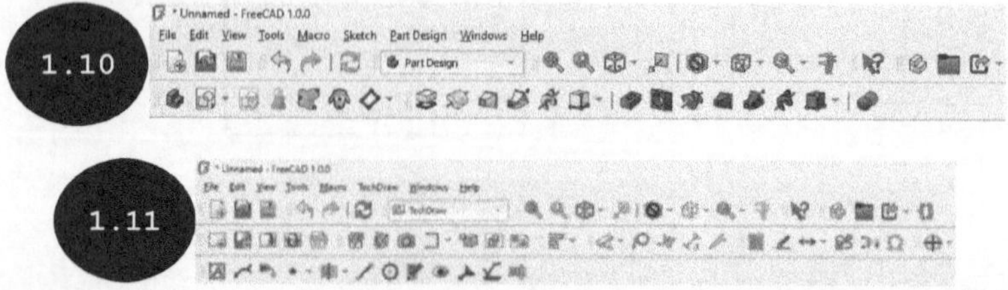

Standard Menu

The **Standard Menu** contains different sets of menus such as **File**, **Edit**, **View**, and **Tools** at the top of the **Toolbar Area**, see Figure 1.12. These menus contain basic tools and commands to operate the program.

1.12

* Unnamed - FreeCAD 1.0.0
File Edit View Tools Macro Sketch Part Design Windows Help

Workbench Selector

The **Workbench Selector** provides a list of available workbenches, see Figure 1.13. You can select the required workbench in the **Workbench Selector** for activating a specific task-oriented environment to meet a particular design objective.

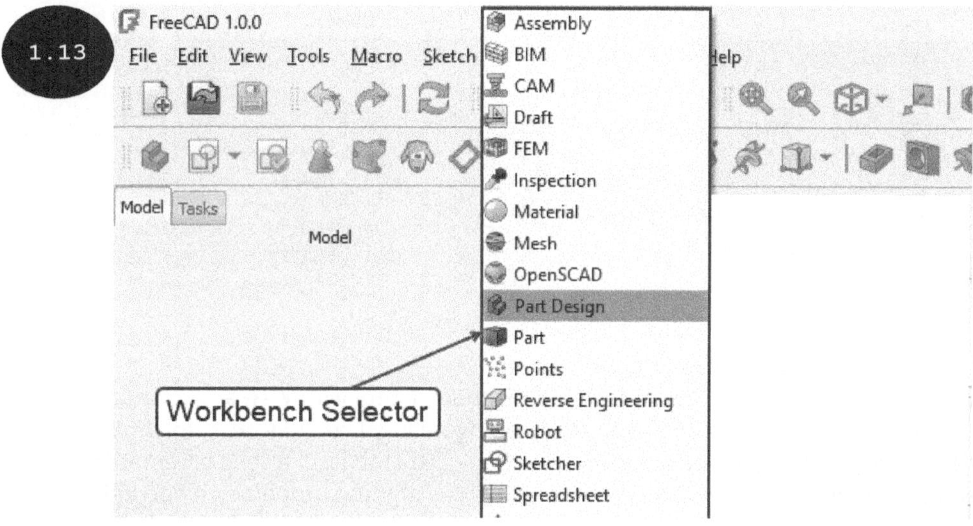

Combo View

The **Combo View** is located on the left side of the 3D View area, by default, see Figure 1.14. It is composed of two sections: the upper section and the lower section.

Upper Section of the Combo View

The upper section of the **Combo View** contains two tabs: **Model** and **Tasks**, see Figure 1.14. The **Model** tab displays the **Tree View**, which keeps a record of all features of a design created in the current document, including 2D sketches, bodies, and datum geometries.

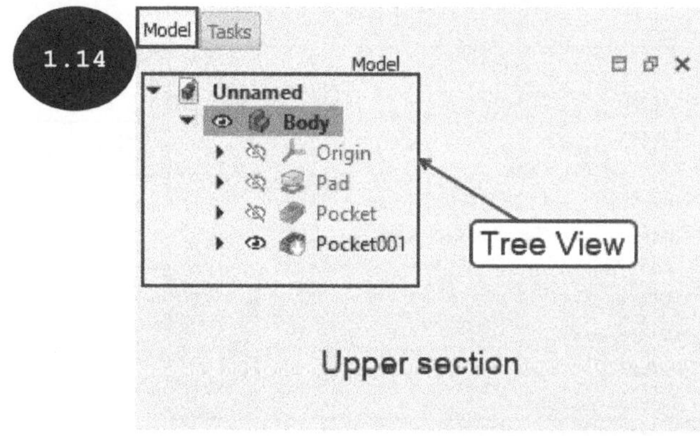

The **Tasks** tab displays the **Task Panel**, which allows you to choose different actions depending on the selected geometry in the 3D View area (see Figure 1.15) or specify parameters depending on the active tool, see Figure 1.16. Figure 1.15 shows the **Task Panel** when a face of a model is selected in the 3D View area and Figure 1.16 shows the **Task Panel** when the **Pad** tool is activated.

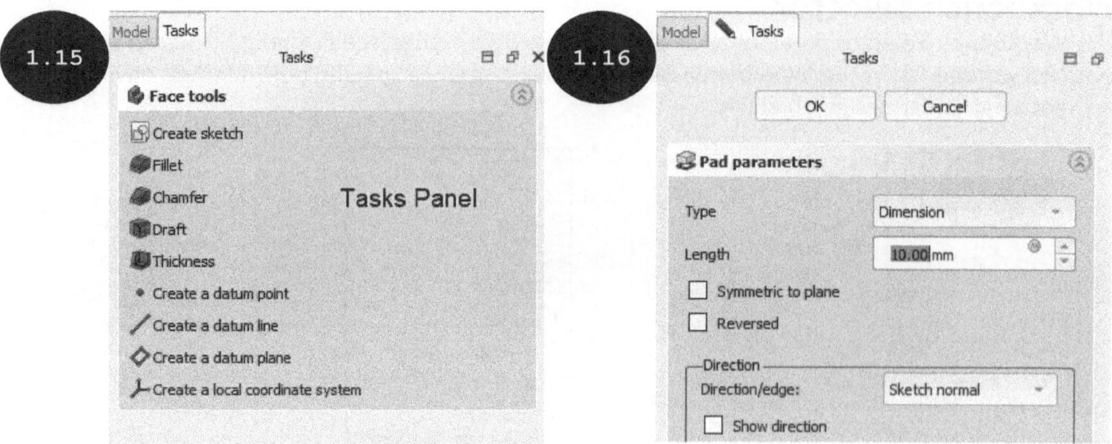

Lower Section of the Combo View

The lower section of the **Combo View** displays the **Property Editor** with **View** and **Data** tabs at its bottom depending on the geometry or feature selected, see Figure 1.17. The **View** tab displays the visualization properties of the selected geometry or feature, and the **Data** tab displays the parametric properties of the selected geometry or feature. You can also edit some of these properties if needed.

Note that the lower section appears only when the **Model** tab is activated in **Combo View** and a geometry or a feature of a model is selected in the 3D View area or the **Tree View**. Figure 1.17 shows the **Property Editor** when a hole feature is selected in the **Tree View**. You will learn about creating different features of a model in later chapters.

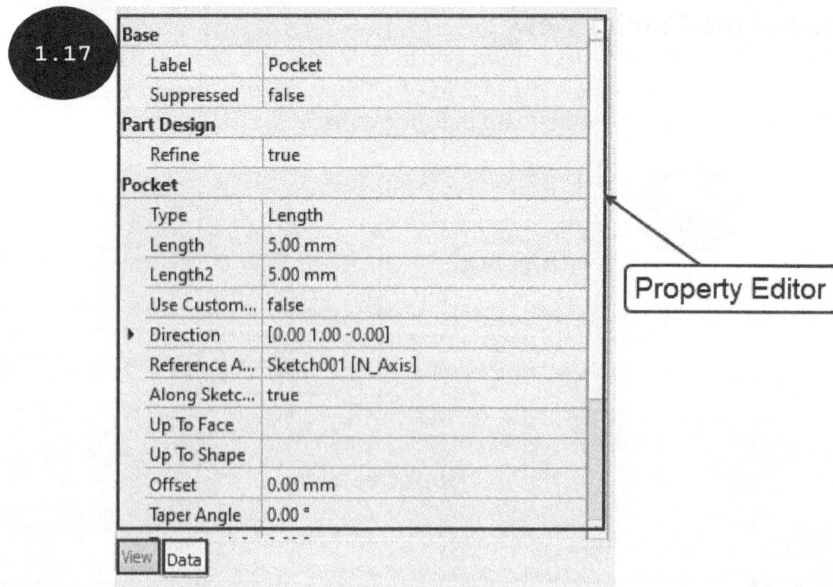

Navigation Cube

The **Navigation Cube** is in the upper right corner of the 3D View area by default, see Figure 1.18. It provides visual information about the current view orientation of a model in the 3D View area. You can also use the **Navigation Cube** to switch between various standard views of a model. You will learn about various components of the **Navigation Cube** and methods for navigating a 3D model by using it in later chapters.

1.18

Status Bar

The **Status Bar** is located at the bottom of the 3D View area. It provides some information based on the active tool as well as displays tooltips.

Invoking a Shortcut Menu

A shortcut menu is displayed when you right-click on the geometry of a model, the empty area, or an item in the **Tree View** or **Toolbar**. It allows quick access to the most used tools or options. Note that the availability of options in the shortcut menu depends on the workbench and the item/geometry selected to invoke the shortcut menu. Figure 1.19 shows a shortcut menu that appears when you right-click on the empty area in the 3D View area of the **Part Design** workbench.

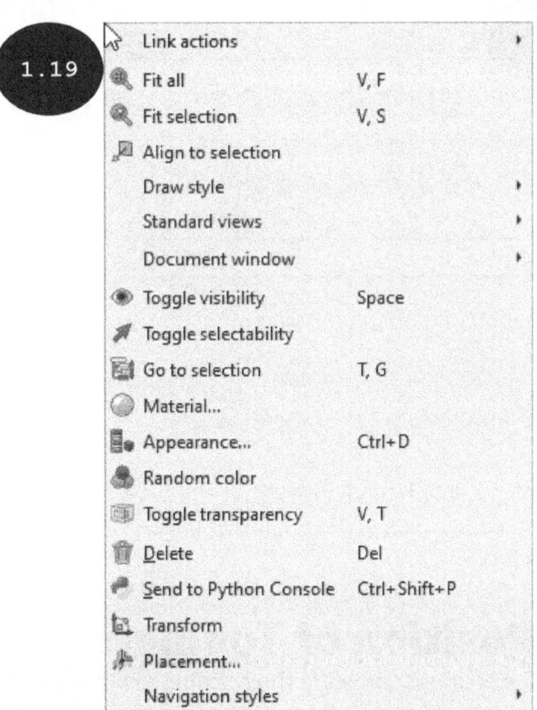

Figure 1.20 shows a shortcut menu that appears when you right-click on a feature in **Tree View**.

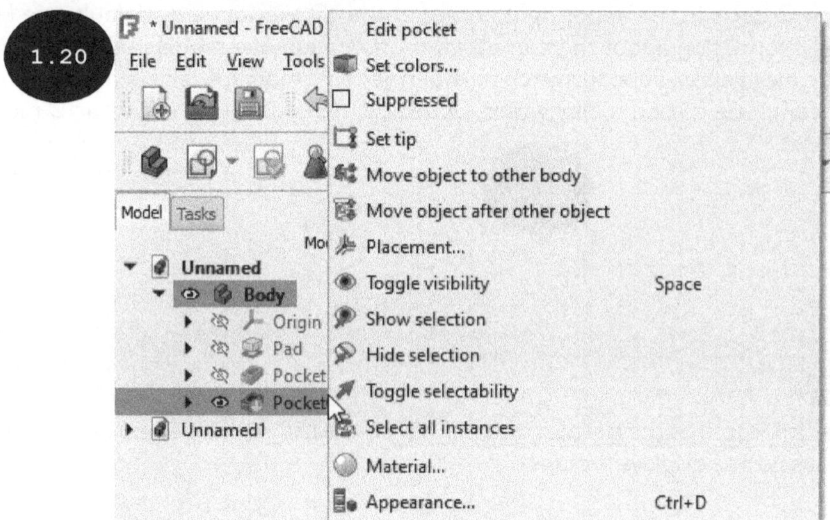

Customizing the Toolbar Area

In FreeCAD, you can customize to add or remove toolbars in the **Toolbar Area** of the active workbench. To do this, right-click anywhere on the **Toolbar Area** (on a tool of a toolbar or an empty area), see Figure 1.21. A shortcut menu appears with the display of all the available toolbars of the active workbench.

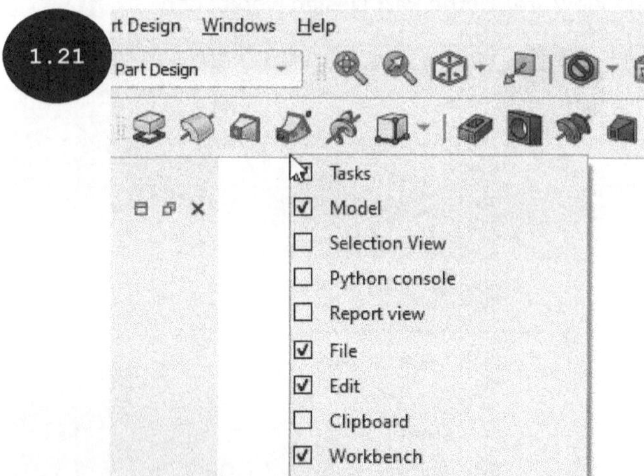

Note that in this shortcut menu, a tick mark in front of the toolbars indicates that these toolbars are already added in the **Toolbar Area**. Click on the required toolbar in the shortcut menu to be added or removed in the **Toolbar Area**.

Defining the Position of Toolbars

In FreeCAD, you can drag the toolbars to define their position in the **Toolbar Area**, as required. To do this, move the cursor on the vertical dots in front of the first tool on the toolbar, see Figure 1.22. The cursor changes to move cursor, see Figure 1.23. Next, drag the toolbar to define its new position on the

Toolbar Area or anywhere on the 3D View area by pressing and holding the left mouse button. After the toolbar position is defined, release the left mouse button. You can also dock the toolbars to the left or right side of the 3D View area by dragging and dropping them.

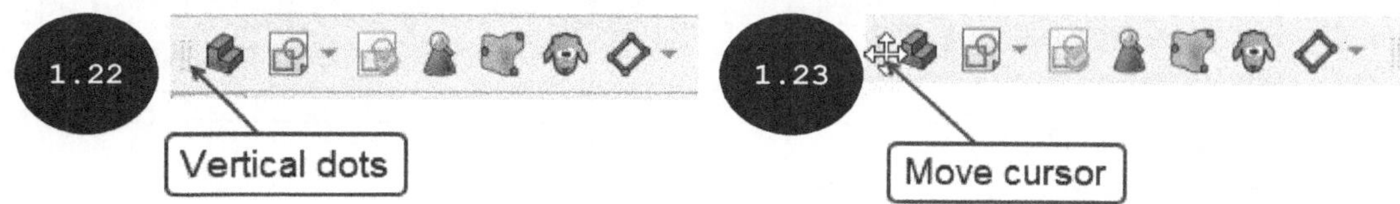

Changing the Background Color

In FreeCAD, you can change the background color of the 3D View area. The method to change the background color is discussed below:

1. Click on **Edit > Preferences** in the **Standard Menu**, see Figure 1.24. The **Preferences** dialog box appears.

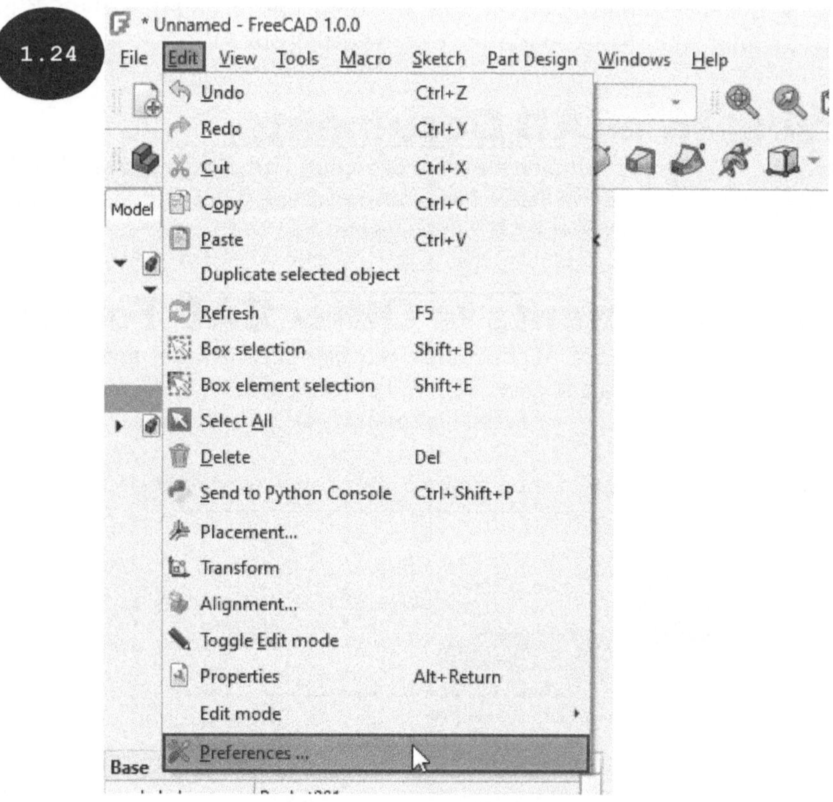

2. Click on the **Display** section in the left panel of the **Preferences** dialog box and then click on the **Colors** tab, see Figure 1.25. The options related to defining color for selections, the background of the 3D View area, and **Tree View** items appear in the dialog box.

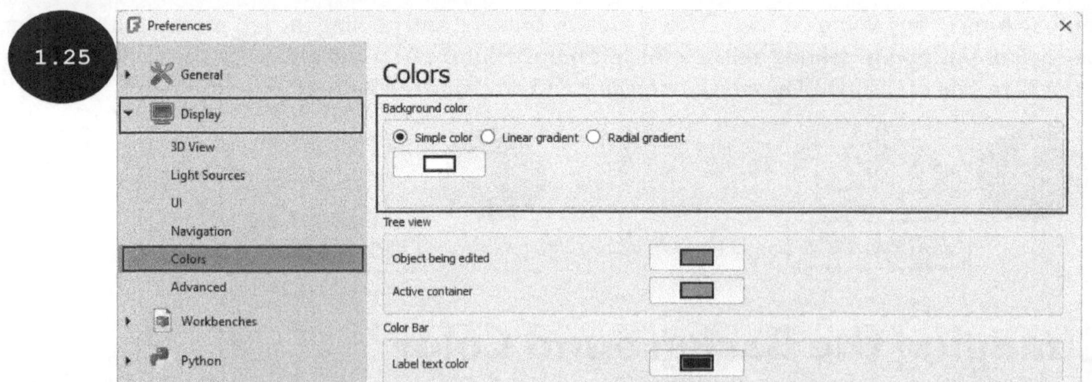

3. Define a color or a color gradient for the background by selecting the required radio button (**Simple color**, **Linear gradient**, or **Radial gradient**) in the **Background color** area of the dialog box, respectively.

4. After defining the background color, click on the **Apply** button and then the **OK** button in the dialog box to confirm the change made and exit the dialog box.

Identifying FreeCAD Documents

Documents created in different workbenches like **Sketcher**, **Part Design**, **Assembly**, **Drawing**, and **TechDraw** of FreeCAD have the same native file extension that is **.FCStd*. It means, when you save a FreeCAD document, it will be saved with **.FCStd* file extension.

Exporting Documents to Other CAD Formats

FreeCAD allows you to export FreeCAD documents or files such as parts and assemblies to other CAD formats or neutral file formats such as STEP, STL, IGES, and SAT. The method for exporting a document to another CAD format or a neutral file format is discussed below:

1. Select a body in the **Tree View** of the **Combo View** in an active workbench to be exported, see Figure 1.26.

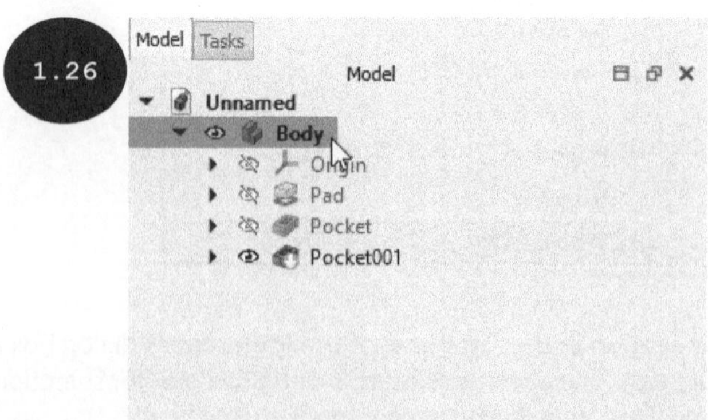

2. Click on **File > Export** in the **Standard Menu** (see Figure 1.27) or press the CTRL + E keys. The **Export file** dialog box appears.

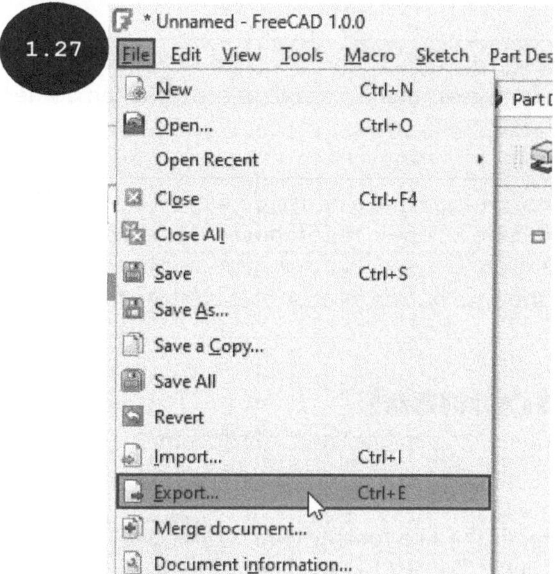

3. In the **Save as type** drop-down list of the **Export file** dialog box, select the required file format such as **3D Manufacturing Format (*.3mf)**, **Autodesk DWG 2D (*.dwg)**, **Alias Mesh (*.obj)**, **Inventor V2.1(*.iv)**, **Open CAD Format (*.oca)**, **STEP with colors (*.step *.stp)**, **STL Mesh (*.stl *.ast)**, and **Technical Drawing (*.svg *.dxf *.pdf)**.

4. Specify the name of the file or object in the **File name** field of the dialog box. Next, browse to the required location and then click on the **Save** button in the **Export file** dialog box. The FreeCAD model or object gets exported to the selected CAD format.

Saving a Document

After creating a design (Part, Assembly, or 2D Drawing), you need to save it in the required location. The method for saving a design document is discussed below:

1. Click on the **Save** tool in the **File** toolbar (see Figure 1.28) or press the CTRL + S keys. The **Save FreeCAD Document** dialog box appears.

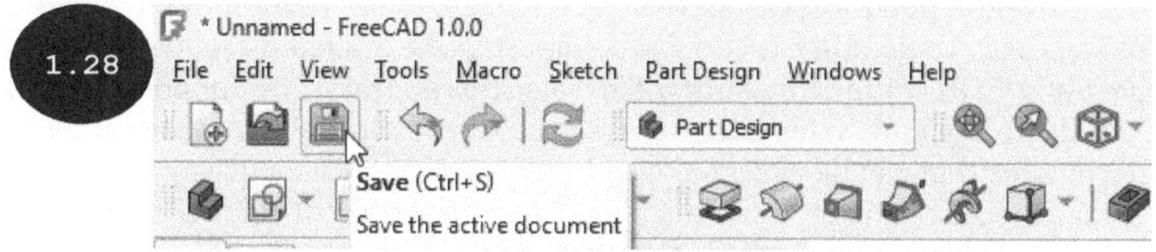

2. Enter the name of the document in the **File name** field of the dialog box and then browse to the required location in the local drive of your system where you want to save the design document.

3. Click on the **Save** button in the dialog box. The design document gets saved at the specified location with the native file extension (**.FCStd*).

Note: After saving a design document, you can close it by clicking on **File > Close** in the **Standard Menu** or click on the cross mark in its tab at the lower left corner of the 3D View area.

Tip: It is also possible to save a copy of a design document with a different name. To do this, click on **File > Save As** or **Save a Copy** in the **Standard Menu**. The **Save FreeCAD Document** dialog box appears. In this dialog box, specify a new name and location for saving the design document and then click on the **Save** button. A copy of the design file gets saved.

Opening a Document

In FreeCAD, you can open an existing native FreeCAD document (*.*FCStd*) or a document created in another CAD application. The method for opening a document is discussed below:

1. Click on the **Open** tool in the **File** toolbar (see Figure 1.29) or press the CTRL + O keys. The **Open document** dialog box appears.

2. In the **Open document** dialog box, browse to the required location where the required document to be opened is saved.

   By default, the **Supported formats (*.FCStd *.3ds *.FCMacro ......)** file extension is selected in the drop-down list of the **Open document** dialog box. As a result, all the supported FreeCAD documents including FCStd (native FreeCAD), STEP, STL, IGES, and SAT files appear in the dialog box. You can also select a specific file extension in the drop-down list depending on the document to be opened in FreeCAD.

3. Select the document to be opened in the dialog box and then click on the **Open** button. The selected document gets opened as a new document in a separate tab of FreeCAD and becomes active by default.

Note: You can also import a file such as STEP, STL, IGES, SAT, etc. into a currently active document of FreeCAD. To do this, click on **File > Import** in the **Standard Menu** (see Figure 1.30) or press the CTRL + I key. The **Import file** dialog box appears. The **Supported formats (*.3ds *.FCMacro *.FCMat ....)** file extension is selected in this dialog box. As a result, all the support documents that can be imported into FreeCAD appear in the dialog box. Browse to the required location and then select a file to be imported into the currently active document of FreeCAD. Next, click on the **Open** button in the dialog box. The selected file gets imported into the currently active document of FreeCAD as a new body.

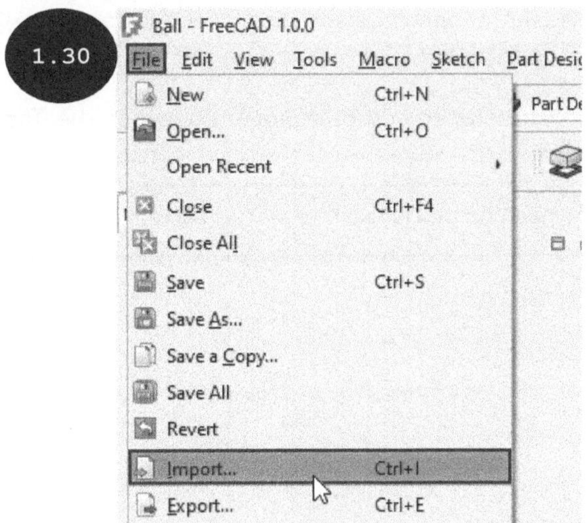

Summary

In this chapter, you have learned about the system requirements for installing FreeCAD, how to start a new document, the different FreeCAD workbenches, user-interface components, and shortcut menus. The chapter also explained the methods to customize the Toolbar Area, specify the position of toolbars, change the background color, identify FreeCAD documents, export documents to other CAD formats, save a document, and open an existing document.

Questions

Complete and verify the following sentences:

- FreeCAD is an _________ 3D CAD software available for free download and installation.
- In FreeCAD, the _________ are defined as task-oriented environments in which different tools and commands are organized according to design objectives.
- The _________ keeps a record of all features of a design created in the current document, including 2D sketches, bodies, and datum geometries.
- The _________ is in the upper right corner of the 3D View area and is used to switch between various standard views of a model.
- The _________ is the native file extension of FreeCAD documents.
- The _________ tool is used for importing a file such as STEP, STL, IGES, and SAT into a currently active document of FreeCAD.

- The _________ tool is used for opening an existing FreeCAD document (**.FCStd*) or a document created in another CAD application.
- In FreeCAD, you can customize to add or remove toolbars in the **Toolbar Area** of the active workbench. (True/False)
- You cannot change the position of the toolbars. (True/False)

CHAPTER

2

Creating and Editing Sketches with FreeCAD

In this chapter, the following topics will be discussed:

- Starting a New Design Document
- Invoking the Sketcher Workbench
- Working with the Selection of Planes
- Specifying Units
- Specifying Grids and Snap Settings
- Drawing a Line
- Drawing an Arc
- Drawing an Elliptical Arc
- Drawing a Hyperbolic Arc
- Drawing a Parabolic Arc
- Drawing a Circle
- Drawing an Ellipse
- Drawing a B-Spline
- Drawing a Polyline
- Drawing a Rectangle
- Drawing Polygons
- Drawing a Slot
- Creating a Fillet
- Trimming, Extending and Splitting Sketch Entities
- Creating Construction Sketch Entities
- Applying Geometric Constraints
- Applying Dimensional Constraints
- Editing and Modifying Dimensions
- Working with Different States of a Sketch
- Exiting the Sketcher Workbench

FreeCAD is an open-source, feature-based, free parametric 3D modeling design, and automation software. Before you start creating 3D models in FreeCAD, you need to understand that to design a 3D model using this software, you need to create all its features one by one, see Figures 2.1 and 2.2. The features are divided into two main categories: sketch-based features and placed features. A feature created by using a sketch is known as a sketch-based feature, whereas a feature created on an existing feature without using a sketch is known as a placed feature. Of the two categories, the sketch-based feature is the first feature of any real-world component to be designed. Therefore, it is important to focus first on drawing a sketch.

Figure 2.1 shows a component consisting of a pad feature and a chamfer. Of these two features, the pad feature is created by using a sketch, refer to Figure 2.2. Therefore, this feature is known as a sketch-based feature. On the other hand, since no sketch is used in creating the chamfer, this feature is known as a placed feature. Figure 2.2 depicts the process of creating the model.

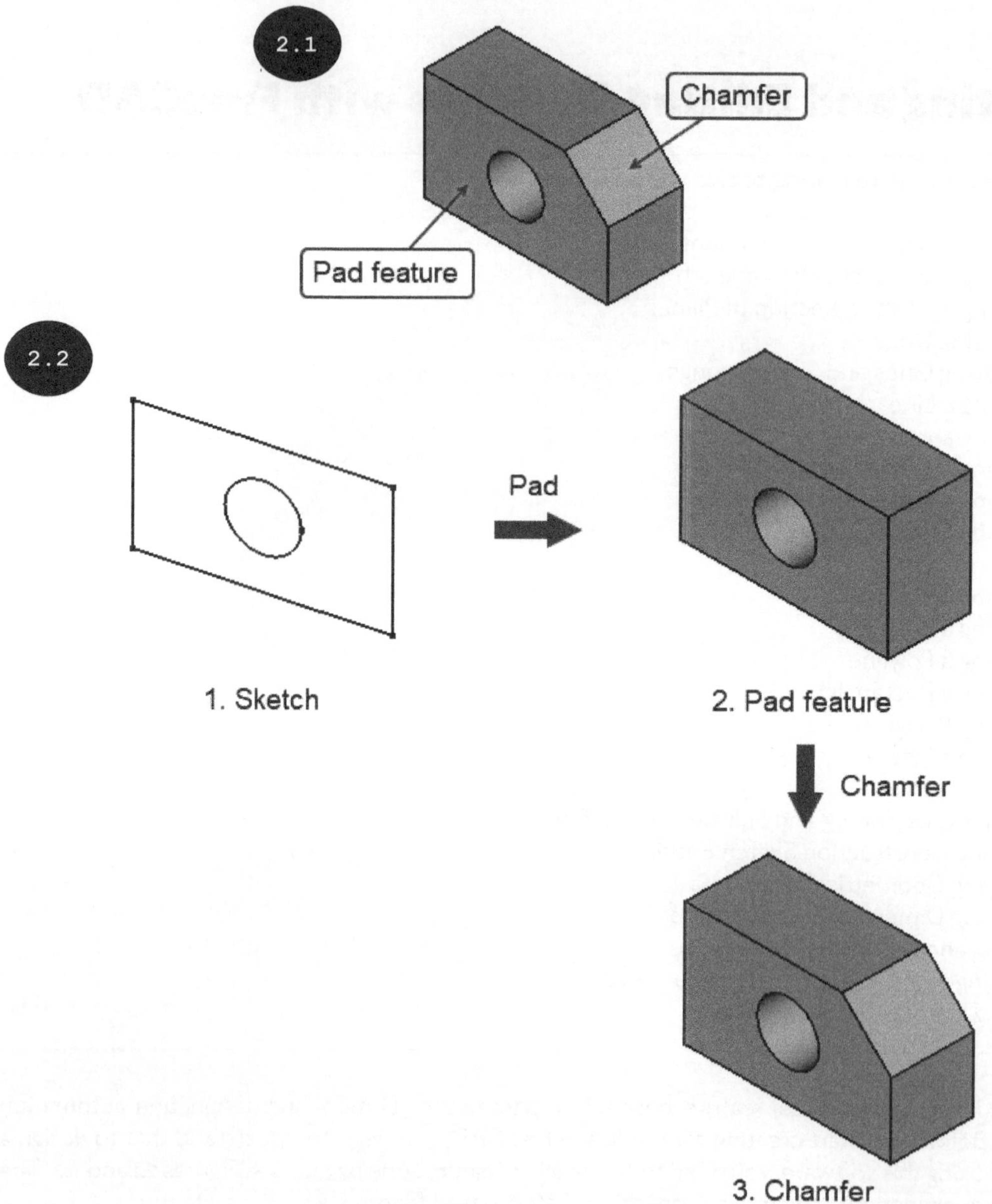

As the first feature of any component is sketch-based, first you need to learn how to create sketches in the **Sketcher** workbench. In FreeCAD, you can create sketches using the various tools available in the **Sketcher** workbench, which is accessible within a design document of the **Part Design** Workbench.

Starting a New Design Document

Start FreeCAD by double-clicking the **FreeCAD 1.0** icon on your desktop. Once all the required files are loaded, the startup user interface appears, displaying the **Start** page, see Figure 2.3.

2.3

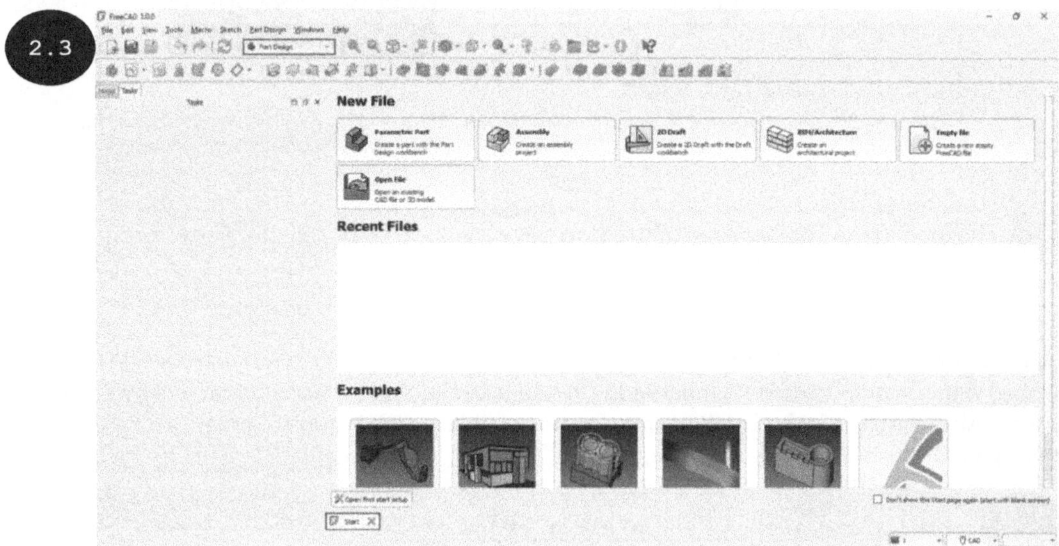

The **Start** page serves as a welcome screen and is divided into three sections: **New File**, **Recent Files**, and **Examples**.

New File: The **New File** section provides options to start a new parametric part design document, assembly document, 2D draft document, BIM/Architecture document, or an empty document. It also allows you to open an existing CAD file or 3D model using the **Open File** button.

Recent Files: The **Recent Files** section displays a list of recently used files for quick access.

Examples: The **Examples** section showcases a collection of FreeCAD example files for reference and learning.

Note: As mentioned earlier, when launching FreeCAD for the first time after installation, the **Welcome to FreeCAD** dialog box appears, allowing you to configure default preferences such as **Language**, **Unit System**, **Navigation Style**, and **Theme**, see Figure 2.4. These options have already been covered in Chapter 1. Click the **Done button** to close the dialog box.

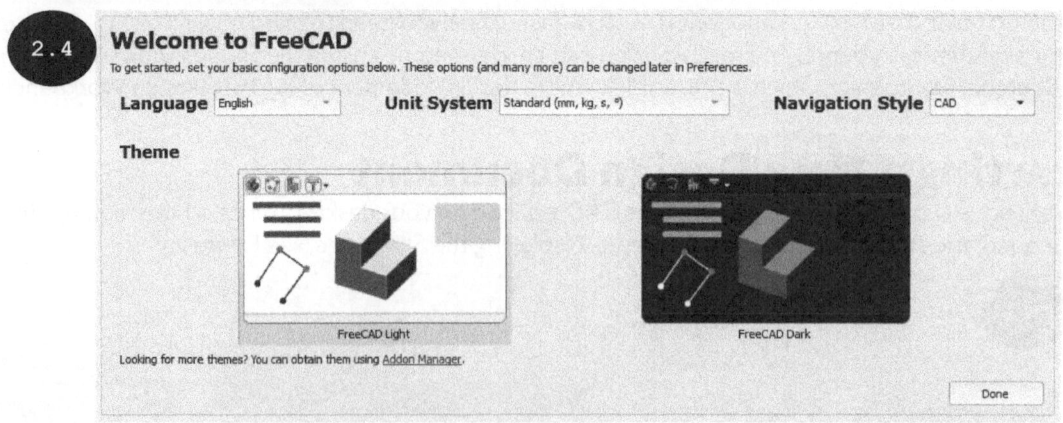

Tip: The tools in the **Toolbar Area** of the **Start** page are disabled by default. They become enabled once you start a new design file.

In the **New File** section of the **Start** page, click the **Parametric Part** button. A new part design document is invoked with the default name "**Unnamed:1**" in a separate tab, and it becomes active by default, see Figure 2.5. Also, the tools in the **Toolbar Area** become enabled, allowing you to create a new parametric part design.

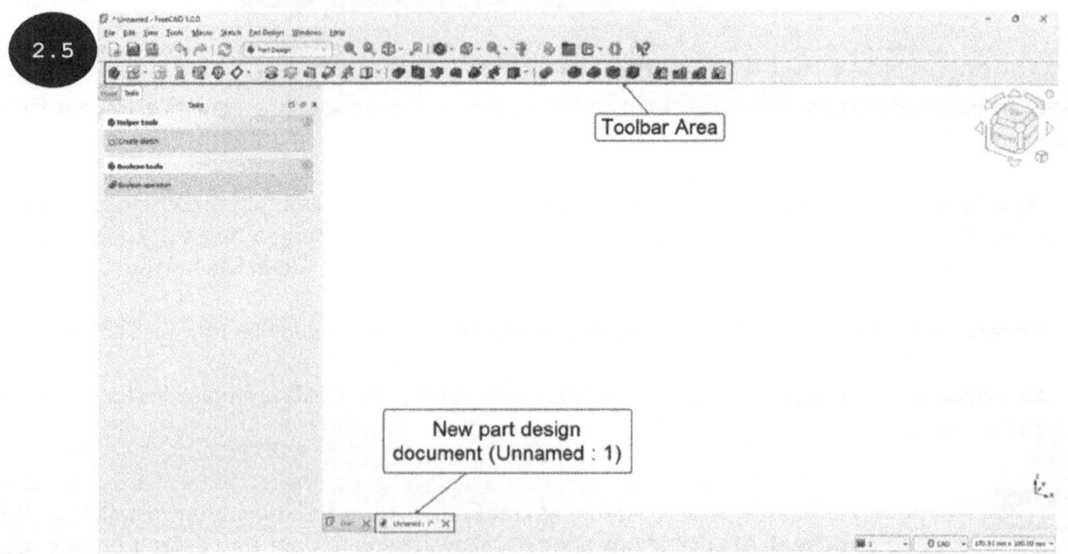

Note: The availability of toolbars in the **Toolbar Area** of a new design document depends on the activated workbench. By default, the **Part Design** workbench is activated. You can switch between different workbenches within a design document by selecting the desired workbench from the **Workbench Selector** in the **Workbench** toolbar, see Figure 2.6.

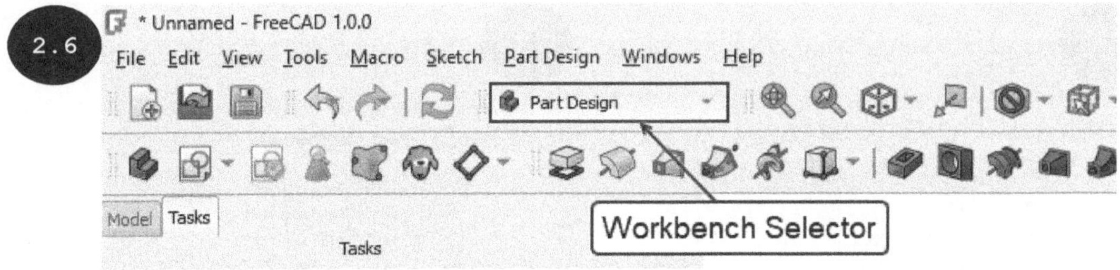

Alternatively, to start a new part document, click the **New** tool in the **File** toolbar of the **Start** page (see Figure 2.7) or select **File > New** from the **Standard Menu**, see Figure 2.8. Then, select the **Part Design** workbench in the **Workbench Selector**.

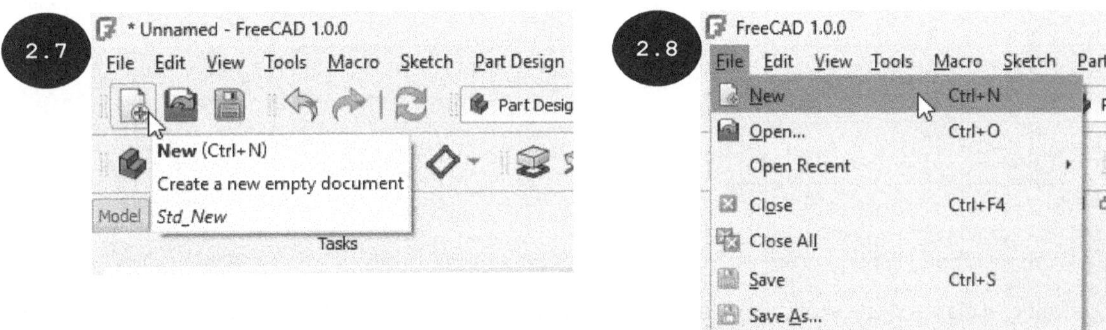

Invoking the Sketcher Workbench

The method for invoking the **Sketcher** workbench within the **Part Design** workbench to create 2D sketches is discussed below:

1. Click on the **Create sketch** tool in the **Part Design Helper** toolbar (see Figure 2.9) or click on **Sketch > Create sketch** in the **Standard Menu** (see Figure 2.10). The three default planes, which are mutually perpendicular to each other appear in the 3D View area, see Figure 2.11. Also, the **Tasks Panel** appears in the **Tasks** tab of the **Combo View** and displays the name of three default planes, see Figure 2.12.

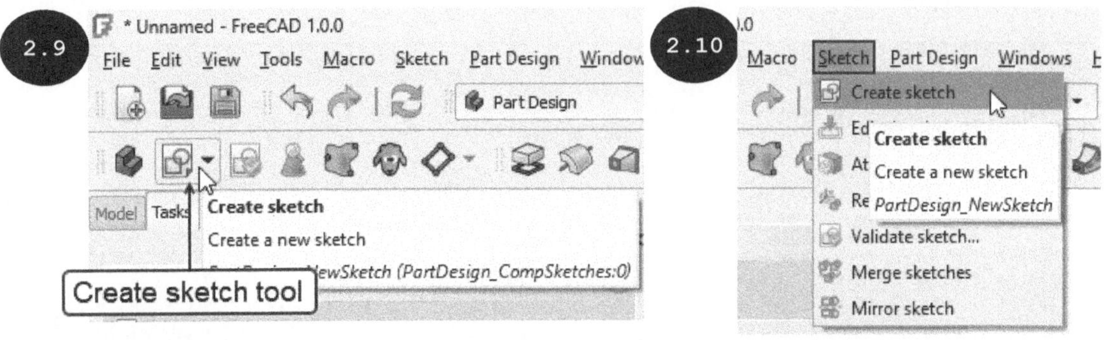

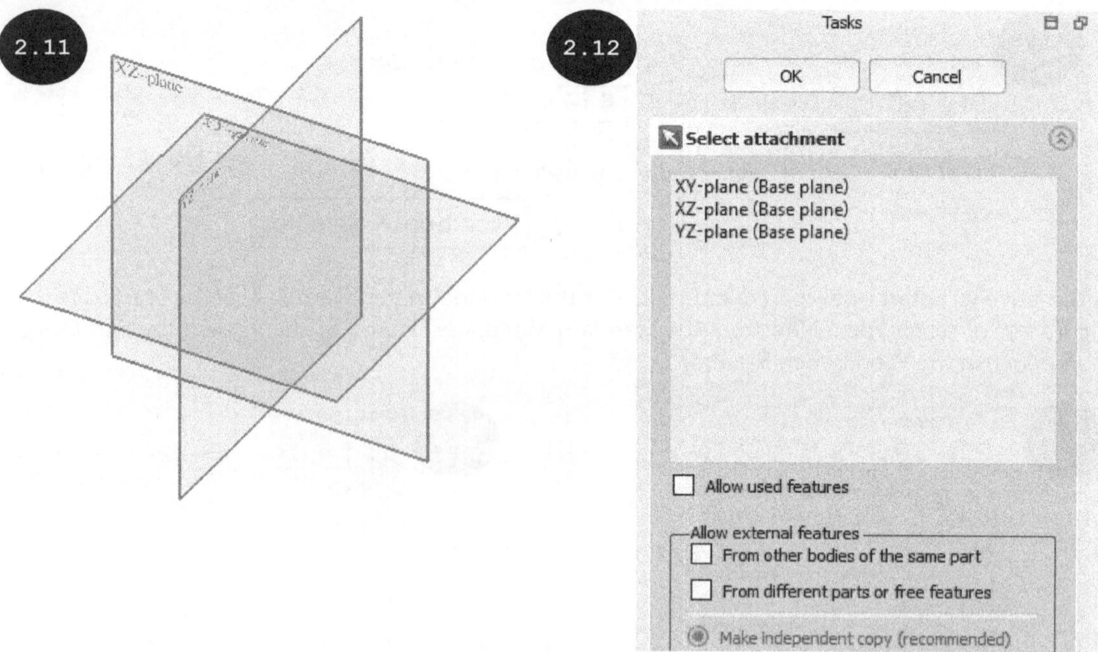

2. Select a plane as the sketching plane for creating a sketch in either the 3D View area or the **Tasks Panel**. The selected plane gets highlighted in the 3D View area.

3. After selecting a plane, click on the **OK** button in the **Tasks Panel**. The Sketch editing mode of the **Sketcher** workbench gets invoked, see Figure 2.13. Also, the selected plane becomes the sketching plane for drawing the sketch and it is oriented normal to the viewing direction so that you can easily create a sketch.

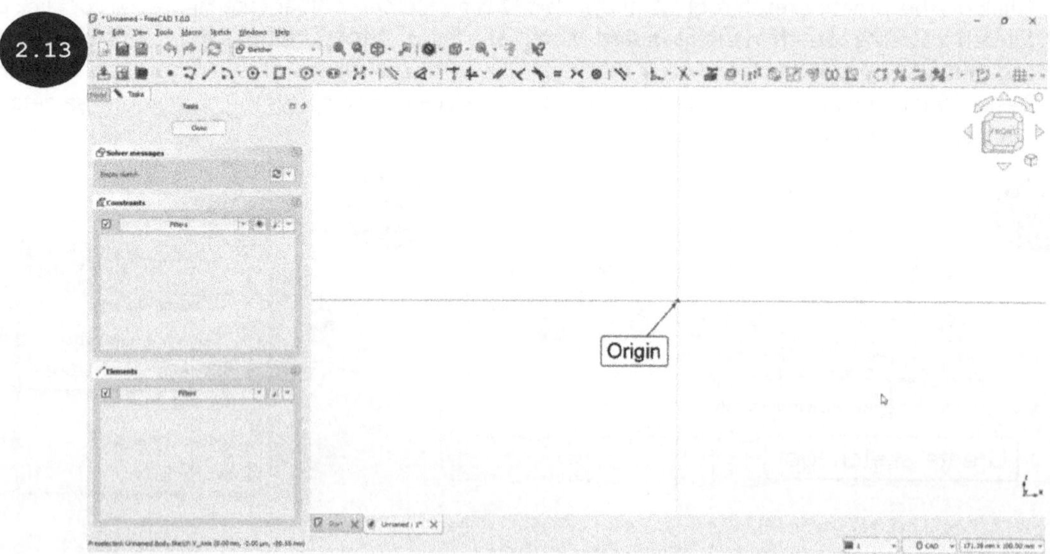

Note: In the Sketch editing mode of the **Sketcher** workbench, a point with two perpendicular axes appears at the center of the 3D View area. It represents the origin (0,0) of the sketching plane.

Now, you can start creating a sketch of a feature by using the sketching tools. However, before you start drawing a sketch, it is important to understand the selection of correct sketching planes, the procedure for setting the unit of measurement, and grid settings.

Working with the Selection of Planes

As discussed earlier, to invoke the Sketch editing mode of the **Sketcher** workbench for creating a sketch, you need to select a plane as the sketching plane. The selection of the correct plane is very important in defining the right orientation of the model. Figure 2.14 shows the isometric view of a model having a length of 200 mm, width of 100 mm, and height of 40 mm. To create this model with the same orientation, you can select the Top plane as the sketching plane and then draw a rectangular sketch of 200 mm X 100 mm. Later, in the **Part Design** workbench, you can extrude this sketch to a depth of 40 mm to create a 3D solid model. You will learn about creating a 3D solid model in later chapters. However, if you select the Front plane as the sketching plane for creating this model, you must draw a rectangular sketch of 200 mm X 40 mm. Likewise, if you select the Right plane as the sketching plane, you must draw a rectangular sketch of 100 mm X 40 mm.

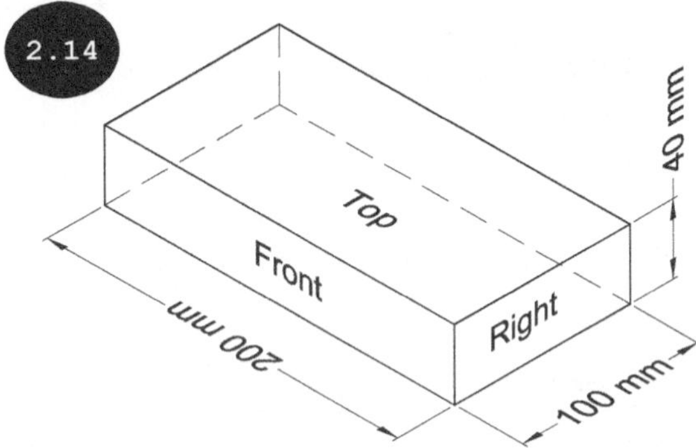

Specifying Units

In FreeCAD, you can define the default units at any point of your design for any document, as required. The method for specifying units is discussed below:

1. Click on **Edit > Preferences** in the **Standard Menu**, see Figure 2.15. The **Preferences** dialog box appears, refer to Figure 2.16.

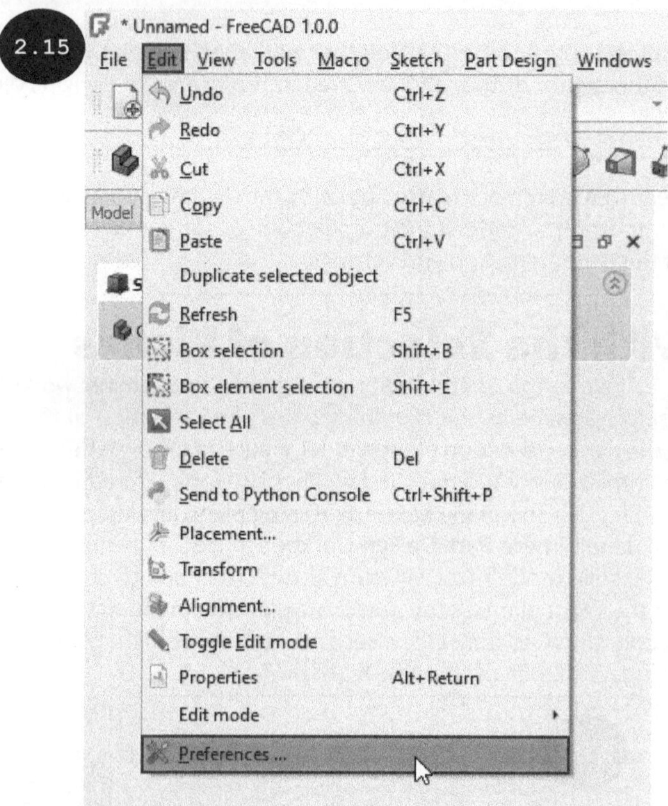

2. Ensure that the **General** section is selected in the left panel of the dialog box, see Figure 2.16. The options to define unit settings appear on the right panel of the dialog box within the **Language and number format** area of the **General** section, see Figure 2.16.

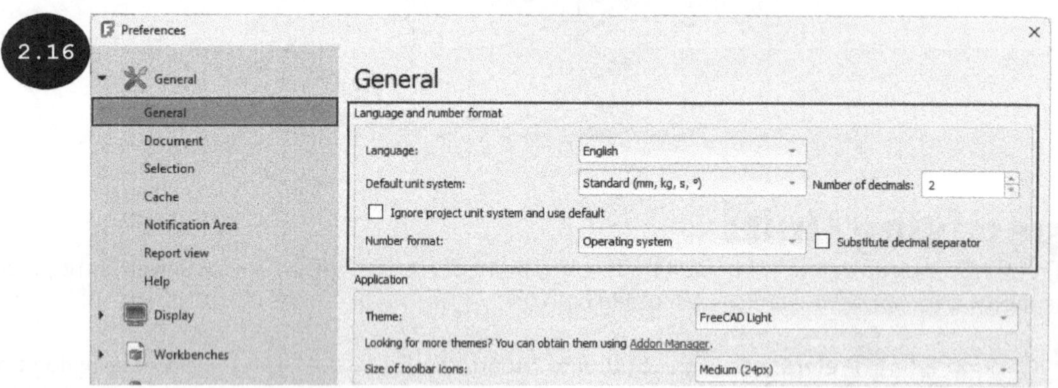

3. Select the required predefined unit system as the default unit system for documents in the **Unit system** drop-down list of the **Language and number format** area in the **General** tab, refer to Figure 2.16. For example, to set the metric unit system, select the **Standard (mm, kg, s, degree)** unit system. In this unit system, length is measured in millimeters, mass is calculated in kilograms, time is represented in seconds, and angle is measured in degrees.

4. In the **Number of decimals** field, specify the required number of unit decimals, as required.

5. After defining the unit settings, click on the **Apply** button and then the **OK** button in the dialog box. The units get defined, and the dialog box gets closed.

Any changes made to the default unit settings will apply to new design documents. The units of the current design document will remain unchanged. To modify the units of the current design document, invoke the **Unit** flyout that appears at the lower right corner of the **Status Bar**, see Figure 2.17. Next, select the desired unit system for your current design document in this flyout.

2.17

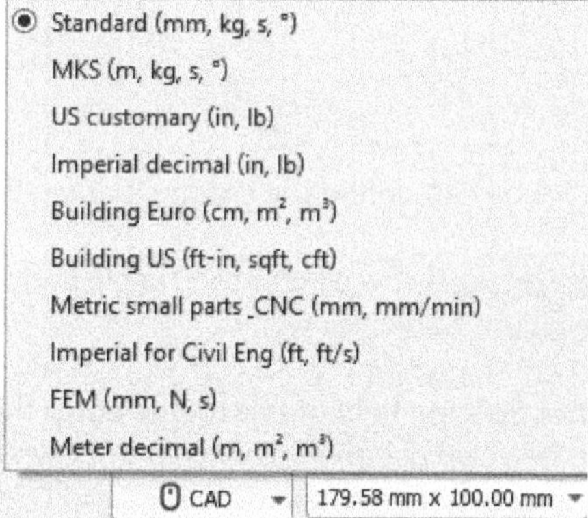

Specifying Grids and Snap Settings

Grids help you specify points in the 3D View area for creating sketch entities and act as reference lines. By default, the display of grids is turned off. You can turn on the display of grids in the 3D View area and the snap mode to snap the movement of the cursor on grid lines. The methods to control the display of grids and the snap mode are discussed below:

1. Click on the **Toggle grid** tool in the **Sketcher edit tools** toolbar, see Figure 2.18. The grids are displayed in the 3D View area with default spacing between the grid lines, see Figure 2.19. Note that this tool is used to toggle the display of grids on or off within the 3D View area.

2.18

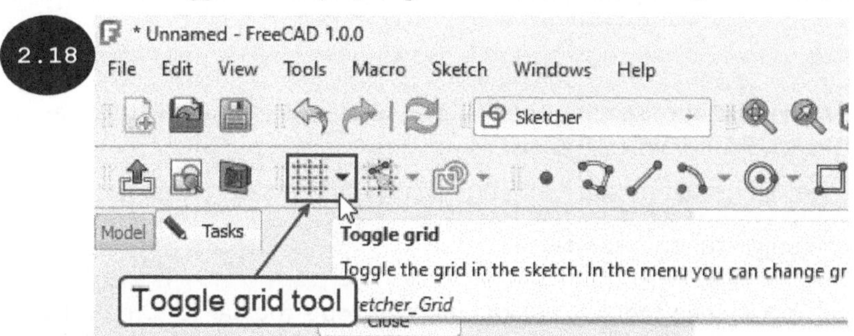

2.19

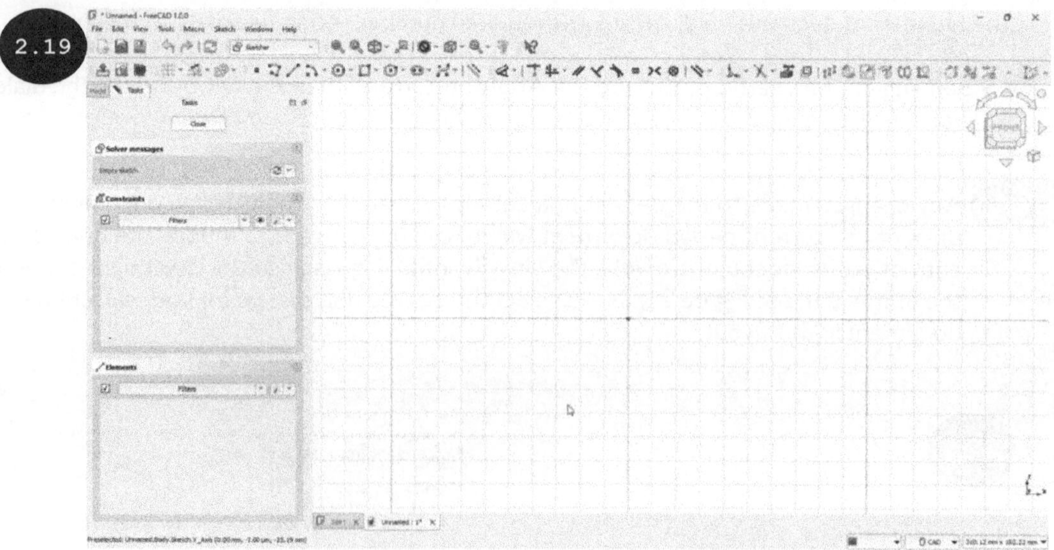

Now, you can define the spacing between two subsequent grid lines, as required.

2. Click on the arrow next to the **Toggle grid** tool in the **Sketcher edit tools** toolbar to display a menu, see Figure 2.20.

3. In the **Spacing** field of this menu, enter the required spacing between two subsequent grid lines. You can also use the Spinner up or down arrows of the **Spacing** field to increase or decrease the spacing between two subsequent grid lines in the 3D View area, see Figure 2.19.

2.20

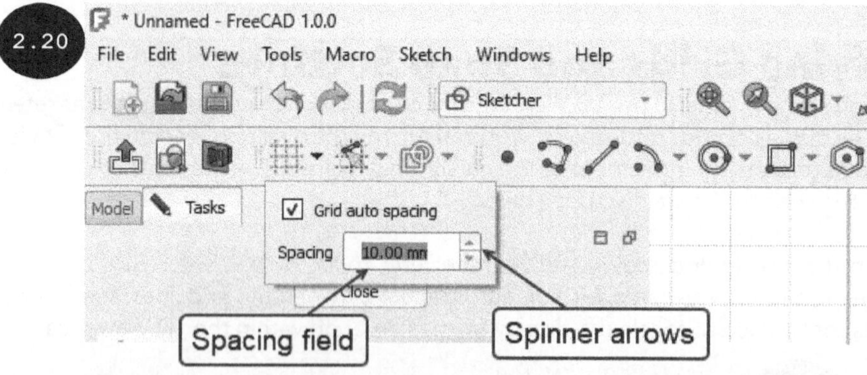

Note: When the **Grid auto spacing** check box is selected in the menu, the spacing between the grid lines will automatically adjust as you zoom in and out of the view in the 3D View area.

Now, you can toggle the snap mode.

4. Click on the **Toggle snap** tool in the **Sketcher edit tools** toolbar to turn on the snap mode for snapping the movement of the cursor on grid lines based on the default snap settings, see Figure 2.21. Note that this tool is used to toggle the snap mode on or off.

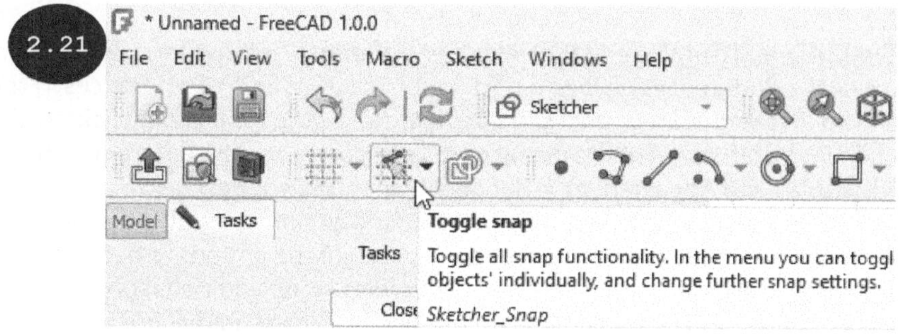

Note: To snap the movement of the cursor to grid lines while drawing a sketch entity, you must turn on the snap mode.

Now, you can control the snap settings.

5. Click on the arrow next to the **Toggle snap** tool in the **Sketcher edit tools** toolbar to display a menu, see Figure 2.22. Note that the options in this menu are enabled only when the snap mode is turned on. The options are discussed below:

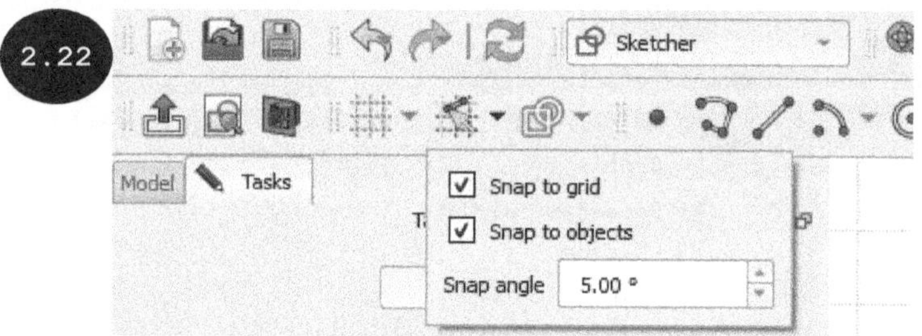

Snap to grid: The **Snap to grid** check box is used to snap the movement of the cursor to the grid lines while drawing a sketch entity. Note that it also works even if the grids are not displayed.

Snap to objects: The **Snap to objects** check box is used to snap the movement of the cursor to objects like edges, vertices, or midpoints of lines and arcs while drawing a sketch entity.

Snap angle: The **Snap angle** field is used to specify an angle value for the angular snap of the cursor while specifically drawing a line. Note that you need to press the CTRL key to enable the angular snap of the cursor.

6. Select the **Snap to grid** and **Snap to objects** check boxes in the menu to snap the movement of the cursor to grid lines and objects, respectively, as discussed above.

Note: In FreeCAD, you can also edit the default grid and snap settings for new sketch documents by using the **Preferences** dialog box. To do this, click on **Edit > Preferences** in the **Standard Menu** to invoke the **Preferences** dialog box, see Figure 2.23. Next, click on the **Sketcher** section in the left panel of the dialog box, see Figure 2.24. The different options (**General, Grid, Display**, and **Appearance**) to define sketch settings appear below the **Sketcher** section in the left panel, see Figure 2.24. Select the **Grid** option to display options to define grid settings on the right panel of the dialog box. Most of the options to define grid settings are the same as discussed earlier, but it also provides some additional options to control the display of minor and major grid lines. After defining the required grid settings, click on the **OK** button. Note that the changes made in the **Preferences** dialog box as the default grid settings will be reflected in the new sketch documents.

2.23

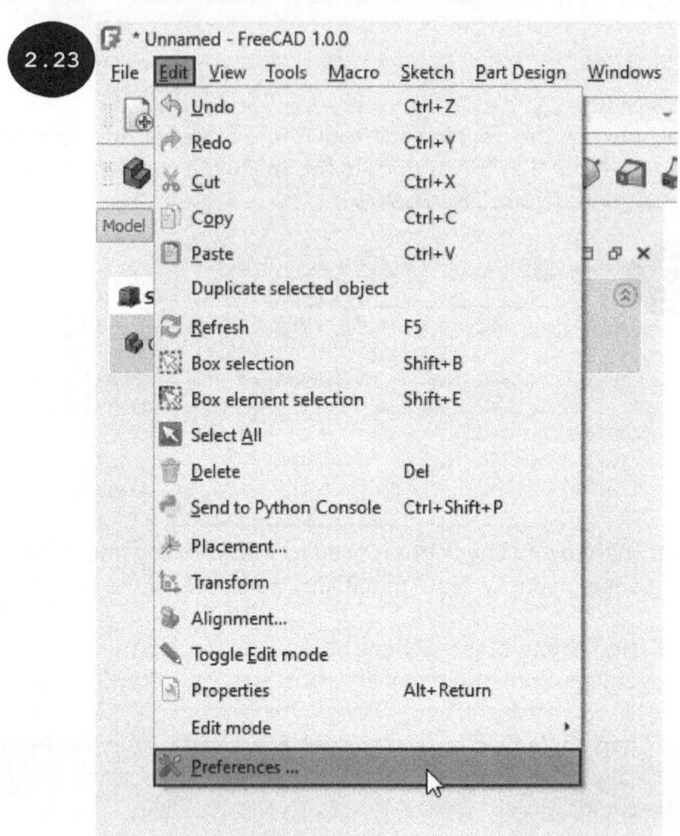

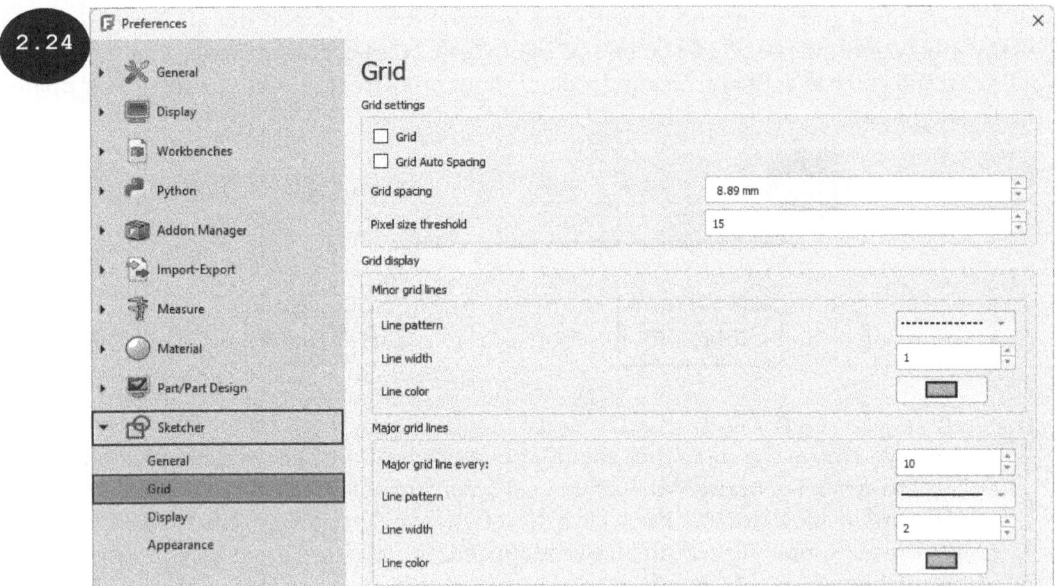

Drawing a Line

A line is defined as the shortest distance between two points. The method for drawing a line is discussed below:

1. Click on the **Create line** tool in the **Sketcher geometries** toolbar, see Figure 2.25. The **Create line** tool gets activated and the appearance of the cursor changes to a cross mark with the display of a red line icon, see Figure 2.26. Also, the coordinates of the current location appear near the cursor.

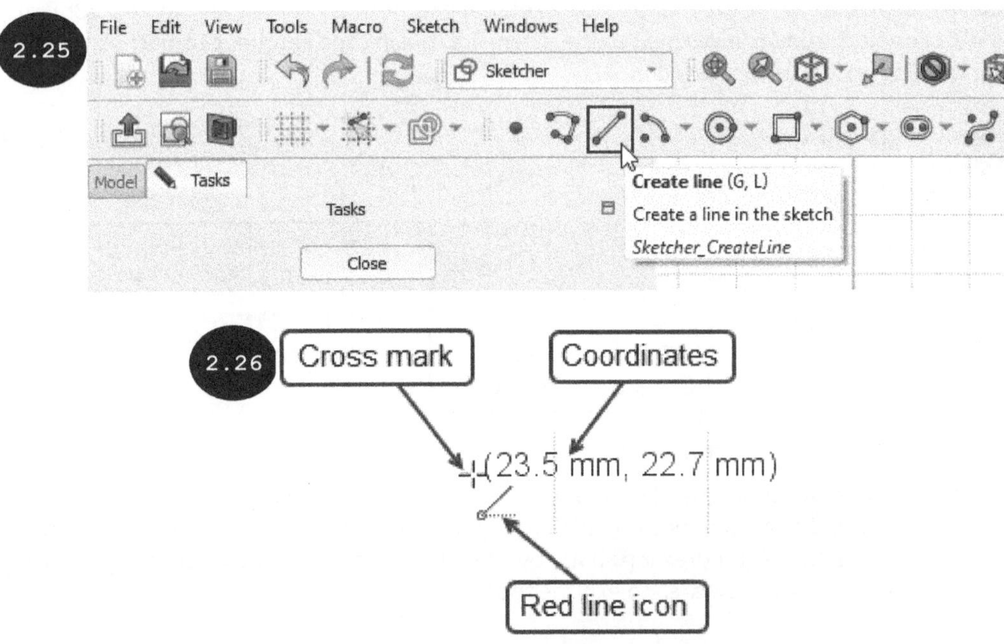

2. Click to specify a start point and an endpoint of a line one by one in the 3D view area. A line is drawn between the specified points, see Figure 2.27. Note that the **Create line** tool remains activated and you can continue creating multiple lines one after the other by specifying points in the drawing area.

2.27

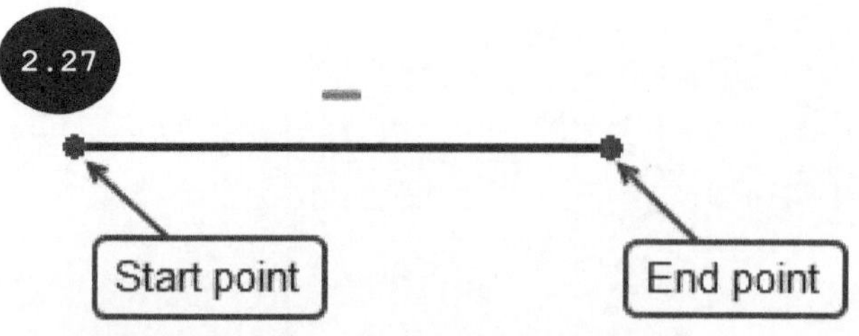

Note: When you move the cursor horizontally or vertically after specifying the start point of the line, the symbol of horizontal — or vertical | constraint appears near the line. The symbol of constraint indicates that if you click the left mouse button to specify the endpoint of the line, the corresponding constraint will be applied. You will learn more about constraints later in this chapter.

3. After creating one or more lines, press the ESC key or right-click in the 3D View area to exit the **Create line** tool.

Drawing an Arc

You can draw an arc using the **Create arc by center** and **Create arc by 3 points** tools. You can access both these tools in the **Create arc** menu of the **Sketcher geometries** toolbar, see Figure 2.28. To invoke this menu, click on the down arrow next to the active arc tool in the **Sketcher geometries** toolbar. The tools for drawing an arc are discussed next.

2.28

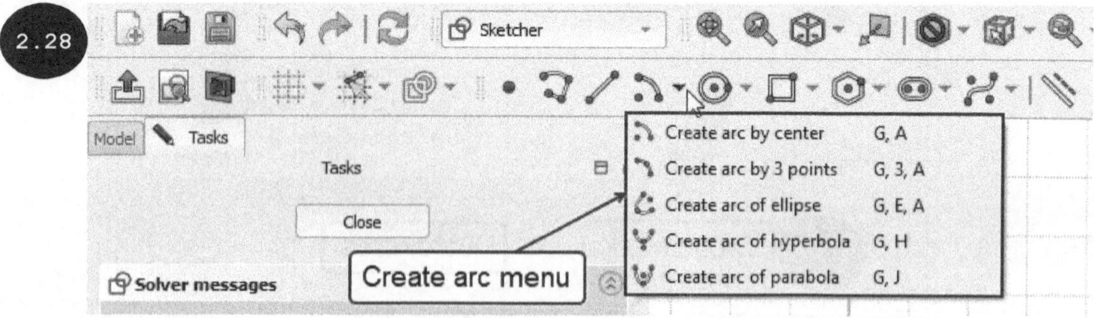

Create arc by center Tool

The **Create arc by center** tool is used for drawing an arc by first specifying its center point, and then the start angle and end angle points along the arc radius by clicking the left mouse button in the 3D View area, see Figure 2.29. After drawing an arc by using the **Create arc by center** tool, press the ESC key or right-click on the 3D View area to exit the tool.

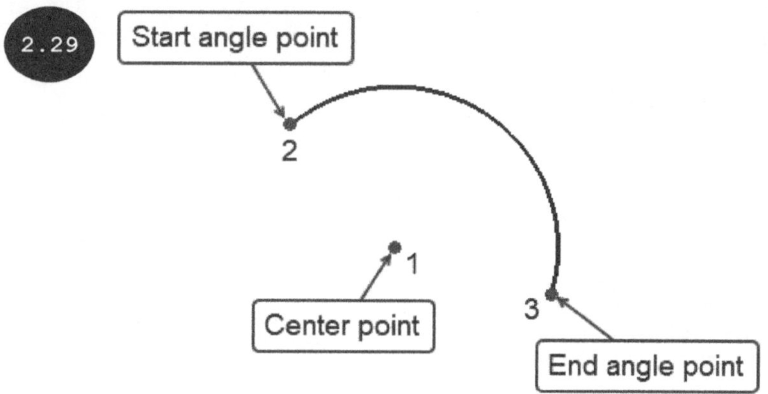

Note: In this textbook, some of the figures are numbered for your reference only, see Figure 2.28. These numbers represent the sequence of points specified in the 3D View area for creating an object by clicking the left mouse button.

Create arc by 3 points Tool

The **Create arc by 3 points** tool is used for drawing an arc by first specifying its start point, and then the endpoint and a point on the arc by clicking the left mouse button in the 3D View area, see Figure 2.30. After creating an arc, press the ESC key or right-click on the 3D View area to exit the tool.

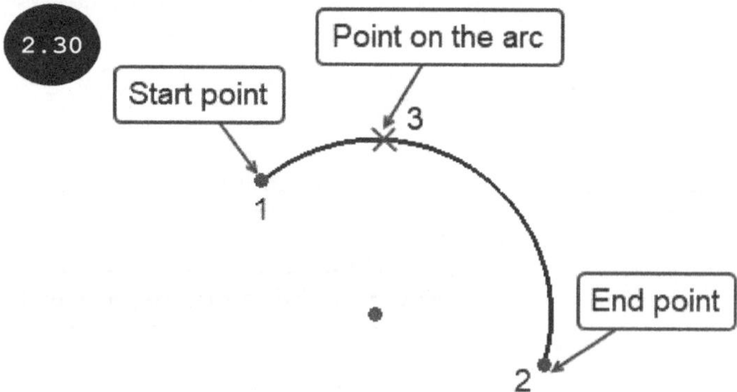

Drawing an Elliptical Arc

The **Create Arc of Ellipse** tool in the **Create arc** menu is used to draw an elliptical arc. To do this, invoke the **Create arc** menu, then click on the **Create Arc of Ellipse** tool. Next, specify the center point of the arc, followed by a point to define its major axis. After selecting these points, move the cursor slightly to display a preview of the ellipse. Next, click to specify the start point, then the end point of the elliptical arc in the 3D View area, see Figure 2.31. The elliptical arc is then created.

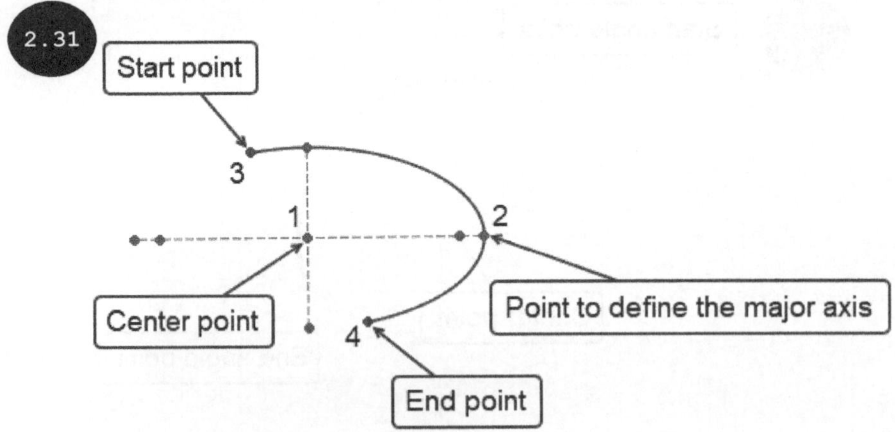

Drawing a Hyperbolic Arc

The **Create arc of hyperbola** tool in the **Create arc** menu is used to draw a hyperbolic arc. After activating the **Create arc of hyperbola** tool, first specify the center point of the major axis of hyperbola in the 3D View area and then a point to define its major axis, refer to Figure 2.32. After defining the center point and the major axis, move the cursor to a distance in the 3D View area. The preview of an imaginary hyperbola appears. Next, click to specify the start point and then the endpoint of the hyperbolic arc in the 3D View area, see Figure 2.32. The hyperbolic arc is created. After creating an arc, press the ESC key or right-click on the 3D View area to exit the tool.

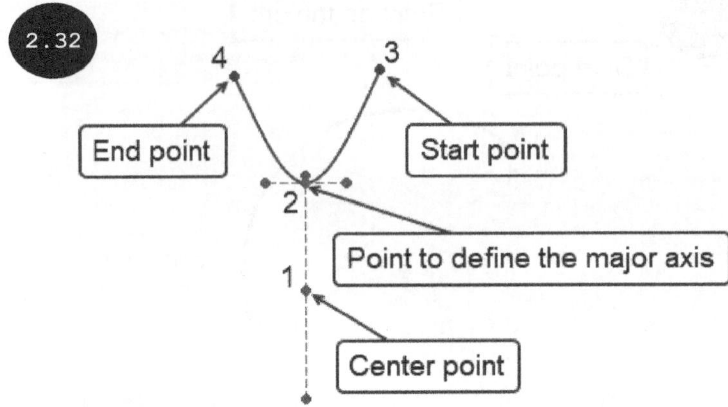

Drawing a Parabolic Arc

The **Create arc of parabola** tool in the **Create arc** menu is used to draw a parabolic arc. After activating the **Create arc of parabola** tool, fist specify the focus point and then an apex point of the parabola, refer to Figure 2.33. After defining the focus and apex points, move the cursor to a distance in the 3D View area. The preview of an imaginary parabola appears. Next, click to specify the start point and then the endpoint of the parabolic arc in the 3D View area, see Figure 2.33. The parabolic arc is created. After creating the arc, press the ESC key or right-click on the 3D View area to exit the tool.

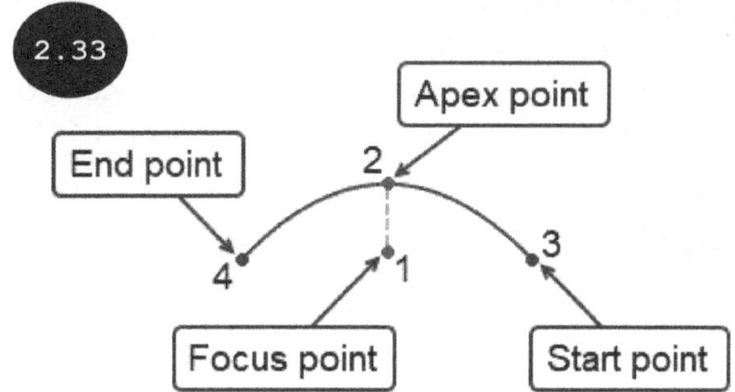

Drawing a Circle

In FreeCAD, you can draw a circle using the **Create circle by center** and **Create circle by 3 points** tools. You can access both these tools in the **Create circle** menu of the **Sketcher geometries** toolbar, see Figure 2.34. To invoke this menu, click on the down arrow next to the active circle tool in the **Sketcher geometries** toolbar. The tools for drawing a circle are discussed next.

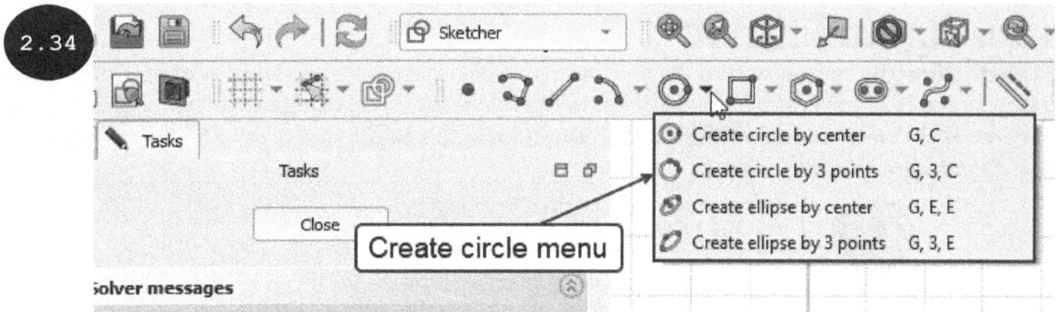

Create circle by center Tool

The **Create circle by center** tool is used for drawing a circle by first specifying its center point and then a point on its circumference by clicking the left mouse button in the 3D View area, see Figure 2.35. After creating a circle, press the ESC key or right-click on the 3D View area to exit the tool.

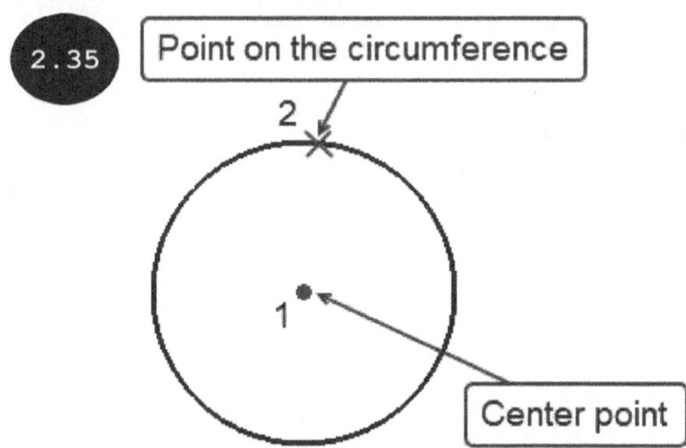

Create circle by 3 points Tool

The **Create circle by 3 points** tool is used for drawing a circle by specifying three points on its circumference by clicking the left mouse button in the 3D View area one by one, see Figure 2.36. After creating a circle, press the ESC key or right-click on the 3D View area to exit the tool.

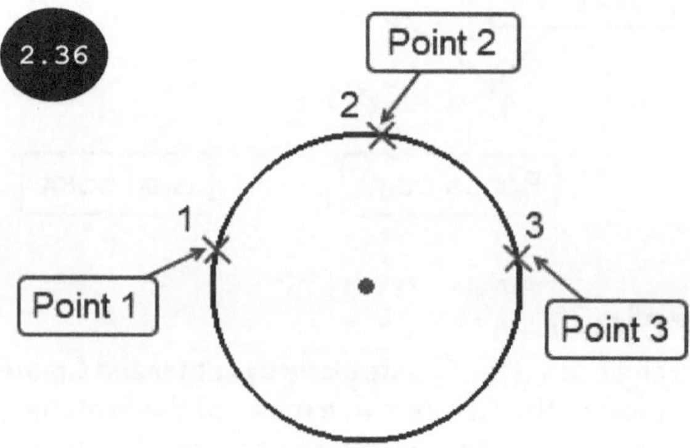

Drawing an Ellipse

The **Create ellipse by center** tool is used for drawing an ellipse by first specifying its center, and then an endpoint of the major axis and a point to define the minor axis by clicking the left mouse button one by one in the 3D View area, see Figure 2.37. After creating an ellipse, press the ESC key or right-click on the 3D View area to exit the tool.

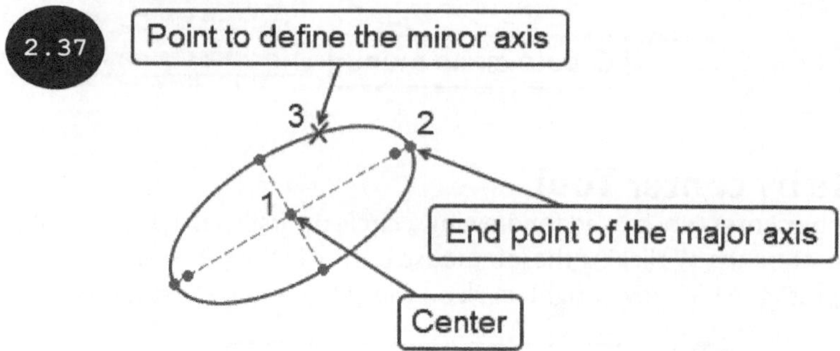

Create ellipse by 3 points Tool

The **Create ellipse by 3 points** tool is used for drawing an ellipse by specifying three points in the 3D View area. The first point defines the periapsis (first endpoint of the major axis), the second point defines the apoapsis (second endpoint of the major axis), and the third point defines the minor axis of the ellipse, see Figure 2.38. After creating an ellipse, press the ESC key or right-click on the 3D View area to exit the tool.

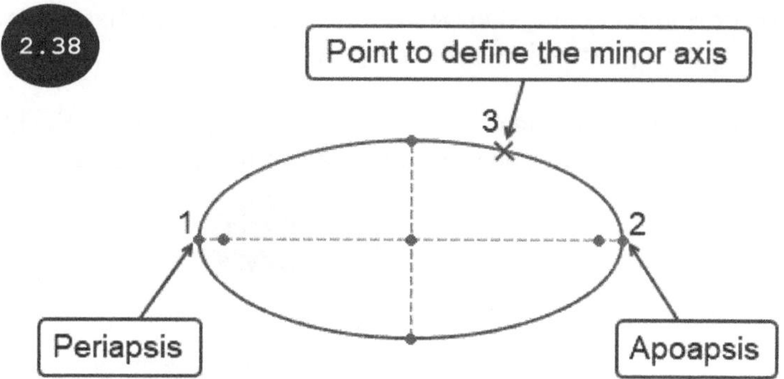

Drawing a B-Spline

A B-spline is defined as a curve having a high degree of smoothness and is used for creating free-form features. You can draw a B-spline by specifying two or more control points in the 3D View area. The different tools for drawing a B-spline are available in the **Create B-spline** menu of the **Sketcher geometries** toolbar (see Figure 2.39) and the same are discussed next.

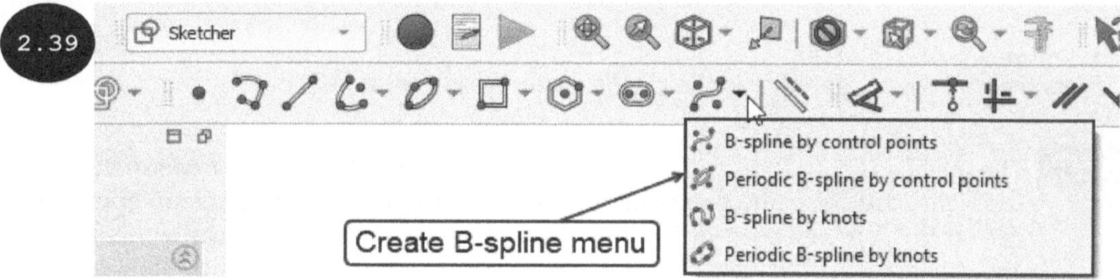

B-spline by control points Tool

The **B-spline by control points** tool is used for drawing a B-spline by specifying two or more control points in the 3D View area by clicking the left mouse button, see Figure 2.40. This figure shows a B-spline drawn by specifying 4 control points. The method for drawing a B-spline is discussed below:

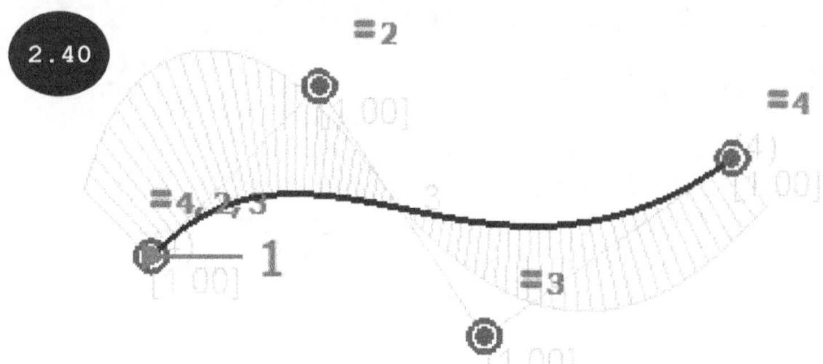

1. Invoke the **Create B-spline** menu and then click on the **B-spline by control points** tool, refer to Figure 2.39.

2. Click to specify control points in the 3D View area one by one. Notice that all the specified control points are connected through straight lines, see Figure 2.41.

3. After specifying the control points, right-click in the 3D View area or press the ESC key. A smooth B-Spline is drawn such that it passes near the specified control points, see Figure 2.42.

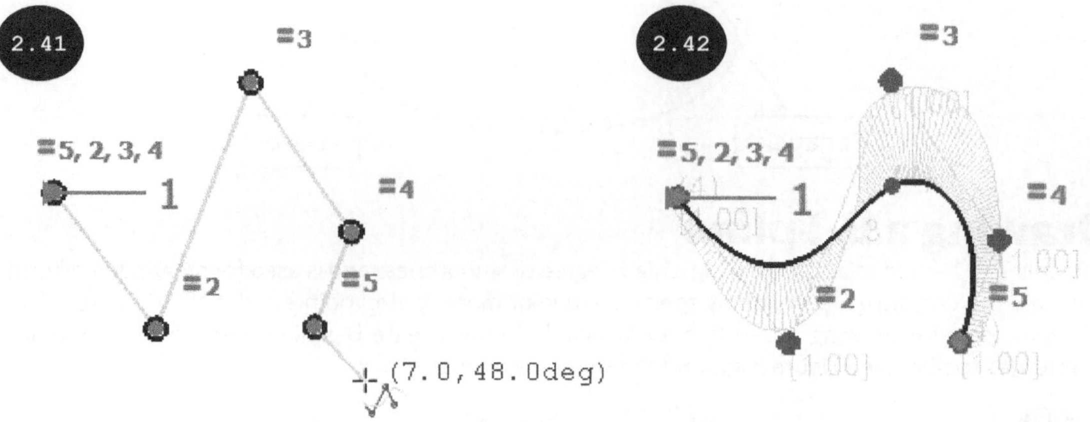

4. Press the ESC key or right-click in the 3D View area again to exit the tool.

Note: The specified control points are connected through control polygons (green straight lines), see Figure 2.41. Also, the green number (digit) at the center of the spline represents its degree. In Figure 2.42, the 3-digit number is displayed at the center of the spline as its degree. You can increase or decrease the degree of a spline. To do this, select the spline in the 3D View area and then click on the **Increases B-spline degree** or **Decreases B-spline degree** tool in the **Sketcher B-spline tools** toolbar, respectively, see Figure 2.43.

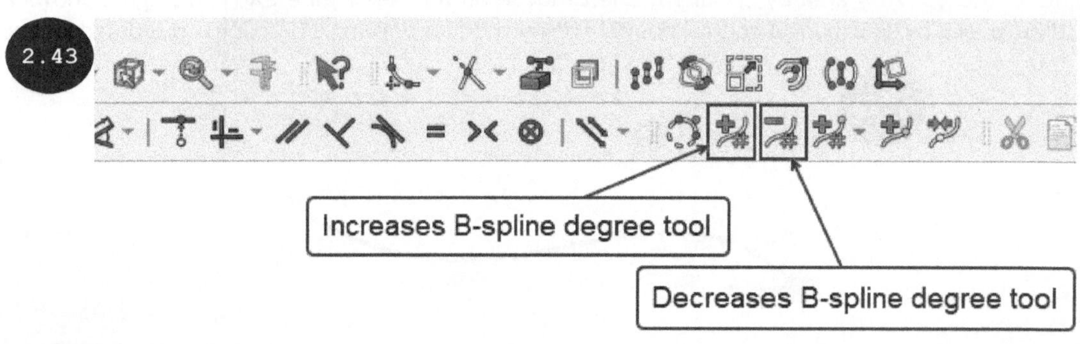

Tip: You can edit or modify a spline by dragging its control points in the 3D View area.

Periodic B-spline by control points Tool

The **Periodic B-spline by control points** tool is used for drawing a closed (periodic) B-spline by specifying three or more control points in the 3D View area, see Figure 2.44. The method for creating a closed B-spline is discussed below:

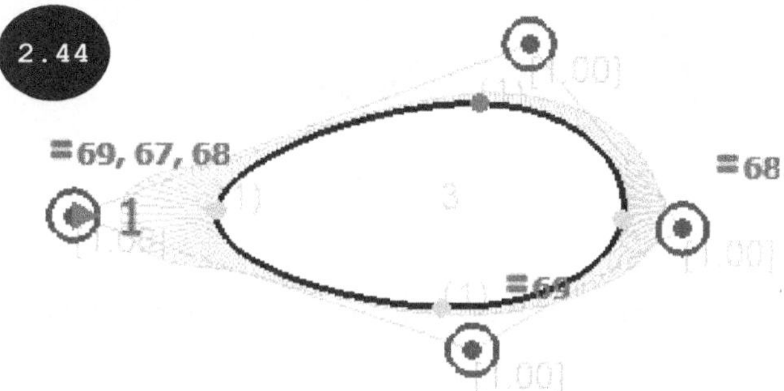

1. Invoke the **Create B-spline** menu and then click on the **Periodic B-spline by control points** tool, see Figure 2.45.

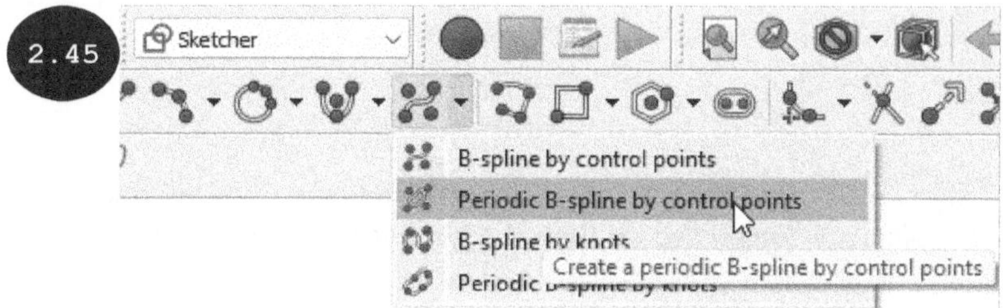

2. Click to specify three or more control points by clicking the left mouse button in the 3D View area. All the specified control points are connected through straight lines in the 3D View area.

3. After specifying the control points, right-click in the 3D View area or press the ESC key. A periodic (closed) B-Spline is drawn such that its end control point coincides or merges with the start control point of the spline, automatically, refer to Figure 2.44. In this figure, a periodic (closed) B-Spline is drawn by specifying 4 control points in the 3D View area.

4. Press the ESC key or right-click in the 3D View area again to exit the tool.

B-spline by Knots Tool

The **B-spline by Knots** tool is used for drawing a B-spline by specifying two or more knots by clicking the left mouse button, in the 3D View area, see Figure 2.46. This figure shows a B-spline drawn by specifying 5 knot points. Note that the knots are the points that pass along the spline to influence its shape. The method for drawing a B-spline by using this tool is discussed below:

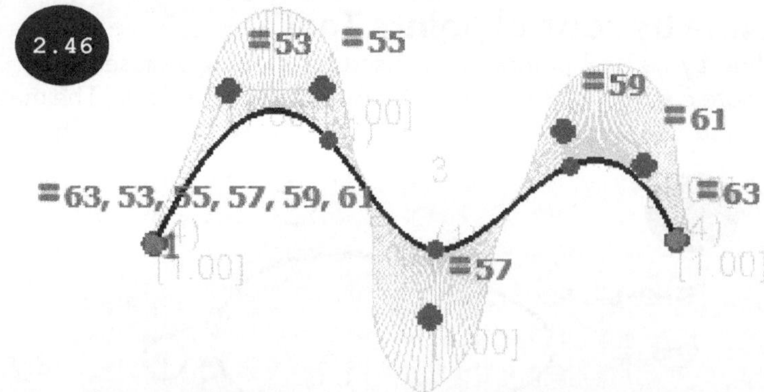

1. Invoke the **Create B-spline** menu and then click on the **B-spline by knots** tool, refer to Figure 2.47.

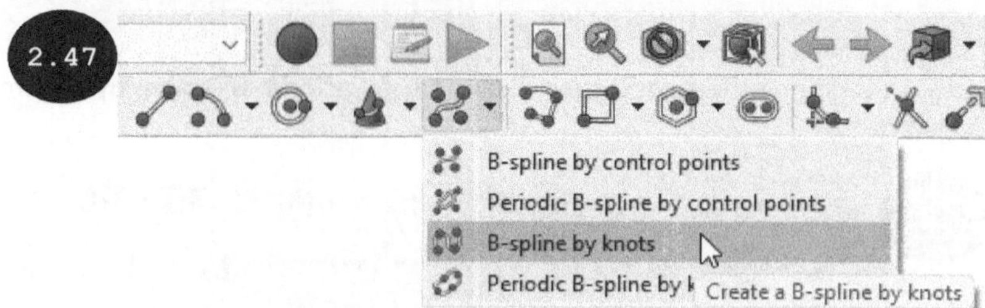

2. Click to specify two or more knot points in the 3D View area one by one. Notice that all the specified knot points are connected through straight lines, see Figure 2.48.

3. After specifying the knot points, right-click in the 3D View area or press the ESC key. A smooth B-Spline is drawn such that it passes through the specified knot points, see Figure 2.49.

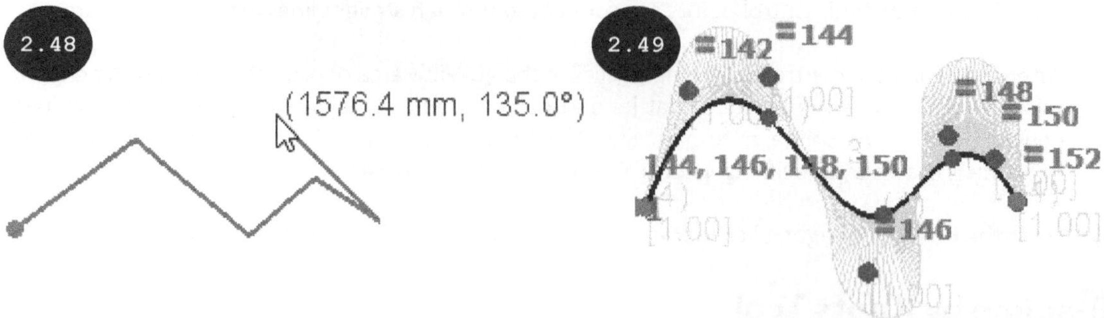

4. Press the ESC key or right-click in the 3D View area again to exit the tool.

Periodic B-spline by Knots Tool

The **Periodic B-spline by Knots** tool is used for drawing a closed (periodic) B-spline by specifying three or more knots in the 3D View area, see Figure 2.50. The method for creating a closed B-spline is discussed below:

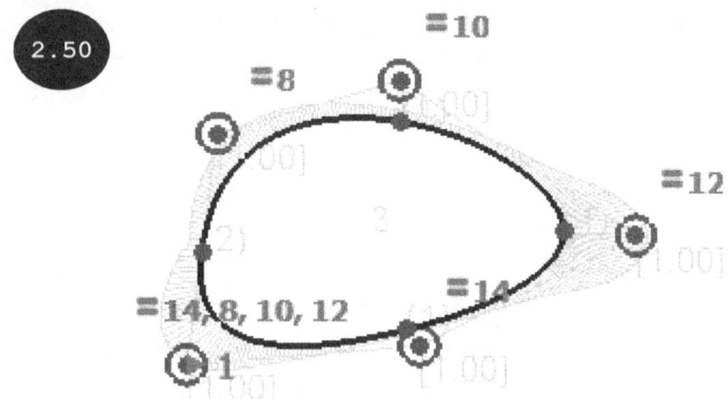

1. Invoke the **Create B-spline** menu and then click on the **Periodic B-spline by Knots** tool, see Figure 2.51.

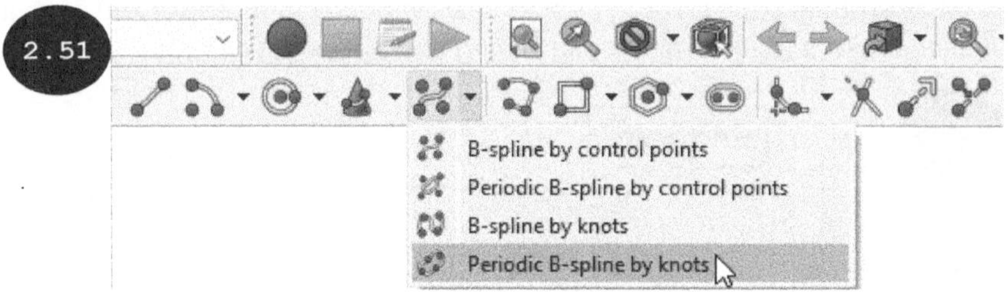

2. Click to specify three or more knot points in the 3D View area. All the specified knots are connected through straight lines in the 3D View area.

3. After specifying the knot points, right-click in the 3D View area or press the ESC key. A periodic (closed) B-Spline is drawn such that its end knot point coincides or merges with the start knot point of the spline, automatically, refer to Figure 2.50. In this figure, a periodic (closed) B-Spline is drawn by specifying 4 knot points in the 3D View area.

4. Press the ESC key or right-click in the 3D View area again to exit the tool.

Drawing a Polyline

A polyline consists of one or more than one line or arc segments, see Figure 2.52. In FreeCAD, you can draw a polyline consisting of a series of perpendicular or tangentially connected lines, arcs, or a combination of line and arc segments. The method for drawing a polyline is discussed below:

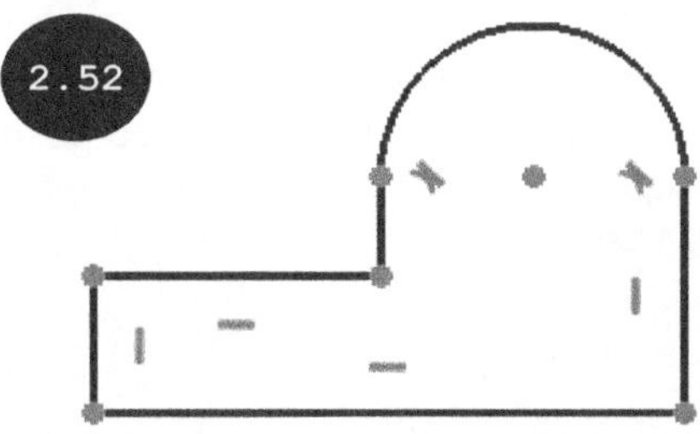

1. Click on the **Create polyline** tool in the **Sketcher geometries** toolbar, see Figure 2.53. The **Create polyline** tool gets activated and the appearance of the cursor changes to cross mark with the display of a red polyline icon. Also, the coordinates of the current location appear near the cursor.

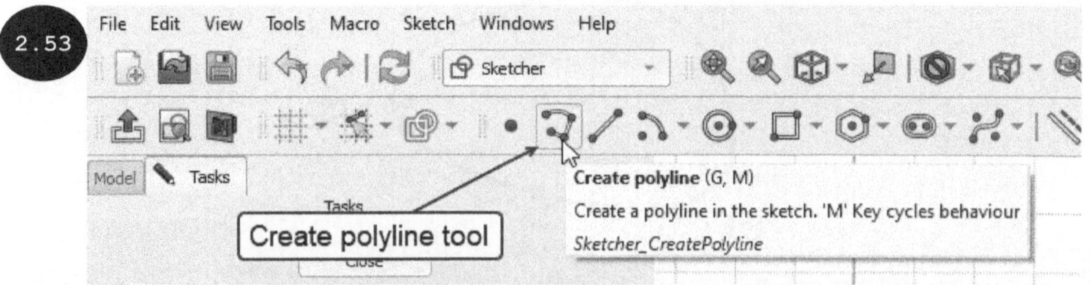

2. Click to specify a start point and then an endpoint of the first line segment of a polyline in the 3D view area. The first line segment of a polyline is drawn between the specified points, see Figure 2.54. Also, a rubber band line segment appears with one of its ends fixed or attached at the last specified endpoint and the other end attached to the cursor, see Figure 2.54.

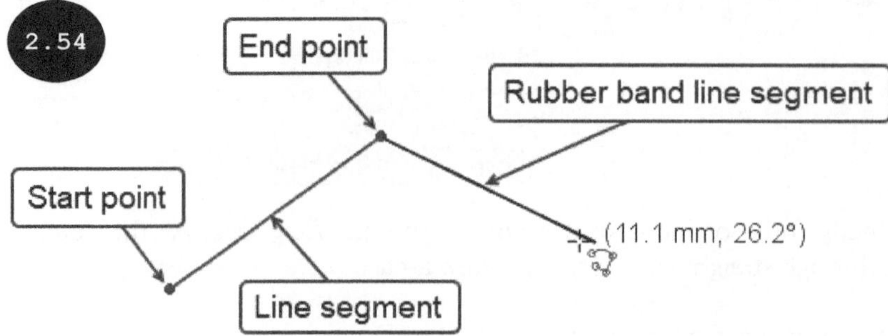

Note that the first segment of a polyline is always a line segment. After creating the first line segment of a polyline, you can create a perpendicular or tangentially connected line or arc segment as the second segment of the polyline. You can cycle through all six different polyline modes (segments) including the default polyline mode by repeatedly pressing the M key in sequential order, as given below:

i. The default polyline mode is a line segment that is connected to its previous segment.
ii. The first polyline mode is a line segment that is perpendicular to its previous segment.
iii. The second polyline mode is a line segment that is tangent to its previous segment.
iv. The third polyline mode is an arc segment that is tangent to its previous polyline segment.
v. The fourth polyline mode is an arc segment that is normal to the left of its previous segment.
vi. The fifth polyline mode is an arc segment that is normal to the right of its previous segment.

3. After creating the first line segment of a polyline, press the **M** key to invoke the required polyline mode, see Figure 2.55. This figure shows an arc mode invoked as the second polyline segment which is tangent to its previous segment. As discussed earlier, you can cycle through six different polyline modes by pressing the M key.

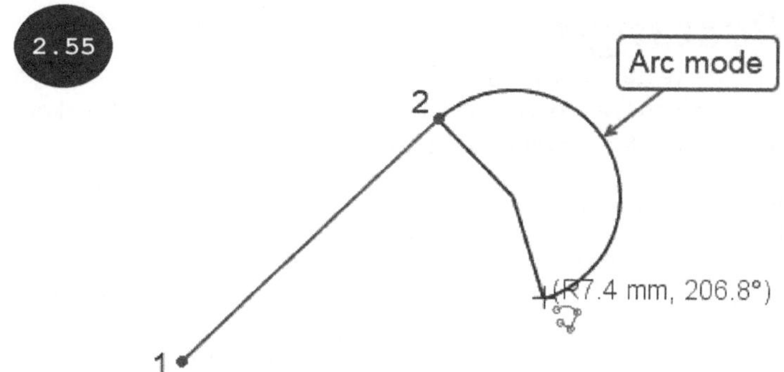

4. Click the left mouse button in the 3D View area to create the respective second polyline segment, see Figure 2.56. In this figure, a tangent arc segment is created as the second segment.

5. After creating the second polyline segment, press the M key again to invoke the required polyline mode, and then click the left mouse button in the 3D View area to create the respective third polyline segment. Similarly, you can create a polyline with a series of connected lines and arc segments one after another by clicking the left mouse button in the 3D View area. After creating all the segments of a polyline, press the ESC key or right-click in the 3D View area. A polyline with multiple lines and arc segments gets created, see Figure 2.57.

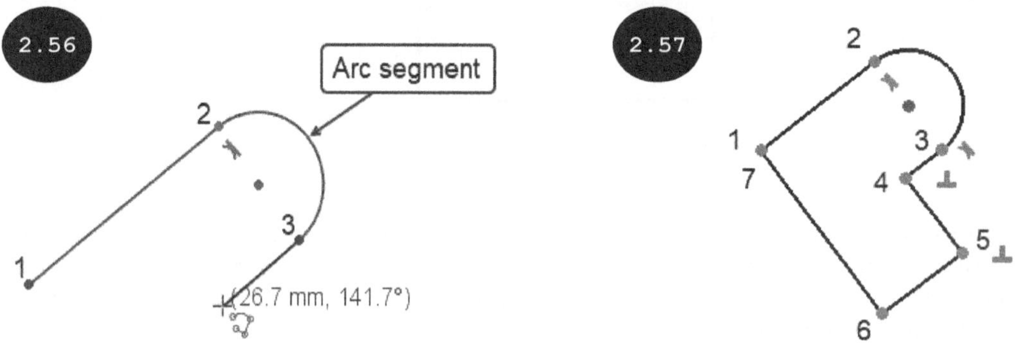

6. Press the ESC key or right-click in the 3D View area to exit the tool.

Tip: To create a closed polyline like the one shown in Figure 2.57, you need to specify the endpoint of the last segment to the start point of the first segment such that both the points get coincident with each other.

Note: As mentioned earlier, some of the figures are numbered for your reference only, refer to Figures 2.55 through 2.57. These numbers represent the sequence of points specified in the 3D View area by clicking the left mouse button.

Drawing a Rectangle

In FreeCAD, you can draw a rectangle by using the **Rectangle**, **Centered rectangle**, and **Rounded rectangle** tools. You can access these tools in the **Create rectangle** menu of the **Sketcher geometries** toolbar, see Figure 2.58. The tools for drawing a rectangle are discussed next.

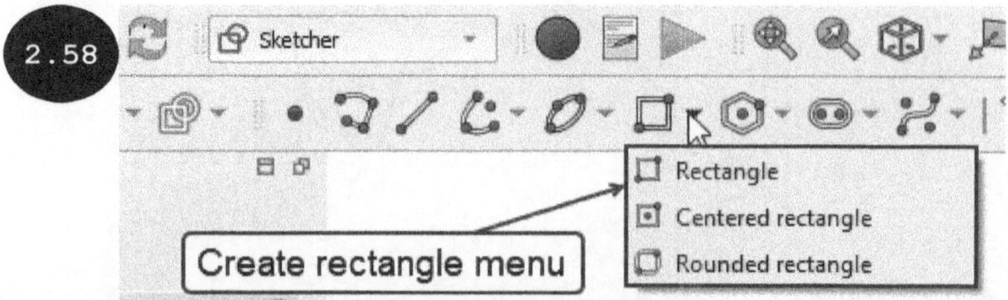

Rectangle Tool

The **Rectangle** tool is used for drawing a rectangle by specifying its two diagonally opposite corners in the 3D View, see Figure 2.59. The method for creating a rectangle by using this tool is discussed below:

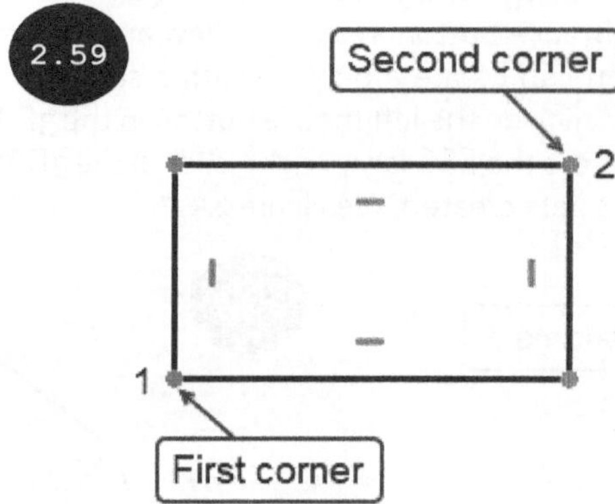

1. Invoke the **Create rectangle** menu in the **Sketcher geometries** toolbar and then click on the **Rectangle** tool, refer to Figure 2.58. The **Rectangle** tool gets activated and the appearance of the cursor changes to a cross mark with the display of a red rectangle icon. Also, the coordinates of the current location appear near the cursor.

2. Click to specify two diagonally opposite corners of a rectangle one by one in the 3D View area, refer to Figure 2.59. Note that the first corner defines the position of the rectangle, and the second corner defines its length and width.

3. After creating a rectangle, the **Rectangle** tool remains active. Press the ESC key or right-click in the 3D View area to exit the tool.

Centered rectangle Tool

The **Centered rectangle** tool is used for drawing a rectangle by specifying its center and a corner point in the 3D View, see Figure 2.60. The method for creating a rectangle by using this tool is discussed below:

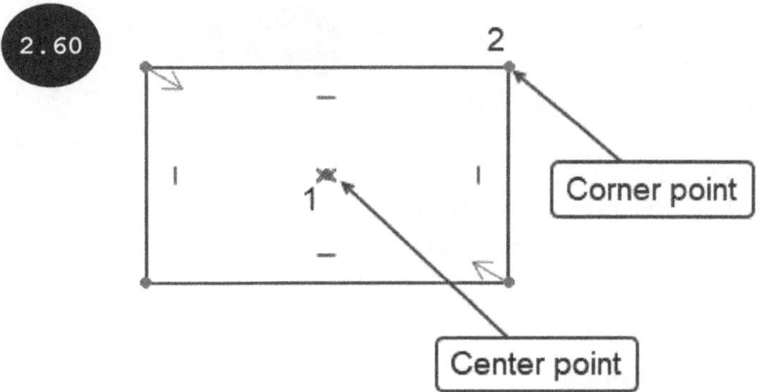

1. Invoke the **Create rectangle** menu in the **Sketcher geometries** toolbar and then click on the **Centered rectangle** tool, refer to Figure 2.61.

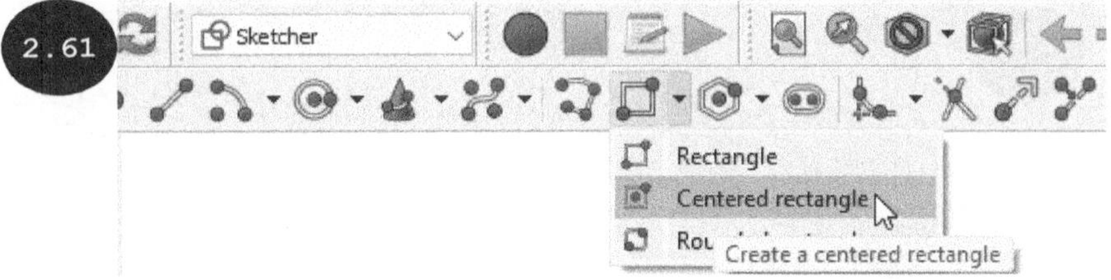

2. Click to specify the center point and then a corner of a rectangle in the 3D View area, refer to Figure 2.60. A rectangle gets drawn. Next, right-click to exit the tool.

Rounded rectangle Tool

The **Rounded rectangle** tool is used for drawing a rectangle with filleted or rounded corners by specifying its two diagonally opposite corners, see Figure 2.62. The method for drawing a rectangle with rounded corners is discussed below:

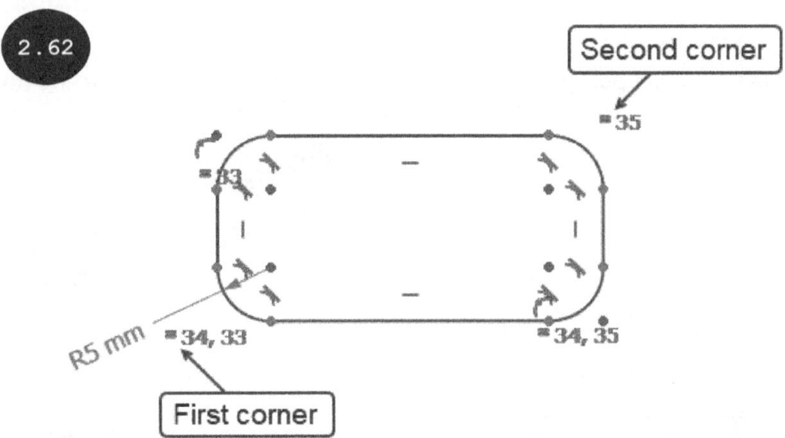

1. Invoke the **Create rectangle** menu in the **Sketcher geometries** toolbar and then click on the **Rounded rectangle** tool, refer to Figure 2.63.

2. Click to specify two diagonally opposite corners of a rectangle one by one in the 3D View area, refer to Figure 2.62. A rectangle with rounded corners is created. Next, right-click to exit the tool.

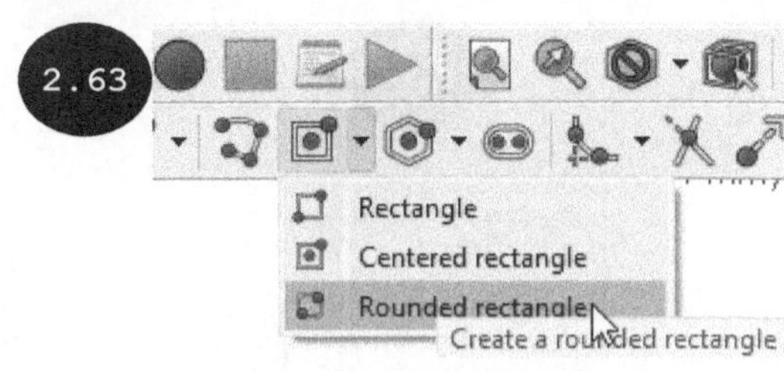

Drawing Polygons

In FreeCAD, you can draw different types of polygons such as triangular, square, pentagon, hexagon, heptagon, etc. by using their respective tools available in the **Create regular polygon** menu of the **Sketcher geometries** toolbar, see Figure 2.64. The tools for drawing polygons are discussed next.

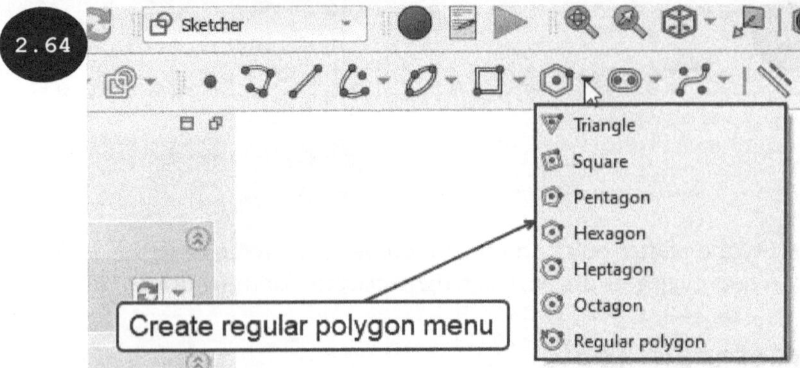

Triangle Tool

The **Triangle** tool is used for drawing an equilateral triangle by specifying its center and a corner, inside an imaginary construction circle, see Figure 2.65. The method for drawing an equilateral triangle is discussed below:

1. Invoke the **Create regular polygon** menu in the **Sketcher geometries** toolbar and then click on the **Triangle** tool, see Figure 2.66. The **Triangle** tool gets activated.

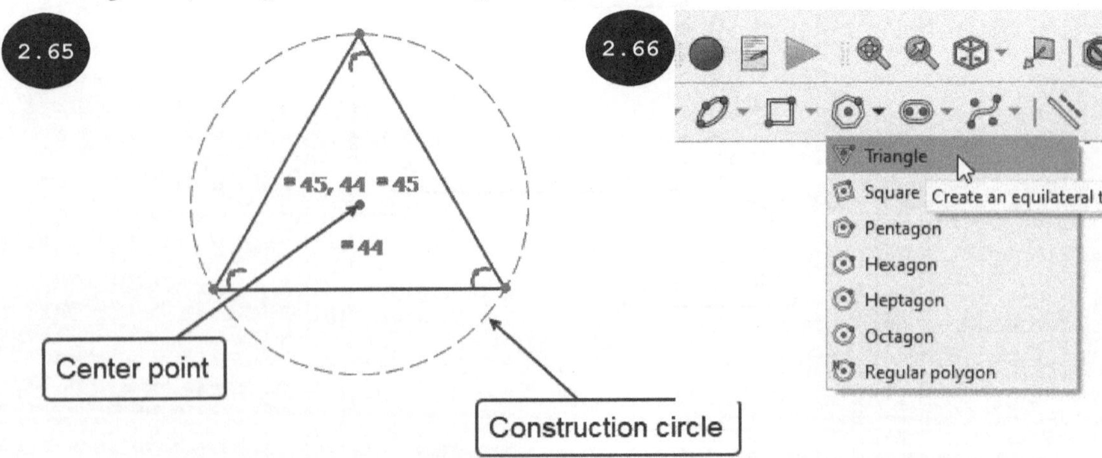

2. Click to specify the center point of a triangle or an imaginary construction circle in the 3D View area, refer to Figure 2.65. The center point is defined and as you move the cursor, the preview of an equilateral triangle appears such that one of its vertices is attached to the cursor.

3. Click to define the position of one of the vertices of the triangle in the 3D View area. An equilateral triangle is drawn inside an imaginary construction circle such that its vertices touch the construction circle, refer to Figure 2.65. Next, press the ESC key or right-click to exit the tool.

Note: The construction entities of a sketch are visible only while creating or editing the sketch in the **Sketcher** workbench.

Square Tool

The **Square** tool is used for drawing a square which is a four-sided polygon by specifying its center and a corner, inside an imaginary construction circle, see Figure 2.67. The method for drawing a square is discussed below:

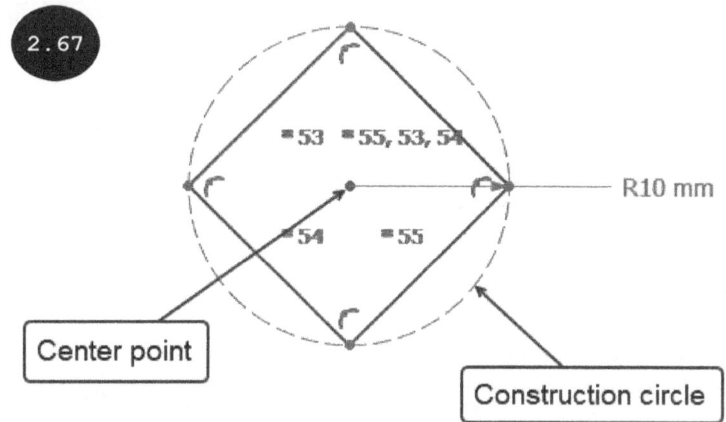

1. Invoke the **Create regular polygon** menu in the **Sketcher geometries** toolbar and then click on the **Square** tool, see Figure 2.68. The **Square** tool gets activated.

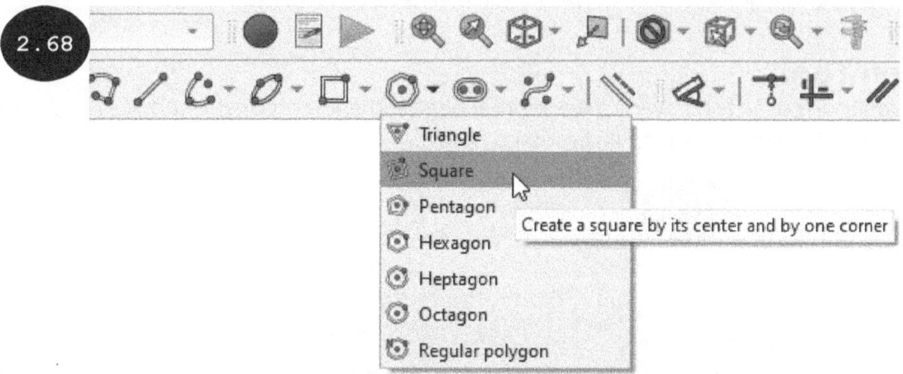

2. Click to specify the center point of a square in the 3D View area. The center point is defined and as you move the cursor, the preview of a square appears such that one of its vertices is attached to the cursor.

3. Click to define the position of one of the vertices of the square in the 3D View area. A square is drawn inside an imaginary construction circle such that its vertices touch the construction circle, refer to Figure 2.67. Next, press the ESC key or right-click in the 3D View area to exit the tool.

Pentagon Tool

The **Pentagon** tool is used for drawing a pentagon, inside an imaginary construction circle, see Figure 2.69. The method for drawing a pentagon is discussed below:

1. Invoke the **Create regular polygon** menu in the **Sketcher geometries** toolbar and then click on the **Pentagon** tool, see Figure 2.70. The **Pentagon** tool gets activated.

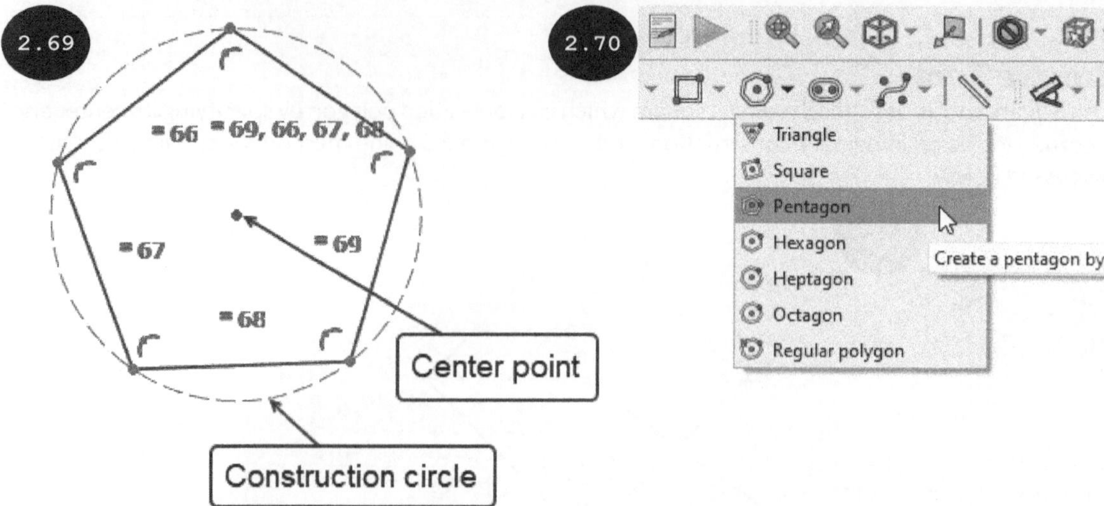

2. Click to specify the center point of a pentagon in the 3D View area. The center point is defined, and the preview of a pentagon appears such that one of its vertices is attached to the cursor.

3. Click to define the position of a vertex in the 3D View area. A pentagon is drawn inside an imaginary construction circle such that its vertices touch the construction circle, refer to Figure 2.69. Next, press the ESC key or right-click in the 3D View area to exit the tool.

Hexagon Tool

The **Hexagon** tool is used for drawing a hexagon, inside an imaginary construction circle, see Figure 2.71. The method for drawing a hexagon is discussed below:

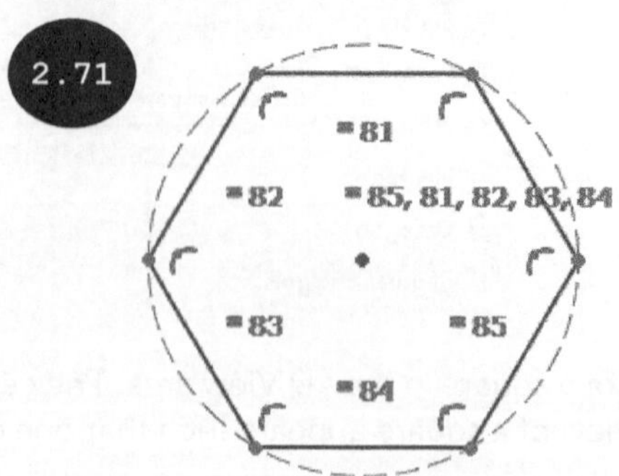

1. Invoke the **Create regular polygon** menu in the **Sketcher geometries** toolbar and then click on the **Hexagon** tool, see Figure 2.72. The **Hexagon** tool gets activated.

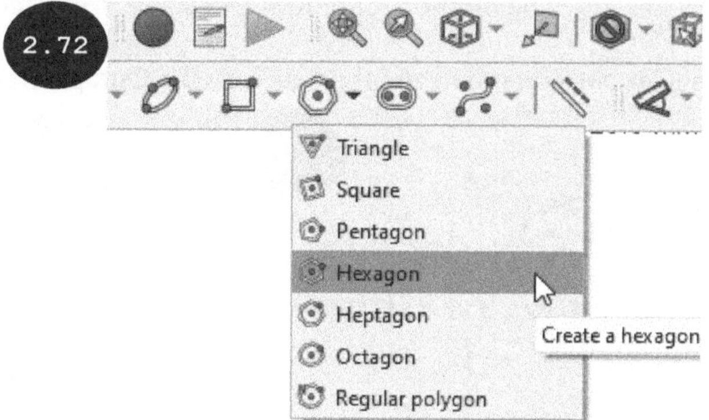

2. Click to specify the center point of a hexagon in the 3D View area. The center point is defined, and as you move the cursor, the preview of a hexagon appears such that one of its vertices is attached to the cursor.

3. Click to define the position of a vertex in the 3D View area. A hexagon is drawn inside an imaginary construction circle such that its vertices touch the construction circle. Next, press the ESC key or right-click in the 3D View area to exit the tool.

Heptagon Tool

The **Heptagon** tool is used for drawing a heptagon which is a seven-sided polygon, inside an imaginary construction circle, see Figure 2.73. The method for drawing a heptagon is discussed below:

1. Invoke the **Create regular polygon** menu and then click on the **Heptagon** tool, see Figure 2.74.

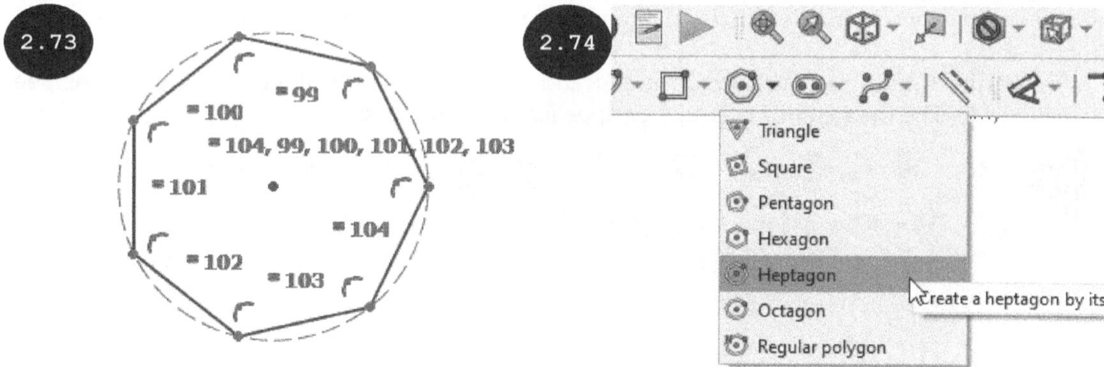

2. Click to specify the center point of a heptagon in the 3D View area. The center point is defined, and the preview of a heptagon appears such that one of its vertices is attached to the cursor.

3. Click to define the position of a vertex in the 3D View area. A heptagon is drawn inside an imaginary construction circle such that its vertices touch the construction circle. Next, press the ESC key or right-click in the 3D View area to exit the tool.

Octagon Tool

The **Octagon** tool is used for drawing an octagon which is an eight-sided polygon, inside an imaginary construction circle, see Figure 2.75. The method for drawing an octagon is discussed below:

1. Invoke the **Create regular polygon** menu and then click on the **Octagon** tool, see Figure 2.76.

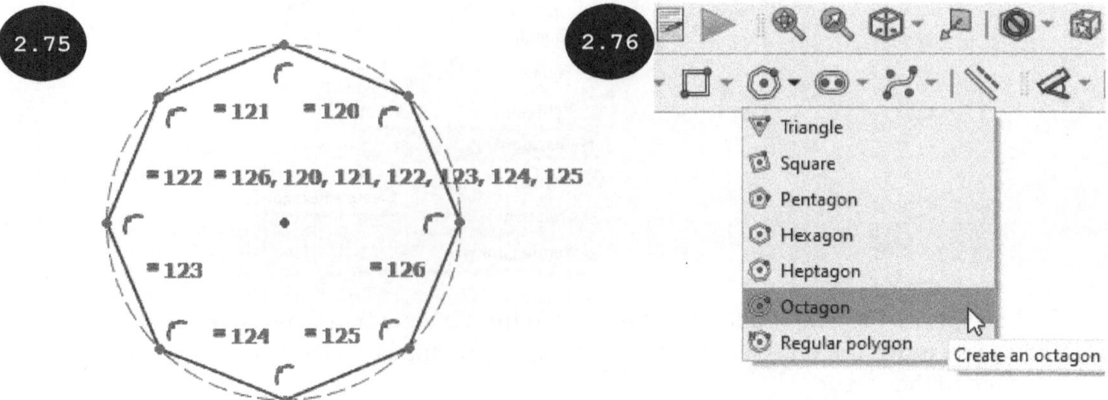

2. Click to specify the center point of an octagon in the 3D View area. The center point is defined, and the preview of an octagon appears such that one of its vertices is attached to the cursor.

3. Click to define the position of a vertex in the 3D View area. An octagon is drawn inside an imaginary construction circle such that its vertices touch the construction circle. Next, press the ESC key or right-click in the 3D View area to exit the tool.

Regular Polygon Tool

The **Regular Polygon** tool is used for drawing a polygon with the number of sides ranging from 3 to 99, inside an imaginary construction circle. The method for drawing a polygon is discussed below:

1. Invoke the **Create regular polygon** menu and then click on the **Regular Polygon** tool, see Figure 2.77. The **Create array** pop-up box appears, see Figure 2.78.

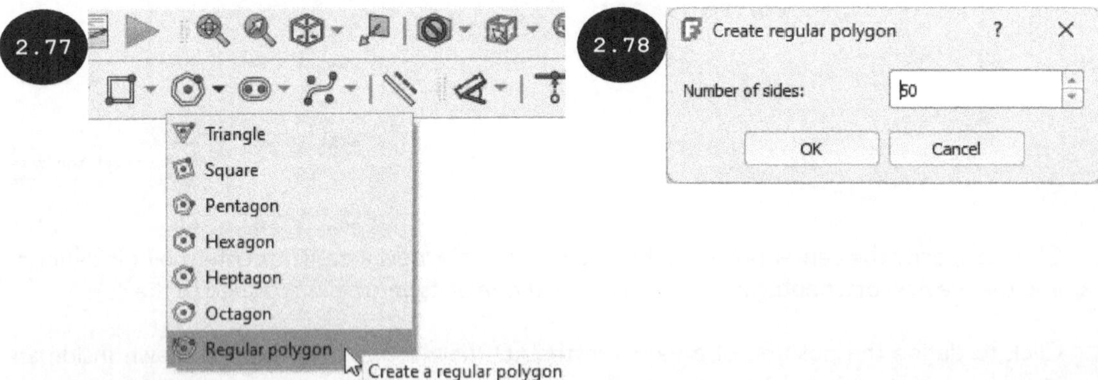

2. Enter the required number of polygon sides to be created in the pop-up box and then click on the **OK** button. Note that you can create a polygon of sides in the range between 3 and 99.

3. Click to specify the center point of a polygon in the 3D View area. The center point is defined and the preview of a polygon with the specified number of sides appears in the 3D View area.

4. Click to define a vertex of a polygon in the 3D View area. A polygon of specified sides is drawn inside an imaginary construction circle. Next, press the ESC key or right-click in the 3D View area to exit the tool.

Drawing a Slot

In FreeCAD, you can draw straight and arc slots using the **Create slot** and **Create arc slot** tools, see Figure 2.79. Both these tools can be accessed from the **Slot** menu and are discussed next.

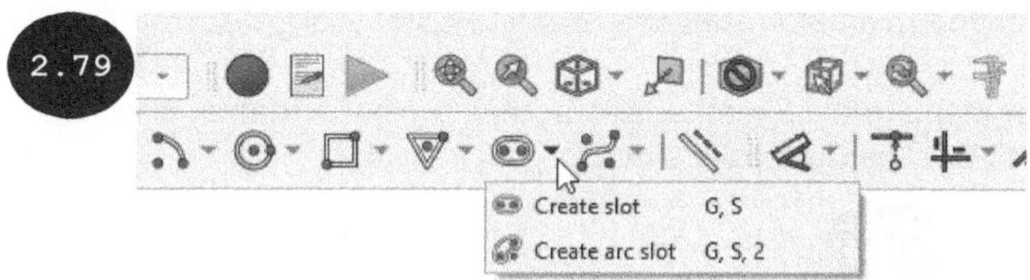

Creating a Straight Slot

In FreeCAD, you can draw a straight slot by specifying the center points of its two semicircles in the 3D View area, see Figure 2.80. The method for drawing a straight slot is discussed below:

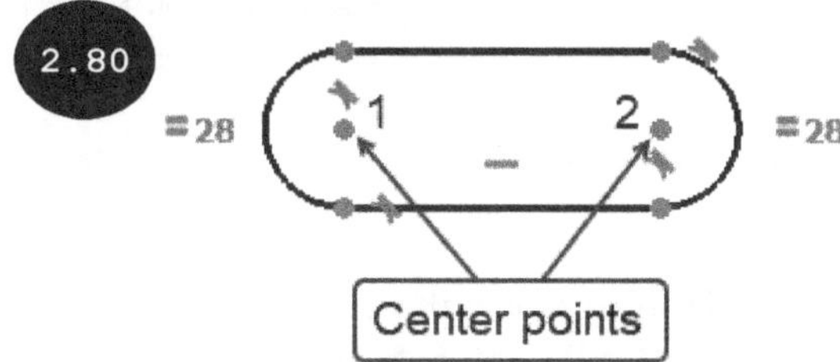

1. Invoke the **Slot** menu and then click on the **Create slot** tool, see Figure 2.81.

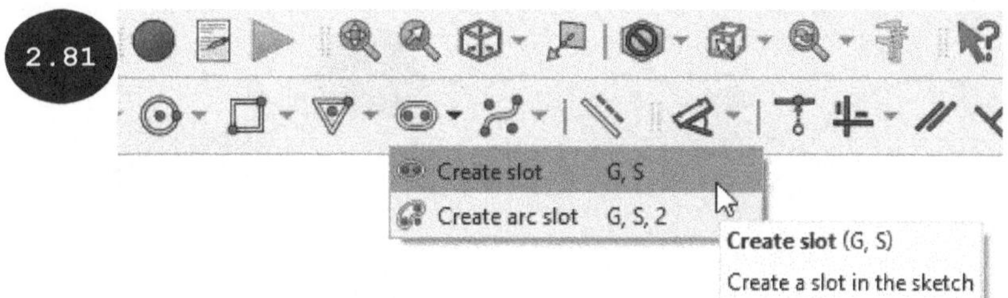

2. Click to specify the center of one of the semi-circles of the slot in the 3D View area. The preview of a straight slot appears such that the center point of its other semicircle is attached to the circle, see Figure 2.82.

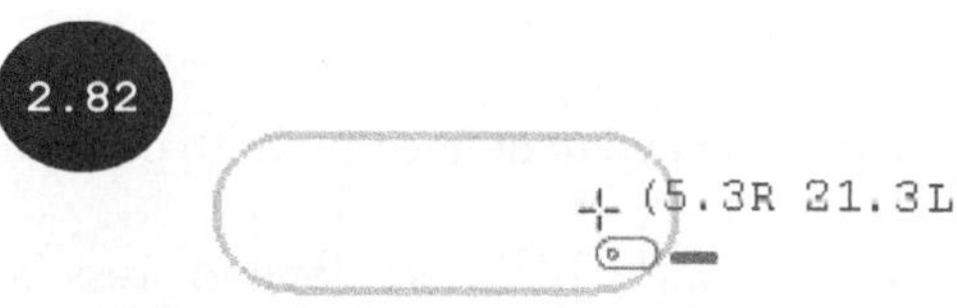

3. Click to specify the center point of the other semicircle of the slot in the 3D View area. A straight slot gets drawn, see Figure 2.83. Next, press the ESC key to exit the tool.

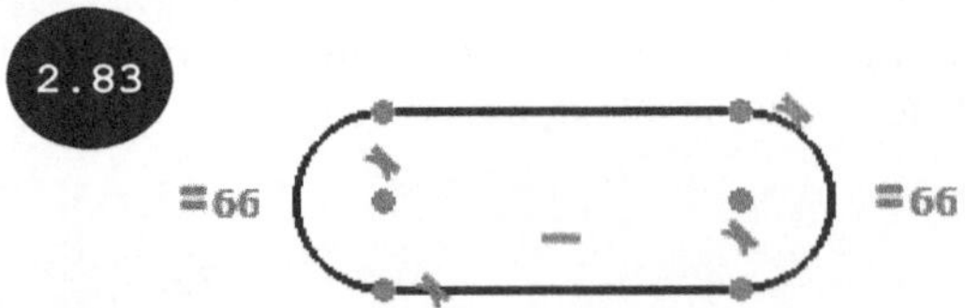

Creating an Arc Slot

The method for creating an arc slot using the **Create arc slot** tool is discussed below:

1. Invoke the **Slot** menu in the **Sketcher geometries** toolbar and then click on the **Create arc slot** tool, see Figure 2.84. The **Create arc slot** tool gets activated.

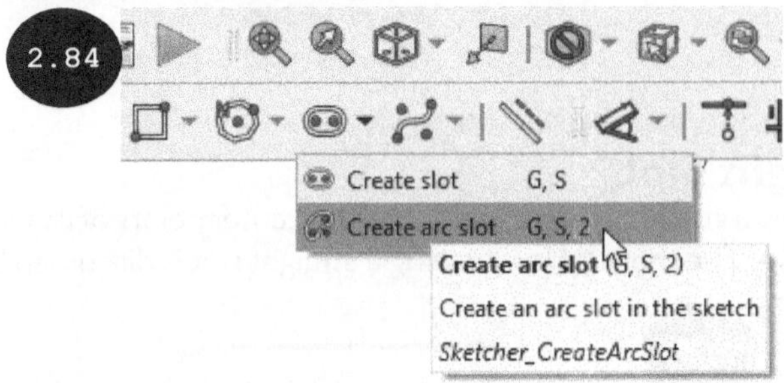

2. Click to specify the center point of the arc slot. A preview of an imaginary circle appears attached to the cursor, see Figure 2.85.

3. Click to define the start point of the arc slot in the 3D View area, which also determines its radius. A preview of the arc slot appears, starting from the specified point.

4. Move the cursor to the desired angle and click to define the end point of the arc slot, see Figure 2.86.

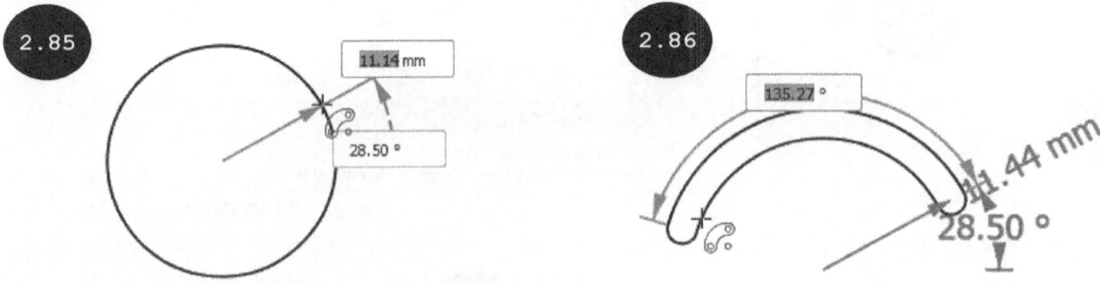

Now, you need to define the width of the arc slot.

5. Enter the width of the arc slot and press ENTER. You can also click in the 3D View area to define the width of the slot, see Figure 2.87. An arc slot is drawn, see figure 2.88.

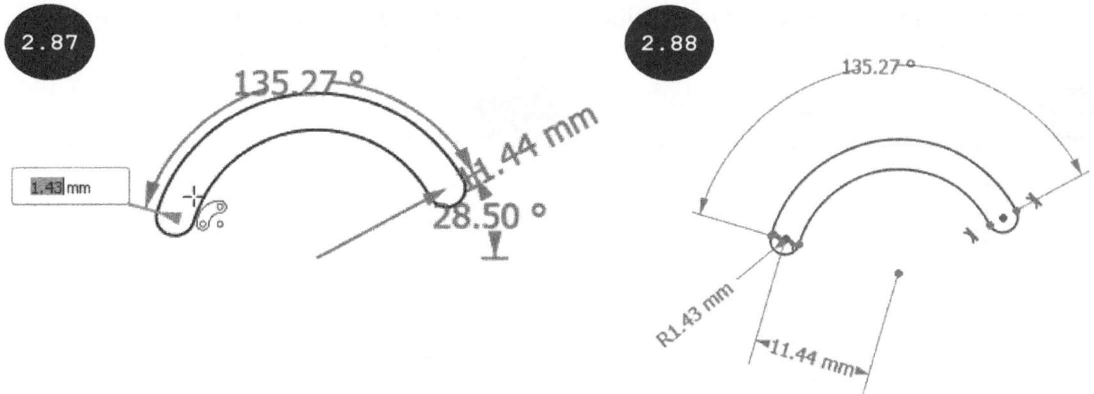

Creating a Fillet

A fillet is created at the intersection of two lines by removing the sharp corner with a tangent arc of constant radius, see Figure 2.89.

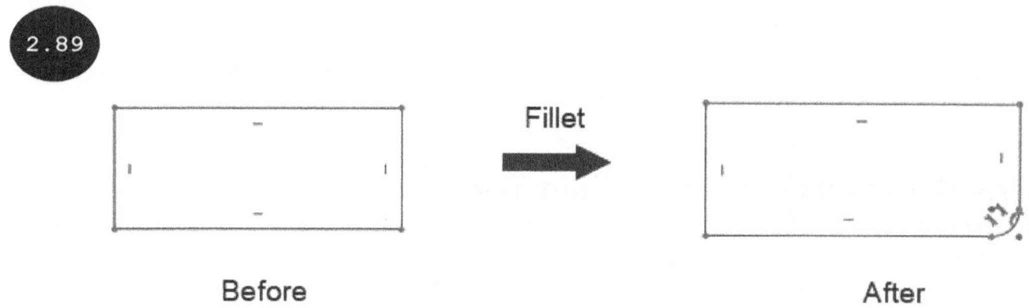

In FreeCAD, you can create a fillet by using the **Sketch fillet** and **Constraint-preserving sketch fillet** tools. You can access both these tools in the **Create fillet** menu of the **Sketcher geometries** toolbar, see Figure 2.90. The tools for creating a fillet are discussed next.

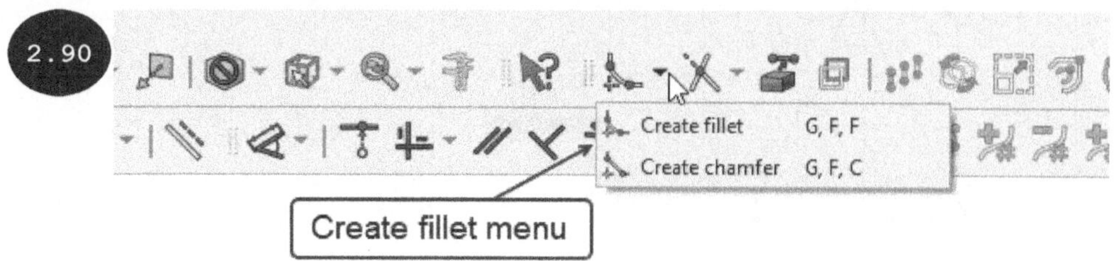

Sketch fillet Tool

The **Sketch fillet** tool is used for creating a fillet between two lines that are joined or intersected at a common point. The method for creating a fillet by using the **Sketch fillet** tool is discussed below:

1. Invoke the **Create fillet** menu in the **Sketcher geometries** toolbar (refer to Figure 2.90) and then click on the **Sketch fillet** tool.

2. Select two joined or intersected line entities one by one in the 3D View area, see Figure 2.91. A fillet of constant radius is created between the selected line entities, see Figure 2.92.

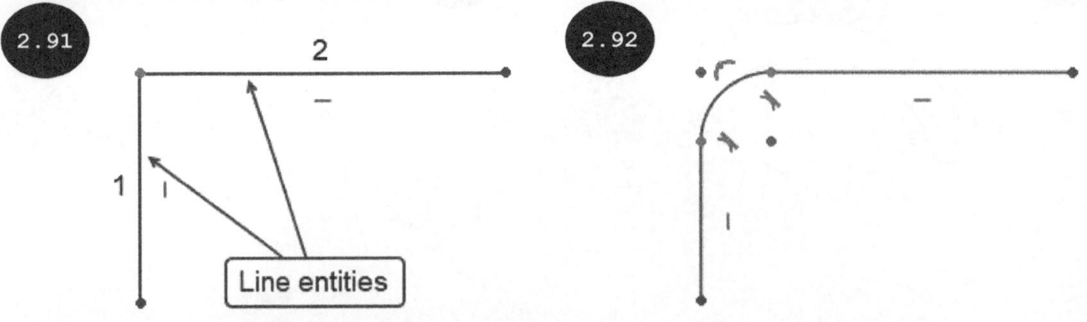

Note: By default, the radius of a fillet is defined based on the distance you click on the first line entity for selecting it from the intersection point with the second line entity. You can control or change the fillet radius by applying the radius dimension. You will learn about applying dimensions later in this chapter.

Tip: Instead of selecting two joined or intersected line entities, you can also select a corner (vertex) created at the intersection of two lines for creating a fillet.

Constraint-preserving sketch fillet Tool

The **Constraint-preserving sketch fillet** tool is used for creating a fillet between two intersecting line entities such that a virtual intersection point is created at the corner to maintain or preserve the already applied constraints and dimensions, see Figure 2.93. The method for creating a fillet by using this tool is the same as discussed earlier by using the **Sketch fillet** tool.

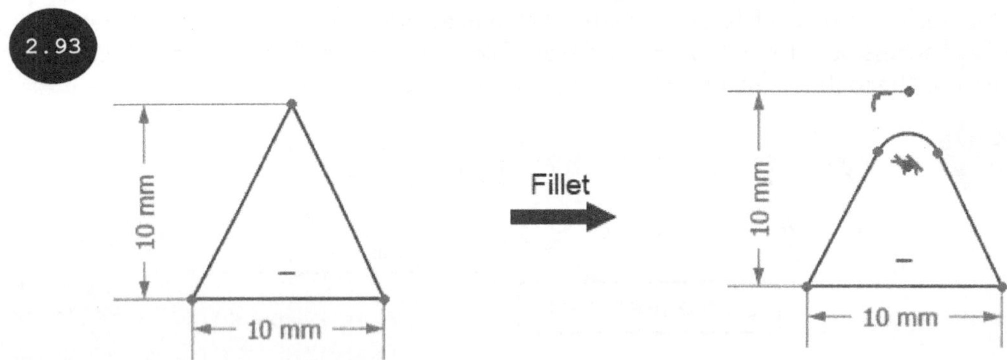

Trimming, Extending, or Splitting Sketch Entities

In FreeCAD, you can trim, extend, and split sketch entities such as lines, circles, and arcs using the respective tools in the **Trim** menu, see Figure 2.94. The methods for performing these operations are discussed next.

Trimming Sketch Entities

1. Invoke the **Trim** menu and then click on the **Trim edge** tool, see Figure 2.95. The **Trim edge** tool gets activated and the appearance of the cursor changes to a cross mark with the display of a red trim icon.

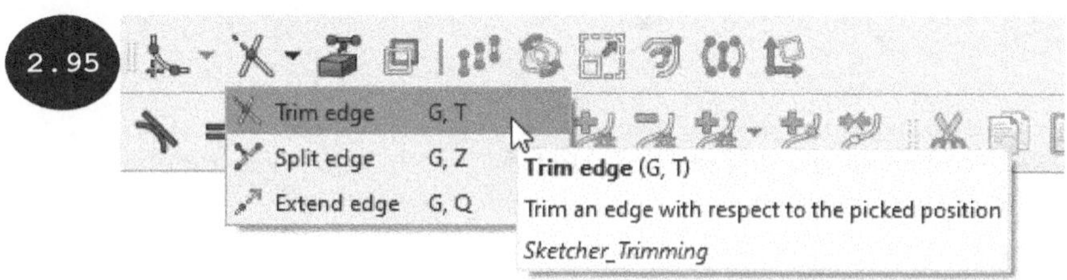

2. Click on a portion of a sketch entity (line, circle, or arc) to be trimmed, see Figure 2.96. The selected portion of the entity gets trimmed from its nearest intersection with the other entity, see Figure 2.97. Also, the **Trim edge** tool remains activated, and you can continue trimming unwanted portions of other sketch entities to their nearest intersection by clicking the left mouse button.

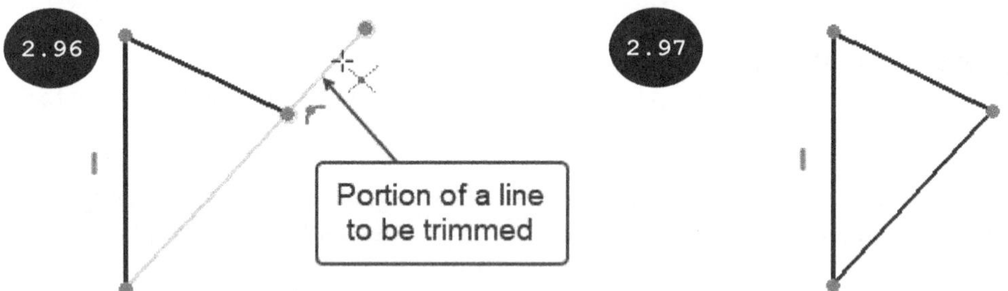

3. After trimming the sketch entities, press the ESC key or right-click to exit the tool.

Split edge Splitting Sketch Entities

You can split a sketch entity into two or more segments using the **Split** tool. The method for splitting a sketch entity is discussed below:

1. Invoke the **Trim** menu, then click on the **Split edge** tool, see Figure 2.98. The **Split edge** tool gets activated.

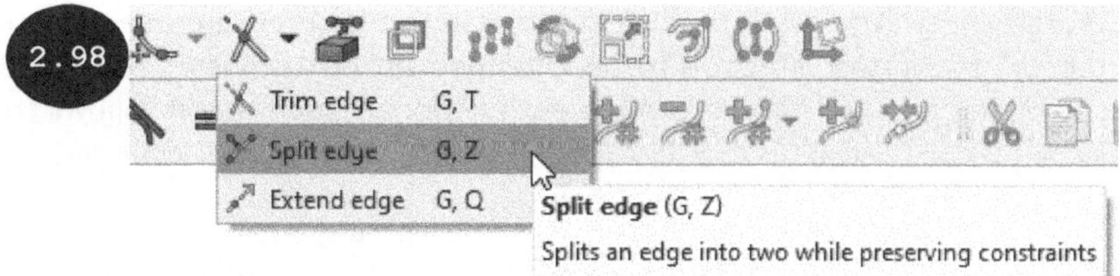

2. Click to define a split point on a sketch entity, see Figure 2.99. The selected entity gets divided into two segments at the specified split point, see Figure 2.100.

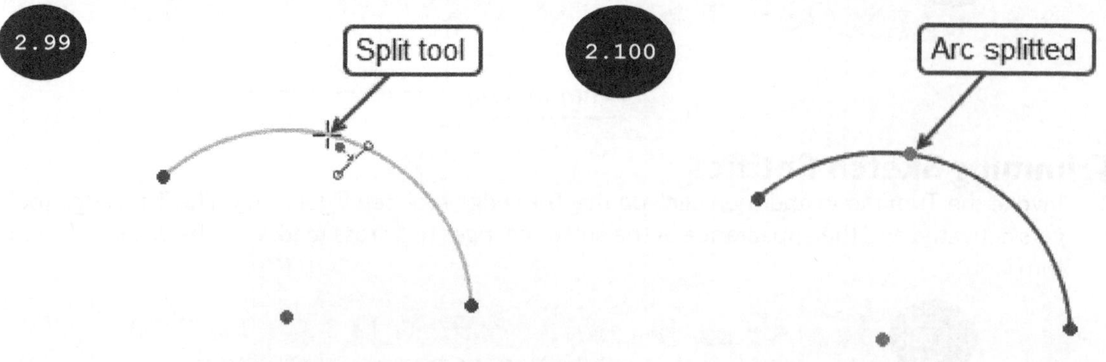

Tip: If the selected entity is a closed curve, such as a circle, you need to define two split points to divide it into two segements.

3. Similarly, you can continue defining split points to divide the entity into multiple segments.

4. After splitting an entity into one or more segments, press the ESC key or right-click to exit the tool.

Extending Sketch Entities

In FreeCAD, you can extend sketch entities up to the nearest intersection using the **Extend edge** tool. The method for extending a sketch entity is discussed below:

1. Invoke the **Trim** menu, then click on the **Extend edge** tool, see Figure 2.101. The **Extend edge** tool gets activated and the appearance of the cursor changes to a cross mark with the display of a red extend icon.

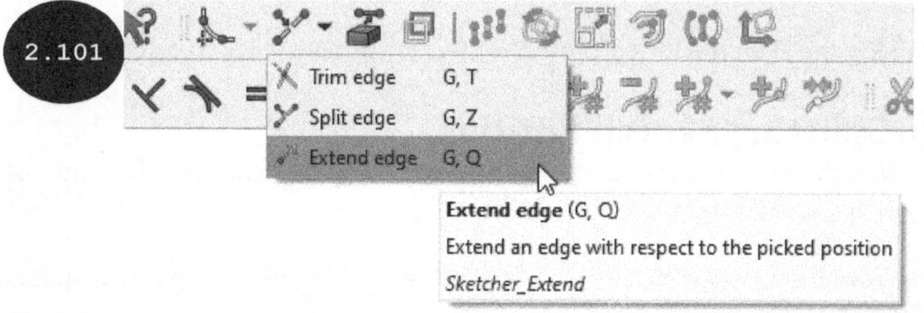

2. Click on a sketch entity (line or arc) to be extended in the 3D View area, see Figure 2.102. Next, move the cursor toward the direction to be extended in the 3D View area. Note that as you move the cursor, the preview of an extended entity appears such that it follows the cursor, see Figure 2.103.

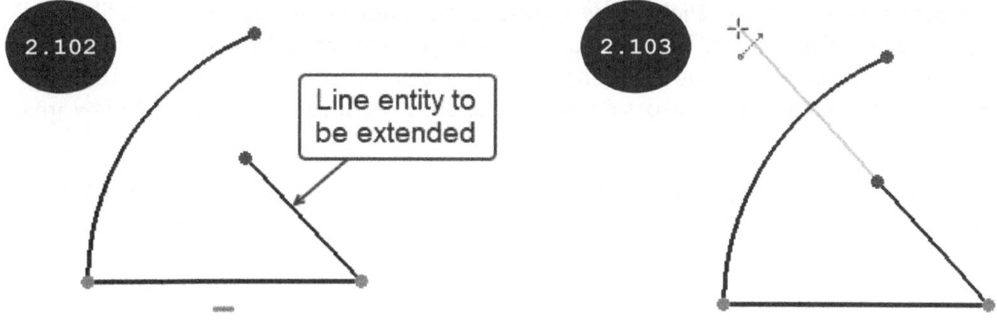

3. Click anywhere in the 3D View area as the endpoint of the resultant extended entity. The selected entity gets extended up to the specified endpoint in the 3D View area, see Figure 2.104.

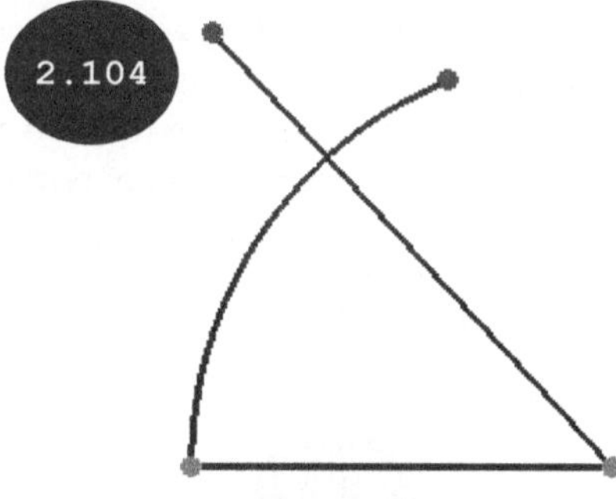

Note: In FreeCAD, you can also extend the selected sketch entity up to another intersecting sketch entity in the 3D View area. To do this, after selecting an entity (line or arc) to be extended, move the cursor over another entity (a line, an arc, an ellipse, an elliptical arc, or a point) up to which you want to extend the selected entity and then click the left mouse button when it gets highlighted. The selected entity gets extended up to the selected sketch entity in the 3D View area.

Creating Construction Sketch Entities

In FreeCAD, you can toggle the creation of solid sketch entities to the construction sketch entities and vice-versa by using the **Toggle construction geometry** tool, see Figure 2.105. By default, this tool is deactivated in the **Sketcher geometries** toolbar. As a result, you can create solid sketch entities by using the sketching tools available in the **Sketcher geometries** toolbar.

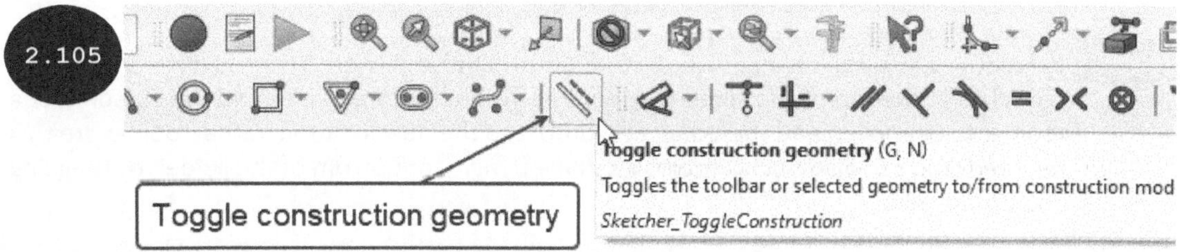

To create construction sketch entities, click on the **Toggle construction geometry** tool in the **Sketcher geometries** toolbar, refer to Figure 2.105. The construction mode gets activated. Now, the sketch entities you create in the drawing area by using the sketching tools will act as construction entities and can only be used as references. Note that the construction entities are shown in blue color in the 3D View area.

Note: The **Toggle construction geometry** tool is a toggle tool. As a result, for creating regular solid sketch entities, you need to click on this tool again to deactivate the construction mode.

Applying Geometric Constraints

Geometric constraints are used to restrict or limit some degrees of freedom of a sketch entity. You can apply a geometric constraint on a sketch entity, between sketch entities, or between a sketch point and the origin. Some of the geometric constraints such as horizontal, vertical, and coincident are applied automatically while drawing sketch entities. For example, while drawing a line, if you move the cursor horizontally toward left or right, an icon of horizontal constraint appears near the cursor, see Figure 2.106. This indicates that if you now specify the endpoint of the line, the horizontal constraint will be applied to the line and the movement of the line will be locked or restricted along the horizontal axis. Likewise, if you move the cursor vertically upward or downward, an icon of vertical constraint appears near the cursor, see Figure 2.107. This indicates that if you now specify the endpoint of the line, the vertical constraint will be applied to the line, and the movement of the line will be locked or restricted along the vertical axis.

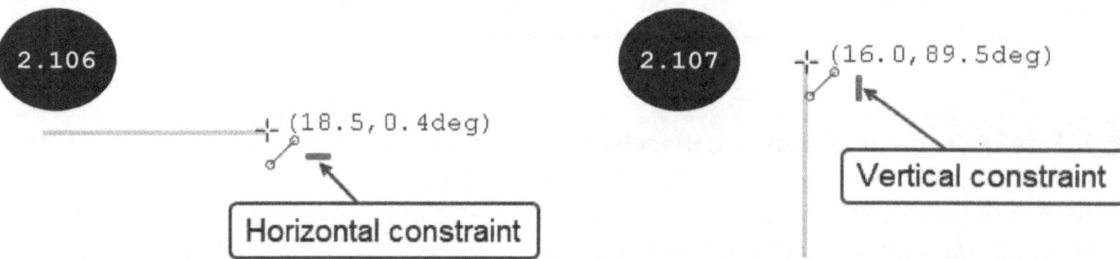

In FreeCAD, you can apply geometric constraints by using the constraints tools available in the **Sketcher constraints** toolbar, see Figure 2.108. The various types of geometric constraints are discussed next.

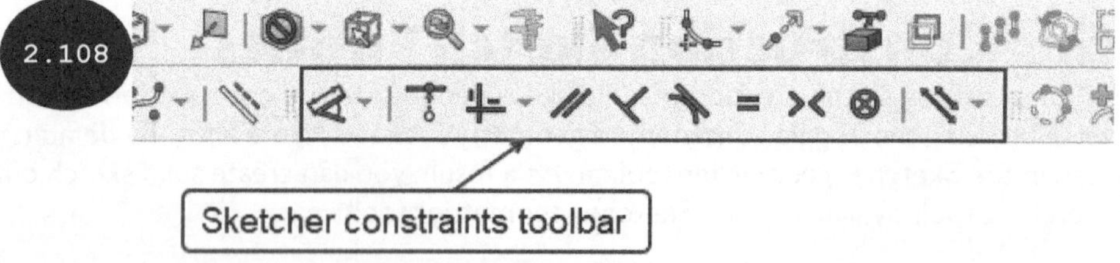

Note: In FreeCAD, you can change the position of a toolbar anywhere in the Toolbar area, which is docked at the top of the screen, by default. To do this, press and hold the cursor over a toolbar to be moved and then drag and drop it to the new location in the Toolbar area, as required. You can also dock a toolbar to the left, right, or bottom of the screen by dragging and dropping it.

Coincident Constraint

A coincident constraint is used for making two sketch points or a sketch point and the origin coincident with each other. To do this, click on the **Constrain coincident** tool in the **Sketcher constraints** toolbar (see Figure 2.109) or press the C key. The **Constrain coincident** tool gets activated and the appearance of the cursor changes to a cross mark with the display of a red coincident constraint icon.

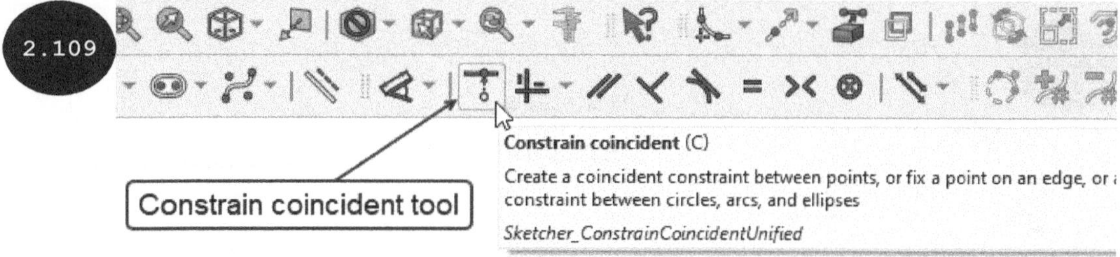

After activating the **Constrain coincident** tool, select two sketch points one by one in the 3D View area, see Figure 2.110. The coincident constraint gets applied, and the selected points become coincident with each other.

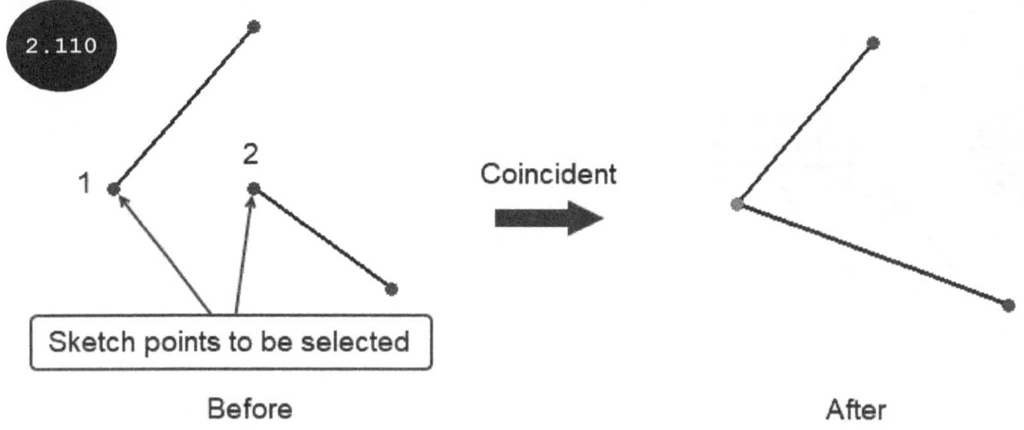

Vertical Constraint

A vertical constraint is used for changing the orientation of a line entity to vertical and forcing it to remain vertical. To do this, click on the **Constrain vertically** tool in the **Sketcher constraints** toolbar or press the V key and then select a line entity in the 3D View area. The vertical constraint gets applied and the orientation of the selected line changes to vertical, see Figure 2.111.

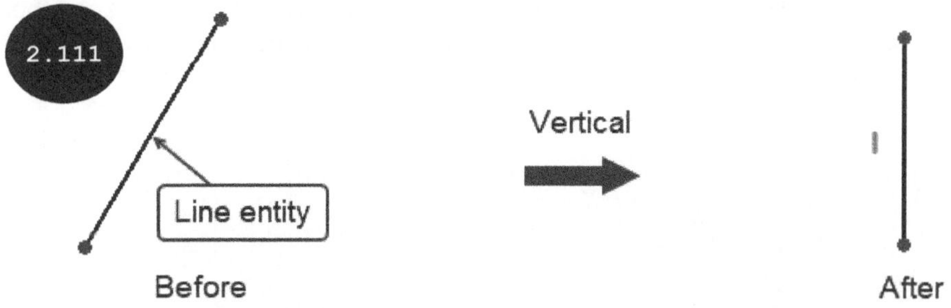

Horizontal Constraint

A horizontal constraint is used for changing the orientation of a line entity to horizontal and forcing it to remain horizontal. To do this, click on the **Constrain horizontally** tool in the **Sketcher constraints** toolbar or press the **H** key and then select a line entity. The horizontal constraint gets applied and the orientation of the selected line changes to horizontal, see Figure 2.112.

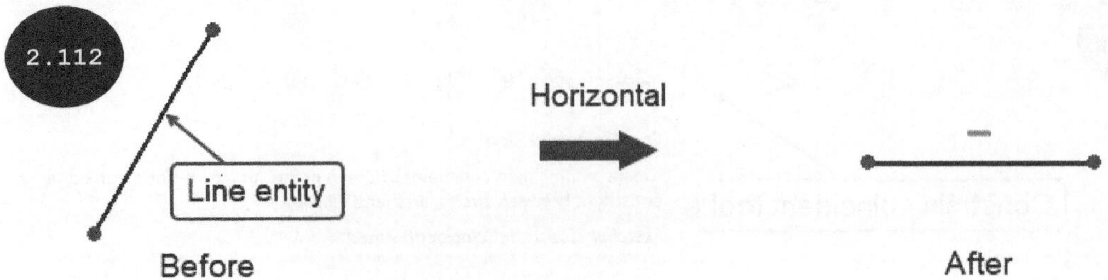

Parallel Constraint

A parallel constraint is used for making two lines parallel to one another. To do this, click on the **Constrain parallel** tool in the **Sketcher constraints** toolbar or press the **P** key. Next, select two lines one by one in the 3D View area. The parallel constraint gets applied, and the selected lines become parallel to each other, see Figure 2.113.

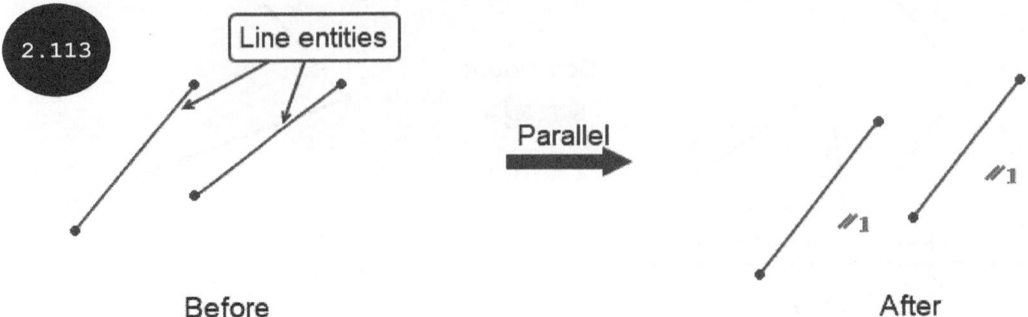

Perpendicular Constraint

A perpendicular constraint is used for making two lines perpendicular to one another. You can also make a line and a circle, an arc, or an ellipse perpendicular at their intersection by using this constraint. To do this, click on the **Constrain perpendicular** tool in the **Sketcher constraints** toolbar or press the **N** key. Next, select two lines or a line and a circle/arc/ellipse one by one in the 3D View area. The perpendicular constraint gets applied, and the selected entities become perpendicular to each other, see Figures 2.114 and 2.115. In Figure 2.114, the perpendicular constraint is applied between two lines. In Figure 2.115, the perpendicular constraint is applied between a line and a circle entity.

2.114

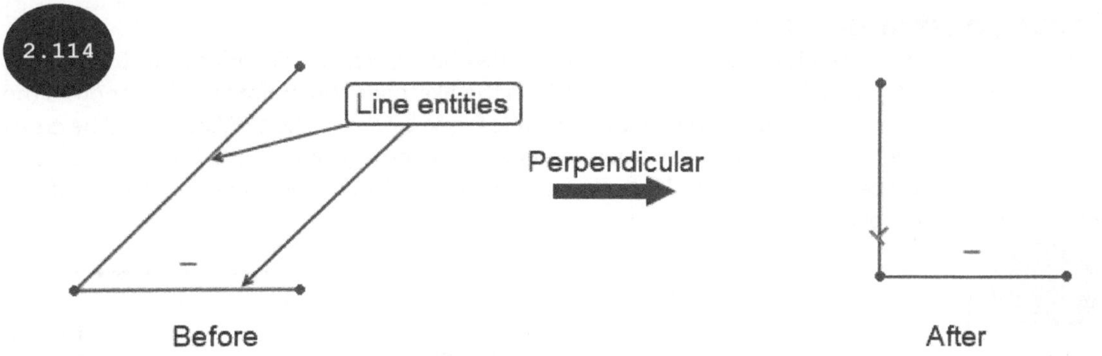

Line entities
Perpendicular
Before
After

2.115

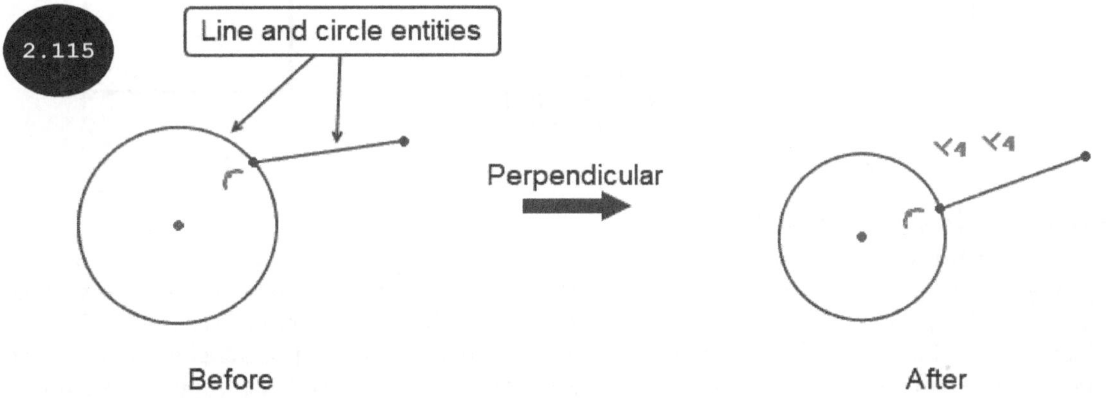

Line and circle entities
Perpendicular
Before
After

Tangent Constraint

A tangent constraint is used for making two sketch entities such as a circle and a line tangent to each other. You can also make two circles, two arcs, two ellipses, or a combination of these sketch entities tangent to each other. To apply a tangent constraint, click on the **Constrain tangent** tool in the **Sketcher constraints** toolbar or press the T key. Next, select two sketch entities one by one in the 3D View area. The tangent constraint gets applied, and the selected entities become tangent to each other, see Figure 2.116.

2.116

Tangent
Before
After

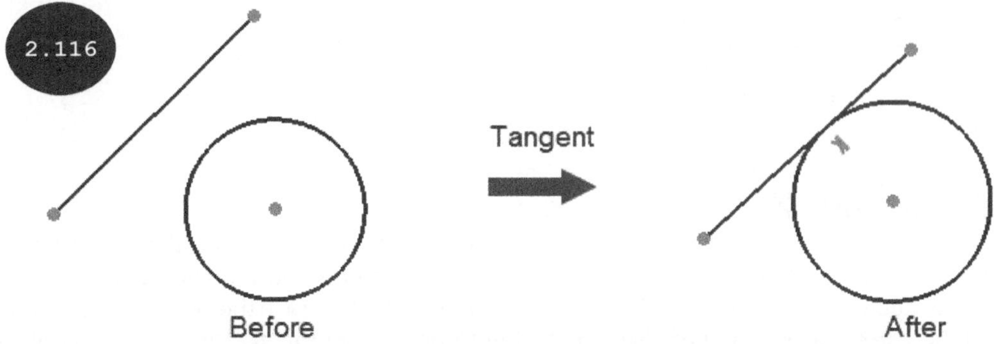

Equal Constraint

An equal constraint is used for making two sketch entities (lines, arcs, or circles) equal. To apply an equal constraint, click on the **Constrain equal** tool in the **Sketcher constraints** toolbar or press the E key. Next, select two sketch entities (lines, arcs, or circles) one by one in the 3D View area. The equal constraint gets applied, and the selected entities become equal, see Figure 2.117. In this figure, the equal constraint is applied between two lines. Note that on applying an equal constraint, the length of line entities and the radii of arc or circle entities become equal.

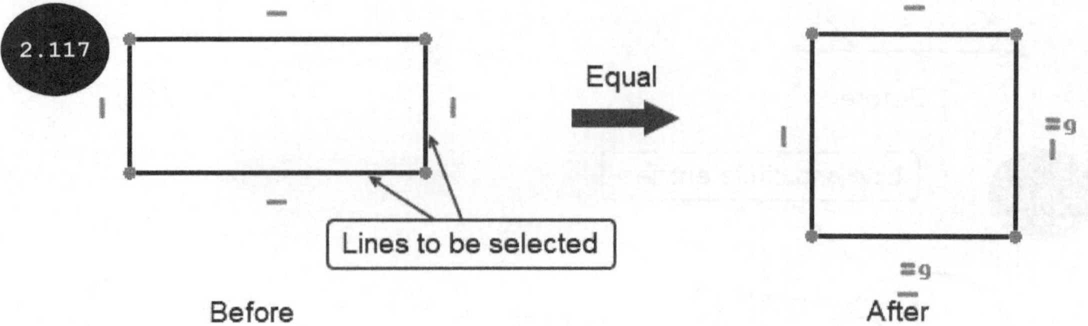

Symmetric Constraint

Symmetric constraint is used for making two points symmetric about a line or another point. To apply a symmetric constraint, click on the **Constrain symmetrical** tool in the **Sketcher constraints** toolbar or press the S key. Next, select two points one by one in the 3D View area, refer to Figure 2.108. After selecting two points, select a line or a third point. The symmetric constraint gets applied, and the first selected two points become symmetric about the line or the third selected point, see Figure 2.118. In this figure, the symmetric constraint is applied between two points and a line entity.

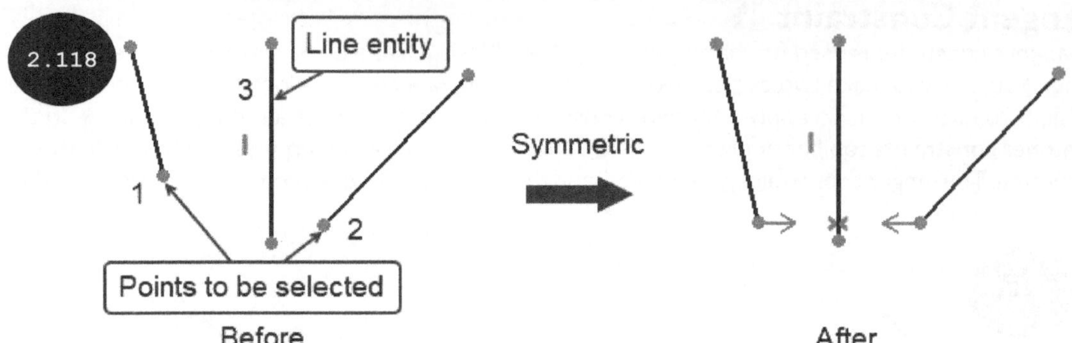

Block Constraint

A block constraint is used for blocking or fixing the current position and size of a sketch entity and making it fully constrained. It is a very useful constraint to fix the current position of a B-spline in the 3D View area. To apply a block constraint, click on the **Constrain block** tool in the **Sketcher constraints** toolbar and then select a sketch entity like a B-Spline to be fixed in the 3D View area. The block constraint gets applied such that its current position and size cannot be changed.

Applying Dimensional Constraints

Once a sketch has been drawn and required geometric constraints are applied, you must apply dimension constraints using the dimension tools. As FreeCAD is a parametric software, the parameters of sketch entities such as the length and angle are controlled or driven by dimension values. When you modify a dimension value, the respective sketch entity also gets modified, accordingly. The various dimension tools are available in the **Dimension** menu (see Figure 2.119) and are discussed next.

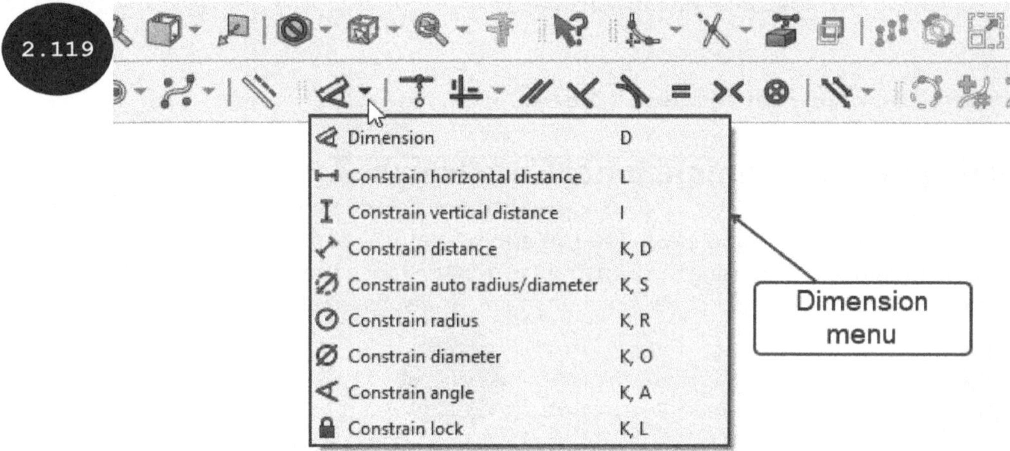

Applying Horizontal Dimensional Constraint

A horizontal dimensional constraint is used for applying the horizontal dimension to a sketch line or between two points, see Figures 2.120 and 2.121. The method for applying a horizontal dimension is discussed below:

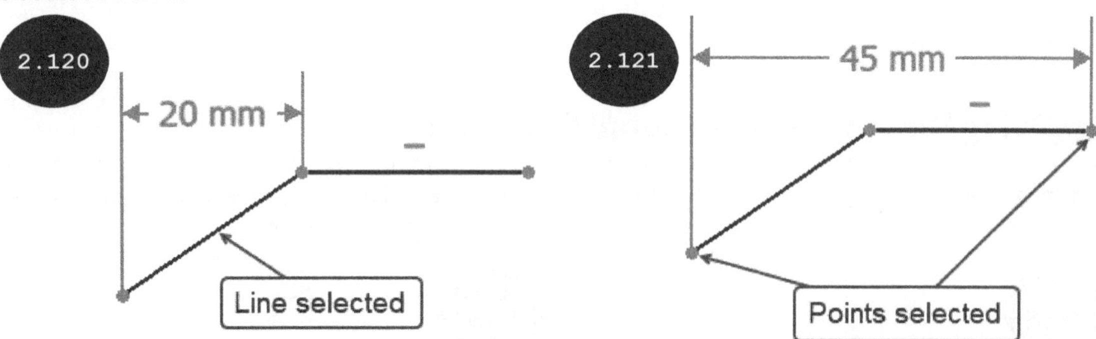

1. Click on the **Constrain horizontal distance** tool in the **Dimension** menu, refer to Figure 2.119. The appearance of the cursor changes to a cross mark with the display of a red horizontal dimensional constraint icon.

2. Select a line entity or two sketch points in the 3D View area. The **Insert length** pop-up dialog box appears with the display of the current dimension value of the selected line entity or points, see Figure 2.122.

3. Enter a new dimension value in the **Length** field of the pop-up dialog box. Next, click on the **OK** button to accept the change made and to exit the pop-up dialog box. The horizontal dimension of the specified dimension value gets applied. Note that the tool remains active, and you can continue applying other horizontal dimensions one by one.

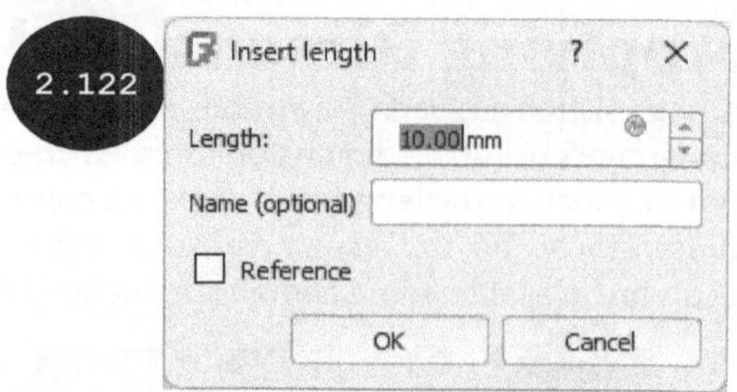

4. Press the ESC key or right-click to exit the tool.

Applying Vertical Dimensional Constraint

A vertical dimensional constraint is used for applying the vertical dimension to a sketch line or between two points, see Figures 2.123 and 2.124. You can apply a vertical dimensional constraint to a line or between two sketch points by using the **Constrain vertical distance** tool of the **Sketcher constraints** toolbar like applying a horizontal dimension constraint, as discussed above.

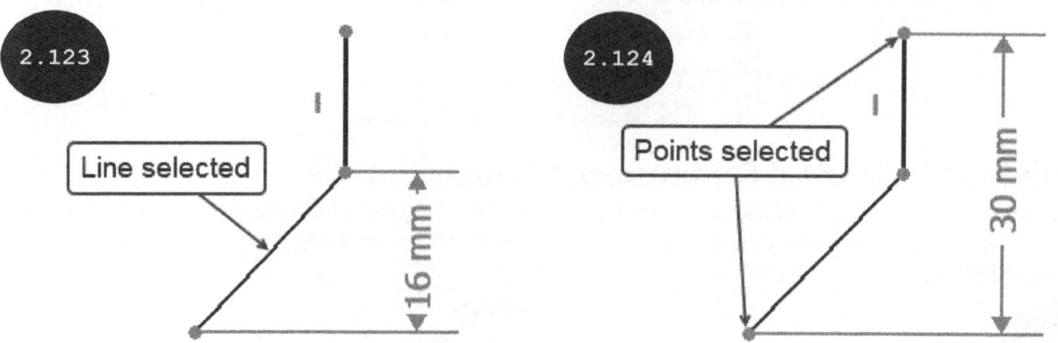

Applying Distance Dimensional Constraint

A distance dimensional constraint is used for applying a horizontal, a vertical, or an aligned dimension to a linear sketch entity (line), between two points, or a point and a line, see Figures 2.125 through 2.127. The method for applying a distance dimensional constraint is discussed below:

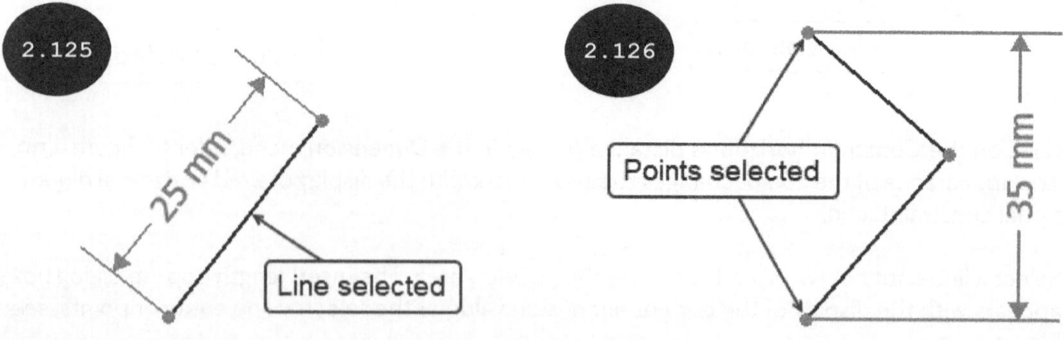

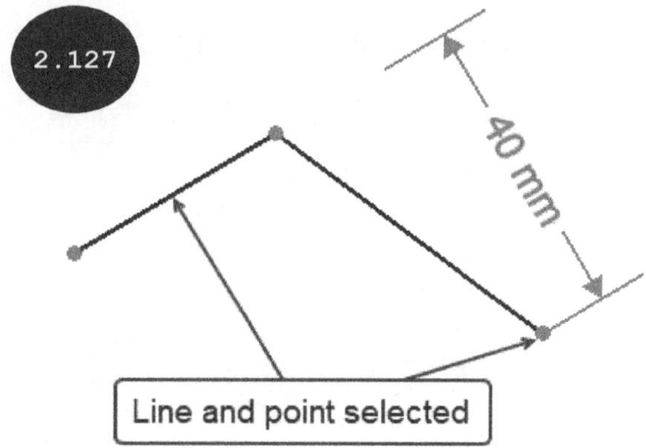

1. Click on the **Constrain distance** tool in the **Dimension** menu.
2. Select a linear sketch entity (line), two points, or a line and a point in the 3D View area. The **Insert length** pop-up dialog box appears with the display of a current dimension value of the selected sketch entity or entities.
3. Enter a new dimension value in the **Length** field of the pop-up dialog box, as required, and then click on the **OK** button to accept the change made, and to exit the pop-up dialog box. A distance dimension of the specified dimension value gets applied to the selected sketch entity or entities. Note that the tool remains active, and you can continue applying other dimensions one by one.
4. Press the ESC key or right-click in the 3D View area to exit the tool.

Applying Radius Dimensional Constraint

A radius dimensional constraint is used for applying a radius dimension to an arc or a circle, see Figures 2.128 and 2.129. The method for applying a radius dimensional constraint is discussed below:

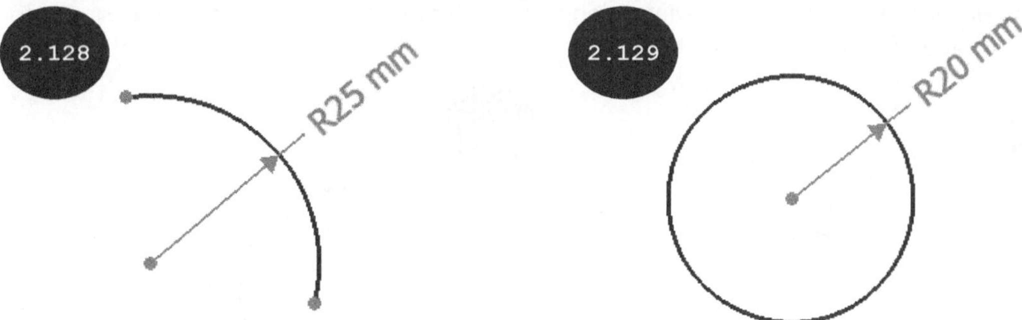

1. Click on the **Constrain radius** tool in the **Dimension** menu, see Figure 2.130.

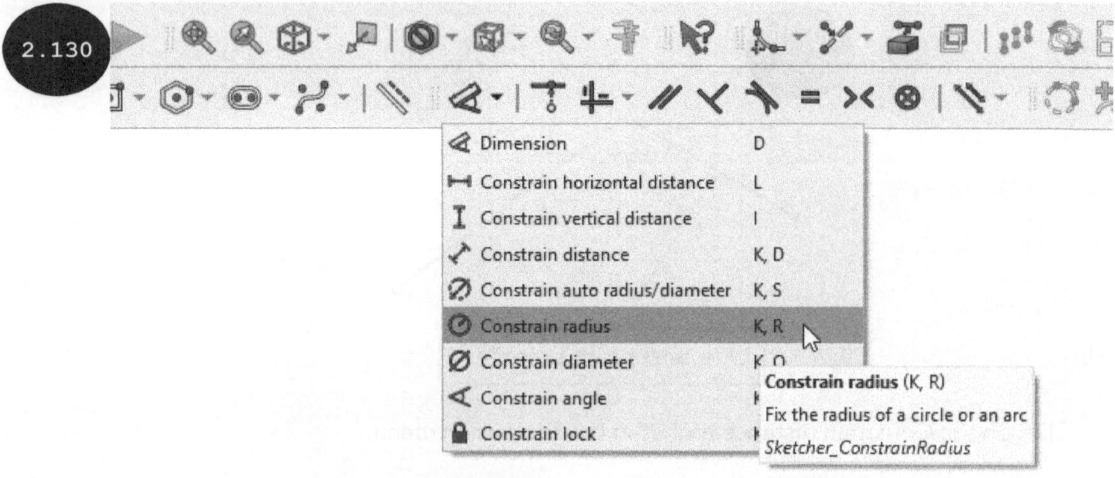

2. Select an arc or a circle in the 3D View area. The **Insert radius** pop-up dialog box appears with the display of the current radius value of the selected entity.

3. Enter a new radius value in the **Radius** field of the pop-up dialog box and then click on the **OK** button to accept the change made and exit the pop-up dialog box. A radius dimension of the specified radius value gets applied to the selected entity. Note that the tool remains active, and you can continue applying other radius dimensions one by one.

4. Press the ESC key or right-click in the 3D View area to exit the tool.

Applying Diameter Dimensional Constraint

A diameter dimensional constraint is used for applying a diameter dimension to a circle or an arc, see Figures 2.131 and 2.132. You can apply a diameter dimensional constraint to a circle or an arc by using the **Constrain diameter** tool of the **Dimension** menu (refer to Figure 2.133) in a manner similar to applying a radius dimensional constraint.

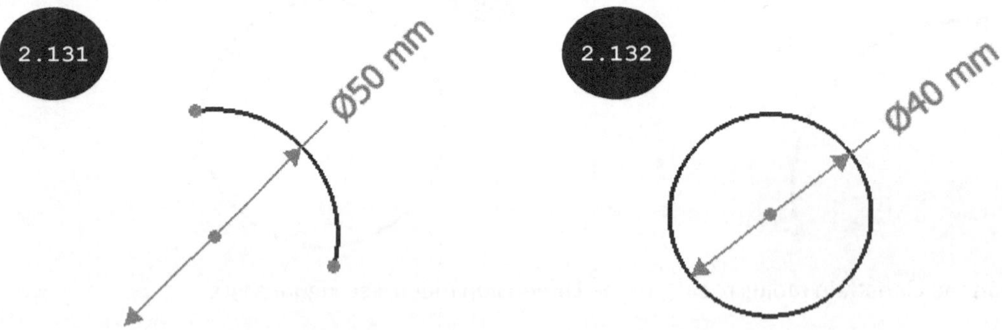

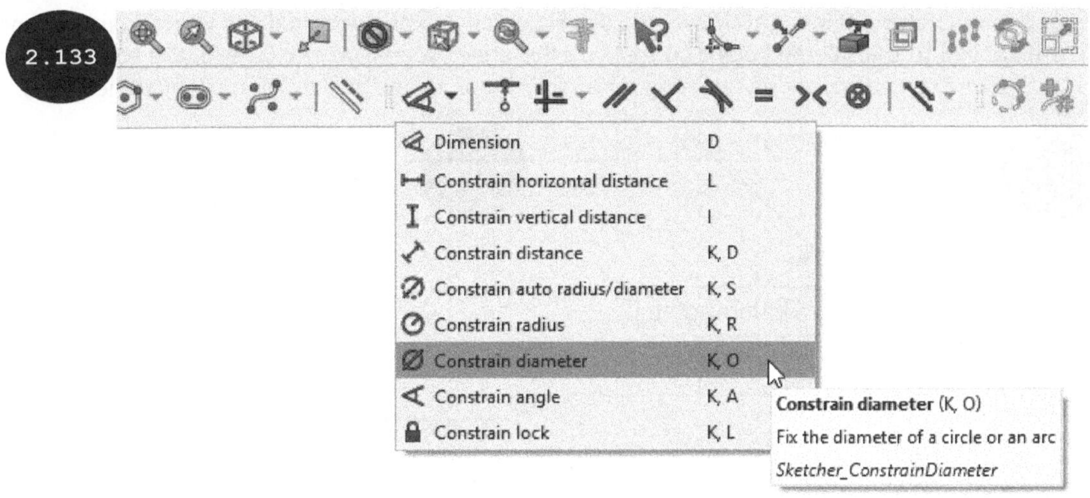

Note: The **Constrain auto radius/diameter** tool in the **Dimension** menu is used for applying a radial or a diameter dimensional constraint depending upon a sketch entity (circle or arc) selected. If you select a circle, then the diameter dimensional constraint will be applied, whereas if you select an arc, then the radial constraint will be applied by using the Constrain auto radius/diameter tool.

Applying Lock Dimensional Constraint

A lock dimensional constraint is used for locking a sketch point by applying horizontal and vertical dimensions to it concerning the origin. The method for applying a lock dimensional constraint is discussed below:

1. Click on the **Constrain lock** tool in the **Dimension** menu, refer to Figure 2.134. The **Constrain lock** tool gets activated.

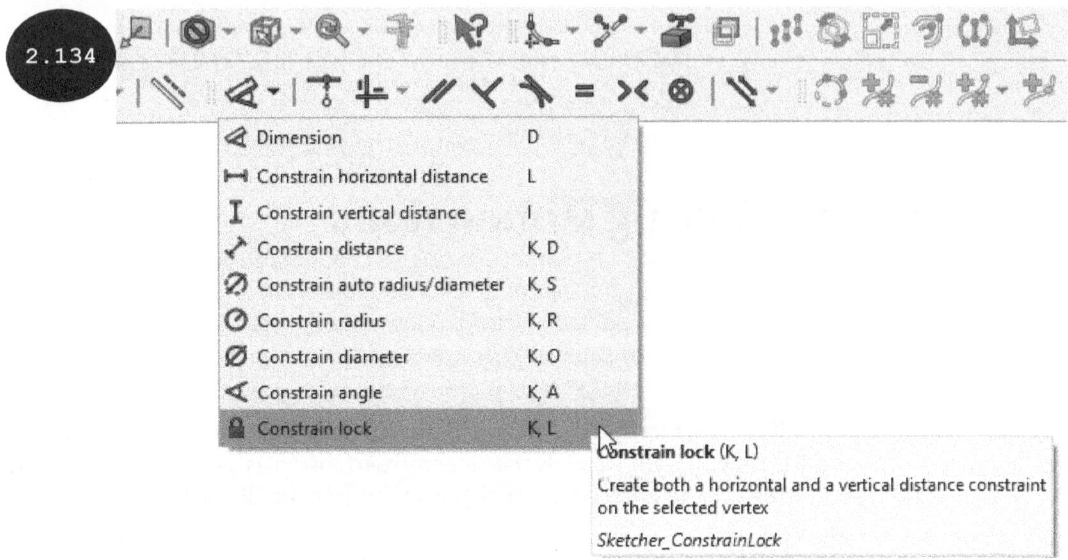

2. Select a sketch point in the 3D View area, see Figure 2.135. The horizontal and vertical dimensions are applied to the selected point concerning the origin, see Figure 2.136. Also, the tool remains active, and you can continue selecting other sketch points one by one for applying dimensions.

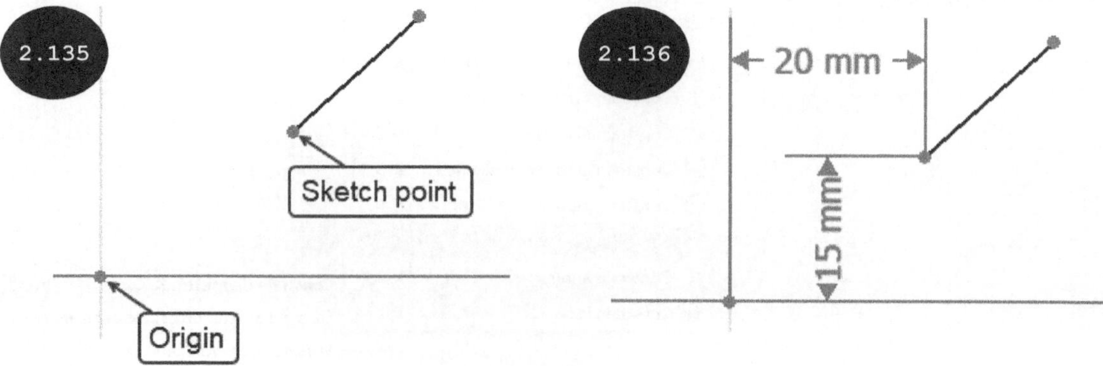

3. Press the ESC key or right-click in the 3D View area to exit the tool.

Note: In FreeCAD 1.0, instead of using separate tools for each type of dimension, you can apply various dimensions using the single **Dimension** tool, see Figure 2.137. This tool intelligently detects the selected sketch entity and automatically assigns the appropriate dimension type. For example, selecting a circle applies a diameter dimension, while selecting a line applies a linear dimension.

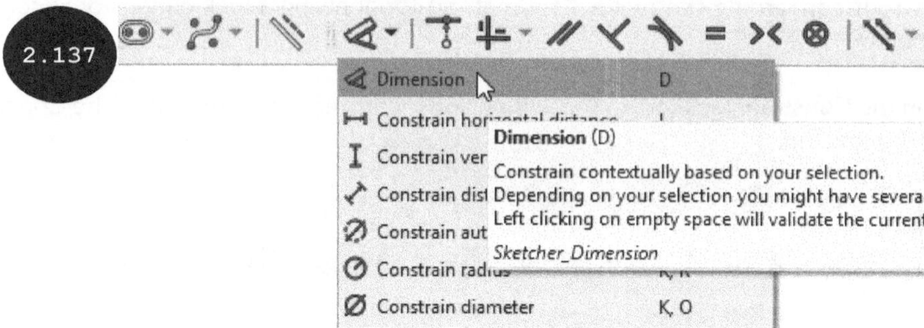

Editing and Modifying Dimensions

After applying dimensions, you may need to modify them due to changes in the design, revisions in the design, and so on. To modify an already applied dimension, double-click on the dimension value (length, angle, radius, or diameter) to be modified in the 3D View area. The respective pop-up dialog box appears, refer to Figure 2.138. In this pop-up dialog box, enter a new dimension value, as desired.

Note: You can also specify a name for the dimension in the **Name** field of the pop-up dialog box. It is an optional field. If you want to apply the selected dimension as a reference dimension only, then you can select the **Reference** check box in this pop-up dialog box.

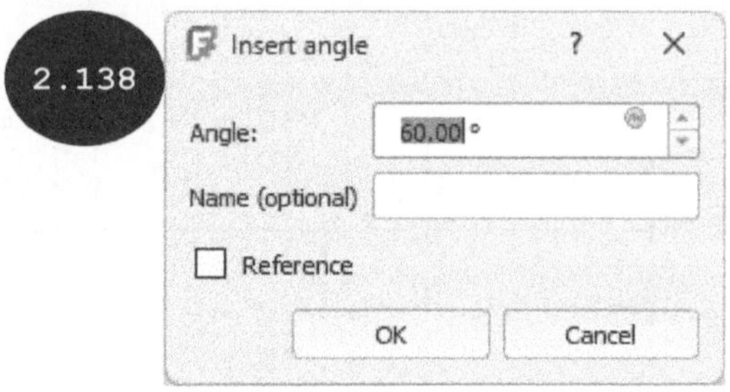

After entering a new dimension value for the selected dimension, click on the **OK** button to accept the change made and exit the pop-up dialog box. The selected dimension value gets modified. Also, the respective length, angle, radius, or diameter of the entity gets changed in the 3D View area, accordingly.

Working with Different States of a Sketch

In FreeCAD, a 2D sketch can be either under constrained, fully constrained, or over constrained. All these states of a sketch are discussed next.

Under Constrained Sketch

An under constrained sketch is a sketch, whose all degrees of freedom are not fixed. This means that the entities of the sketch can change their shape, size, and position upon being dragged. Figure 2.139 shows a rectangular sketch in which the length of the rectangle is defined as 50 mm. However, the width and the position of the rectangle concerning the origin are not defined. This means that the width and position of the rectangle can be changed by dragging the respective entities of the rectangle.

Note: The status of a sketch appears in the **Solver messages** sub-windows of the **Tasks Panel** that appears in the **Tasks** tab of the **Combo View**, see Figure 2.140.

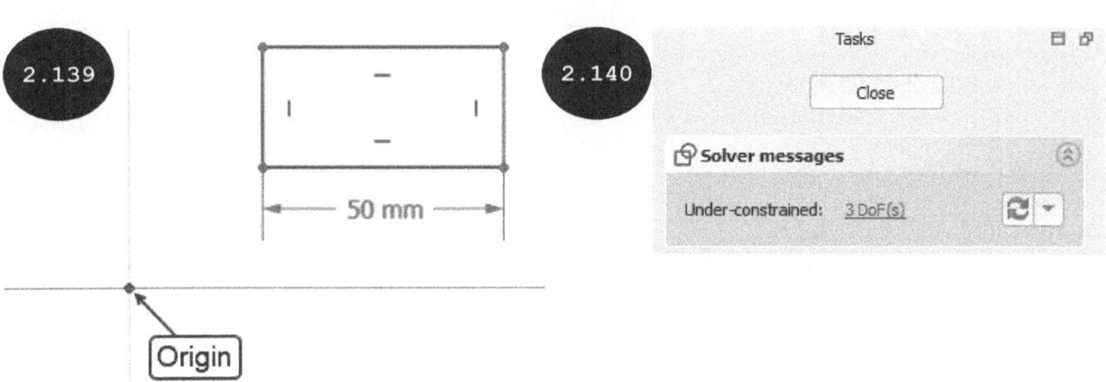

Fully Constrained Sketch

A fully constrained sketch is a sketch, whose all degrees of freedom are fixed by applying the required geometrical and dimensional constraints. This means that the entities of the sketch cannot change their shape, size, and position by being dragged. Figure 2.141 shows a rectangular sketch in which the length, width, and position of the sketch are defined.

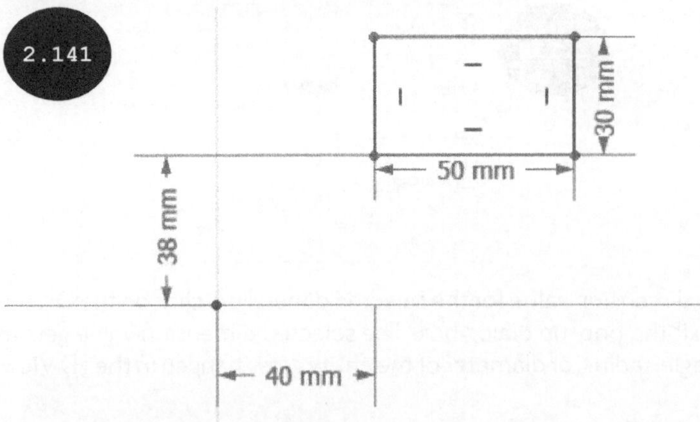

Note: The sketch shown in Figure 2.141 is fully constrained as all its entities are dimensioned. Also, the required geometrical constraints have been applied such that the horizontal and vertical constraints are applied to horizontal and vertical line entities, respectively. Note that these constraints are applied automatically to the entities while they are being drawn.

Over Constrained Sketch

An over constrained sketch is a sketch that is over-defined by applying an extra geometrical or dimensional constraint. Figure 2.142 shows an over constrained line entity. Note that in this figure, on applying a vertical constraint to the line entity, it becomes an over constrained entity.

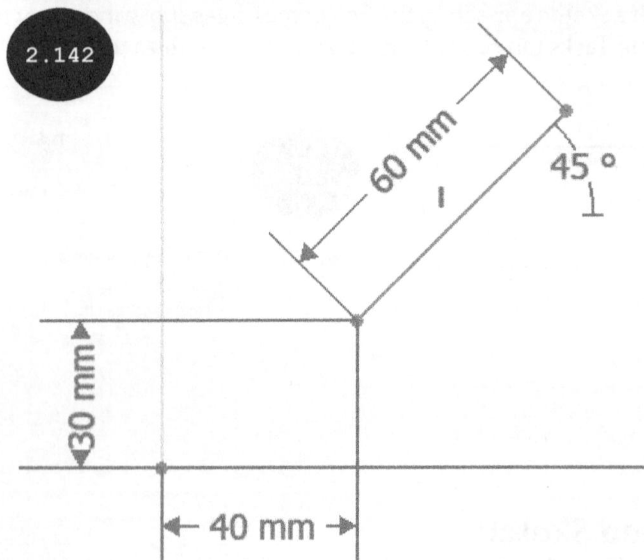

Exiting the Sketcher Workbench

After creating a sketch, you need to exit the Sketch editing mode of the **Sketcher** workbench and switch back to the **Part Design** workbench, where you can create a 3D solid feature by using the sketch. You will learn about creating 3D solid features in later chapters. To exit the Sketch editing mode of the **Sketcher** workbench, click on the **Leave sketch** tool in the **Sketcher** toolbar, see Figure 2.143.

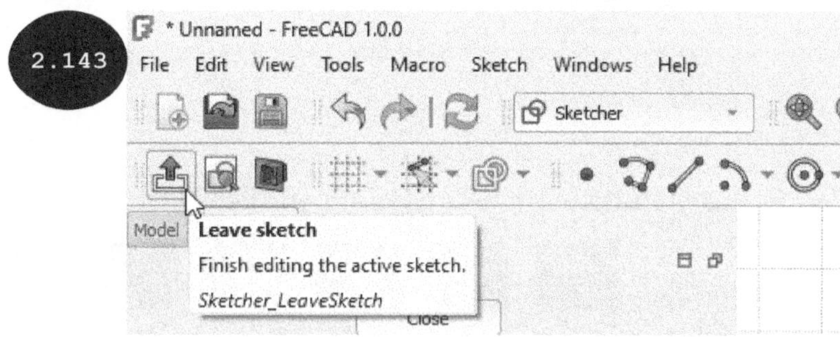

Tutorial 1

Create the sketch shown in Figure 2.144 and make it fully constrained by applying all the required geometric constraints and dimensions. The model shown in this figure is for your reference only. You will learn about creating 3D models in later chapters. All dimensions are in mm.

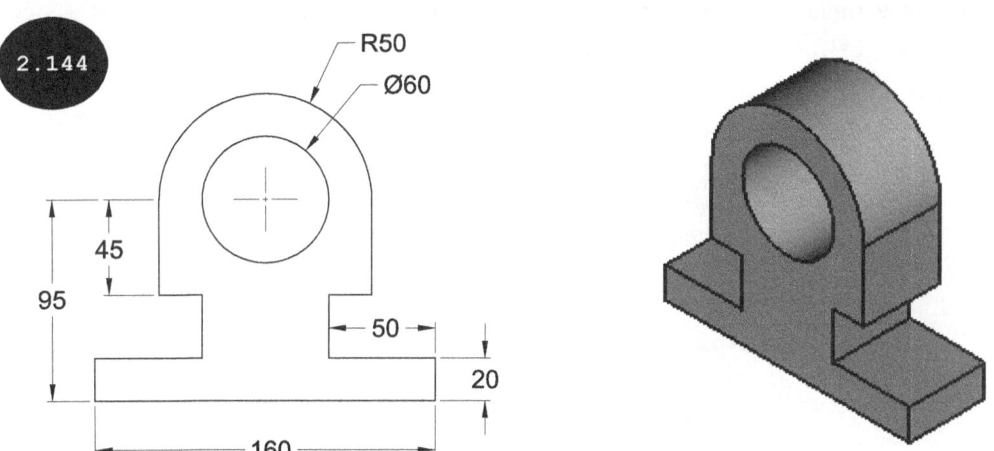

Section 1: Starting FreeCAD and a New Empty Document

1. Start FreeCAD by double-clicking on the **FreeCAD 1.0** icon on your desktop. The startup user interface of FreeCAD appears, see Figure 2.145.

2.145

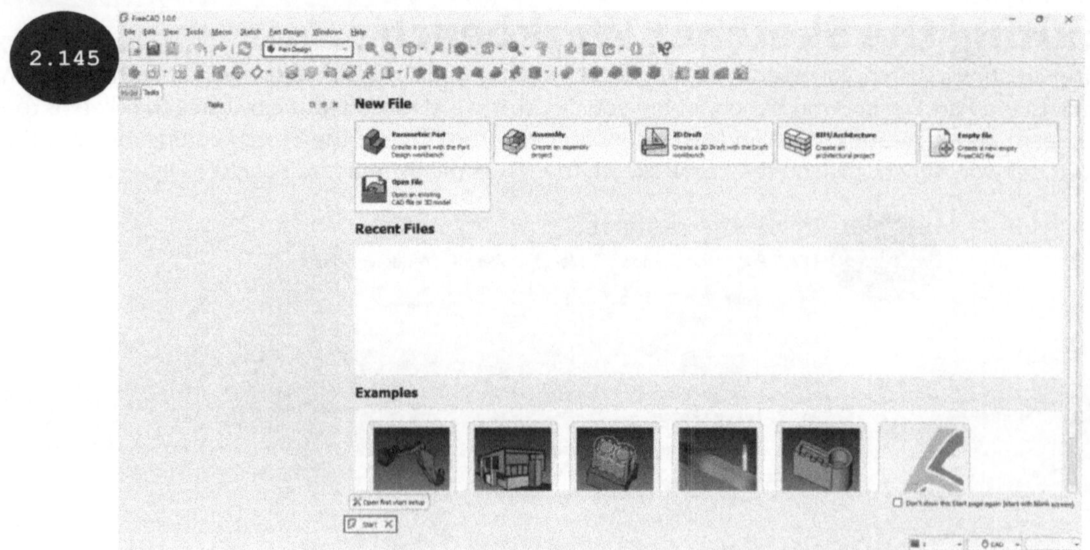

Note: Every time you start FreeCAD, the **Start** workbench is invoked with the display of the **Start** page, by default. The **Start** page acts as a welcome screen that displays recently opened documents, example files, help documentation, the latest activity in FreeCAD, and so on.

2. Click on the **New** tool in the **File** toolbar (see Figure 2.146) or press the **CTRL + N** keys. A new design document gets invoked with the default name "**unnamed: 1**" and it becomes active by default.

2.146

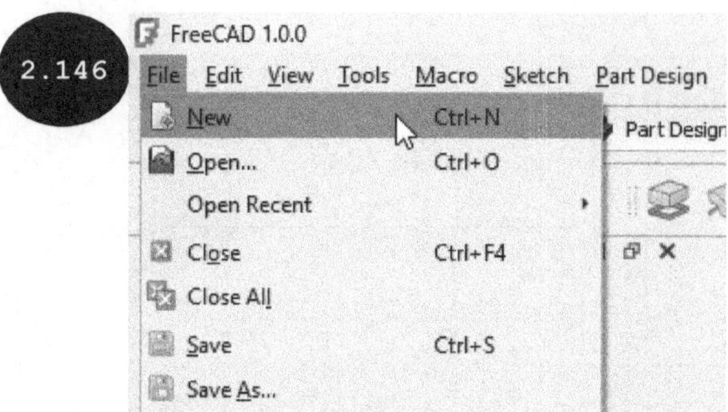

Section 2: Invoking the Sketcher Workbench

Now, you can invoke the **Sketcher** workbench.

1. Click on the **Create sketch** tool in the **Part Design Helper** toolbar, see Figure 2.147. The three default planes appear in the 3D View area. Also, the **Tasks Panel** appears in the **Tasks** tab of **Combo View** and displays the names of the three default planes, see Figure 2.148.

2. Select the **XZ_Plane** as the sketching plane in the 3D View area for creating the sketch. The Sketch editing mode of the **Sketcher** workbench gets invoked, see Figure 2.149. Also, the selected plane becomes the sketching plane for drawing the sketch and it is oriented normal to the viewing direction.

Tip: Alternatively, you can select the **XZ_Plane** in the **Tasks Panel** and then click on the **OK** button for invoking the Sketch editing mode of the **Sketcher** workbench.

Section 3: Specifying Units, Grids, and Snap Settings

Now, you need to specify units, grids, and snap settings for creating the sketch.

1. Invoke the **Unit** flyout that appears at the lower right corner of the **Status Bar**, see Figure 2.150.

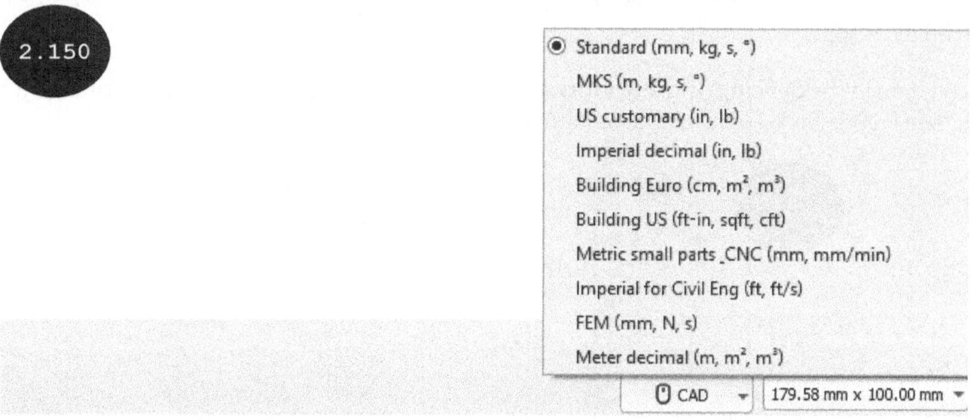

2. In this flyout, ensure that **Standard (mm, kg, s,°)** is selected as the unit system for the current design document.

3. Click on the **Toggle grid** tool in the **Sketcher edit tools** toolbar to display the grids in the 3D View area, see Figure 2.151. Figure 2.152 shows the 3D View area with the display of grids turned on.

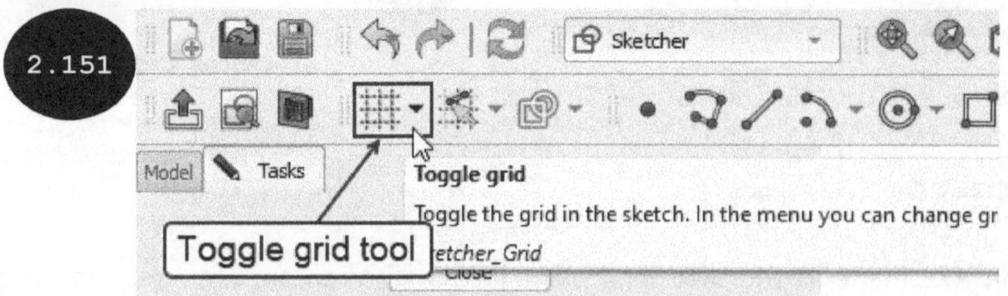

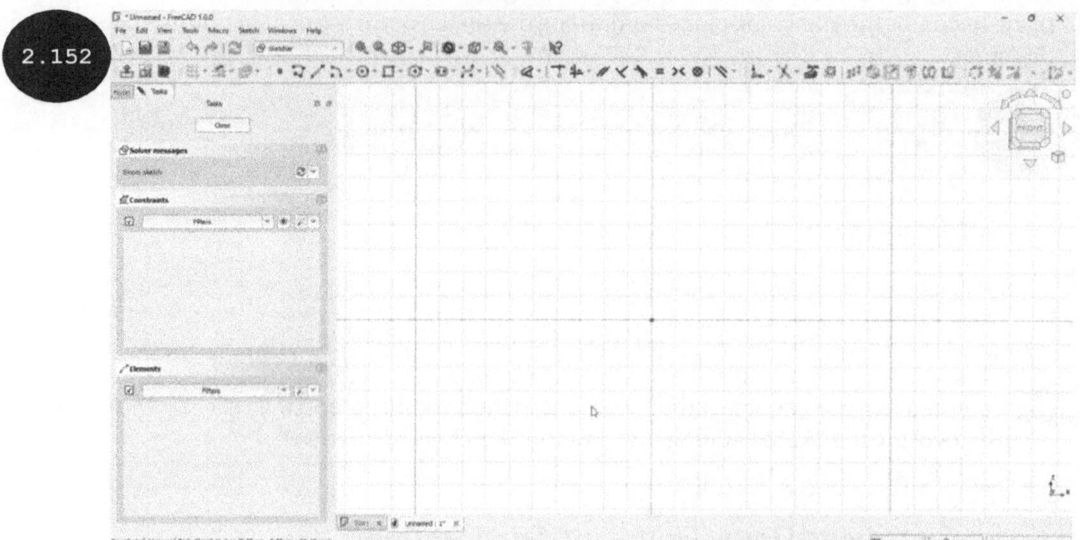

Now, you can define the spacing between two subsequent grid lines.

4. Click on the arrow next to the **Toggle grid** tool in the **Sketcher edit tools** toolbar to display a menu, see Figure 2.153.

5. Enter **5 mm** in the **Spacing** field as the distance between two subsequent grid lines in the 3D View area, see Figure 2.153. Next, click anywhere in the 3D View area.

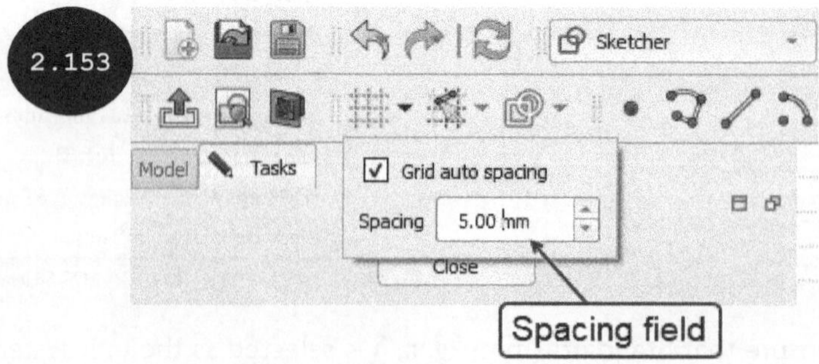

Now, you need to define the snap settings.

6. Click on the **Toggle snap** tool in the **Sketcher edit tools** toolbar to turn on the snap mode for snapping the movement of the cursor on grid lines based on the default snap settings, see Figure 2.154.

7. Click on the arrow next to the **Toggle snap** tool in the **Sketcher edit tools** toolbar to display a menu, see Figure 2.155. Note that the options in this menu are enabled only when the snap mode is turned on.

8. Select the **Snap to grid** check box to snap the movement of the cursor on grid lines, see Figure 2.155. Next, click anywhere in the 3D View area.

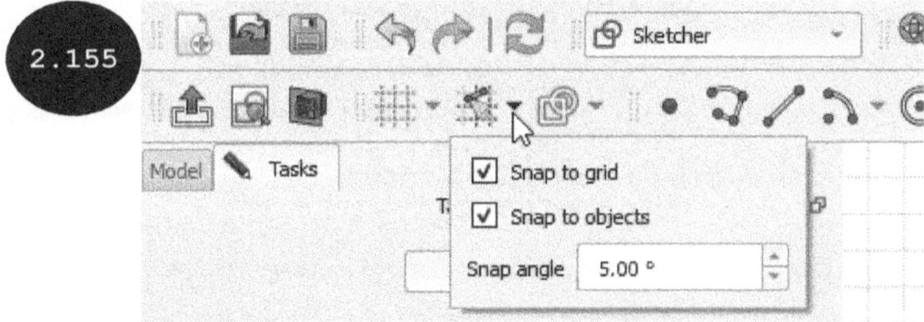

Section 4: Drawing the Sketch

1. Invoke the **Create circle** menu in the **Sketcher geometries** toolbar and then click on the **Center circle by center** tool, see Figure 2.156.

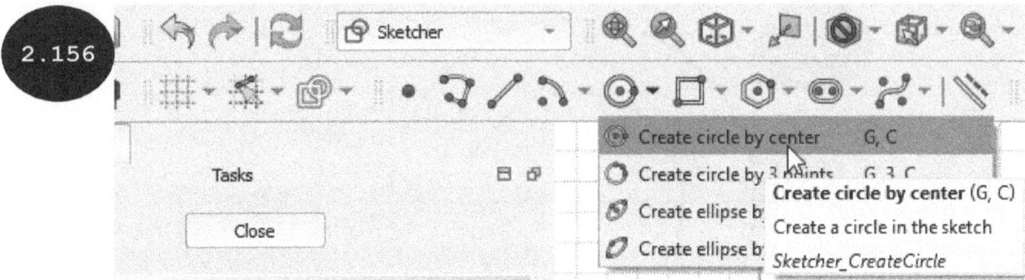

2. Click to specify the center point of the circle at the origin in the drawing area, refer to Figure 2.157.

3. Move the cursor horizontally toward the right and then click to specify a point when the diameter of the circle appears as 60 mm near the cursor, see Figure 2.157. A circle of diameter 60 mm is drawn. Next, press the **ESC** key or right-click in the 3D View area to exit the tool.

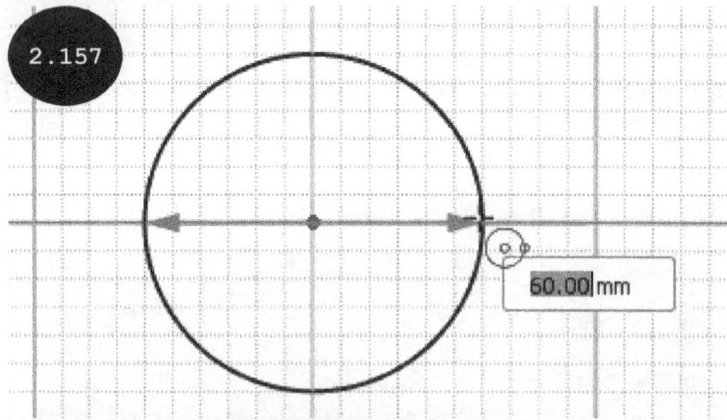

Now, you need to create an arc of the sketch.

4. Invoke the **Create arc** menu in the **Sketcher geometries** toolbar and then click on the **Create arc by center** tool, see Figure 2.158.

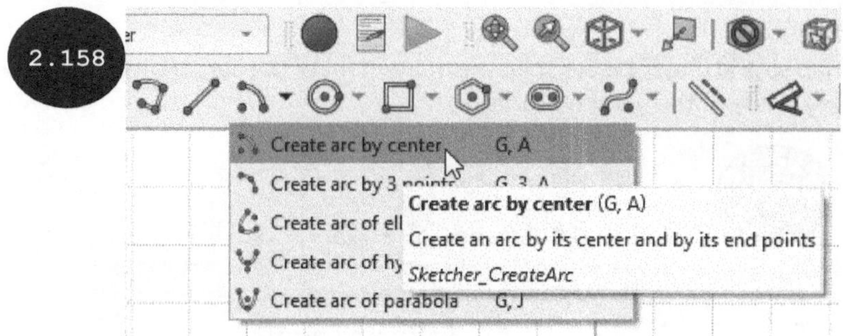

5. Click to specify the center point of the arc at the origin in the 3D View area.

6. Move the cursor horizontally toward the right. The preview of an imaginary circle appears, see Figure 2.159. Next, click to specify the start point of the arc when the radius of the imaginary circle appears as 50 mm and the start angle value appears as 0 degrees near the cursor, see Figure 2.159.

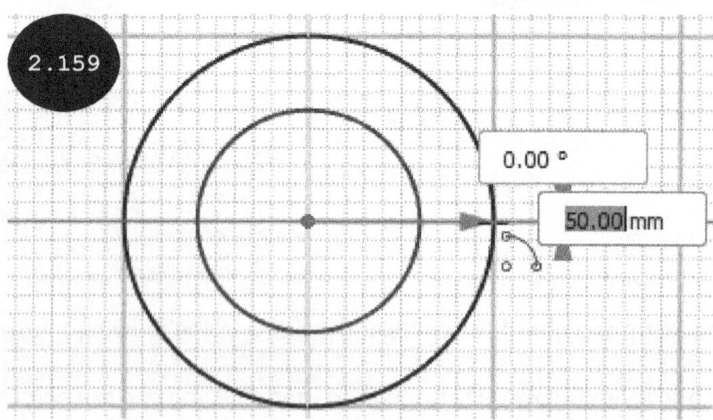

7. Move the cursor in the anti-clockwise direction in the 3D View area and then click to specify the endpoint of the arc when the angle value appears as 180 degrees near the cursor, see Figure 2.160. An arc is drawn. Next, right-click in the 3D View area or press the ESC key to exit the tool. Now, you need to draw a continuous chain of line entities of the sketch.

8. Click on the **Create polyline** tool in the **Sketcher geometries** toolbar, see Figure 2.161. The **Create polyline** tool gets activated.

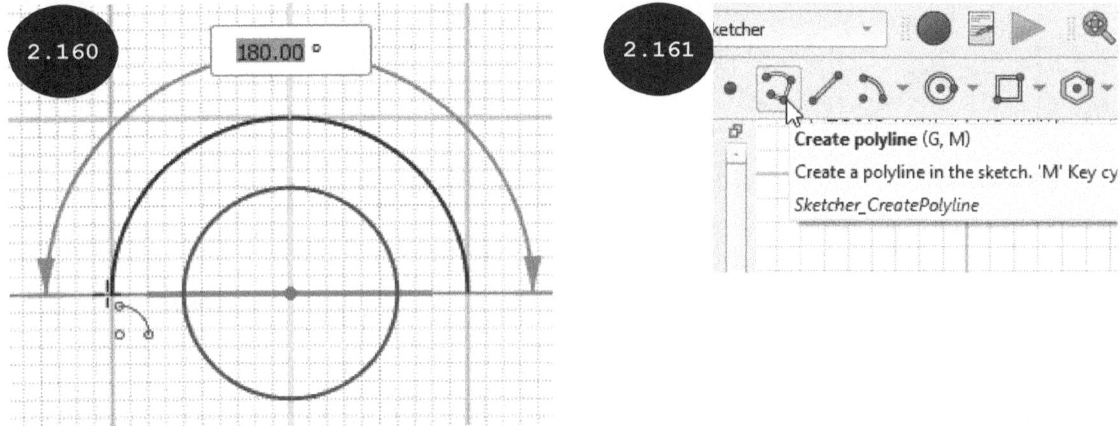

9. Click to specify the start point of the first line segment at the endpoint of the previously drawn arc, see Figure 2.162.

10. Move the cursor vertically downward and then click to specify the endpoint of the line when the length of the line appears as 45 mm, see Figure 2.163. The first line segment of length 45 mm is drawn. Also, a rubber band line segment appears attached to the cursor and the **Create polyline** tool remains active.

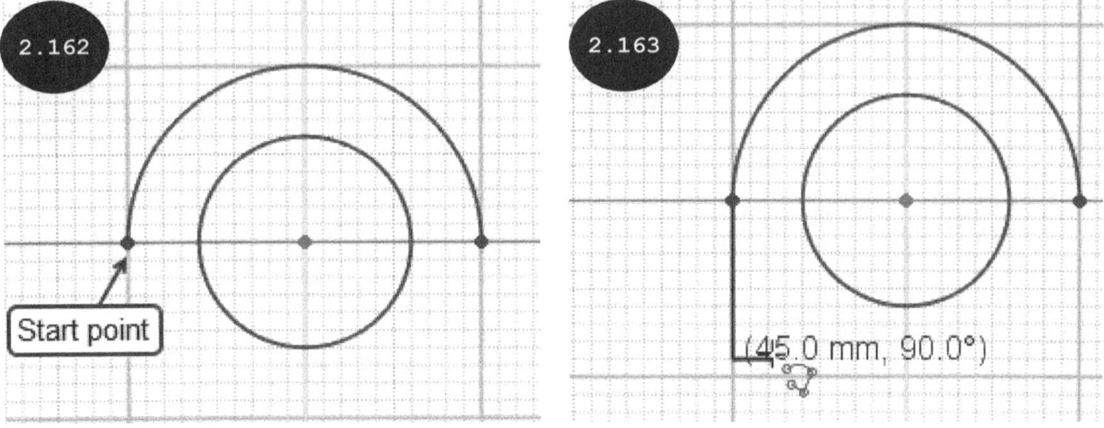

11. Move the cursor horizontally toward the right and then click to specify the endpoint of the second line segment when the length of the line appears as 20 mm, see Figure 2.164.

12. Move the cursor vertically downward and then click the left mouse button when the length of the third line segment appears as 30 mm, see Figure 2.165.

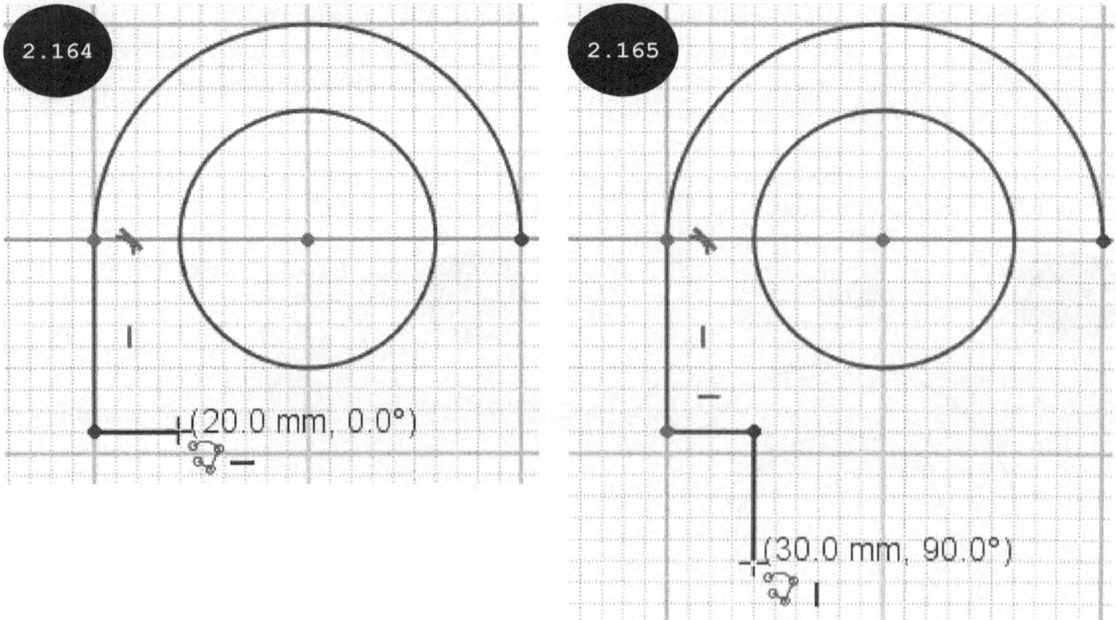

13. Move the cursor horizontally toward the left and click when the length of the fourth line segment appears as 50 mm, see Figure 2.166.

14. Move the cursor vertically downward and click when the length of the fifth line segment appears as 20 mm, see Figure 2.167.

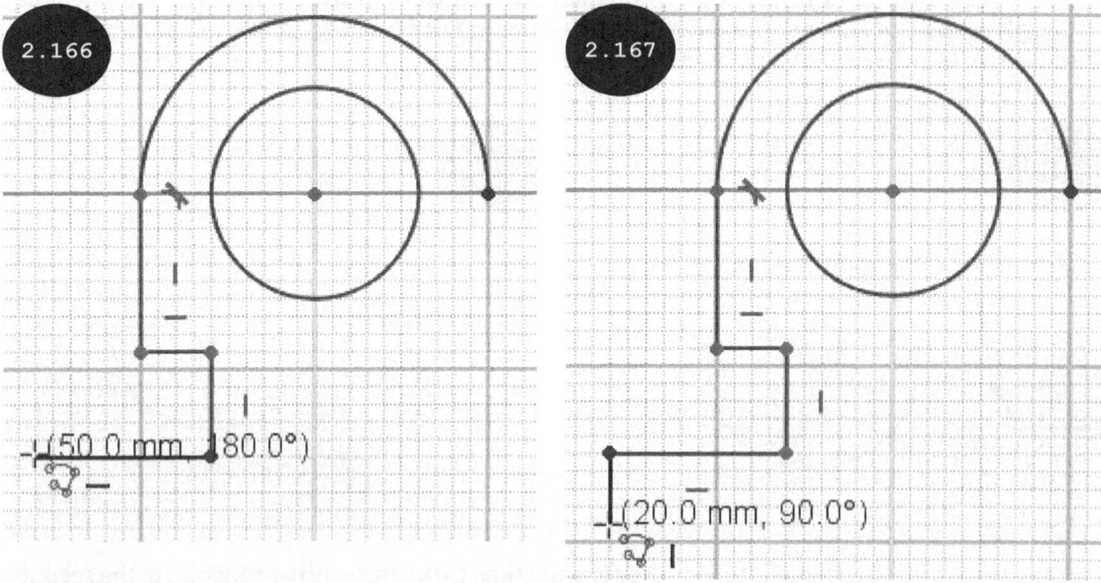

15. Move the cursor horizontally toward the right and click when the length of the sixth line segment appears as 160 mm, see Figure 2.168.

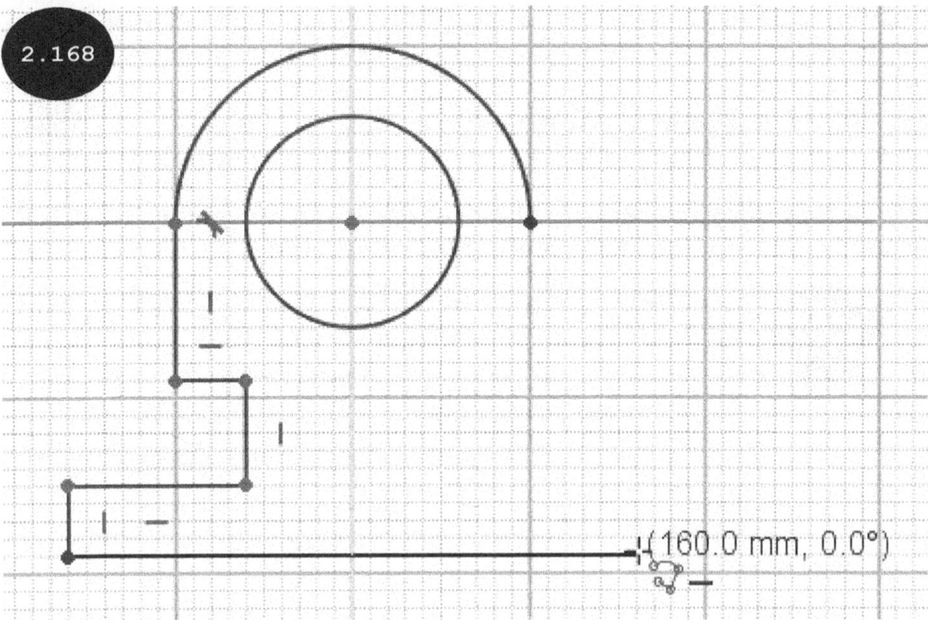

Note: You can zoom in or zoom out the drawing display area by scrolling the middle mouse button up or down, respectively. You will learn more about navigating a sketch or a model in later chapters.

16. Similarly, continue drawing the remaining line segments of the sketch one after the other by specifying points in the 3D View area, see Figure 2.169. Note that the endpoint of the last (eleventh) line segment is specified on the start point of the arc. Also, a rubber band line segment remains attached to the cursor.

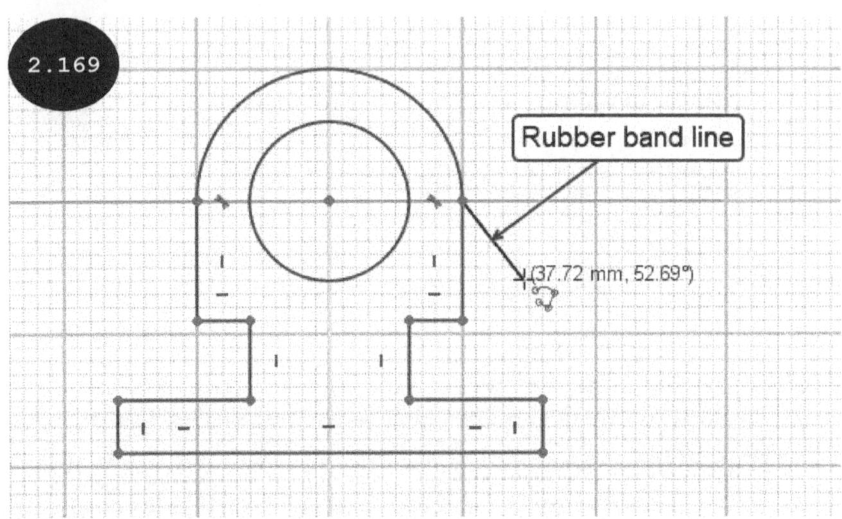

17. Right-click in the 3D View area to end the creation of a continuous chain of lines. Next, right-click again in the 3D View area or press the ESC key to exit the **Create polyline** tool.

Section 5: Applying Geometric Constraints

Now, you need to make the sketch fully constrained by applying the required constraints.

1. Click on the **Constrain equal** tool in the **Sketcher constraints** toolbar (see Figure 2.170) or press the E key to apply equal constraints between lines of equal length.

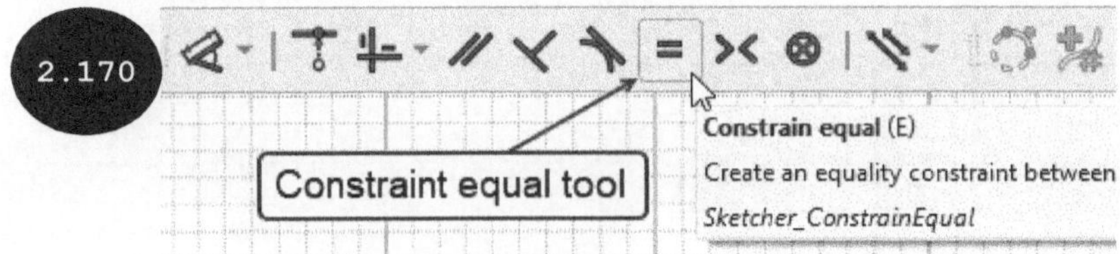

2. Select the first line segment (1) and the eleventh line segment (11) of the sketch one by one, refer to Figure 2.171. An equal constraint gets applied between the selected lines. Also, the **Constrain equal** tool remains active.

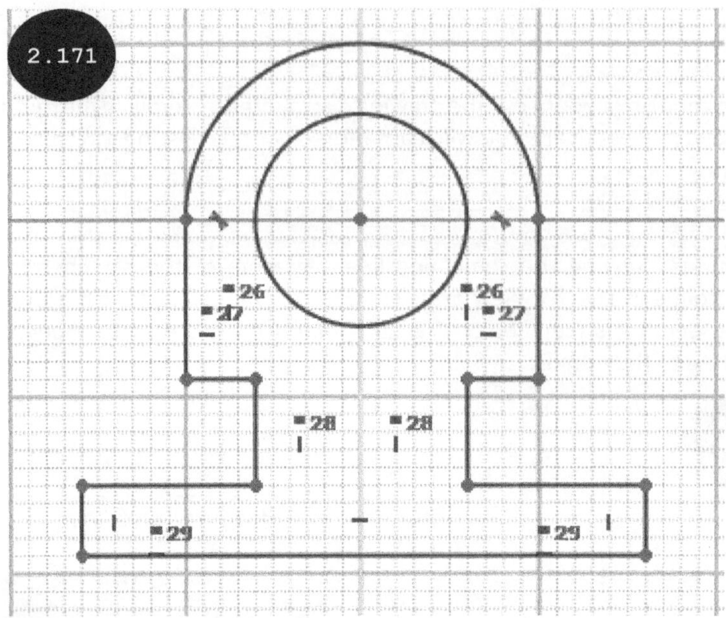

Note: In Figure 2.171, the line segments are labeled 1 to 11 for your reference only.

3. Select the second line segment (2) and the tenth line segment (10) of the sketch one by one, refer to Figure 2.171. An equal constraint gets applied between the selected lines. Also, the **Constrain equal** tool remains active.

4. Select the third line segment (3) and the ninth line segment (9) of the sketch one by one, refer to Figure 2.172. An equal constraint gets applied between the selected lines.

5. Select the fourth line segment (4) and the eighth line segment (8) of the sketch one by one, refer to Figure 2.171. An equal constraint gets applied between the selected lines.

6. After applying the equal constraint between lines of equal length, press the ESC key or right-click in the 3D View area to exit the **Constrain equal** tool.

Section 6: Applying Dimensions

Now, you need to apply the required dimensions to make the sketch fully defined.

1. Invoke the **Dimension** menu and then click on the **Constrain auto radius/diameter** tool, see Figure 2.172.

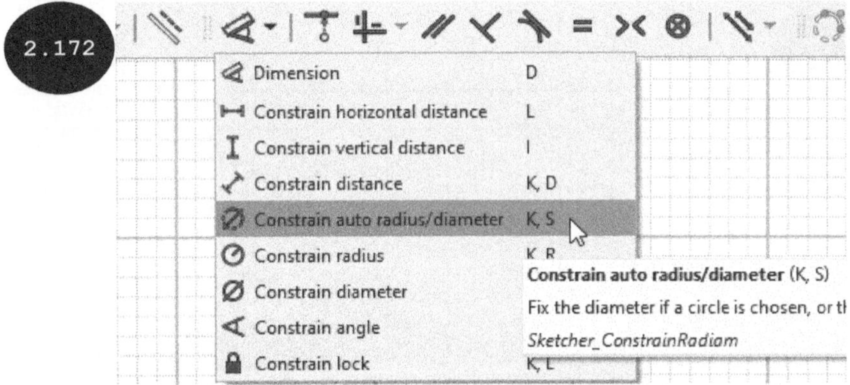

2. Select the circle of the sketch in the 3D View area. The **Insert diameter** pop-up dialog box appears with the display of its current diameter value, see Figure 2.173.

3. Ensure that the diameter of the circle is entered as **60 mm** in the **Diameter** field of the dialog box.

4. Click on the **OK** button in the pop-up dialog box. A diameter dimension gets applied to the selected circle, see Figure 2.174. The **Constrain auto radius/diameter** tool remains active.

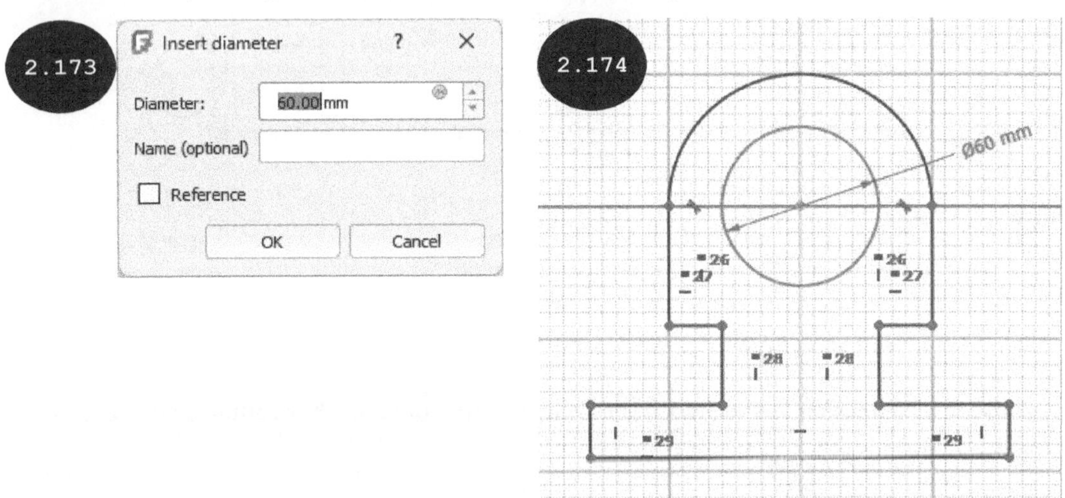

5. Select the arc of the sketch in the 3D View area. The **Insert radius** pop-up dialog box appears with the display of its current radius value, see Figure 2.175.

2.175

Insert radius ? ×
Radius: 50.00 mm
Name (optional)
Reference
OK Cancel

6. Ensure that the radius of the arc is entered as **50 mm** in the **Radius** field of the dialog box.

7. Click on the **OK** button in the pop-up dialog box.
The radius dimension gets applied to the arc, see Figure 2.176. Next, press the ESC key or right-click to exit the tool.

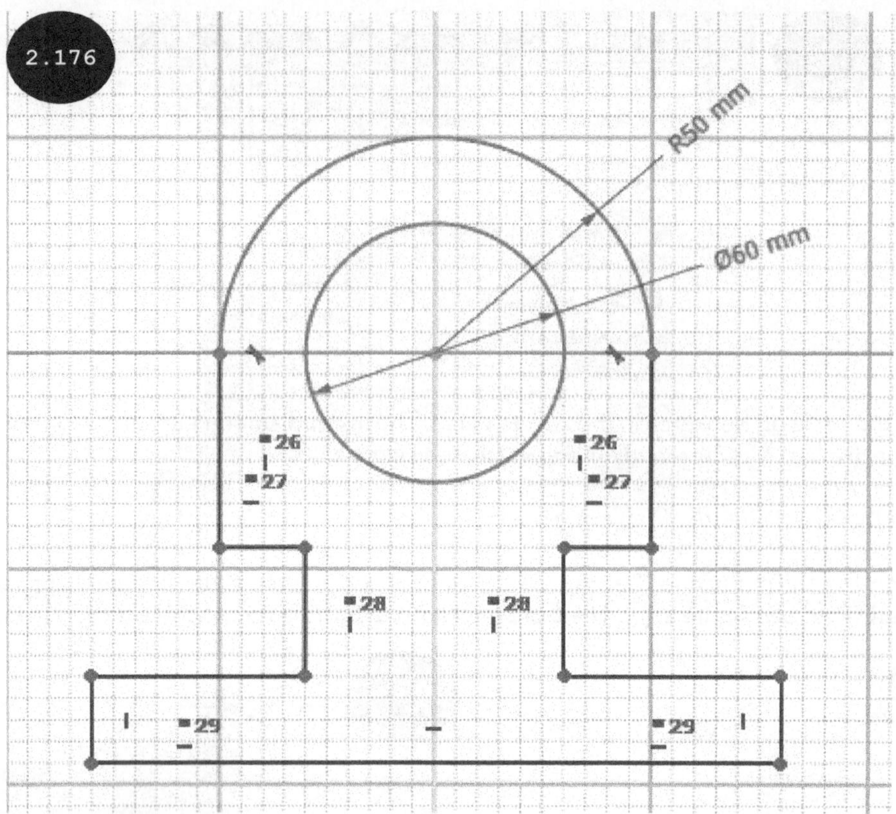

Tip: You can change the position of applied dimensions in the drawing area by dragging and dropping them to the required location in the 3D View area.

Now, you need to apply horizontal dimensions to the sketch entities.

8. Invoke the **Dimension** menu and then click on the **Constrain horizontal distance** tool, see Figure 2.177.

2.177

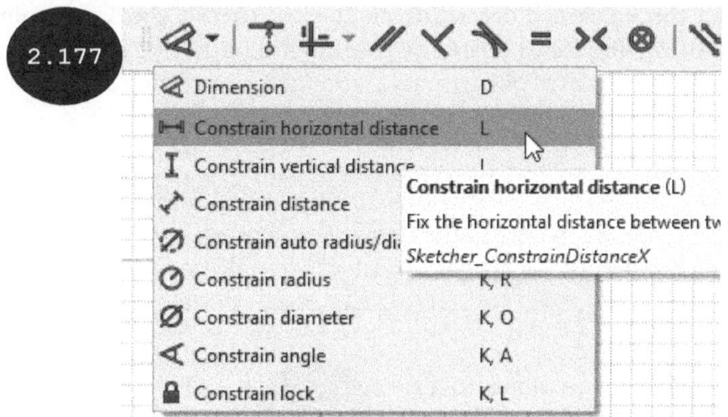

9. Select the bottom-most horizontal line of the sketch measuring a length of 160 mm. The **Insert length** pop-up dialog box appears with the display of its current dimension value.

10. Ensure that the length of the line is entered as **160 mm** in the pop-up dialog box.

11. Click on the **OK** button in the pop-up dialog box. The horizontal dimension of 160 mm gets applied to the selected line, refer to Figure 2.178. Also, the **Constrain horizontal distance** tool remains active.

12. Similarly, apply the horizontal dimension to the other horizontal line entity of length 50 mm, refer to Figure 2.178. Next, right-click in the 3D View area to exit the tool.

    Now, you need to apply vertical dimensions to the sketch entities.

13. Click on the **Constrain vertical distance** tool in the **Sketcher constraints** toolbar and then apply all the vertical dimensions to the sketch, refer to Figure 2.178.

2.178

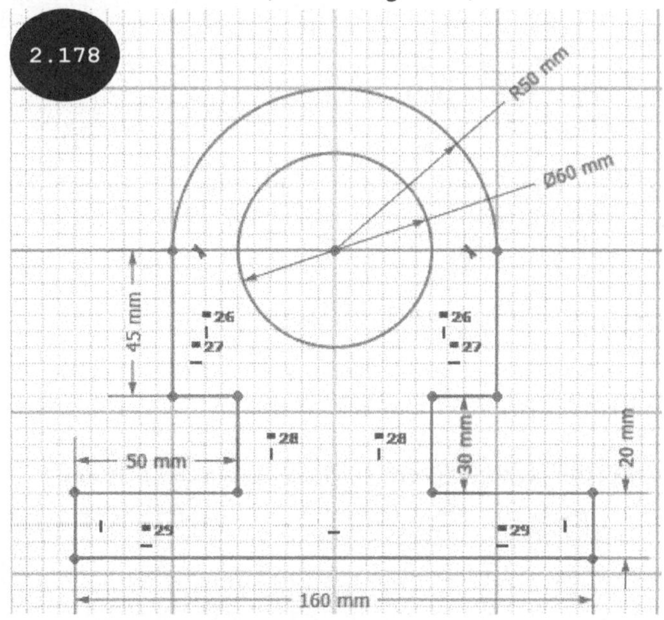

14. After applying all the vertical dimensions, right-click to exit the **Constrain vertical distance** tool. Figure 2.179 shows the fully constrained sketch after applying all geometric constraints and dimensions. Also, the position of dimensions is arranged by dragging and dropping them in the 3D View area.

Tip: In Figure 2.179, the vertical dimensions 20 mm and 45 mm are applied by selecting their respective vertical lines, whereas the vertical dimension 95 mm is applied by selecting the origin and an endpoint of the bottom-most horizontal line of the sketch.

After creating a sketch, you need to exit the Sketch editing mode of the **Sketcher** workbench.

15. Click on the **Leave sketch** tool in the **Sketcher** toolbar to exit the Sketch editing mode of the **Sketcher** workbench and switch back to the **Part Design** workbench, see Figure 2.179.

Section 7: Saving the Sketch

Now, you can save the sketch.

1. Click on the **Save** tool in the **File** toolbar (see Figure 2.180) or press the CTRL + S keys. The **Save FreeCAD Document** dialog box appears.

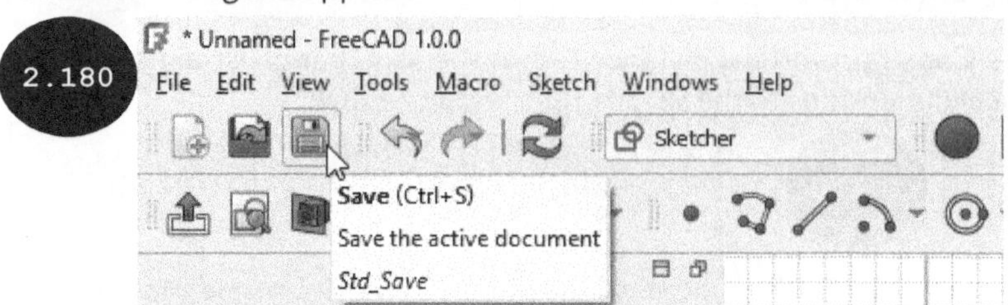

2. Browse to the local drive of your system and then create a folder with the name **FreeCAD**. Next, create another folder with the name **Chapter 2** inside the **FreeCAD** folder and then double-click to access it to save the files of Chapter 2 inside this folder.

3. Enter **Ch02-Tutorial 1** in the **File name** field of the dialog box.

4. Click on the **Save** button in the dialog box. The sketch gets saved with the name **Ch02-Tutorial 1** at the specified location (> *FreeCAD* > *Chapter 02*).

5. Click on **File** > **Close** in the **Standard Menu** to close the current document.

Tutorial 2

Create the sketch shown in Figure 2.181 and make it fully constrained by applying all geometric constraints and dimensions. The model shown in this figure is for your reference only. You will learn how to create 3D models in the later chapters. All dimensions are in inches.

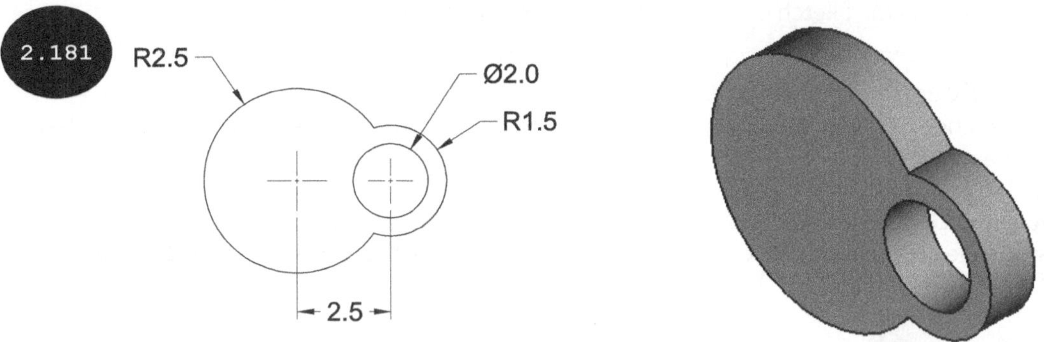

Section 1: Invoking a New Empty Document

1. Start FreeCAD by double-clicking on the **FreeCAD 1.0** icon on your desktop. The startup user interface of FreeCAD appears.

2. Click on the **Parametric Part** button in the **New File** section of the **Start** page, see Figure 2.182. A new design document is invoked with the default name "**Unnamed: 1**".

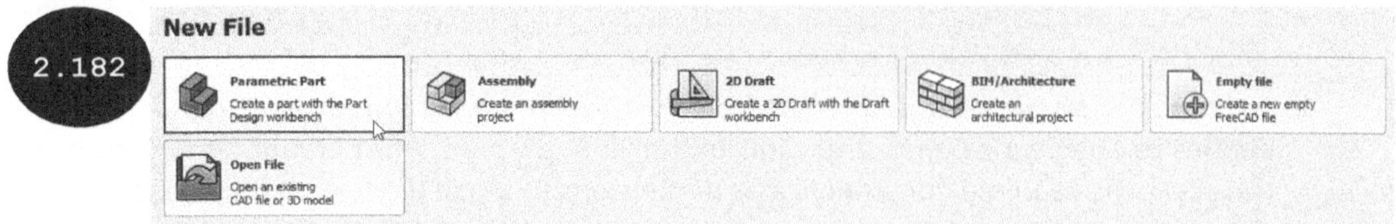

Section 2: Invoking the Sketcher Workbench

Now, you will invoke the **Sketcher** workbench to create a sketch.

1. Click on the **Create sketch** tool in the **Part Design Helper** toolbar, see Figure 2.183. The three default planes, which are mutually perpendicular to each other appear. Also, the **Tasks Panel** appears in the **Combo View** and displays the names of the three default planes, see Figure 2.184.

2. Select the **XZ_Plane** as the sketching plane in the 3D View area. The Sketch editing mode of the **Sketcher** workbench gets invoked. Also, the selected plane becomes the sketching plane for drawing the sketch and it is oriented normal to the viewing direction.

Tip: Alternatively, you can select the **XZ_Plane** in the **Tasks Panel** and then click on the **OK** button for invoking the Sketch editing mode of the **Sketcher** workbench.

Section 3: Specifying the Units

Now, you need to specify Imperial decimal as the unit of measurement for the current design document.

1. Invoke the **Unit** flyout that appears at the lower right corner of the **Status Bar** and ensure that **Imperial decimal (in, lb)** is selected as the unit system for the current design document, see Figure 2.185.

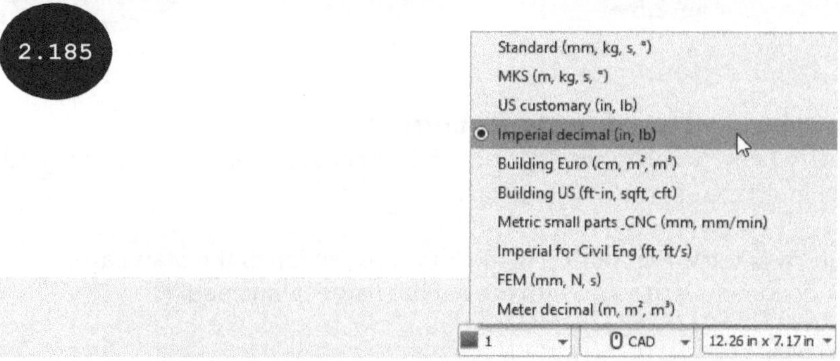

Note: As FreeCAD is a parametric software, you can turn off the snap mode and create the sketch entities by specifying points arbitrarily in the 3D View area. After creating the sketch, you can apply the required constraints and dimensions to make the sketch fully constrained.

2. Click on the **Toggle grid** tool and **Toggle snap** tool in the **Sketcher edit tools** to turn off the grids and snap mode, respectively, see Figure 2.186. Note that these are the toggle tools.

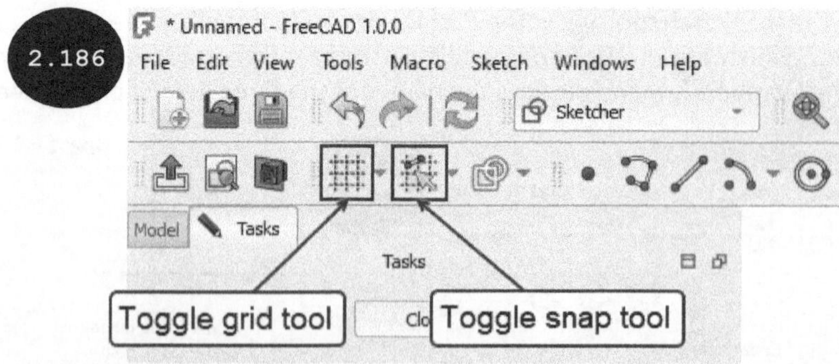

Section 4: Drawing the Sketch

Now, you can draw the sketch entities by specifying points arbitrarily in the 3D View area.

1. Invoke the **Create circle** menu in the **Sketcher geometries** toolbar and then click on the **Create circle by center** tool, see Figure 2.187.

2. Click to specify the center point of the circle at the origin in the 3D View area, refer to Figure 2.188.

3. Move the cursor horizontally toward the right and then click to create a circle of any diameter, see Figure 2.188. A circle gets created and the **Create circle by center** tool remains active.

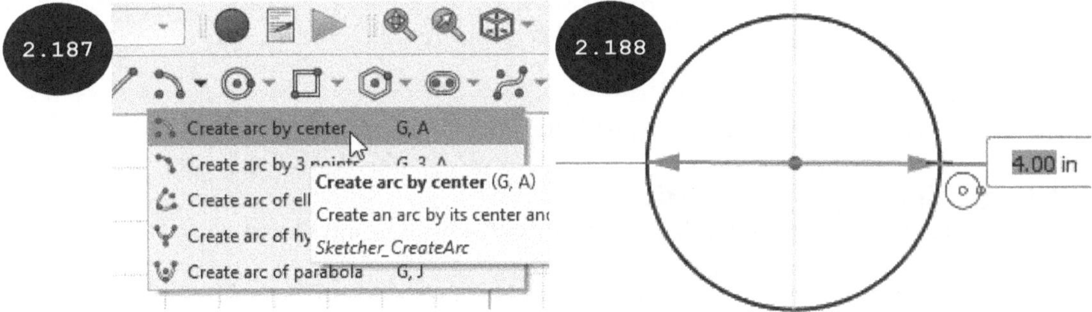

Now, you need to create two more circles on the right quadrant of the previously created circle.

4. Move the cursor toward the right quadrant of the previously created circle and then click to specify the center point when the circle gets highlighted, see Figure 2.189.

5. Move the cursor horizontally toward the right and then click to create a circle of any diameter like the one shown in Figure 2.190. A circle gets created and the **Create circle by center** tool remains active.

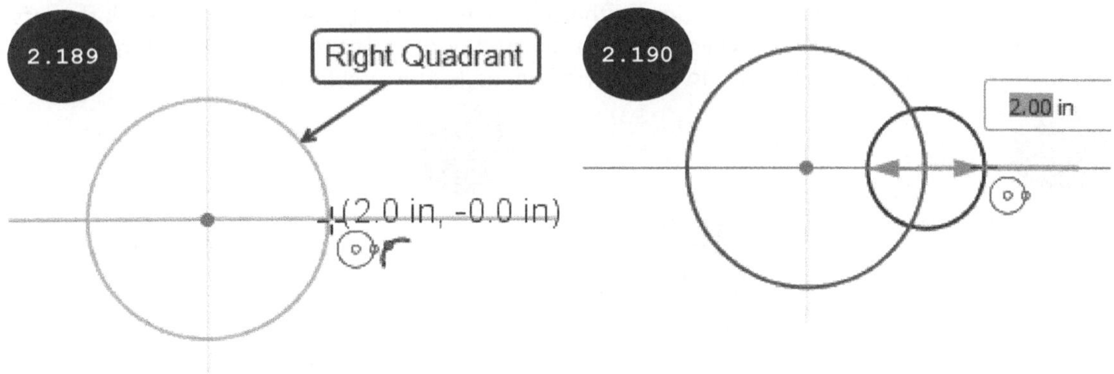

6. Move the cursor to the center point of the previously created circle and then click to specify the center point of another circle when the cursor snaps to it.

7. Move the cursor horizontally toward the right and click to create a circle of any radius inside the previously created circle, see Figure 2.191. Another circle gets created.

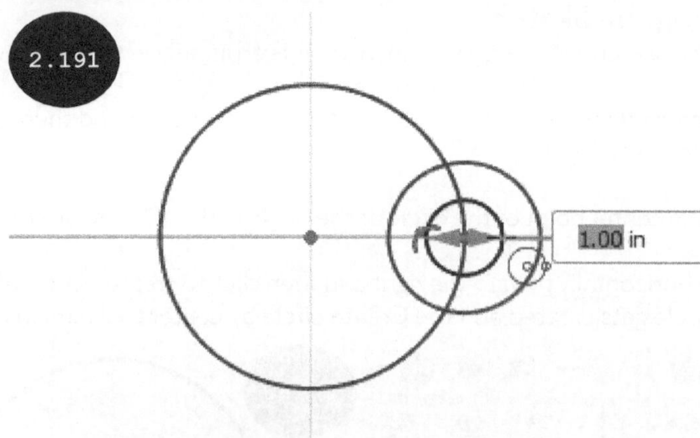

8. Right-click in the 3D View area to exit the **Center and rim point** tool.

Section 5: Trimming Sketch Entities

Now, you need to trim the unwanted sketch entities to their nearest intersection.

1. Click on the **Trim edge** tool in **Trim** menu in the **Sketcher geometries** toolbar, see Figure 2.192. The **Trim edge** tool gets activated and the appearance of the cursor changes to cross mark with the display of a red trim icon.

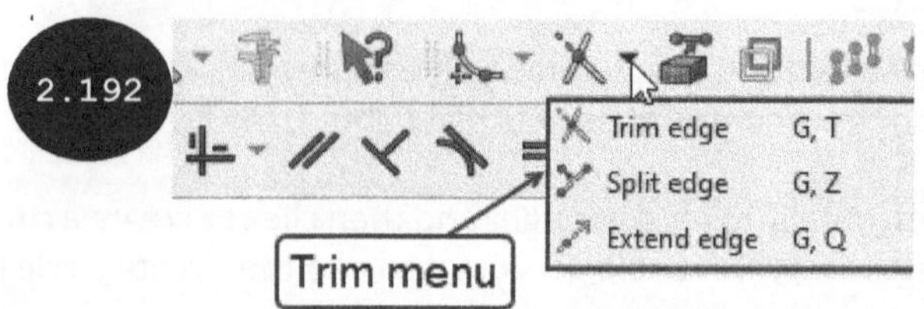

2. Move the cursor over the left portion of the outer circle, see Figure 2.193. Next, click the left mouse button when it gets highlighted. The selected portion of the circle gets trimmed to its nearest intersection, see Figure 2.194. Also, the **Trim edge** tool remains active.

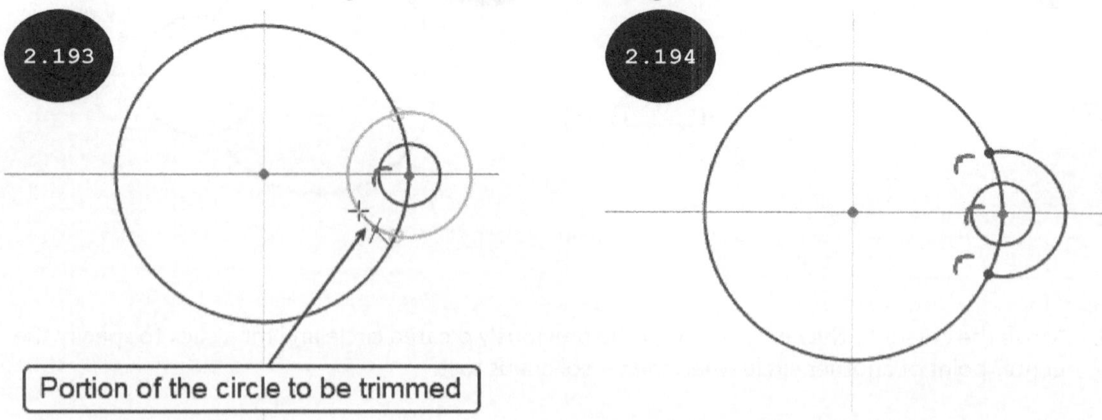

3. Similarly, click on the other unwanted entities of the sketch one by one to trim them. Figure 2.195 shows the sketch after trimming all the unwanted entities of the sketch.

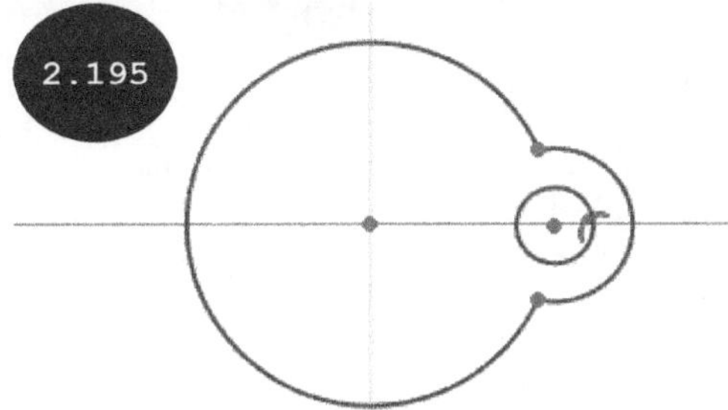

4. Right-click in the 3D View area to exit the **Trim edge** tool.

Section 6: Applying Dimensions

Now, you need to apply the required dimensions to make the sketch fully defined.

1. Invoke the **Dimension** menu and then click on the **Constrain auto radius/diameter** tool, see Figure 2.196. The **Constrain auto radius/diameter** tool gets activated.

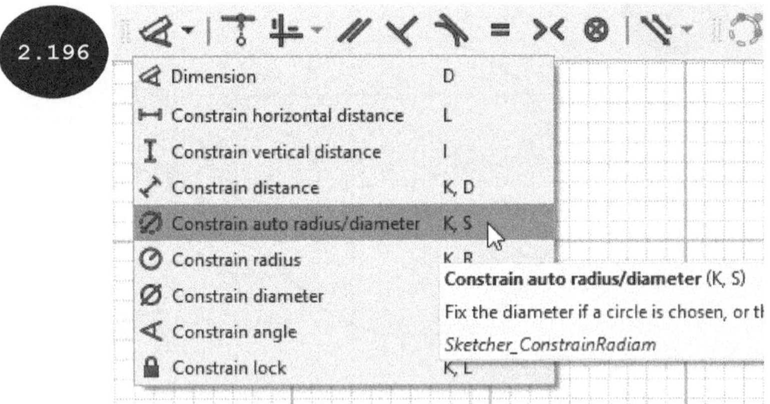

2. Select the left arc of the sketch. The **Insert radius** pop-up dialog box appears with the display of its current radius value.

3. Enter **2.5** inches in the **Radius** field of the dialog box and then click on the **OK** button in the pop-up dialog box. A radius dimension gets applied to the selected arc, see Figure 2.197. The **Constrain auto radius/diameter** tool remains active.

4. Select the right arc of the sketch. The **Insert radius** pop-up dialog box appears.

5. Enter **1.5** inches in the **Radius** field of the dialog box and then click on the **OK** button. A radius dimension gets applied to the selected arc, see Figure 2.198. The **Constrain auto radius/diameter** tool remains active.

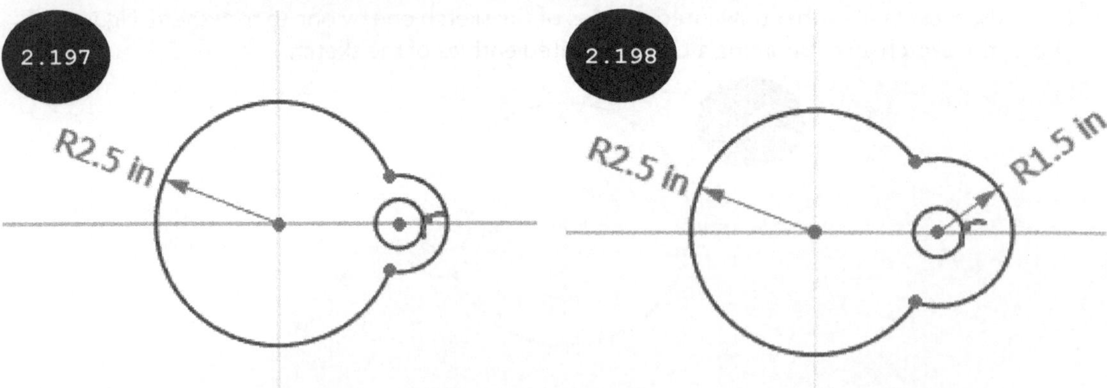

6. Select the inner circle of the sketch. The **Insert diameter** pop-up dialog box appears.

7. Enter **2** inches in the **Diameter** field of the dialog box and then click on the **OK** button. A diameter dimension gets applied to the selected circle, see Figure 2.199. Next, right-click to exit the **Constrain auto radius/diameter** tool.

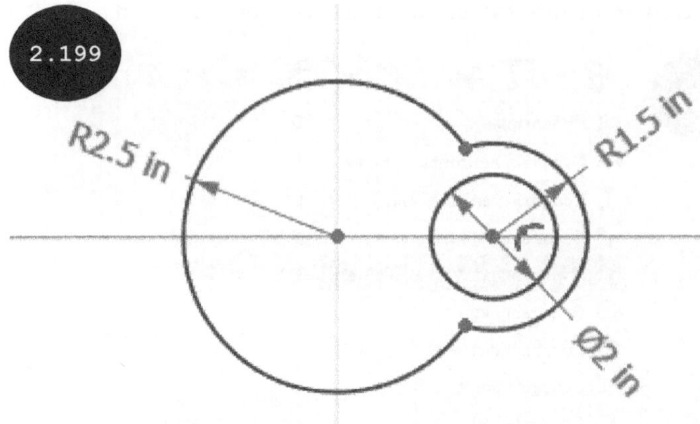

Tip: You can change the position of applied dimensions in the drawing area by dragging and dropping them to the required location in the 3D View area.

Section 7: Applying Geometric Constraints

After applying the dimensions, if the sketch is not fully constrained then you need to apply the required geometric constraints to make it a fully constrained sketch.

1. Invoke the **Constrain horizontal/vertical** menu and then click on the **Constrain horizontally** tool (see Figure 2.200) or press the H key to apply a horizontal constraint.

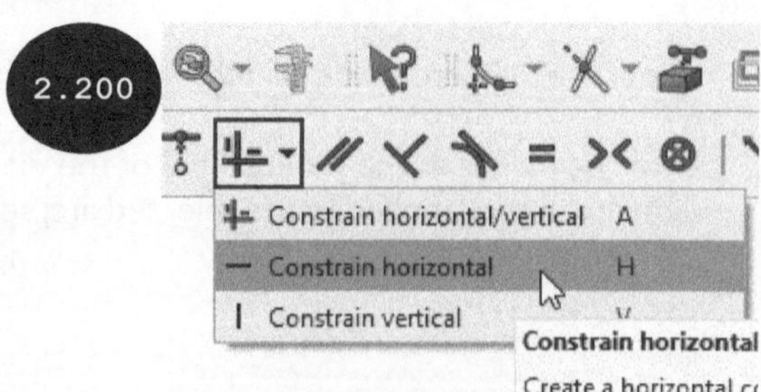

2. Select the origin and then the center point of the right circle of the sketch one by one to make them horizontally aligned to each other, see Figure 2.201. The horizontal constraint gets applied, and the sketch becomes fully constrained, see Figure 2.202. Next, right-click to exit the tool.

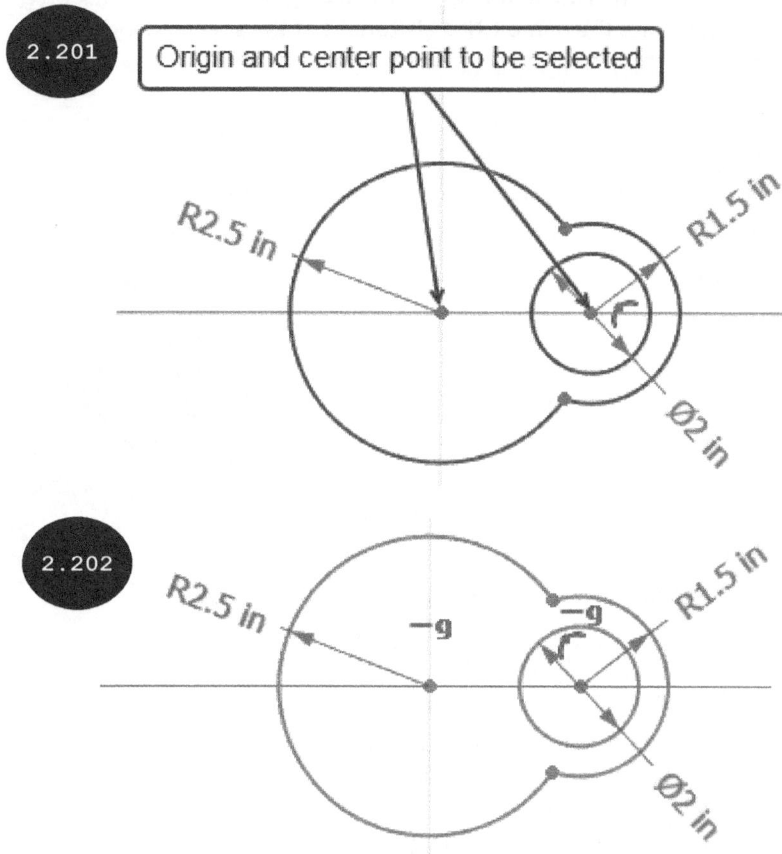

After creating a sketch, you need to exit the Sketch editing mode of the **Sketcher** workbench.

3. Click on the **Leave sketch** tool in the **Sketcher** toolbar to exit the Sketch editing mode of the **Sketcher** workbench (see Figure 2.203) and switch back to the **Part Design** workbench.

Section 8: Saving the Sketch

1. Click on the **Save** tool in the **File** toolbar or press the CTRL + S keys. The **Save FreeCAD Document** dialog box appears.

2. Browse to the **FreeCAD > Chapter 2** folders in the local drive of your system. You need to create these folders if not created earlier.

3. Enter **Ch02-Tutorial 2** in the **File name** field of the dialog box and then click on the **Save** button. The sketch gets saved with the name **Ch02-Tutorial 2** at the specified location.

Hands-on Test Drive 1

Create a sketch of the model shown in Figure 2.204 and make it fully constrained. The model shown in this figure is for your reference only. All dimensions are in mm.

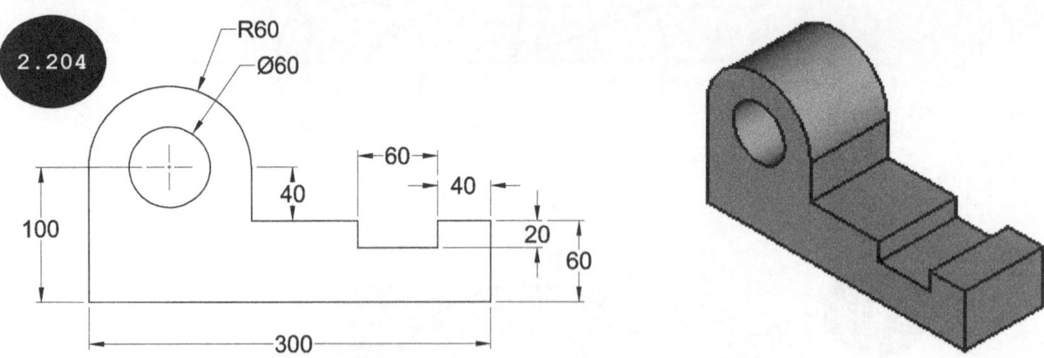

Hands-on Test Drive 2

Create a sketch of the model shown in Figure 2.205 and make it fully constrained. The model shown in this figure is for your reference only. All dimensions are in inches (in).

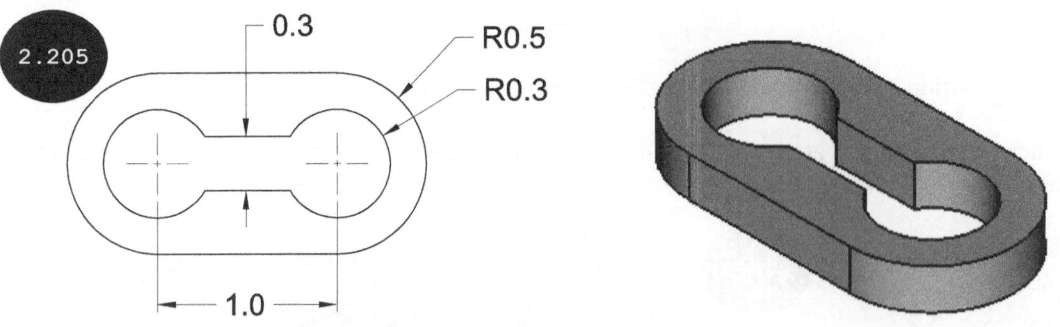

Hands-on Test Drive 3

Create a sketch of the model shown in Figure 2.206 and make it fully constrained. The model shown in this figure is for your reference only. All dimensions are in mm.

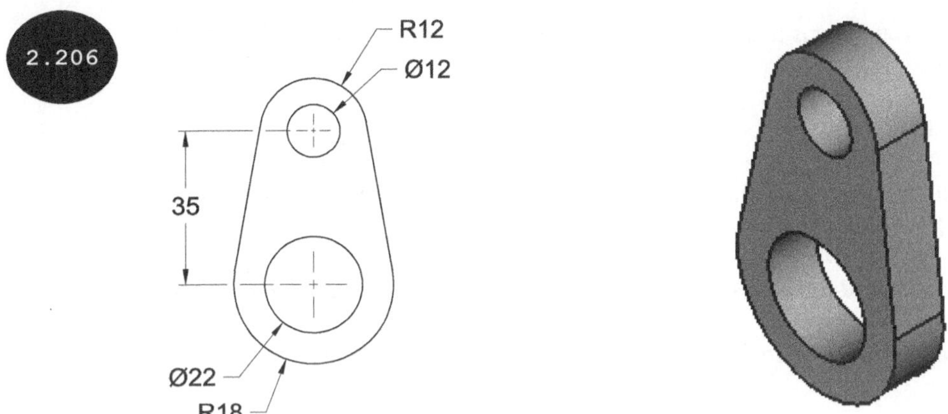

Summary

This chapter discussed how to invoke the **Sketcher Workbench** within the **Part Design** workbench by selecting a sketching plane for creating a sketch. It explained how to specify units as well as the grids and snap settings. The chapter discussed different methods for drawing lines, arcs, circles, ellipses, elliptical arcs, hyperbolic arcs, parabolic arcs, B-splines, polylines, rectangles, polygons, and slots by using the respective sketching tools. Methods for creating fillets, trimming sketch entities, extending sketch entities, and creating construction sketch entities are also discussed, in addition to the application of geometric and dimensional constraints, editing and modifying dimensions, and different states of a sketch.

Questions

Complete and verify the following sentences:

- Features are divided into two main categories: _________ and _________.
- Every time you start FreeCAD, the _________ workbench is invoked with **Start** page, by default.
- The _________ tool is used for drawing a circle by specifying three points on its circumference.
- The _________ key is used for cycling through all six different polyline modes (segments).
- The _________ tool is used for drawing a polygon with the number of sides ranging from _________ to _________.

- The ______ tool is used for creating a fillet between two sketch entities.
- ________ help you specify points in the 3D View area for creating sketch entities and act as reference lines.
- The ______ constraint is used for making two sketch entities such as a circle and a line tangent to each other.
- In FreeCAD, a 2D sketch can be either ______, ______, and ______.
- The availability of toolbars in the Toolbar Area of a new document depends upon the activated workbench. (True/False)
- A fully constrained sketch is a sketch, whose all degrees of freedom are fixed. (True/False)
- You cannot apply a reference dimension to a sketch entity. (True/False)

CHAPTER

3

Creating Base Feature of a 3D Solid Model

This chapter discusses the following topics:

- Creating a Pad Feature
- Creating a Revolution Feature
- Navigating a 3D Model in the 3D View Area
- Displaying Standard Views of a Model
- Working with Navigation Cube
- Changing the Display Style of a Model

Once a sketch has been created and fully constrained, you can convert it into a 3D solid feature in the Part Design workbench, see Figure 3.1. In this figure, the display of dimensions and constraints of the sketch is turned off for the clarity of the image.

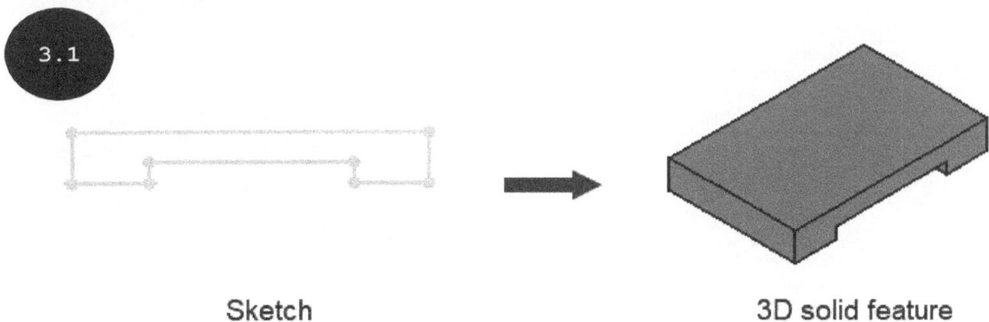

In the Part Design workbench, you can convert a sketch into a 3D solid feature by using the feature modeling tools available in the **Part Design Modeling** toolbar, see Figure 3.2. Note that to create a complete 3D solid model, you need to create all its features one by one using the feature modeling tools, see Figure 3.3. The first created feature of a model is known as the base feature or the parent feature of the model.

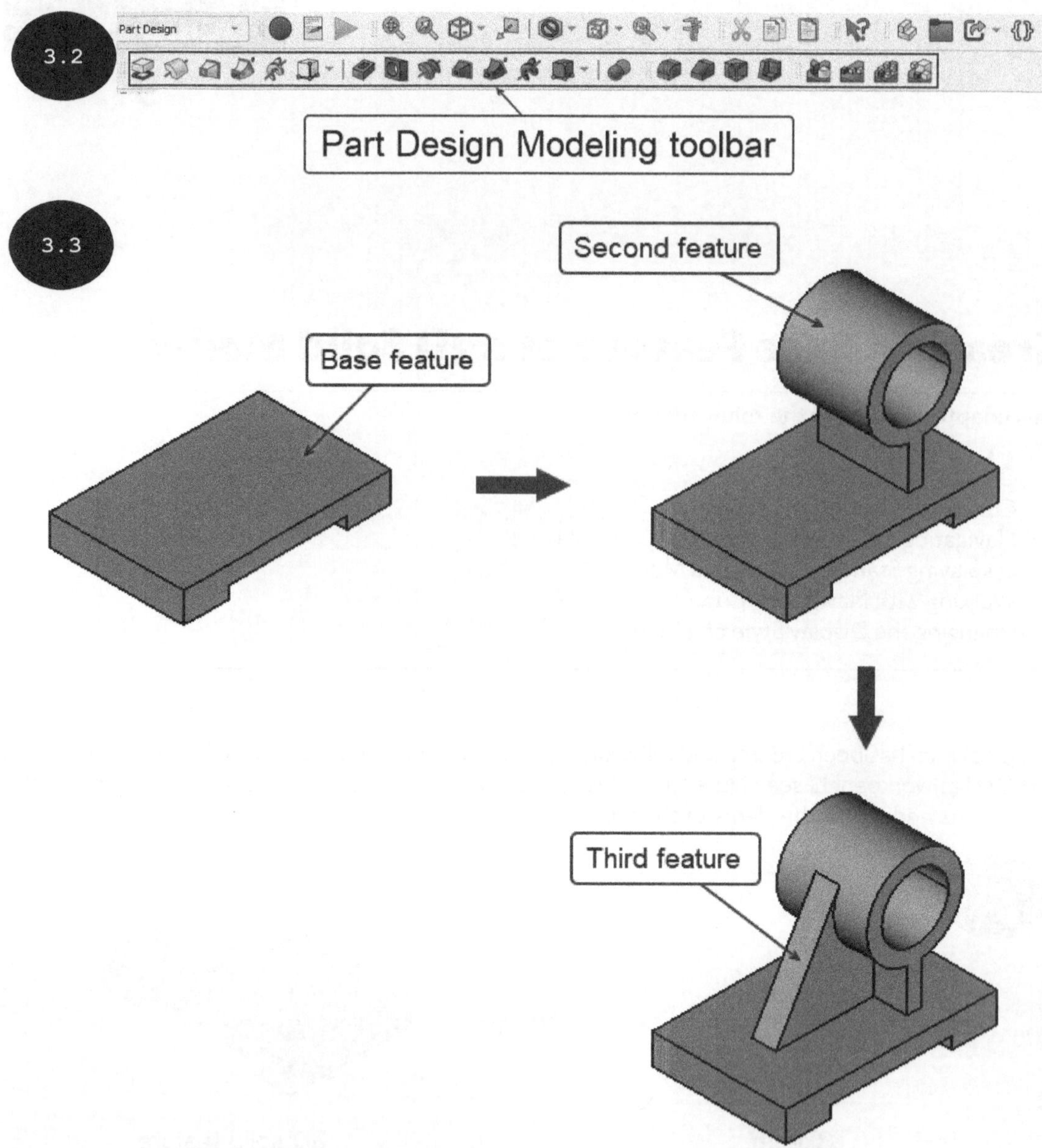

In FreeCAD, you can create the base feature of a model using various feature modeling tools such as **Pad**, **Revolution**, **Additive loft**, **Additive pipe**, and **Additive helix**. In this chapter, you will learn how to create a base feature of a model using the **Pad** and **Revolution** tools. The other tools will be discussed in later chapters.

Creating a Pad Feature

A pad feature is created by extruding a sketch normal to the sketching plane, see Figure 3.4. In FreeCAD, you can create a pad feature using the **Pad** tool.

3.4

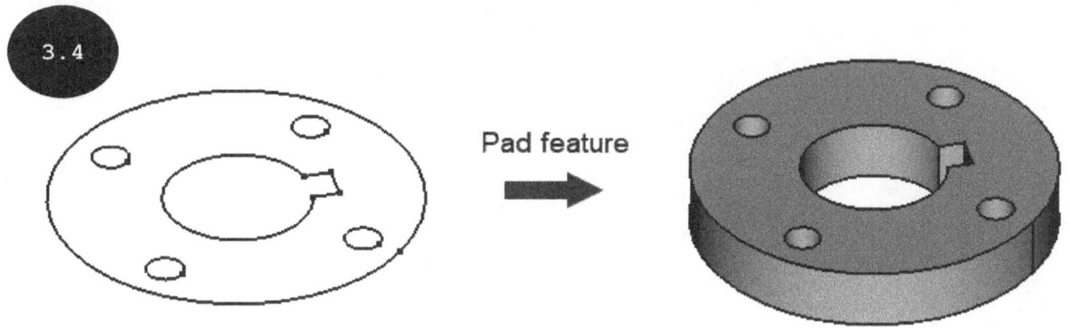

Note: The sketch of a pad feature should be closed. A closed sketch can have single or multiple enclosed profiles. Figure 3.4 shows a sketch that has six closed profiles.

1. After creating a closed sketch of a pad feature, exit the **Sketcher** workbench and switch back to the **Part Design** workbench. You can exit the Sketcher workbench by clicking on the **Leave sketch** tool in the **Sketcher** toolbar, see Figure 3.5.

3.5

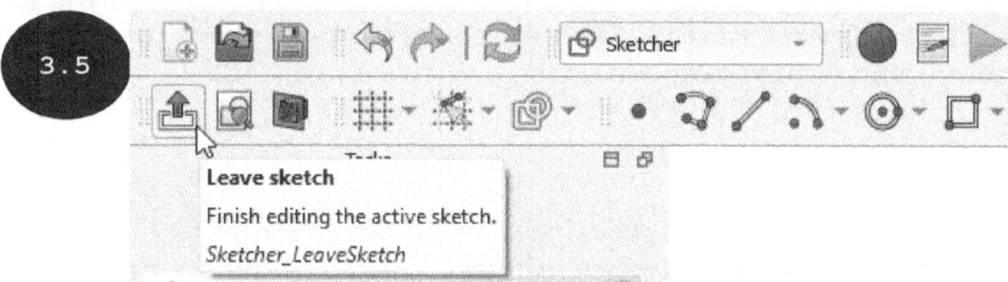

2. In the **Part Design** workbench, click on the **Pad** tool in the **Part Design Modeling** toolbar, see Figure 3.6. The preview of a pad feature appears in the 3D View area with default parameters since the sketch to be extruded gets selected automatically. Also, the **Pad parameters** sub-window appears in the **Tasks Panel** of the **Tasks** tab in **Combo View**, see Figure 3.7.

3.6

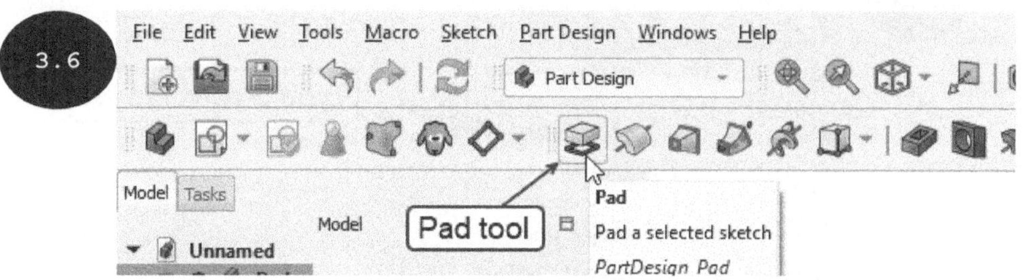

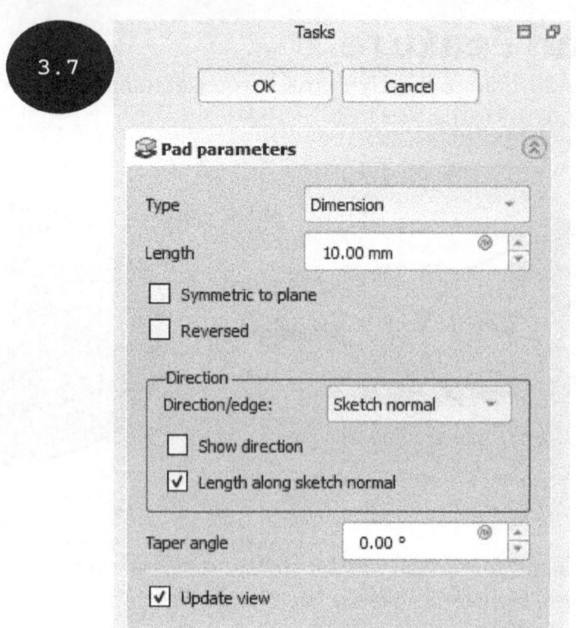

Note: If only one closed sketch is available in the 3D View area, then on invoking the **Pad** tool, it will be selected automatically as the sketch to be extruded and the preview of the pad feature appears. However, if two or more closed sketches are available in the 3D View area, then on invoking the **Pad** tool, you need to select a sketch to be extruded, manually. You can select a sketch to be extruded in the 3D View area or in the **Select feature** sub-window that will appear in the **Tasks Panel**.

The options in the **Pad parameters** sub-window of the **Tasks Panel** (refer to Figure 3.7) are used for specifying the required parameters to create a pad feature and the same are discussed below:

Type: The **Type** drop-down list is used for selecting an option to define the length of the pad feature, see Figure 3.8. The various options available in this drop-down list are discussed below:

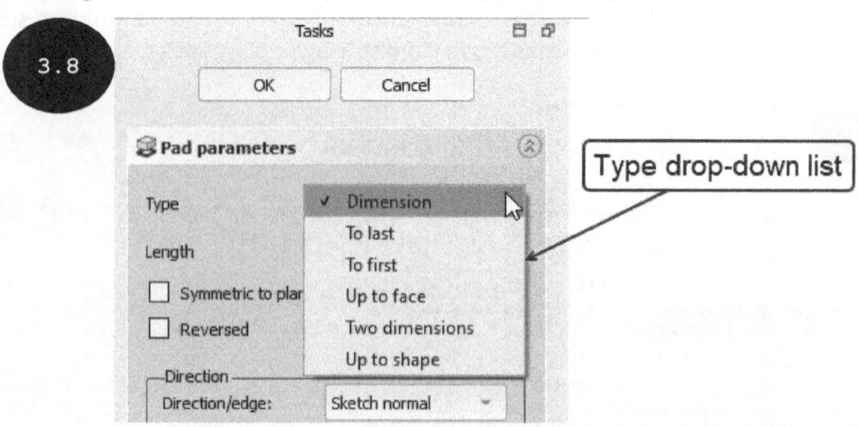

Dimension: The **Dimension** option in the **Type** drop-down list is used for extruding the sketch of a pad feature on one side of the sketching plane by specifying its length value in the **Length** field of the **Pad parameters** sub-window, see Figures 3.9 and 3.10. You can also reverse the direction of extrusion to the other side of the sketching plane by selecting the **Reversed** check box in the **Pad parameters** sub-window.

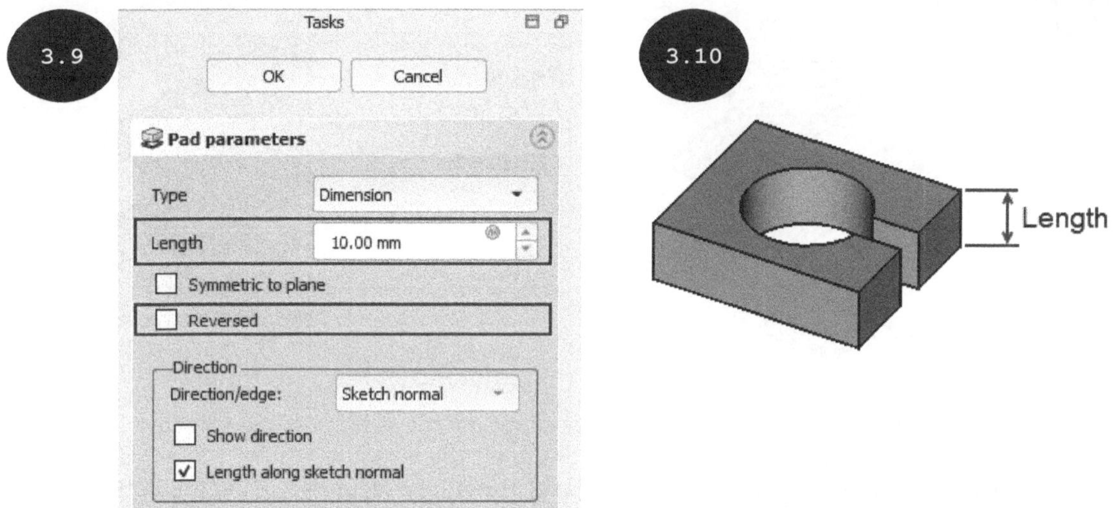

To last: The **To last** option is used for extruding the sketch up to its last intersection with a face of an existing feature of the model along the direction of extrusion. Figure 3.11 shows a sketch (circle) and the preview of a resultant pad feature extruded up to its last intersection.

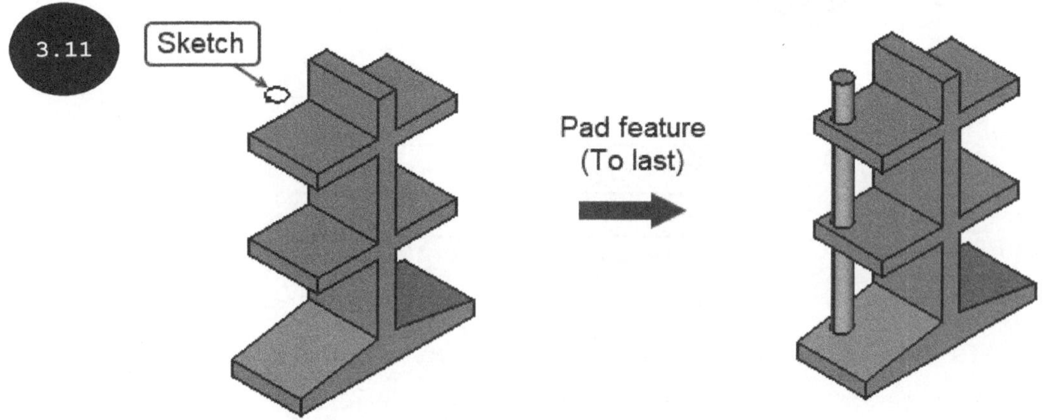

Note: The **To last** option can be used while creating second or further features of a model where the sketch of the pad feature can extrude up to its last intersecting face of an existing feature. This option cannot be used while creating a base feature of a model. You will learn how to build a multi-feature model in later chapters.

Tip: To extrude a sketch up to its last intersecting face of an existing feature, you may need to reverse the direction of extrusion to the other side of the sketching plane by selecting the **Reversed** check box in the **Pad parameters** sub-window of the **Tasks Panel**.

To first: The **To first** option is used for extruding the sketch up to its first or nearest intersecting face of an existing feature along the direction of extrusion. Figure 3.12 shows a sketch (circle) and the preview of a resultant pad feature extruded up to its first intersection.

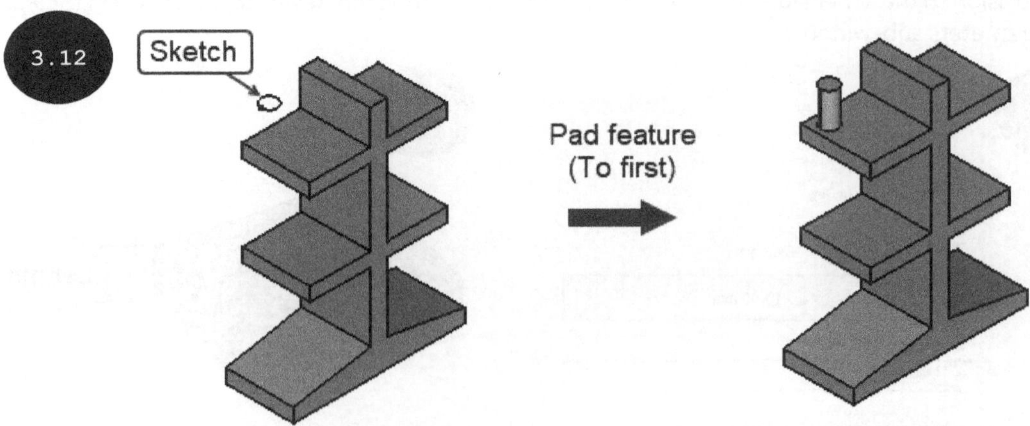

Up to face: The **Up to face** option is used for extruding the sketch up to a selected face of an existing feature or a plane. When you select this option, the **Select face** button and a field appear in the **Pad parameters** sub-window of the **Tasks Panel** (see Figure 3.13) and are activated, by default. Consequently, you can select a face of an existing feature or a plane up to which you would like to extrude the sketch of the pad feature, see Figure 3.14.

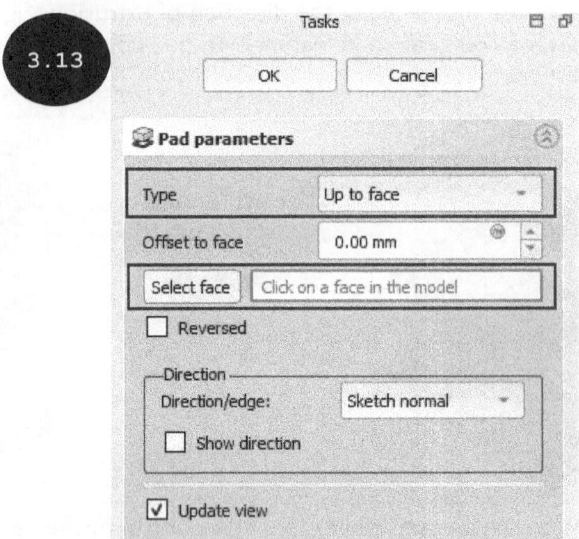

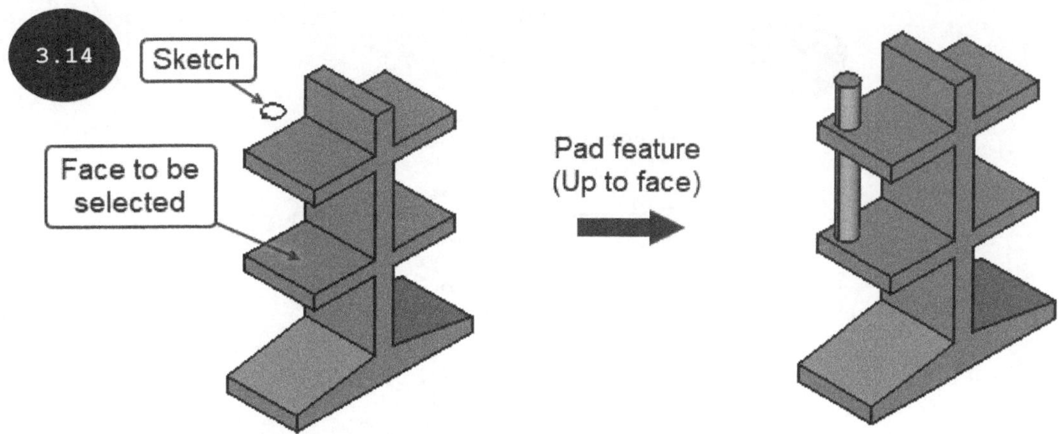

Tip: If you want to replace an already selected face/plane with another face/plane for extruding the sketch, click on the **Select face** button in the **Pad parameters** sub-window and then select a new face/plane of the model up to which you want to extrude the sketch.

Note: The **To last**, **To first**, and **Up to face** options work while creating second or further features of a model. You cannot use these options while creating a base feature of a model. You will learn how to build a multi-feature model in the later chapters.

Two dimensions: The **Two dimensions** option is used for extruding the sketch asymmetrically on both sides of the sketching plane with different extrusion lengths, see Figure 3.15. When the **Two dimensions** option is selected in the **Type** drop-down list, the **Length** and **2nd length** fields are enabled in the **Pad parameters** sub-window, see Figure 3.16. In these fields, you can specify different extrusion lengths on both sides (first and second) of the sketching plane, respectively. You can also switch between the extrusion directions (first and second) by selecting the **Reversed** check box in the **Pad parameters** sub-window.

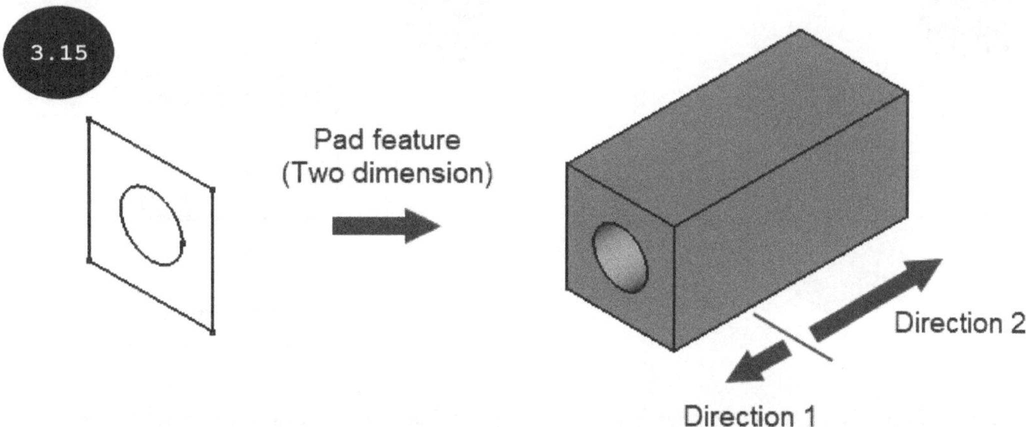

3.16

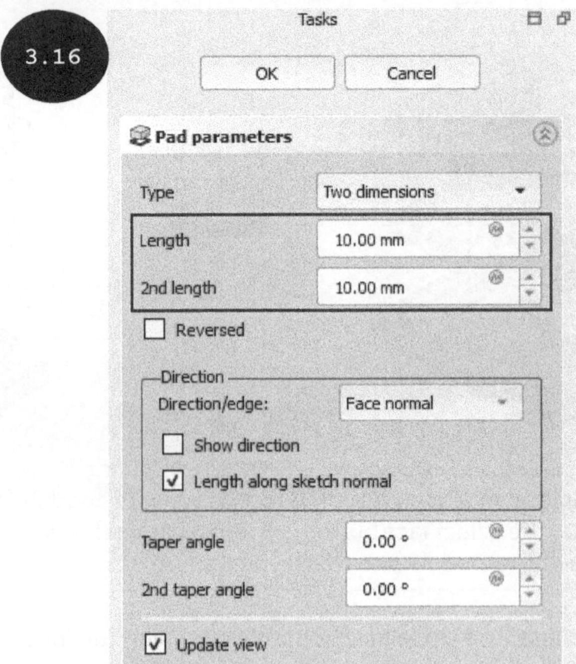

Up to Shape: The Up to Shape option allows you to extrude a sketch up to one or more nearest intersecting faces of an existing feature. By default, when this option is selected, the sketch extrudes to all the nearest intersecting faces, as the **Select all faces** check box is selected by default, see Figure 3.17.

To extrude the sketch to a specific face, first, clear the **Select all faces** check box. Then, click the **Select** button that appears below it and choose the desired face on the model. After selecting a face, click the **Preview** button to visualize the extrusion in the 3D View area, see Figure 3.18.

3.17 3.18

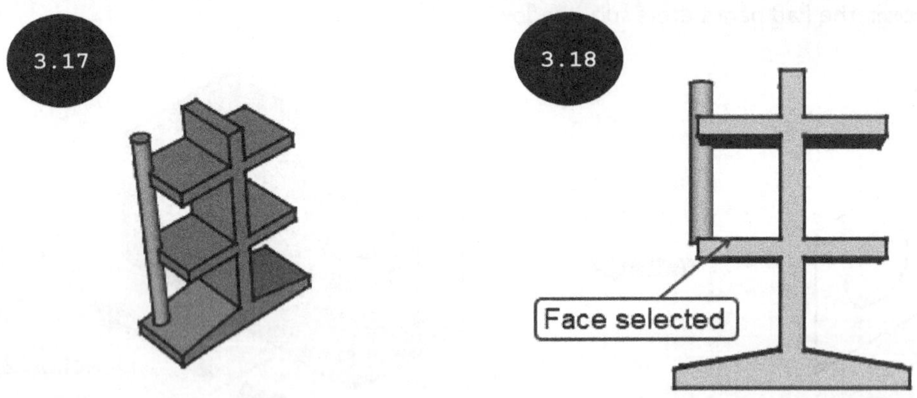

Offset to face: The Offset to face field is used for defining the termination or end of extrusion at an offset distance from face of a model, see Figure 3.19. Note that the **Offset to face** field is enabled in the **Pad parameters** sub-window when the **To last**, **To first**, or **Up to face** option is selected in the **Type** drop-down list for creating a pad feature, as discussed earlier.

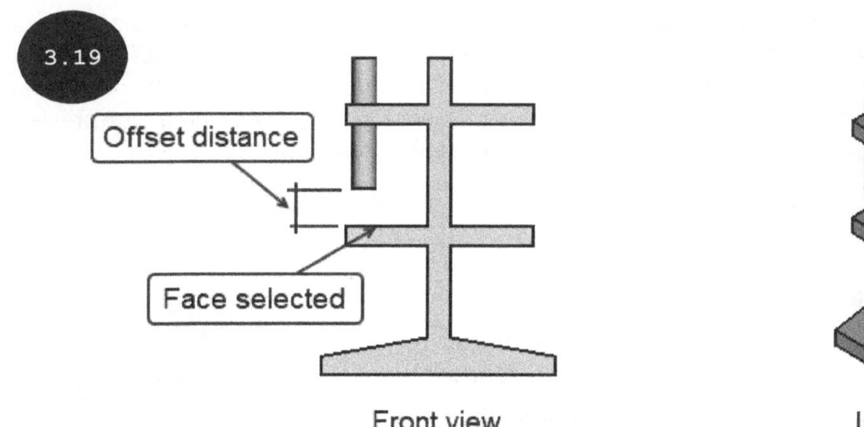

Note: By default, the 0 offset value is entered in the **Offset to face** field. Consequently, the end of extrusion is defined exactly on the face/plane of a model depending upon whether the **To last**, **To first**, or **Up to face** option is selected in the **Type** drop-down list.

Direction/edge: The options in the **Direction/edge** drop-down list of the **Direction** area are used for defining a direction of extrusion of the pad feature, see Figure 3.20. The options in this drop-down list are discussed below:

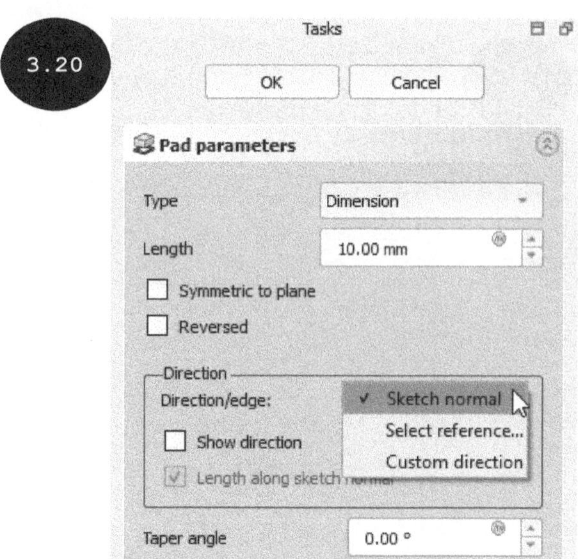

Sketch normal: By default, the **Sketch normal** option is selected in the **Direction/edge** drop-down list. Consequently, the default direction of extrusion of a pad feature is defined as normal to the sketching plane.

Select reference: The **Select reference** option is used for defining the direction of extrusion of a pad feature along a selected direction reference, see Figure 3.21. To do this, select the **Select reference** option in the **Direction/edge** drop-down list and then select a linear sketch entity (line) or a linear edge of an existing feature as the direction reference in the 3D View area. The preview of a pad feature appears along the selected direction reference, see Figure 3.21.

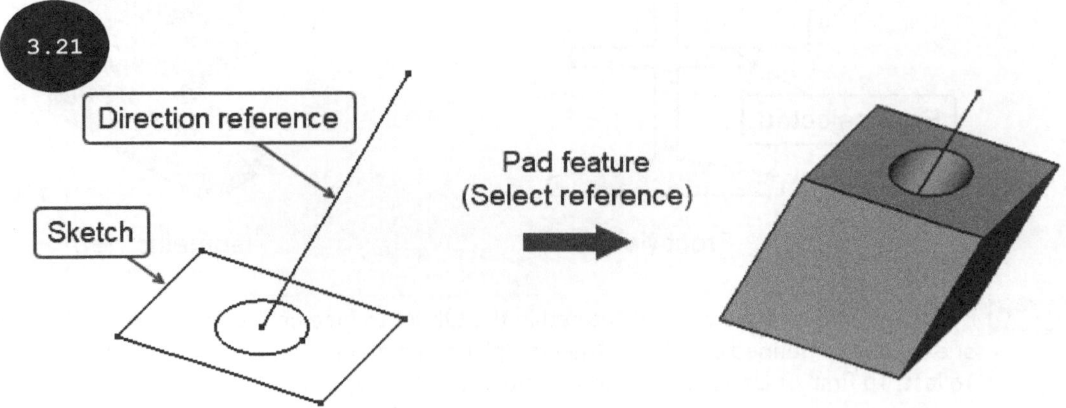

Custom direction: The **Custom direction** option is used for defining the direction of extrusion of a pad feature by specifying X, Y, and Z vector values. To do this, select the **Custom direction** option in the **Direction/edge** drop-down list and then enter X, Y, and Z vector values in the respective **x**, **y**, and **z** fields that appear in the **Pad parameters** sub-window of the **Tasks Panel**, see Figure 3.22.

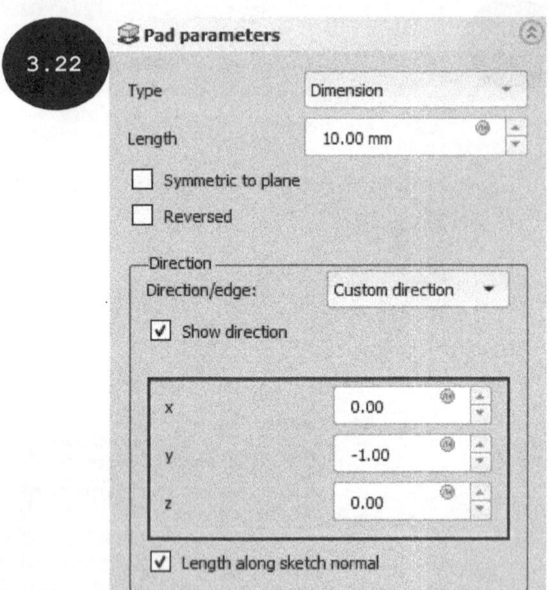

Length along sketch normal: When the **Length along sketch normal** check box is selected in the **Direction** area of the **Pad parameters** sub-window, the extrusion length of the pad feature is measured along the normal direction to the sketching plane, see Figure 3.23. However, when this check box is cleared, the extrusion length is measured along the specified custom direction of the pad feature, see Figure 3.24.

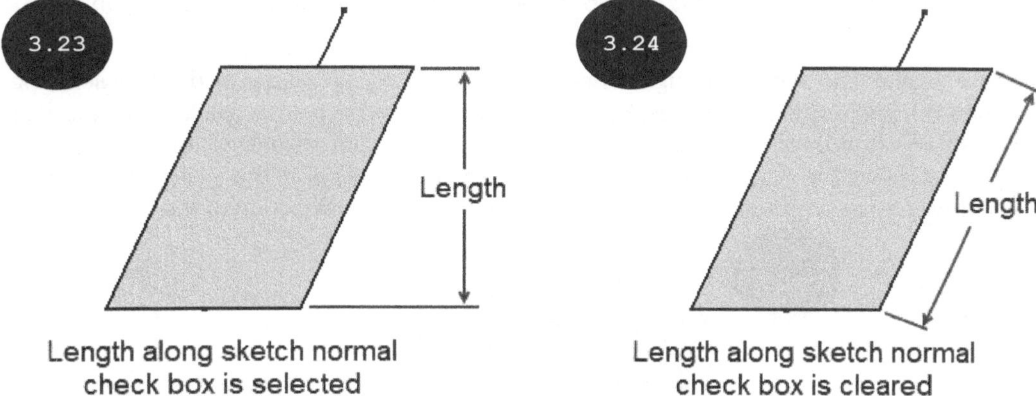

Symmetric to plane: The **Symmetric to plane** check box is used for extruding the sketch of a pad feature symmetrically on both sides of the sketching plane. On selecting the **Symmetric to plane** check box, the extrusion length of the pad feature specified in the **Length** field gets divided equally into both sides of the sketching plane and creates a symmetrical pad feature. For example, if the extrusion length is specified as 100 mm, then the resultant pad feature will be created by adding 50 mm of material to each side of the sketching plane. Note that this check box is available only when the **Dimension** option is selected in the **Type** drop-down list of the **Pad parameters** sub-window for creating a pad feature.

Reversed: The **Reversed** check box is used for reversing the direction of the extrusion of a pad feature to the other side of the sketching plane.

Taper angle: The **Taper angle** field is used for specifying a taper or draft angle along the direction of extrusion for creating a tapered pad feature. By default, the **0** draft angle is entered in this field. Therefore, the resultant pad feature is created without having any tapering in it. You can enter the required draft angle in the **Taper angle** field. Note that a negative draft angle adds taper in the inward direction of the sketch (see Figure 3.25), whereas a positive draft angle adds draft in the outward direction of the sketch (see Figure 3.26), or vice-versa depending upon whether the **Reversed** check box is selected or cleared, respectively.

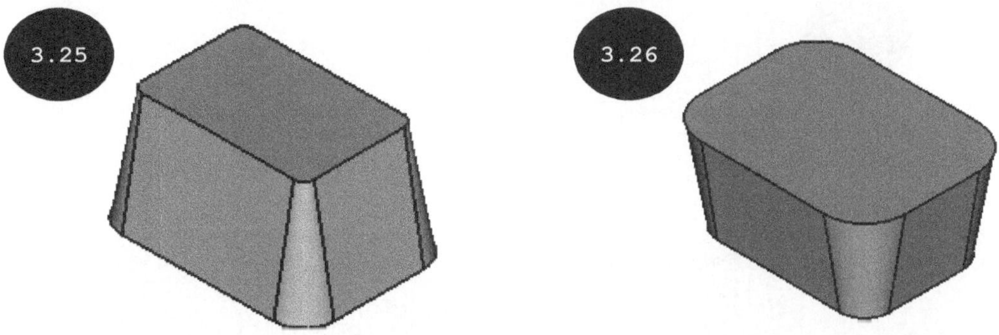

Note: The **Taper angle** field is available in the **Pad parameters** sub-window of the **Tasks Panel** when the **Dimension** or **Two dimensions** option is selected in the **Type** drop-down list.

2nd taper angle: The **2nd taper angle** field is used for specifying a taper or draft angle along the second direction of extrusion, see Figure 3.27. Note that this field is available in the **Pad parameters** sub-window of the **Tasks Panel** only when the **Two dimensions** option is selected in the **Type** drop-down list. Also, a negative draft angle value adds taper in the inward direction of the sketch, whereas a positive draft angle adds draft in the outward direction of the sketch.

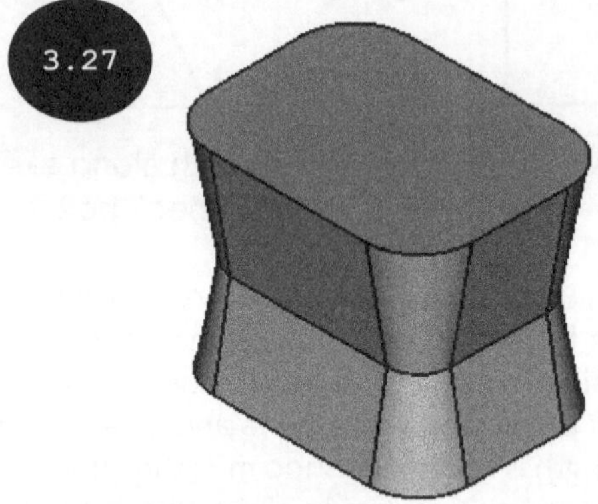

Update view: By default, the **Update view** check box is selected in the **Pad parameters** sub-window of the **Tasks Panel**. Therefore, the pad feature being created gets updated in real-time in the 3D View area by specifying or editing its parameters in the **Pad parameters** sub-window of the **Tasks Panel**.

3. Specify the required parameters in the **Pad parameters** sub-window of the **Tasks Panel** for creating a pad feature, as discussed above.

4. Click on the **OK** button in the **Tasks Panel** of the **Tasks** tab, see Figure 3.28. The pad feature of specified parameters gets created in the 3D View area. Also, its default name gets added under the **Body** node of the **Tree View** in the **Model** tab, see Figure 3.29. You can click on the **Model** tab of the **Tasks Panel** to display the **Tree View**.

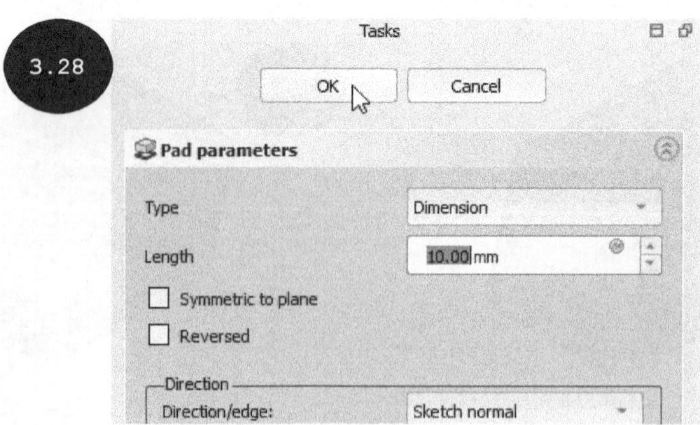

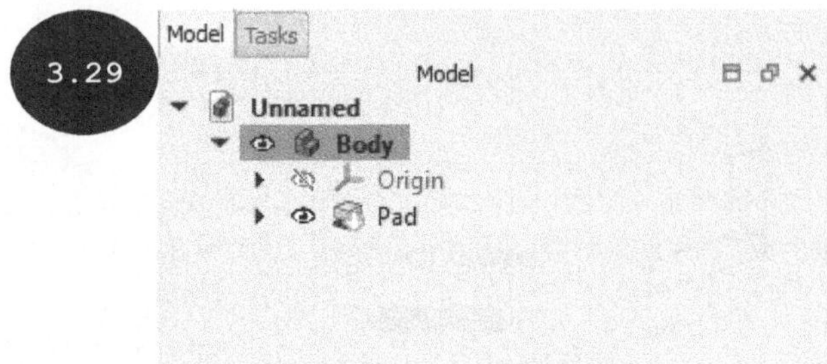

Creating a Revolution Feature

A revolution feature is created by revolving a closed sketch around an axis, see Figure 3.30. In this figure, the sketch revolved 270 degrees around an axis to create a revolution feature. In FreeCAD, you can create a revolution feature by using the **Revolution** tool. The method for creating a revolution feature is discussed below:

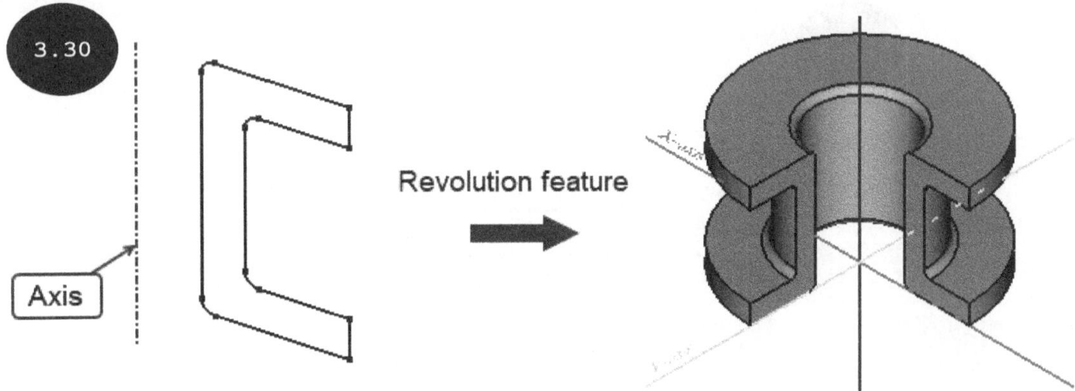

1. After creating a sketch of a revolution feature, exit the **Sketcher** workbench and switch back to the **Part Design** workbench by clicking on the **Leave sketch** tool in the **Sketcher** toolbar. Note that the sketch of the revolution feature should be closed and on either side of its axis of revolution.

2. Click on the **Revolution** tool in the **Part Design Modeling** toolbar, see Figure 3.31. The preview of a revolution feature appears by revolving the sketch around its vertical axis in the 3D View area, see Figure 3.32. It is because the **Vertical sketch axis** option is selected, by default in the **Axis** drop-down list of the **Revolution parameters** sub-window that appears in the **Tasks Panel**, see Figure 3.33.

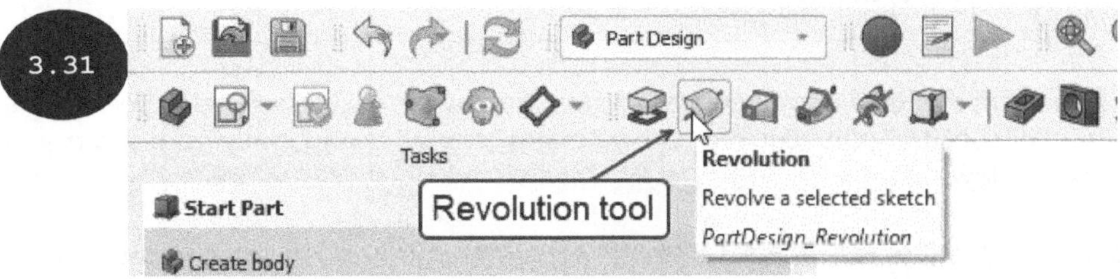

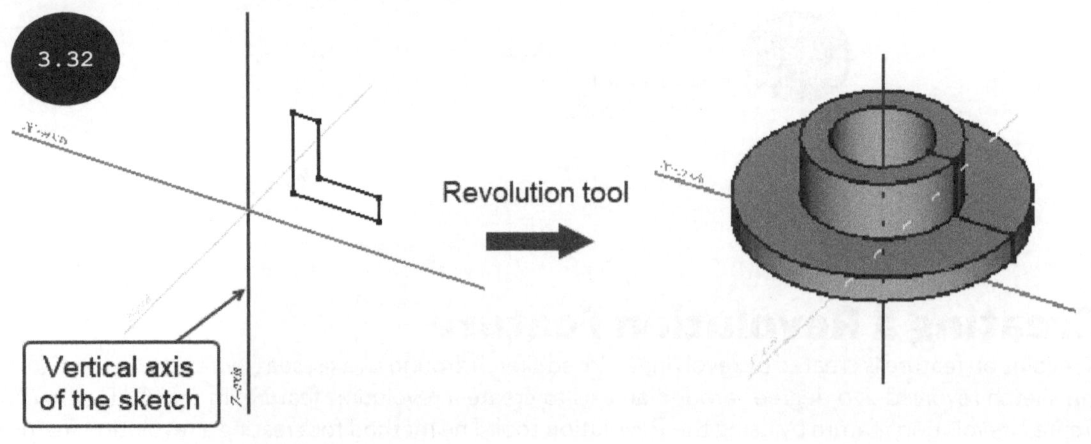

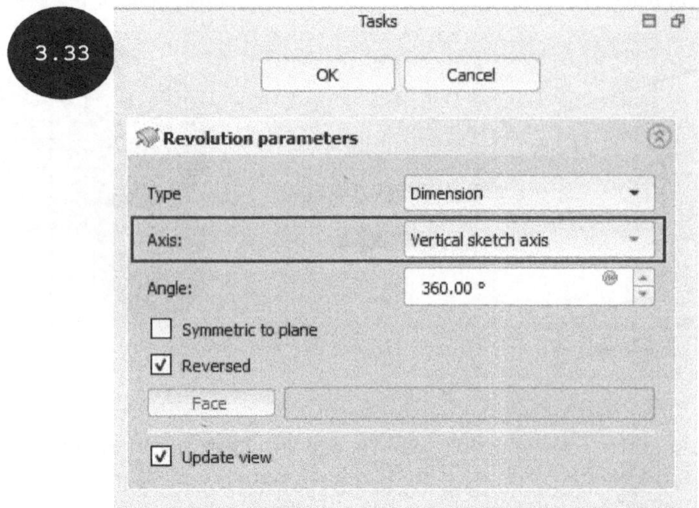

Note: If the sketch of the revolution feature is not on either side of its vertical axis, then on invoking the **Revolution** tool, an error will occur, and a preview of the revolution feature does not appear in the 3D View area. It is because the sketch cannot be revolved around the vertical axis that intersects with it. In this case, you need to define an axis of revolution for the sketch other than its vertical axis by selecting the required option in the **Axis** drop-down list of the **Revolution parameters** sub-window.

The options in the **Revolution parameters** sub-window of the **Tasks Panel** (refer to Figure 3.33) are used for specifying the required parameters to create a revolution feature and the same are discussed below:

Type: The **Type** drop-down list is used to select an option to define the end condition of the revolution feature. The various options available in this drop-down list are discussed below:

Dimension: The **Dimension** option enables you to revolve a sketch on one side of the sketching plane by specifying an angle of revolution. By default, this option is selected in the **Type** drop-down list, making the **Angle** field available in the sub-window. You can enter the desired angle value in this field. The default angle is set to 360 degrees, allowing the sketch to complete a full revolution around the selected axis.

To last: The **To last** option is used to revolve the sketch up to its last intersection face of an existing feature of the model along the direction of revolution.

Note: The **To last** option can be used when creating second or subsequent features in a model, allowing the sketch of the revolution feature to revolve up to its last intersecting face of an existing feature. However, this option cannot be used for creating a base feature. You will learn how to build multi-feature models in later chapters.

To first: The **To first** option is used to revolve the sketch up to its first or nearest intersecting face of an existing feature along the direction of revolution.

Up to face: The **Up to face** option is used to revolve the sketch up to a selected face of an existing feature or a plane. When you select this option, the **Face** button and a field become active in **the Tasks Panel**. You can then choose a face of an existing feature or a plane up to which you would like to revolve the sketch of the revolution feature.

Note: The **To last**, **To first**, and **Up to face** options work while creating second or subsequent features of a model. You cannot use these options while creating a base feature of a model. You will learn how to build a multi-feature model in the later chapters.

Two dimensions: The **Two dimensions** option allows you to revolve a sketch asymmetrically on both sides of the sketching plane with different revolution angles, see Figure 3.34. When this option is selected in the **Type** drop-down list, the **Angle** and **2nd angle** fields become available in the sub-window, see Figure 3.35. You can specify different revolution angles for each side of the sketching plane. Additionally, you can switch the revolution directions by selecting or clearing the **Reversed** check box in the sub-window.

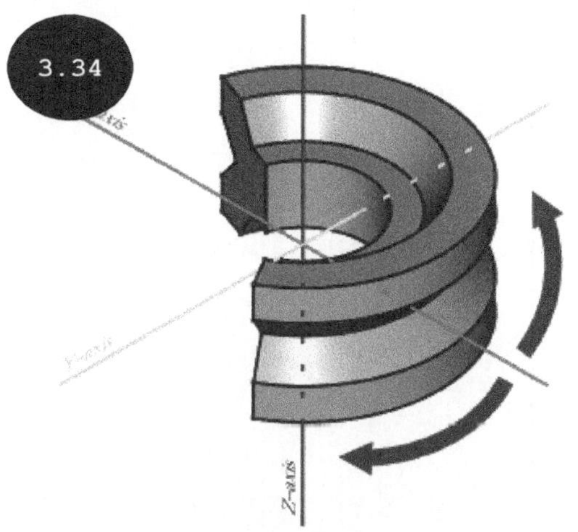

3.34

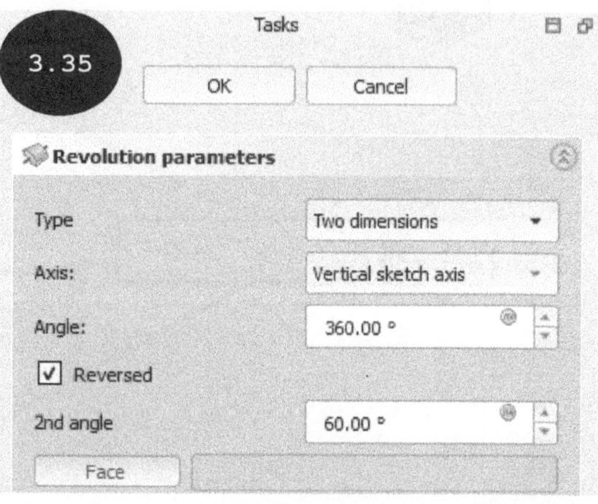

3.35

Axis: The Axis drop-down list is used for selecting an option to define the axis of revolution of the revolution feature (see Figure 3.36) and the options are discussed below:

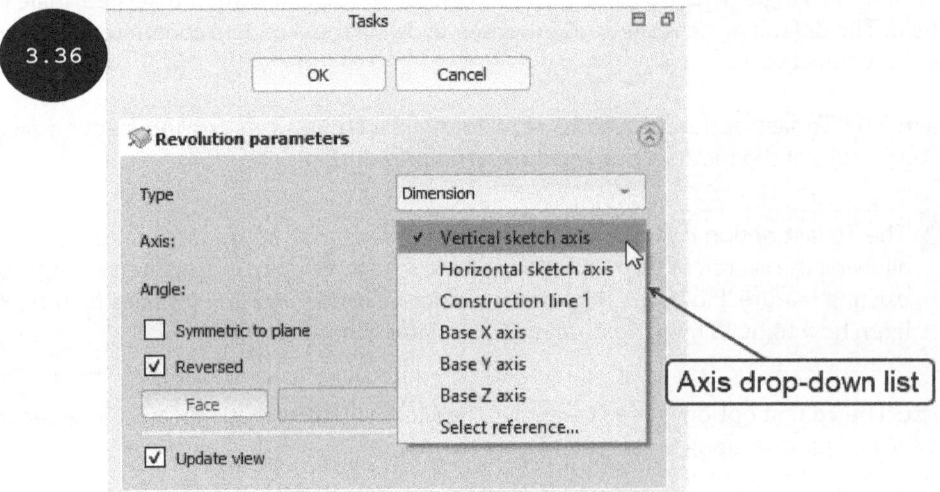

Vertical sketch axis: The **Vertical sketch axis** option is used for revolving the sketch around its vertical axis. A vertical axis of a sketch is an imaginary axis that is vertical to the sketch on its sketching plane.

Horizontal sketch axis: The **Horizontal sketch axis** option is used for revolving the sketch around its horizontal axis. A horizontal axis of a sketch is an imaginary axis that is horizontal to the sketch on its sketching plane.

Base X axis: The **Base X axis** option is used for revolving the sketch around the default X axis of the model, see Figure 3.37.

Base Y axis: The **Base Y axis** option is used for revolving the sketch around the default Y axis of the model, see Figure 3.37.

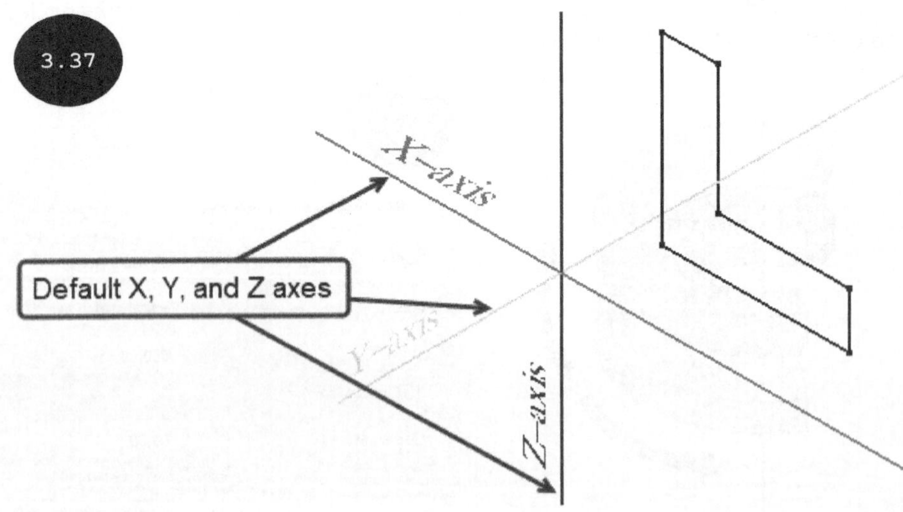

Base Z axis: The **Base Z axis** option is used for revolving the sketch around the default Z axis of the model, refer to Figure 3.37.

Select reference: The **Select reference** option is used for selecting a linear sketch entity (line) of an existing sketch, an axis, or a linear edge of an existing feature as the axis of revolution for creating a revolution feature.

Angle: The **Angle** field in the **Revolution parameters** sub-window of the **Tasks Panel** is used for specifying the required angle value for revolving the sketch around the axis.

Symmetric to plane: On selecting the **Symmetric to plane** check box, the sketch revolves symmetrically on both sides of the sketching plane, around the axis of revolution, see Figure 3.38. Note that when this check box is selected, the angle value specified in the **Angle** field is divided equally into both sides of the sketching plane and creates a symmetrical revolution feature.

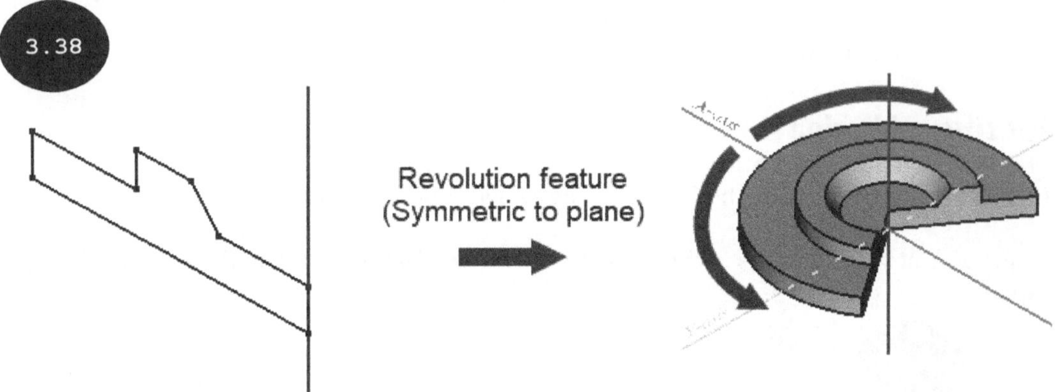

Reversed: The **Reversed** check box is used for reversing the direction of revolution to the other side of the sketching plane.

Update view: By default, the **Update view** check box is selected in the **Revolution parameters** sub-window of the **Tasks Panel**. As a result, the revolution feature being created gets updated in real-time in the 3D View area by specifying or editing its parameters.

3. Specify the required option in the **Axis** drop-down list of the **Revolution parameters** sub-window for defining the axis of revolution of the revolution feature.

4. Enter the required angle of revolution in the **Angle** field of the **Revolution parameters** sub-window.

5. Specify other parameters for creating a revolution feature and then click on the **OK** button in the **Tasks Panel** of the **Tasks** tab, see Figure 3.39. The revolution feature of specified parameters gets created in the 3D View area. Also, its default name gets added under the **Body** node of the **Tree View** in the **Model** tab. You can click on the **Model** tab of the **Combo View** to display the **Tree View**.

3.39

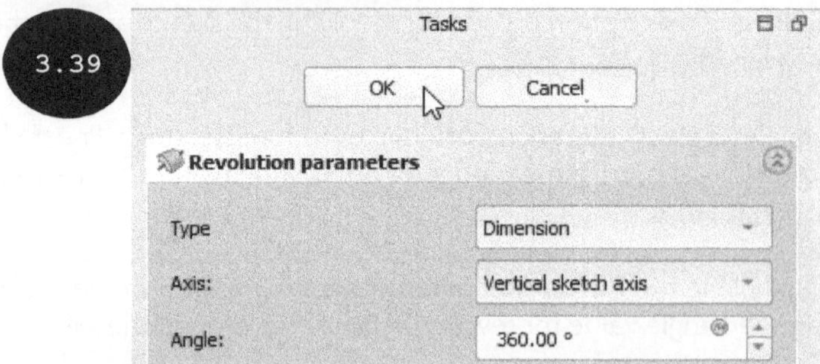

Navigating a 3D Model in the 3D View Area

In FreeCAD, you can navigate a model by using mouse buttons depending upon the active navigation style. A navigation style controls mouse shortcuts for panning, zooming, and rotating a model in the 3D View area. FreeCAD supports multiple navigation styles for navigating a model such as CAD, Revit, Blender, Touchpad, OpenSCAD, and TinkerCAD. The methods for selecting a navigation style and navigating a 3D model in the 3D View area are discussed next.

Selecting a Navigation Style

In FreeCAD, you can select a navigation style that controls the navigation settings by using the **Preferences** dialog box. The method for selecting a navigation style is discussed below:

1. Click on **Edit > Preferences** in the **Standard Menu**, see Figure 3.40. The **Preferences** dialog box appears.

3.40

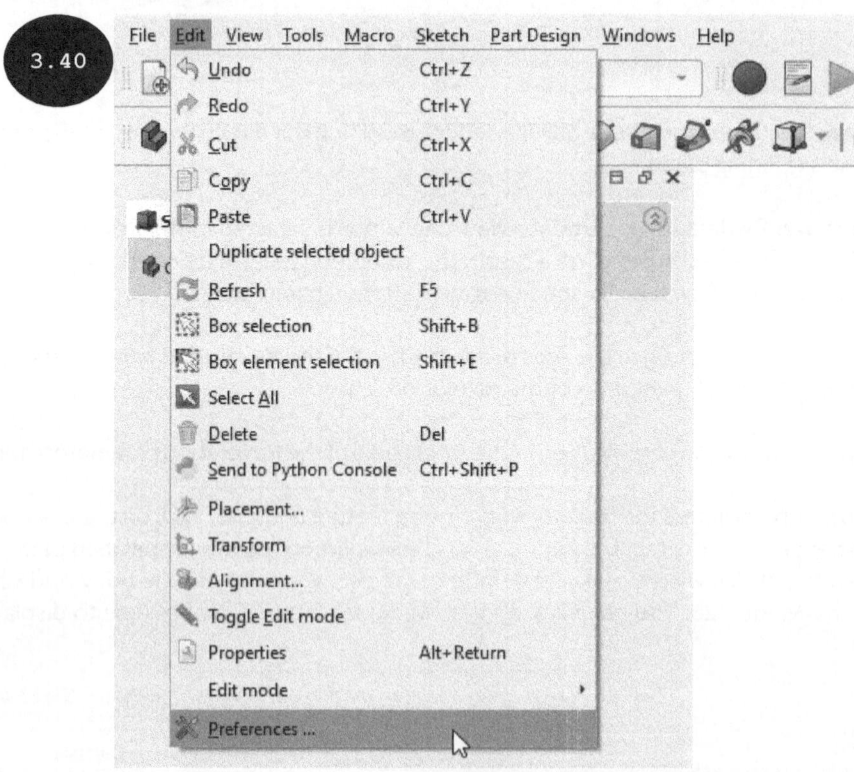

2. Select the **Display** section in the left panel of the **Preferences** dialog box and then click on the **Navigation** tab, see Figure 3.41. The options to control the navigation settings appear in the dialog box.

3.41

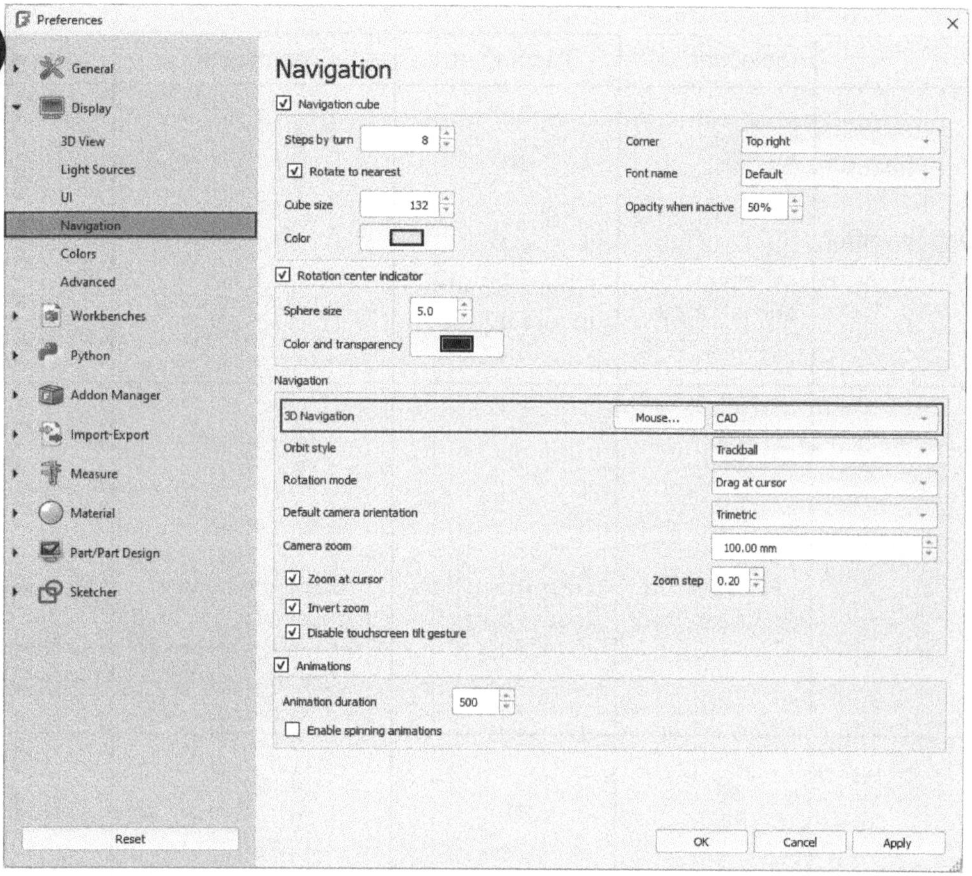

3. In the **3D Navigation** drop-down list of the dialog box, select the required navigation style, see Figure 3.42. By default, the **CAD** navigation style is selected.

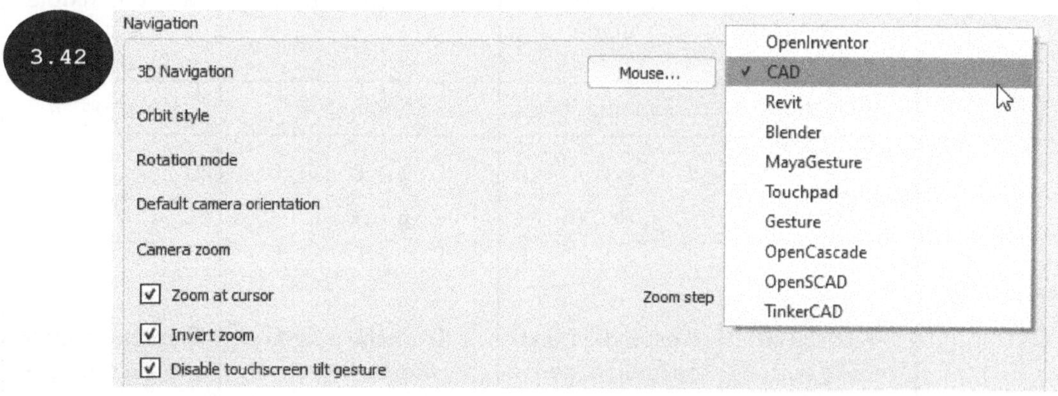

3.42

Note that depending upon the navigation style selected in the **3D Navigation** drop-down list, you can navigate a model by using the respective mouse configuration. Some of the navigation styles and the respective mouse configurations are given in the below table:

	Selection	Panning	Zooming	Rotation
OpenInventor	Press CTRL and left mouse button + drag	Press the middle mouse button + drag	Scroll the middle mouse button	Press the left mouse button + drag
CAD	Press the left mouse button + drag	Press the middle mouse button + drag	Scroll the middle mouse button or hold the middle and then click the left/right mouse button once	Press the middle and left or middle and right buttons + drag
Revit	Press the left mouse button + drag	Press the middle mouse button + drag	Scroll the middle mouse button	Press SHIFT and the middle mouse button + drag
	Selection	Panning	Zooming	Rotation
Blender	Press the left mouse button + drag	Press SHIFT and the middle mouse button + drag	Scroll the middle mouse button	Press the middle mouse button + drag

Touchpad	Press the left mouse button + drag	Press the SHIFT button + move mouse	Press the CTRL and SHIFT buttons + move the mouse	Press the ALT button + move the mouse
OpenSCAD	Press the left mouse button + drag	Press the right mouse button + drag	Press the middle mouse button or SHIFT and the right mouse button + drag	Press the left mouse button + drag
TinkerCAD	Press the left mouse button + drag	Press the middle mouse button + drag	Scroll the middle mouse button	Press the right mouse button + drag

Tip: After selecting a navigation style, you can view its mouse configuration for selection, panning, zooming, and rotation by click on the **Mouse** button available in front of the **3D Navigation** drop-down list in the dialog box.

Note: If needed, you can also define an orbit style and a rotation mode by selecting the required option in the **Orbit style** and **Rotation mode** drop-down lists in the **Navigation** tab of the **Preferences** dialog box, respectively.

4. After selecting the required navigation style, click on the **Apply** button and then on the **OK** button in the **Preferences** dialog box.

Tip: Alternatively, to select a navigation style, right-click on an empty area in the 3D View area and then move the cursor over the **Navigation styles** option in the shortcut menu that appears, see Figure 3.43. A cascading menu appears with the display of all the navigation styles. You can select the required navigation style in this cascading menu.

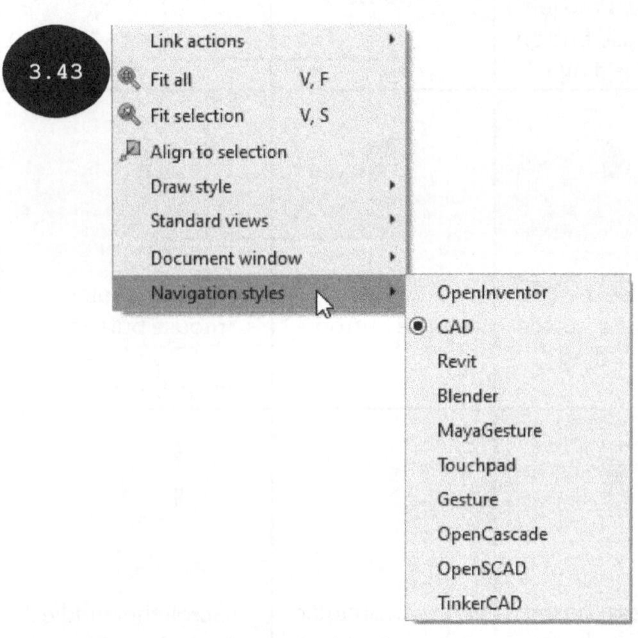

Note: In this textbook, the default **CAD** navigation style is used for panning, zooming, and rotating a model.

Now, you can navigate a model as per the navigation style specified in the **Preferences** dialog box. The method for navigating a model using the **CAD** navigation style is discussed next.

Pan

To pan or move a model in the 3D View area, press and hold the middle mouse button and then drag the cursor.

Zoom

To zoom into or out of the view of a model dynamically, scroll the middle mouse button up or down, respectively. On scrolling the middle mouse button up, the view gets enlarged, whereas on scrolling the middle mouse button down, the view gets reduced.

Alternatively, press and hold the middle mouse button and then click the right or left mouse button. Next, drag the cursor upward or downward in the 3D View area to enlarge or reduce the view of a model, respectively.

Rotate

To rotate a model in the 3D view area, press and hold the middle mouse button and right or left mouse button and then drag the cursor.

Fit All

You can fit all objects/bodies available in the current document completely inside the 3D View area (screen) by using the **Fit all** tool. This tool is available in the **View** toolbar, see Figure 3.44.

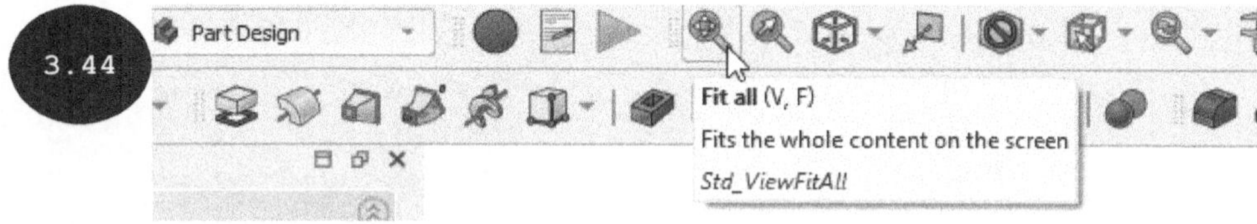

Fit selection

You can fit a selected geometry or object of the document completely in the 3D View area by using the **Fit selection** tool. This tool is available in the **View** toolbar, see Figure 3.45.

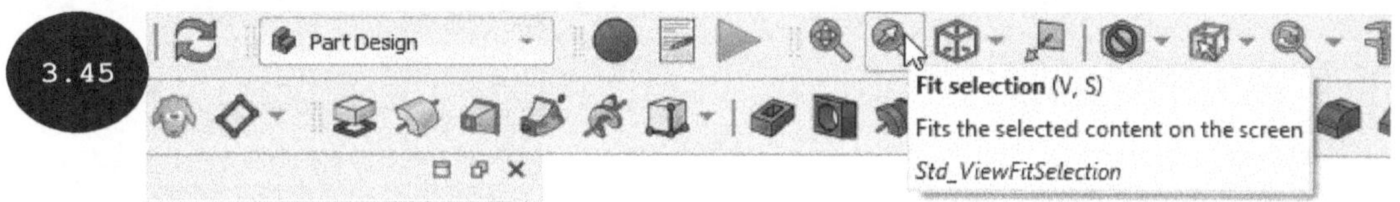

Displaying Standard Views of a Model

In FreeCAD, you can display a 3D model in various standard views such as Front, Top, Right, Rear, Bottom, and Isometric by using the respective tools available in the **View** toolbar, see Figure 3.46.

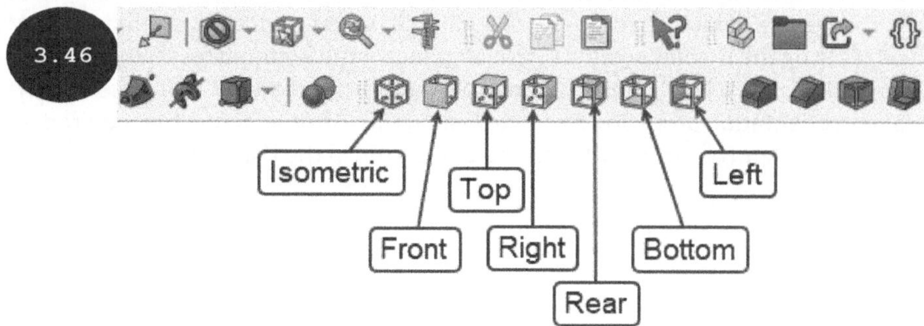

You can also access these tools to switch among different standard views such as Front, Top, Right, Rear, Bottom, and Isometric by clicking on the **View > Standard views** in the **Standard Menu,** see Figure 3.47. The tools are discussed next.

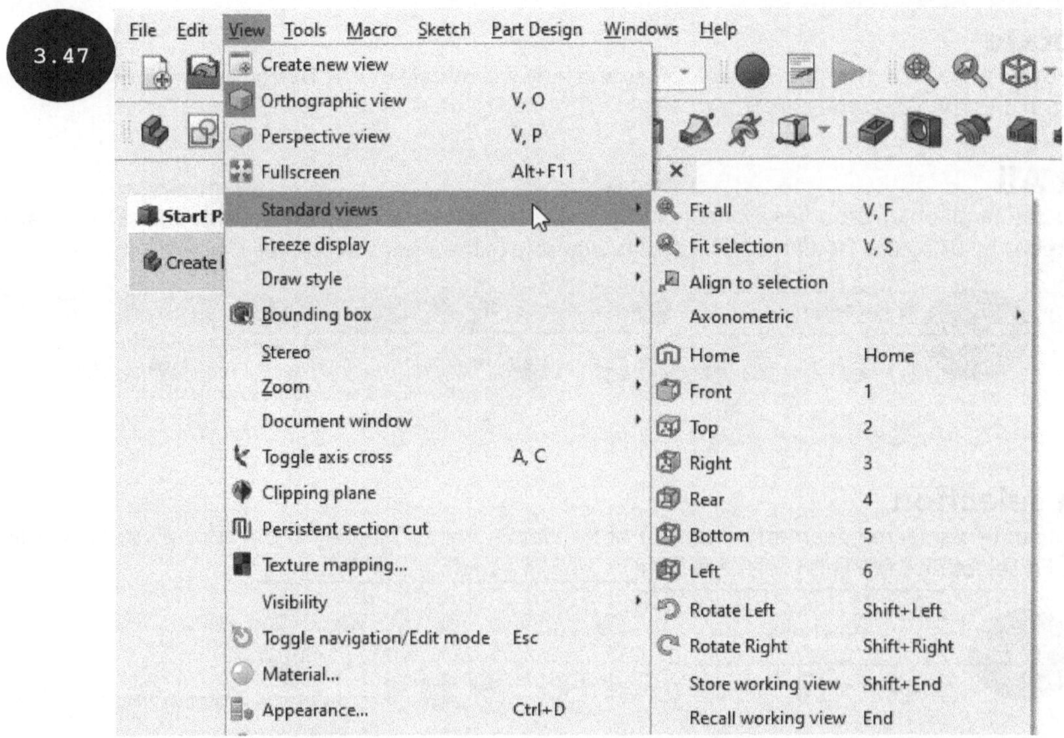

Home Tool

The Home tool is used to switch the view orientation of a model to the default home view, which is the trimetric view, by default.

Note: To change the default home view, click on **Edit > Preferences** in the **Standard Menu** and then click on the **Display** section in the left panel of the **Preferences** dialog box that appears. Next, click on the **Navigation** tab and then select the required home view in the **Default camera orientation** drop-down list, see Figure 3.48. After selecting the required home view, click on the **Apply** button and then the **OK** button in the dialog box.

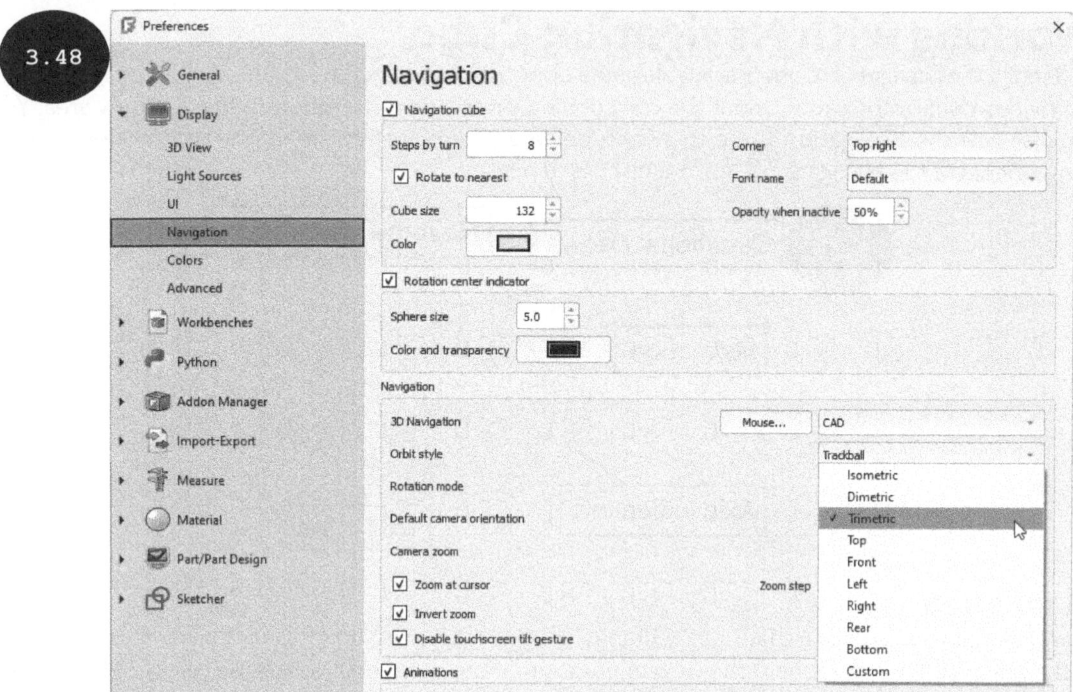

Front, Top, Right, Rear, Bottom, and Left Tools

The **Front**, **Top**, **Right**, **Rear**, **Bottom**, and **Left** tools are used to switch the view orientation of a model to the respective predefined standard view: Front, Top, Right, Rear, Bottom, and Left.

Isometric, Dimetric, and Trimetric Tools

The **Isometric**, **Dimetric**, and **Trimetric** tools are used to switch the view orientation of a model to the isometric, dimetric, and trimetric view, respectively. To access these tools, click on **View > Standard views > Axonometric** in the **Standard Menu**, see Figure 3.49.

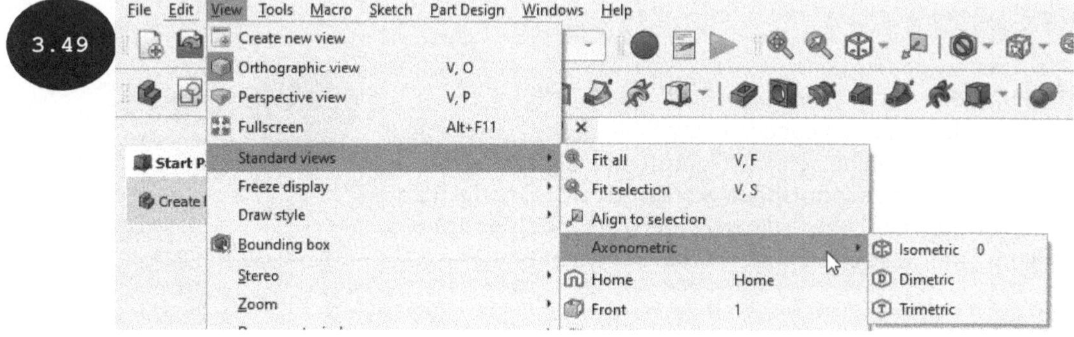

Working with Navigation Cube

By default, the **Navigation Cube** is available at the upper right corner of the 3D View area, see Figure 3.50. It provides visual information about the current view orientation of a model in the 3D View area. You can also use the **Navigation Cube** to switch between various standard views of a model. Various components of the **Navigation Cube** are discussed next.

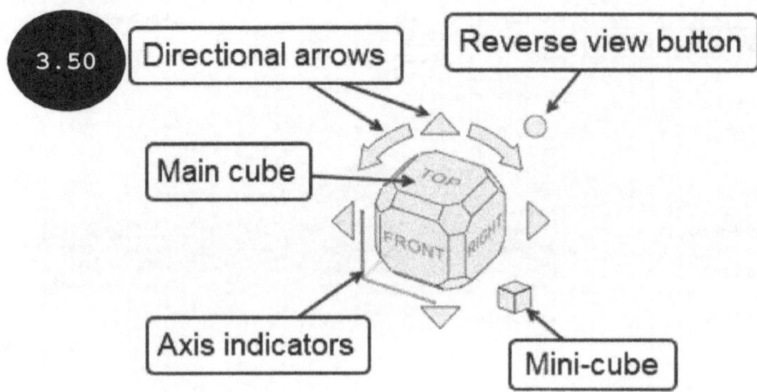

Main cube

The Main cube has 6 square faces, 12 rectangular edge faces, and 8 triangular corner faces. You can click on any of them to reorient the view orientation of the model normal to the selected face of the Main cube.

Directional arrows

The **Navigation Cube** consists of a total of 6 direction arrows. Out of which, 4 are triangular arrowheads and 2 are curved arrows. On clicking a triangular arrowhead, the view orientation of a model rotates 45 degrees around a line normal to the direction of the selected arrow. Similarly, on clicking a curved arrow, the view orientation of a model rotates 45 degrees around the view direction.

Reverse view button

The **Reverse view button** is used to rotate the view orientation of a model 180 degrees around the vertical axis of the view.

Mini-cube

The **Mini-cube** is a small cube icon available at the bottom right corner of the Main cube, refer to Figure 3.51. It is used to display additional options to control the view orientation of a model. To do this, click on the **Mini-cube** to display a menu with addition options, see Figure 3.51. These options are discussed next.

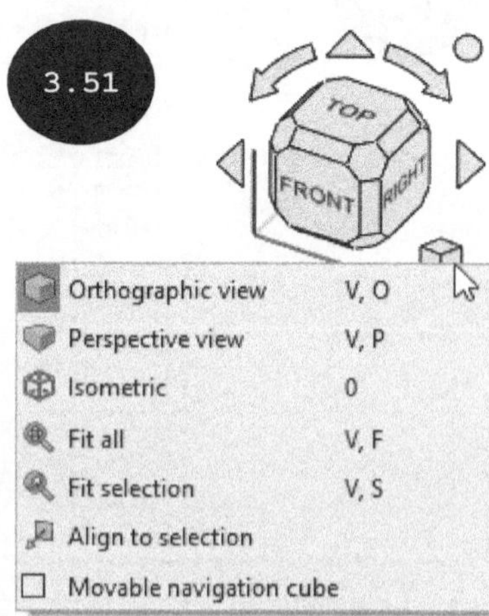

Orthographic view
The **Orthographic view** option is used to change the view of a model to an orthographic view.

Perspective view
The **Perspective view** option is used to change the view of a model to a perspective view.

Isometric
The **Isometric** option is used to change the view of a model to an isometric view.

Fit all
The **Fit all** option is used to fit all the objects available in the 3D View area completely inside the screen.

Movable navigation cube
The **Movable navigation cube** option is used to dock or undock the position of the **Navigation Cube**. When this option is activated, you can change the location of the **Navigation Cube** anywhere on the 3D View area by pressing and holding the left mouse button on the Main cube and then dragging it to a new location.

Note: By default, the **Navigation Cube** is available at the upper right corner of the 3D View area. To change the default position of the **Navigation Cube**, invoke the **Preferences** dialog box and then click on the **Display** section on the left panel of the dialog box. Next, click on the **Navigation** option and then select the required option in the **Corner** drop-down list of the dialog box to define a default location of the **Navigation Cube** on the 3D View area, see Figure 3.52. You can also define other navigation settings by using the options available in this dialog box. After defining the required settings, exit the dialog box.

3.52

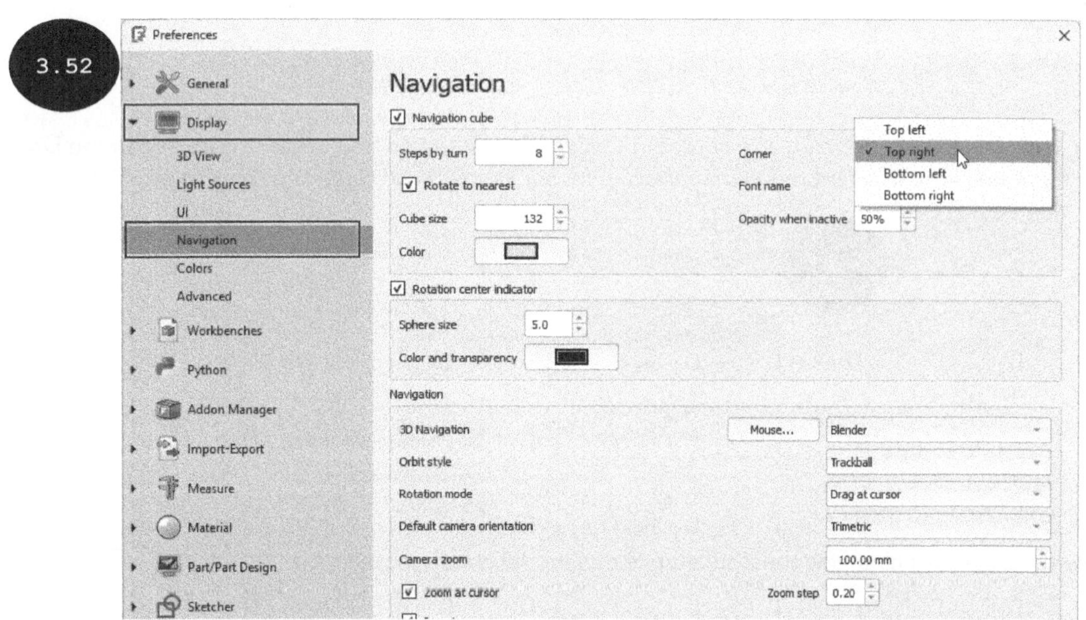

Changing the Display Style of a Model

You can change the display style of a model to Points, Wireframe, Hidden line, No shading, Shaded, and Flat lines. You can access these tools to change the display style of a model in the **Draw style** menu of the **View** toolbar, see Figure 3.53.

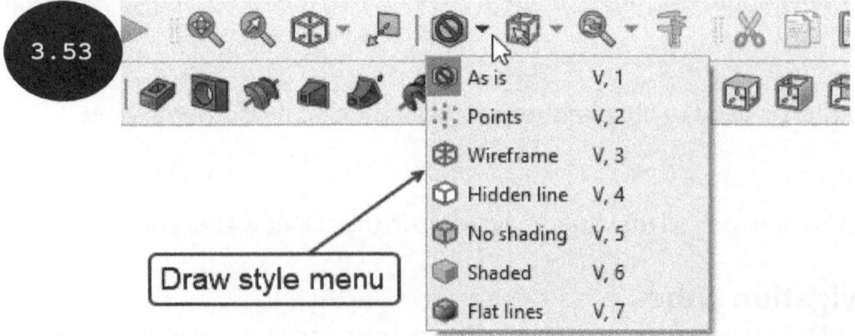

Alternatively, click on **View > Draw style** in the **Standard Menu** to access tools for changing the display style of a model, see Figure 3.54.

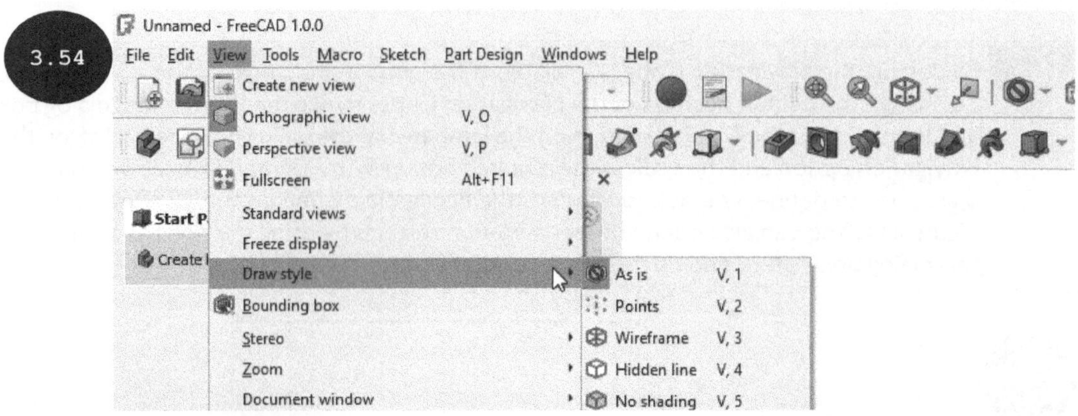

You can also right-click on an empty area in the 3D View area and then move the cursor to the **Draw style** option in the shortcut menu that appears for accessing these tools, see Figure 3.55.

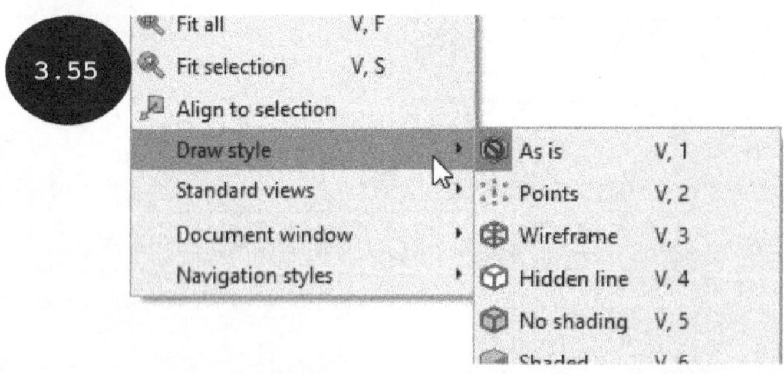

The tools used for changing the display style of a model are discussed next.

As is

The **As is** tool is used for displaying a model in the 'As is' display style. In this style, the model is displayed in its default or custom-specified display mode.

Note: To define a display mode for a model, click on the **Model** tab in the **Combo View** and then select the **Body** node in the **Tree View** that appears, see Figure 3.56. The **Property Editor** appears in its lower section with **View** and **Data** tabs, see Figure 3.57. Click on the **View** tab for displaying the visualization properties of the selected body, see Figure 3.57. Next, click on the **Display Mode** field of the **View** tab. An arrow appears in this field. Click on this arrow and then select the required display mode in the drop-down list that appears. The selected display mode gets defined as the 'As is' display style of the model.

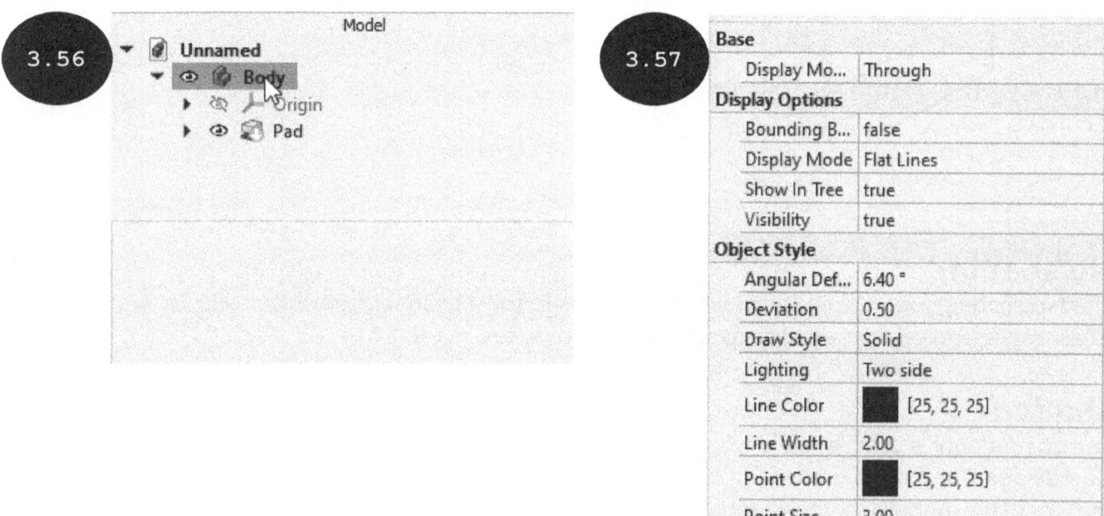

Points

The **Points** tool is used for displaying a model in the 'Points' display style. In this display style, the vertices of a model are displayed in a solid color (dots), while the edges and faces of the model become invisible, see Figure 3.58.

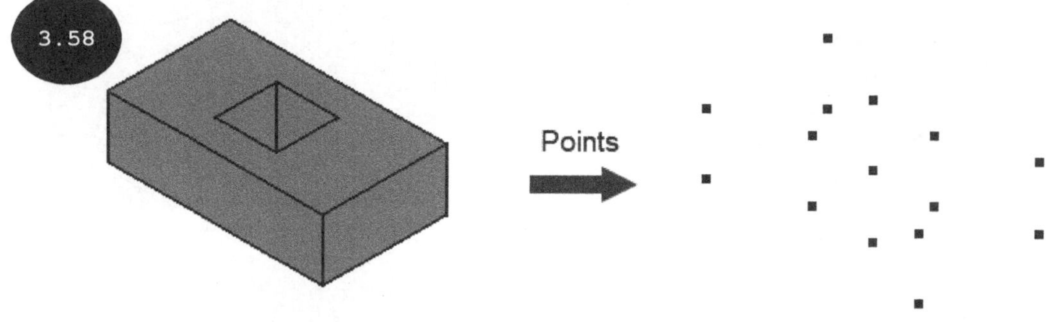

Wireframe

The **Wireframe** tool is used for displaying a model in the 'Wireframe' display style. In this style, all the edges and vertices of a model are displayed in a solid color, while the faces of the model become invisible, see Figure 3.59.

Hidden line

The **Hidden line** tool is used for displaying a model in the 'Hidden line' display style. In this style, the faces of the model are displayed in triangular meshes, while the hidden edges of the model become invisible, see Figure 3.60.

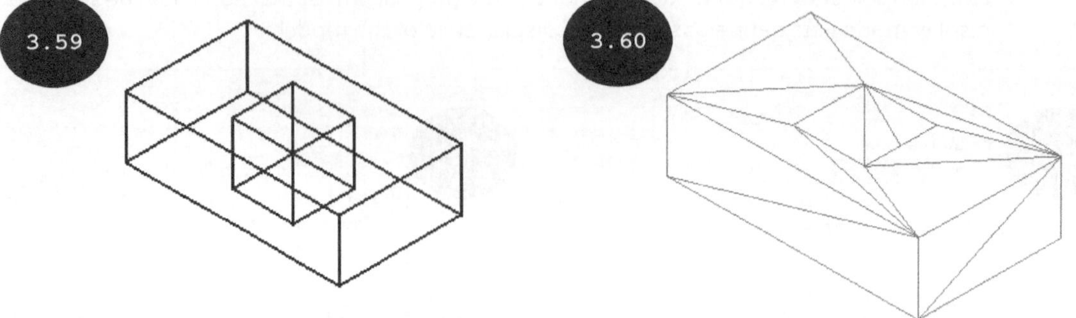

No shading

The **No shading** tool is used for displaying a model in the 'No shading' display style. In this style, the faces, edges, and vertices are displayed in a solid color, see Figure 3.61.

Shaded

The **Shaded** tool is used for displaying a model in the 'Shaded' display style. In this style, the faces of a model are illuminated depending upon their orientation in the 3D View area, while the edges and vertices of the model become invisible, see Figure 3.62. In this figure, the model is displayed in trimetric view orientation.

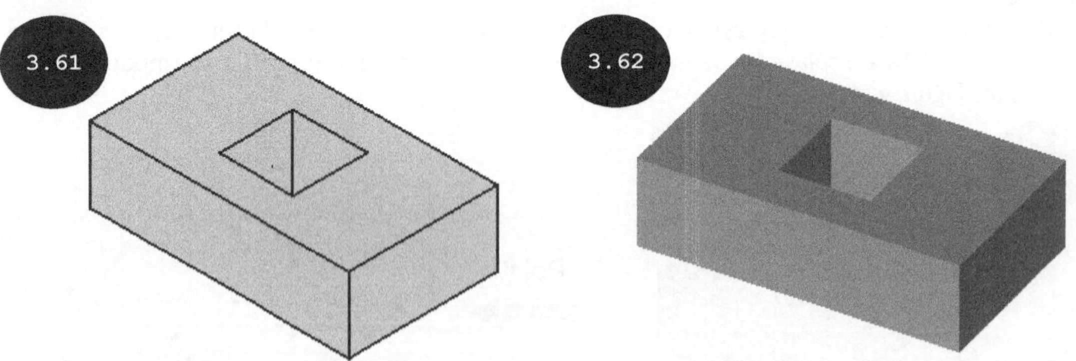

Flat lines

The **Flat lines** tool is used for displaying a model in the 'Flat lines' display style. In this style, the edges and vertices of a model are displayed in a solid color, while the faces of the model are illuminated depending upon their orientation in the 3D View area, see Figure 3.63.

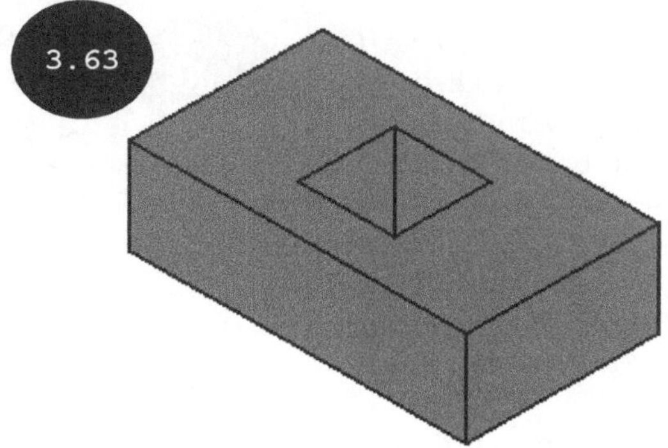

Tutorial 1

Create a sketch of the model shown in Figure 3.64 and then extrude it to a depth of 16 mm symmetrically about the sketching plane. All dimensions are in mm.

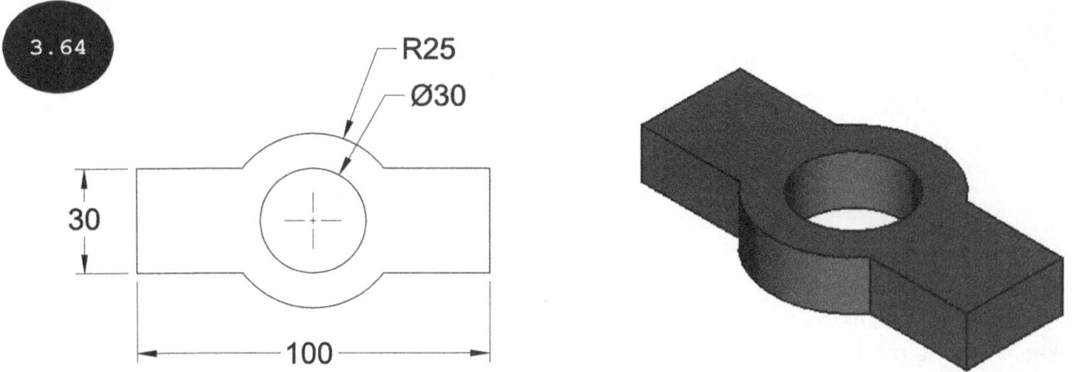

Section 1: Starting FreeCAD and a New Part Document

1. Start FreeCAD by double-clicking on the **FreeCAD 1.0** icon on your desktop. The startup user interface of FreeCAD appears, see Figure 3.65.

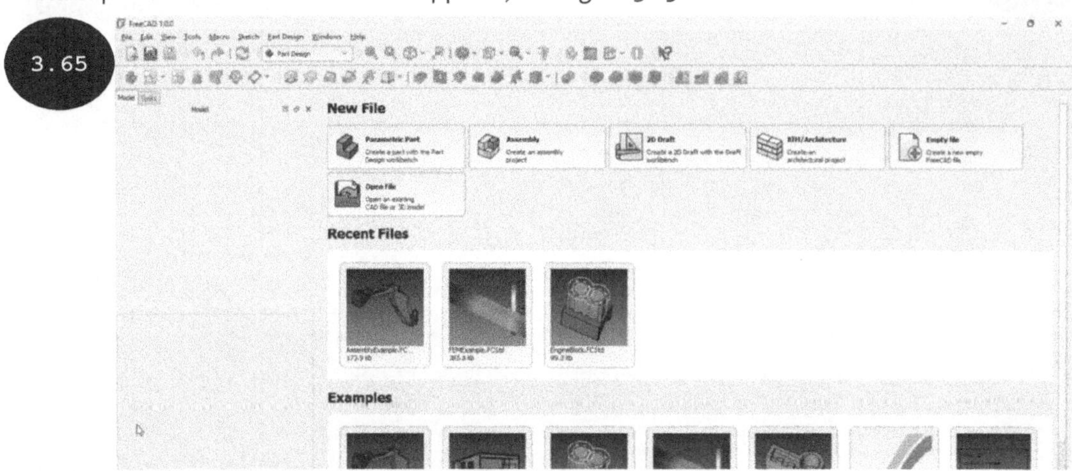

2. Click on the **New** tool in the **File** toolbar (see Figure 3.66) or press the **CTRL + N** keys. A new part document gets invoked with the default name "**unnamed: 1**" and it becomes active by default. Additionally, the tools in the Toolbar Area are enabled, allowing you to start designing a parametric part. This is because the Part Design workbench is selected in the Workbench Selector by default.

3.66

Section 2: Invoking the Sketcher Workbench

Now, you need to invoke the **Sketcher** workbench to create a sketch of the base feature.

1. Click on the **Create sketch** tool in the **Part Design Helper** toolbar, see Figure 3.67. The three default planes appear in the 3D View area. Also, the **Tasks Panel** appears in the **Tasks** tab of the **Combo View** and displays the name of the three default planes, see Figure 3.68.

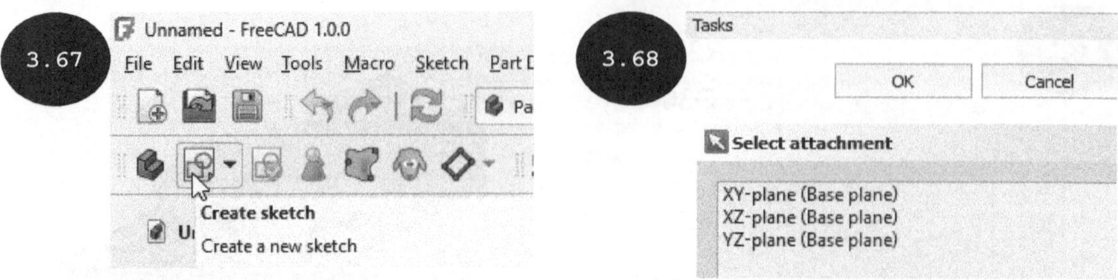

3.67

3.68

2. Select the **XY_Plane** as the sketching plane in the 3D View area for creating the sketch. The Sketch editing mode of the **Sketcher** workbench gets invoked, see Figure 3.69. Note that the selected plane becomes the sketching plane for drawing the sketch and it is oriented normal to the viewing direction.

3.69

Section 3: Specifying Units, Grids, and Snap Settings

Now, you need to specify millimeters (mm) as the measurement unit for the document. Also, you need to turn off the display of grids and snap mode for creating the sketch by specifying points arbitrarily in the 3D View area.

1. Invoke the **Unit** flyout that appears at the lower right corner of the **Status Bar** and ensure that **Standard (mm, kg, s,*)** is selected as the unit system for the current design document, see Figure 3.70.

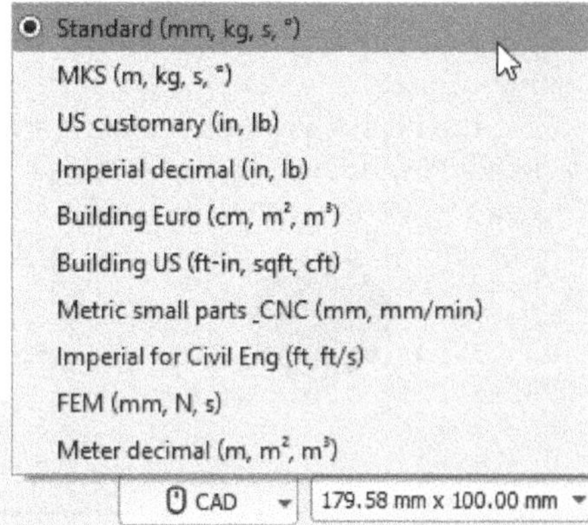

Note: As FreeCAD is a parametric software, you can turn off the snap mode and create the sketch entities by specifying points arbitrarily in the 3D View area. After creating the sketch, you can apply the required constraints and dimensions to make the sketch fully constrained.

---

2. Click on the **Toggle grid** tool and **Toggle snap** tool in the **Sketcher edit tools** to turn off the grids and snap mode, respectively, see Figure 3.71. Note that these are the toggle tools.

Section 4: Creating the Sketch

Now, you can create a sketch of the pad feature by specifying points arbitrarily in the 3D View area.

1. Invoke the **Create rectangle** menu in the **Sketcher geometries** toolbar and then click on the **Centered rectangle** tool, see Figure 3.72.

3.72

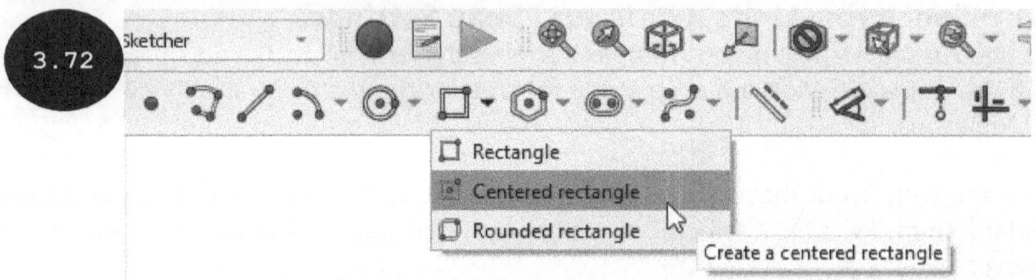

2. Click to specify the center of the rectangle at the origin in the 3D View area, refer to Figure 3.73.

3. Move the cursor towards the right and then click to specify a corner of the rectangle when its length and width values appear close to 100 mm and 30 mm in the input fields, respectively., see Figure 3.73. A rectangle is created.

3.73

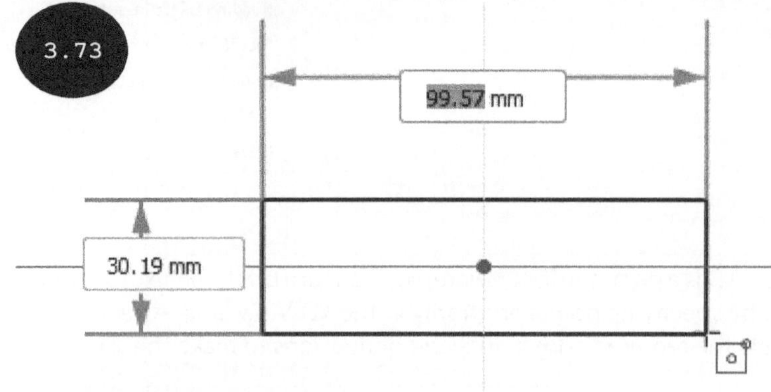

4. Press ESC or right-click to exit the **Centered rectangle** tool.

   Now, you need to create two circles.

5. Invoke the **Create circle** menu in the **Sketcher geometries** toolbar and then click on the **Create circle by center** tool, see Figure 3.74. The **Create circle by center** tool gets activated.

3.74

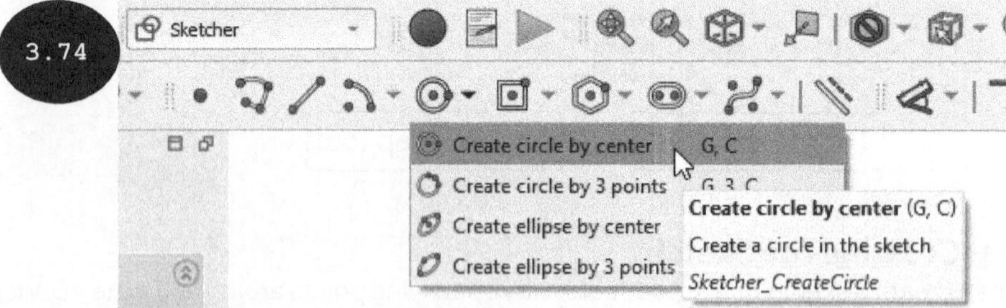

6. Click to specify the center point of the circle at the origin, refer to Figure 3.75.

7. Move the cursor horizontally toward the right and then click to specify a point when the diameter of the circle appears close to 50 mm near the cursor, see Figure 3.75. A circle gets drawn. Also, the **Create circle by center** tool remains active.

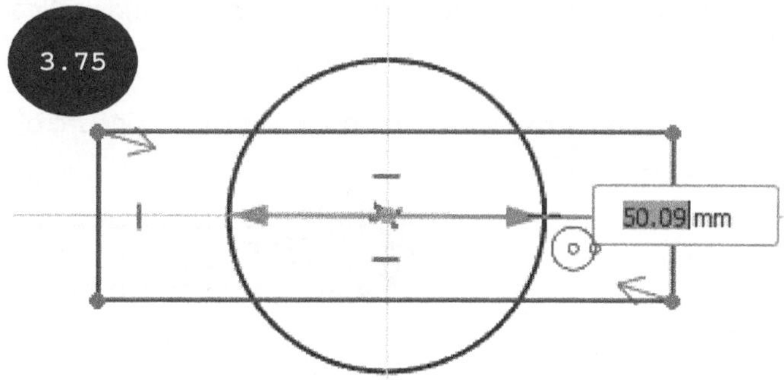

Now, you need to create another circle.

8. Click to specify the center point of the circle at the origin and then click to specify a point when the diameter of the circle appears close to 30 mm near the cursor, see Figure 3.76. A circle gets drawn. Next, right-click to exit the **Create circle by center** tool.

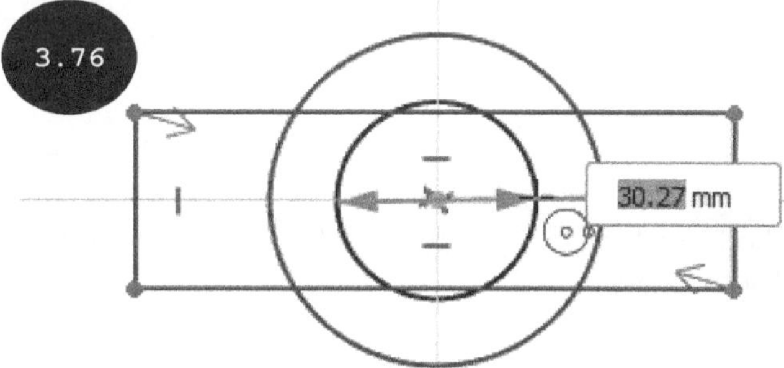

Now, you need to trim the unwanted sketch entities to their nearest intersection.

9. Invoke the **Trim** menu and click on the **Trim edge** tool, see Figure 3.77. The **Trim edge** tool gets activated and the appearance of the cursor changes to cross mark with the display of a red trim icon.

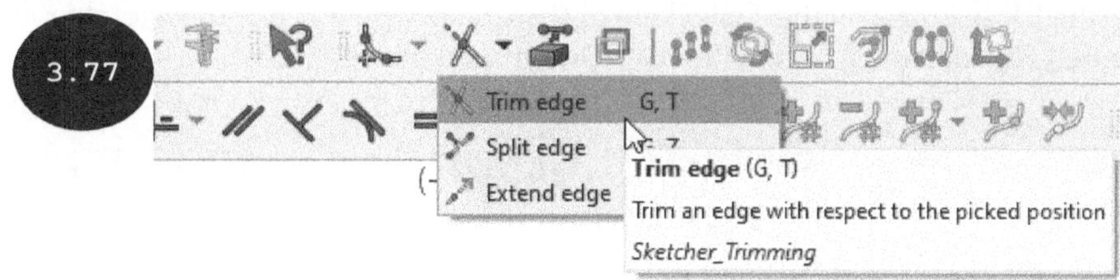

10. Click to trim the unwanted entities of the sketch to their nearest intersection one by one. Figure 3.78 shows the final sketch after trimming all the unwanted entities of the sketch. Next, right-click in the 3D View area to exit the **Trim edge** tool.

Now, you need to apply the required geometric constraints and dimensions to make the sketch fully defined.

11. Apply the horizontal and vertical constraints to all the horizontal and vertical lines of the sketch, if not applied by default.

12. Apply the horizontal constraint between the endpoints of the upper arc of the sketch to make them aligned horizontally, see Figure 3.79.

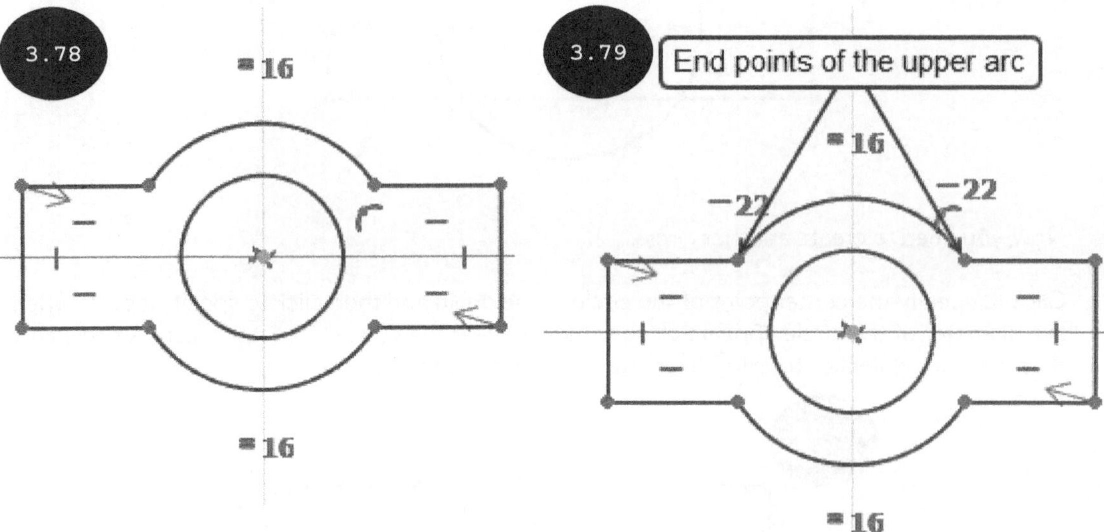

13. Similarly, apply the horizontal constraint between the endpoints of the lower arc of the sketch to make them aligned horizontally.

    Now, you need to apply the required dimensions.

14. Apply all the required dimensions to the sketch using the respective dimension tools. Figure 3.80 shows a fully defined sketch after applying all the required dimensions.

    After creating the sketch, you need to exit the Sketch editing mode of the **Sketcher** workbench.

15. Click on the **Close** button in the **Task Plane** of the **Combo View** to exit the **Sketcher** workbench (see Figure 3.81) and switch back to the **Part Design** workbench.

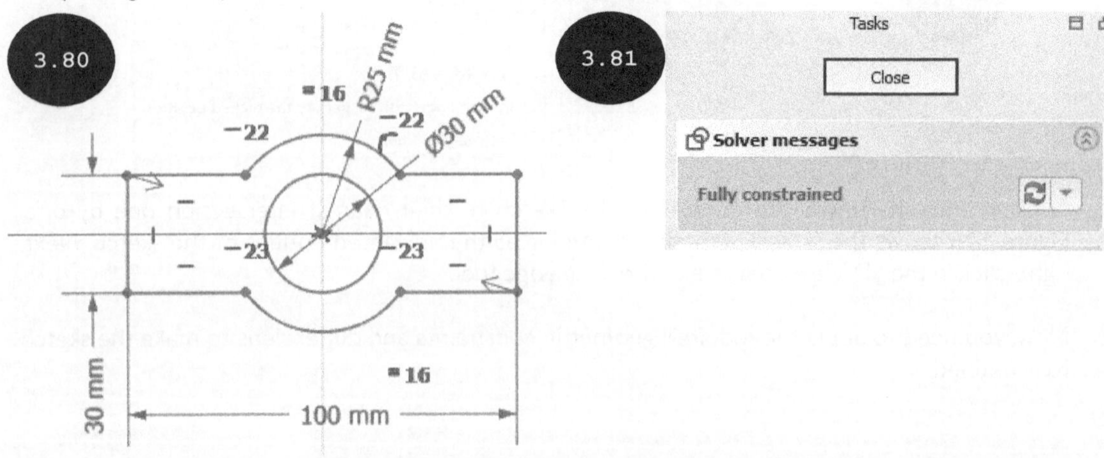

Section 5: Creating a Pad Feature

Now, you need to create a pad feature by extruding the sketch to a depth of 16 mm symmetrically on both sides of the sketching plane.

1. Click on the **Pad** tool in the **Part Design Modeling** toolbar, see Figure 3.82. The preview of a pad feature appears in the 3D View area with default parameters since the sketch gets selected automatically. Also, the **Pad parameters** sub-window appears in the **Tasks Panel** of the **Combo View**, see Figure 3.83.

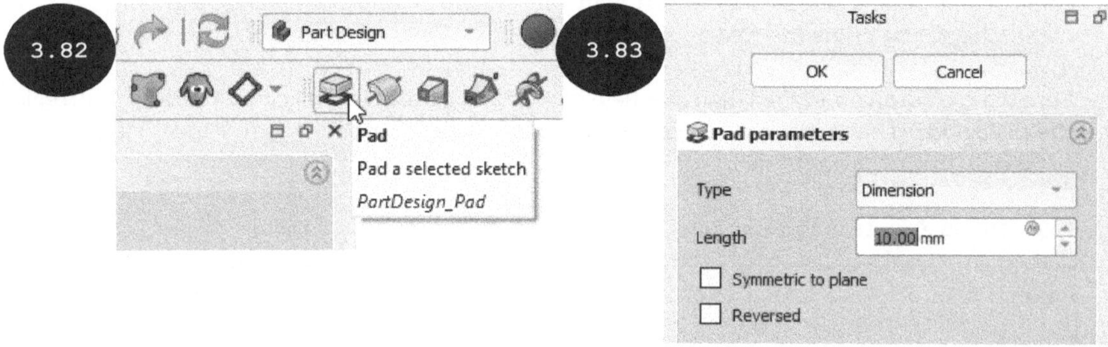

2. Ensure that the **Dimension** option is selected in the **Type** drop-down list of the **Pad parameters** sub-window in the **Tasks Panel**.

3. Enter **16** mm in the **Length** field of the **Pad parameters** sub-window as the extrusion length of the pad feature.

4. Select the **Symmetric to plane** check box in the **Pad parameters** sub-window for extruding the sketch symmetrically on both sides of the sketching plane, see Figure 3.84.

5. Click on the **OK** button in the **Tasks Panel**. The pad feature of specified parameters gets created in the 3D View area, see Figure 3.85.

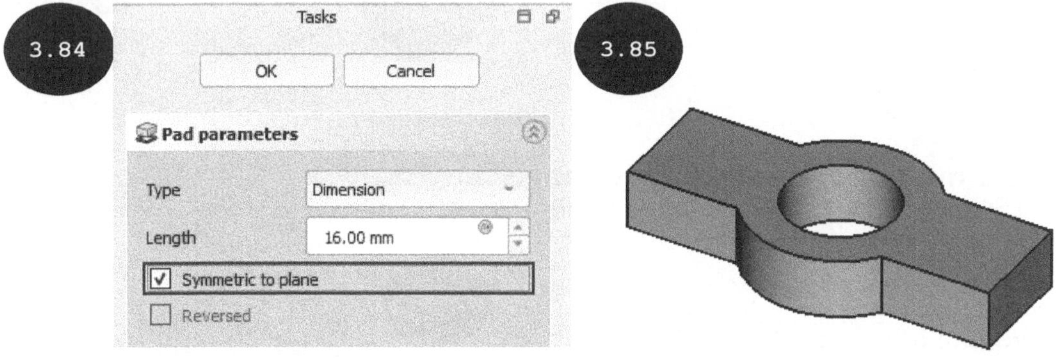

Section 6: Saving the Model

Now, you can save the model.

1. Click on the **Save** tool in the **File** toolbar (see Figure 3.86) or press the CTRL + S keys. The **Save FreeCAD Document** dialog box appears.

2. Browse the **FreeCAD** folder in the local drive of your system. Next, create a new folder with the name **Chapter 03** inside this folder.

3. Enter **Ch03-Tutorial 1** in the **File name** field of the dialog box. Next, click on the **Save** button in the dialog box. The model gets saved with the name **Ch03-Tutorial 1** at the specified location (*> FreeCAD > Chapter 03*).

4. Click on **File** > **Close** in the **Standard Menu** to close the current document.

Tutorial 2

Create a sketch of the model shown in Figure 3.87 and then revolve it around the vertical axis at an angle of 270 degrees. All dimensions are in inches (in).

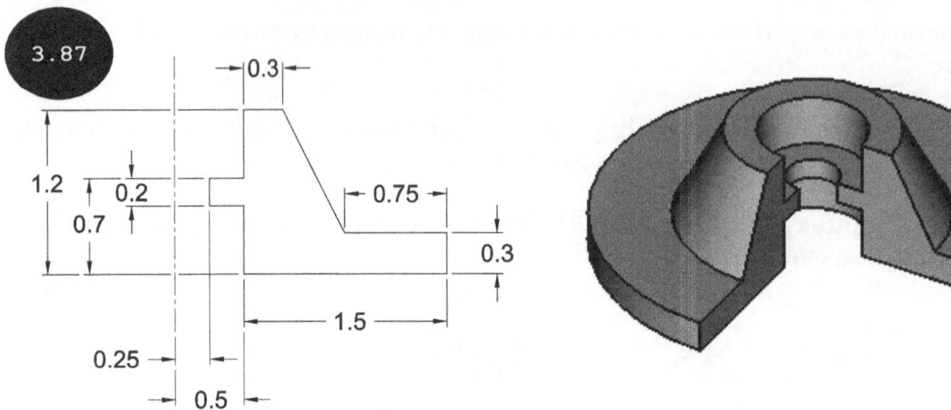

Section 1: Invoking a New Part Document

1. Start FreeCAD by double-clicking on the **FreeCAD 1.0** icon on your desktop. The startup user interface of FreeCAD appears.

2. Click on the **New** tool in the **File** toolbar (see Figure 3.88) or press the **CTRL + N** keys. A new

part document gets invoked with the default name "**unnamed: 1**" and it becomes active by default. Additionally, the tools in the **Toolbar Area** are enabled, allowing you to start designing a parametric part, see Figure 3.89. This is because the **Part Design** workbench is selected in the **Workbench Selector**, by default.

Section 2: Invoking the Sketcher Workbench and Specifying Units

Now, you need to invoke the **Sketcher** workbench to create a sketch of the base feature.

1. Click on the **Create sketch** tool in the **Part Design Helper** toolbar, see Figure 3.90. The three default planes appear in the 3D View area. Also, the **Tasks Panel** appears in the **Tasks** tab of **Combo View** and displays the name of the three default planes, see Figure 3.91.

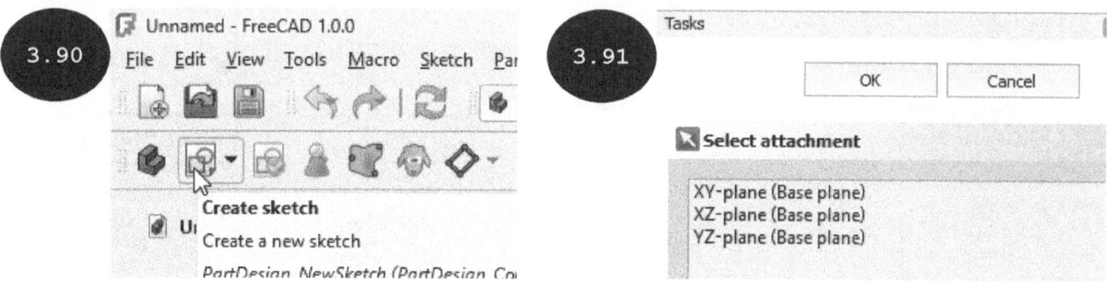

2. Select the **XZ_Plane** as the sketching plane in the **Tasks Panel** and then click on the **OK** button. You can also select the sketching plane in the 3D View area. The **Sketcher** workbench gets invoked and the selected plane gets oriented normal to the viewing direction.

Section 3: Specifying the Units

1. Invoke the **Unit** flyout that appears at the lower right corner of the **Status Bar** and ensure that **Imperial decimal (in,lb)** is selected as the unit system for the current design document, see Figure 3.92.

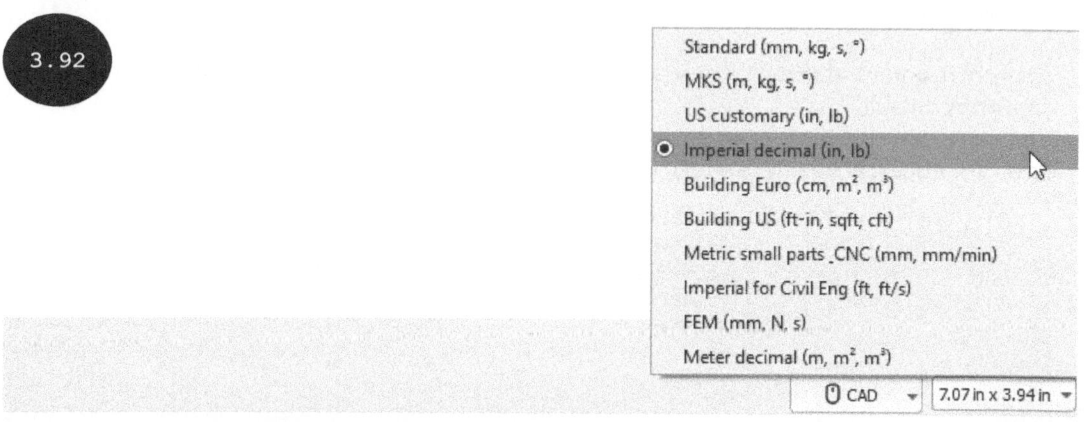

Section 4: Creating the Sketch

Now, you can create a sketch of the revolution feature.

1. Click on the **Create polyline** tool in the **Sketcher geometries** toolbar for drawing a continuous chain of line entities, see Figure 3.93. The **Create polyline** tool gets activated.

2. Move the cursor over the horizontal axis, at a small distance from the origin and then click to specify the start point of the first line segment, refer to Figure 3.94.

3. Move the cursor vertically upward and then click anywhere to specify the endpoint of the vertical line, refer to Figure 3.94. A vertical line of any length gets created and the **Create polyline** tool remains activated.

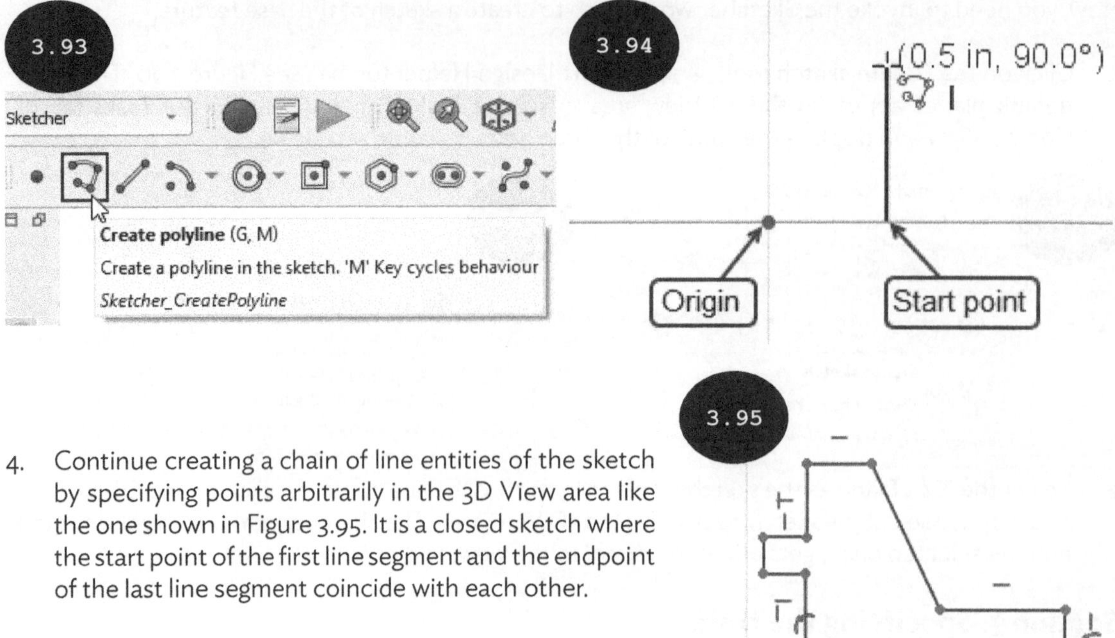

4. Continue creating a chain of line entities of the sketch by specifying points arbitrarily in the 3D View area like the one shown in Figure 3.95. It is a closed sketch where the start point of the first line segment and the endpoint of the last line segment coincide with each other.

5. Right-click twice to exit the **Create polyline** tool.

   Now, you need to apply the required geometric constraints and dimensions to make the sketch fully defined.

6. Apply horizontal and vertical constraints to the horizontal and vertical lines of the sketch, if not applied by default.

7. Apply the equal constraint between the lines of equal length, see Figure 3.96.

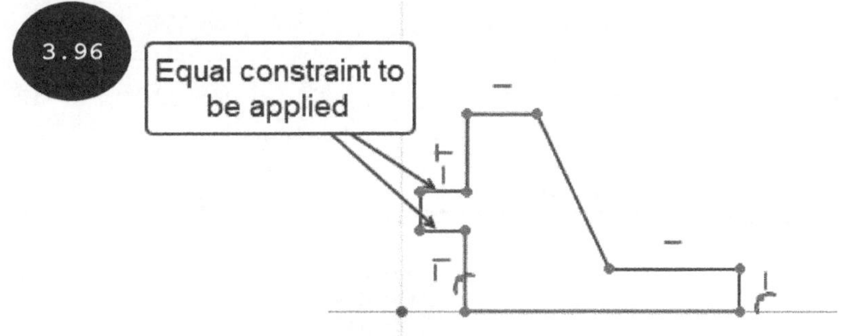

8. After applying the required geometric constraints, apply dimensions to the sketch by using the dimension tools. Figure 3.97 shows a fully defined sketch after applying the required dimensions.

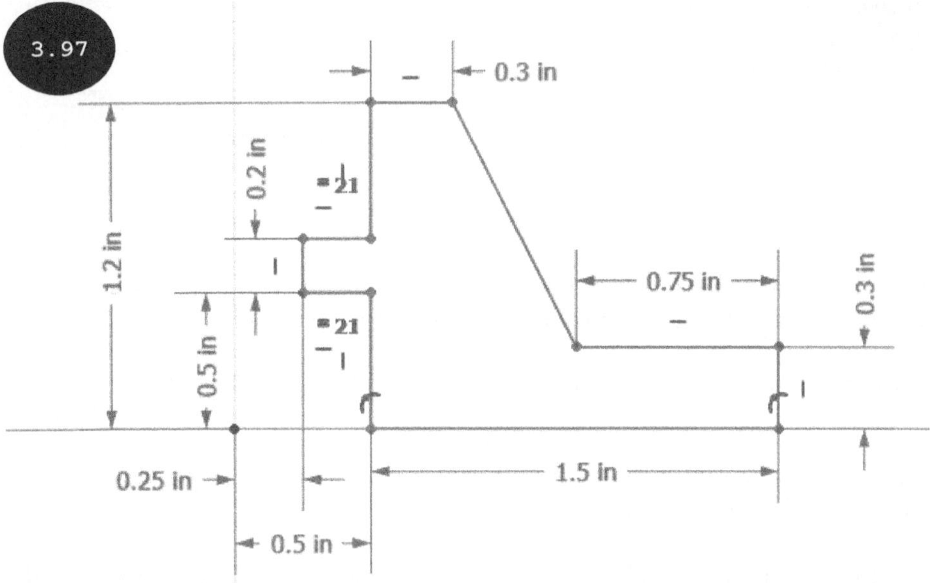

Now, you can exit the **Sketcher** workbench.

9. Click on the **Close** button in the **Task Plane** of the **Combo View** to exit the **Sketcher** workbench and switch back to the **Part Design** workbench.

Section 5: Creating a Revolution Feature

Now, you need to create a revolution feature by revolving the sketch at an angle of 270 degrees around the vertical axis.

1. Click on the **Revolution** tool in the **Part Design Modeling** toolbar, see Figure 3.98. The preview of a revolution feature appears in the 3D View area with the default angle of revolution, see Figure 3.99. Also, the **Revolution parameters** sub-window appears in the **Tasks Panel** of the **Combo View**, see Figure 3.100.

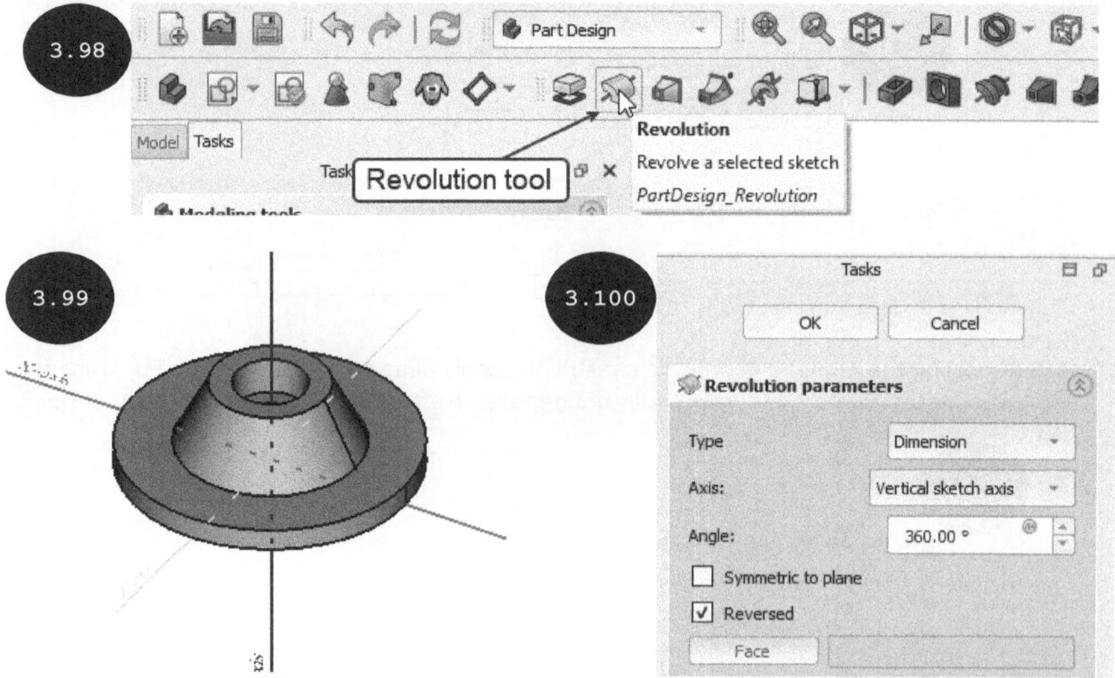

2. Ensure that the **Vertical sketch axis** option is selected in the **Axis** drop-down list of the **Tasks Panel** to define the vertical axis of the sketch as the axis of revolution.

3. Enter 270 degrees as the angle of revolution in the **Angle** field of the **Tasks Panel**. A preview of the revolution feature appears by revolving the sketch 270 degrees around the axis of the revolution.

4. If needed, clear the **Reversed** check box in the **Tasks Panel** to define the direction of revolution of the feature like the one shown in Figure 3.101.

5. Click on the **OK** button in the **Tasks Panel**. The revolution feature of the specified angle of revolution gets created in the 3D View area, see Figure 3.102.

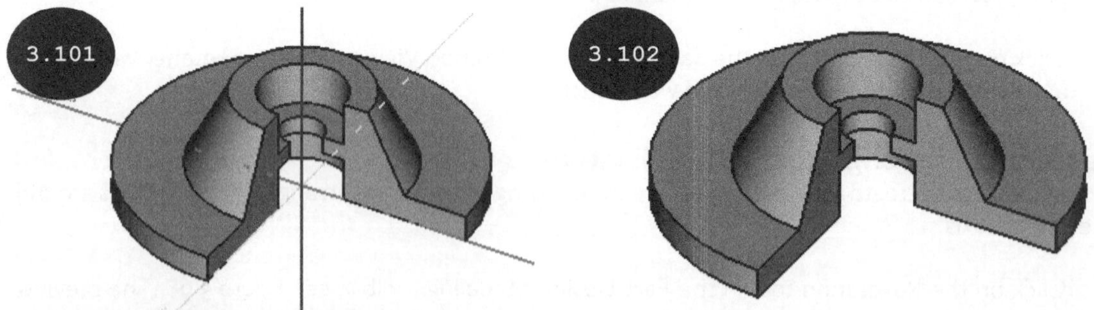

Section 6: Saving the Model

1. Click on the **Save** tool in the **File** toolbar (see Figure 3.103) or press the CTRL + S keys. The **Save FreeCAD Document** dialog box appears.

2. Browse to the *FreeCAD* > *Chapter 03* folder in the local drive of your system. You need to create these folders, if not created earlier.

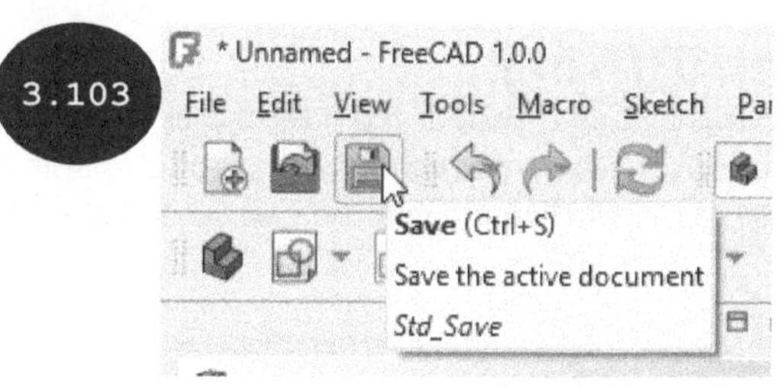

3. Enter **Ch03-Tutorial 2** in the **File name** field of the dialog box. Next, click on the **Save** button in the dialog box. The model gets saved at the specified location. Next, close the document by clicking on **File > Close** in the **Standard Menu**.

Hands-on Test Drive 1

Create the revolution model shown in Figure 3.104. The angle of revolution is 360 degrees around the vertical axis. All dimensions are in mm.

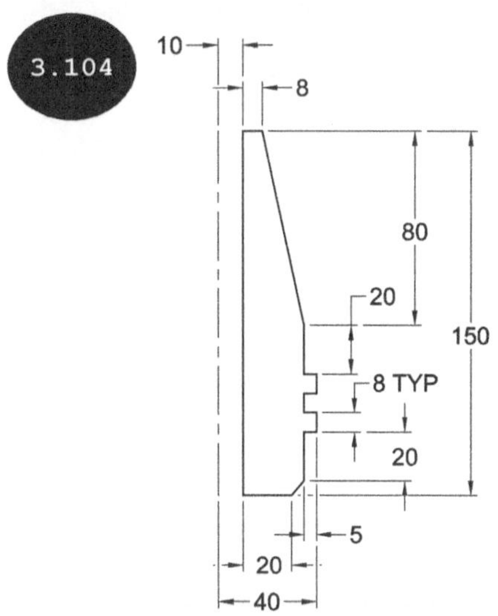

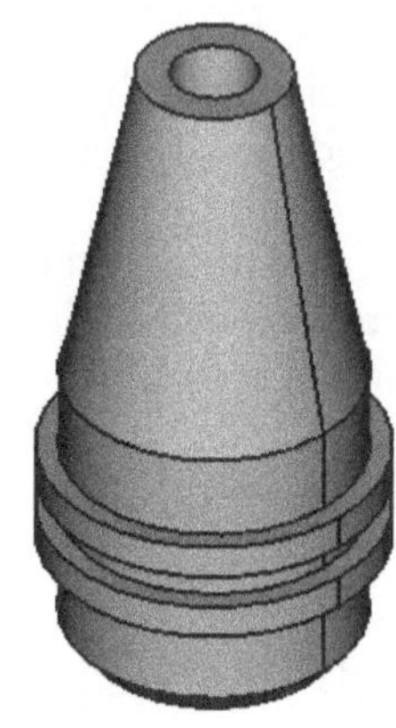

Hands-on Test Drive 2

Create the pad model shown in Figure 3.105. The depth of extrusion is 1.5 inches, symmetrically about the sketching plane. All dimensions are in inches (in).

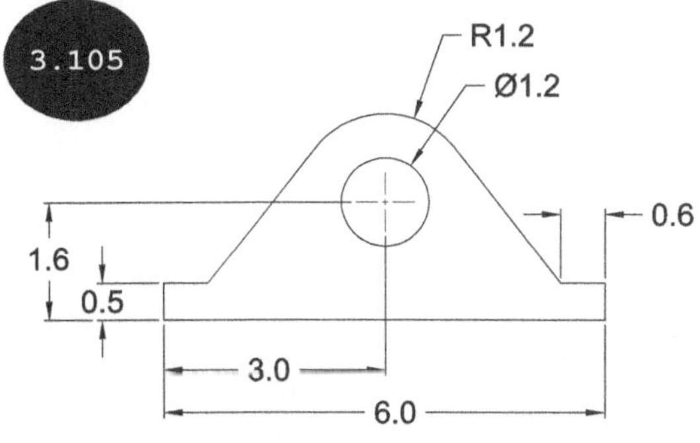

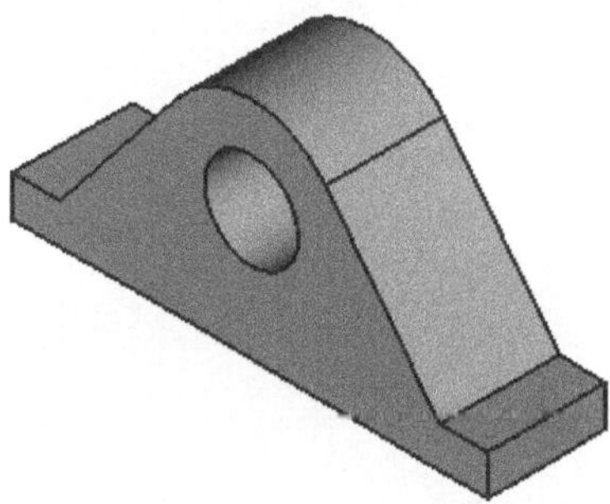

Summary

In this chapter, you learned how to create pad and revolution features. Additionally, the chapter covered various methods for navigating a model, displaying standard views, and changing the display style. You also explored the Navigation Cube and its applications in model manipulation.

Questions

Complete and verify the following sentences:

- A _________ feature is created by extruding a sketch normal to the sketching plane.
- The _________ tool is used for creating a feature by revolving a sketch around an axis.
- The _________ tool is used for fitting a model completely inside the graphics area.
- The _________ is used to switch between various standard views of a model.
- In _______ display style, the edges and vertices of a model are displayed in a solid color, while the faces of the model are illuminated depending upon their orientation in the 3D View area.
- The _______ option is used for extruding a sketch on both sides of the sketching plane with different extrusion lengths.
- The _________ option is used for extruding a sketch up to its nearest intersection.
- By default, the direction of extrusion of a pad feature is normal to the sketching plane. (True/False)
- The position of the Navigation Cube is fixed at the upper right corner of the 3D View area. (True/False)

4

Creating Datum Geometries

This chapter discusses the following topics:

- Creating Datum Planes
- Creating Datum Lines/Axes
- Creating Datum Points
- Creating a Local Coordinate System

Datum geometries such as datum planes, datum lines, and datum points are used as references to create sketches, features, or other datum geometries. In FreeCAD, the three default datum planes (**XY_Plane**, **XZ_Plane**, and **YZ_Plane**) and three datum axes (**X_Axis**, **Y_Axis**, and **Z_Axis**) are available, by default. You can use these datum geometries for creating sketches and 3D solid features of a model, as discussed in earlier chapters. However, to create a real-world model having multiple features, you may need additional datum geometries, since the default datum geometries may not be enough for creating all features of a 3D model. FreeCAD allows you to create datum planes, datum axes, datum lines, and a local coordinate system by using the respective tools available in the **Datum** menu of the **Part Design Helper** toolbar, see Figure 4.1.

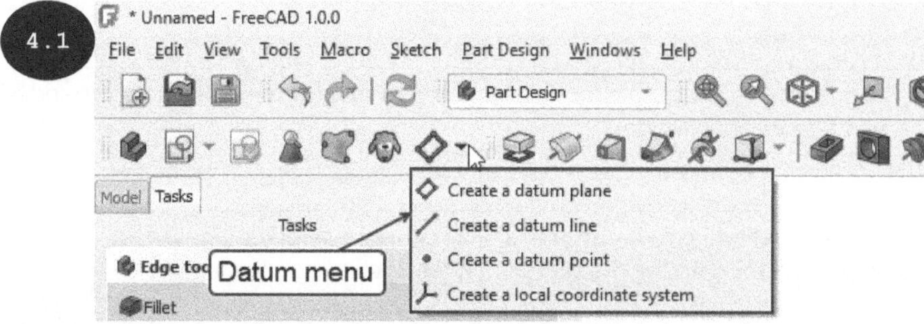

Consider the case of a 3D model shown in Figure 4.2, which consists of four features. Its first feature is a pad feature created on the **YZ_Plane**. The second feature of the model is a pocket feature created on the right planar face of the model by removing material. The third feature is a datum plane created at an angle by using the **Create a datum plane** tool. The fourth feature is a pad feature created on the datum plane. Figure 4.3 illustrates the model creation process.

4.2

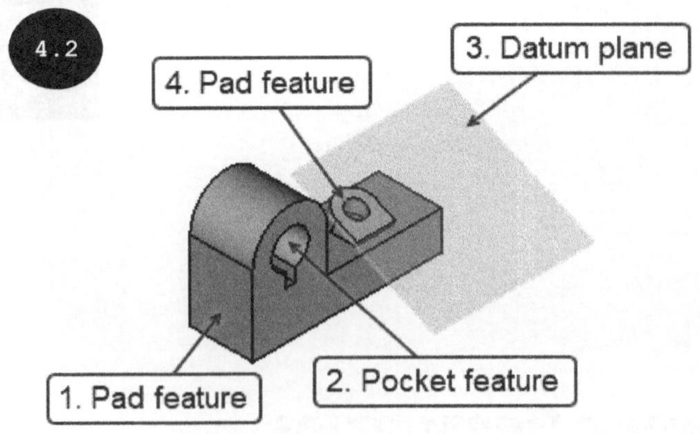

4.3

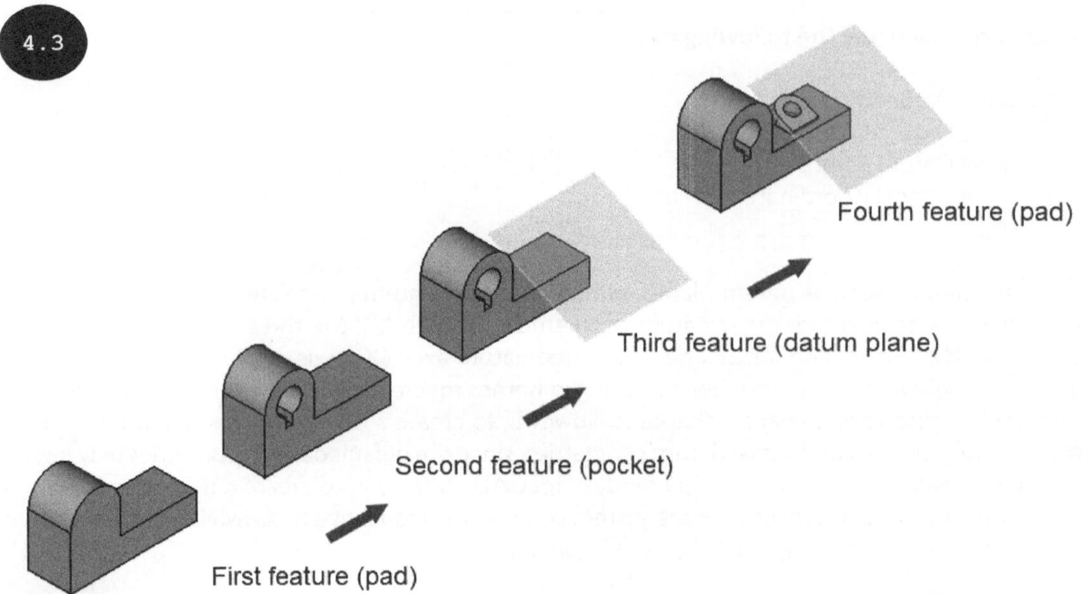

Note: It is evident from the above model that additional datum planes may be needed to create certain features of a model.

Tip: In addition to selecting a datum plane, you can also select a planar face of a model as the sketching plane for creating the sketch of a feature.

Creating Datum Planes

In FreeCAD, you can create datum planes normal to an edge, passing through three vertices, passing through the first two vertices and normal to the third vertex, tangent to a face at a vertex, aligned to a planar face, aligned to the default XY plane, and so on using the **Create a datum plane** tool.

To create a datum plane, click on the **Create a datum plane** tool in **Datum** menu, see Figure 4.4. The **Datum Plane parameters** sub-window appears in the **Tasks Panel** of the **Combo View**, see Figure 4.5. Also, you are prompted to select the first reference for creating a datum plane. The options in the **Tasks Panel** are used for creating various types of datum planes.

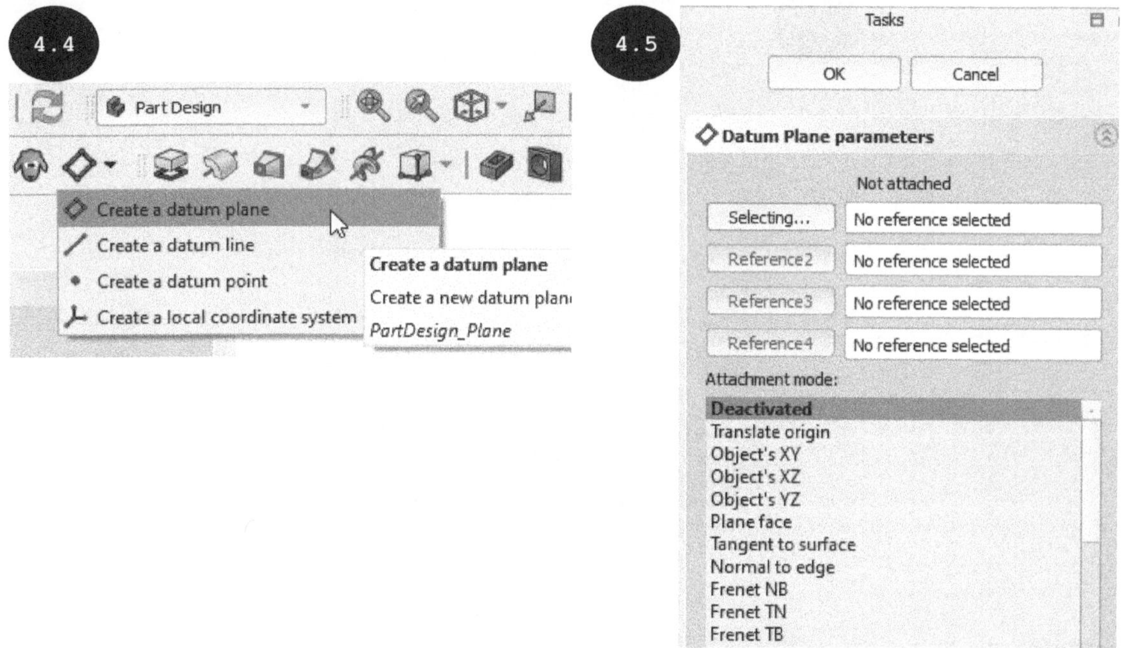

By default, the **Reference1** button is activated and labeled as **Selecting** in the **Tasks Panel**, indicating that you can select the first reference in the 3D View area for creating a datum plane. You can select an edge, a vertex, a plane, a face, a curve, a circle, or a conic sketch entity as the first reference for creating a datum plane.

After selecting the first reference, the **Reference2** button gets activated automatically in the **Tasks Panel** and labeled as **Selecting**, indicating that you can select the second reference for creating the datum plane.

Tip: The selection of references depends upon the type of datum plane to be created. For example, to create a datum plane normal to an edge and passing through a vertex, you need to select a linear edge as the first reference and a vertex as the second reference for creating the datum plane.

Depending upon the type of first reference selected, the list of attachment modes gets filtered in the **Attachment mode** area of the **Tasks Panel** for creating a datum plane. Also, among them, the most suitable attachment mode is applied to the selected first reference and is highlighted in the **Attachment mode** area of the **Tasks Panel**. Moreover, the name of the applied attachment mode appears as "**Attached with mode** <*name of the mode*>" at the top of the **Datum Plane parameters** sub-window in the **Tasks Panel** in green color, see Figure 4.6. The green color indicates that the application of the applied attachment mode is passed. However, if it appears in red, it indicates that the application of the applied attachment mode to the selected reference geometries of the model failed. Figure 4.6 shows a list of attachment modes displayed in the **Attachment mode** area when a linear edge is selected as the first reference for creating a datum plane. The methods for creating some of the different types of datum planes are discussed next.

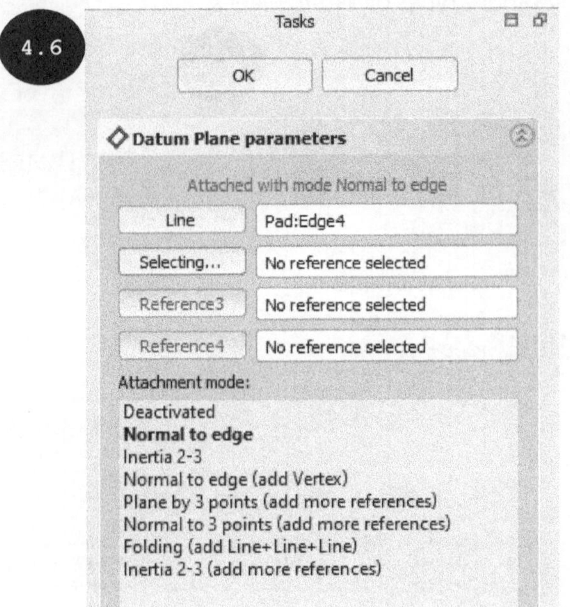

Note: An attachment mode is used to attach a plane being created to the selected reference geometries of the model. It creates an association with each other such that if any modification is made to the reference geometries of the model, then the associated datum plane will also be modified accordingly. Various attachment modes are discussed next.

Creating a Datum Plane Coplanar to the Default XY Plane

You can create a datum plane coplanar to the default XY Plane by using the **Deactivated** attachment mode and the method for creating the same is discussed below:

1. Invoke the **Datum** menu and then click on the **Create a datum plane** tool, see Figure 4.7. The **Datum Plane parameters** sub-window appears in the **Tasks Panel**, see Figure 4.8. Also, the preview of a datum plane appears coplanar to the default XY Plane in the 3D View area since, the **Deactivated** mode is activated in the **Attachment mode** area of the **Tasks Panel**, by default.

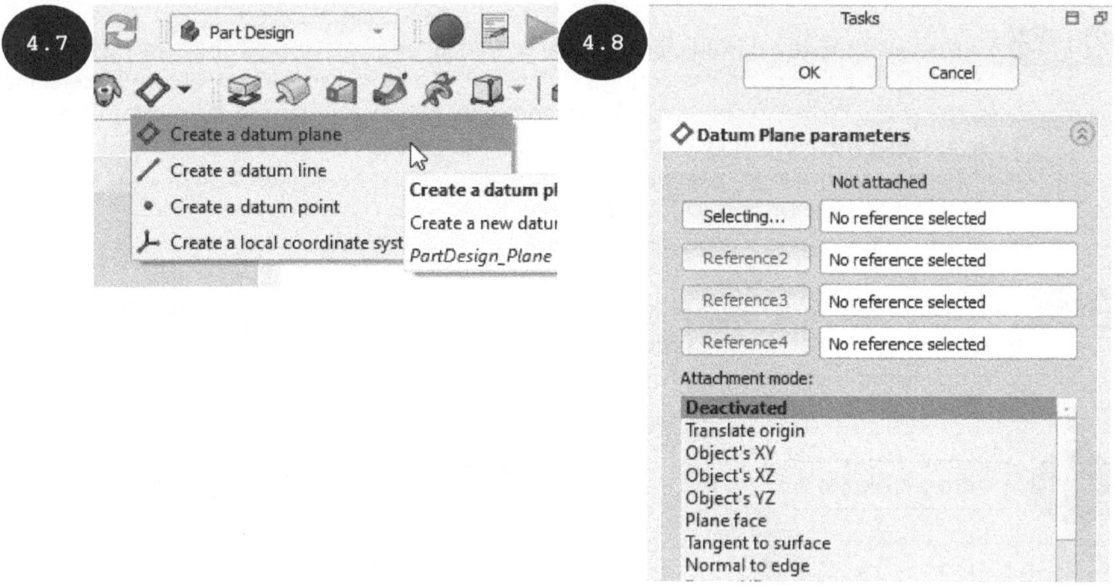

Note: The **Deactivated** mode is used for creating a datum plane coplanar to the default XY Plane. It is the default mode, and the selection of a reference geometry is not required for creating a datum plane by using this attachment mode.

2. Click on the OK button in the **Tasks Panel**. The **Incompatible reference set** window appears, informing that no attachment mode fits the current set of references. Click on the **Yes** button in this window to confirm the creation of the datum plane.

Creating a Datum Plane Normal to an Edge

You can create a datum plane normal to a linear edge of a model by using the **Normal to edge** attachment mode and the method for creating the same is discussed below:

1. Invoke the **Datum** menu in the **Part Design Helper** toolbar and then click on the **Create a datum plane** tool, refer to Figure 4.7. The **Datum Plane parameters** sub-window appears in the **Tasks Panel**. Also, you are prompted to select a first reference for creating a datum plane.

2. Select a linear edge of a model as the first reference. The preview of a datum plane appears normal to the selected edge of the model, see Figure 4.9. Also, the **Normal to edge** mode gets activated in the **Attachment mode** area of the **Tasks Panel**.

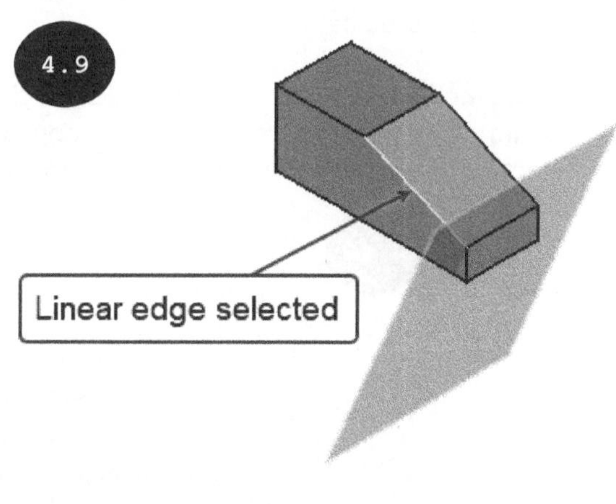

Note: You can also create a datum plane normal to a linear edge of a model and passing through a vertex. For doing so, after selecting a linear edge of a model as the first reference, select a vertex of the model as the second reference, see Figure 4.10. Ignore, if an error appears. Next, select the **Normal to edge** mode in the **Attachment mode** area of the **Tasks Panel**. The preview of a datum plane appears normal to the selected edge and passing through the selected vertex in the 3D View area, see Figure 4.10.

Tip: You can further control the placement and orientation of the datum plane in the 3D View area by specifying translational and rotational values in the respective fields of the **Attachment Offset** area of the **Tasks Panel**, see Figure 4.11.

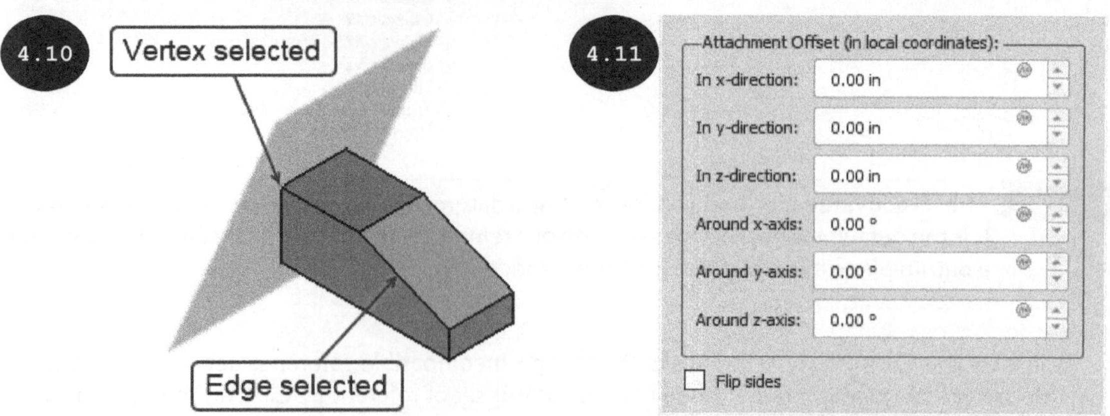

3. Click on the **OK** button in the **Tasks Panel** to confirm the creation of the datum plane and exit the **Tasks Panel**.

Creating a Datum Plane Passing through a Vertex

The method for creating a datum plane passing through a vertex of a model and parallel to the default XY Plane is discussed below:

1. Invoke the **Datum** menu and then click on the **Create a datum plane** tool, see Figure 4.12. The **Datum Plane parameters** sub-window appears in the **Tasks Panel**. Also, you are prompted to select a first reference for creating a datum plane.

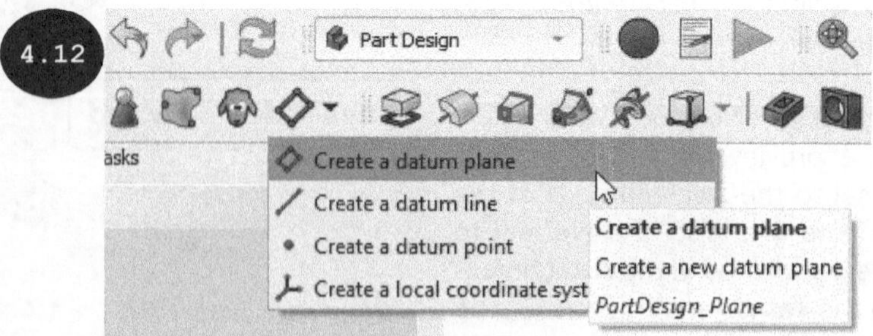

2. Select a vertex of a model as the first reference in the 3D View area. The preview of a datum plane appears passing through the selected vertex and parallel to the default XY Plane in the 3D View area, see Figure 4.13. Also, the **Translate origin** mode gets activated automatically in the **Attachment mode** area of the **Tasks Panel**.

Tip: You can further control the placement of the datum plane in the 3D View area by specifying translational or offset distance values in the respective fields of the **Attachment Offset** area of the **Tasks Panel**, see Figure 4.14.

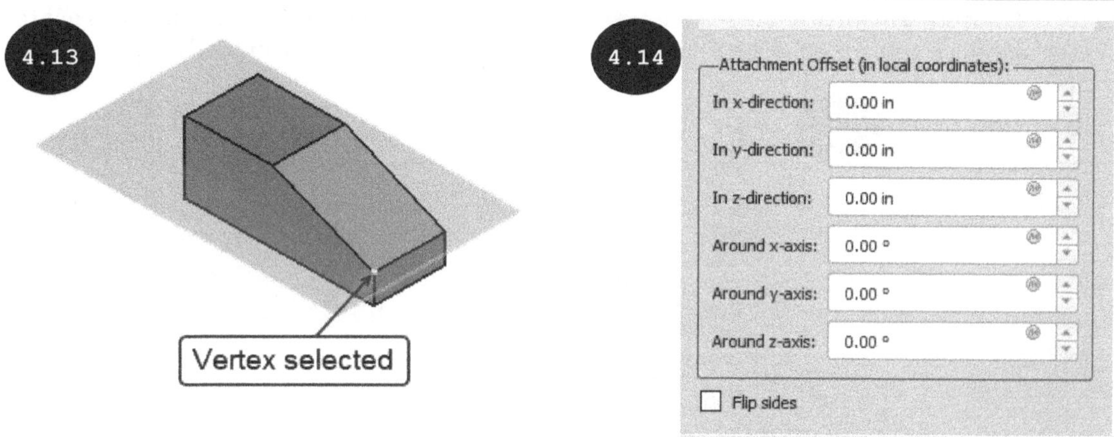

3. Click on the **OK** button in the **Tasks Panel** to confirm the creation of the datum plane and exit the **Tasks Panel**.

Creating a Datum Plane Coincident to a Planar Face

The method for creating a datum plane coincident to a plane or a planar face of a model is discussed below:

1. Invoke the **Datum** menu and then click on the **Create a datum plane** tool. The **Datum Plane parameters** sub-window appears in the **Tasks Panel**. Also, you are prompted to select a first reference for creating a datum plane.

2. Select a plane or a planar face of a model as the first reference in the 3D View area. The preview of a datum plane appears to coincide with the selected plane or planar face in the 3D View area, see Figure 4.15. Also, the **Plane face** mode gets activated automatically in the **Attachment mode** area of the **Tasks Panel**.

3. Click on the **OK** button in the **Tasks Panel** to confirm the creation of the datum plane and exit the **Tasks Panel**.

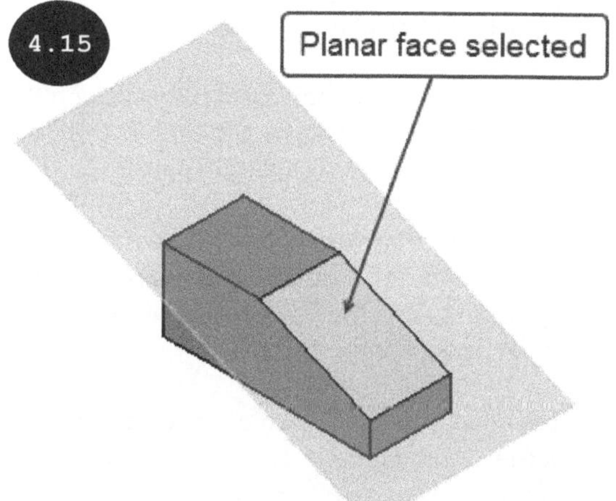

Creating a Datum Plane Tangent to a Face

The method for creating a datum plane tangent to the face of a model at a vertex is discussed below:

1. Invoke the **Datum** menu and then click on the **Create a datum plane** tool. The **Datum Plane parameters** sub-window appears in the **Tasks Panel**. Also, you are prompted to select a first reference for creating a datum plane.

2. Select the face of a model as the first reference and then a vertex as the second reference in the 3D View area. The preview of a datum plane appears such that it is tangent to the selected face of the model and normal to the selected vertex of the model, see Figure 4.16. Also, the **Tangent to surface** mode gets activated automatically in the **Attachment mode** area of the **Tasks Panel**.

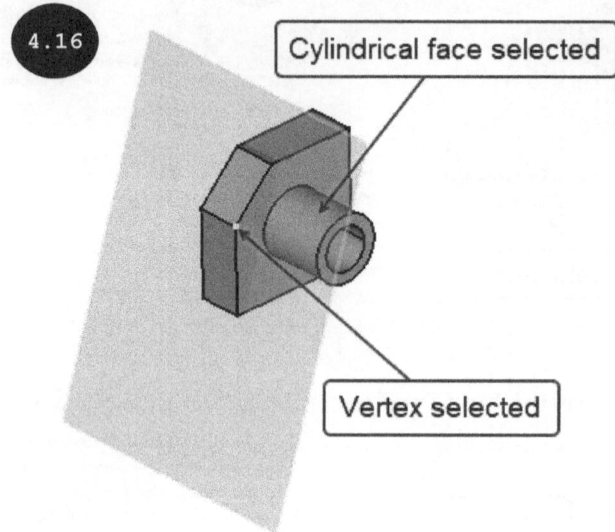

3. Click on the OK button in the **Tasks Panel** to confirm the creation of the datum plane and exit the **Tasks Panel**.

Creating a Datum Plane Aligned to the Plane of an Entity

The method for creating a datum plane aligned to the plane of a circular sketch entity (circle), a curve, or a circular edge of a model is discussed below:

1. Invoke the **Datum** menu and then click on the **Create a datum plane** tool. The **Datum Plane parameters** sub-window appears in the **Tasks Panel**. Also, you are prompted to select a first reference for creating a datum plane.

2. Select a circular sketch entity (circle), a curve, or a circular edge of a model as the first reference. The preview of a datum plane appears aligned to the plane of the selected reference, see Figure 4.17. Also, the **Concentric** mode gets activated automatically in the **Attachment mode** area of the **Tasks Panel**.

3. If needed, you can also select a vertex or a point as the second reference to define the orientation of the datum plane.

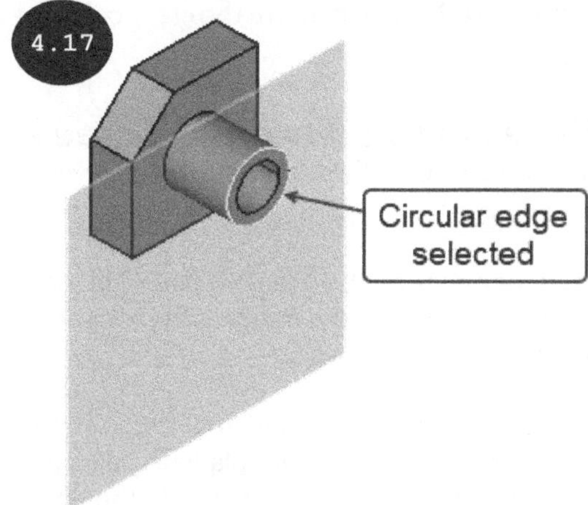

4. Click on the **OK** button in the **Tasks Panel** to confirm the creation of the datum plane and exit the **Tasks Panel**.

Creating a Datum Plane Normal to the Plane of an Entity

The method for creating a datum plane normal to the plane of a circular sketch entity (circle), a curve, or a circular edge of a model is discussed below:

1. Invoke the **Datum** menu and then click on the **Create a datum plane** tool. The **Datum Plane parameters** sub-window appears in the **Tasks Panel**. Also, you are prompted to select a first reference for creating a datum plane.

2. Select a circular sketch entity (circle), a curve, or a circular edge of a model as the first reference in the 3D View area.

3. Select the **Revolution Section** mode in the **Attachment mode** area of the **Tasks Panel**. The preview of a datum plane appears normal to the plane of the selected reference, see Figure 4.18.

4. If needed, you can select a vertex or an endpoint of a curve as the second reference for creating a datum plane normal to the plane of the first reference and passing through the vertex selected as the second reference, see Figure 4.19.

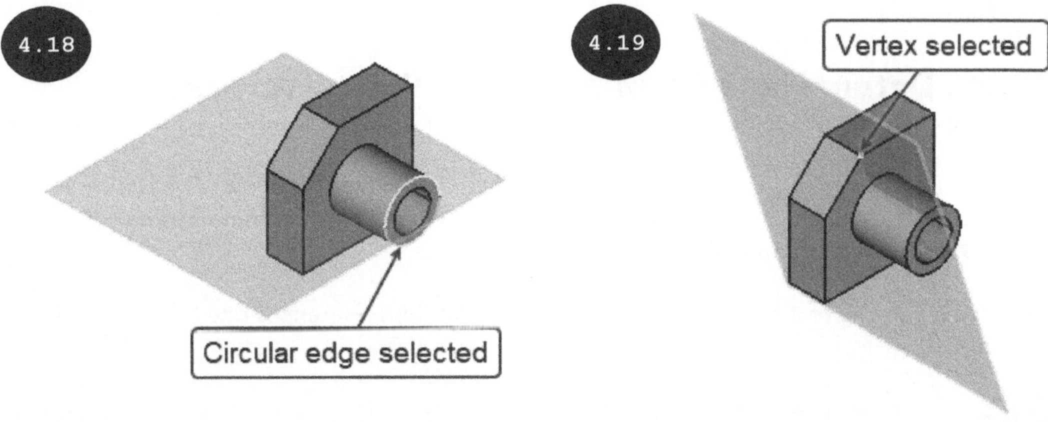

5. Click on the **OK** button in the **Tasks Panel** to confirm the creation of the datum plane and exit the **Tasks Panel**.

Creating a Datum Plane Passing Through Three Points/Vertices

The method for creating a datum plane passing through three points or vertices of a model is discussed below:

1. Invoke the **Datum** menu and then click on the **Create a datum plane** tool. The **Datum Plane parameters** sub-window appears in the **Tasks Panel**. Also, you are prompted to select a first reference for creating a datum plane.

2. Select three vertices of a model as the first, second, and third references one by one in the 3D View area, see Figure 4.20. The preview of a datum plane appears passing through the selected vertices. Also, the **Plane by 3 points** mode gets selected in the **Attachment mode** area of the **Tasks Panel**.

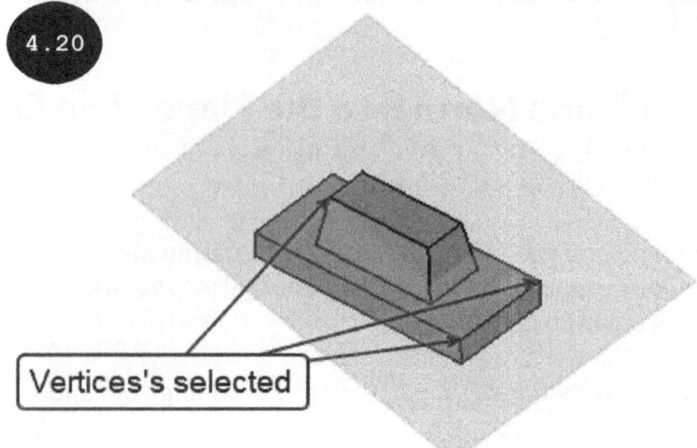

Note: Alternatively, you can also select a linear edge and a vertex or two linear edges as the first and second references for creating a datum plane passing through the selections using the **Plane by 3 points** attachment mode.

3. Click on the **OK** button in the **Tasks Panel** to confirm the creation of the datum plane and exit the **Tasks Panel**.

Creating a Datum Plane Normal to Three Points/Vertices

The method for creating a datum plane normal to three points or vertices of a model is discussed below:

1. Invoke the **Datum** menu and then click on the **Create a datum plane** tool. The **Datum Plane parameters** sub-window appears in the **Tasks Panel**. Also, you are prompted to select a first reference for creating a datum plane.

2. Select three vertices of a model as the first, second, and third references one by one in the 3D View area.

3. Select the **Normal to 3 points** mode in the **Attachment mode** area of the **Tasks Panel**. The preview of a datum plane appears normal to selected references in the **3D View** area.

Note: Alternatively, you can also select a linear edge and a vertex or two linear edges as the first and second references for creating a datum plane normal to the selections using the **Normal to 3 points** attachment mode.

4. Click on the **OK** button in the **Tasks Panel** to confirm the creation of the datum plane and exit the **Tasks Panel**.

Creating a Datum Plane Normal to a Curve

The method for creating a datum plane normal to a curve is discussed below:

1. Invoke the **Datum** menu and then click on the **Create a datum plane** tool. The **Datum Plane parameters** sub-window appears in the **Tasks Panel**. Also, you are prompted to select a first reference for creating a datum plane.

2. Select a curve or a circular edge as the first reference in the 3D View area. The **Frenet NB** mode gets activated in the **Attachment mode** area of the **Tasks Panel**, automatically. Also, the preview of a datum plane appears normal to the selected curve such that the normal-binormal (NB) axes of the frenet-serret coordinate get aligned at an endpoint of the curve or the center of the circular edge, see Figures 4.21 and 4.22. Figure 4.21 shows the preview of a datum plane normal to a curve and Figure 4.22 shows the axes (N, B, and T) of the frenet-serret coordinate for your reference.

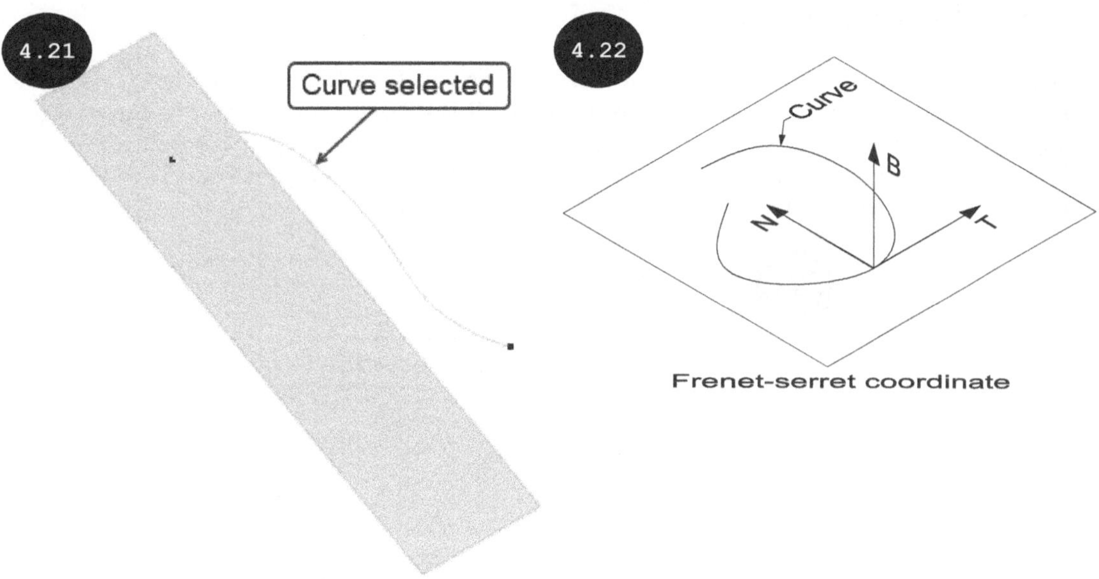

Tip: After selecting a curve as the first reference, you can also select a point as the second reference to define the location of the datum plane along the curve, if needed.

3. Click on the **OK** button in the **Tasks Panel** to confirm the creation of the datum plane and exit the **Tasks Panel**.

Creating a Datum Plane Coincident to the Plane of a Curve

The method for creating a datum plane coincident to the plane of a curve is discussed below:

1. Invoke the **Datum** menu and then click on the **Create a datum plane** tool. The **Datum Plane parameters** sub-window appears in the **Tasks Panel**. Also, you are prompted to select a first reference for creating a datum plane.

2. Select a curve or a circular edge as the first reference in the 3D View area. Next, select the **Frenet TN** mode in the **Attachment mode** area of the **Tasks Panel.** The preview of a datum plane appears coincident with the plane of the curve such that the tangent-normal (TN) axes of the frenet-serret coordinate get aligned to the plane of the curve. Refer to Figure 4.22 for the axes (N, B, and T) of the frenet-serret coordinate.

3. Click on the **OK** button in the **Tasks Panel** to confirm the creation of the datum plane and exit the **Tasks Panel**.

Creating a Datum Plane Tangent to an Endpoint of a Curve

The method for creating a datum plane tangent to an endpoint of a curve is discussed below:

1. Invoke the **Datum** menu and then click on the **Create a datum plane** tool. The **Datum Plane parameters** sub-window appears in the **Tasks Panel**. Also, you are prompted to select a first reference for creating a datum plane.

2. Select a curve or a circular edge as the first reference in the 3D View area. Next, select the **Frenet TB** mode in the **Attachment mode** area of the **Tasks Panel.** The preview of a datum plane appears tangent to an endpoint of the selected curve such that the tangent-binormal (TB) axes of the frenet-serret coordinate get aligned at an endpoint of the curve, see Figure 4.23. Refer to Figure 4.22 for the axes (N, B, and T) of the frenet-serret coordinate.

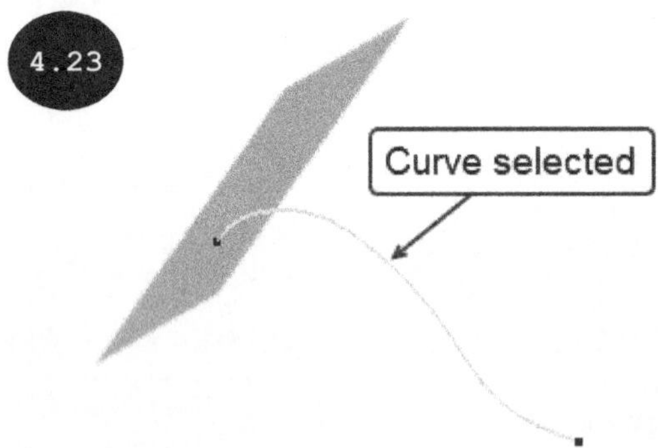

Tip: You can also select a point or a vertex as the second reference to define an endpoint of the curve for creating a datum plane tangent to it.

3. Click on the **OK** button in the **Tasks Panel** to confirm the creation of the datum plane and exit the **Tasks Panel**.

Creating a Datum Plane Aligned to the XY Plane of a Conic Curve

The method for creating a datum plane aligned to the local XY plane of a conic curve or edge is discussed below:

1. Invoke the **Datum** menu and then click on the **Create a datum plane** tool . The **Datum Plane parameters** sub-window appears in the **Tasks Panel**. Also, you are prompted to select a first reference for creating a datum plane.

2. Select a conical edge or a conic curve (sketch) such as an ellipse, a hyperbolic arc, or a parabolic arc as the first reference in the 3D View area. The preview of a datum plane appears aligned to the local XY plane of the selected entity, see Figure 4.24. Also, the **Object's XY** mode gets selected in the **Attachment mode** area of the **Tasks Panel**.

3. Click on the **OK** button in the **Tasks Panel** to confirm the creation of the datum plane and exit the **Tasks Panel**.

Creating a Datum Plane Aligned to the XZ Plane of a Conic Curve

The method for creating a datum plane aligned to the local XZ plane of a conic curve or edge is discussed below:

1. Invoke the **Datum** menu and then click on the **Create a datum plane** tool . The **Datum Plane parameters** sub-window appears in the **Tasks Panel**. Also, you are prompted to select a first reference for creating a datum plane.

2. Select a conical edge or a conic curve (sketch) such as an ellipse, a hyperbolic arc, or a parabolic arc as the first reference in the 3D View area. Next, select the **Object's XZ** mode in the **Attachment mode** area of the **Tasks Panel**. The preview of a datum plane appears aligned to the local XZ plane of the selected entity, see Figure 4.25.

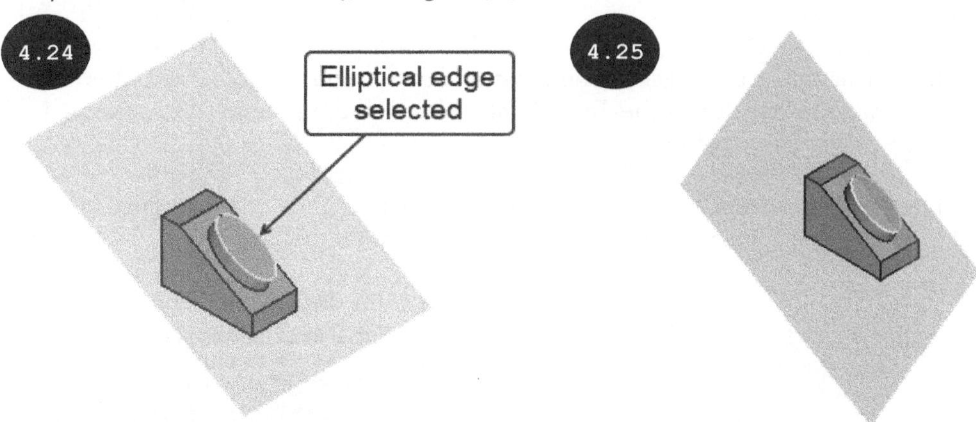

3. Click on the **OK** button in the **Tasks Panel** to confirm the creation of the datum plane and exit the **Tasks Panel**.

Creating a Datum Plane Aligned to the YZ Plane of a Conic Curve

The method for creating a datum plane aligned to the local YZ plane of a conic curve or edge is discussed below:

1. Invoke the **Datum** menu and then click on the **Create a datum plane** tool. The **Datum Plane parameters** sub-window appears in the **Tasks Panel**. Also, you are prompted to select a first reference for creating a datum plane.

2. Select a conical edge or a conic curve (sketch) such as an ellipse, a hyperbolic arc, or a parabolic arc as the first reference in the 3D View area. Next, select the **Object's YZ** mode in the **Attachment mode** area of the **Tasks Panel**. The preview of a datum plane appears aligned to the local YZ plane of the selected entity, see Figure 4.26.

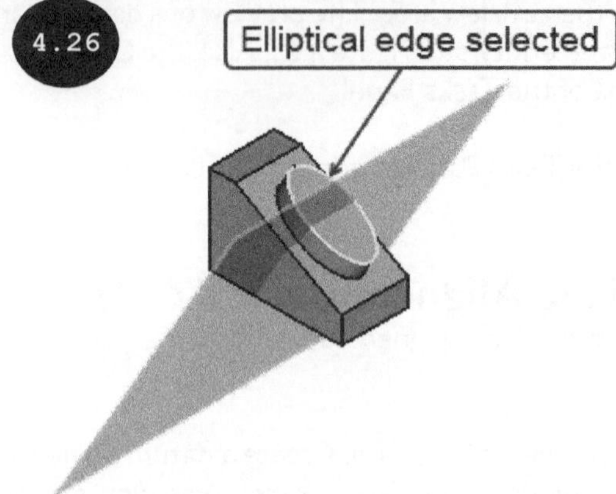

3. Click on the **OK** button in the **Tasks Panel** to confirm the creation of the datum plane and exit the **Tasks Panel**.

Creating a Datum Plane Passing Through 2 and 3 Axes of Inertia

The method for creating a datum plane passing through the second and third principal axes of inertia is discussed below:

1. Invoke the **Datum** menu and then click on the **Create a datum plane** tool. The **Datum Plane parameters** sub-window appears in the **Tasks Panel**. Also, you are prompted to select a first reference for creating a datum plane.

2. Select an object such as a plane, a face, an edge, a vertex, or a sketch as the first reference. The preview of a datum plane appears depending on the type of entity selected.

3. Select the **Inertia 2-3** mode in the **Attachment mode** area of the **Tasks Panel**. The preview of a datum plane appears passing through the second and third principal axes of inertia of the selected entity.

4. Similarly, you can select an object as the second reference or second and third references one by one in the 3D View area, if needed. The preview of a datum plane appears passing through the second and third principal axes of inertia (center of mass) of the selected entities, accordingly.

5. Click on the **OK** button in the **Tasks Panel** to confirm the creation of the datum plane and exit the **Tasks Panel**.

Creating Datum Lines/Axes

You can also create datum lines that can be used as axes of revolution for creating features such as revolution, groove, and polar patterns similar to creating datum planes. To create a datum line/axis, invoke the **Datum** menu in the **Part Design Helper** toolbar and then click on the **Create a datum line** tool, see Figure 4.27. The **Datum Line parameters** sub-window appears in the **Tasks Panel** of the **Combo View**, see Figure 4.28. Also, you are prompted to select the first reference for creating a datum line/axis. The options in the **Tasks Panel** are used for creating various types of datum lines. The methods for creating some of the different types of datum lines/axes are discussed next.

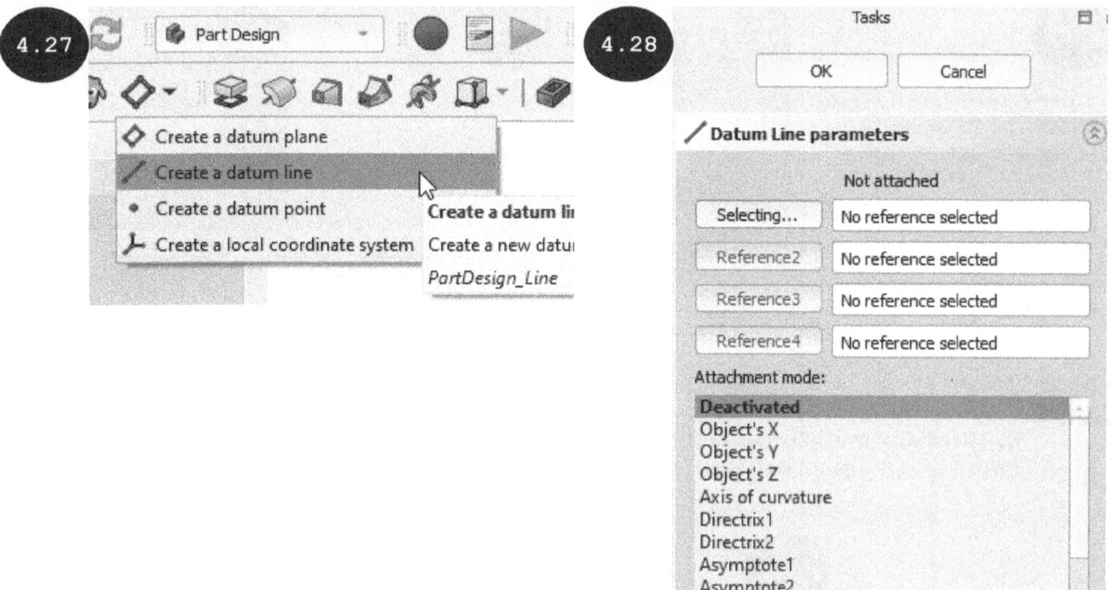

Creating a Datum Line Along the Default Z Axis

The method for creating a datum plane along the default Z axis is discussed below:

1. Invoke the **Datum** menu and then click on the **Create a datum line** tool, refer to Figure 4.27. The **Datum Line parameters** sub-window appears in the **Tasks Panel**. Also, the preview of a datum line appears along the default Z axis in the 3D View area since the **Deactivated** mode is activated in the **Attachment mode** area of the **Tasks Panel**, by default.

2. Click on the **OK** button in the **Tasks Panel**. The **Incompatible reference set** window appears, informing that no attachment mode fits the current set of references. Click on the **Yes** button in this window to continue with the creation of the datum axis along the default Z axis.

Creating a Datum Line Passing Through Two Points

The method for creating a datum line passing through two points or along an edge is discussed below:

1. Invoke the **Datum** menu and then click on the **Create a datum line** tool. The **Datum Line parameters** sub-window appears in the **Tasks Panel**, and you are prompted to select the first reference.

2. Select two vertices of a model as the first and second references one by one in the 3D View area. The preview of a datum axis/line appears passing through the selected vertices, see Figure 4.29. Also, the **Through two points** mode gets activated in the **Attachment mode** area of the **Tasks Panel**.

Note: Instead of selecting two vertices, you can also select a linear edge of a model as the first reference for creating a datum axis along it by using the **Through two points** attachment mode, see Figure 4.30.

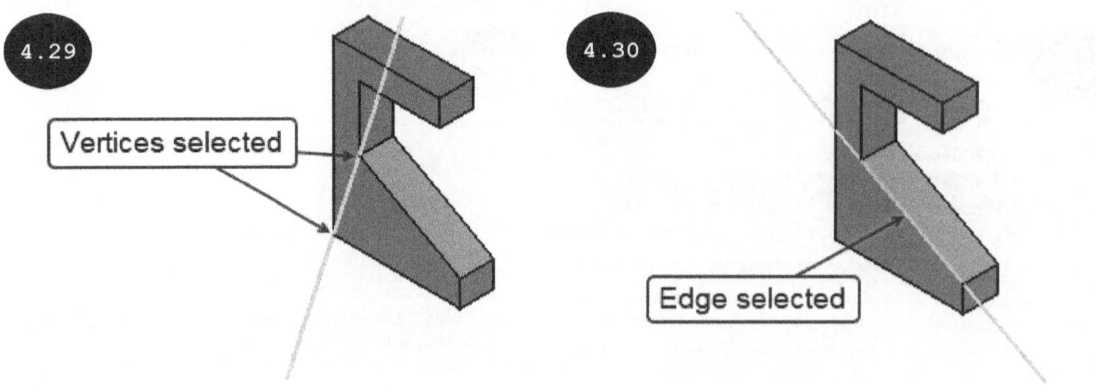

Tip: You can further control the placement and orientation of the datum line in the 3D View area by specifying translational and rotational values in the respective fields of the **Attachment Offset** area in the **Tasks Panel**, see Figure 4.31.

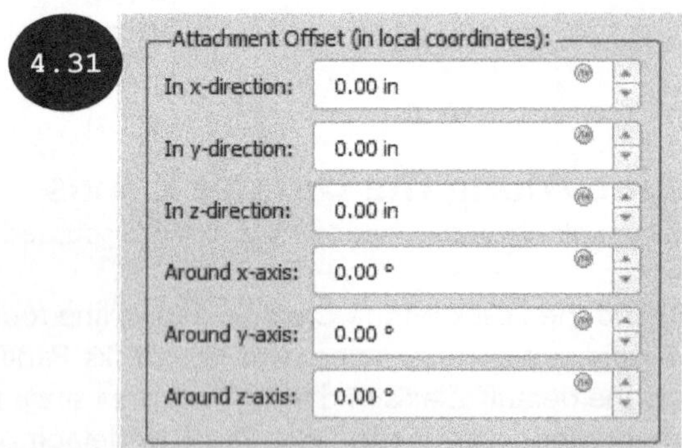

3. Click on the **OK** button in the **Tasks Panel** to confirm the creation of the datum axis and exit the **Tasks Panel**.

Creating a Datum Line Along the Axis of Curvature

The method for creating a datum line along the axis of curvature of a curved edge is discussed below:

1. Invoke the **Datum** menu and then click on the **Create a datum line** tool. The **Datum Line parameters** sub-window appears in the **Tasks Panel**, and you are prompted to select the first reference.

2. Select a curved edge of a model as the first reference in the 3D View area. The preview of a datum axis/line appears along the axis of curvature of the selected entity, see Figure 4.32. Also, the **Axis of Curvature** mode gets activated in the **Attachment mode** area of the **Tasks Panel**.

Tip: You can further control the placement and orientation of the datum line/axis in the 3D View area by specifying translational and rotational values in the respective fields of the **Attachment Offset** area in the **Tasks Panel**, see Figure 4.33.

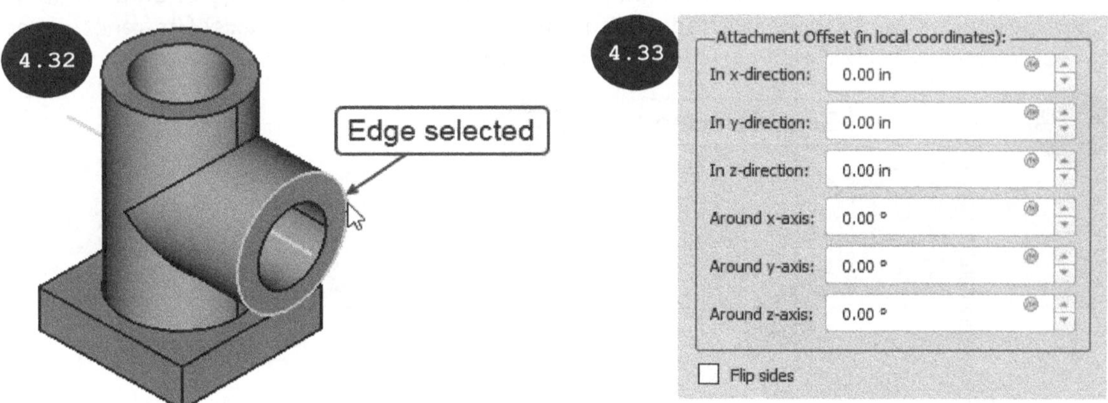

3. Click on the **OK** button in the **Tasks Panel** to confirm the creation of the datum axis and exit the **Tasks Panel**.

Creating a Datum Line Tangent to an Edge

The method for creating a datum line tangent to an edge at a vertex is discussed below:

1. Invoke the **Datum** menu and then click on the **Create a datum line** tool. The **Datum Line parameters** sub-window appears in the **Tasks Panel**, and you are prompted to select the first reference.

2. Select a curved edge of a model as the first reference in the 3D View area. Next, select the **Tangent** mode in the **Attachment mode** area of the **Tasks Panel**. The preview of a datum line appears tangent to the selected circular edge of the model, see Figure 4.34.

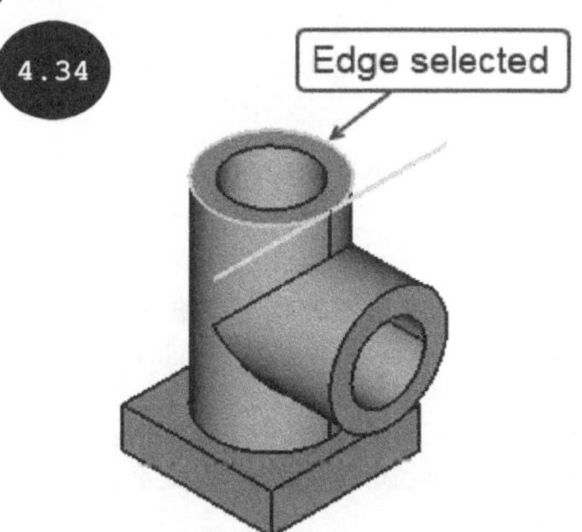

Tip: If needed, you can also select a vertex as the second reference to define the location of the datum line tangent to the selected edge of the model.

3. Click on the **OK** button in the **Tasks Panel** to confirm the creation of the datum axis and exit the **Tasks Panel**.

Creating a Datum Line Normal to a Curved Edge

The method for creating a datum line normal to a curved edge is discussed below:

1. Invoke the **Datum** menu and then click on the **Create a datum line tool**. The **Datum Line parameters** sub-window appears in the **Tasks Panel**.

2. Select a curved edge of a model as the first reference in the 3D View area. Next, select the **Normal to edge** mode in the **Attachment mode** area of the **Tasks Panel**. The preview of a datum plane appears normal to the selected edge such that it gets aligned to the N axis of its frenet-serret coordinate in the 3D View area, see Figures 4.35 and 4.36.

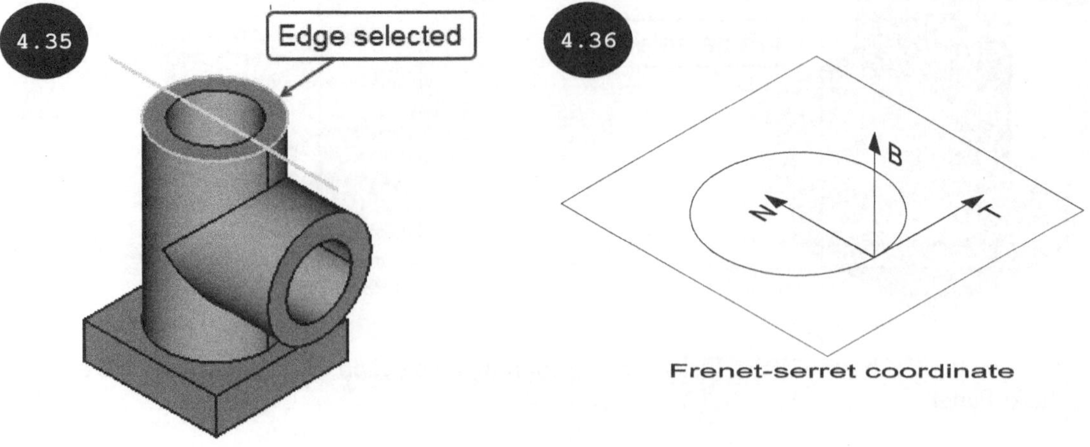

Tip: If needed, you can also select a vertex as the second reference to define the location of the datum line normal to the selected edge of the model.

3. Click on the **OK** button in the **Tasks Panel** to confirm the creation of the datum axis and exit the **Tasks Panel**.

Creating a Datum Line Binormal to a Curved Edge

The method for creating a datum line normal to a curved edge is discussed below:

1. Invoke the **Datum** menu and then click on the **Create a datum line tool**. The **Datum Line parameters** sub-window appears in the **Tasks Panel**, and you are prompted to select the first reference.

2. Select a curved edge of a model as the first reference in the 3D View area. Next, select the **Binormal** mode in the **Attachment mode** area of the **Tasks Panel**. The preview of a datum plane appears normal to the selected edge such that it gets aligned to the B axis of its frenet-serret coordinate in the 3D View area, see Figure 4.37. Refer to Figure 4.36 for the frenet-serret coordinate.

Tip: If needed, you can also select a vertex as the second reference to define the location of the datum line normal to the selected edge of the model.

3. Click on the **OK** button in the **Tasks Panel** to confirm the creation of the datum axis and exit the **Tasks Panel**.

Creating a Datum Line along the First Principal Axis of Inertia

The method for creating a datum line along the first principal axis of inertia is discussed below:

1. Invoke the **Datum** menu and then click on the **Create a datum line** tool. The **Datum Line parameters** sub-window appears in the **Tasks Panel**, and you are prompted to select the first reference.

2. Select a planar or curved face of a model as the first reference in the 3D View area. The preview of a datum plane appears such that it follows the first principal axis of inertia, see Figure 4.38. Also, the **1st principal axis** mode gets activated in the **Attachment mode** area of the **Tasks Panel**.

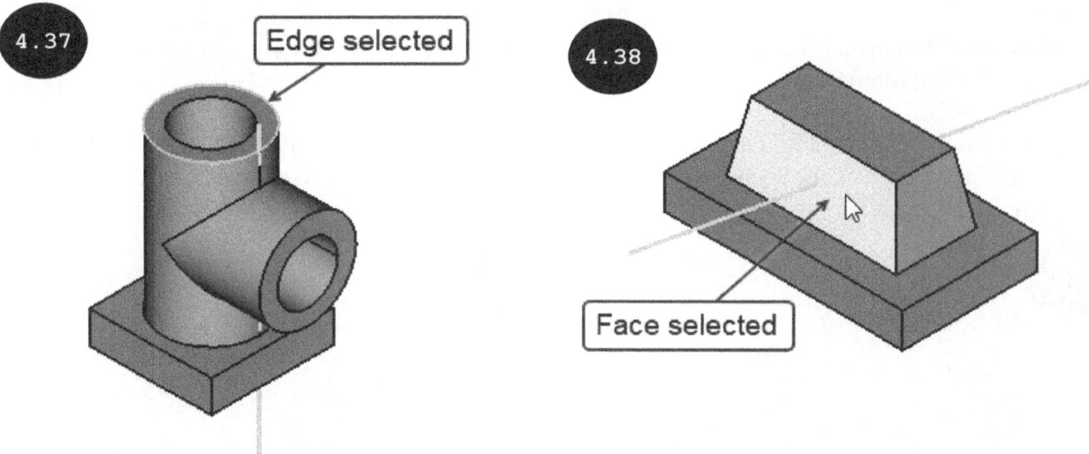

Note: You can also select second, third, and/or fourth references (faces) one by one in the 3D View area for creating a datum line following the first principal axis of inertia of the selected references (faces).

3. Click on the **OK** button in the **Tasks Panel** to confirm the creation of the datum axis and exit the **Tasks Panel**.

Creating a Datum Line along the Second Principal Axis of Inertia

The method for creating a datum line along the second principal axis of inertia is discussed below:

1. Invoke the **Datum** menu and then click on the **Create a datum line** tool . The **Datum Line parameters** sub-window appears in the **Tasks Panel**, and you are prompted to select the first reference.

2. Select a planar or curved face of a model as the first reference in the 3D View area. Next, select the **2nd principal axis** mode in the **Attachment mode** area of the **Tasks Panel**. The preview of a datum plane appears such that it follows the second principal axis of inertia, see Figure 4.39.

Note: You can also select the faces as the second, third, and/or fourth references one by one in the 3D View area for creating a datum line following the second principal axis of inertia of the selected references. After selecting the references, you need to activate the **2nd principal axis** mode in the **Attachment mode** area of the **Tasks Panel**.

3. Click on the **OK** button in the **Tasks Panel** to confirm the creation of the datum axis and exit the **Tasks Panel**.

Creating a Datum Line along the Third Principal Axis of Inertia

The method for creating a datum line along the third principal axis of inertia is discussed below:

1. Invoke the **Datum** menu and then click on the **Create a datum line** tool . You are prompted to select the first reference.

2. Select a planar or curved face of a model as the first reference in the 3D View area. Next, select the **3rd principal axis** mode in the **Attachment mode** area of the **Tasks Panel**. The preview of a datum plane appears such that it follows the third principal axis of inertia, see Figure 4.40.

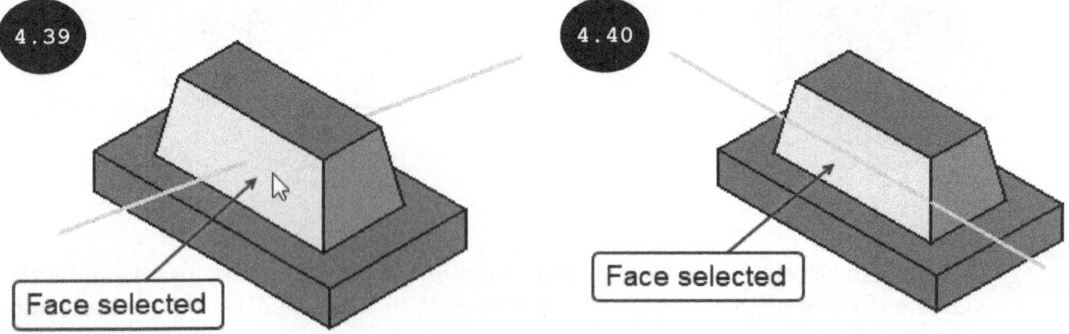

Note: You can also select the faces as the second, third, and/or fourth references one by one in the 3D View area for creating a datum line following the third principal axis of inertia of the selected references. After selecting the references, you need to activate the **3rd principal axis** mode in the **Attachment mode** area of the **Tasks Panel**.

3. Click on the **OK** button in the **Tasks Panel** to confirm the creation of the datum axis and exit the **Tasks Panel**.

Creating a Datum Line Along the Local X-Axis of a Conic Curve

The method for creating a datum line along the local X-axis of a conic curve/edge is discussed below:

1. Invoke the **Datum** menu and then click on the **Create a datum line** tool. The **Datum Line parameters** sub-window appears in the **Tasks Panel**.

2. Select a conical edge or a conic curve (sketch) such as an ellipse, a hyperbolic arc, or a parabolic arc as the first reference in the 3D View area. Next, select the **Object's X** mode in the **Attachment mode** area of the **Tasks Panel**. The preview of a datum line appears aligned to the local X-axis of the selected reference, see Figure 4.41.

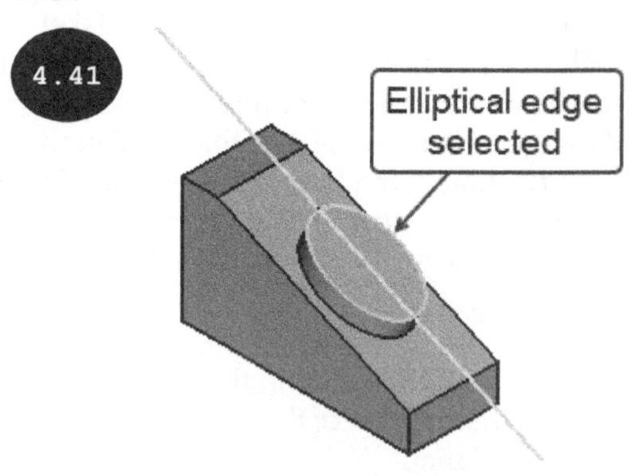

3. Click on the **OK** button in the **Tasks Panel** to confirm the creation of the datum axis and exit the **Tasks Panel**.

Tip: As discussed earlier, you can further control the placement and orientation of the datum line in the 3D View area by specifying translational and rotational values in the respective fields of the **Attachment Offset** area in the **Tasks Panel**.

Creating a Datum Line Along the Local Y-Axis of a Conic Curve

The method for creating a datum line aligned along the local Y-axis of a conic curve or edge is discussed below:

1. Invoke the **Datum** menu and then click on the **Create a datum line** tool. The **Datum Line parameters** sub-window appears in the **Tasks Panel**, and you are prompted to select the first reference.

2. Select a conical edge or a conic curve (sketch) such as an ellipse, a hyperbolic arc, or a parabolic arc as the first reference in the 3D View area. Next, select the **Object's Y** mode in the **Attachment mode** area of the **Tasks Panel**. The preview of a datum line appears aligned to the local Y-axis of the selected reference, see Figure 4.42.

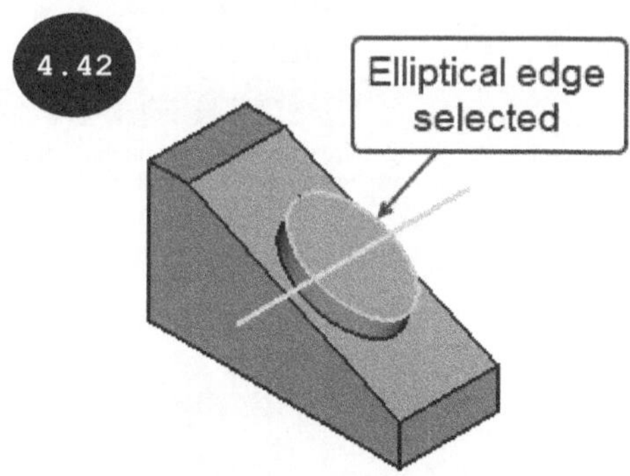

3. Click on the **OK** button in the **Tasks Panel** to confirm the creation of the datum axis and exit the **Tasks Panel**.

Creating a Datum Line Along the Local Z-Axis of a Conic Curve

The method for creating a datum line aligned along the local Z-axis of a conic curve or edge is discussed below:

1. Invoke the **Datum** menu and then click on the **Create a datum line** tool. The **Datum Line parameters** sub-window appears in the **Tasks Panel**, and you are prompted to select the first reference.

2. Select a conical edge or a conic curve (sketch) such as an ellipse, a hyperbolic arc, or a parabolic arc as the first reference in the 3D View area. Next, select the **Object's Z** mode in the **Attachment mode** area of the **Tasks Panel**. The preview of a datum line appears aligned to the local Z-axis of the selected reference, see Figure 4.43.

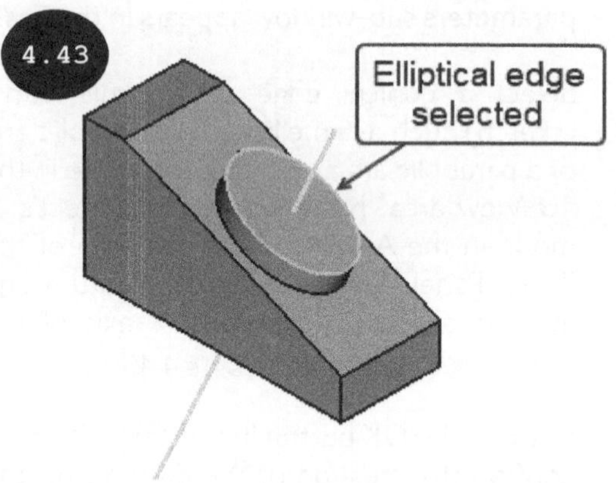

3. Click on the **OK** button in the **Tasks Panel** to confirm the creation of the datum axis and exit the **Tasks Panel**.

Creating Datum Points

A datum point can be created anywhere on a 3D model or space. It can be used as a reference point for measuring distances, creating sketches and datum geometries, and so on. To create a datum point, invoke the **Datum** menu in the **Part Design Helper** toolbar and then click on the **Create a datum point** tool, see Figure 4.44. The **Datum Point parameters** sub-window appears in the **Tasks Panel** of the **Combo View**, see Figure 4.45. Also, you are prompted to select the first reference for creating a datum point. The options in the **Tasks Panel** are used for creating various types of datum points. The methods for creating some of the different types of datum points are discussed next.

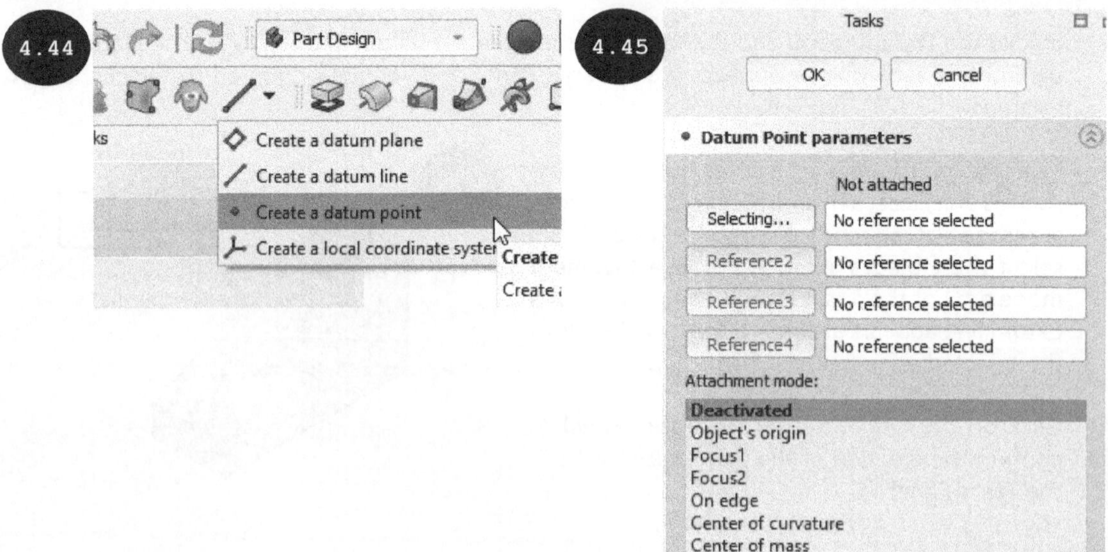

Creating a Datum Point at the Origin

The method for creating a datum point at the origin is discussed below:

1. Invoke the **Datum** menu and then click on the **Create a datum point** tool, refer to Figure 4.44. The **Datum Point parameters** sub-window appears in the **Tasks Panel**. Also, the preview of a datum point appears at the origin in the 3D View area since the **Deactivated** mode is activated in the **Attachment mode** area of the **Tasks Panel**, by default.

2. Click on the **OK** button in the **Tasks Panel**. The **Incompatible reference set** window appears, informing that no attachment mode fits the current set of references. Click on the **Yes** button in this window to continue with the creation of the datum point at the origin.

Creating a Datum Point at the Center of Mass

The method for creating a datum point at the center of mass of the selected references (faces, edges, or vertices) is discussed below:

1. Invoke the **Datum** menu and then click on the **Create a datum point** tool. The **Datum Point parameters** sub-window appears in the **Tasks Panel**.

2. Select a face, an edge, or a vertex of a model as the first reference. The preview of a datum point appears at the center of mass of the selected reference, see Figures 4.46 and 4.47. Ensure that the **Center of mass** mode gets activated in the **Attachment mode** area of the **Tasks Panel** for creating a datum point at the center of mass of the selected reference.

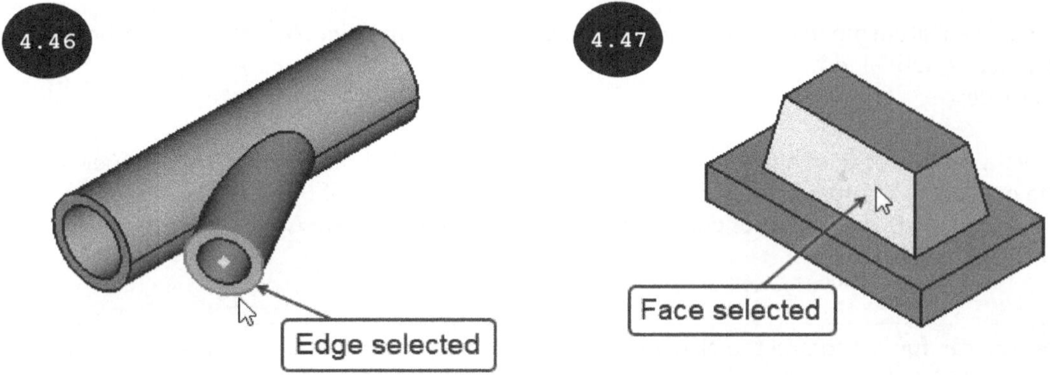

Note: When you select a vertex or an edge of a model as the first reference, you need to select the **Center of mass** mode manually in the **Attachment mode** area of the **Tasks Panel** for creating a datum point at the center of mass of the selected reference.

3. If needed, you can also select the second, third, and/or fourth references for creating a datum point at the center of mass of the selected references. You can select faces, edges, or vertices of a model as references in the 3D View area. After selecting the required references, ensure that the **Center of mass** mode is activated in the **Attachment mode** area of the **Tasks Panel**.

Tip: You can further control the placement and orientation of the datum point in the 3D View area by specifying translational and rotational values in the respective fields of the **Attachment Offset** area in the **Tasks Panel**, see Figure 4.48.

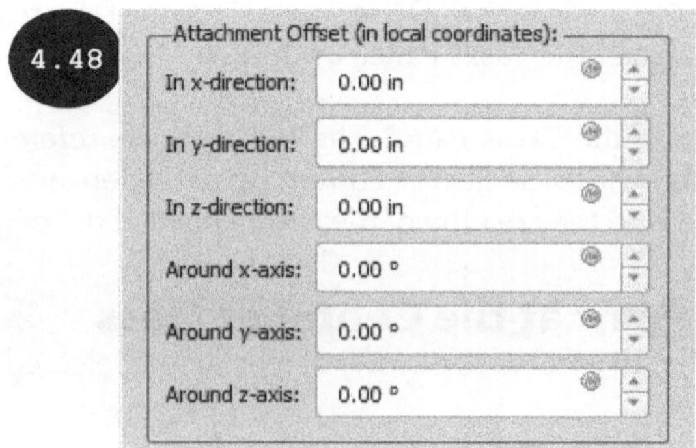

4. Click on the **OK** button in the **Tasks Panel** to confirm the creation of the datum point and exit the **Tasks Panel**.

Creating a Datum Point at the Center of Curvature

The method for creating a datum point at the center of curvature of a circular edge, a circle, or a curve is discussed below:

1. Invoke the **Datum** menu and then click on the **Create a datum point** tool •. The **Datum Point parameters** sub-window appears in the **Tasks Panel**, and you are prompted to select the first reference.

2. Select a circular edge of a model, a circle, or a curve as the first reference in the 3D View area. The preview of a datum point appears at the center of curvature of the selected reference, see Figure 4.49. Also, the **Center of curvature** mode gets activated in the **Attachment mode** area of the **Tasks Panel**.

Tip: You can further control the placement of the datum point in the 3D View area by specifying translational and rotational values in the respective fields of the **Attachment Offset** area in the **Tasks Panel**.

3. Click on the **OK** button in the **Tasks Panel** to confirm the creation of the datum point and exit the **Tasks Panel**.

Creating a Datum Point onto a Vertex

The method for creating a datum point onto a vertex of a model is discussed below:

1. Invoke the **Datum** menu and then click on the **Create a datum point** tool •. The **Datum Point parameters** sub-window appears in the **Tasks Panel**, and you are prompted to select the first reference.

2. Select a vertex of a model as the first reference in the 3D View area. The preview of a datum point appears on the selected vertex of the model, see Figure 4.50. Next, select the **Vertex** mode in the **Attachment mode** area of the **Tasks Panel**.

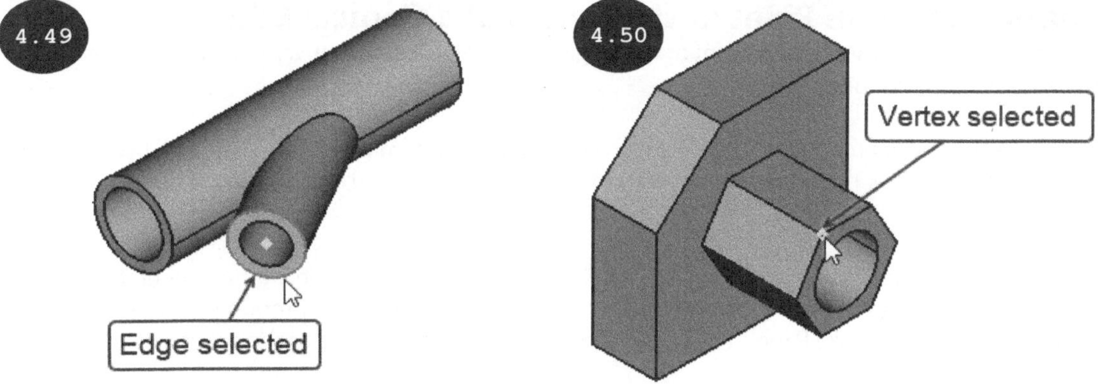

Note: Instead of selecting a vertex, you can select an edge or a line as the first reference for creating a datum point onto a vertex of the selected edge/line by using the **Vertex** attachment mode.

3. Click on the **OK** button in the **Tasks Panel** to confirm the creation of the datum point and exit the **Tasks Panel**.

Creating a Datum Point onto an Edge

The method for creating a datum point on to an edge of a model is discussed below:

1. Invoke the **Datum** menu and then click on the **Create a datum point** tool . The **Datum Point parameters** sub-window appears in the **Tasks Panel**, and you are prompted to select the first reference.

2. Select an edge of a model as the first reference in the 3D View area. The preview of a datum point appears on an endpoint of the selected edge of the model.

3. Select a vertex of the model as the second reference in the 3D View area. The preview of a datum point appears by projecting the selected vertex onto the edge of the model, see Figure 4.51.

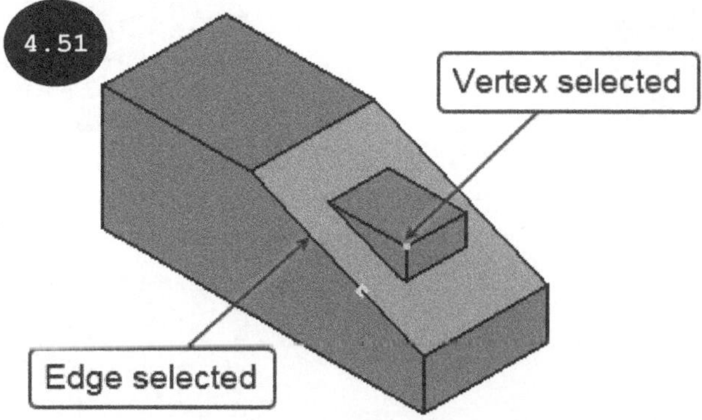

4. Click on the **OK** button in the **Tasks Panel** to confirm the creation of the datum point and exit the **Tasks Panel**.

Creating a Datum Point at the Origin of a Conical Edge

The method for creating a datum point at the origin of a conical edge such as an ellipse, a parabola, or a hyperbola is discussed below:

1. Invoke the **Datum** menu and then click on the **Create a datum point** tool . The **Datum Point parameters** sub-window appears in the **Tasks Panel**, and you are prompted to select the first reference.

2. Select a conical edge of a model such as an ellipse, a parabola, or a hyperbola as the first reference in the 3D View area, see Figure 4.52. Next, select the Object's origin mode in the **Attachment mode** area of the **Tasks Panel**. The preview of a datum point appears at the origin of the selected conical edge.

3. Click on the **OK** button in the **Tasks Panel** to confirm the creation of the datum point and exit the **Tasks Panel**.

Creating a Datum Point on a Focus of a Conical Edge

The method for creating a datum point on a focus of an ellipse, a parabola, or a hyperbola edge of a model is discussed below:

1. Invoke the **Datum** menu and then click on the **Create a datum point** tool . The **Datum Point parameters** sub-window appears in the **Tasks Panel**.

2. Select an ellipse, a parabola, or a hyperbola edge of a model as the first reference in the 3D View area. The preview of a datum point appears on a focus of the selected conical edge, see Figure 4.53.

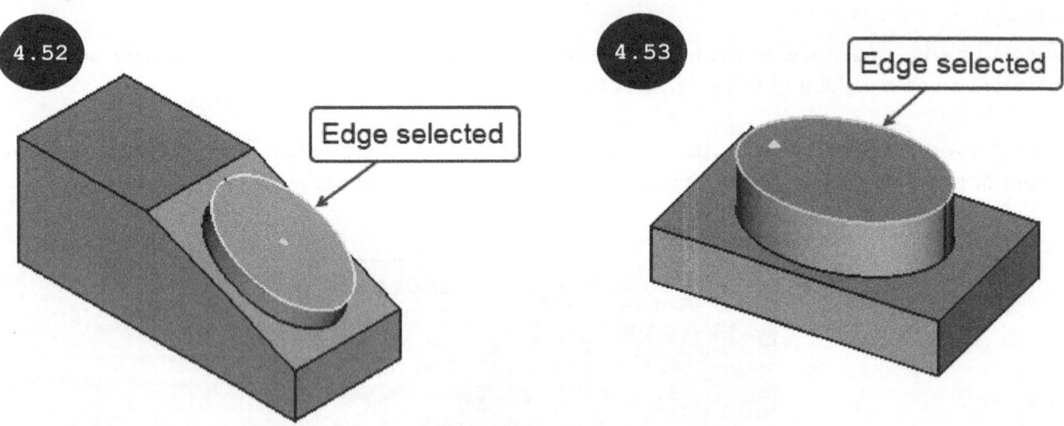

Note: After selecting an edge, if the **Focus2** mode gets activated in the **Attachment mode** area of the **Tasks Panel** by default, then you can select the **Focus1** mode for creating a datum point on the other focus of the selected edge or vice-versa.

3. Click on the **OK** button in the **Tasks Panel** to confirm the creation of the datum point and exit the **Tasks Panel**.

Creating a Local Coordinate System

In addition to creating a datum plane, a datum line, and a datum point, you can also create a local coordinate system by using the **Create a local coordinate system** tool of the **Datum** menu, see Figure 4.54.

A local coordinate system can be used as a reference for creating other datum geometries. It can also be used for machining or analyzing a model by positioning the origin of the model relative to its features, identifying the orientation of the attached datum geometry, and so on. The method for creating a local coordinate system is discussed below:

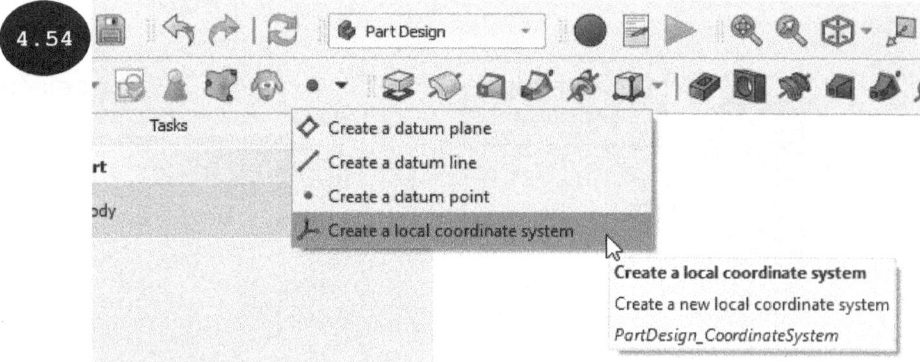

1. Invoke the **Datum** menu and then click on the **Create a local coordinate system** tool. The **Local Coordinate System parameters** sub-window appears in the **Tasks Panel**.

2. Select a plane, a planar face, a linear edge, a vertex, a conical edge (ellipse, parabola, or hyperbola), a circular edge, a curve, or a circle as the first reference geometry in the 3D View area. The preview of a local coordinate system appears depending upon the selected reference geometry, refer to Figure 4.55. Also, the respective mode gets activated automatically in the **Attachment mode** area of the **Tasks Panel**.

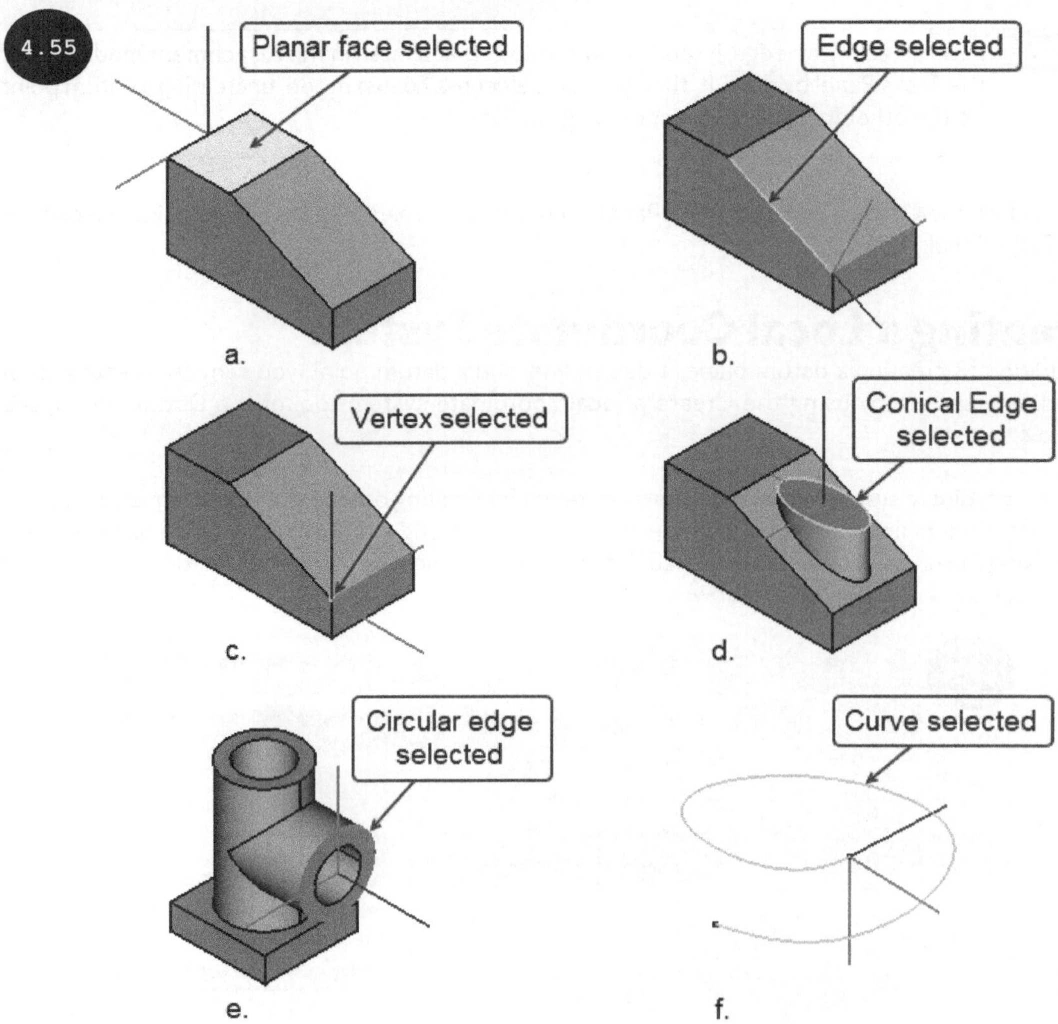

3. Ensure that the required attachment mode is activated in the **Attachment mode** area of the **Tasks Panel**.

Tip: You can further control the placement and orientation of the local coordinate system in the 3D View area by specifying translational and rotational values in the respective fields of the **Attachment Offset** area in the **Tasks Panel**, see Figure 4.56.

4. If needed, you can also select second, third, and/or fourth references for creating a local coordinate system. For example, to create a local coordinate system by aligning its XY plane passing through three vertices, you need to select three vertices as the first, second, and third references.

5. Click on the **OK** button in the **Tasks Panel** to confirm the creation of the local coordinate system and exit the **Tasks Panel**.

4.56

Attachment Offset (in local coordinates):

In x-direction: 0.00 in

In y-direction: 0.00 in

In z-direction: 0.00 in

Around x-axis: 0.00 °

Around y-axis: 0.00 °

Around z-axis: 0.00 °

Flip sides

Tutorial 1

Create a multi-feature model, as shown in Figure 4.57. You need to create the model by creating all its features one by one. All dimensions are in mm.

4.57

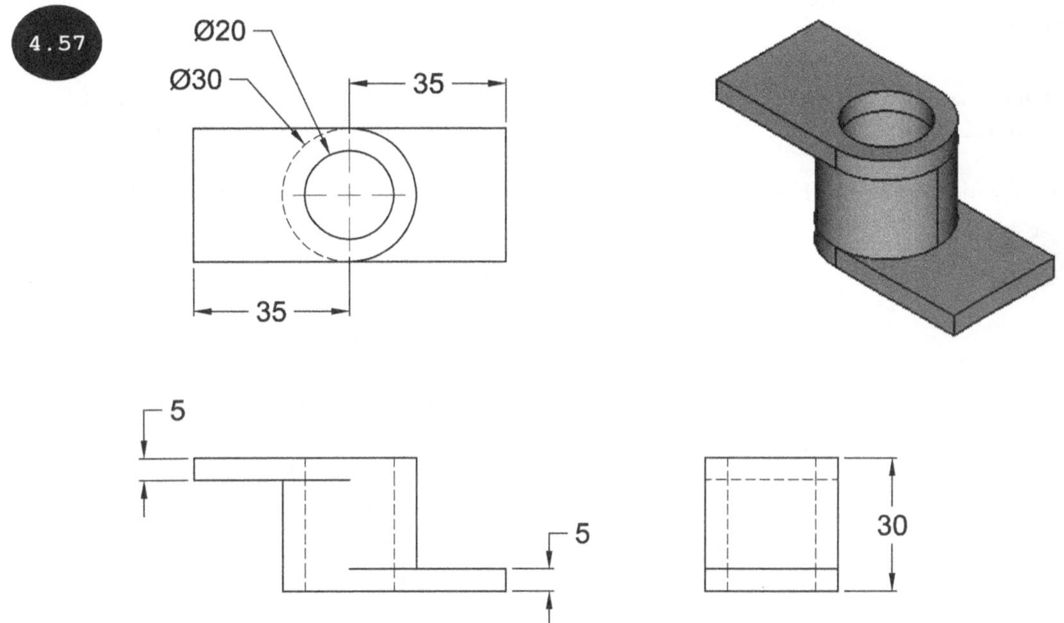

Section 1: Starting FreeCAD and a New Part Document

1. Start FreeCAD by double-clicking on the **FreeCAD 1.0** icon on your desktop. The startup user interface of FreeCAD appears, see Figure 4.58.

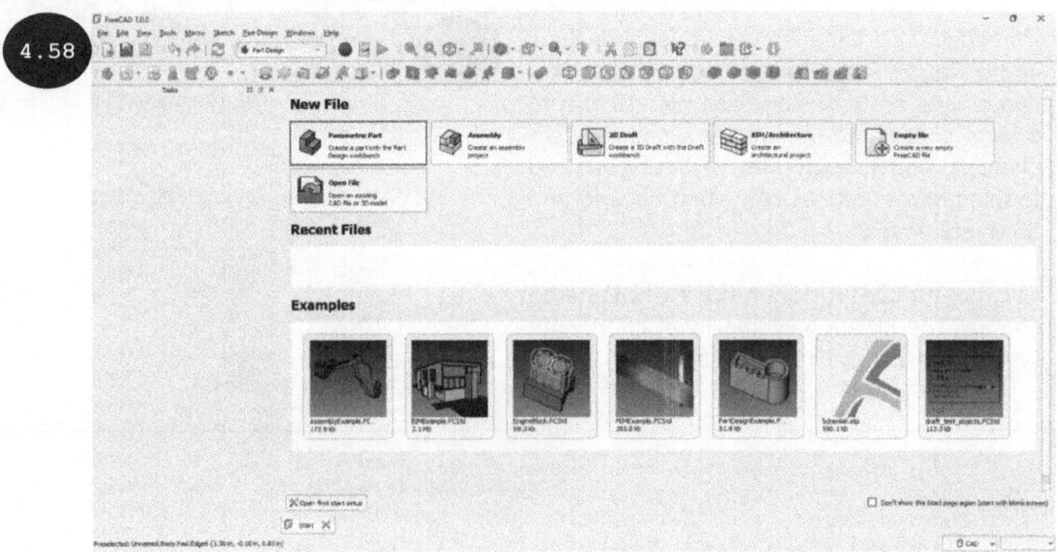

2. Click on the **Parametric Part** icon on the **Start** page (see Figure 4.58) or press the **CTRL + N** keys. A new part document gets invoked with the default name "**unnamed: 1**" and it becomes active by default.

Section 2: Specifying the Unit

Now, you need to specify millimeters (mm) as the measurement unit for the document.

1. Invoke the **Unit** flyout that appears at the lower right corner of the **Status Bar**, see Figure 4.59.

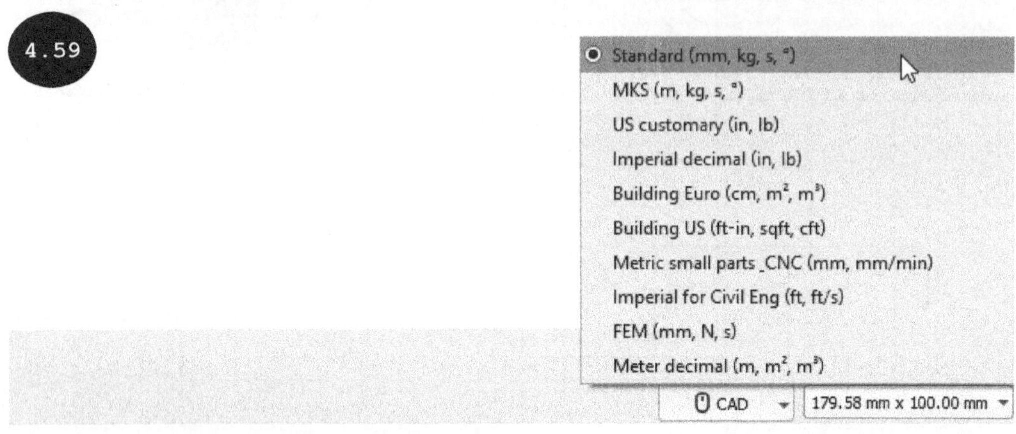

2. In this flyout, ensure that **Standard (mm, kg, s,*)** is selected as the unit system for the current design document.

Section 3: Creating the Base Feature

Now, you can create the base feature of the model, which is a pad feature.

1. Click on the **Create sketch** tool in the **Part Design Helper** toolbar, see Figure 4.60. The three default planes appear in the 3D View area. Also, the **Tasks Panel** appears in the **Tasks** tab of the **Combo View** with a list of three default planes.

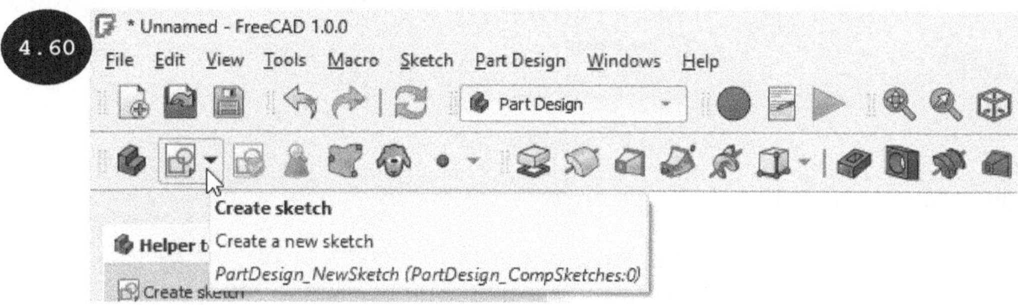

2. Select the **XY_Plane** as the sketching plane in the 3D View area for creating the sketch of the base feature. The **Sketcher** workbench gets invoked. Note that the selected plane becomes the sketching plane for drawing the sketch and is oriented normal to the viewing direction.

   Now, you can create a sketch of the base feature.

3. Create the sketch of the base feature and then apply the required constraints and dimensions to the sketch, see Figure 4.61.

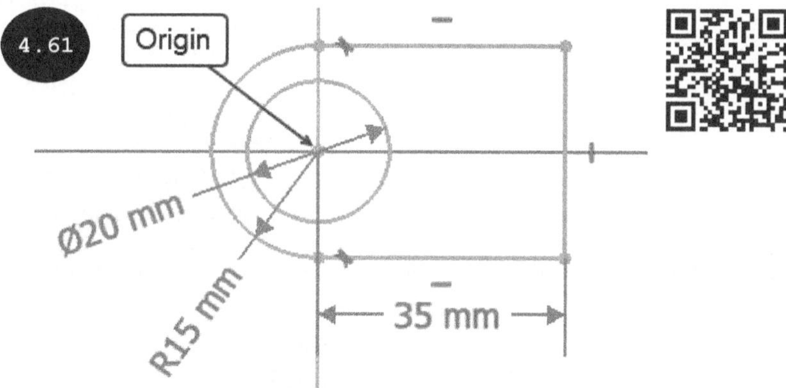

Note: In Figure 4.63, a tangent constraint is applied between each set of connected arc and line entities to make the sketch fully constrained.

After creating the sketch, you need to exit the **Sketcher** workbench.

4. Click on the **Close** button in the **Tasks Plane** of the **Combo View** to exit the **Sketcher** workbench (see Figure 4.62) and switch back to the **Part Design** workbench.

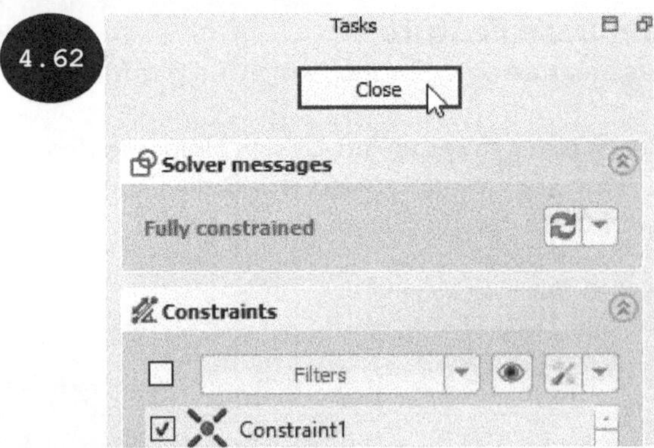

Now, you need to create a pad feature.

5. Click on the **Pad** tool in the **Part Design Modeling** toolbar, see Figure 4.63. The preview of a pad feature appears in the 3D View area with default parameters. Also, the **Pad parameters** sub-window appears in the **Tasks Panel** of **Combo View**, see Figure 4.64.

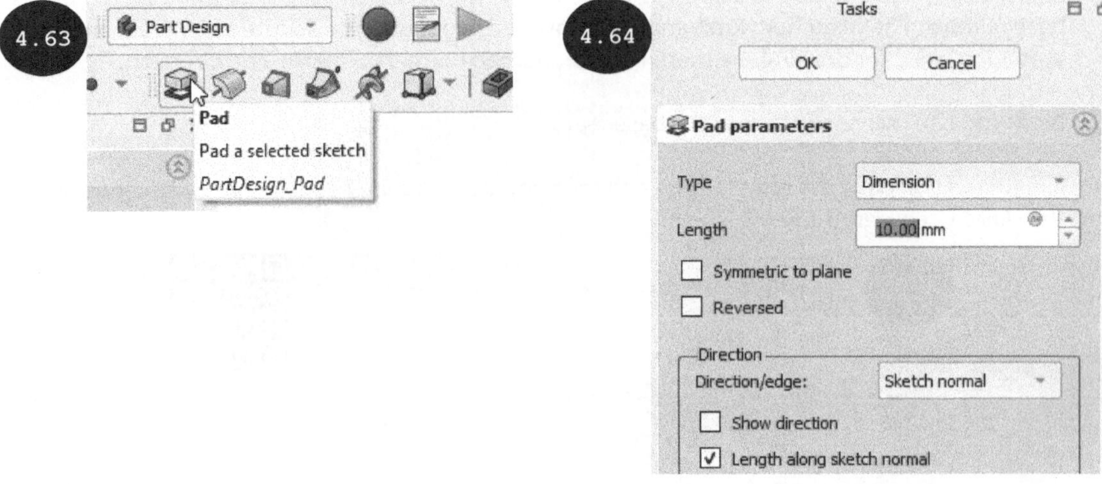

6. Ensure that the **Dimension** option is selected in the **Type** drop-down list for creating a pad feature by specifying its length.

7. Enter **5** mm as the length of the pad feature in the **Length** field of the **Tasks Panel**. Next, press the TAB key or click anywhere in the 3D View area to update the preview of the pad feature.

8. Click on the **OK** button in the **Tasks Panel** to confirm the creation of the pad feature and exit the **Tasks Panel**. The pad feature gets created, see Figure 4.65.

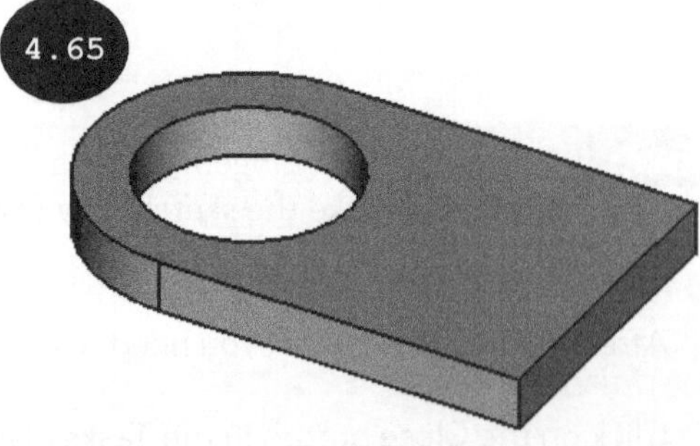

Section 4: Creating the Second Feature

Now, you can create the second feature of the model.

1. Click to select the top planar face of the base feature as the sketching plane for creating the sketch of the second feature of the model, see Figure 4.66.

2. Click on the **Create sketch** tool in the **Part Design Helper** toolbar, see Figure 4.67. The **Sketcher** workbench gets invoked and the top planar face of the base feature gets oriented normal to the viewing direction.

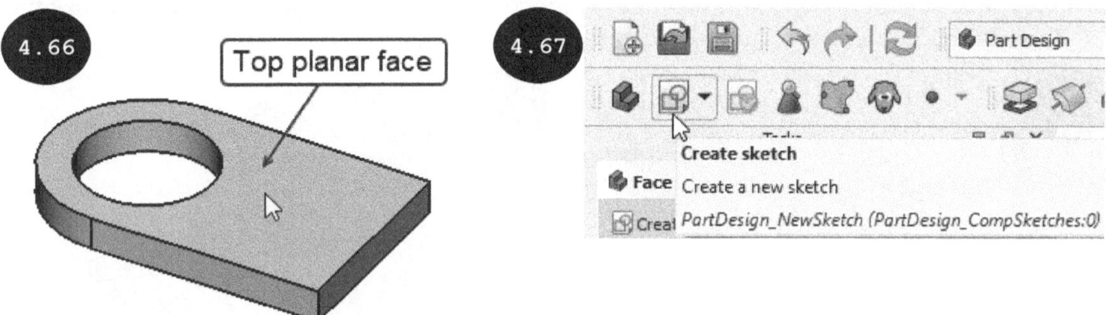

3. Create two circles as the sketch of the second feature and then apply the required dimensions, see Figure 4.68.

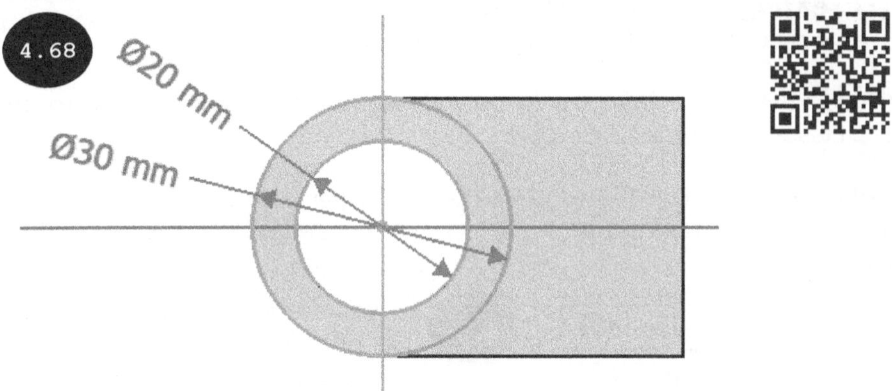

4. After creating the sketch, click on the **Close** button in the **Tasks Plane** of the **Combo View** to exit the **Sketcher** workbench (see Figure 4.69) and switch back to the **Part Design** workbench.

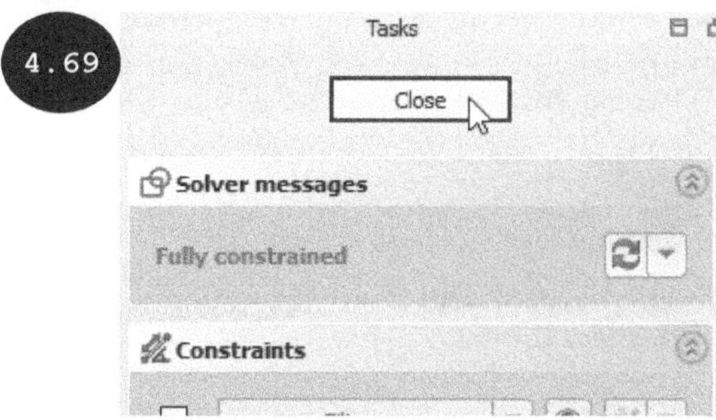

Now, you can convert the sketch into a pad feature.

5. Click on the **Pad** tool in the **Part Design Modeling** toolbar, see Figure 4.70. The preview of a pad feature appears in the 3D View area with default parameters. Also, the **Pad parameters** sub-window appears in the **Tasks Panel** of **Combo View**.

6. Enter **20** mm as the length of the pad feature in the **Length** field of the **Tasks Panel**. Next, press the TAB key or click anywhere in the 3D View area to update the preview of the pad feature.

7. Click on the **OK** button in the **Tasks Panel** to confirm the creation of the pad feature and exit the **Tasks Panel**. The second feature gets created, see Figure 4.71.

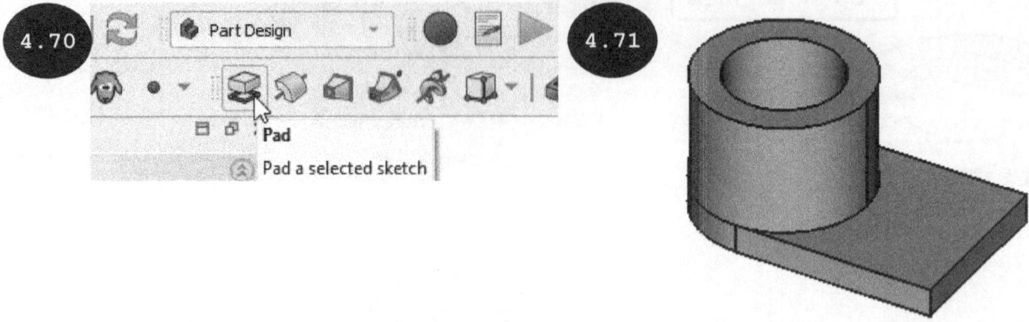

Section 5: Creating the Third Feature

Now, you need to create the third feature of the model.

1. Click to select the top planar face of the second feature as the sketching plane for creating the sketch of the third feature, see Figure 4.72.

2. Click on the **Create sketch** tool in the **Part Design Helper** toolbar, see Figure 4.73. The **Sketcher** workbench gets invoked and the top planar face of the model gets oriented normal to the viewing direction.

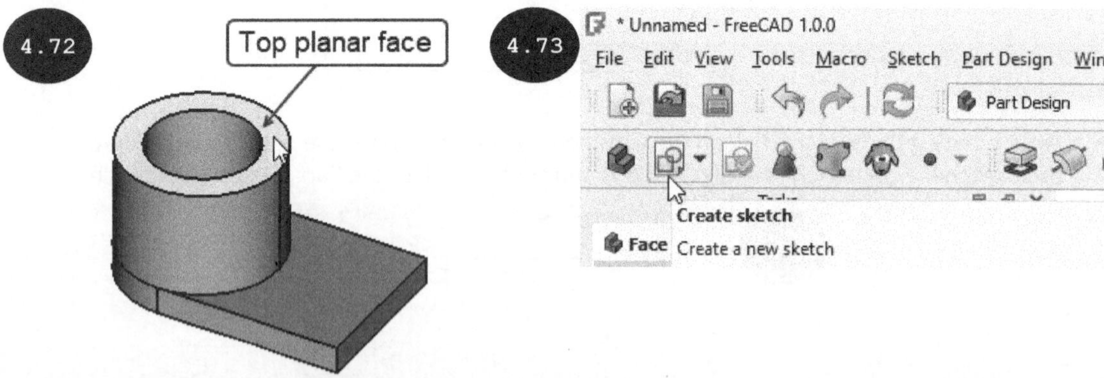

3. Create the sketch of the third feature and then apply the required constraints and dimensions, see Figure 4.74.

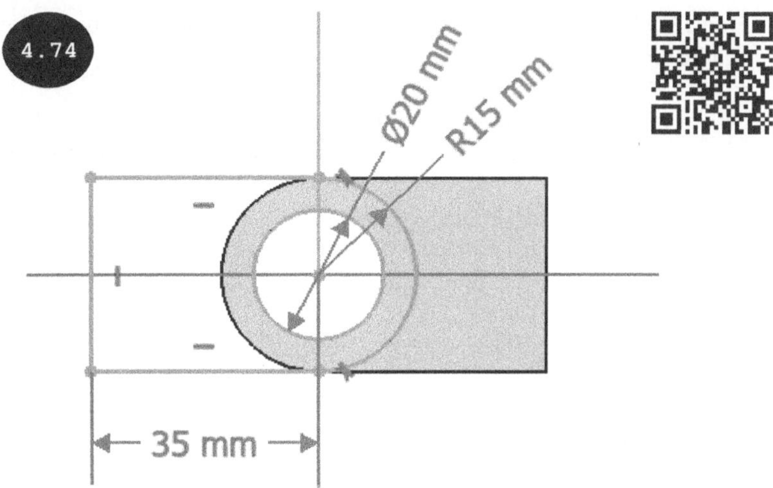

4. After creating the sketch, click on the **Close** button in the **Tasks Plane** of the **combo view** to exit the **Sketcher** workbench and switch back to the **Part Design** workbench.

5. Click on the **Pad** tool in the **Part Design Modeling** toolbar, see Figure 4.75. The preview of a pad feature appears in the 3D View area with default parameters. Also, the **Pad parameters** sub-window appears in the **Tasks Panel** of the **Combo View**.

6. Enter **5** mm as the length of the pad feature in the **Length** field of the **Tasks Panel**. Next, press the TAB key or click anywhere in the 3D View area to update the preview of the pad feature.

7. Click on the **OK** button in the **Tasks Panel** to confirm the creation of the feature and exit the **Tasks Panel**. Figure 4.76 shows the final model after creating all its features.

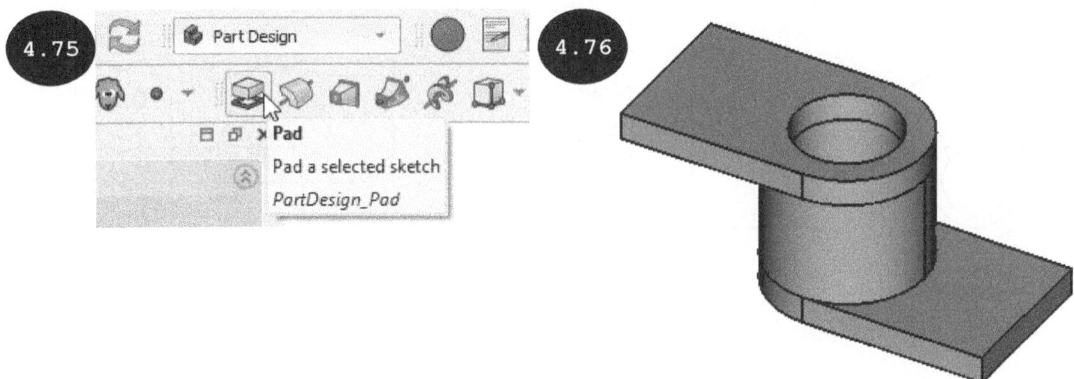

Section 6: Saving the Model

1. Click on the **Save** tool in the **File** toolbar (see Figure 4.77) or press the CTRL + S keys. The **Save FreeCAD Document** dialog box appears.

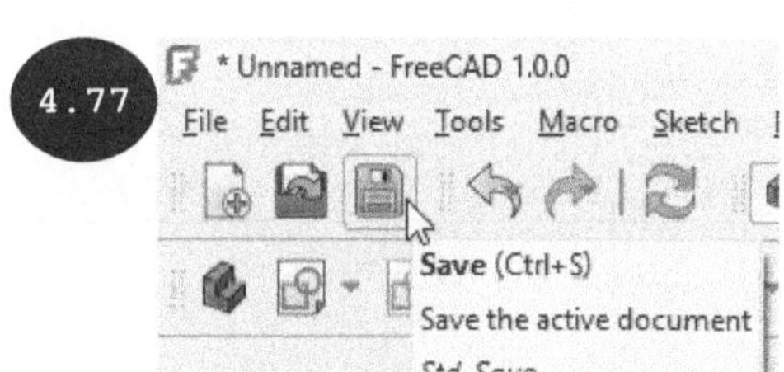

2. Browse to the **FreeCAD** folder in the local drive of your system. Next, create a new folder with the name **Chapter 04** inside it.

3. Enter **Ch04-Tutorial 1** in the **File name** field of the dialog box. Next, click on the **Save** button in the dialog box. The mode gets saved with the name **Ch04-Tutorial 1** at the specified location (*> FreeCAD > Chapter 04*).

4. Click on **File > Close** in the **Standard Menu** to close the current document.

Tutorial 2

Create a multi-feature model, as shown in Figure 4.78. You need to create the model by creating all its features one by one. All dimensions are in inches (in).

4.78

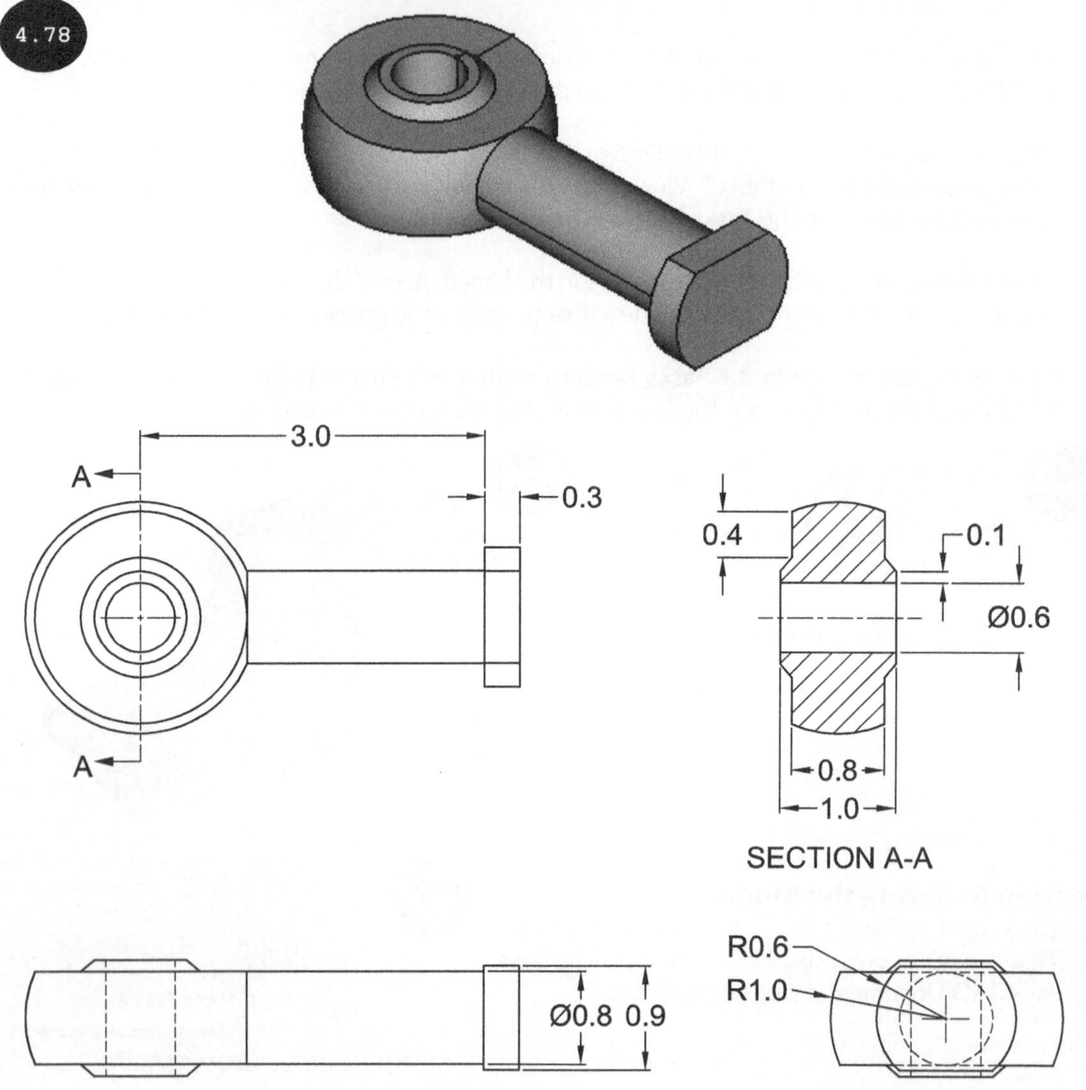

Section 1: Starting FreeCAD and a New Empty Document

1. Start FreeCAD by double-clicking on the **FreeCAD 0.21** icon on your desktop, if not started already. The startup user interface of FreeCAD appears.

2. Click on the **New** tool in the **File** toolbar (see Figure 4.79) or press the **CTRL + N** keys. A new Part document gets invoked with the default name and gets activated, by default.

4.79

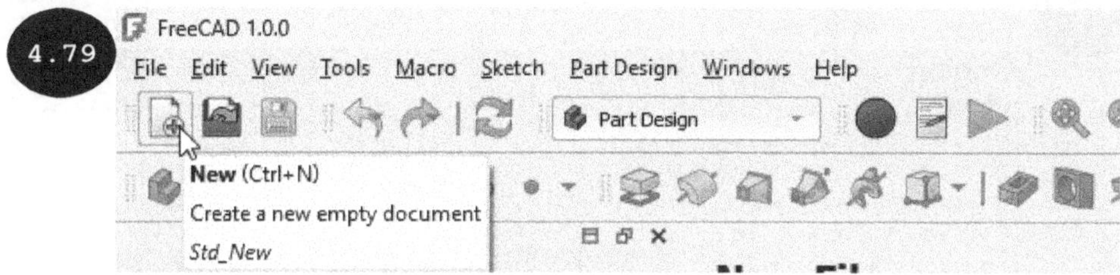

Section 2: Specifying the Unit

Now, you need to specify inches (in) as the measurement unit for the document.

1. Invoke the **Unit** flyout that appears at the lower right corner of the **Status Bar**, see Figure 4.80.

4.80

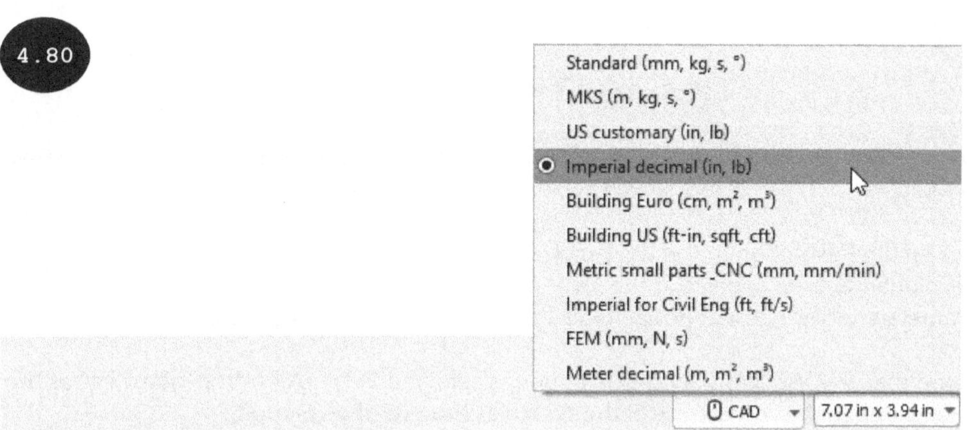

2. In this flyout, ensure that **Imperial decimal (in,lb)** is selected as the unit system for the current design document.

Section 3: Creating the Base Feature

Now, you can create the base feature of the model, which is a revolution feature.

1. Click on the **Create sketch** tool in the **Part Design Helper** toolbar, see Figure 4.81. The three default planes appear in the 3D View area. Also, the **Tasks Panel** appears in the **Tasks** tab of the **Combo View**.

4.81

2. Select the **YZ_Plane** as the sketching plane in the 3D View area. The **Sketcher** workbench gets invoked and the selected plane gets oriented normal to the viewing direction.

3. Create the sketch of the base feature of the model and then apply the required constraints and dimensions, see Figure 4.82.

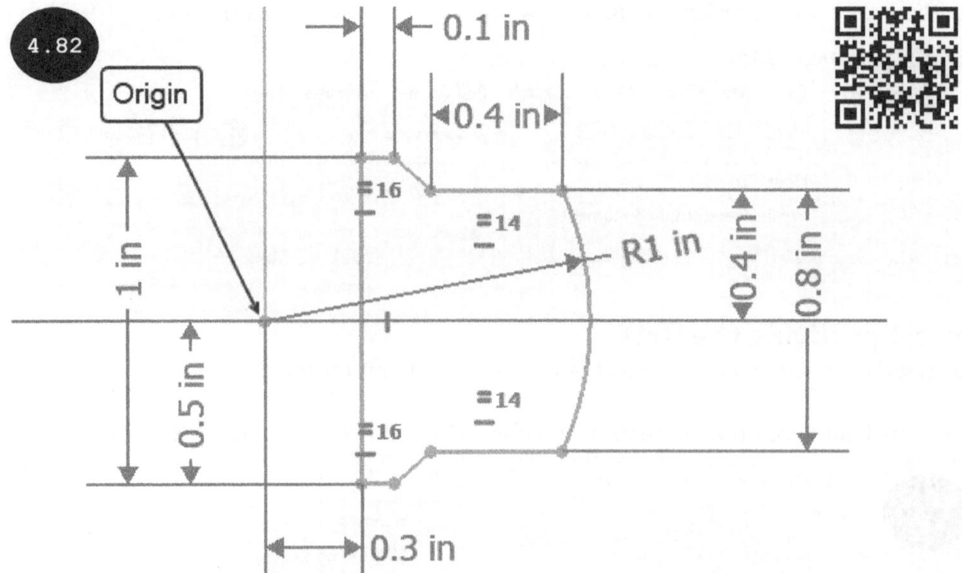

4. After creating the sketch, click on the **Close** button in the **Tasks Plane** of the **Combo View** to exit the **Sketcher** workbench and switch back to the **Part Design** workbench.

5. Click on the **Revolution** tool in the **Part Design Modeling** toolbar, see Figure 4.83. The preview of a revolution feature appears in the 3D View area with default parameters. Also, the **Revolution parameters** sub-window appears in the **Tasks Panel** of the **Combo View**.

6. Ensure that the **Vertical sketch axis** option is selected in the **Axis** drop-down list of the **Tasks Panel** to define the vertical axis of the sketch as the axis of revolution.

7. Ensure that the **360** degrees is specified as the angle of revolution in the **Angle** field of the **Tasks Panel**.

8. Click on the **OK** button in the **Tasks Panel**. The revolution feature gets created in the 3D View area, see Figure 4.84.

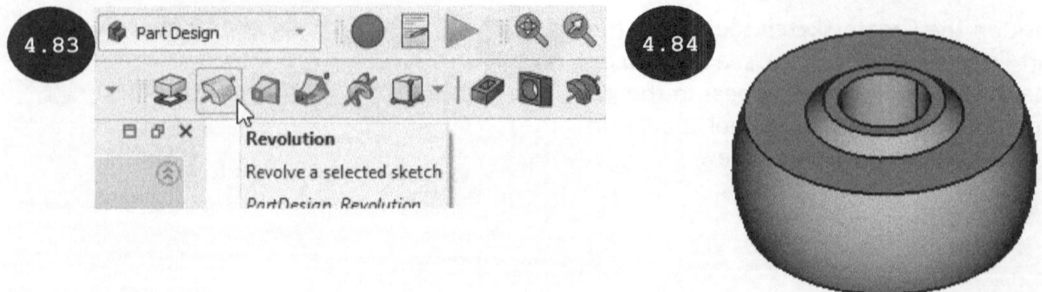

Section 4: Creating the Second Feature

Now, you can create the second feature of the model, which is a pad feature. To create the second feature of the model, you first need to create a datum plane at an offset distance of 3 inches from the YZ_Plane.

1. Invoke the **Datum** menu, then click on the **Create a datum plane** tool. The **Datum Plane parameters** sub-window appears in the **Tasks Panel**. Also, you are prompted to select a first reference for creating a datum plane.

2. Select the top circular edge of the base feature as the first reference, see Figure 4.85. The preview of a datum plane appears aligned to the plane of the selected reference, see Figure 4.86. Also, the **Concentric** mode gets activated automatically in the **Attachment mode** area of the **Tasks Panel**.

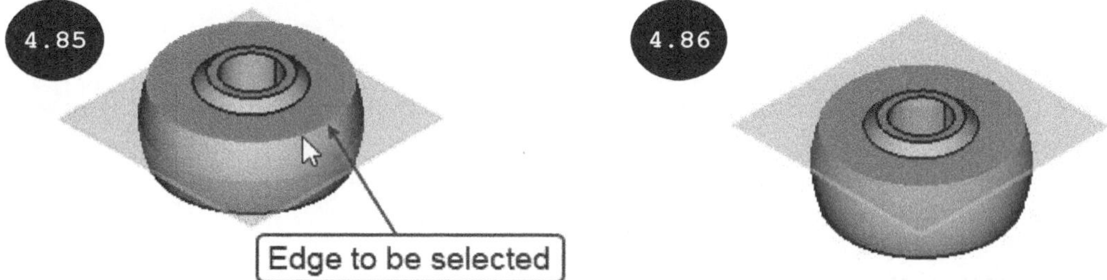

3. Select the **Revolution Section** mode in the **Attachment mode** area of the **Tasks Panel**. The preview of a datum plane appears normal to the plane of the selected reference, see Figure 4.87.

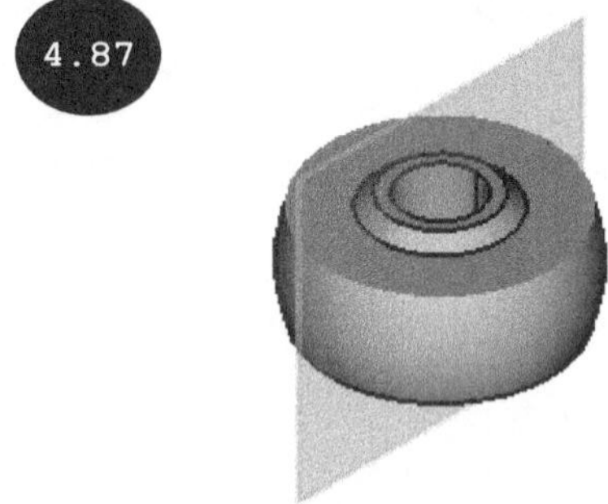

4. Enter **3** inches in the **In z-direction** field of the **Attachment Offset** area of the **Tasks Panel** as the offset distance along the z-axis, see Figure 4.88.

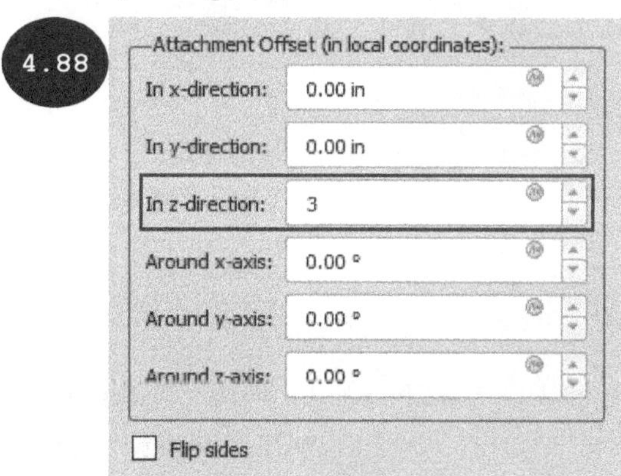

5. Select the **Flip sides** check box in the **Attachment Offset** area of the **Tasks Panel** to reverse the direction of the datum plane like the one shown in Figure 4.89.

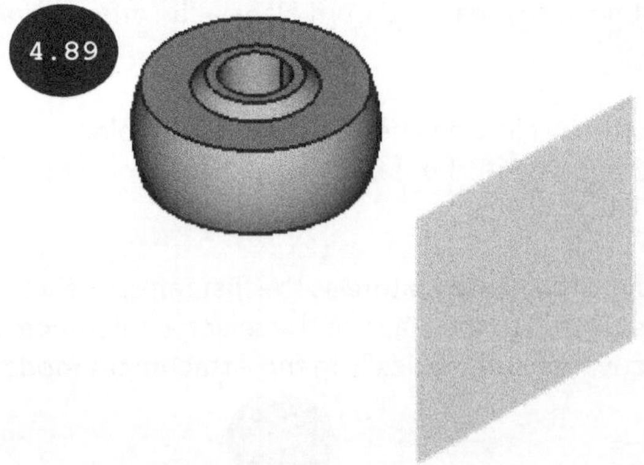
4.89

6. Click on the **OK** button in the **Tasks Panel** to confirm the creation of the datum plane and exit the **Tasks Panel**.

   Now, you can create the second feature of the model.

7. Click on the **Create sketch** tool in the **Part Design Helper** toolbar, see Figure 4.90. The three default planes appear in the 3D View area. Also, the **Tasks Panel** appears in the **Tasks** tab of **Combo View**.

4.90

8. Select the newly created datum plane as the sketching plane in the 3D View area. The **Sketcher** workbench gets invoked and the selected plane gets oriented normal to the viewing direction.

9. Create a circle of diameter 0.8 inches as the sketch of the second feature and then apply the required dimensions, see Figure 4.91.

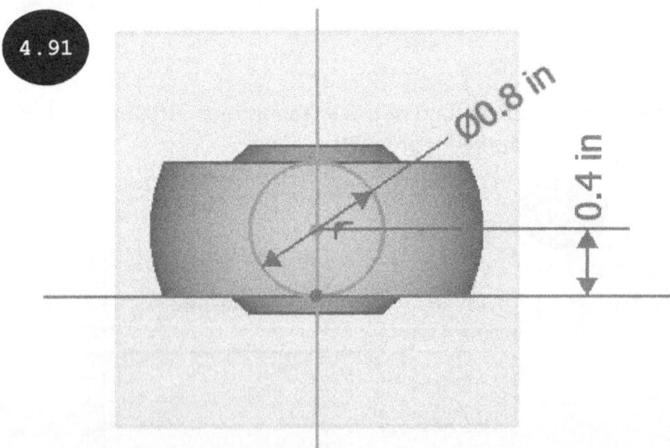

4.91

10. After creating the sketch, click on the **Close** button in the **Tasks Plane** of the **Combo View** to exit the **Sketcher** workbench and switch back to the **Part Design** workbench.

11. Click on the **Pad** tool in the **Part Design Modeling** toolbar, see Figure 4.92. The **Pad parameters** sub-window appears in the **Tasks Panel** of the **Combo View**. Also, an error appears informing that the creation of a feature has failed.

12. Select the **Reversed** check box in the **Tasks Panel** to reverse the direction of extrusion towards the base feature of the model.

13. Select the **To first** option in the **Type** drop-down list of the **Tasks Panel**. The preview of a pad feature appears up to its next intersection in the 3D View area, see Figure 4.93.

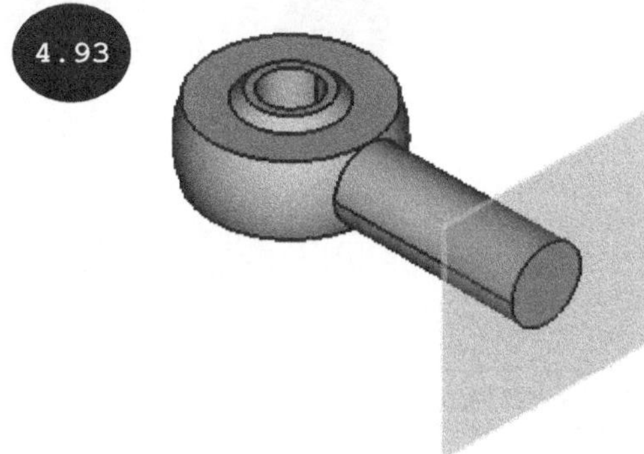

14. Click on the **OK** button in the **Tasks Panel** to confirm the creation of the pad feature and exit the **Tasks Panel**. The second feature gets created.

Section 5: Hiding the Datum Plane

Now, you can hide the datum plane in the 3D View area.

1. Click to select the datum plane in the 3D View area or the **Model** tab of the **Tasks Panel** and then press the SPACEBAR key. The datum plane gets hidden in the 3D View area, see Figure 4.94.

Tip: In FreeCAD, you can toggle the display of a datum plane or a feature in the 3D View area by selecting it in the **Model** tab of the **Tasks Panel** and then pressing the SPACEBAR key. You can select a datum plane or a feature in the 3D View area, if its current display status is turned on.

Section 6: Creating the Third Feature

Now, you need to create the third feature of the model.

1. Select the right planar face of the model as the sketching plane for creating the sketch of the third feature, see Figure 4.95.

2. Click on the **Create sketch** tool in the **Part Design Helper** toolbar, see Figure 4.96. The **Sketcher** workbench gets invoked and the right planar face of the model gets oriented normal to the viewing direction.

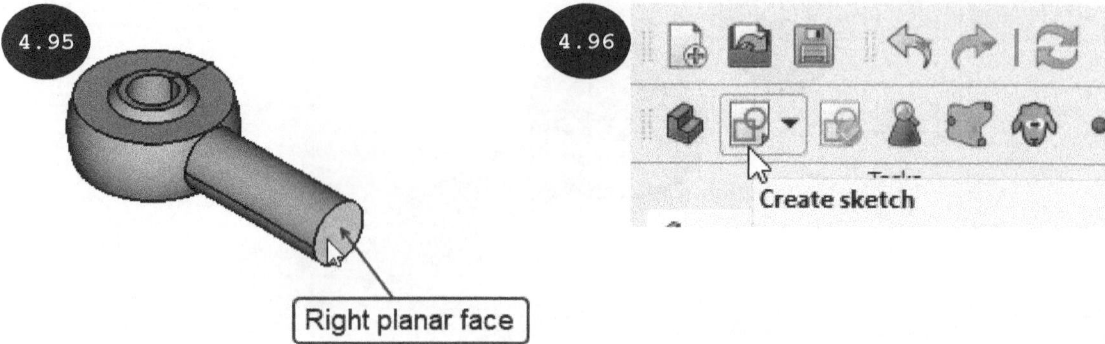

3. Create the sketch of the third feature and then apply the required constraints and dimensions, see Figure 4.97.

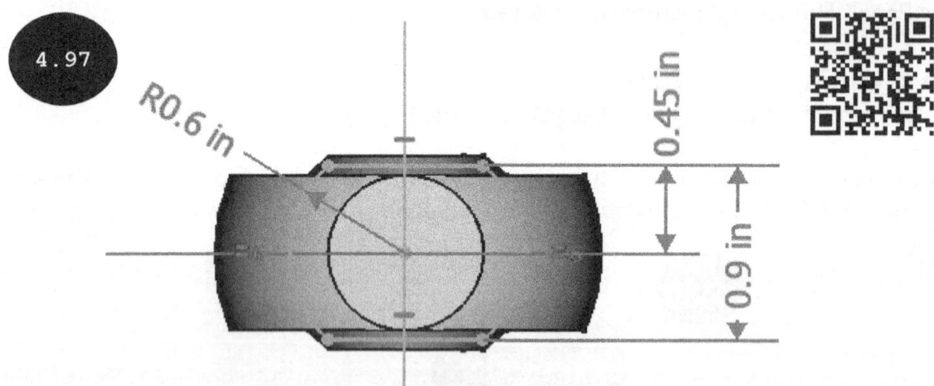

4. After creating the sketch, click on the **Close** button in the **Tasks Plane** of **Combo View** to exit the **Sketcher** workbench and switch back to the **Part Design** workbench.

5. Click on the **Pad** tool in the **Part Design Modeling** toolbar, see Figure 4.98. The preview of a pad feature appears in the 3D View area with default parameters. Also, the **Pad parameters** sub-window appears in the **Tasks Panel** of the **Combo View**.

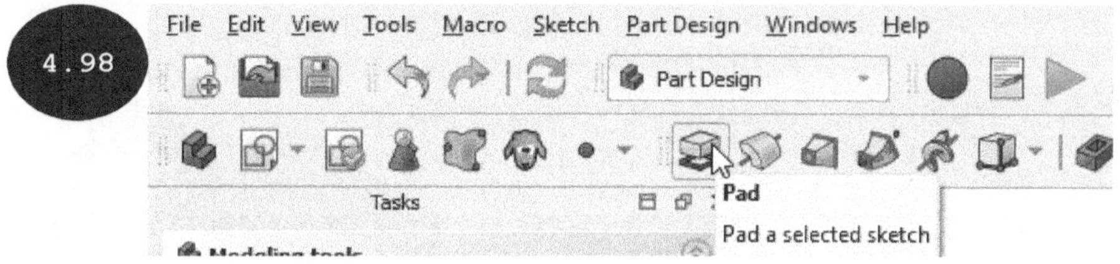

6. Enter **0.3** inches as the length of the pad feature in the **Length** field of the **Tasks Panel**. Next, press the TAB key or click anywhere in the 3D View area to update the preview of the pad feature.

7. Click on the **OK** button in the **Tasks Panel** to confirm the creation of the feature and exit the **Tasks Panel**. Figure 4.99 shows the final model after creating all its features.

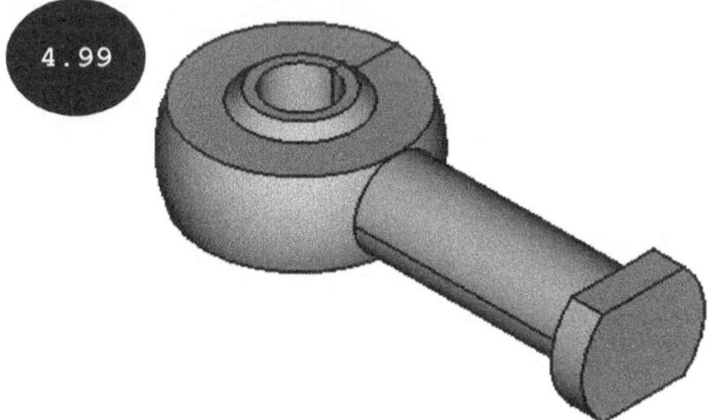

Section 7: Saving the Model

Now, you can save the model.

1. Click on the **Save** tool in the **File** toolbar (see Figure 4.100) or press the CTRL + S keys. The **Save FreeCAD Document** dialog box appears.

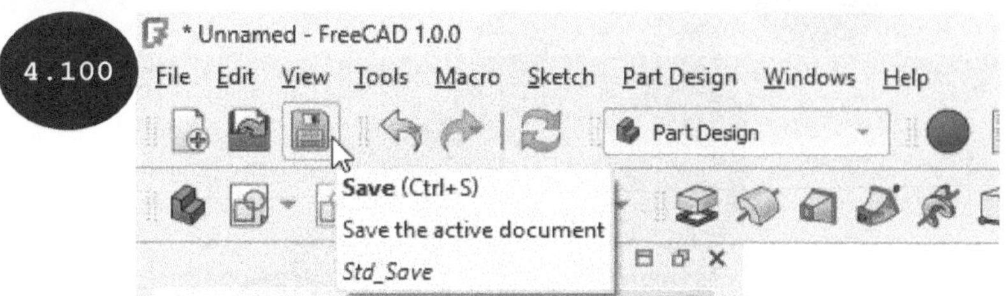

2. Browse to the *FreeCAD > Chapter 04* folder in the local drive of your system. You need to create these folders, if not created earlier.

3. Enter **Ch04-Tutorial 2** in the **File name** field of the dialog box. Next, click on the **Save** button in the dialog box. The mode gets saved with the name **Tutorial 2** at the specified location. Next, close the document by clicking on **File > Close** in the **Standard Menu**.

Hands-on Test Drive 1

Create the model shown in Figure 4.101. You need to create the model by creating all its features one by one. All dimensions are in inches (in).

4.101

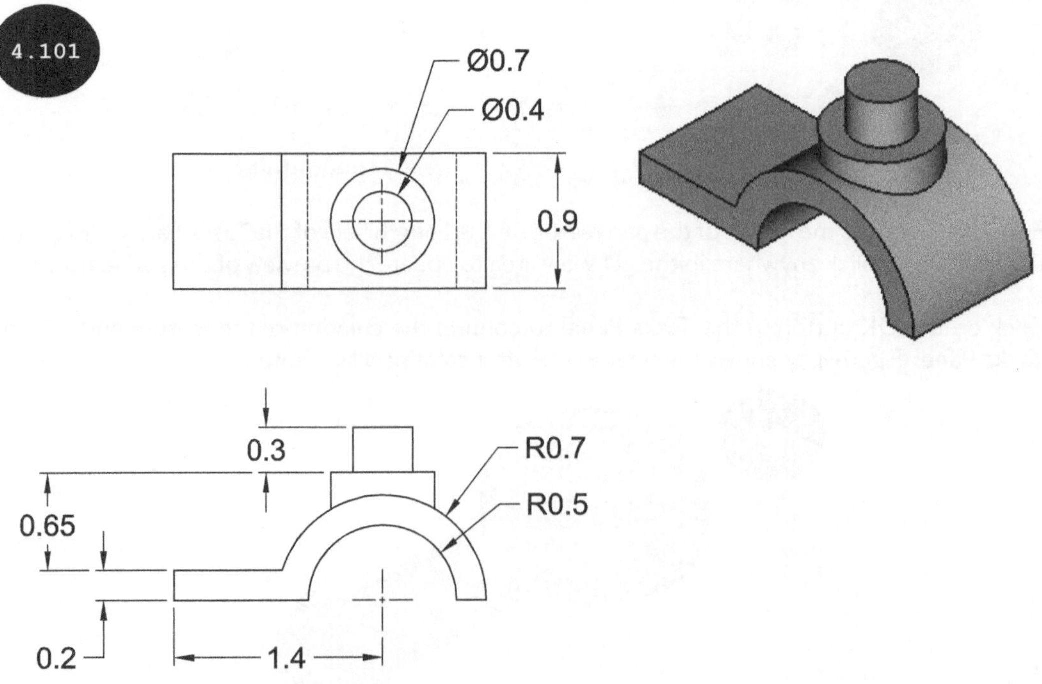

Hands-on Test Drive 2

Create the model shown in Figure 4.102. The different views and dimensions for creating the model are shown in Figure 4.103. All dimensions are in mm.

4.102

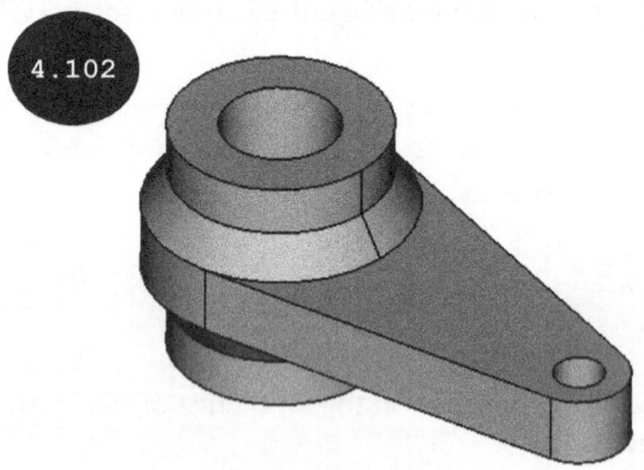

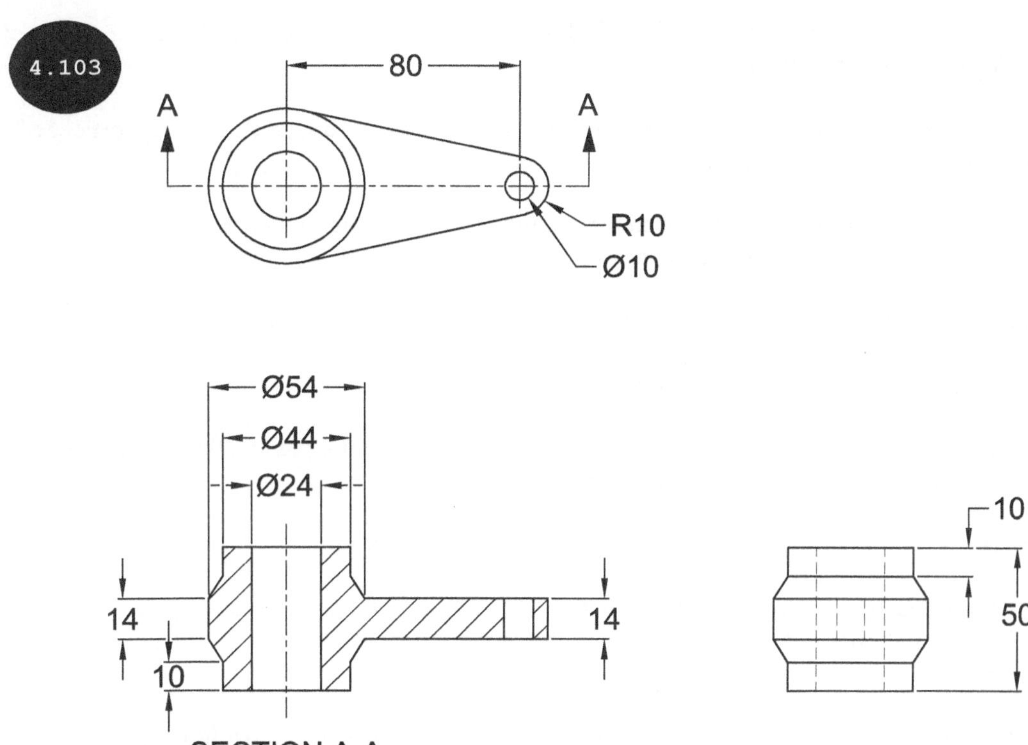

Hint: While creating a sketch of a feature, you may need to take references from the edges of an existing feature of the model for applying constraints and dimensions. In FreeCAD, you can project the edges of an existing feature onto the current sketching plane to take references by using the ***Create external geometry*** *tool. You will learn about projecting the edges of a model onto the current sketching plane as reference entities in Chapter 7.*

Summary

In this chapter, you have learned various methods for creating additional datum planes, axes, and points by using the respective tools.

Questions

Complete and verify the following sentences:

- In FreeCAD, you can create various types of datum planes by using the ________ tool.
- ________, ________, and ________ are the three default datum planes of a document.

- To create a datum plane normal to a linear edge of a model, you need to select a _________ of a model as the first reference.
- To create a datum plane passing through three vertices, you need to select _______ vertices of a model as the _______, _______, and _______ references.
- The _______ attachment mode is used for creating a datum plane aligned to the local XZ plane of a conical edge or curve (ellipse, hyperbola, or parabola).
- You can create various types of datum lines by using the _________ tool.
- The _________ tool is used for creating a datum point.
- The _______ attachment mode is used for creating a datum plane passing through the second and third principal axes of inertia of the selected entity.
- The _________ tool is used for creating a local coordinate system.
- In FreeCAD, you can control the placement and orientation of a datum plane by specifying the required translational and rotational values in the respective fields of the _________ area in the **Tasks Panel**.
- An attachment mode is used to attach a plane being created to the selected reference geometries of the model such that if any modification is made to the reference geometries, then the associated datum plane will also be modified accordingly. (True/False)
- The **Deactivated** attachment mode is used for creating a datum plane, coplanar with the default XY Plane without selecting any reference geometry. (True/False)

CHAPTER
5

Creating Pocket and Groove Features

This chapter discusses the following topics:

- Creating a Pocket Feature
- Creating a Groove Feature
- Projecting External Geometries onto the Sketch
- Displaying Section View in the Sketch Model
- Displaying an Earlier State of a Model
- Reordering Features of a Model
- Deleting a Feature of a Model
- Editing Features and Sketches
- Defining Display Properties or Appearance
- Measuring Distance Between Two Geometries

In the previous chapters, you have learned about creating pad features and revolution features by adding material. In this chapter, you will learn about creating pocket and groove features by subtracting material from an existing body. Besides, you will also learn about displaying an earlier state of a model, editing features and sketches, measuring distance, and assigning appearance to a body.

Creating a Pocket Feature

A pocket feature is created by subtracting material from an existing body, see Figure 5.1. You can create a pocket feature by using the **Pocket** tool in the **Part Design Modeling** toolbar. Note that the sketch of a pocket feature should be closed. The method for creating a pocket feature is discussed below:

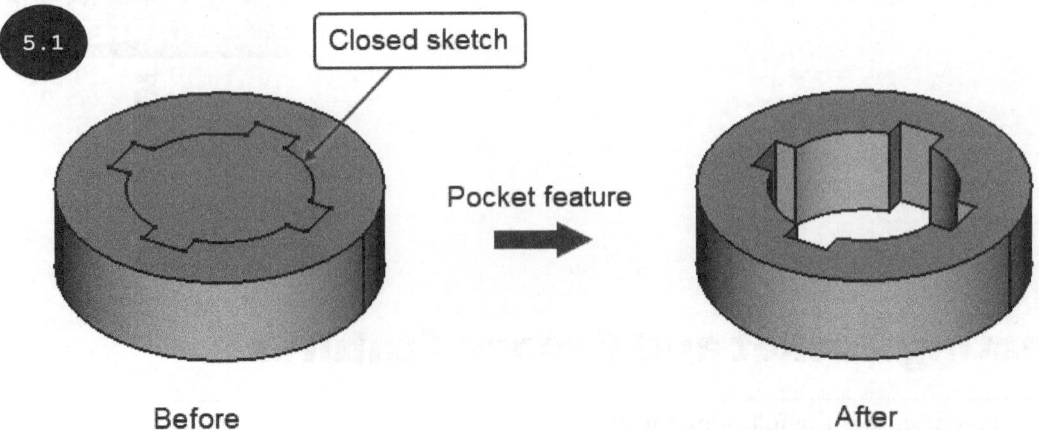

1. Invoke the **Sketcher** workbench by selecting a plane or a planar face as the sketching plane and then create a closed sketch of a pocket feature. After creating a sketch, exit the **Sketcher** workbench to switch back to the **Part Design** workbench.

2. In the **Part Design** workbench, click on the **Pocket** tool in the **Part Design Modeling** toolbar, see Figure 5.2. The preview of a pocket feature appears in the 3D View area, since the sketch of the pocket feature gets selected automatically, refer to Figure 5.3. Also, the **Pocket parameters** sub-window appears in the **Tasks Panel** of the **Tasks** tab in **Combo View**, see Figure 5.4.

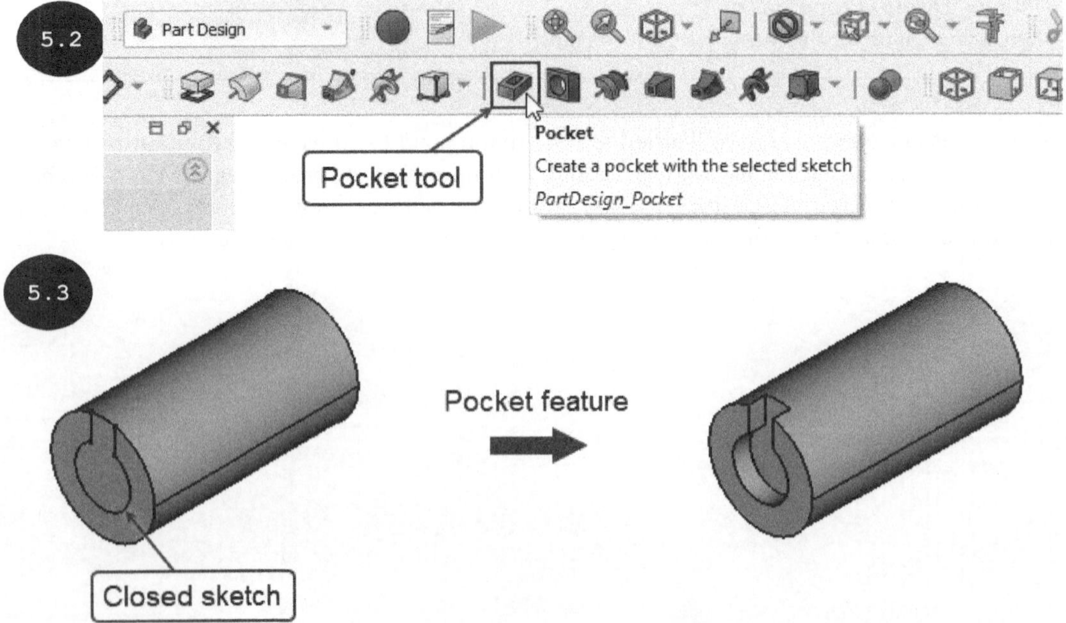

5.4

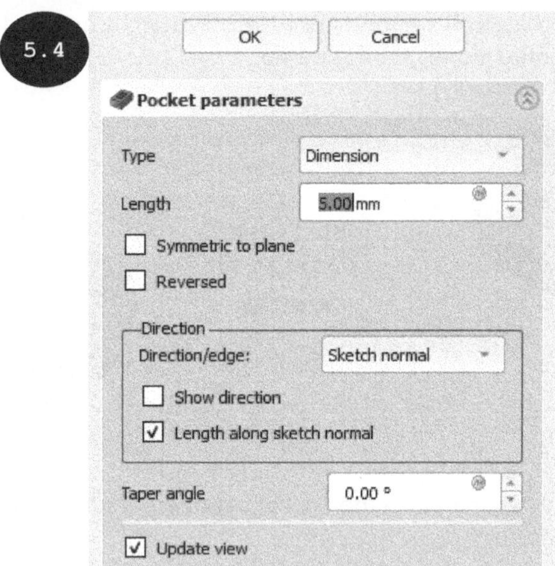

Note: If only one closed sketch is available in the 3D View area, then on invoking the **Pocket** tool, it will be selected automatically, and the preview of a pocket feature appears. However, if two or more closed sketches are available in the 3D View area, then on invoking the **Pocket** tool, you need to select a sketch of the pocket feature, manually. You can select a sketch in the 3D View area or in the **Select feature** sub-window that appears in the **Task Panel**.

3. Select the required option in the **Type** drop-down list of the **Tasks Panel** for specifying the depth of the pocket feature. The options in this drop-down list are the same as discussed earlier while creating a pad feature by adding material except the **Through all** option (see Figure 5.5), which is discussed next.

5.5

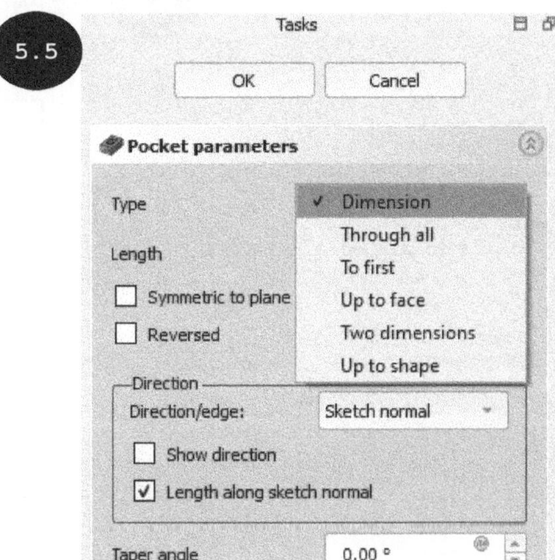

Through all: The **Through all** option is used for creating a pocket feature by removing the material through the entire model, see Figure 5.6.

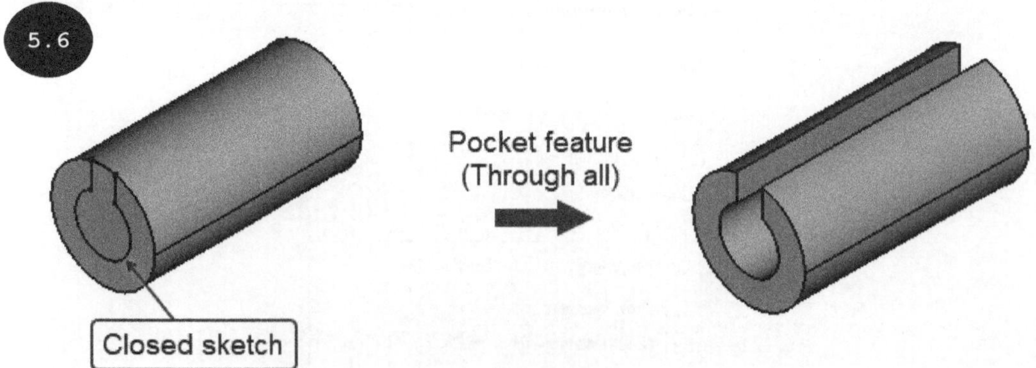

4. Specify all the required parameters in the **Pocket parameters** sub-window of the **Tasks Panel** for creating the pocket feature.

Note: The options in the **Pocket parameters** sub-window are the same as those discussed earlier while creating a pad feature with the only difference being that the options in the **Pocket parameters** sub-window are used for creating a pocket feature by removing material from the model.

5. After specifying all the required parameters for creating a pocket feature, click on the **OK** button in the **Tasks Panel**, see Figure 5.7. The pocket feature of specified parameters gets created. Also, its default name gets added under the **Body** node of the **Tree View** in the **Model** tab, see Figure 5.8. You can click on the **Model** tab of the **Combo View** to display the **Tree View**.

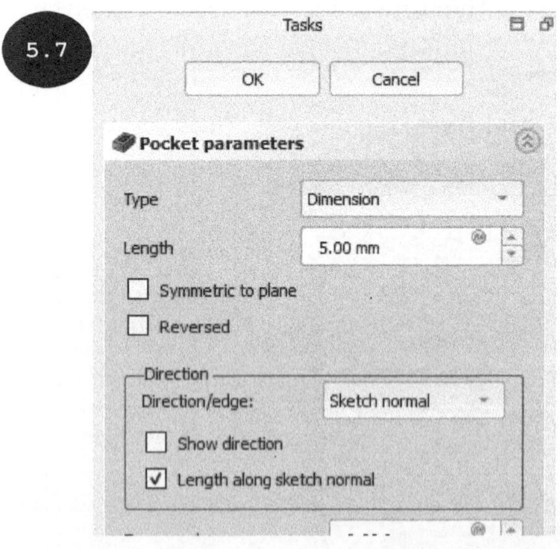

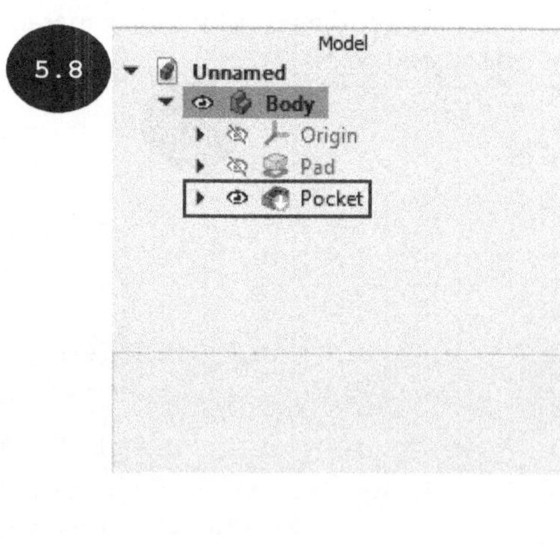

Creating a Groove Feature

A groove feature is created such that the material is subtracted from an existing body by revolving a sketch around an axis, see Figure 5.9. In FreeCAD, you can create a groove feature by using the **Groove** tool in the **Part Design Modeling** toolbar. The method for creating a groove feature is discussed below:

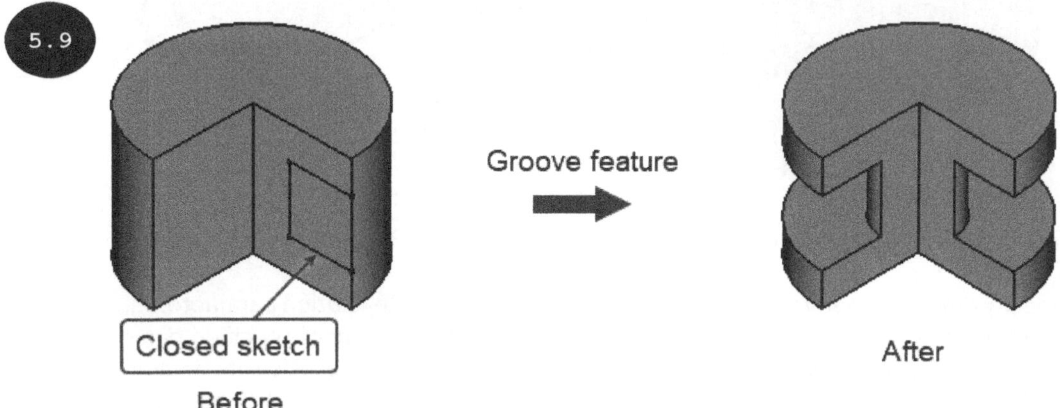

1. Invoke the **Sketcher** workbench by selecting a plane or a planar face as the sketching plane and then create a closed sketch of a groove feature. After creating a sketch, exit the **Sketcher** workbench to switch back to the **Part Design** workbench. Note that the sketch of a groove feature should be closed. Also, it should be on either side of its axis of revolution.

2. Click on the **Groove** tool in the **Part Design Modeling** toolbar, see Figure 5.10. Ignore if an error message is displayed since the vertical axis is chosen by default as the axis of revolution.

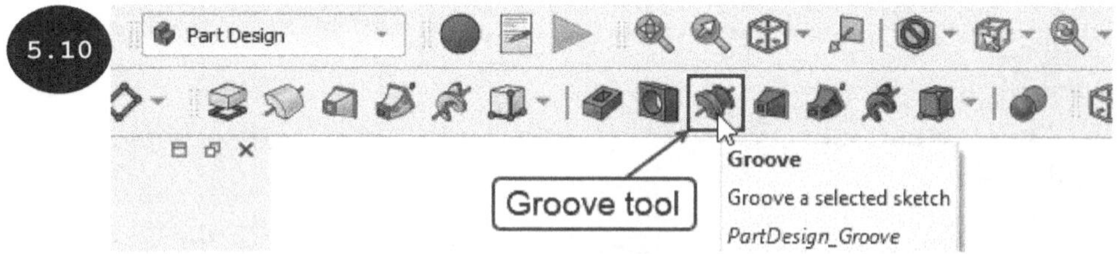

3. Select the required axis of rotation in the **Axis** drop-down list of the **Revolution parameters** sub-window that appears in the **Tasks Panel**, see Figure 5.11. The preview of a groove feature appears such that the material is removed from the existing body by revolving the sketch around the selected axis of revolution in the 3D View area, see Figure 5.12. In this figure, the **Horizontal sketch axis** option is selected as the axis of revolution for creating the groove feature. Note that the options in the **Axis** drop-down list are the same as discussed earlier while creating a revolution feature.

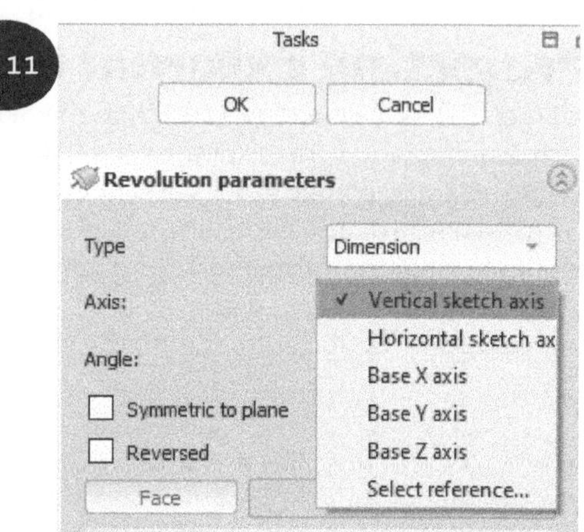

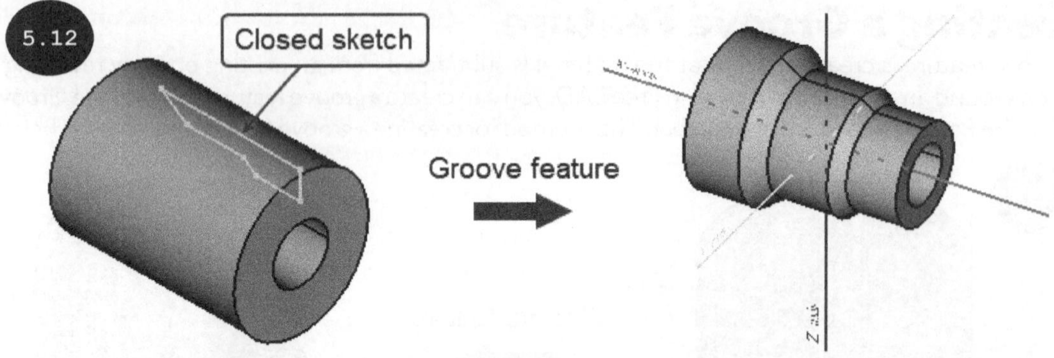

4. Enter the required angle of revolution in the **Angle** field of the **Revolution parameters** sub-window.

5. Specify other parameters for creating a groove feature in the **Revolution parameters** sub-window and then click on the **OK** button, see Figure 5.13. A groove feature of specified parameters gets created in the 3D View area by removing material from the model. Also, its default name gets added under the **Body** node of the **Tree View**, see Figure 5.14. You can click on the **Model** tab of the **Combo View** to display the **Tree View**.

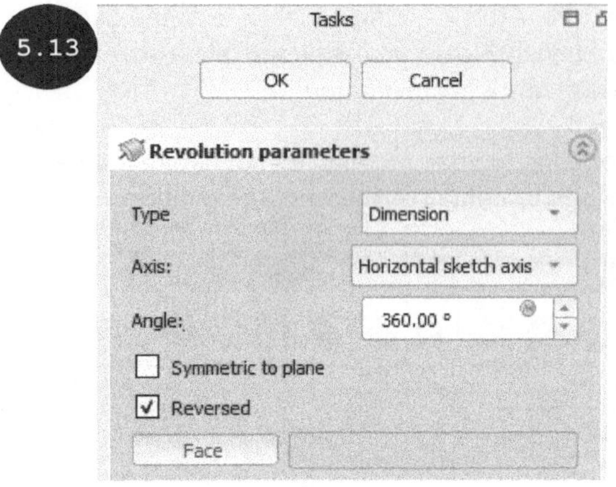

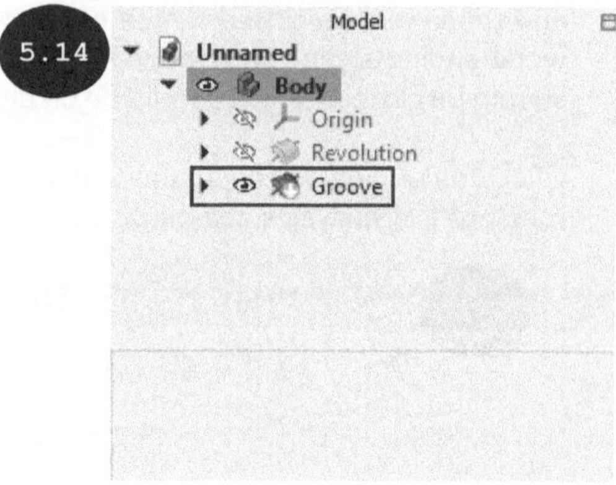

Projecting External Geometries onto the Sketch

In FreeCAD, while creating a sketch in the **Sketcher** workbench, you can project external geometries such as edges and vertices of the model as linked construction entities onto the sketch by using the **Create external geometry** tool, see Figure 5.15. In this figure, the external edges of the model are projected as linked construction entities onto the sketch. You can use these construction entities as reference entities for applying geometrical and dimensional constraints to the sketch entities. By default, the linked construction entities are displayed in magenta color. The method for projecting external geometries as linked construction entities onto the sketch is discussed below:

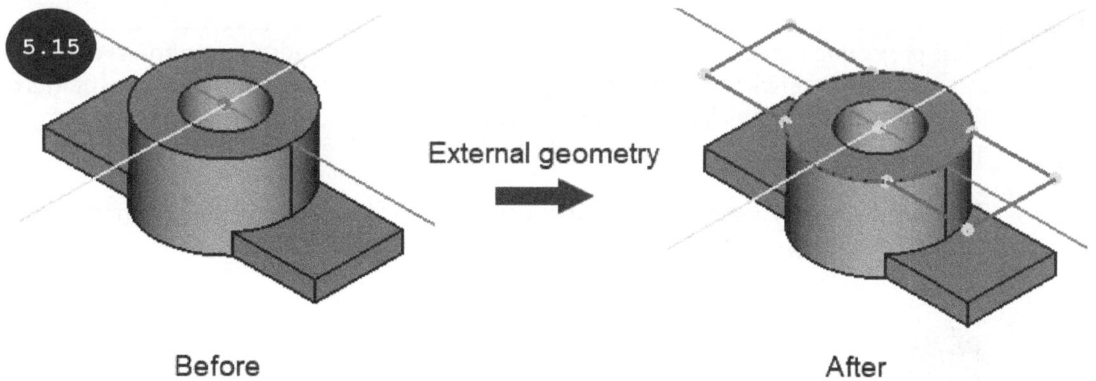

1. Invoke the **Sketcher** workbench by selecting a plane or a planar face as the sketching plane using the **Create sketch** tool, see Figure 5.16.

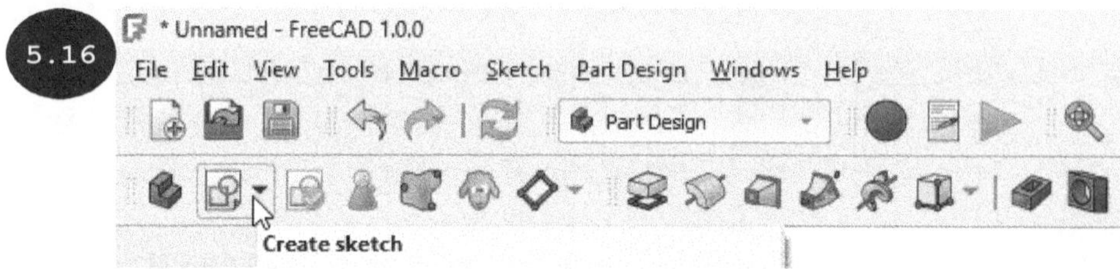

2. In the **Sketcher** workbench, click on the **Create external geometry** tool in the **Sketcher geometries** toolbar, see Figure 5.17. The **Create External geometry** tool gets activated.

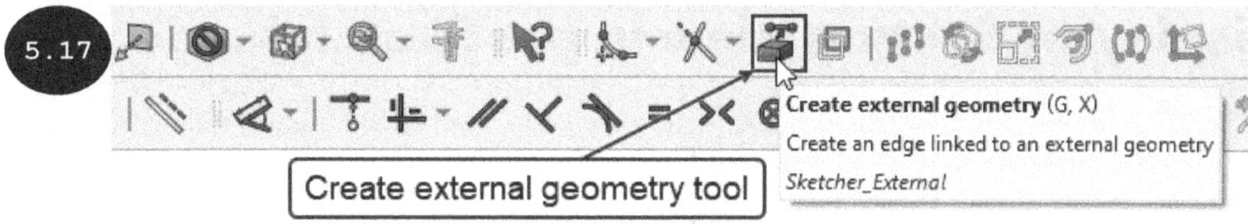

3. Select one or more edges or vertices of the existing features of the body to be projected as the linked construction entities onto the sketch. The selected external geometries (edges or vertices) get projected as linked construction entities onto the sketch, see Figure 5.18. You can also select sketch entities and points of an existing sketch to be projected as the linked construction entities onto the current sketch. Note that the linked construction entities are displayed in magenta color, by default. In Figure 5.18, the outer edges of the body are projected as linked construction entities onto the sketch.

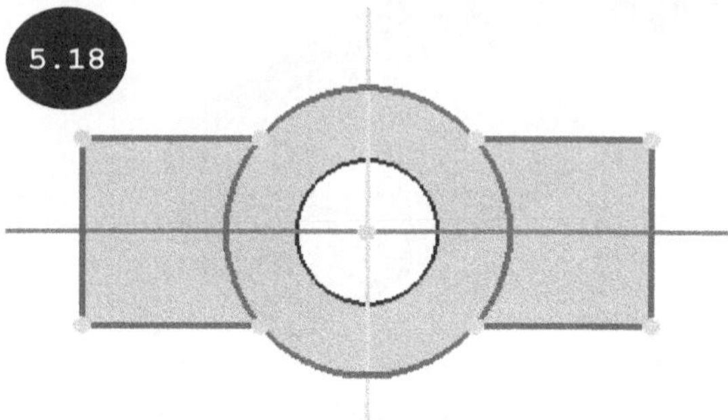

4. Press the ESC key to exit the **Create External geometry** tool.

Note: After projecting external geometries as linked construction entities onto the sketch, you can use them as reference entities for applying geometrical and dimensional constraints to the sketch entities, see Figure 5.19. In this figure, two horizontal dimensions of 12 mm are applied to the sketch by using the linked construction entities.

The linked construction entities are only visible in the **Sketcher** workbench when you are creating or editing a sketch.

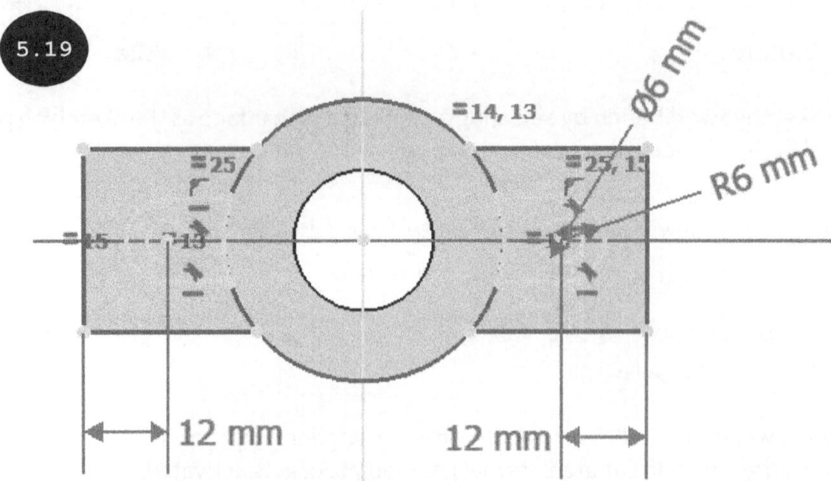

Displaying Section View in the Sketch Mode

In FreeCAD, you can switch between the section view and the full view in the Sketch editing mode of the **Sketcher** workbench, see Figure 5.20. A section view is created by temporarily hiding the material in front of the current sketching plane so that the sketch appears in front.

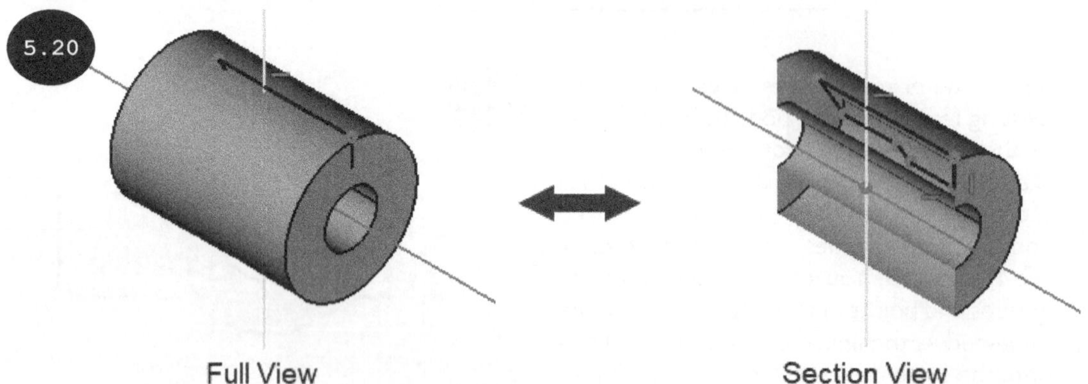

To display a section view of a model in the Sketch editing mode of the **Sketcher** workbench, click on the **View Section** tool in the **Sketcher** toolbar, see Figure 5.21. The section view of the model appears in the 3D View area by temporarily hiding the material that is in front of the sketching plane. Note that it is a toggle tool. As a result, to display the model back to its original full-view state, you need to click on this tool again.

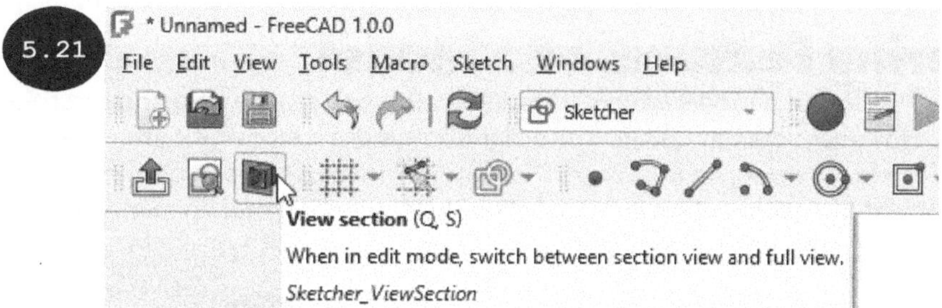

Displaying an Earlier State of a Model

In FreeCAD, when you create a new feature of a model, it gets added at the end of the feature list in **Tree View** and is activated as the last feature of the model, see Figure 5.22. Also, the model is displayed in the 3D View area with all its features.

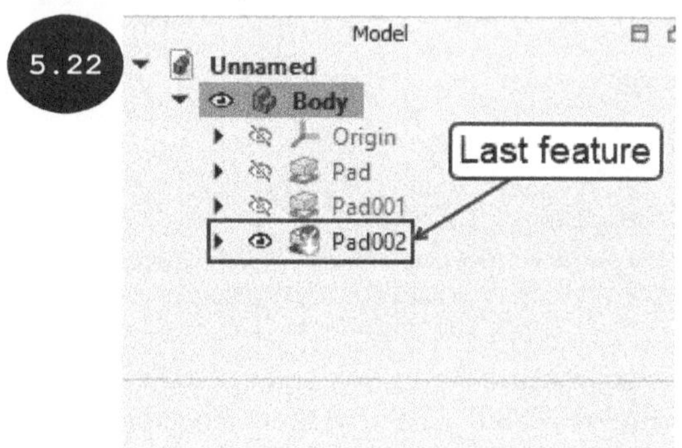

To display the earlier state of a model, click on the feature to be activated as the last feature of the model in **Tree View** (see Figure 5.23) and then press SPACEBAR. The selected feature gets activated as the last feature of the model, see Figure 5.24. Also, the earlier state of the model appears in the 3D View area such that all the features that are below the activated feature are not displayed in the model.

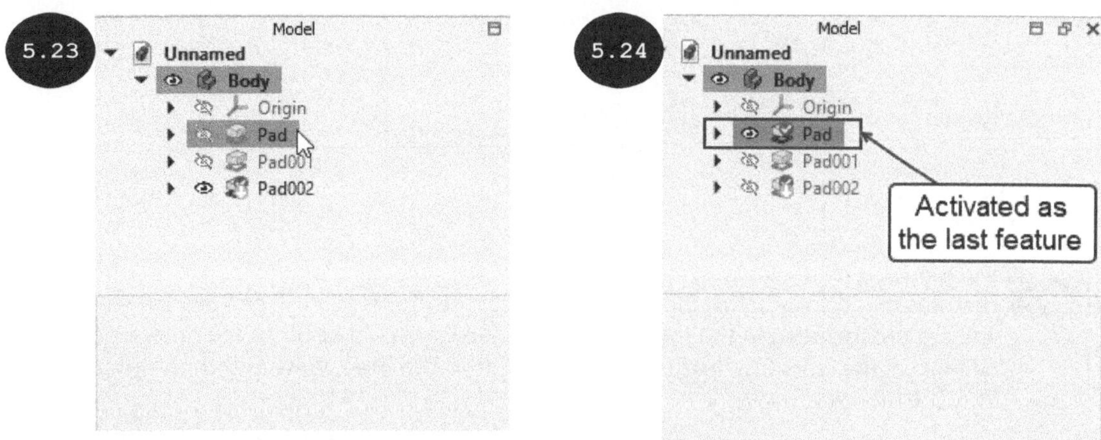

To display the complete model in its original state, select the last feature of the model in **Tree View** and then press SPACEBAR to activate it. The model is displayed in the 3D View area including all its features.

Reordering Features of a Model

By default, the features of a model are organized one after the other in the order of their creation in the **Tree View**. However, you may change the order of a feature by moving it after the other feature of the model, if desired. To do so, right-click on the feature whose order is to be changed and then click on the **Move object after other object** option in the shortcut menu that appears, see Figure 5.25. The **Select feature** dialog box appears, see Figure 5.26.

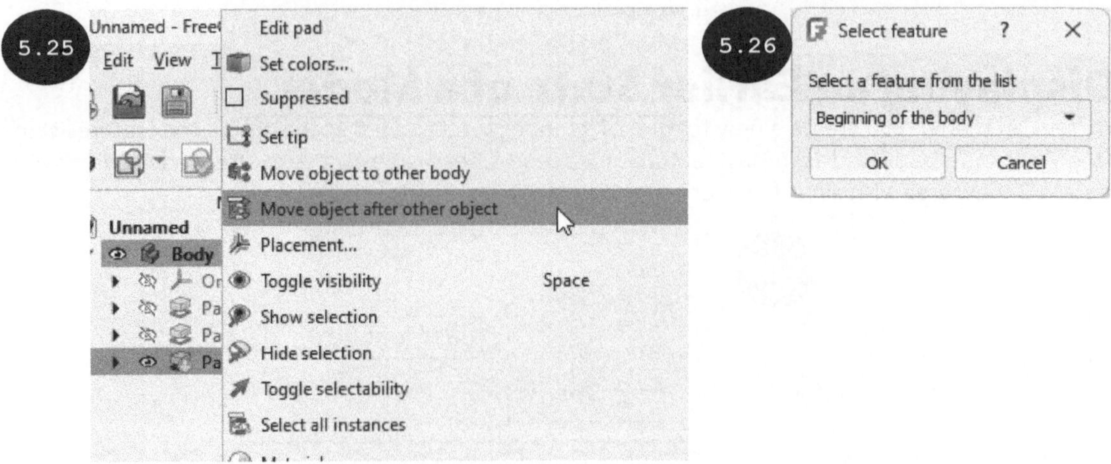

In the drop-down list of the **Select feature** dialog box, select a desired feature of the model after which the selected feature is to be moved, see Figure 5.27. Next, click on the **OK** button. The feature gets moved after the selected feature of the model in **Tree View**. Also, it gets activated as the last feature of the model. Note that you cannot move a child feature above its parent feature in the **Tree View**.

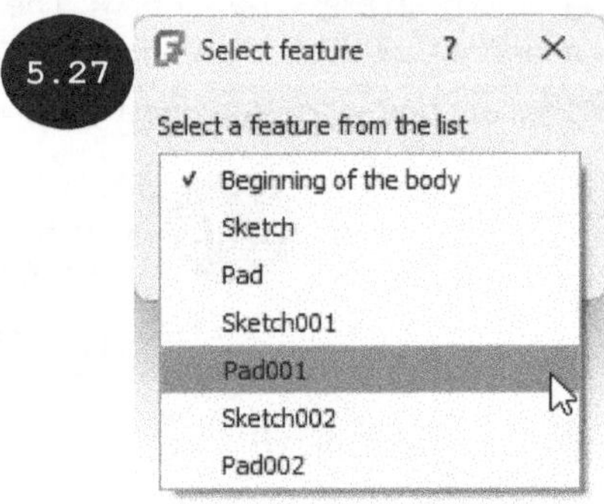

Note: Features that display below the active feature of the model in the **Tree View** are greyed out and are not included in the model in the 3D View area. To display the entire model, you need to activate its last feature by selecting it in the **Tree View** and then pressing the SPACEBAR key.

Deleting a Feature of a Model

To delete an existing feature of a model, select the feature to be deleted in **Tree View** and then right-click to display a shortcut menu, see Figure 5.28. In this shortcut menu, select the **Delete** option. The selected feature gets deleted from the model.

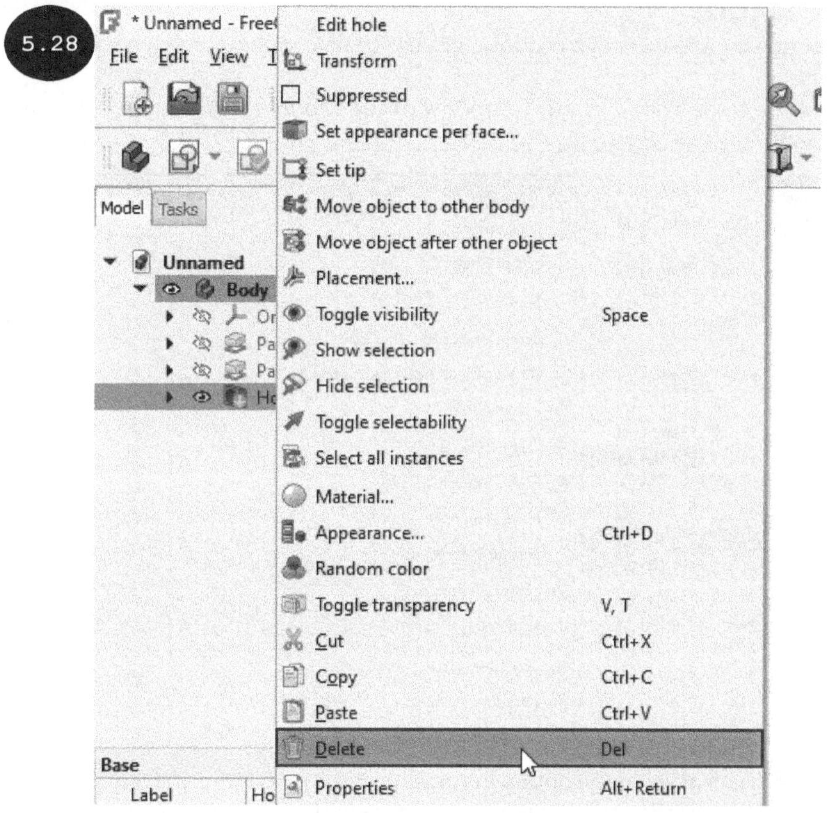

Note: If the selected feature has some dependent features, then while deleting it, the **Object dependencies** dialog box appears, see Figure 5.29. This dialog box displays a list of all dependent/child features of the feature being deleted. You can confirm or decline to delete the selected feature by clicking on the **Yes** or **No** button in the dialog box, respectively.

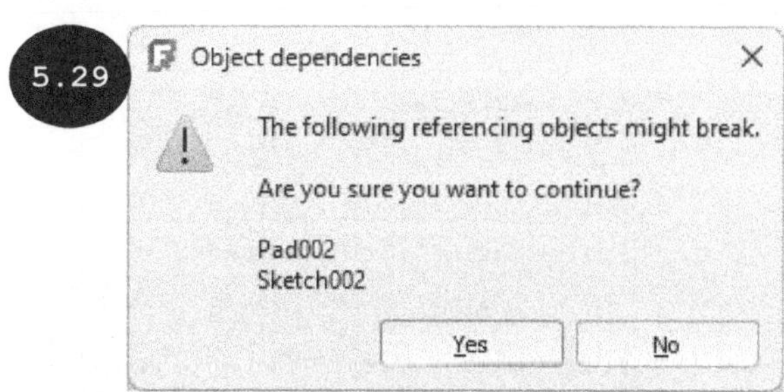

Editing Features and Sketches

FreeCAD lets you edit the individual features of a model and their sketches at any point in the design. The methods for editing a feature and its sketch are discussed next.

Editing a Feature

The method for editing a feature of a model is discussed below:

1. Select a feature to be edited in the **Tree View** of the **Model** tab and then right-click to display a shortcut menu, see Figure 5.30.

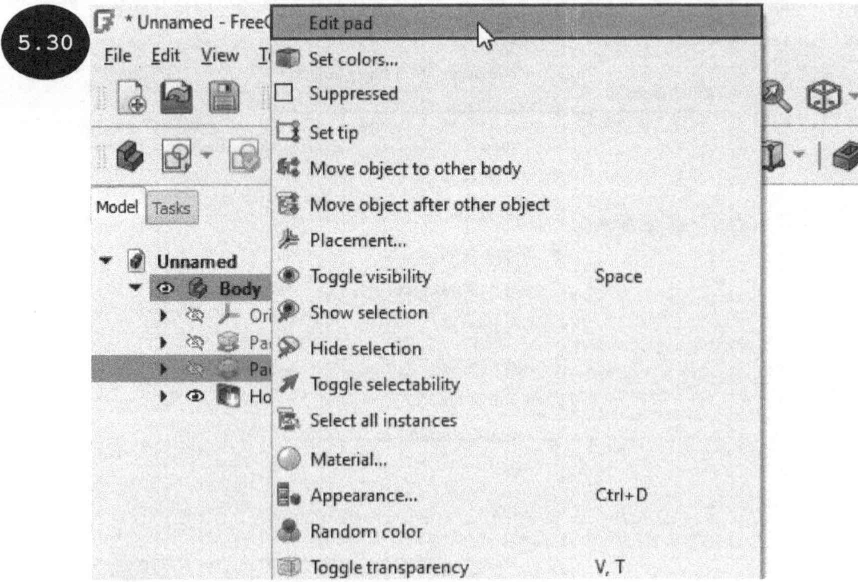

2. Click on the **Edit *<feature type>*** option in the shortcut menu, refer to Figure 5.30. The options to edit the parameters of the selected features appear in the **Tasks Panel**, see Figure 5.31.

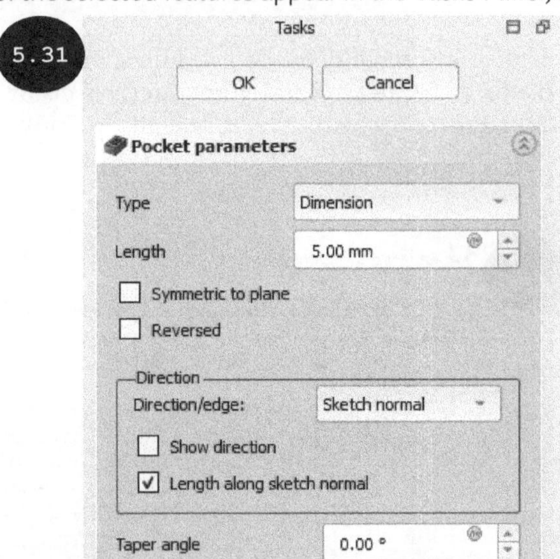

3. Edit the required parameters of the selected feature by using the respective options in the **Tasks Panel**.

4. After editing the required parameters, click on the **OK** button in the **Tasks Panel**. The selected feature of the model gets modified, accordingly.

5. Similarly, you can edit the other features of the model one by one.

Editing a Sketch

The method for editing a sketch of a feature or an individual sketch is discussed below:

1. Select the sketch of a feature or an individual sketch to be edited in the **Tree View** of the **Model** tab and then right-click to display a shortcut menu, see Figure 5.32. Note that to select the sketch of a feature, you need to expand its feature node in **Tree View**.

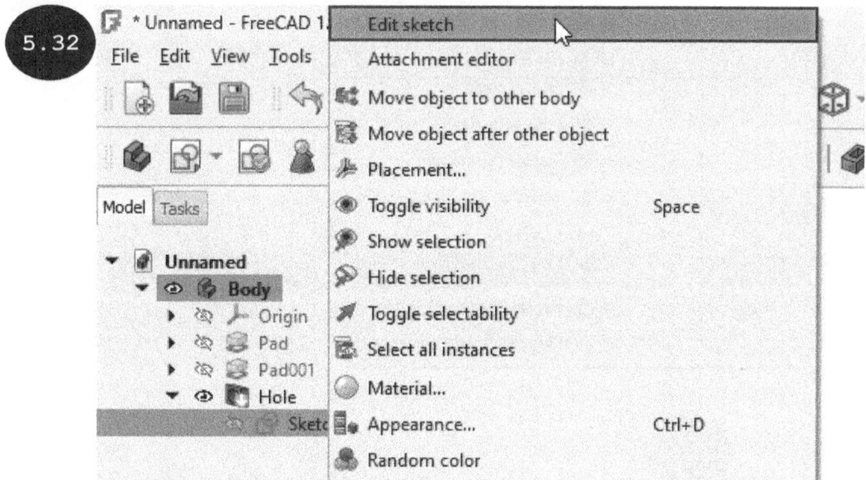

2. Click on the **Edit sketch** option in the shortcut menu. The Sketch editing mode gets invoked with the display of the selected sketch normal to the viewing direction.

3. Edit the sketch by using the sketching tools, as required.

4. After editing the sketch, exit the Sketch editing mode by clicking on the **Close** button in the **Tasks Panel**. The sketch gets modified.

5. Similarly, you can edit the other sketches of the model one by one.

Defining Display Properties or Appearance

In FreeCAD, you can define the required display properties or appearance of a model. The method for defining the display properties of a model is discussed below:

1. Right-click on the **Body** node in the **Tree View** and then click on the **Appearance** option in the shortcut menu that appears, see Figure 5.33. The **Display properties** sub-window appears in the

Tasks Panel, see Figure 5.34. Alternatively, select the **Body** node in the **Tree View** or a face of the model in the 3D View area and then click on **View > Appearance** in the **Standard Menu** or press the CTRL + D keys to invoke the **Display properties** sub-window in the **Tasks Panel**.

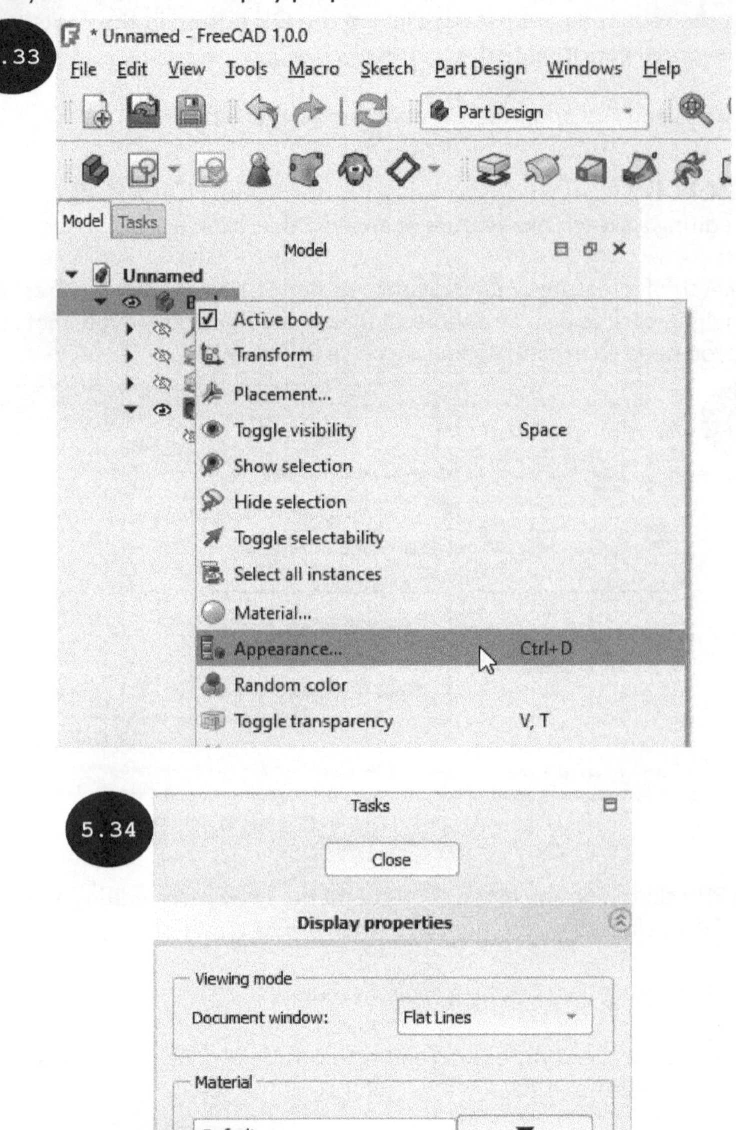

2. Select the required option (**Flat Lines**, **Shaded**, **Wireframe**, or **Points**) as the display style of the model in the **Document window** drop-down list in the **Tasks Panel**, see Figure 5.35.

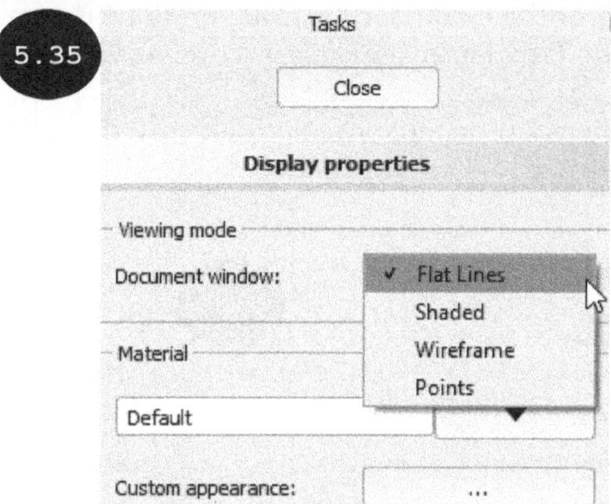

3. Click the down arrow next to the **Material** drop-down list in the **Tasks Panel** to view a list of predefined materials, such as Aluminum, Brass, Bronze, Copper, and Chrome, see Figure 5.36.

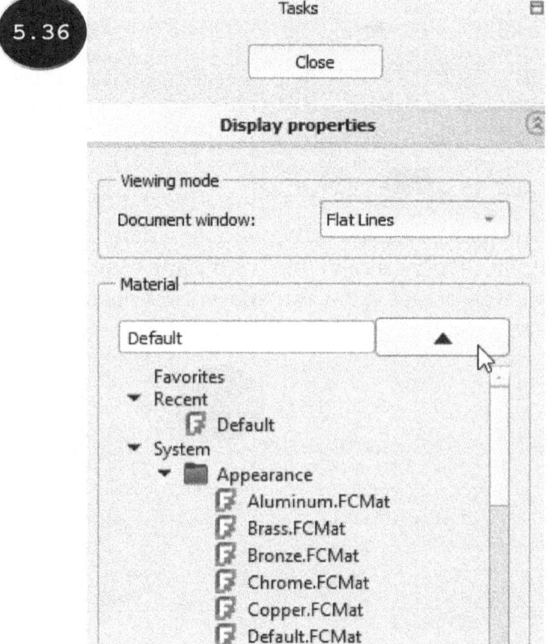

4. Select the desired material from the list, then click the arrow again to collapse the drop-down list.

5. If needed, you can edit the predefined line and point colors for the selected material by clicking the respective color swatches (**Line color**, and **Point color**) in the **Material** area of the **Tasks Panel**. Note that when you click on a color swatch (**Line color**, or **Point color**), the **Select Color** dialog box appears. In this dialog box, you can select the required color to be assigned and then click on the **OK** button to exit the dialog box.

Note: You can also customize the properties such as ambient, diffuse, emissive, specular, shininess and transparency of the material by clicking on the **Custom appearance** button in the **Material** area of the **Tasks Panel**, see Figure 5.37. When you click on this button, the **Material properties** dialog box appears, see Figure 5.38. In this dialog box, edit the material properties as required and then click on the **Close** button to exit the dialog box. The custom material properties get assigned to the selected model.

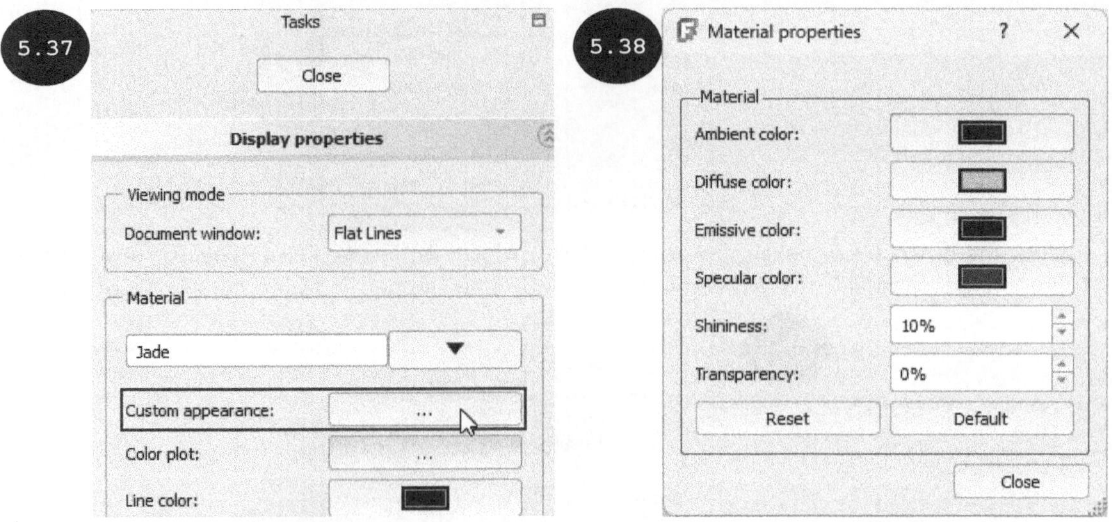

6. Accept or edit the default point size, line width, and transparency display settings of the model in the respective fields of the **Display** area in the **Tasks Panel**, see Figure 5.39. You can also edit the transparency of the model by dragging the **Transparency** slider available in the **Display** area of the **Tasks Panel**. In Figure 5.40, the transparency of the model is changed to 75%.

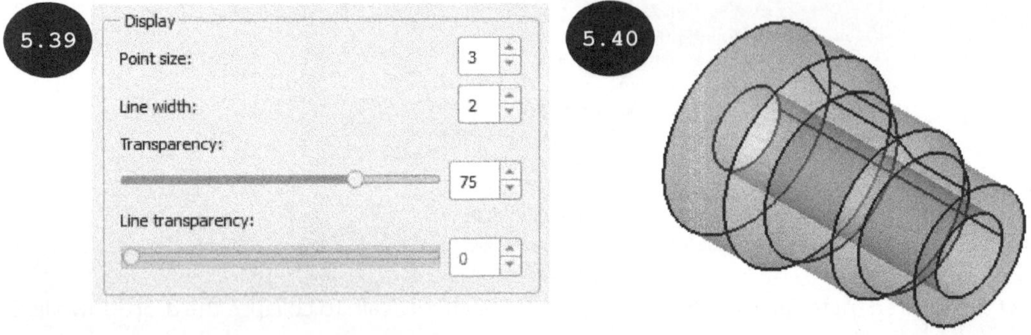

7. After defining the required display properties, click on the **Close** button in the **Tasks Panel**. The defined display properties or appearance get assigned to the model. Click anywhere in the 3D View area to exit the current selection set.

Measuring Parameters of Geometries

You can measure various parameters, such as angle, length, position, and area, for one or more geometries, including vertices, edges, and faces of a model, see Figure 5.41. In this figure, the distance between two linear edges is measured. The methods for measuring different parameters are discussed below:

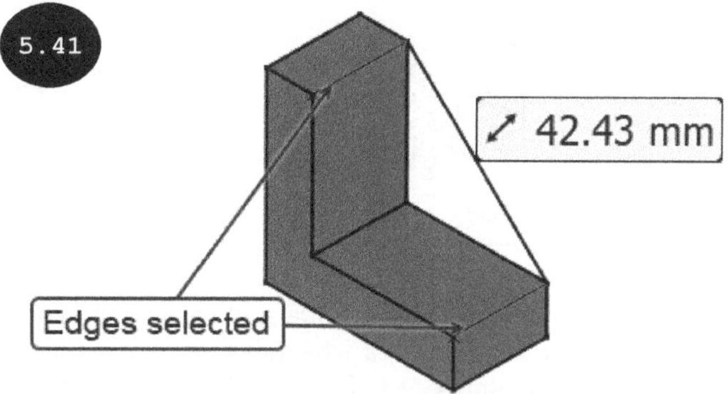

1. Click on the **Measure** tool in the **View** toolbar, see Figure 5.42. The **Measurement** sub-window appears in the **Tasks Panel**, see Figure 5.43.

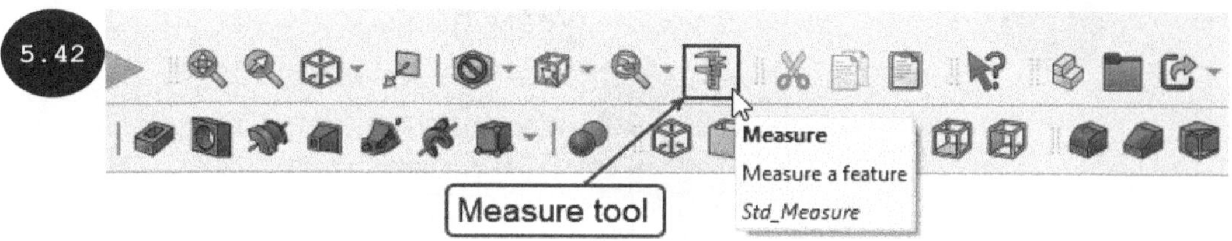

2. Select the required option such as **Distance**, **Angle**, **Length**, **Position**, or **Area** in the **Mode** drop-down list as the parameter to be measured, see Figure 5.44. By default, the **Auto** option is selected, allowing the software to automatically measure the parameter based on the selected geometry or geometries.

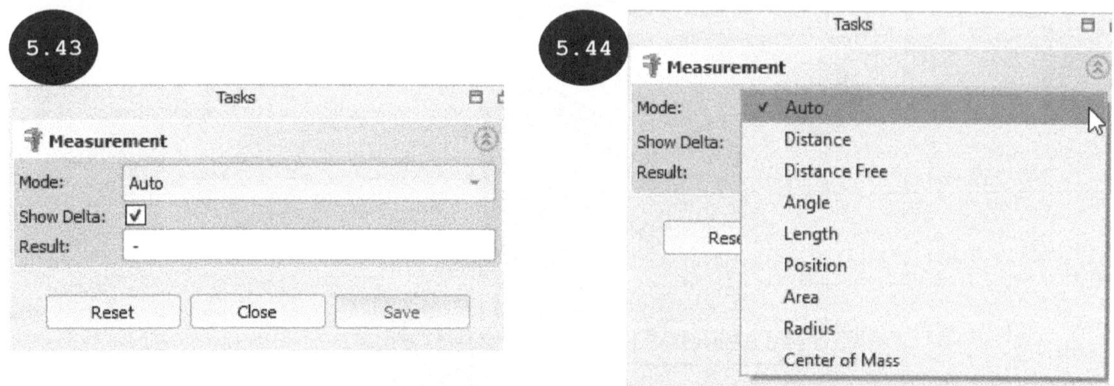

3. Select the first geometry of the model in the 3D View area. You can select a vertex, an edge, or a face of a model as the geometry. The measurement results of the selected geometry appear in

the 3D View area (see Figure 5.45) as well as in the **Result** field of the **Measurement** sub-window in the **Tasks Panel**. In Figure 5.45, a face is selected.

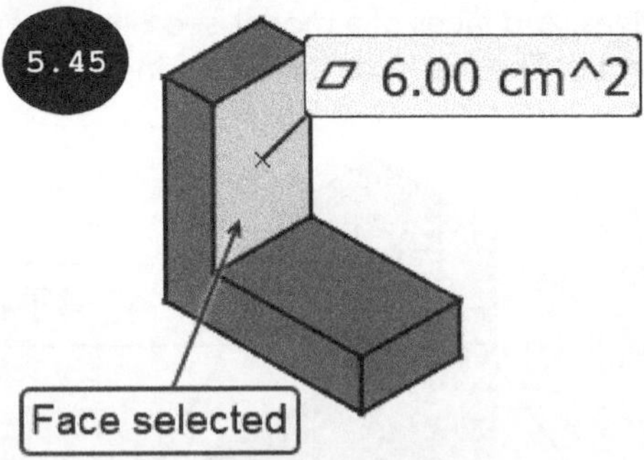

4. After selecting the first geometry, you can continue and select the second geometry (vertex, edge, or face) of the model in the 3D View area. The measurement results between the selected geometries appear, see Figures 5.46 and 5.47. In Figure 5.46, two vertices are selected to measure the distance between them, while in Figure 5.47 two non-parallel linear edges are selected to measure angle between them.

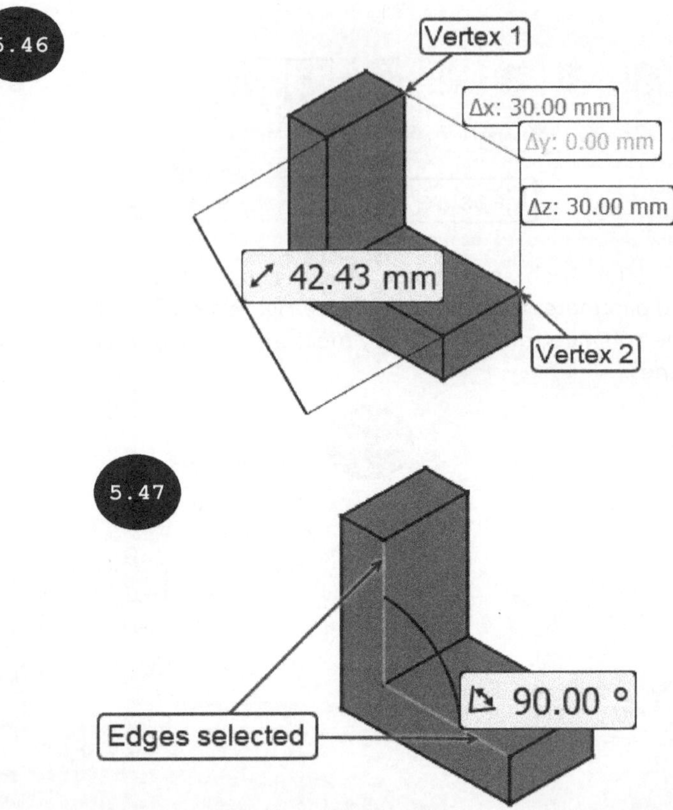

5. If needed, you can save or tag the measurement results of the selected geometry or geometries in the 3D View area by clicking on the **Save** button.

6. Click the **Reset** button to clear the current selection set, enabling you to select a new set of geometries for measurement.

7. Similarly, you can measure the distance, angle, area, and other parameters for additional sets of geometries one by one.

Note: The shortest (direct) distance between the two selected geometries and the delta measurement (orthogonal dimensions) parallel to the global X, Y, and Z axes are displayed in the 3D View area, refer to Figure 5.48. In this figure, two linear edges of the model are selected as the geometries to measure the distance between them.

8. After measuring the required parameters of one or more geometries, click the **Close** button to exit the **Tasks Panel**.

Note: The saved measurement results will remain visible in the 3D View area. Additionally, a **Measurements** node will be added to the **Tree View** in the **Model** tab, see Figure 5.49. To toggle the display of these measurement results in the 3D View area, click the **Show/Hide** button that appears in front of the **Measurements** node in the **Tree View**.

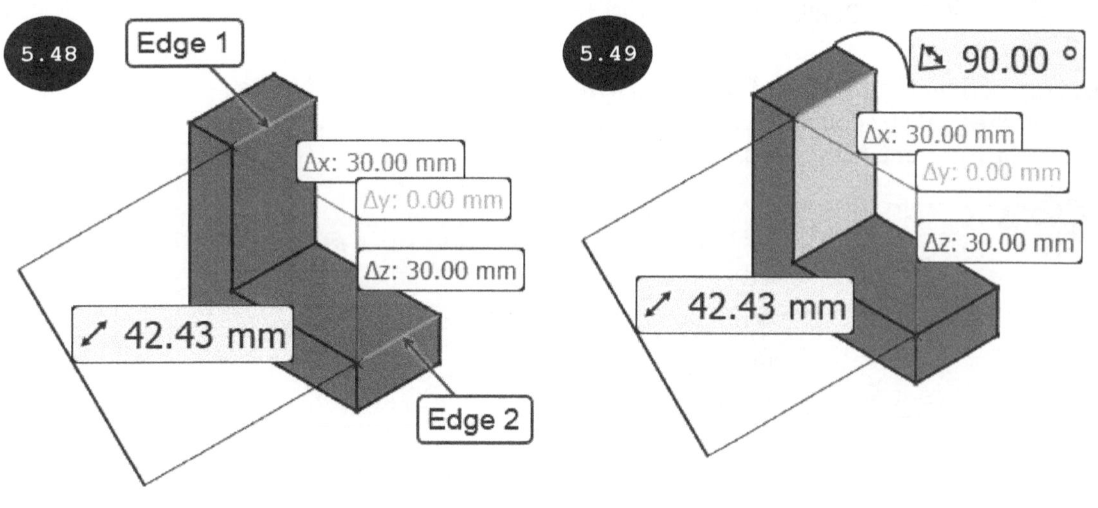

Tutorial 1

Create a model, as shown in Figure 5.50. Different views and dimensions of the model are given in the same figure. All dimensions are in mm.

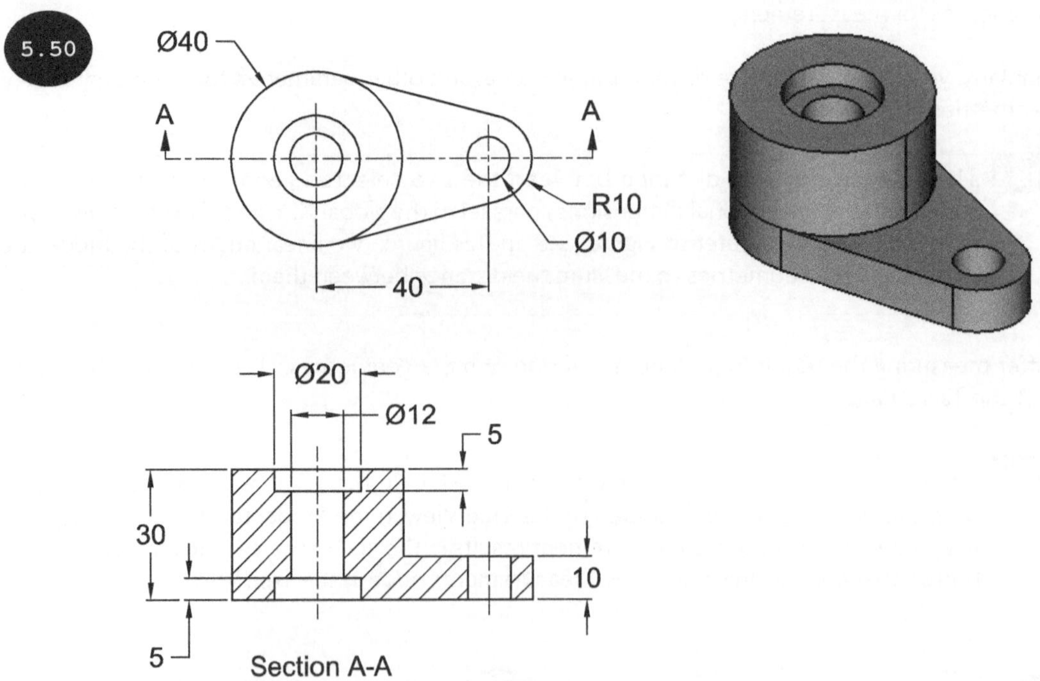

Section 1: Starting a New Part Document and Specifying Units

1. Start FreeCAD by double-clicking on the **FreeCAD 1.0** icon on your desktop. The startup user interface of FreeCAD appears, see Figure 5.51.

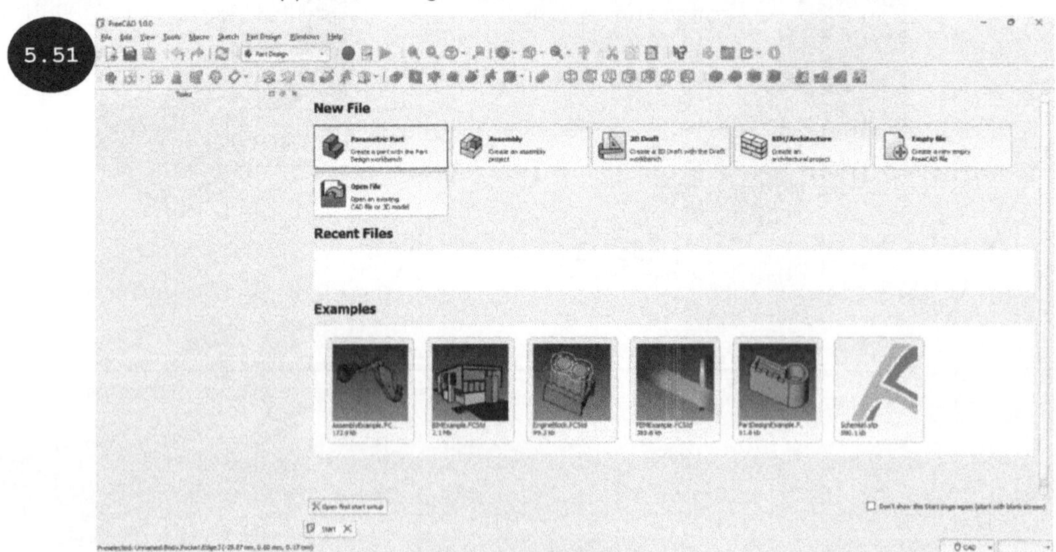

2. Click on the **Parametric Part** icon on the **Start** page (refer to Figure 5.51) or press the **CTRL + N** keys. A new part document gets invoked with the default name "**unnamed:** 1" and it becomes active by default.

   Now, you need to specify millimeters (mm) as the measurement unit for the document.

3. Invoke the **Unit** flyout that appears at the lower right corner of the **Status Bar**, see Figure 5.52.

5.52

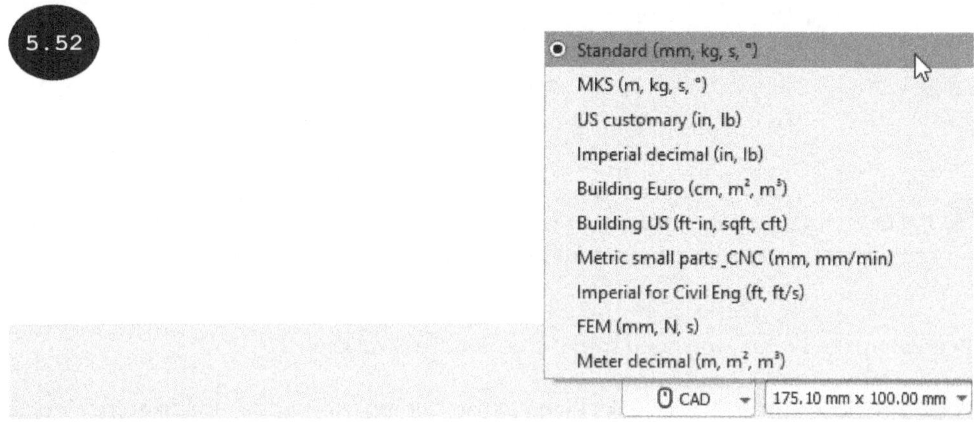

4. In this flyout, ensure that **Standard (mm, kg, s,*)** is selected as the unit system for the current design document.

Section 2: Creating the Base Feature

Now, you can create the base feature of the model, which is a pad feature.

1. Click on the **Create sketch** tool in the **Part Design Helper** toolbar, see Figure 5.53. The three default planes appear in the 3D View area. Also, the **Tasks Panel** appears in the **Tasks** tab of **Combo View** with a list of three default planes.

5.53

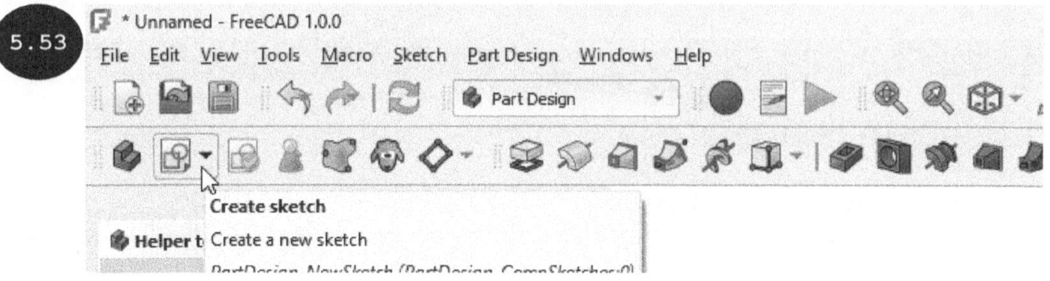

2. Select the **XY_Plane** as the sketching plane in the 3D View area for creating the sketch of the base feature. The **Sketcher** workbench gets invoked. Also, the selected plane becomes the sketching plane for drawing the sketch and is oriented normal to the viewing direction.

   Now, you can create a sketch of the base feature.

3. Create the sketch of the base feature and then apply the required constraints and dimensions to the sketch, see Figure 5.54.

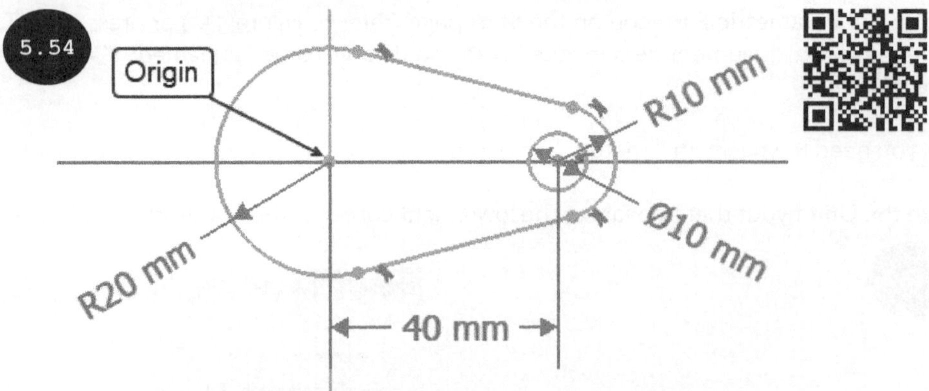

Note: In Figure 5.54, a tangent constant is applied between each set of connected arc and line entities of the sketch to make it fully constrained.

After creating the sketch, you need to exit the **Sketcher** workbench.

4. Click on the **Close** button in the **Tasks Plane** of the **Combo View** to exit the **Sketcher** workbench (see Figure 5.55) and switch back to the **Part Design** workbench.

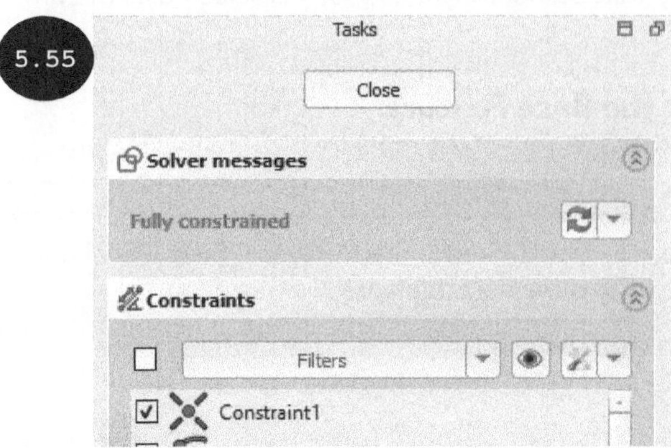

Now, you need to create a pad feature.

5. Click on the **Pad** tool in the **Part Design Modeling** toolbar, see Figure 5.56. The preview of a pad feature appears in the 3D View area with default parameters. Also, the **Pad parameters** sub-window appears in the **Tasks Panel**, see Figure 5.57.

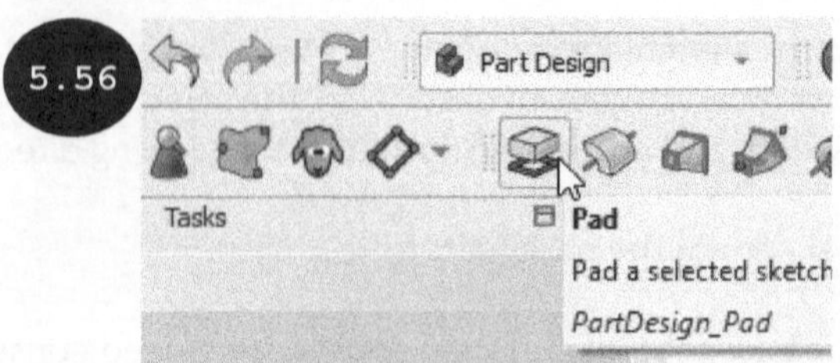

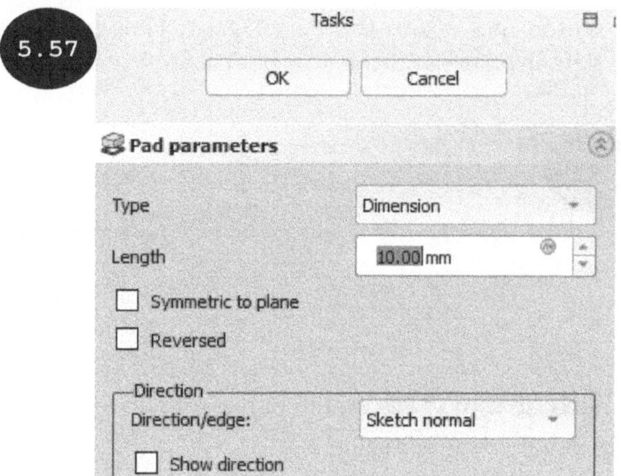

6. Ensure that the **Dimension** option is selected in the **Type** drop-down list for creating a pad feature by specifying its length.

7. Enter **10** mm as the length of the pad feature in the **Length** field of the **Tasks Panel**. Next, press the TAB key or click anywhere in the 3D View area to update the preview of the pad feature.

8. Click on the **OK** button in the **Tasks Panel** to confirm the creation of the pad feature and exit the **Tasks Panel**. The pad feature gets created, see Figure 5.58.

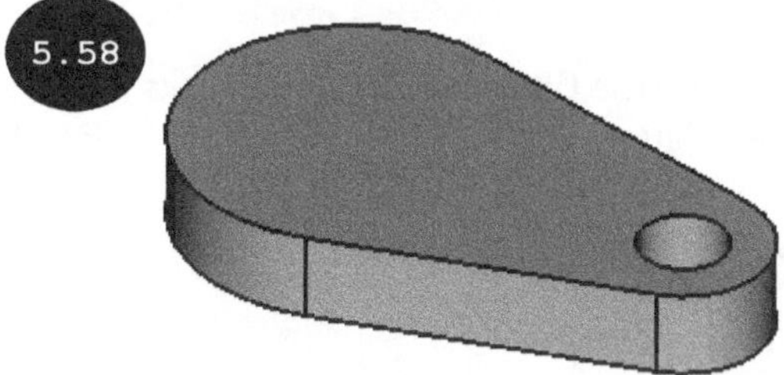

Section 3: Creating the Second Feature

Now, you can create the second feature of the model.

1. Click to select the top planar face of the base feature as the sketching plane for creating the sketch of the second feature of the model, see Figure 5.59.

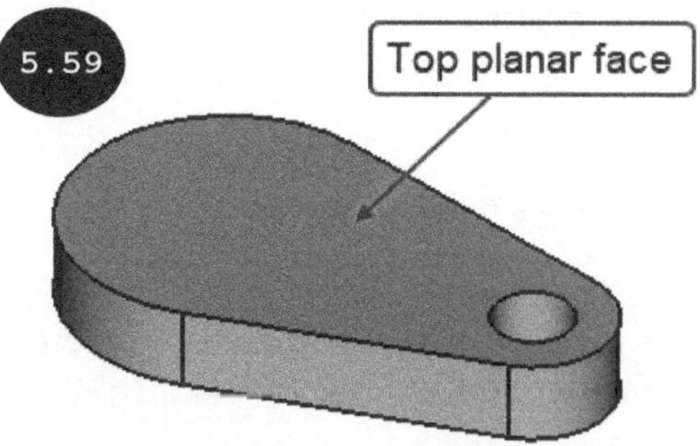

2. Click on the **Create sketch** tool in the **Part Design Helper** toolbar, see Figure 5.60. The **Sketcher** workbench gets invoked and the top planar face of the base feature gets oriented normal to the viewing direction.

3. Create a circle of diameter 40 mm as the sketch of the second feature, see Figure 5.61. Note that the center point of the circle is at the origin.

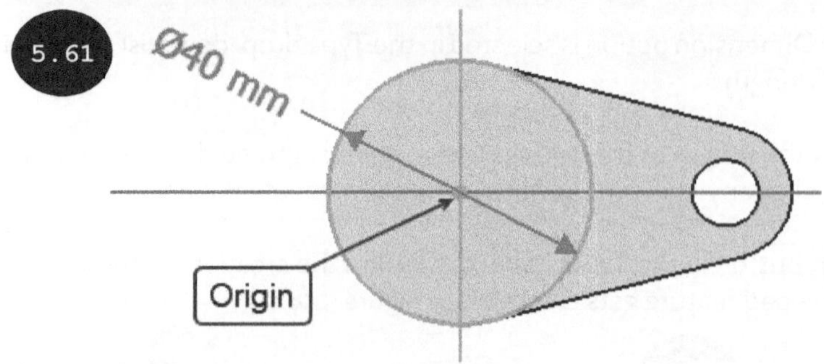

4. After creating the sketch, click on the **Close** button in the **Tasks Plane** of the **Combo View** to exit the **Sketcher** workbench (see Figure 5.62) and switch back to the **Part Design** workbench.

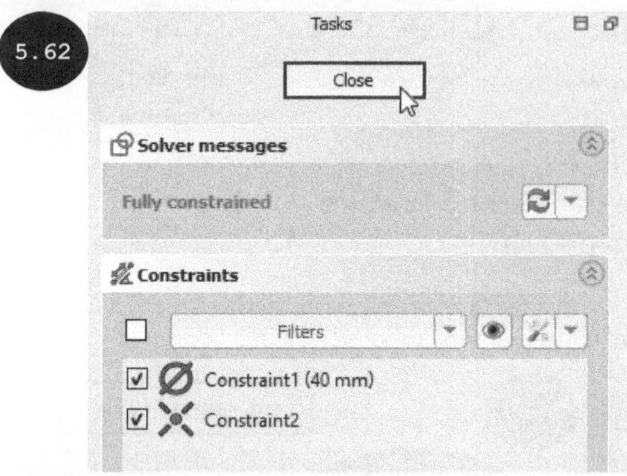

Now, you can extrude the sketch to create a pad feature.

5. Click on the **Pad** tool in the **Part Design Modeling** toolbar, see Figure 5.63. The preview of a pad feature appears in the 3D View area with default parameters. Also, the **Pad parameters** sub-window appears in the **Tasks Panel**.

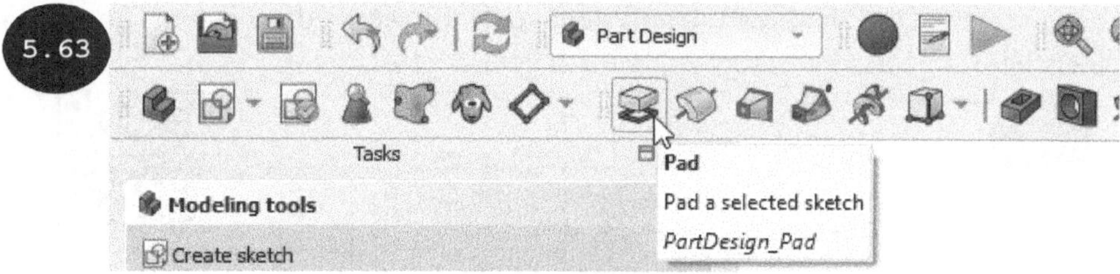

6. Enter **20** mm as the length of the pad feature in the **Length** field of the **Tasks Panel**. Next, press the TAB key or click anywhere in the 3D View area to update the preview of the pad feature.

7. Click on the **OK** button in the **Tasks Panel** to confirm the creation of the pad feature and exit the **Tasks Panel**. The second feature gets created, see Figure 5.64. Click anywhere in the 3D View area to exit the current selection set.

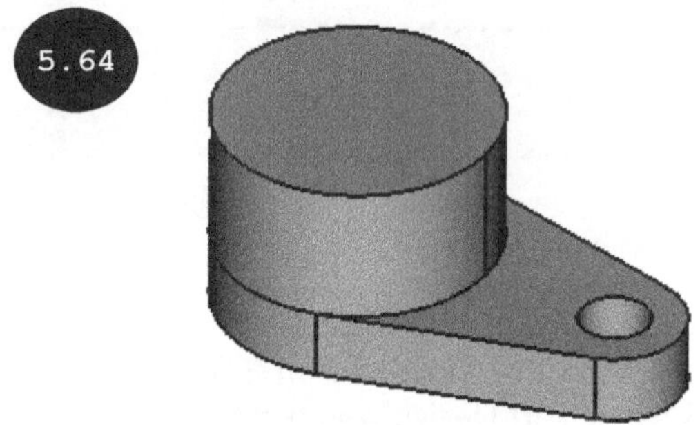

Section 4: Creating the Third Feature

Now, you need to create the third feature of the model, which is a groove feature.

1. Click on the **Create sketch** tool in the **Part Design Helper** toolbar, see Figure 5.65. The three default planes appear in the 3D View area, and you are prompted to select a sketching plane for creating the sketch of the third feature.

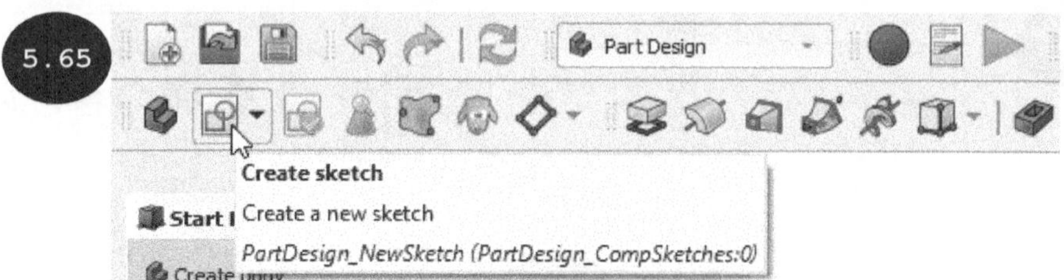

2. Select the **XZ_Plane** as the sketching plane in the 3D View area for creating the sketch of the third feature. The **Sketcher** workbench gets invoked. Also, the selected plane gets oriented normal to the viewing direction.

3. Select the **View section** tool in the **Sketcher** toolbar, see Figure 5.66. The section view of the model appears in the 3D View area by temporarily hiding the material that is in front of the sketching plane.

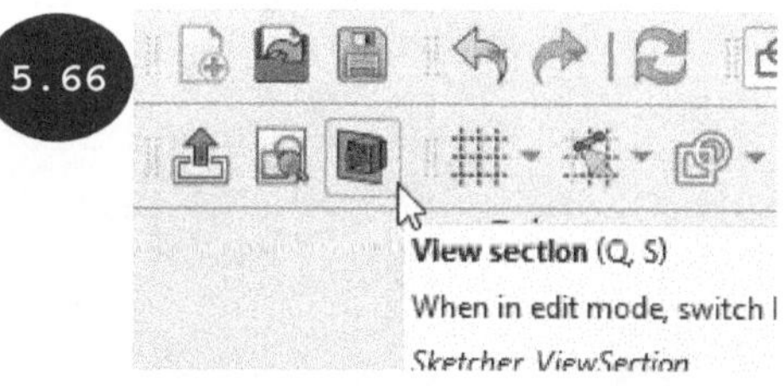

4. Create the sketch of the third feature and then apply the required constraints and dimensions, see Figure 5.67.

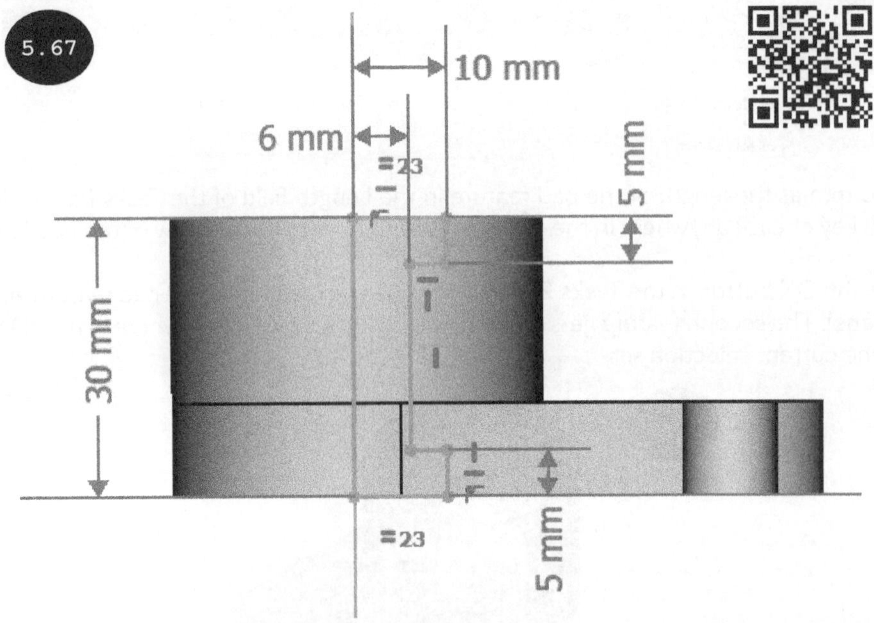

5. After creating the sketch, click on the **Close** button in the **Tasks Plane** to exit the **Sketcher** workbench and switch back to the **Part Design** workbench.

6. Click on the **Groove** tool in the **Part Design Modeling** toolbar, see Figure 5.68. The preview of a groove feature appears such that the material is removed from the model by revolving the sketch around its vertical axis in the 3D View area, see Figure 5.69. Since the **Vertical sketch axis** option is selected by default in the **Axis** drop-down list of the **Revolution parameters** sub-window that appears in the **Tasks Panel**, see Figure 5.70.

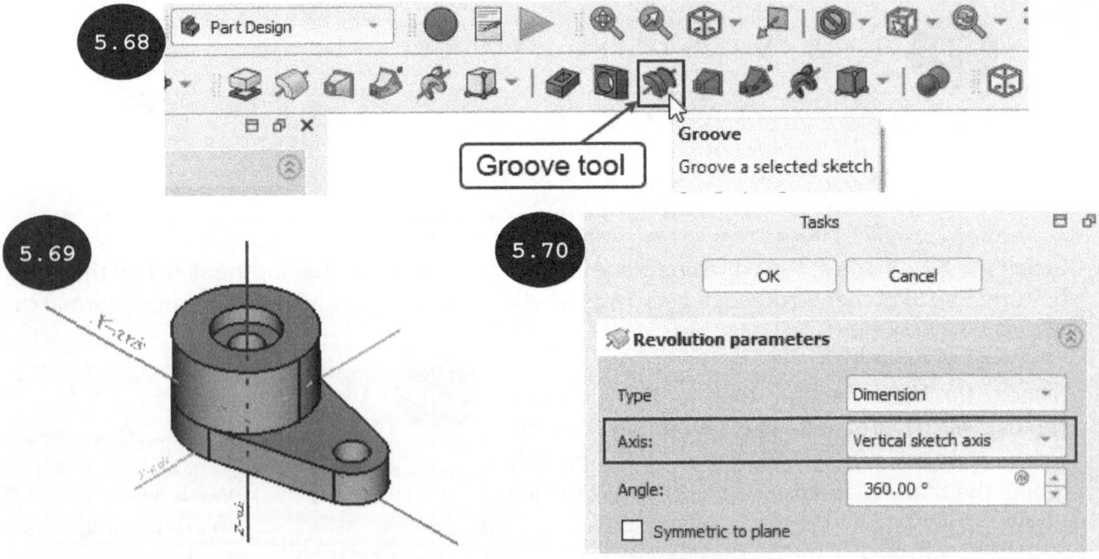

7. Ensure that the **360**-degree is specified as the angle of revolution in the **Angle** field of the **Tasks Panel**.

8. Click on the **OK** button in the **Tasks Panel** to confirm the creation of the feature and exit the **Tasks Panel**. Figure 5.71 shows the final model after creating all its features.

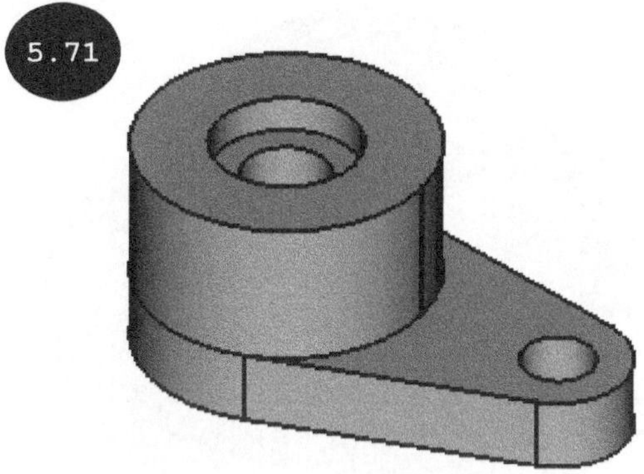

Section 5: Saving the Model

1. Click on the **Save** tool in the **File** toolbar (see Figure 5.72) or press the CTRL + S keys. The **Save FreeCAD Document** dialog box appears.

2. Browse to the required folder (:*FreeCAD > Chapter 05*) in the local drive of your system. Note that you need to create the Chapter 05 sub-folder inside the FreeCAD folder.

3. Enter **Ch05-Tutorial 1** in the **File name** field of the dialog box. Next, click on the **Save** button in the dialog box. The model gets saved with the name **Tutorial 1** at the specified location (:*FreeCAD > Chapter 05*).

4. Click on **File > Close** in the **Standard Menu** to close the current document.

Tutorial 2

Create a model, as shown in Figure 5.73. Different views and dimensions of the model are given in Figure 5.74. All dimensions are in inches (in).

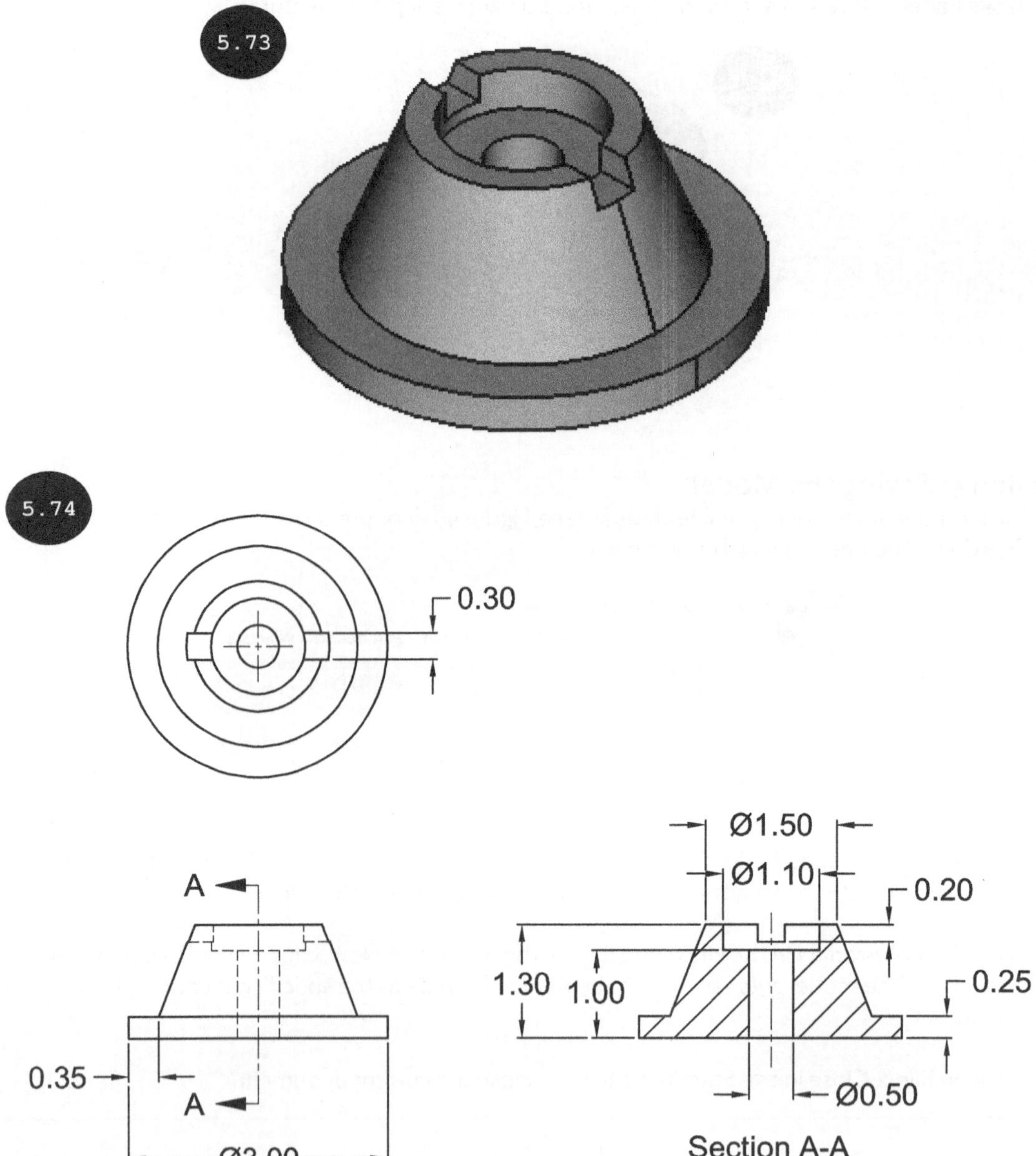

Section 1: Starting a New Part Document and Specifying Units

1. Start FreeCAD by double-clicking on the **FreeCAD 1.0** icon on your desktop, if not started already. The startup user interface of FreeCAD appears.

2. Click on the **New** tool in the **File** toolbar (see Figure 5.75) or press the **CTRL + N** keys. A new part document gets invoked with the default name and gets activated, by default.

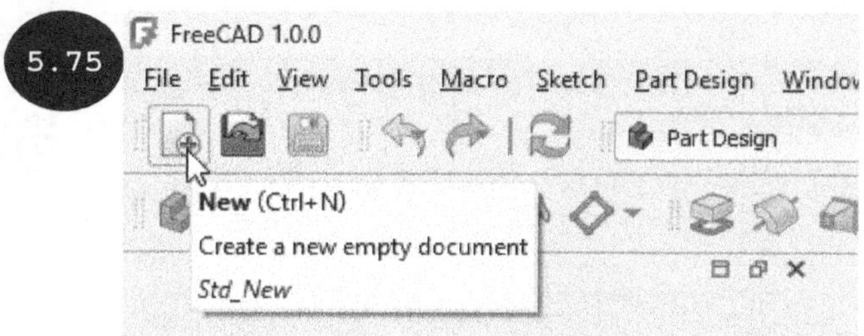

Now, you need to specify inches (in) as the measurement unit for the document.

3. Invoke the **Unit** flyout that appears at the lower right corner of the **Status Bar**, see Figure 5.76.

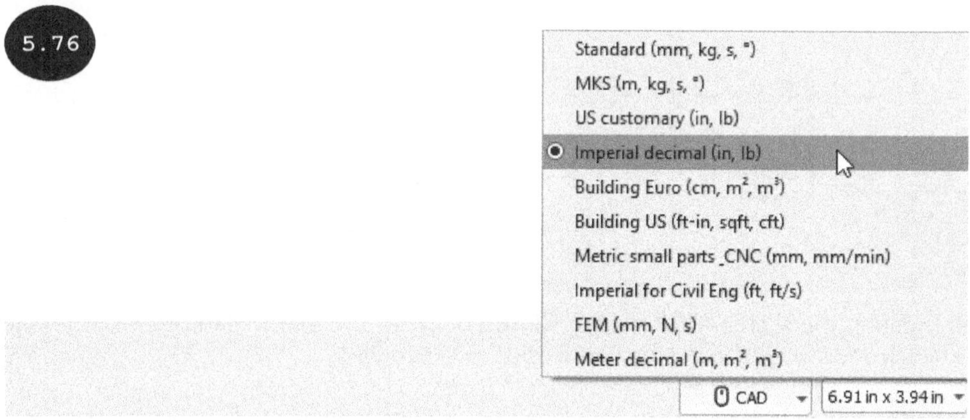

4. In this flyout, ensure that **Imperial decimal (in, lb)** is selected as the unit system for the current design document.

Section 2: Creating the Base Feature

Now, you can create the base feature of the model, which is a revolution feature.

1. Click on the **Create sketch** tool in the **Part Design Helper** toolbar, see Figure 5.77. The three default planes appear in the 3D View area. Also, the **Tasks Panel** appears in the **Tasks** tab of **Combo View**.

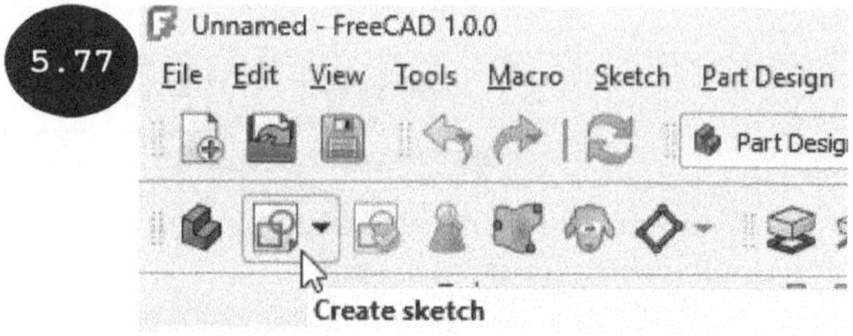

2. Select the **XZ_Plane** as the sketching plane in the 3D View area. The **Sketcher** workbench gets invoked and the selected plane gets oriented normal to the viewing direction.

3. Create the sketch of the base feature of the model and then apply the required constraints and dimensions, see Figure 5.78.

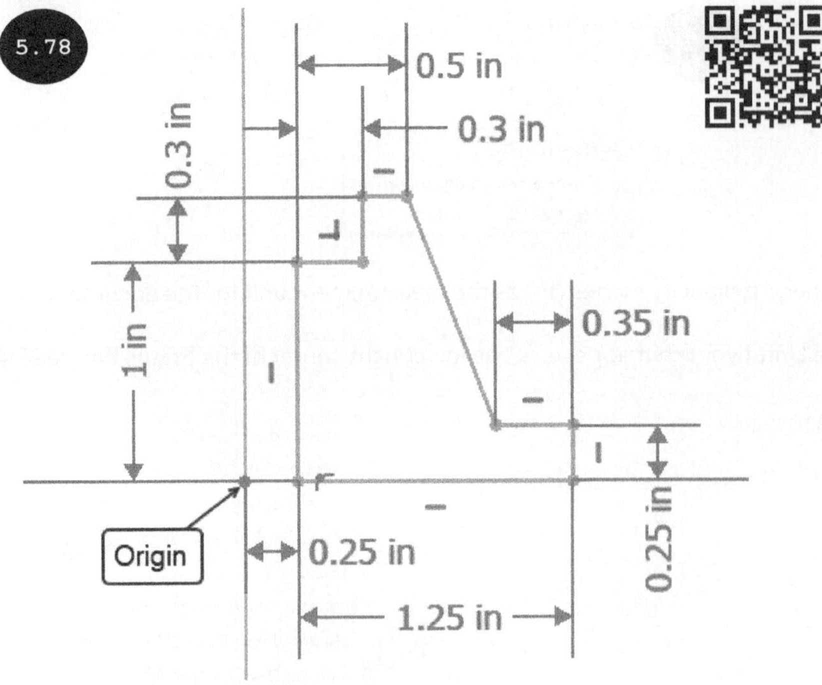

4. After creating the sketch, click on the **Close** button in the **Tasks Plane** to exit the **Sketcher** workbench and switch back to the **Part Design** workbench.

5. Click on the **Revolution** tool in the **Part Design Modeling** toolbar, see Figure 5.79. The preview of a revolution feature appears in the 3D View area with default parameters. Also, the **Revolution parameters** sub-window appears in the **Tasks Panel** of the **Combo View**.

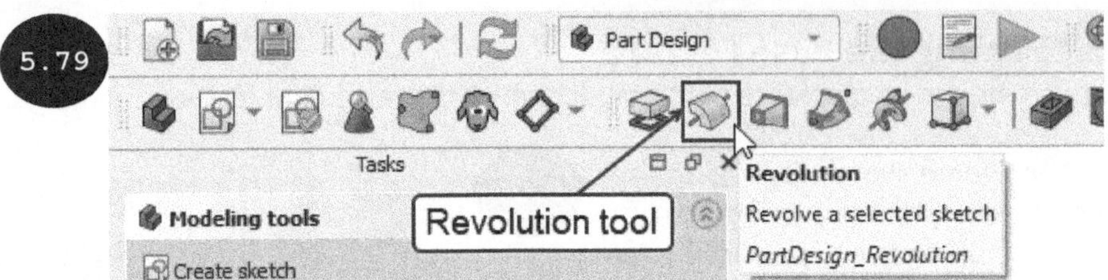

6. Ensure that the **Vertical sketch axis** option is selected in the **Axis** drop-down list of the **Tasks Panel** as the axis of revolution.

7. Ensure that the **360** degrees is specified as the angle of revolution in the **Angle** field of the **Tasks Panel**.

8. Click on the **OK** button in the **Tasks Panel**. The revolution feature gets created in the 3D View area, see Figure 5.80.

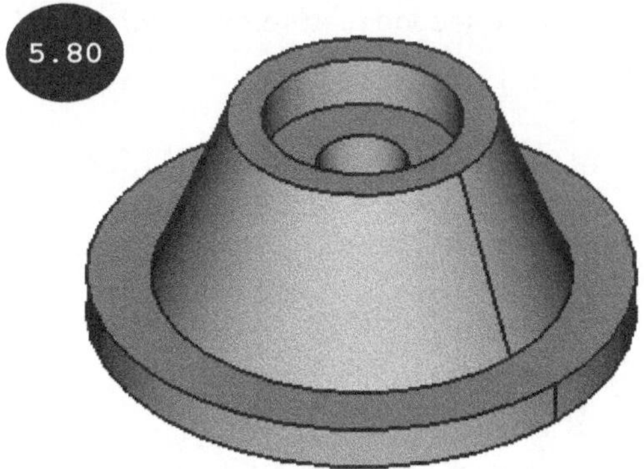

Section 3: Creating the Second Feature

Now, you can create the second feature of the model, which is a pocket feature.

1. Select the top planar face of the base feature as the sketching plane for creating the sketch of the second feature, see Figure 5.81.

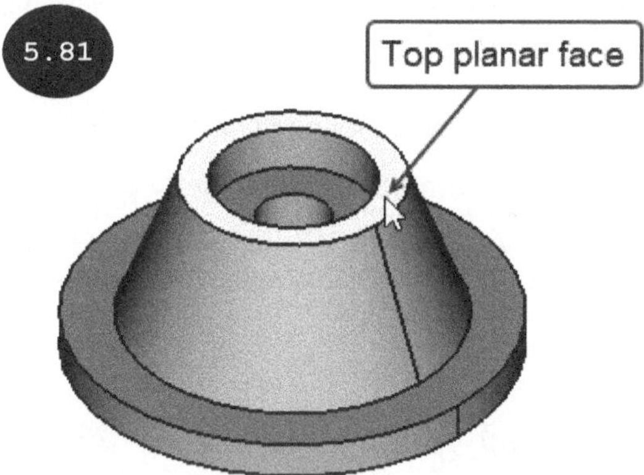

2. Click on the **Create sketch** tool in the **Part Design Helper** toolbar, see Figure 5.82. The **Sketcher** workbench gets invoked and the top planar face of the base feature gets oriented normal to the viewing direction.

3. Create a rectangle as the sketch of the second feature, see Figure 5.83. Note that the center point of the rectangle is at the origin.

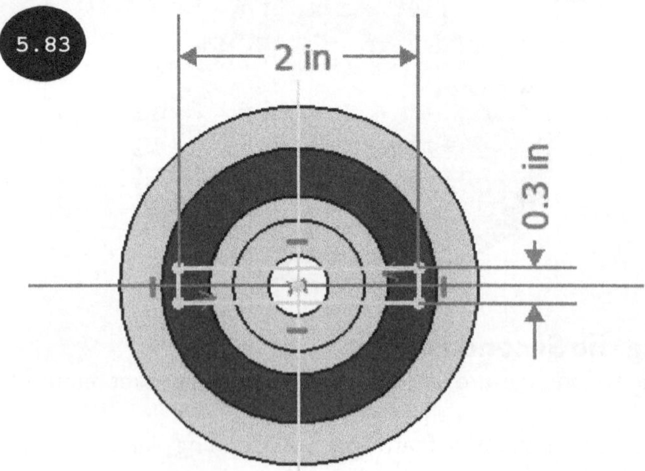

4. After creating the sketch, click on the **Close** button in the **Tasks Plane** to exit the **Sketcher** workbench and switch back to the **Part Design** workbench.

   Now, you can create a pocket feature by removing the material from the model.

5. Click on the **Pocket** tool in the **Part Design Modeling** toolbar, see Figure 5.84. The preview of a pocket feature appears in the 3D View area by removing material from the model up to a default length. Also, the **Pocket parameters** sub-window appears in the **Tasks Panel**.

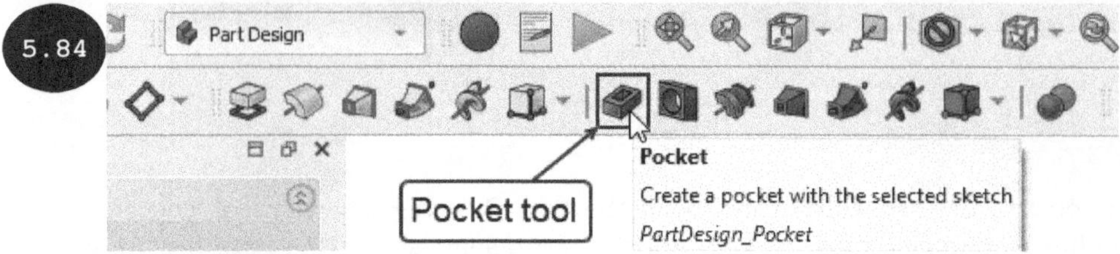

6. Ensure that the **Dimension** option is selected in the **Type** drop-down list of the **Tasks Panel** for extruding the sketch up to a specified length.

7. Enter **0.2** inches in the **Length** field of the Tasks Panel as the length of extrusion and then press the TAB key to update the preview of the pocket feature in the 3D View area.

8. Accept the remaining default options and then click on the **OK** button in the **Tasks Panel** to confirm the creation of the pocket feature by removing the material from the model. Figure 5.85 shows the final model after creating all its features.

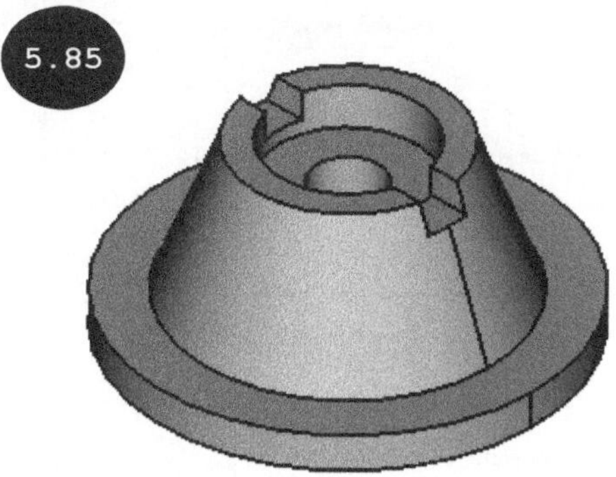

Section 4: Assigning the Material/Appearance

Now, you can assign the chrome material/appearance to the model.

1. Right-click on the **Body** node in the **Model** tab of the **Combo View** and then click on the **Appearance** option in the shortcut menu that appears, see Figure 5.86. The **Display properties** sub-window appears in the **Tasks Panel**, see Figure 5.87.

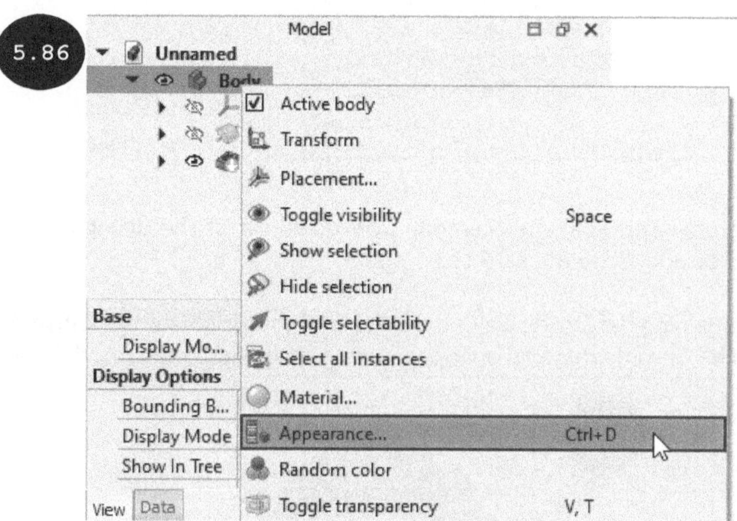

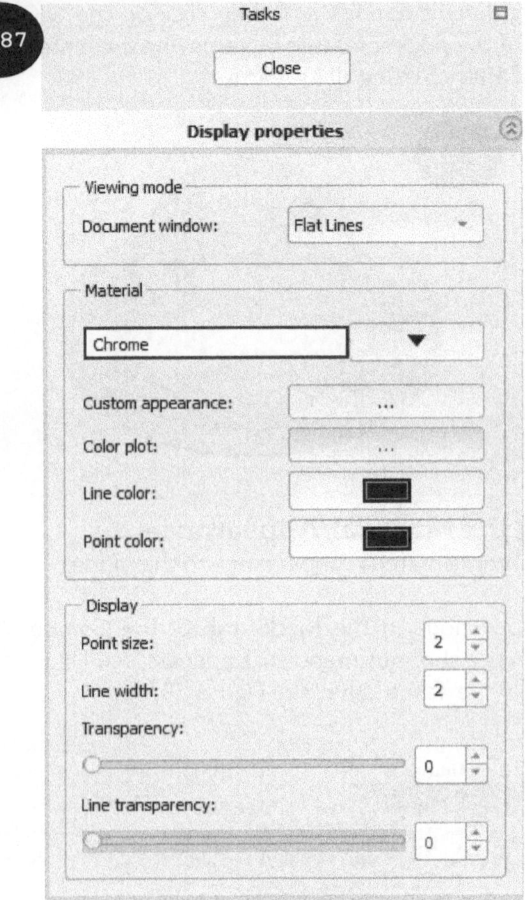

2. Select the **Chrome** option in the Material drop-down list of the dialog box as the material or appearance to be applied to the selected model.

3. Accept the remaining default display properties and then click on the **Close** button to exit the **Tasks Panel**. The Chrome material or appearance gets applied to the model, see Figure 5.88.

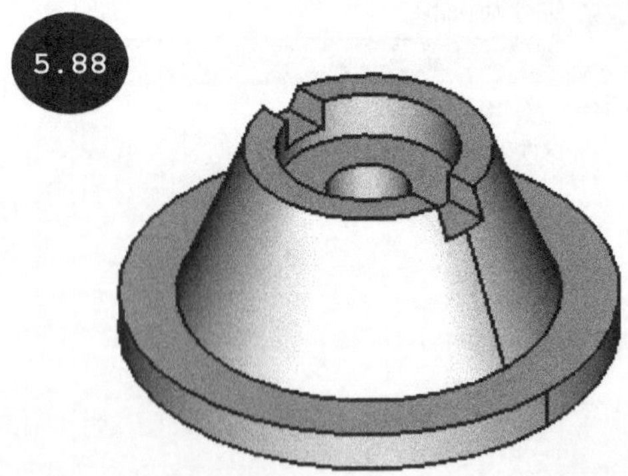

Section 5: Saving the Model

Now, you can save the model.

1. Click on the **Save** tool in the **File** toolbar (see Figure 5.89) or press the CTRL + S keys. The **Save FreeCAD Document** dialog box appears.

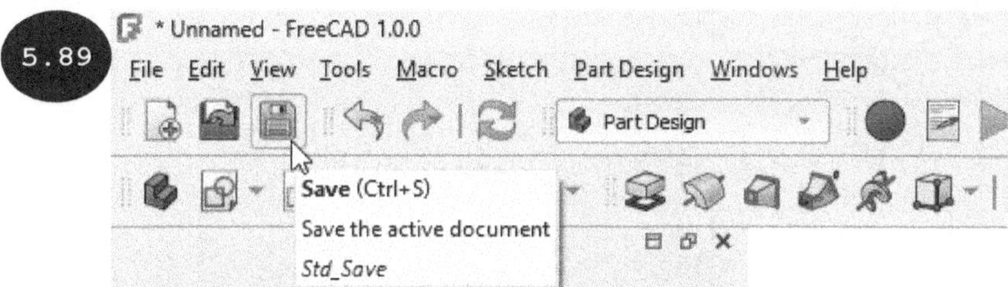

2. Browse to the *FreeCAD > Chapter 05* folder in the local drive of your system. You need to create these folders, if not created earlier.

3. Enter **Ch05-Tutorial 2** in the **File name** field of the dialog box. Next, click on the **Save** button in the dialog box. The mode gets saved at the specified location.

4. Close the document by clicking on **File > Close** in the **Standard Menu**.

Hands-on Test Drive 1

Create the model shown in Figure 5.90. The different views and dimensions for creating this model are shown in Figure 5.91. You need to create the model by creating all its features one by one. All dimensions are in mm.

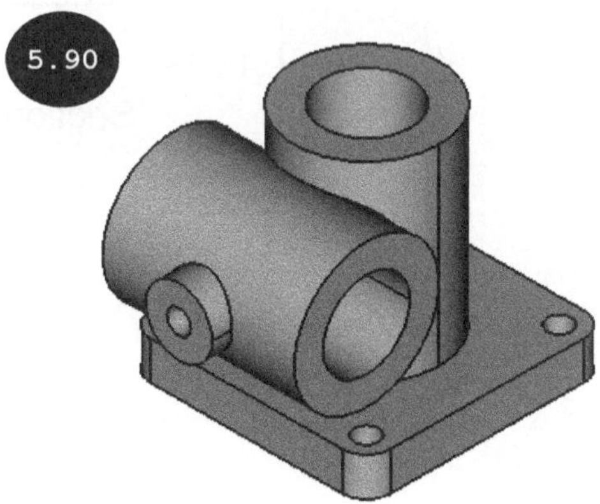

5.91

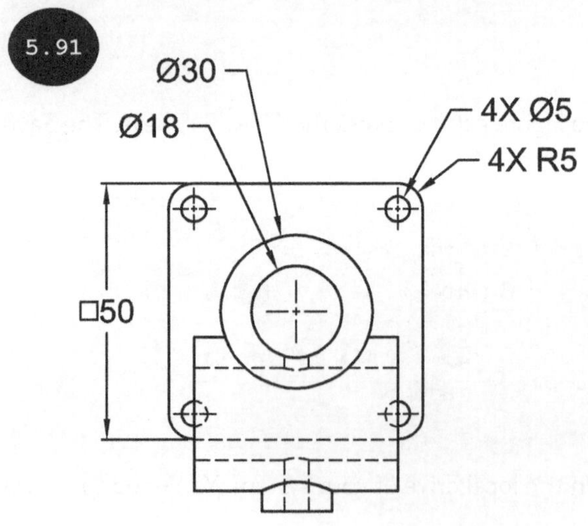

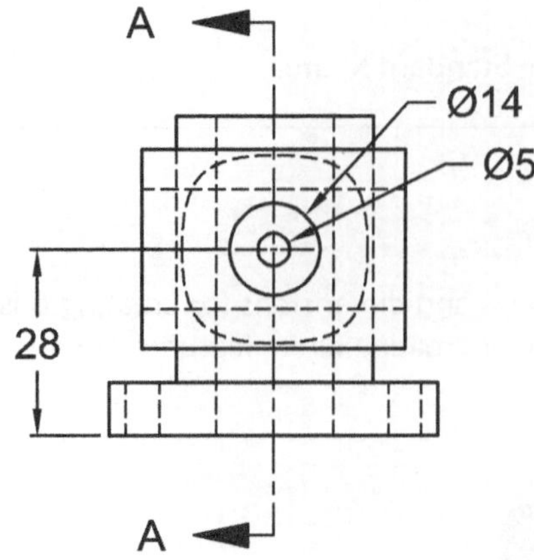

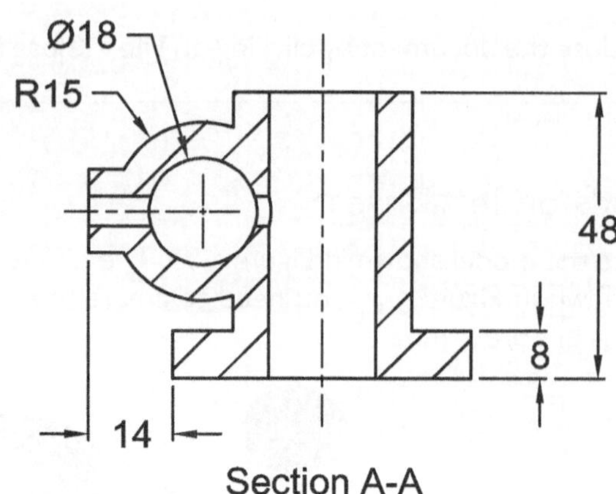

Section A-A

Hands-on Test Drive 2

Create the model shown in Figure 5.92. You need to create the model by creating all its features one by one. All dimensions are in inches.

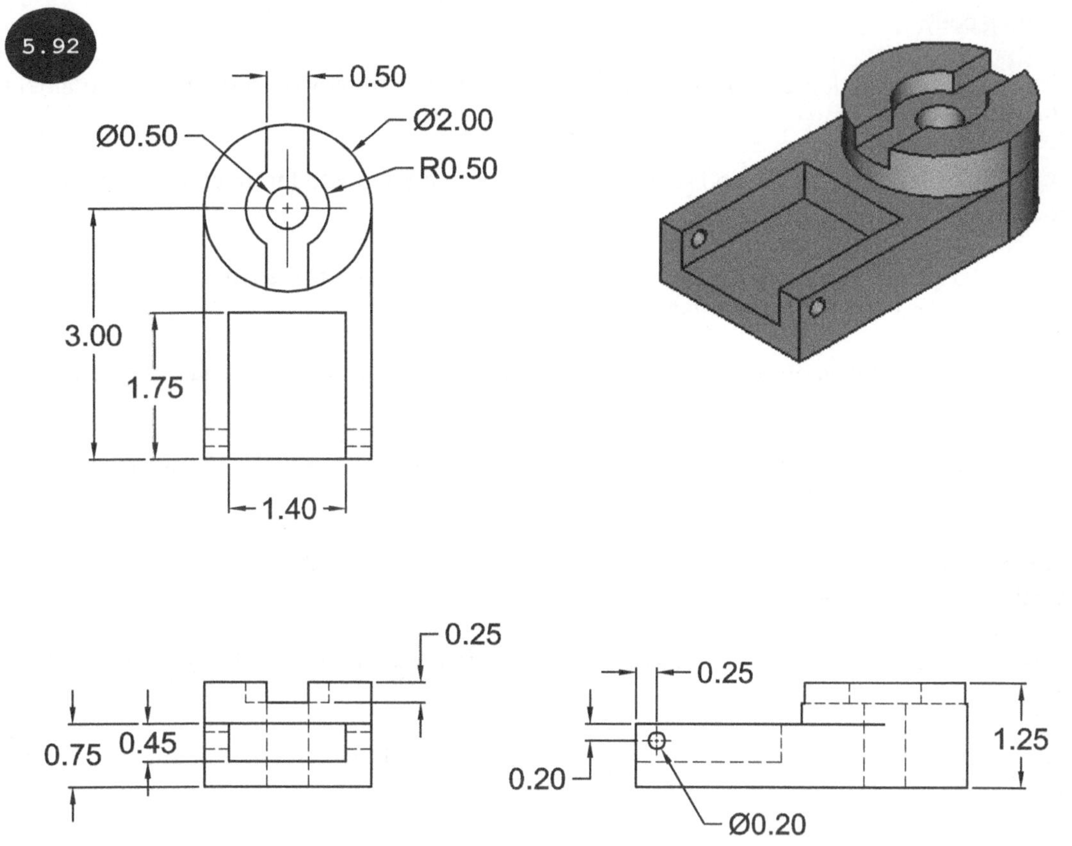

Summary

In this chapter, you have learned how to create pocket and groove features by removing the material from the model. The chapter also described methods for projecting external geometries onto the sketch, displaying section view and an earlier state of a model, reordering features, deleting, and editing features, and defining display properties to the model. It also discussed how to measure the distance between two geometries of a model.

Questions

Complete and verify the following sentences:

- A _________ feature is created by subtracting material, normal to the sketching plane from an existing body.
- The _________ option is used for creating a pocket feature by removing the material throughout the entire model.
- A _________ feature is created such that the material is subtracted from an existing body by revolving a sketch around an axis.
- The _________ tool is used for projecting external geometries such as edges and vertices of the model as linked construction entities onto the sketch.
- The _______ entities are only visible in the **Sketcher** workbench while creating or editing a sketch.
- In the **Sketcher** workbench, you can create a _________ view by temporarily hiding the material in front of the current sketching plane.
- You can measure the _________ and _________ distances between two geometries such as vertices, edges, or faces of a model.
- The _______ tool is used for creating a section view of a model in the Sketch editing mode of the **Sketcher** workbench.
- FreeCAD lets you edit the individual features of a model and their sketches at any point in the design. (True/False)
- The linked construction entities of a sketch can be only used as reference entities for applying geometrical and dimensional constraints to the sketch entities. (True/False)
- In the **Tree View**, you can change the order of a feature by moving it above its parent feature. (True/False)

CHAPTER 6

Creating Pipe, Loft, and Helix Features

This chapter discusses the following topics:

- Creating an Additive Pipe Feature
- Creating a Multi-section Additive Pipe Feature
- Creating a Subtractive Pipe Feature
- Creating an Additive Loft Feature
- Creating a Subtractive Loft Feature
- Creating an Additive Helix Feature
- Creating a Subtractive Helix Feature
- Creating a Helical Curve

In the previous chapters, you have learned about the primary modeling tools that are used for creating features like pad, revolution, pocket, and groove. You have also learned about the basic workflow of creating models, which is to first create the base feature of a model and then create the remaining features of the model one after the other.

In this chapter, you will explore some of the advanced modeling features such as additive pipe, additive loft, additive helix, subtractive pipe, subtractive loft, and subtractive helix.

Creating an Additive Pipe Feature

An additive pipe feature is created by adding material by sweeping a profile (closed sketch) along a path (open or closed sketch). Figure 6.1 shows a profile and a path as well as the resultant additive pipe feature.

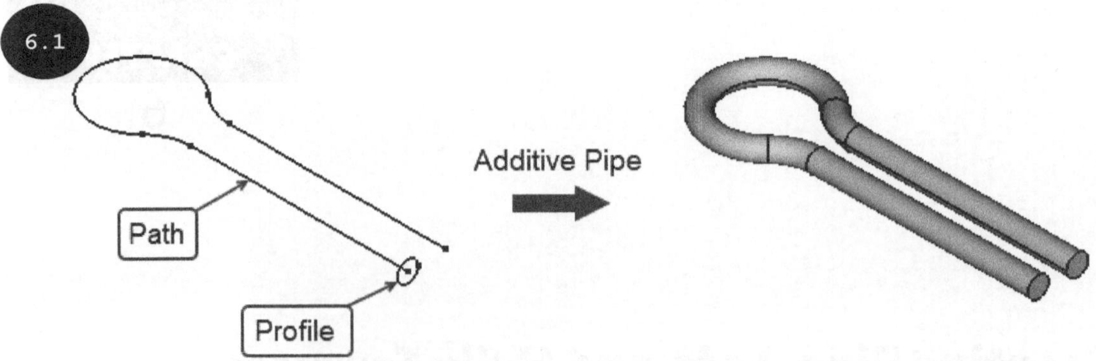

It is evident from the above figures that to create an additive pipe, you first need to create a path and a profile where the profile follows the path and creates an additive pipe feature. The profile defines the cross-section of the feature, and the path defines the route taken by the profile for creating the pipe feature. In FreeCAD, you can create an additive pipe feature by using the **Additive Pipe** tool. Note that for creating an additive pipe feature, you need to be sure of the following:

- The profile must be a closed sketch.
- The path can be an open or a closed sketch, which is made up of a set of end-to-end connected sketched entities, a curve, or a set of model edges.
- The path should start or pass through the plane of the profile to get better results.
- The profile and path as well as the resultant pipe feature must not be self-intersected.

The method for creating an additive pipe feature is discussed below:

1. Create a path and a profile as separate sketches in the **Sketcher** workbench, refer to Figure 6.2.

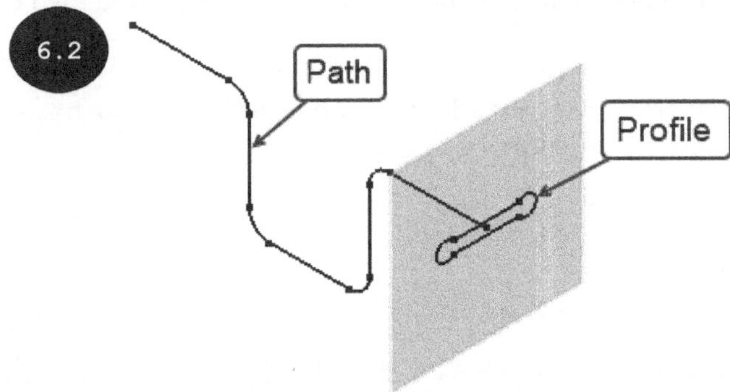

Note: In Figure 6.2, the path is created on the XZ Plane (front plane), and the profile is created on a datum plane that is normal to the right horizontal entity of the path as separate sketches one by one. The methods for creating datum planes are discussed in Chapter 4.

2. After creating a path and a profile, click on the **Additive pipe** tool in the **Part Design Modeling** toolbar, see Figure 6.3. The **Select feature** sub-window appears in the **Tasks Panel** and displays a list of sketches available in the 3D View area, see Figure 6.4. Also, you are prompted to select a sketch as the profile of the feature.

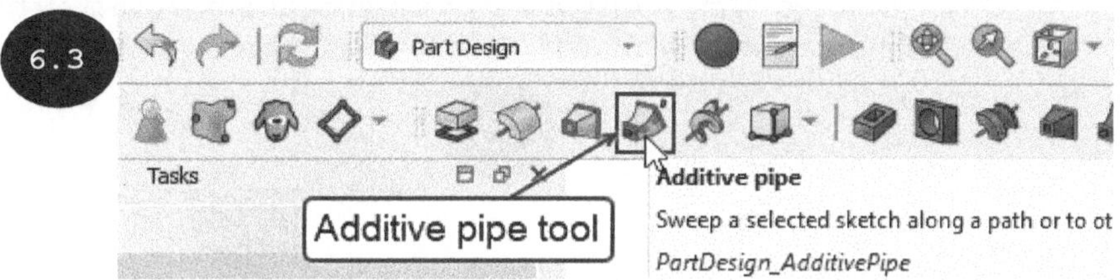

Note: You can also first select the profile and then the path by pressing the CTRL key in the **Task Panel** before invoking the **Additive pipe** tool. On doing so, the preview of the resultant additive pipe feature appears in the 3D View area, directly. Also, the names of the selected profile and the path get displayed in the respective fields of the **Task Panel** that appears.

3. Select a closed sketch as the profile of the feature in the 3D View area or the **Select feature** sub-window of the **Tasks Panel** and then click on the **OK** button. The options for creating an additive pipe feature appear in the **Tasks Panel**, see Figure 6.5. Also, the name of the selected sketch appears in the **Profile** field of the **Pipe parameters** sub-window in the **Tasks Panel**. Ignore the error message that may appear in the **Report view** window at the bottom of the screen after selecting the profile of the additive pipe feature. You can close the **Report view** window by clicking on the cross mark × that appears in its top right corner.

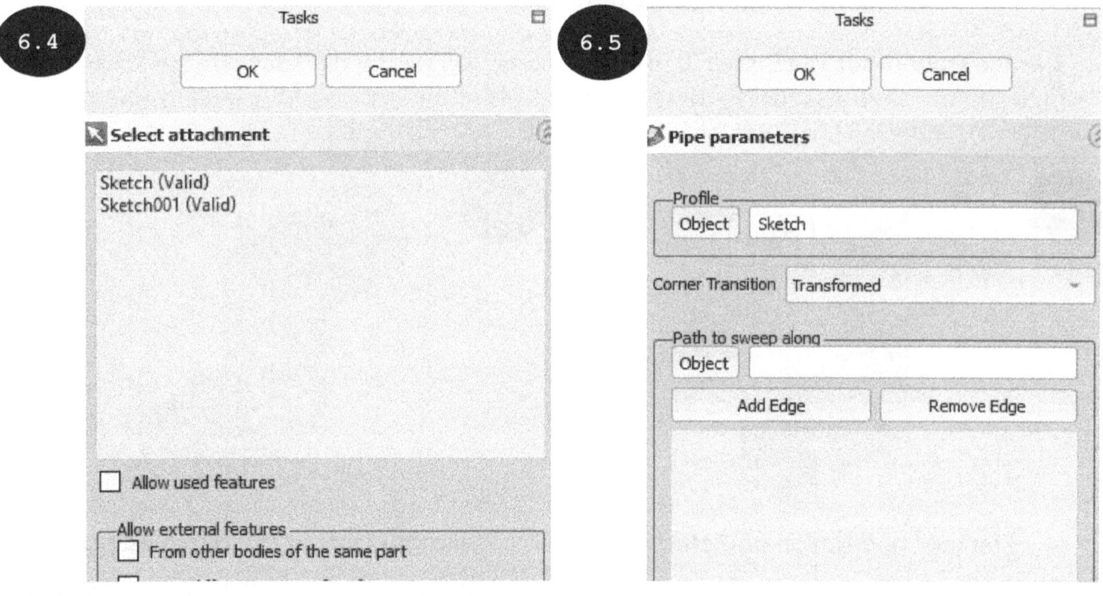

Tip: You can also select a closed sketch or a face of a 3D model as the profile of an additive feature prior to invoking the **Additive pipe** tool.

4. Click on the **Object** button in the **Path to sweep along** area of the **Pipe parameters** sub-window in the **Tasks Panel** (see Figure 6.6) for selecting a path of the additive pipe feature.

5. Select an open or closed sketch as the path of the feature. A preview of the additive pipe feature appears in the 3D View area, see Figure 6.7. Note that on selecting an entity of a sketch, the whole sketch gets selected as the path of the feature.

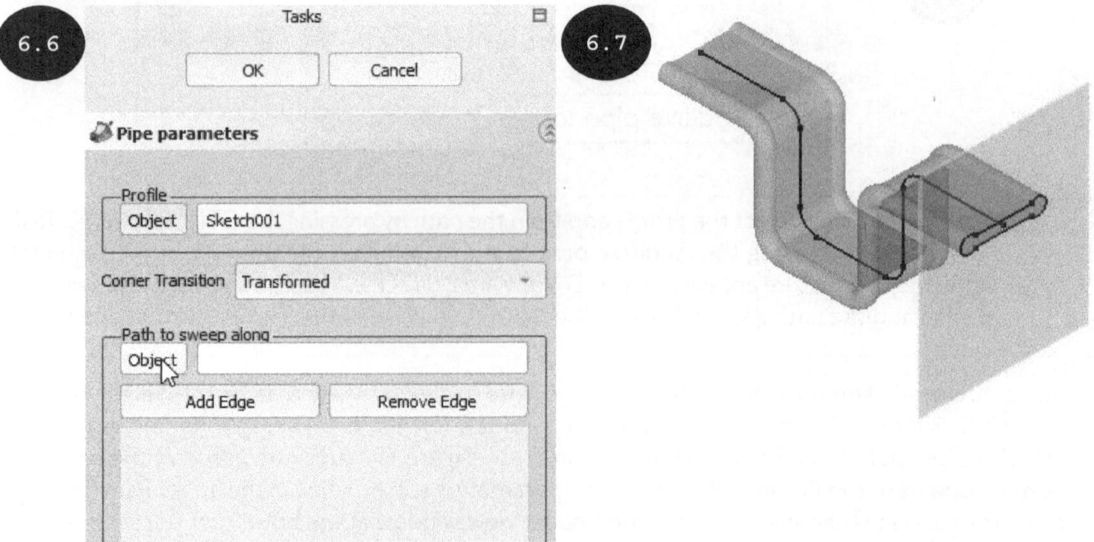

The options to control other settings such as corner transition and orientation of an additive pipe feature in the **Tasks Panel** are discussed next.

Corner Transition: The **Corner Transition** drop-down list is used for defining the transformed, right corner, or round corner transition of the profile at the corners of the path by selecting the respective options, see Figures 6.8 through 6.10.

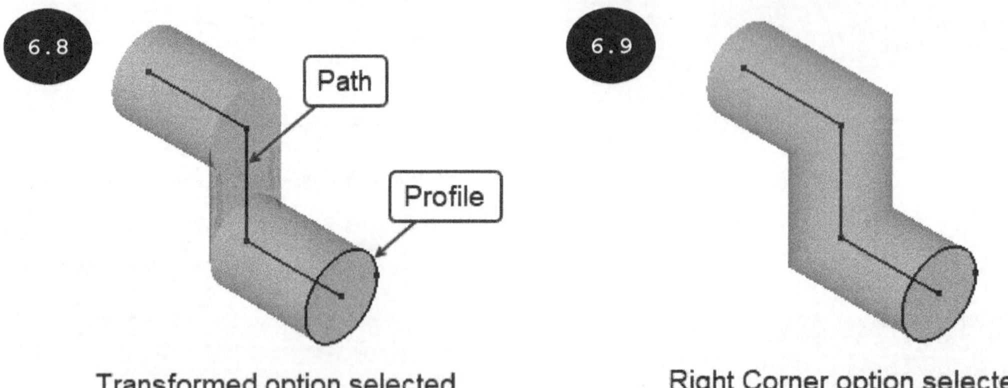

Transformed option selected

Right Corner option selected

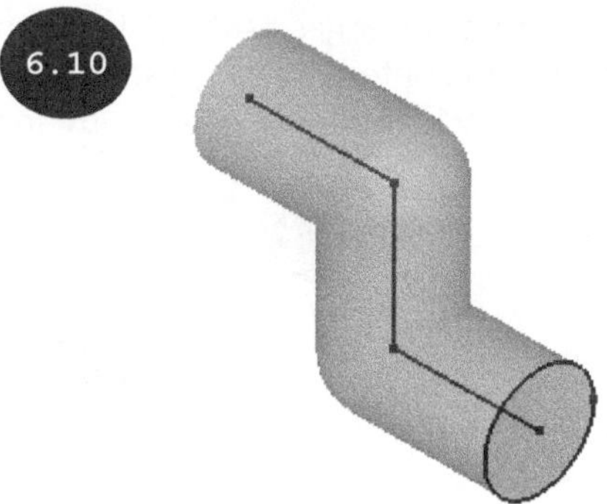

Round Corner option selected

Add Edge: The **Add Edge** button is used for selecting a single sketch entity or an edge of a 3D model as the path of an additive pipe feature. To do so, click on the **Add Edge** button in the **Tasks Panel** and then select a sketch entity or an edge of a 3D model as the path of the additive pipe feature in the 3D View area, see Figures 6.11 and 6.12. The preview of an additive pipe feature appears such that the profile follows only the selected sketch entity or the edge, see Figures 6.11 and 6.12. Also, the name of the selected sketch entity or edge appears in the selection field that appears below the **Add Edge** button in the **Tasks Panel**.

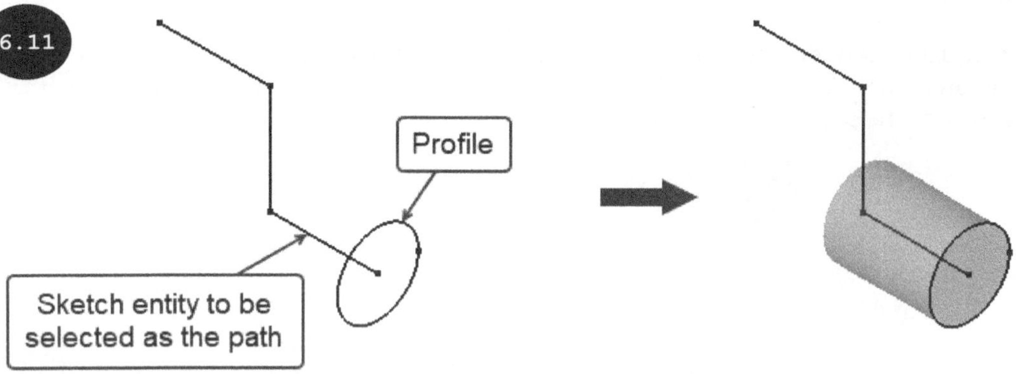

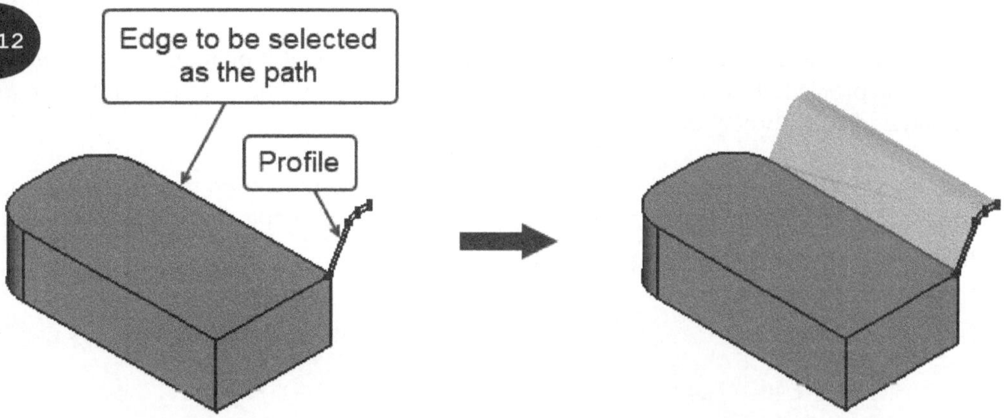

You can also select multiple sketch entities or edges as the path of an additive pipe feature by clicking on the **Add Edge** button every time before making a selection, see Figures 6.13 and 6.14. Note that you must select continuous sketch entities or edges with no branches.

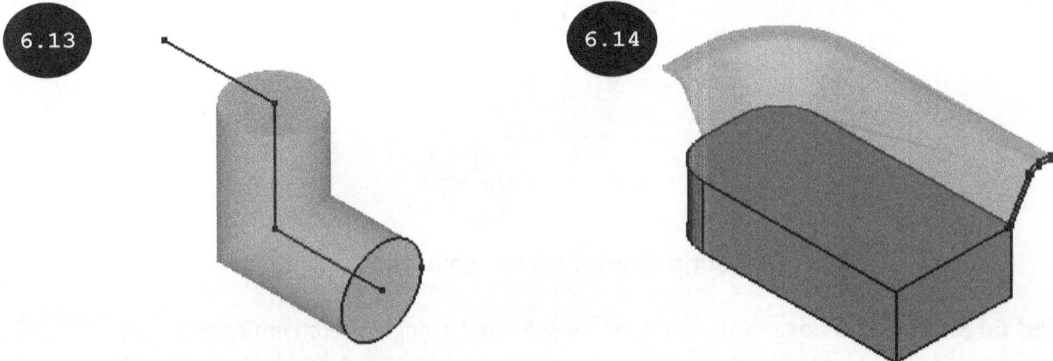

Remove Edge: The **Remove Edge** button is used for removing a sketch entity or an edge from the list of entities/edges selected as the path of the additive pipe feature. To do so, click on the **Remove Edge** button in the **Tasks Panel** and then click on a sketch entity or edge in the 3D View area to be removed from the path selection set. Note that you need to click on the **Remove Edge** button every time before removing a sketch entity or edge from the path selection set.

Orientation mode: The options in the **Orientation mode** drop-down list of the **Section orientation** sub-window are used for controlling the orientation of the profile along the path, see Figure 6.15. The options are discussed next.

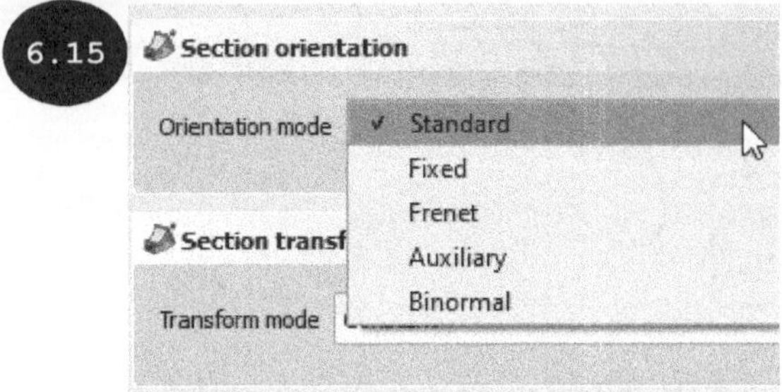

Standard: By default, the **Standard** option is selected in the **Orientation mode** drop-down list. As a result, the profile follows the path such that the cross-section shape of the resultant feature is kept perpendicular throughout the path, see Figure 6.16.

Fixed: On selecting the **Fixed** option, the profile follows the path such that it remains parallel throughout the path, see Figure 6.17. It means the cross-section shape of the resultant feature will not be rotated with the path and kept constant throughout.

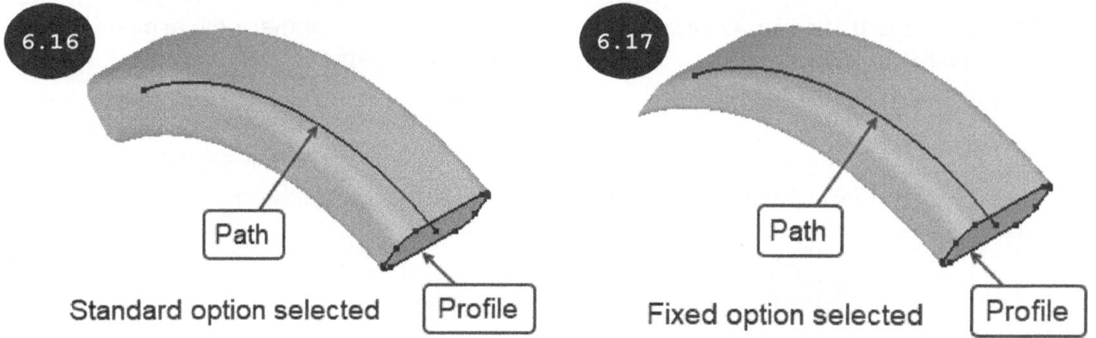

Frenet: On selecting the **Frenet** option, a minimum possible twisting is applied to the profile while following the path, see Figure 6.18. This figure shows a path, a profile, and the preview of the resultant additive pipe feature when the **Frenet** option is selected. Figure 6.19 shows the preview of an additive pipe feature when the **Standard** option is selected to better understand the difference between the **Frenet** and **Standard** options.

6.18

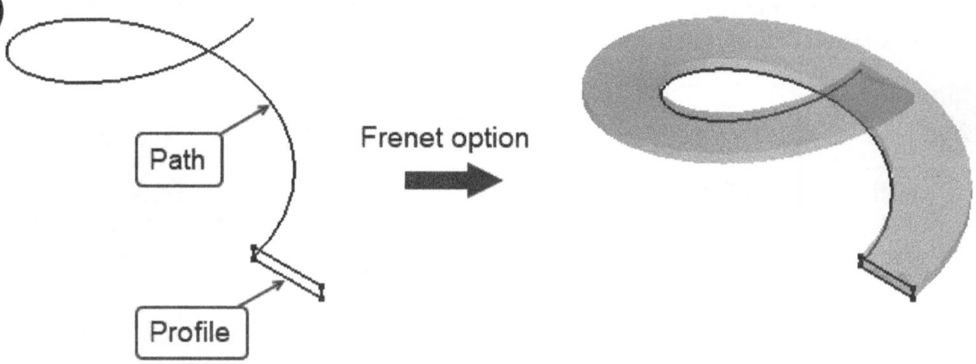

Path

Frenet option

Profile

6.19

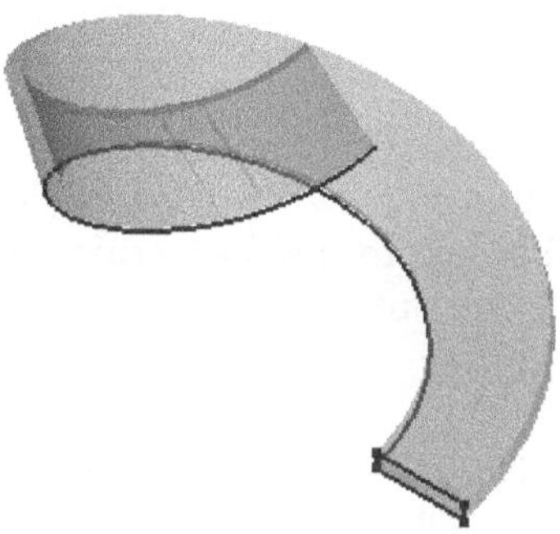

Note: In Figures 6.18 and 6.19, a helical curve is selected as the path of the additive pipe feature. You will learn about creating a helical curve later in this chapter.

Auxiliary: On selecting the **Auxiliary** option, the **Profile** area appears in the **Section orientation** sub-window of the **Tasks Panel** for selecting a secondary path to guide the profile of the additive pipe feature, see Figure 6.20.

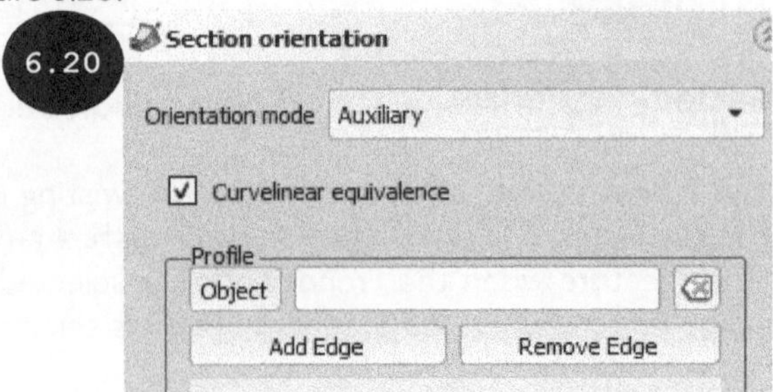

After selecting the **Auxiliary** option in the **Orientation mode** drop-down list, click on the **Object** button in the **Profile** area that appears and then select a secondary path (guide curve) to guide the orientation of the profile while following the path, see Figure 6.21.

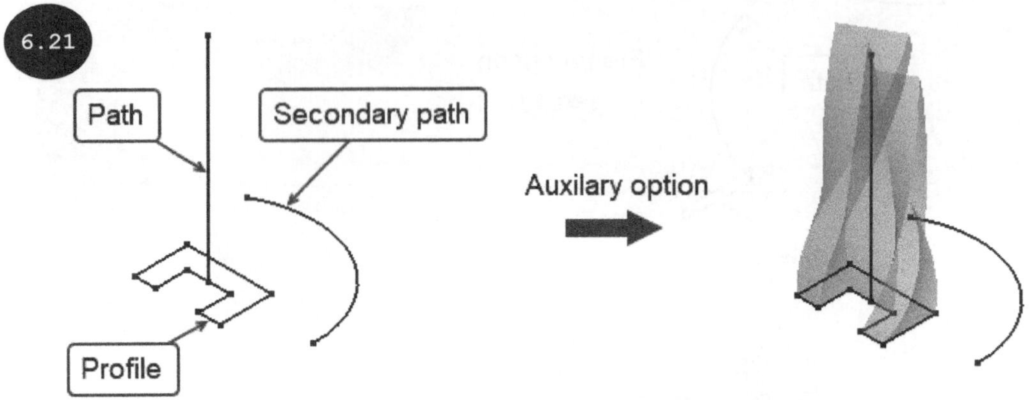

Tip: In Figure 6.21, an arc is created on the XY Plane (top plane) as the secondary path to guide the orientation of the profile. Also, the profile is created on the XY Plane (top plane), and the path is created on the XZ Plane (front plane) as separate sketches.

Binormal: On selecting the **Binormal** option, the **X**, **Y**, and **Z** fields appear in the **Selection orientation** sub-window of the **Tasks Panel** (see Figure 6.22) for specifying the respective binormal vector to define the orientation of the profile.

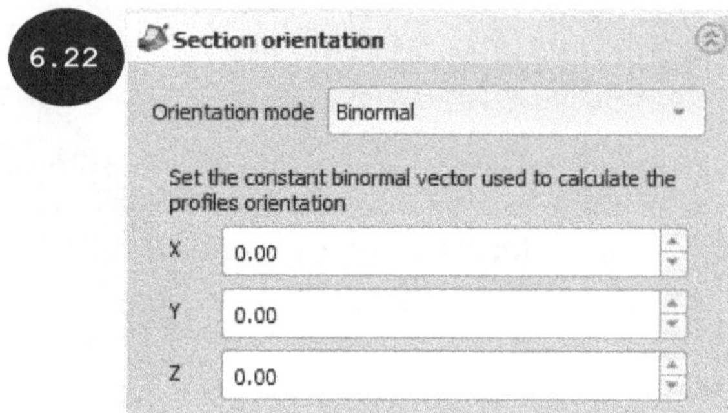

Transform mode: By default, the **Constant** option is selected in the **Transform mode** drop-down list of the **Section transformation** sub-window in the **Tasks Panel**, see Figure 6.23. As a result, you can create an additive pipe feature by using a single profile, see Figure 6.24. This figure shows an additive pipe feature created by using a single profile. Note that it has a constant cross-section.

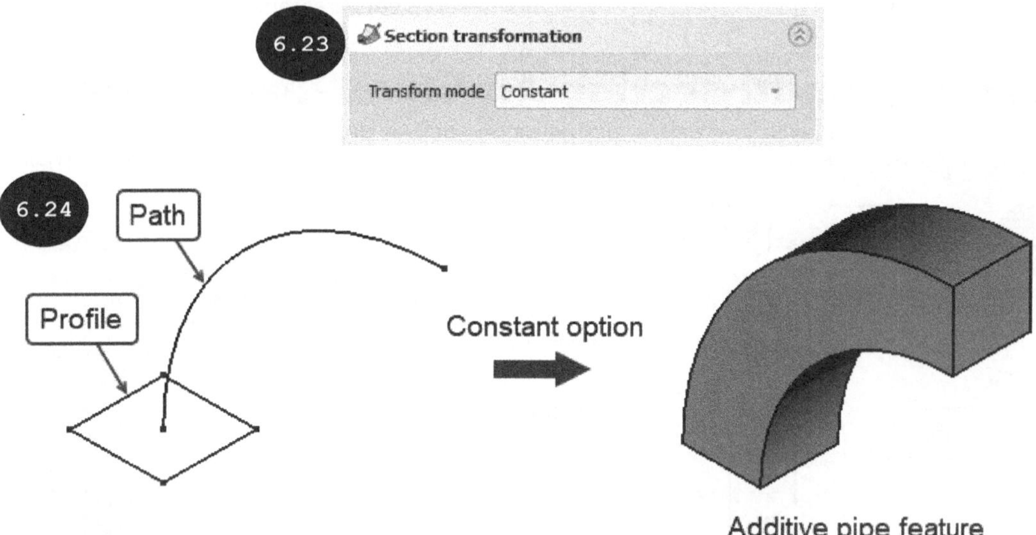

On selecting the **Multisection** option in the **Transform mode** drop-down list of the **Section transformation** sub-window (see Figure 6.25), you can create an additive pipe feature by using multiple profiles, see Figure 6.26. In this figure, an additive pipe feature is created by using two different profiles. You will learn about creating a multi-section additive pipe feature later in this chapter.

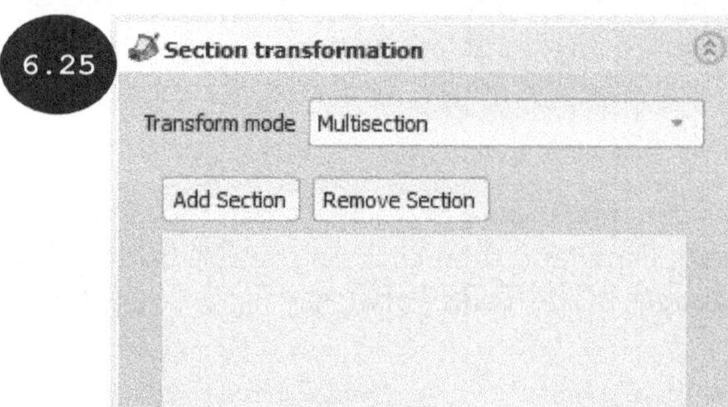

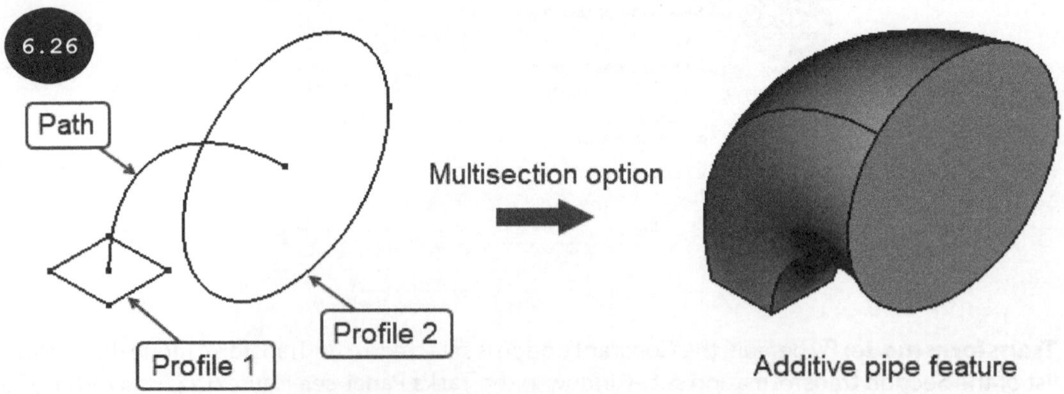

6. After selecting the required options for creating an additive pipe feature, click on the **OK** button in the **Tasks Panel**. An additive feature of specified settings gets created.

Creating a Multi-section Additive Pipe Feature

As discussed earlier, you can also create a multi-section additive pipe feature by using two or more profiles, see Figure 6.27. The method for creating a multi-section additive pipe feature is discussed below:

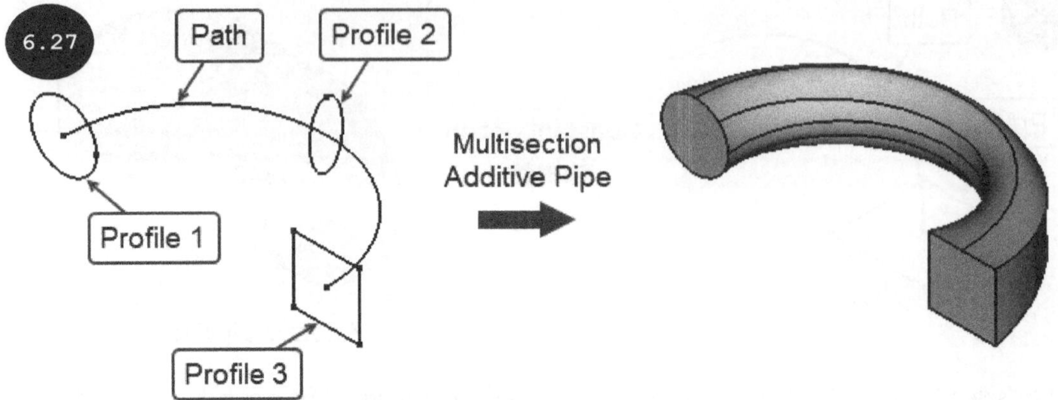

1. Create a path and the required number of profiles as separate sketches for creating a multi-section additive pipe feature, refer to Figure 6.27.

2. After creating a path and the required profiles, click on the **Additive pipe** tool in the **Part Design Modeling** toolbar, see Figure 6.28. The **Select feature** sub-window appears in the **Tasks Panel** and displays a list of sketches available in the 3D View area. Also, you are prompted to select a sketch as the profile of the feature.

3. Select a closed sketch as the first profile of the feature in the 3D View area or the **Select feature** sub-window of the **Tasks Panel** and then click on the **OK** button. The options for creating an additive pipe feature appear in the **Tasks Panel**, see Figure 6.29. Ignore the error message that

may appear in the **Report view** window at the bottom of the screen after selecting a profile. You can close the **Report view** window by clicking on the cross mark × that appears in its top right corner.

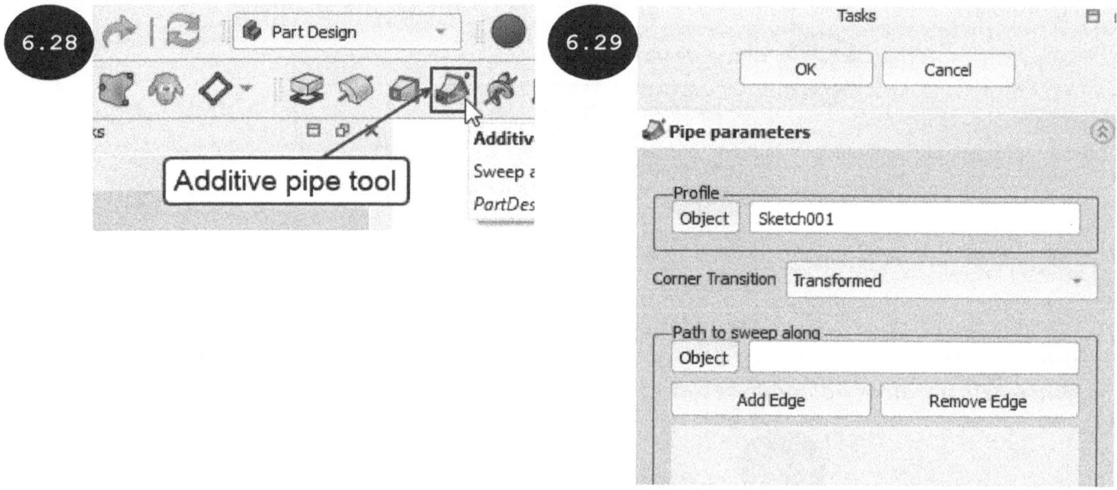

4. Click on the **Object** button in the **Path to sweep along** area of the **Pipe parameters** sub-window in the **Tasks Panel** (see Figure 6.30) and then select an open or a closed sketch as the path of the feature in the 3D View area. A preview of the additive pipe feature appears such that the profile follows the path, see Figure 6.31.

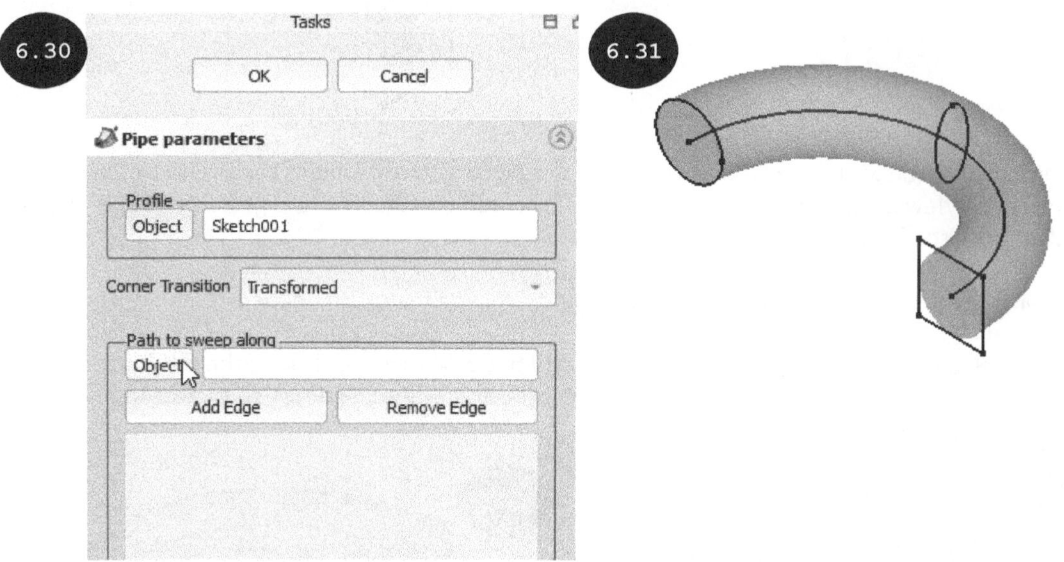

5. Select the **Multisection** option in the **Transform mode** drop-down list of the **Section transformation** sub-window for selecting multiple profiles to create a multi-section additive pipe feature, see Figure 6.32.

Now, you can select multiple profiles for creating a multi-section additive pipe feature.

6. Click on the **Add Section** button that appears below the **Transform mode** drop-down list, refer to Figure 6.32.

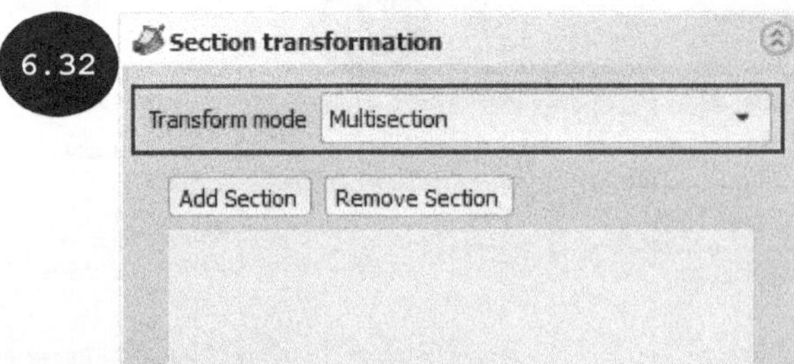

6.32

7. Select a closed sketch as the second profile of the additive pipe feature in the 3D View area. The preview of the additive pipe feature gets updated in the 3D View area such that its cross-sectional shape gets transformed from one profile to another while following the path, see Figure 6.33.

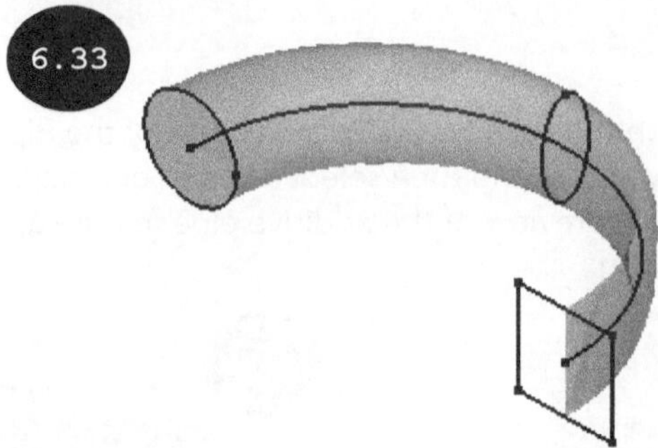
6.33

8. Click on the **Add Section** button again and then select the third profile of the additive pipe feature in the 3D View area, if needed. The preview of the additive pipe feature gets updated in the 3D View area, see Figure 6.34.

9. Similarly, you can select other profiles of the additive pipe feature, if needed.

10. After selecting all the required profiles of the additive pipe feature, click on the **OK** button in the **Tasks Panel**. A multi-section additive pipe feature of specified settings gets created in the 3D View area, see Figure 6.35.

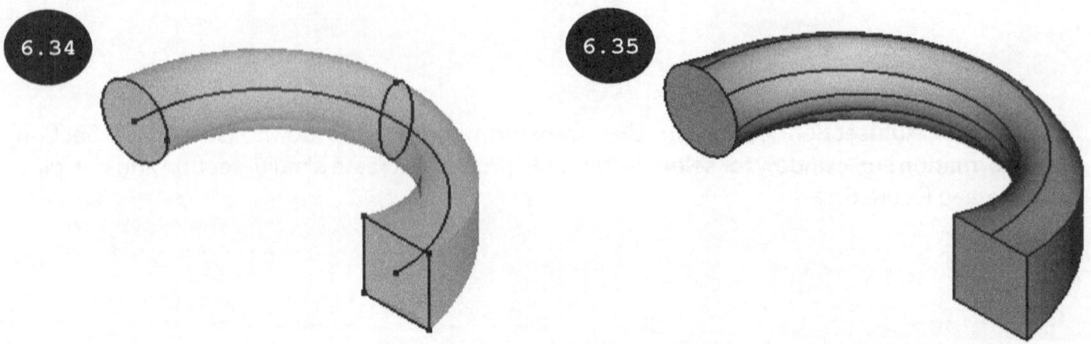
6.34 6.35

Creating a Subtractive Pipe Feature

In FreeCAD, you can create a subtractive pipe feature like that of creating an additive pipe feature with the only difference being that the subtractive pipe feature is created by subtracting or removing material from an existing body, see Figure 6.36. The method for creating a subtractive pipe feature is discussed below:

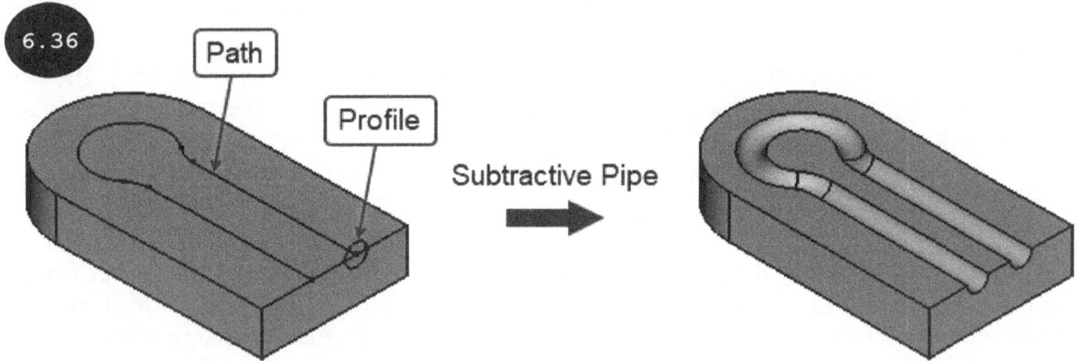

1. Create a path and a profile of a subtractive pipe feature as separate sketches one by one in the **Sketcher** workbench, refer to Figure 6.37.

Note: In Figure 6.37, the path is created on the top planar face of the model and the profile is created on the right planar face of the model as separate sketches.

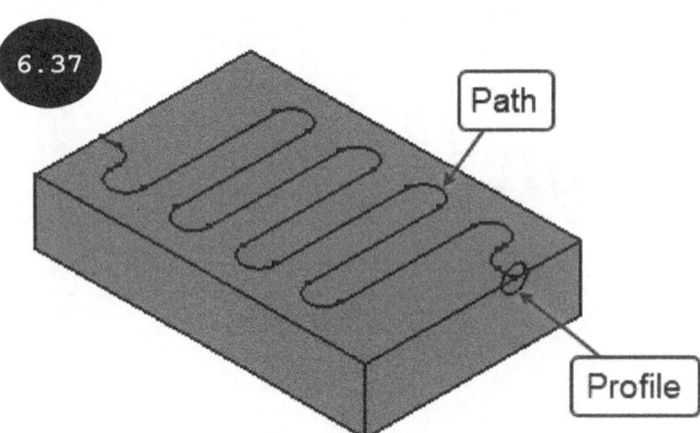

2. After creating a path and a profile, click on the **Subtractive pipe** tool in the **Part Design Modeling** toolbar, see Figure 6.38. The **Select feature** sub-window appears in the **Tasks Panel** and displays a list of sketches available in the 3D View area. Also, you are prompted to select a sketch as the profile of the feature.

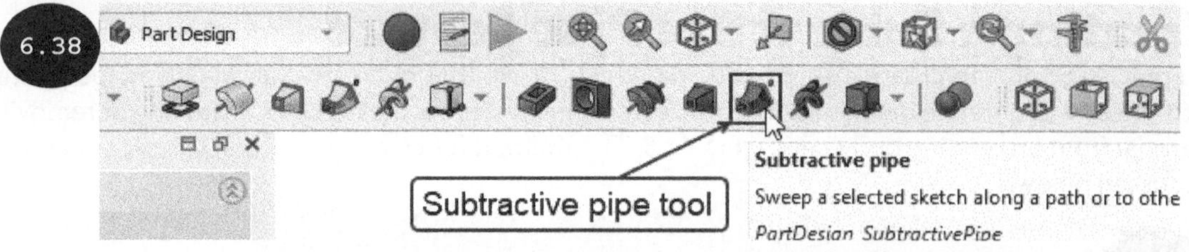

Note: You can also first select the profile and then the path by pressing the CTRL key in the **Task Panel** before invoking the **Subtractive pipe** tool. On doing so, the preview of the resultant subtractive pipe feature appears in the 3D View area, directly. Also, the names of the selected profile and the path get displayed in the respective fields of the **Task Panel** that appears.

3. Select a closed sketch as the profile of the feature in the 3D View area or the **Select feature** sub-window of the **Tasks Panel** and then click on the **OK** button. The options for creating a subtractive pipe feature appear in the **Tasks Panel**, see Figure 6.39. Also, the name of the selected sketch appears in the **Profile** field of the **Pipe parameters** sub-window in the **Tasks Panel**. Ignore the error message that may appear in the **Report view** window at the bottom of the screen after selecting the profile of the subtractive pipe feature. You can close the **Report view** window by clicking on the cross mark × that appears in its top right corner.

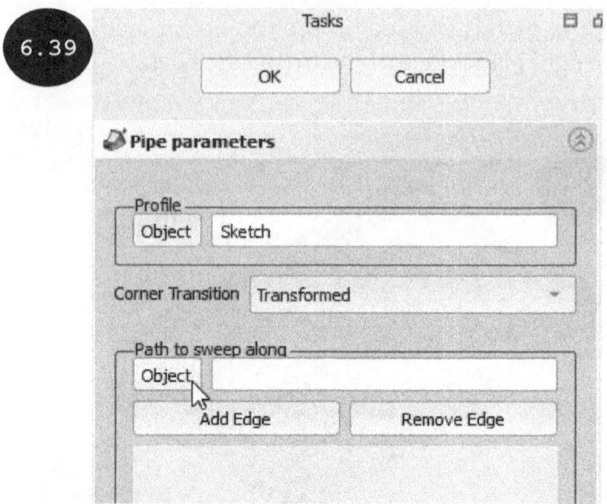

4. Click on the **Object** button in the **Path to sweep along** area of the **Pipe parameters** sub-window in the **Tasks Panel** (refer to Figure 6.39) for selecting a path of the subtractive pipe feature.

5. Select an open or closed sketch as the path of the feature. A preview of the subtractive pipe feature appears in the 3D View area, see Figure 6.40. Note that on selecting an entity of a sketch, the whole sketch gets selected as the path of the feature.

6. Click on the **OK** button in the **Tasks Panel**. A subtractive pipe feature is created by removing the material from the model, see Figure 6.41.

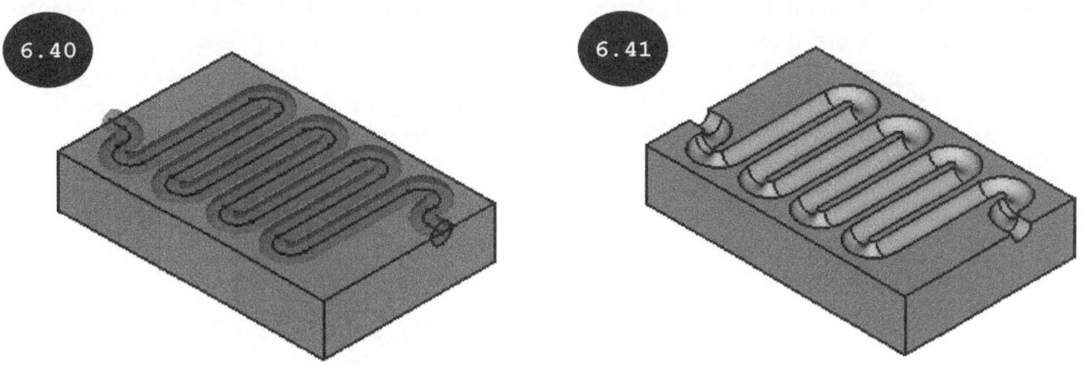

Note: In the **Task Panel**, the options to control the corner transition and orientation settings of a subtractive pipe feature are the same as discussed earlier.

Creating an Additive Loft Feature

An additive loft feature is created by making a transition between two or more profiles. Figure 6.42 shows three different profiles and the resultant additive loft feature.

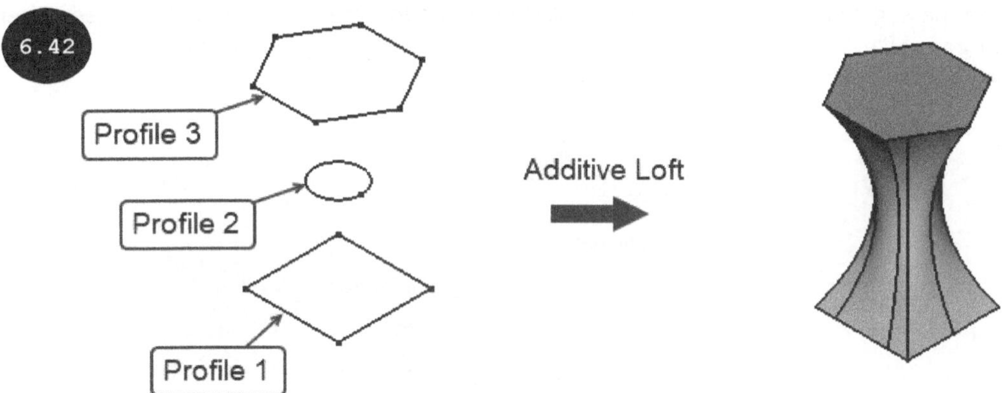

To create an additive loft feature, you first need to create all its profiles that define its cross-sectional shape. In FreeCAD, you can create an additive loft feature by using the **Additive Loft** tool. Note that for creating an additive loft feature, you need to be sure of the following:

- Two or more similar or dissimilar sketch profiles must be available in the 3D View area before invoking the **Additive Loft** tool.
- Profiles must be closed sketches. You can also select faces or edges as profiles.
- All sketch profiles must be created as separate sketches.
- The profiles and the resultant loft feature must not be self intersect.

The method for creating an additive loft feature is discussed below:

1. Create all profiles of the loft feature as separate sketches one by one in the 3D View Area, refer to Figure 6.43. In this figure, three closed sketches are created as profiles on different planes.

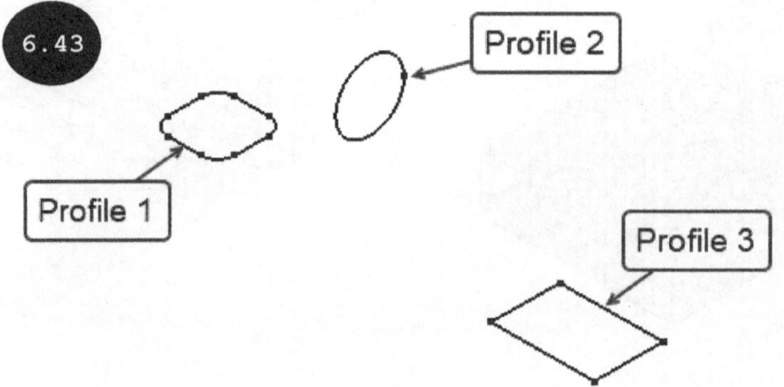

2. After creating the profiles, click on the **Additive loft** tool in the **Part Design Modeling** toolbar, see Figure 6.44. The **Select feature** sub-window appears in the **Tasks Panel** and displays a list of sketches available in the 3D View area.

3. Select a closed sketch as the profile of the feature in the 3D View area or the **Select feature** sub-window of the **Tasks Panel** and then click on the **OK** button. The options for creating an additive loft feature appear in the **Tasks Panel**, see Figure 6.45. Also, the name of the selected sketch appears in the **Profile** field of the **Loft parameters** sub-window in the **Tasks Panel**. Ignore the error message that may appear in the **Report view** window at the bottom of the screen after selecting a profile. You can close the **Report view** window by clicking on the cross mark × that appears in its top right corner.

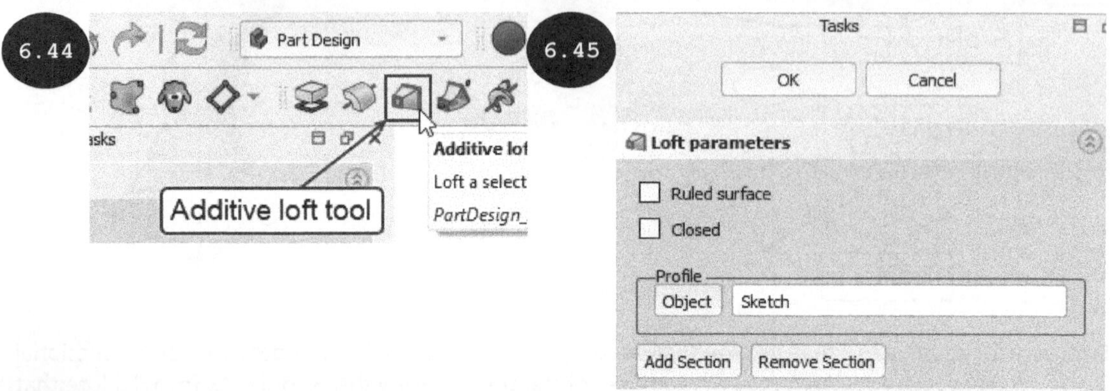

Tip: You can also select two or more sketches as the profiles of an additive loft feature prior to invoking the **Additive loft** tool.

Moreover, you can also select a face as the profile of a loft feature.

4. Click on the **Add Section** button in the **Loft parameters** sub-window (see Figure 6.46) and then select the second profile of the loft feature. The preview of an additive loft feature appears in the

3D View area, see Figure 6.47. Note that you can select a closed sketch or a face of an existing feature as the profile of a loft feature.

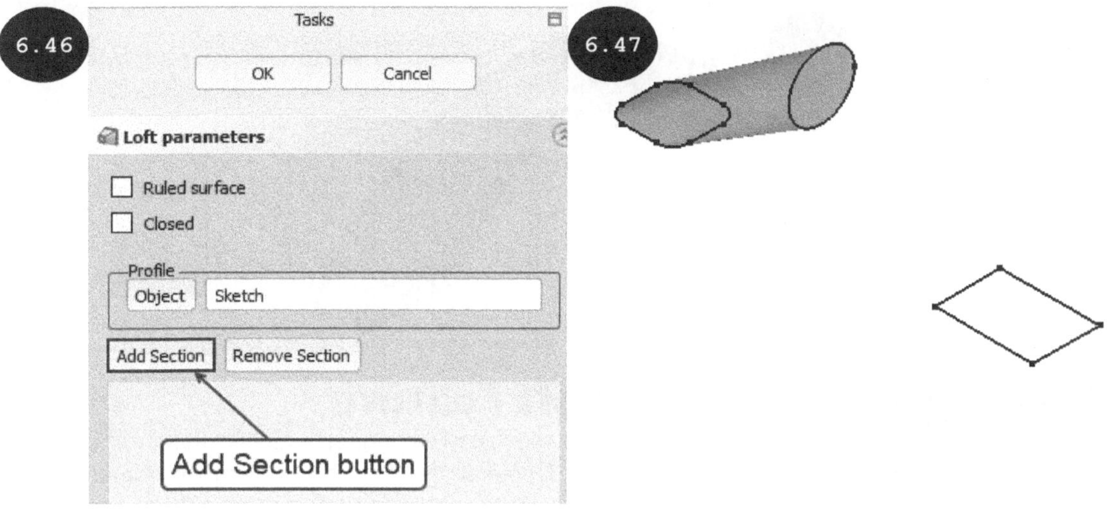

5. Click on the **Add Section** button again in the **Loft parameters** sub-window and then select the third profile of the loft feature in the 3D View area, if needed. The preview of the loft feature gets updated in the 3D View area, see Figure 6.48.

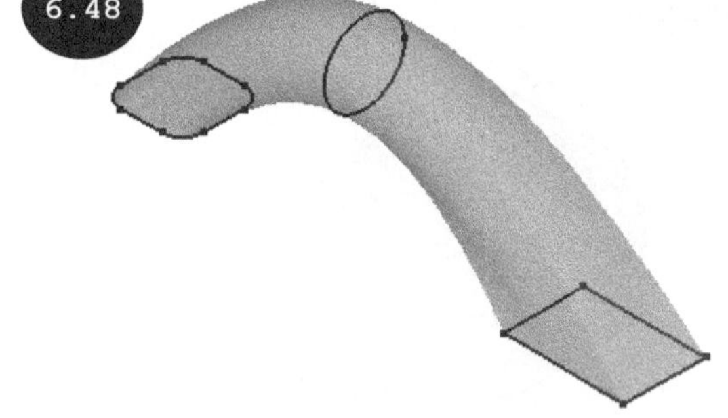

6. Similarly, you can select other profiles of the additive loft feature by using the **Add Section** button, if needed.

7. Ensure that the **Ruled surface** check box is cleared in the **Tasks Panel** for creating an additive loft feature with smooth transitions between its profiles, see Figure 6.49. On selecting this **Ruled surface** check box, the additive loft feature will be created with straight transitions between its profiles or cross-sections, see Figure 6.50.

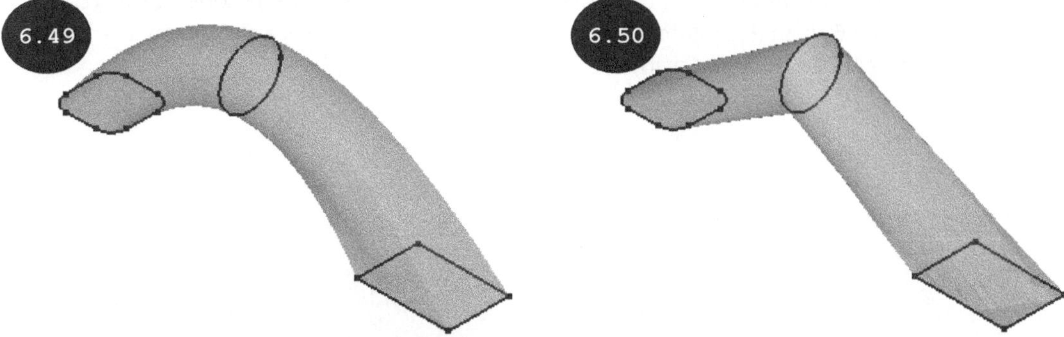

Ruled surface check box is cleared

Ruled surface check box is selected

8. After selecting all the profiles (sections) of the additive loft feature, click on the **OK** button in the **Tasks Panel**. The additive loft feature gets created, see Figure 6.51.

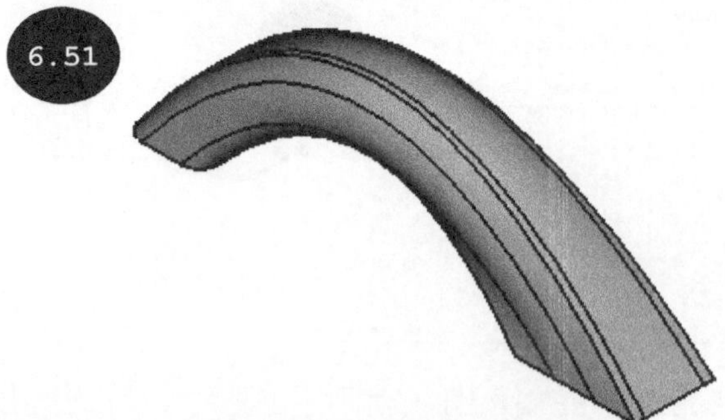

Creating a Subtractive Loft Feature

In FreeCAD, you can create a subtractive loft feature like that of creating an additive loft feature with the only difference being that the subtractive loft feature is created by subtracting or removing material from an existing body, see Figure 6.52. The method for creating a subtractive loft feature is discussed below:

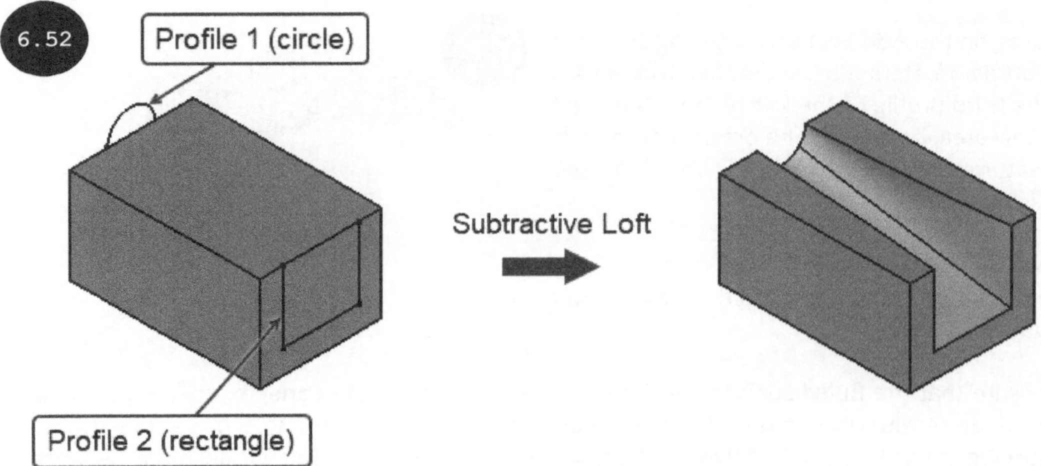

1. Create all profiles of a subtractive loft feature as separate sketches one by one in the 3D View Area, refer to Figure 6.53. In this figure, three closed sketches (an ellipse, a circle, and a rectangle) are created as profiles on different planes.

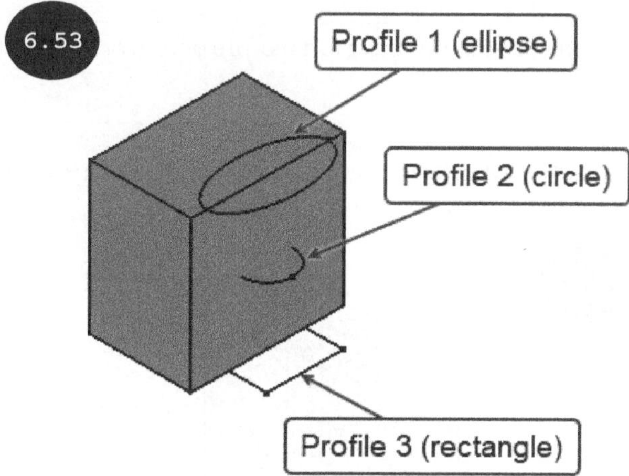

Note: In Figure 6.53, half a portion of Profile 2 (circle) and Profile 3 (rectangle) overlap or pass into the existing object, so they are not completely visible.

Now, you can create the subtractive loft feature.

2. Select all the profiles in the **Tasks Panel** by pressing the CTRL key and then click on the **Subtractive loft** tool in the **Part Design Modeling** toolbar, see Figure 6.54. The preview of a subtractive loft feature appears in the 3D View area, see Figure 6.55. Also, the **Loft parameters** sub-window appears in the **Tasks Panel**. The options in this sub-window are the same as discussed earlier.

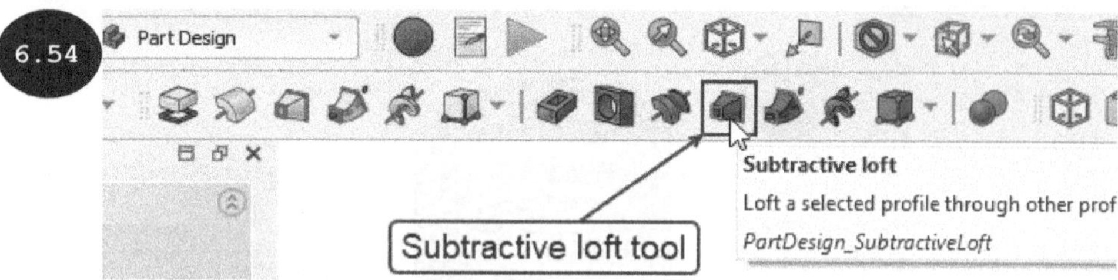

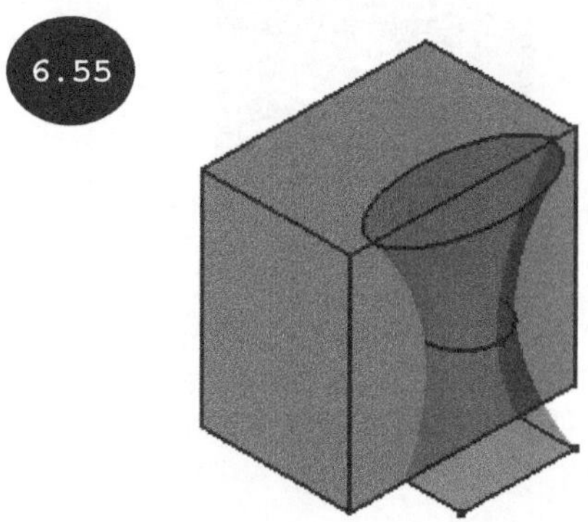

Tip: You can select the profiles of a subtractive loft feature before or after invoking the **Subtractive loft** tool.

3. Click on the **OK** button in the **Tasks Panel**. The subtractive loft feature is created by removing the material from the model, see Figure 6.56.

6.56

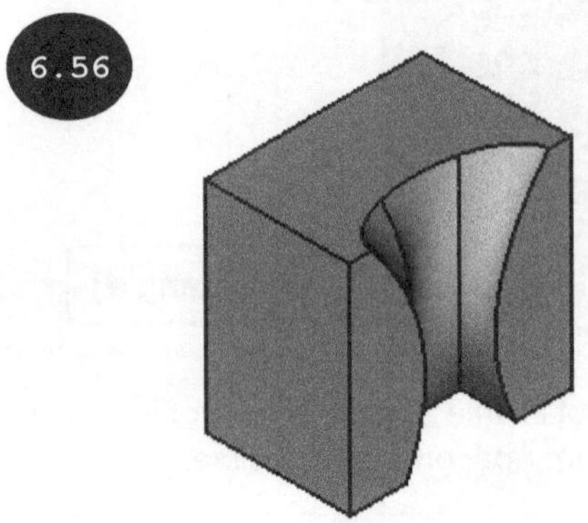

Creating an Additive Helix Feature

In FreeCAD, you can create an additive helix feature by sweeping a closed sketch (profile) along a helix path around an axis, see Figure 6.57. In this figure, an additive helix feature (helical coil) is created by sweeping a rectangular sketch around the vertical axis. The method for creating an additive helix feature is discussed below:

6.57

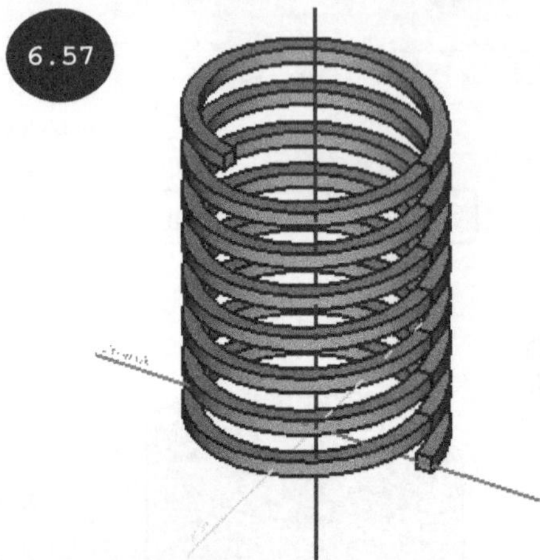

1. Create a closed sketch as the profile of an additive helix feature in the **Sketcher** workbench, see Figure 6.58. In this figure, a circle is created as the profile of the helix feature. After creating a sketch, exit the **Sketcher** workbench to switch back to the **Part Design** workbench.

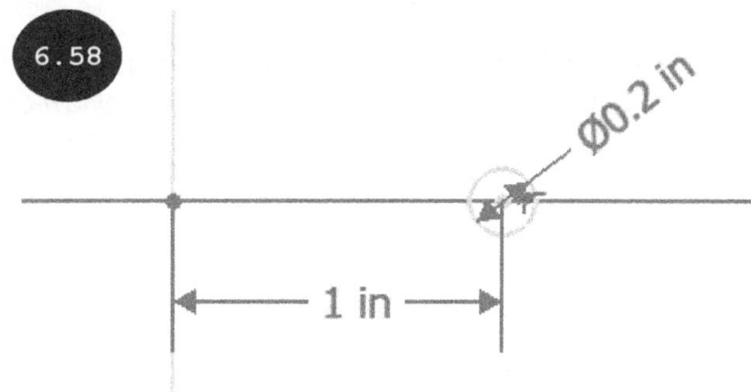

Note: The sketch of an additive helix feature should be a closed sketch and on either side of its axis of revolution.

2. Click on the **Additive helix** tool in the **Part Design Modeling** toolbar, see Figure 6.59. The preview of an additive helix feature appears in the 3D View area by revolving the sketch along a helix path around the vertical axis of the sketch, see Figure 6.60. It is because the **Vertical sketch axis** option is selected, by default in the **Axis** drop-down list of the **Helix parameters** sub-window that appears in the **Tasks Panel**, see Figure 6.61.

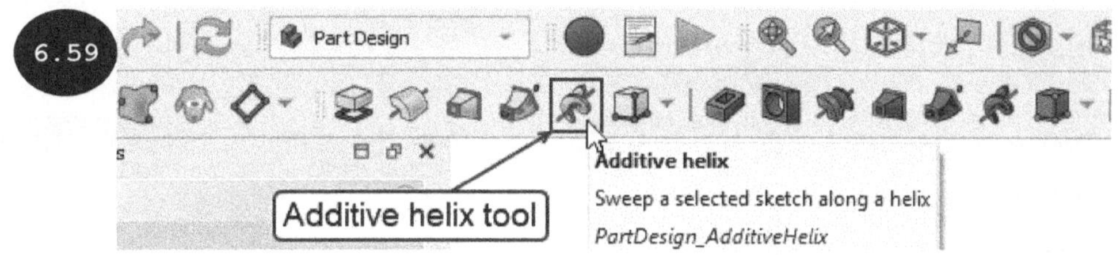

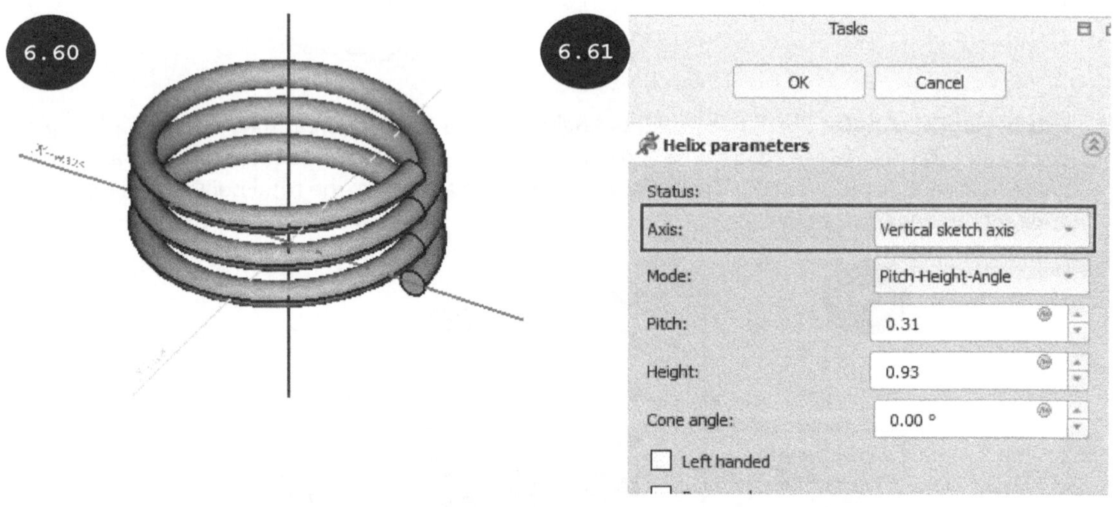

Note: If the sketch of an additive helix feature is not on either side of its vertical axis, then on invoking the **Additive helix** tool, an error will occur, and a preview of the feature does not appear in the 3D View area. This happens because the sketch cannot be revolved about its vertical axis that intersects it. In this case you need to define an axis of revolution for the sketch other than its vertical axis by selecting the required option in the **Axis** drop-down list of the **Helix parameters** sub-window.

3. Specify the required option in the **Axis** drop-down list of the **Helix parameters** sub-window for defining the axis of revolution of the feature, see Figure 6.62. The options in this drop-down list are the same as discussed in earlier chapters while creating a revolution feature.

4. Specify the required option in the **Mode** drop-down list of the **Helix parameters** sub-window for creating a helix by specifying the respective set of parameters, see Figure 6.63. The options are discussed next.

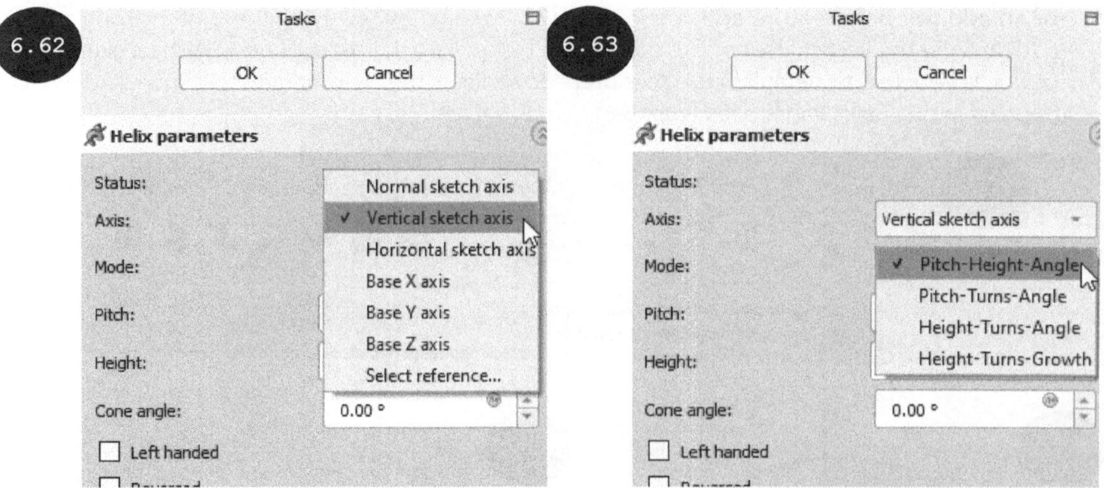

Pitch-Height-Angle: The Pitch-Height-Angle option is used for creating a helix by defining its pitch and total height, see Figure 6.64. When this option is selected, the **Pitch**, **Height**, and **Cone angle** fields are displayed in the **Tasks Panel** for defining the pitch, the total height, and the taper angle of the helix, respectively.

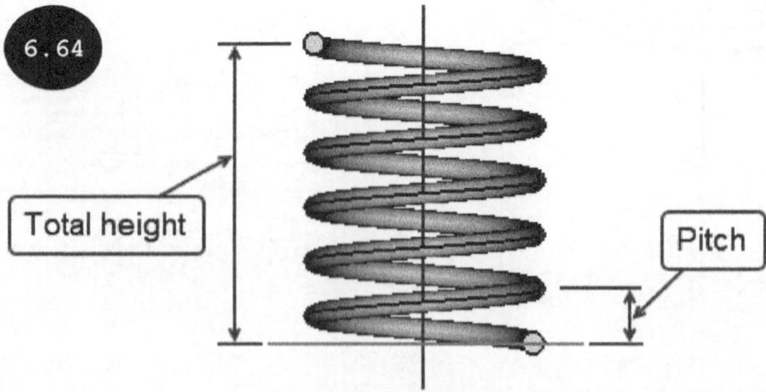

Note: On specifying a taper angle value in the **Cone angle** field of the **Task Panel**, you can create a tapered helix of a defined angle, see Figure 6.65.

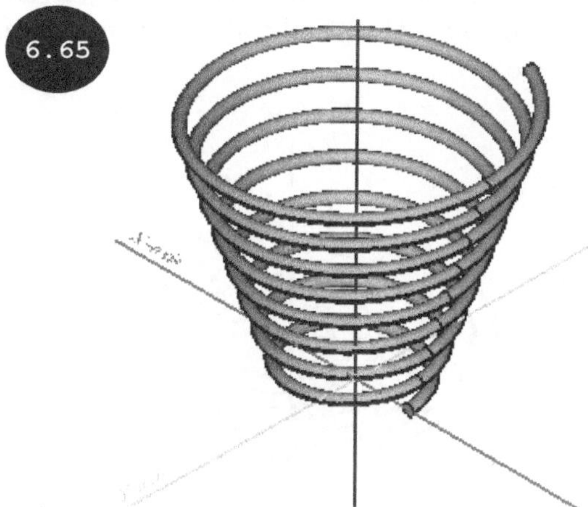
6.65

Pitch-Turns-Angle: The **Pitch-Turns-Angle** option is used for creating a helix by defining its pitch and number of revolutions (turns). When this option is selected, the **Pitch**, **Turns**, and **Cone angle** fields get enabled in the dialog box for defining the pitch, the number of revolutions, and the taper angle of the helix, respectively.

Height-Turns-Angle: The **Height-Turns-Angle** option is used for creating a helix by defining its total height and number of revolutions (turns). When this option is selected, the **Height**, **Turns**, and **Cone angle** fields get enabled in the dialog box for defining the total height, the number of revolutions (turns), and the taper angle of the helix, respectively.

Height-Turns-Growth: The **Height-Turns-Growth** option is used for creating a helix by defining its total height, number of revolutions (turns), and incremental growth of the helical radius, see Figure 6.66. When this option is selected, the **Height**, **Turns**, and **Radial growth** fields get enabled in the **Tasks Panel** for defining the total height, the number of revolutions (turns), and the incremental growth value of the helical radius of the helix, respectively.

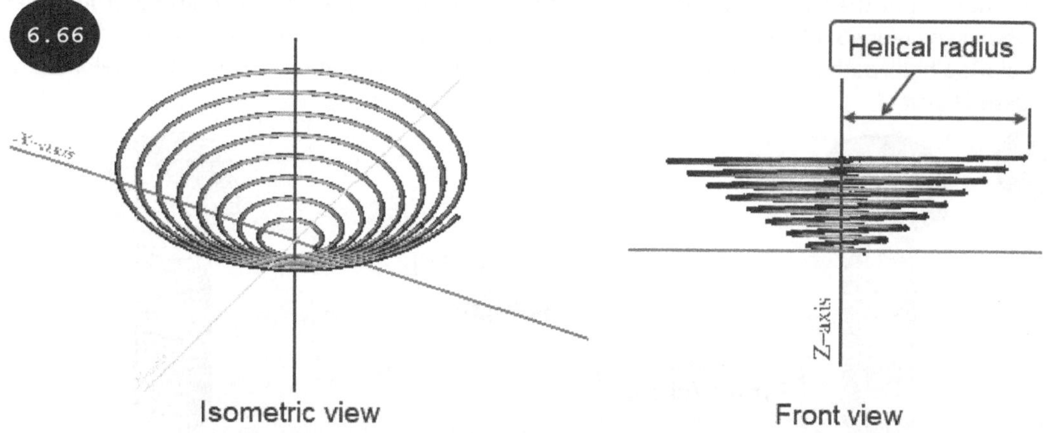

6.66

Note: You can also create a spiral coil by using the **Height-Turns-Growth** option, see Figure 6.67. For doing so, after selecting the **Height-Turns-Growth** option in the **Mode** drop-down list, enter **0** in the **Height** field and then enter the required number of revolutions (turns) and the incremental growth of the helical radius in the respective **Turns** and **Radial growth** fields of the **Task Panel**. The preview of a spiral coil of specified parameters appears in the 3D View area, see Figure 6.67.

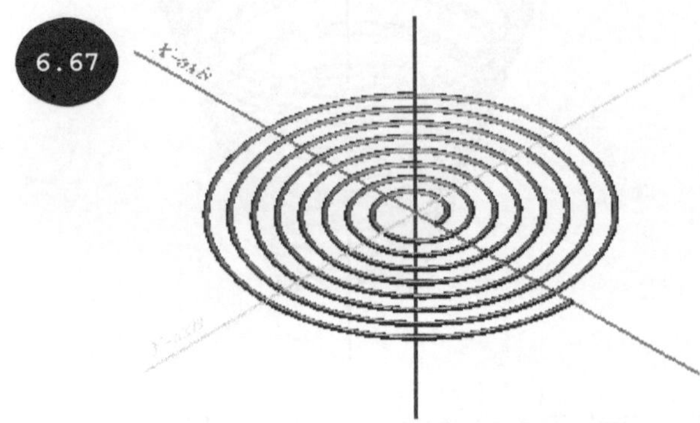
6.67

5. Specify the required parameters for creating an additive helix feature depending upon the option selected in the **Mode** drop-down list of the **Tasks Panel**, as discussed above.

6. Select the **Left handed** check box to reverse the direction of the helix from default clockwise to counterclockwise if needed.

7. Select the **Reversed** check box to reverse the axis direction of the helix to its other side, if needed.

8. After specifying all the required parameters for creating an additive helix feature, click on the **OK** button in the **Tasks Panel**. The additive helix feature of specified parameters gets created.

Creating a Subtractive Helix Feature

In FreeCAD, you can create a subtractive helix like that of creating an additive helix feature with the only difference that the subtractive helix is created by subtracting or removing material from an existing body, see Figure 6.68. In this figure, a subtractive helix feature is created by sweeping a circular profile along a helix path around the vertical axis. The method for creating a subtractive helix feature is discussed below:

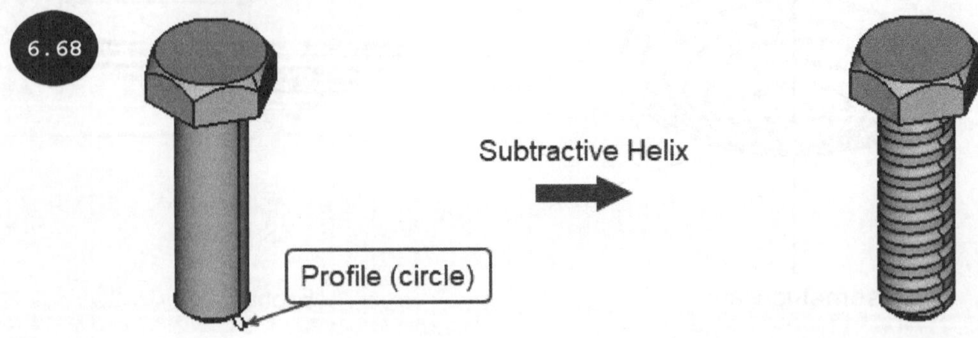

6.68

1. Create a closed sketch as the profile of a subtractive helix feature, see Figure 6.69. In this figure, a rectangle is created as the profile of the helix feature.

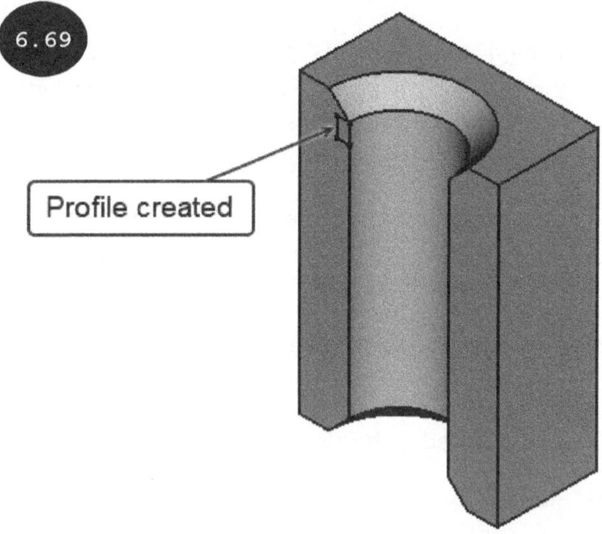

2. Click on the **Subtractive helix** tool in the **Part Design Modeling** toolbar, see Figure 6.70. The preview of a subtractive helix feature appears with default parameters in the 3D View area, see Figure 6.71. Also, the **Helix parameters** sub-window appears in the **Tasks Panel** with the **Vertical sketch axis** option selected in its **Axis** drop-down list, by default. As a result, the preview of a subtractive helix feature appears by revolving the profile around the vertical axis.

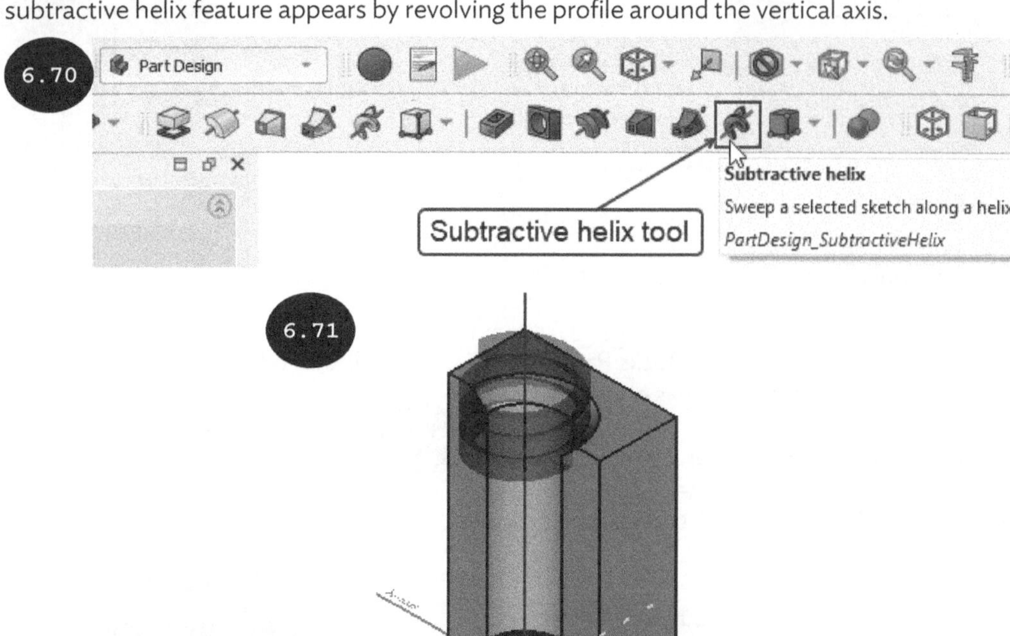

3. Specify the required option in the **Axis** drop-down list of the **Helix parameters** sub-window for defining the axis of revolution. The options in this drop-down list are the same as discussed earlier.

4. Specify the required option (**Pitch-Height-Angle**, **Pitch-Turns-Angle**, **Height-Turns-Angle**, or **Height-Turns-Growth**) in the **Mode** drop-down list of the **Helix parameters** sub-window for creating a helix, see Figure 6.72. The options in this drop-down list are the same as discussed earlier.

5. Specify the required parameters for creating a subtractive helix feature in the respective fields of the **Tasks Panel.** Note that the availability of fields for specifying the parameters depends upon the option selected in the **Mode** drop-down list of the **Tasks Panel**.

6. Select the **Left handed** check box to reverse the direction of the helix, if needed.

7. Select the **Reversed** check box to reverse the axis direction of the helix to its other side, if needed. The preview of the feature gets updated in the 3D View area, see Figure 6.73.

6.72

6.73

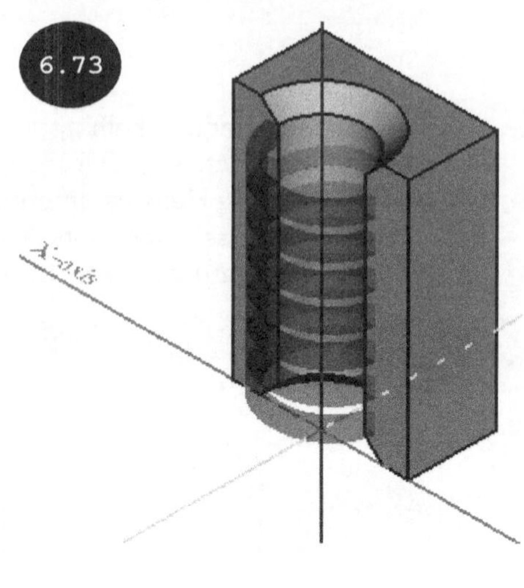

Note that all the options in the **Tasks Panel** are the same as discussed earlier except the **Remove outside of profile** option, which is discussed next.

Remove outside of profile: On selecting the **Remove outside of profile** check box, only the intersection of the helix and the existing body will be retained in the resultant feature.

6.74

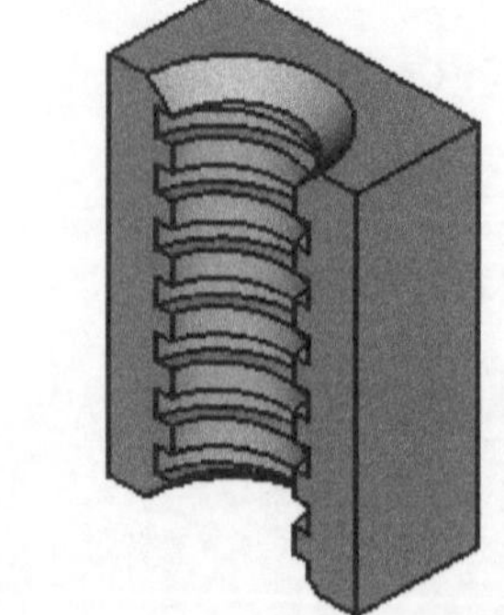

8. After specifying all the required parameters, click on the **OK** button in the **Tasks Panel**. The subtractive helix feature of specified parameters gets created, see Figure 6.74.

Creating a Helical Curve

In FreeCAD, you can create a helical curve as a primitive in the **Part** workbench. The method for creating a helical curve in the **Part** workbench is discussed below:

1. Invoke the **Part** workbench by selecting the **Part** option in the **Workbench Selector**.

2. In the **Part** workbench, click on the **Create primitives** tool of the **Solid** toolbar, see Figure 6.75. The **Geometric Primitives** and **Location** sub-windows appear in the **Tasks Panel** with options to create various types of primitives such as box, cylinder, cone, sphere, prism, helix, and spiral, refer to Figure 6.76.

3. Select the **Helix** option in the **Primitives** drop-down list of the **Geometric Primitives** sub-window, see Figure 6.76. The options to create a helical curve appear.

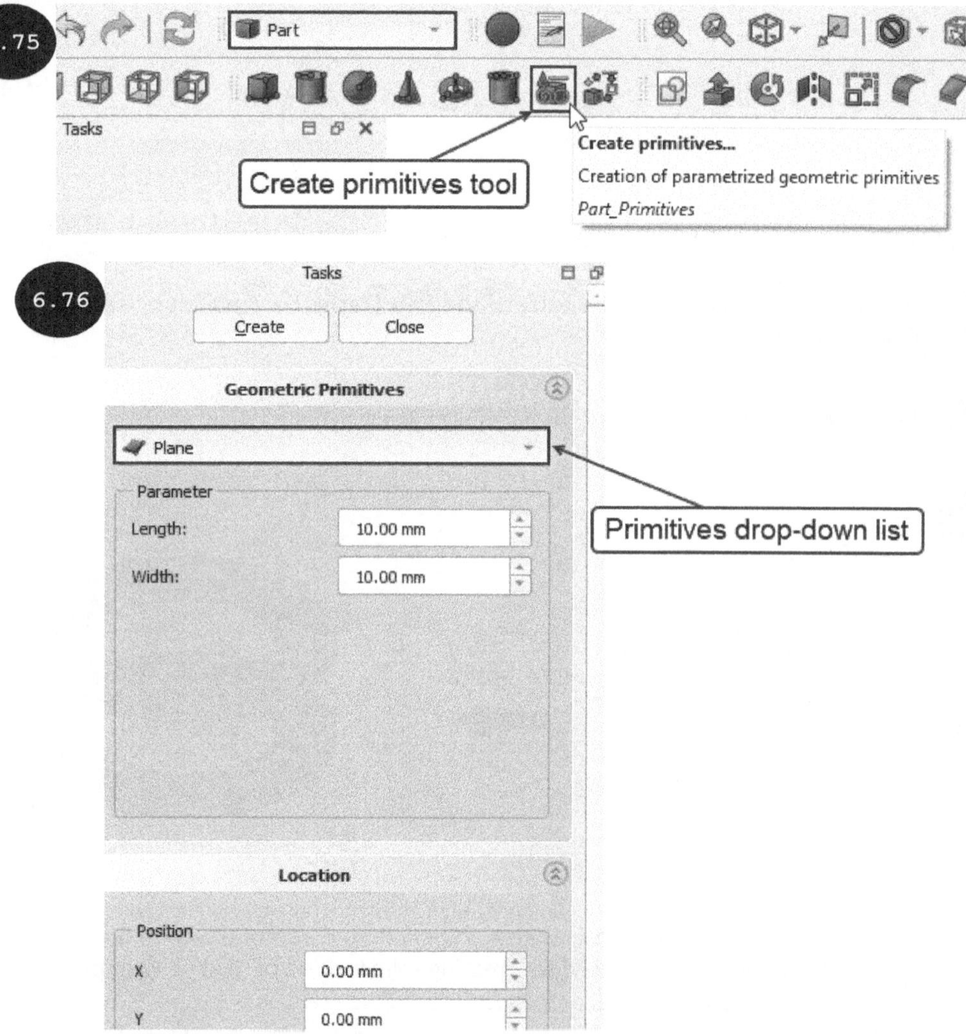

4. Specify the required parameters such as pitch, height, radius, and angle of the helical curve in the respective fields of the **Tasks Panel**. You can also define the position of the helical curve in the 3D View area by specifying the required X, Y, and Z coordinates in the **Location** sub-window of the **Tasks Panel**.

5. After specifying the required parameters, click on the **Create** button in the Tasks Panel. A helical curve of specified parameters gets created in the 3D View area, see Figure 6.77.

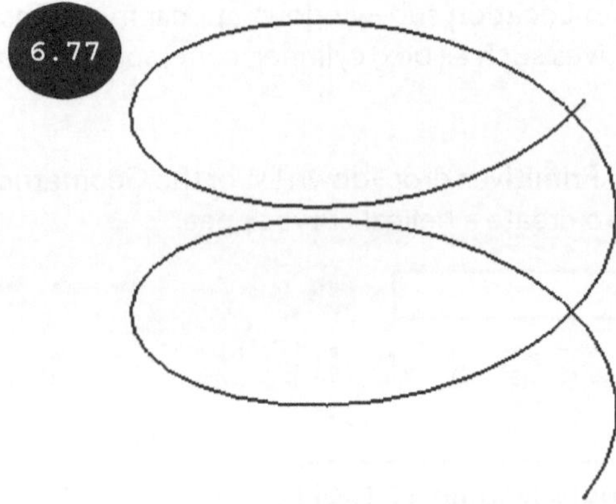

6. Exit the **Tasks Panel** by clicking on the **Close** button.

7. After creating a helical curve, switch back to the **Part Design** workbench by selecting it in the **Workbench Selector**.

Tip: You can use a helical curve as a path to create a feature like pipe, refer to Figure 6.78.

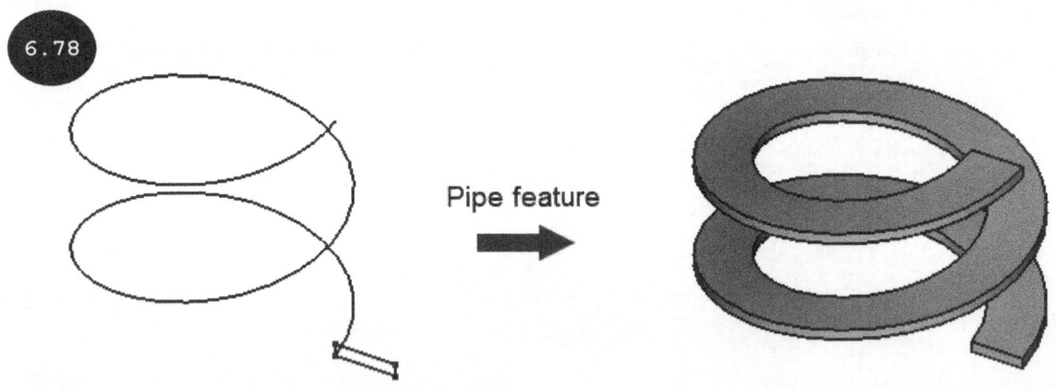

Note: This textbook covers the **Part Design** workbench for creating 3D solid parametric models. The **Part** workbench is also used for creating solid models of relatively simple shapes.

Tutorial 1

Create a model, as shown in Figure 6.79. The different views and dimensions are given in the same figure. All dimensions are in mm.

6.79

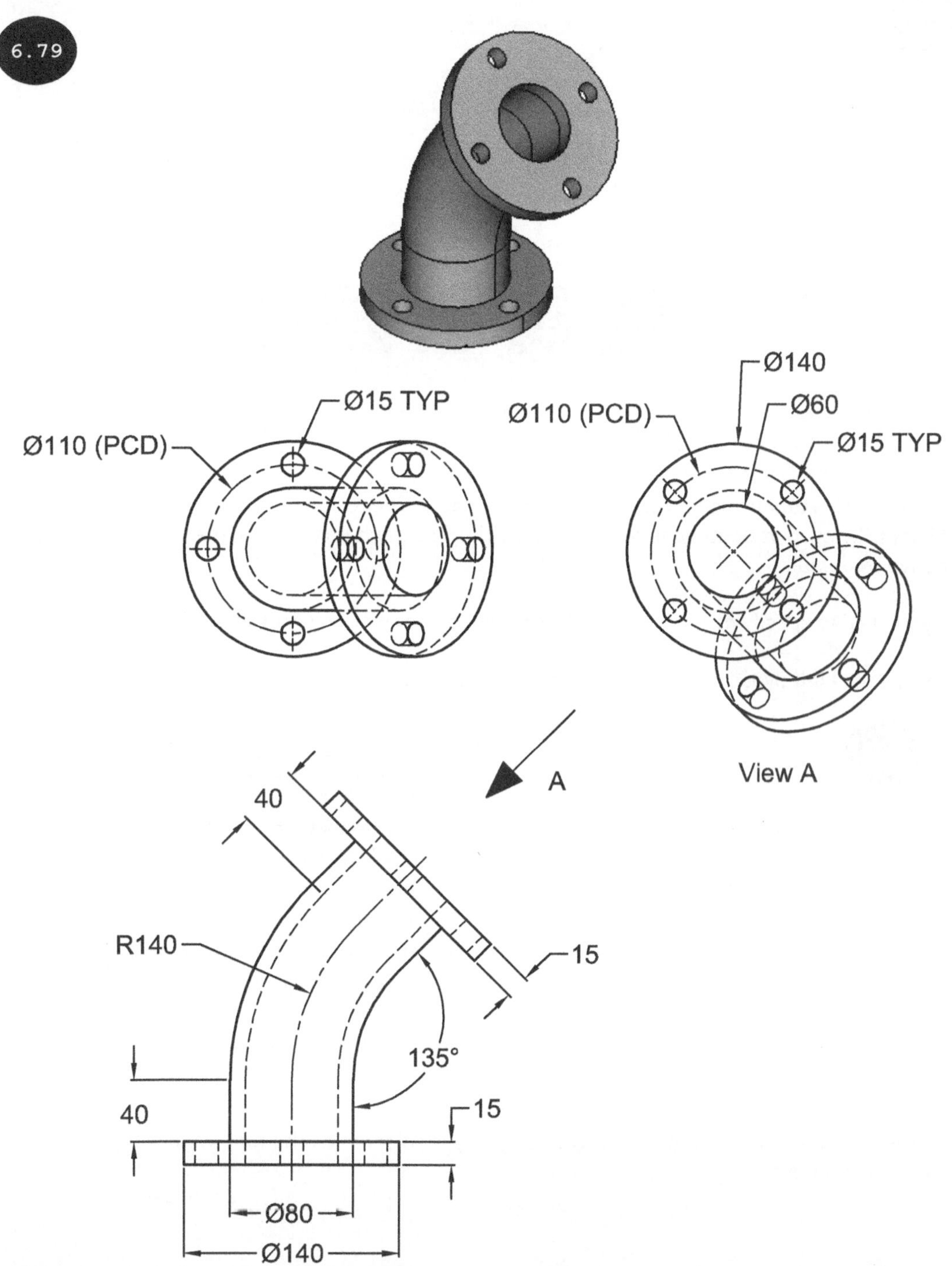

Section 1: Starting a New Part Document and Specifying Units

1. Start FreeCAD by double-clicking on the **FreeCAD 1.0** icon on your desktop. The startup user interface of FreeCAD appears, see Figure 6.80.

6.80

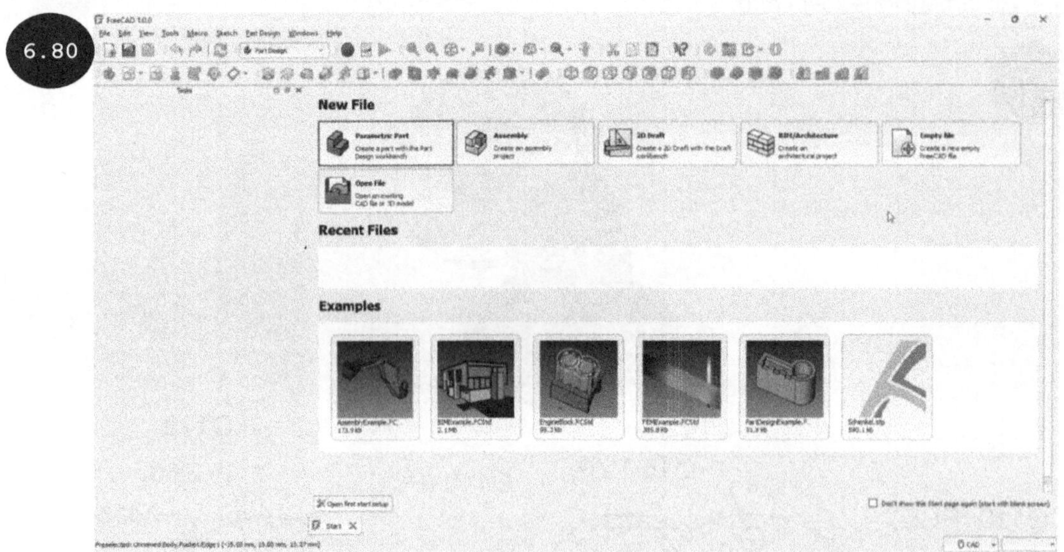

2. Click on the **Parametric Part** icon on the **Start** page (refer to Figure 6.80) or press the **CTRL + N** keys. A new part document gets invoked with the default name "**unnamed: 1**" and it becomes active by default.

Now, you need to specify millimeters (mm) as the measurement unit for the document.

3. Invoke the **Unit** flyout that appears at the lower right corner of the **Status Bar**, see Figure 6.81.

6.81

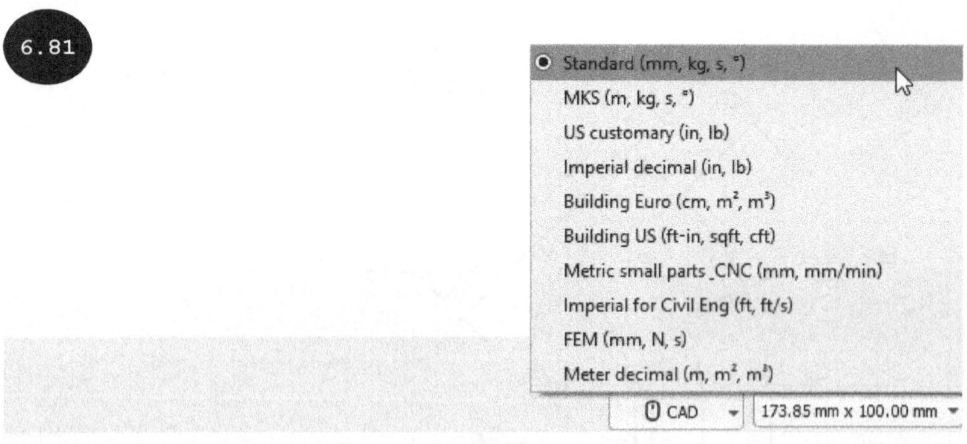

4. In this flyout, ensure that **Standard (mm, kg, s,*)** is selected as the unit system for the current design document.

Section 2: Creating the Base Feature

Now, you can create the base or first feature of the model, which is an additive pipe feature.

1. Invoke the **Sketcher** workbench by selecting the **XZ_Plane** as the sketching plane and then create a sketch, which consists of an arc and two-line entities as the path, see Figure 6.82. Note that the connected line and arc entities of the sketch are tangent to each other. After creating the sketch, exit the **Sketcher** workbench to switch back to the **Part Design** workbench.

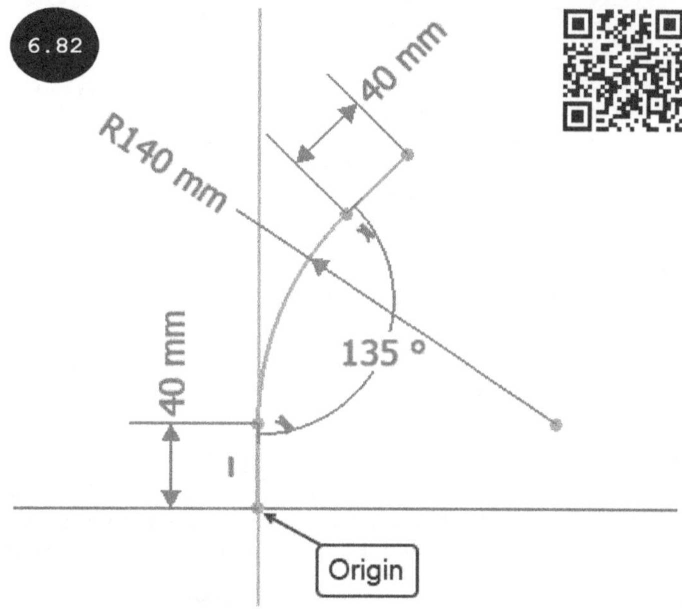

Note: You need to apply the required dimensions and constraints to make the sketch (path) fully constrained.

Now, you need to create the profile of the additive pipe feature.

2. Invoke the **Sketcher** workbench by selecting the **XY_Plane** as the sketching plane and then create a sketch (two concentric circles) as the profile of the additive pipe feature, see Figure 6.83. Note that the center point of both circles is at the origin.

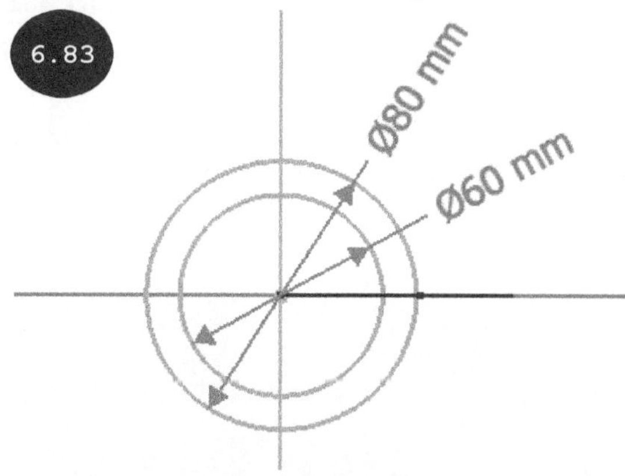

3. After creating the profile, exit the **Sketcher** workbench and then change the view orientation to isometric, see Figure 6.84. Click anywhere in the 3D View area to exit the current selection set.

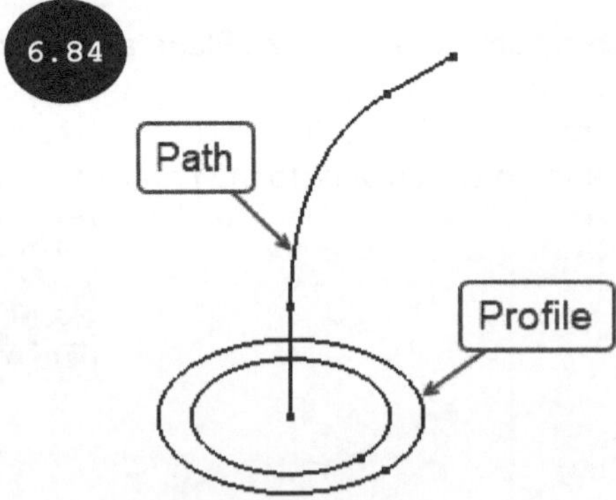

Now, you can create the additive pipe feature.

4. Select the sketch of the profile and then the sketch of the path in the **Tree View** of the **Model** tab in the **Tasks Panel** by pressing the CTRL key. Next, release the CTRL key.

5. After selecting the profile and the path in the **Tree View**, click on the **Additive pipe** tool in the **Part Design Modeling** toolbar, see Figure 6.85. The preview of the additive pipe feature appears in the 3D View area such that the profile follows the path, see Figure 6.86. Also, the **Pipe parameters** sub-window appears in the **Tasks Panel** with the options to create an additive pipe feature.

Note: You can also select the profile and the path of the feature after invoking the **Additive pipe** tool.

6. Accept the default settings in the **Pipe parameters** sub-window of the **Tasks Panel** and then click on the **OK** button. The additive pipe feature gets created, see Figure 6.87.

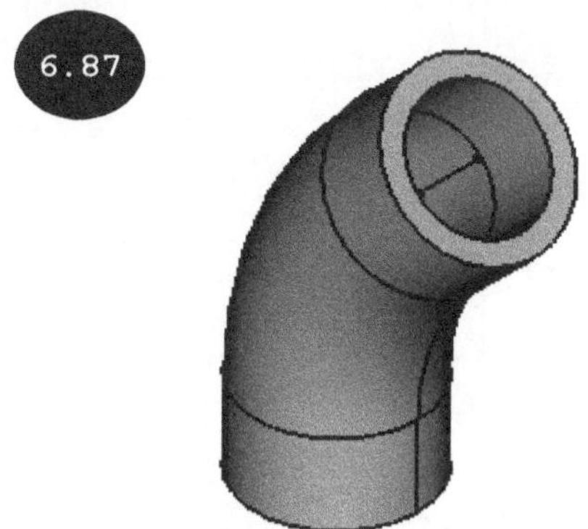

Section 3: Creating the Second Feature

Now, you can create the second feature of the model, which is a pad feature.

1. Click on the **Create sketch** tool in the **Part Design Helper** toolbar (see Figure 6.88) and then select the **XY_Plane** as the sketching plane. The **Sketcher** workbench gets invoked and the selected plane gets oriented normal to the viewing direction.

2. Select the **View section** tool in the **Sketcher** toolbar, see Figure 6.89. The section view of the model appears in the 3D View area by temporarily hiding the material that is in front of the sketching plane.

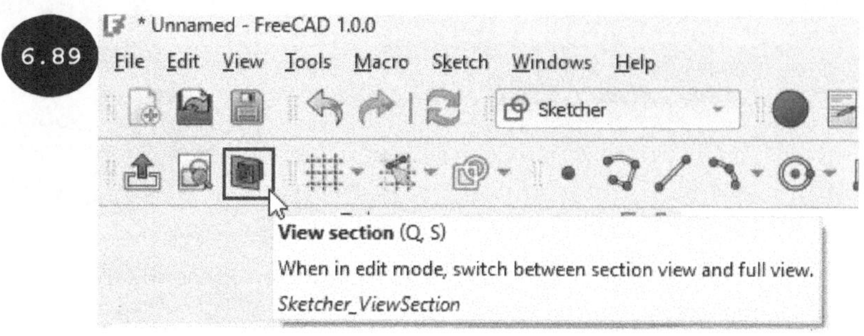

3. Create the sketch of the pad feature by using the sketching tools, see Figure 6.90.

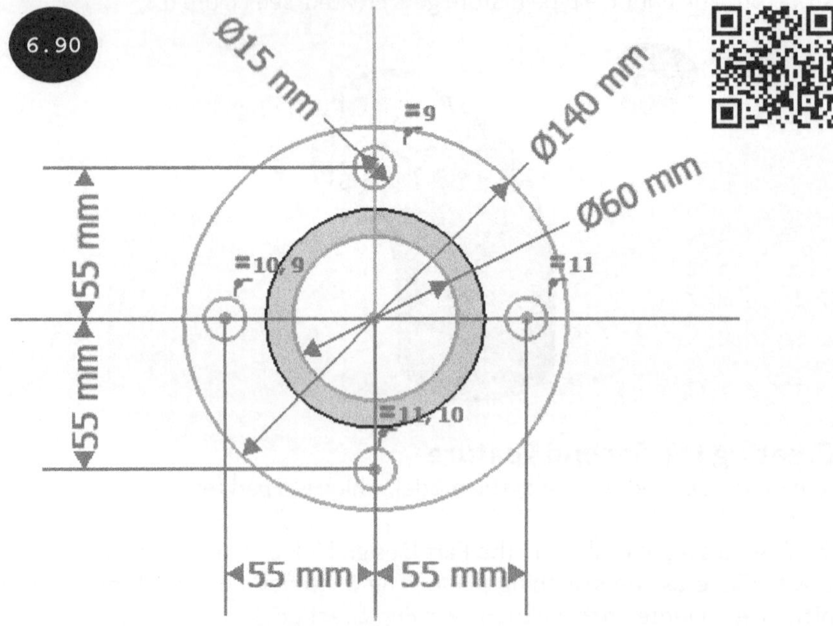

4. After creating the sketch, exit the **Sketcher** workbench to switch back to the **Part Design** workbench.

   Now, you can extrude the sketch to create a pad feature.

5. Click on the **Pad** tool in the **Part Design Modeling** toolbar, see Figure 6.91. The preview of a pad feature appears in the 3D View area with default parameters, see Figure 6.92. Also, the **Pad parameters** sub-window appears in the **Tasks Panel**.

6. Enter **15** mm in the **Length** field of the **Tasks Panel** and then press the TAB key to update the preview of the pad feature.

7. Select the **Reversed** check box in the **Pad parameters** sub-windows of the **Tasks Panel** to reverse the direction of extrusion downward.

8. Click on the **OK** button in the **Tasks Panel** to confirm the creation of the pad feature and exit the **Tasks Panel**. The second feature gets created, see Figure 6.93.

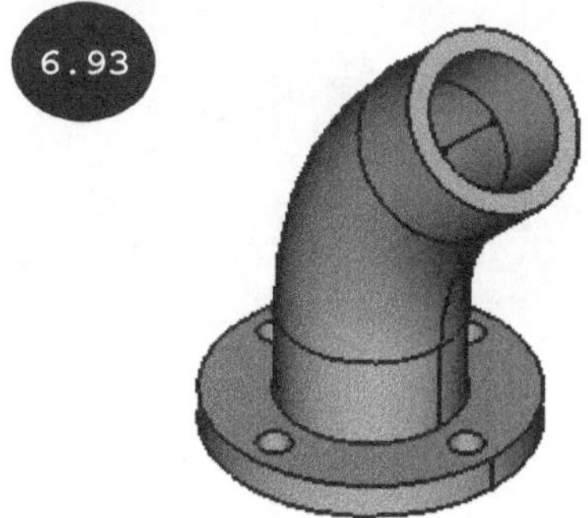

Section 4: Creating the Third Feature

Now, you can create the third feature of the model, which is also a pad feature.

1. Select the top planar face of the base feature (additive pipe) as the sketching plane (see Figure 6.94) and then click on the **Create sketch** tool in the **Part Design Helper** toolbar, see Figure 6.95. The **Sketcher** workbench gets invoked and the selected planar face gets oriented normal to the viewing direction.

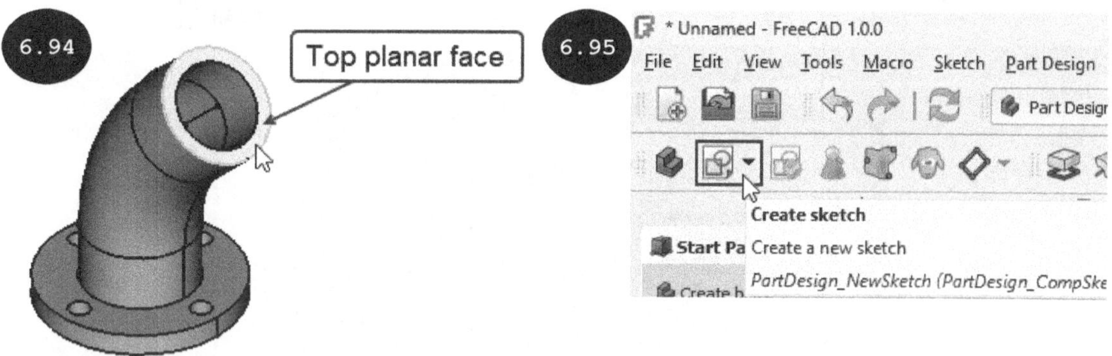

2. Click on the **Create external geometry** tool in the **Sketcher geometries** toolbar (see Figure 6.96) to project the edges of existing features as the linked construction entities onto the sketch.

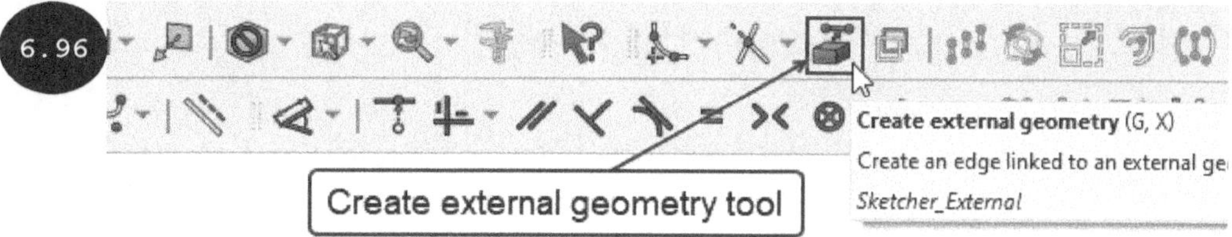

3. Select the inner circular edge of the top planar face of the base feature to be projected as the linked construction entity onto the sketch, see Figure 6.97. Next, press the ESC key to exit the tool.

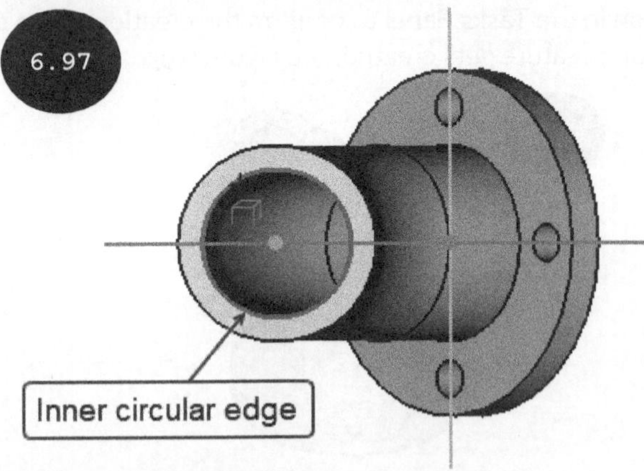

Now, you can take reference of the linked construction entity for creating the sketch of the pad feature.

4. Create the sketch of the pad feature by using the sketching tools, see Figure 6.98.

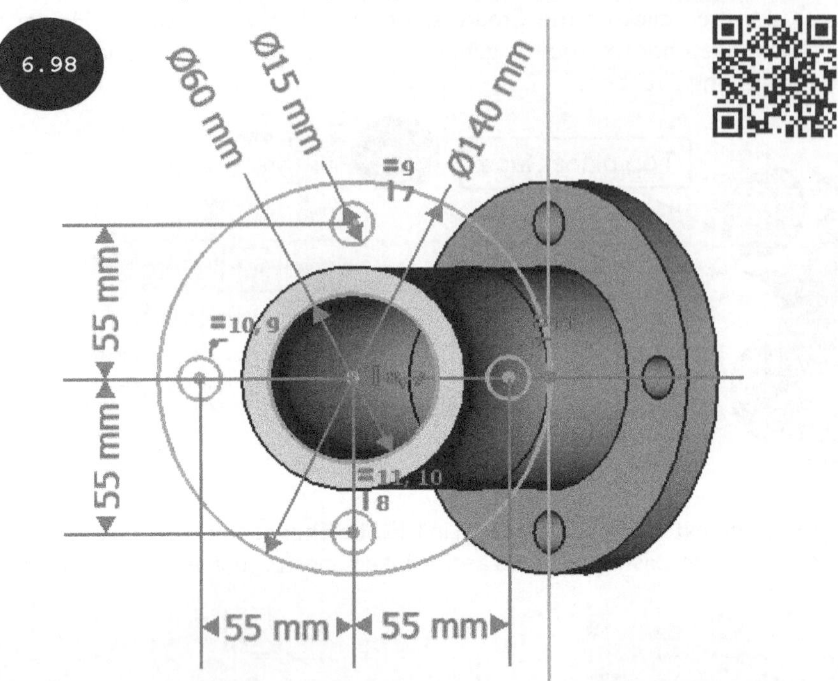

5. After creating the sketch, exit the **Sketcher** workbench to switch back to the **Part Design** workbench.

Now, you can extrude the sketch to create a pad feature.

6. Click on the **Pad** tool in the **Part Design Modeling** toolbar, see Figure 6.99. The preview of a pad feature appears in the 3D View area with default parameters. Also, the **Pad parameters** sub-window appears in the **Tasks Panel**.

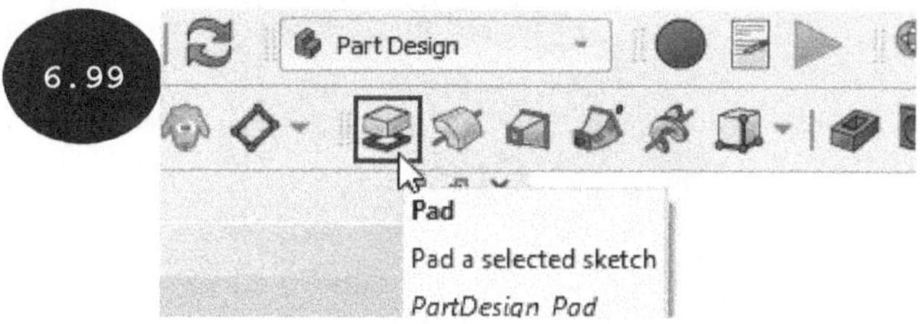

7. Enter **15** mm in the **Length** field of the **Tasks Panel** and then press the TAB key to update the preview of the pad feature.

8. Click on the **OK** button in the **Tasks Panel** to confirm the creation of the pad feature and exit the **Tasks Panel**. The pad feature of specified length gets created, see Figure 6.100.

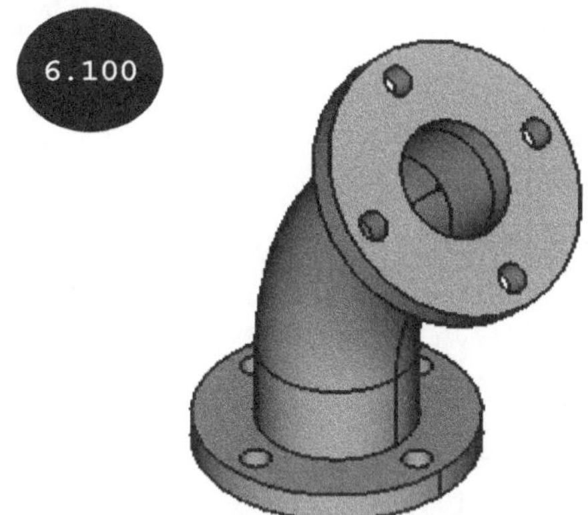

Section 5: Saving the Model

1. Click on the **Save** tool in the **File** toolbar or press the CTRL + S keys. The **Save FreeCAD Document** dialog box appears.

2. Browse to the required folder (:*FreeCAD > Chapter 06*) in the local drive of your system. Note that you need to create the Chapter 06 sub-folder inside the FreeCAD folder.

3. Enter **Chapter 06-Tutorial 1** in the **File name** field of the dialog box. Next, click on the **Save** button in the dialog box. The model gets saved at the specified location (:*FreeCAD > Chapter 06*).

4. Click on **File > Close** in the **Standard Menu** to close the current document.

Tutorial 2

Create the model shown in Figure 6.101. All dimensions are in inches (in).

6.101

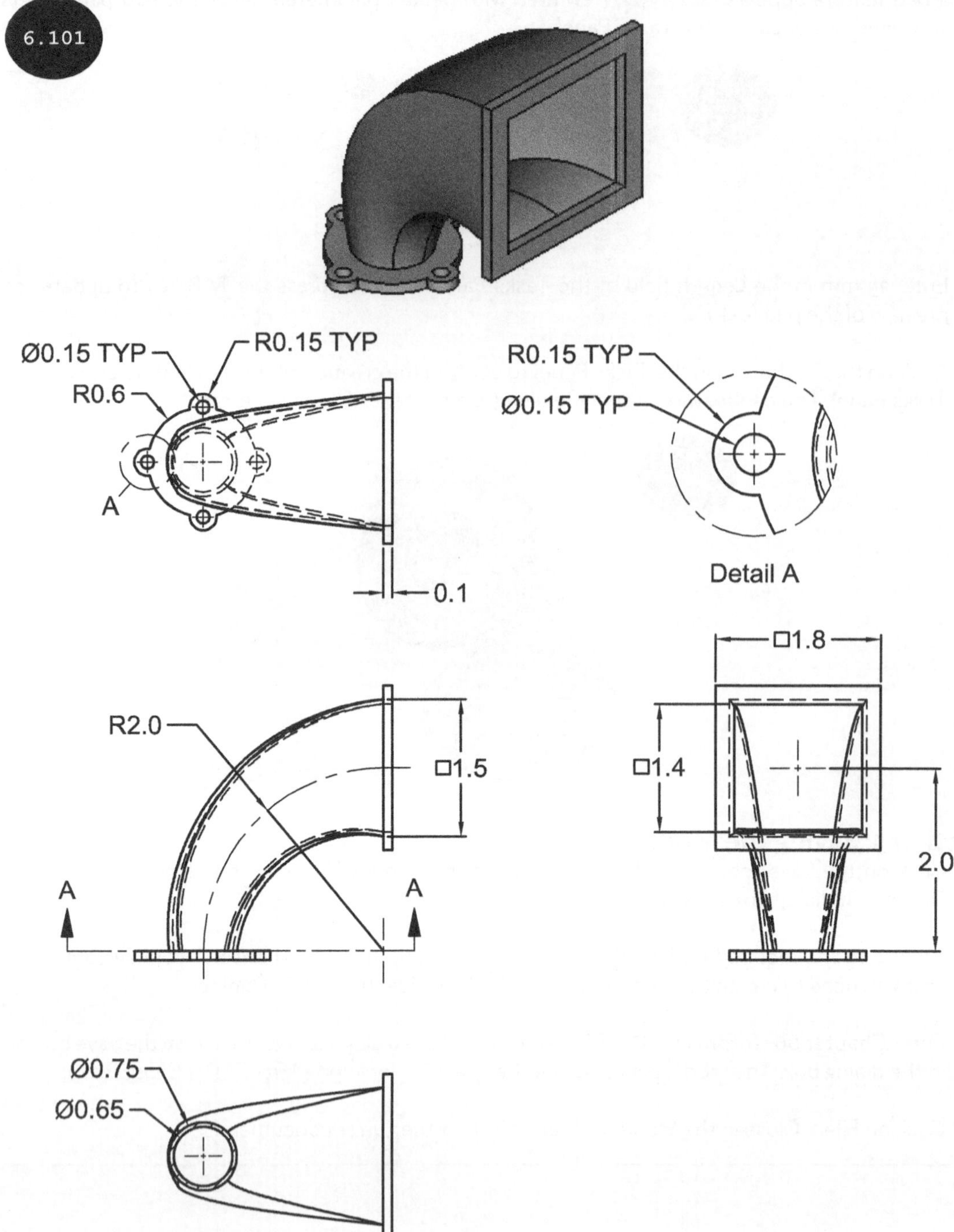

Section 1: Starting a New Part Document and Specifying Units

1. Start FreeCAD by double-clicking on the **FreeCAD 1.0** icon on your desktop. The startup user interface of FreeCAD appears, see Figure 6.102.

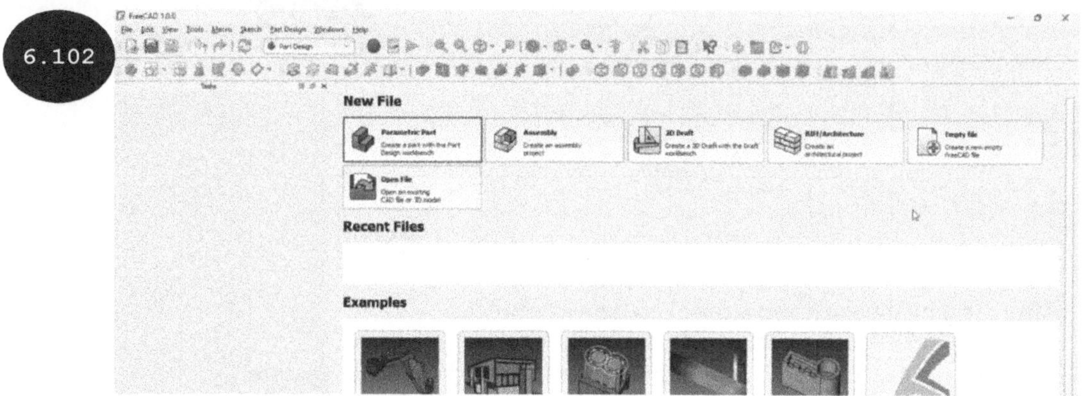

2. Click on the **Parametric Part** icon on the **Start** page (refer to Figure 6.102) or press the **CTRL + N** keys. A new part document gets invoked with the default name "**unnamed: 1**" and it becomes active by default.

3. Invoke the **Unit** flyout that appears at the lower right corner of the **Status Bar**, see Figure 6.103.

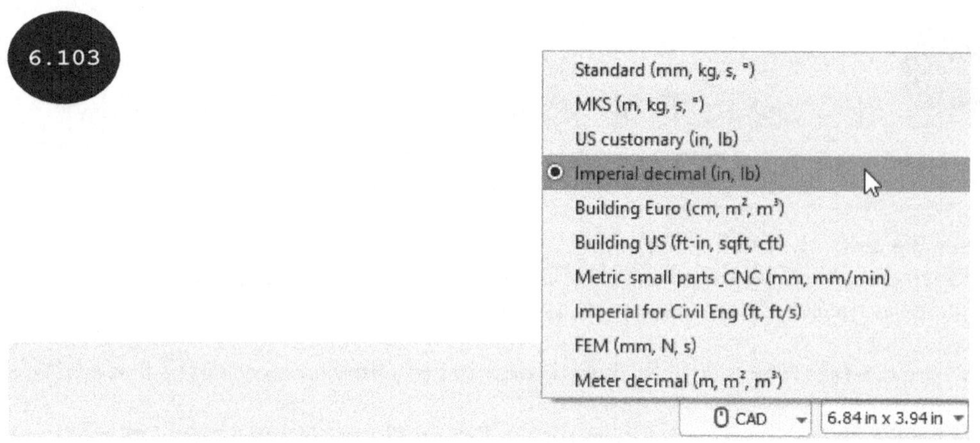

4. Select the **Imperial decimal (in, lb)** as the unit system for the current document in this flyout.

Section 2: Creating the Base Feature

Now, you can create the base or first feature of the model, which is an additive pipe feature.

1. Invoke the **Sketcher** workbench by selecting the **XZ_Plane** as the sketching plane and then create an arc as the path of the additive pipe feature, see Figure 6.104.

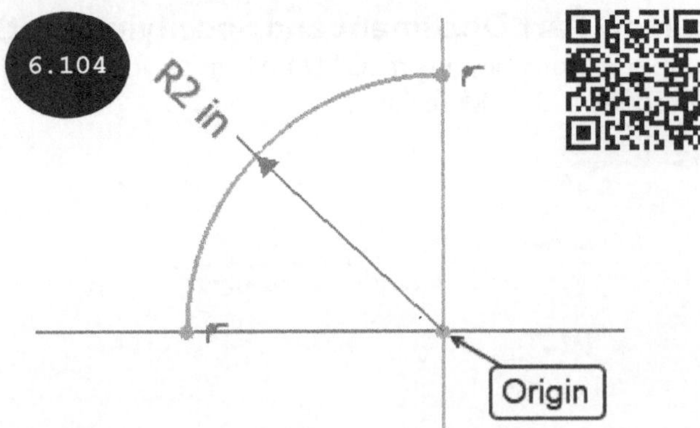

2. After creating the sketch, exit the **Sketcher** workbench.

   Now, you need to create two different profiles of the additive pipe feature.

3. Invoke the **Sketcher** workbench by selecting the **XY_Plane** as the sketching plane for creating the first profile of the additive pipe feature.

4. Click on the **Create external geometry** tool in the **Sketcher geometries** toolbar (see Figure 6.105) to project the existing sketch (path) as the linked construction entities onto the sketch.

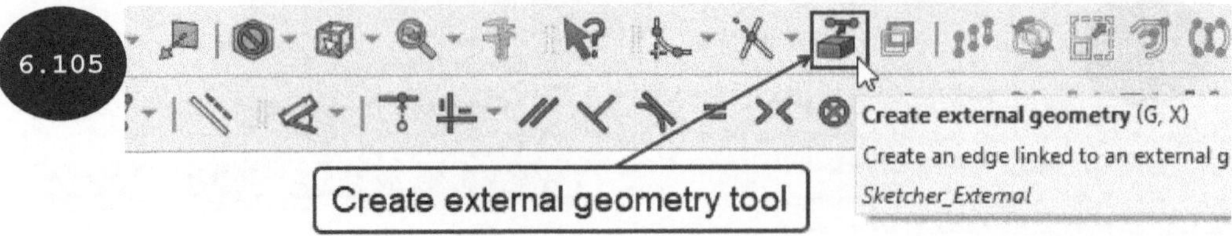

5. Select the existing sketch to be projected as the linked construction entity onto the sketch and then press the ESC key to exit the **Create external geometry** tool. The existing sketch gets projected as the linked construction entity onto the sketch.

   Now, you can take reference of the linked construction entity for creating the first profile.

6. Create a sketch (two concentric circles) as the first profile, see Figure 6.106. Note that the center point of both circles is at the left endpoint of the linked construction entity.

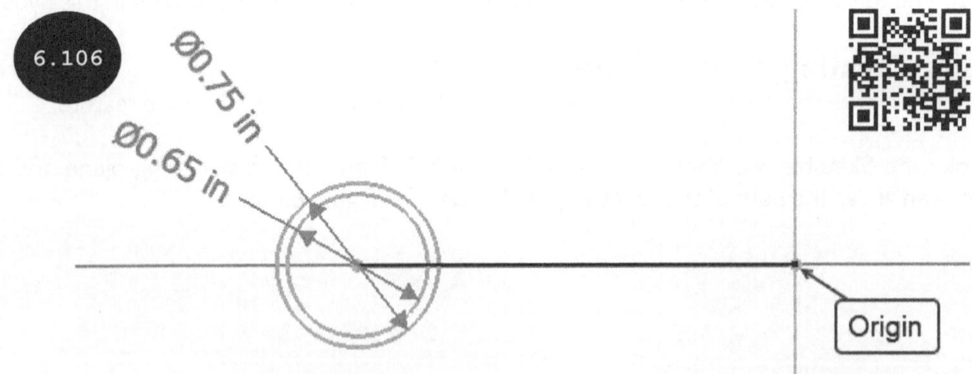

7. After creating the profile, exit the **Sketcher** workbench and then change the view orientation to isometric, see Figure 6.107. Click anywhere in the 3D View area to exit the current selection set.

   Now, you need to create second profile of the additive pipe feature.

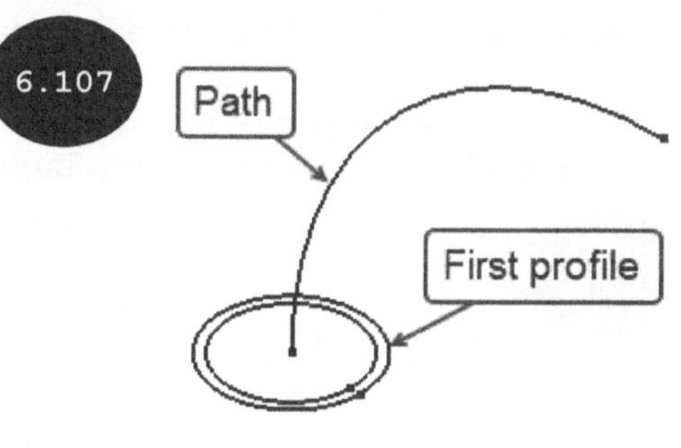

8. Invoke the **Sketcher** workbench by selecting the **YZ_Plane** as the sketching plane and then create the sketch (two concentric rectangles) of the second profile of the additive pipe feature, see Figure 6.108.

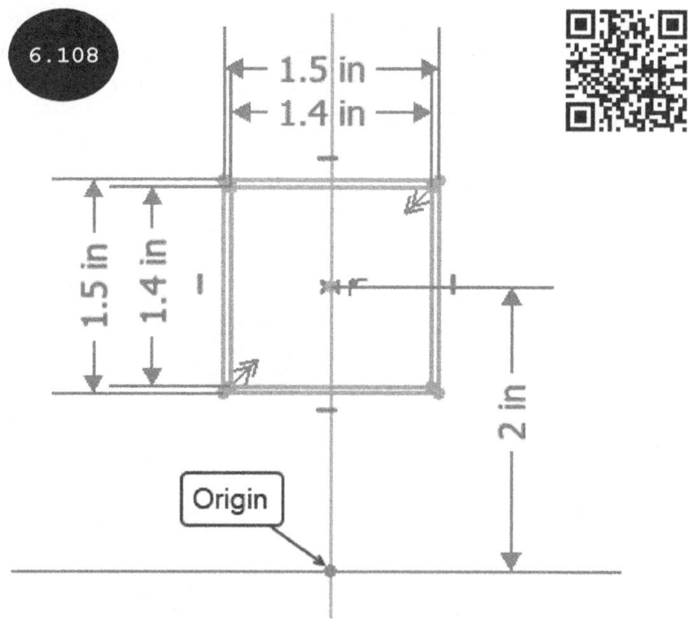

9. After creating the second profile, exit the **Sketcher** workbench and then change the view orientation to isometric, see Figure 6.109. Click anywhere in the 3D View area to exit the current selection set.

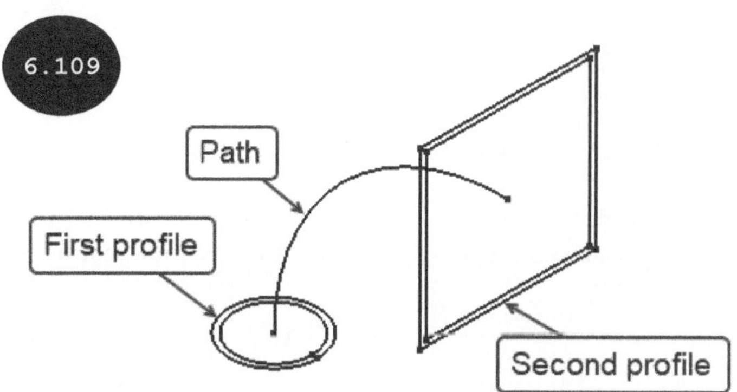

Now, you can create the additive pipe feature.

10. Click on the **Additive pipe** tool in the **Part Design Modeling** toolbar, see Figure 6.110. The **Select feature** sub-window appears in the **Tasks Panel**.

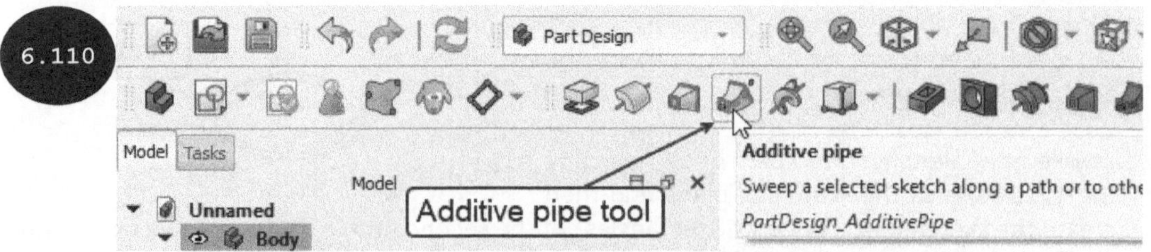

11. Select the sketch of the first profile in the 3D View area. The options to create an additive pipe feature appear in the **Pipe parameters** sub-window of the **Tasks Panel**. Also, the name of the selected sketch appears in its **Profile** field. Ignore the error message that may appear in the **Report view** window at the bottom of the screen. You can close the **Report view** window by clicking on the cross mark × that appears in its top right corner.

12. Click on the **Object** button in the **Path to sweep along** area of the **Pipe parameters** sub-window in the **Tasks Panel** (see Figure 6.111) and then select the path of the additive feature in the 3D View area. The preview of an additive pipe feature appears such that the first selected profile follows the path, see Figure 6.112.

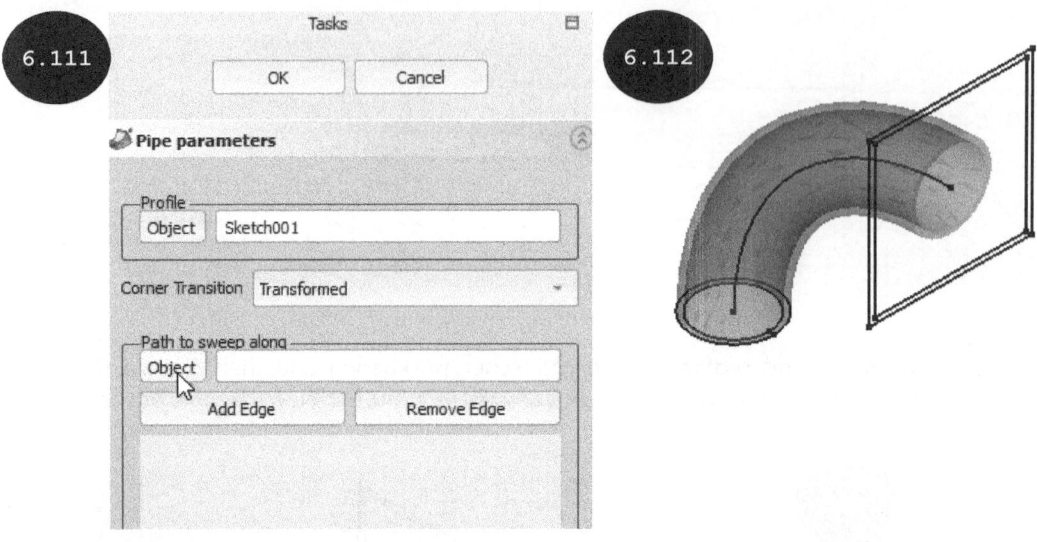

Now, you can select the section profile of the additive pipe feature.

13. Select the **Multisection** option in the **Transform mode** drop-down list of the **Section transformation** sub-window to create a multi-section additive pipe feature, see Figure 6.113.

6.113

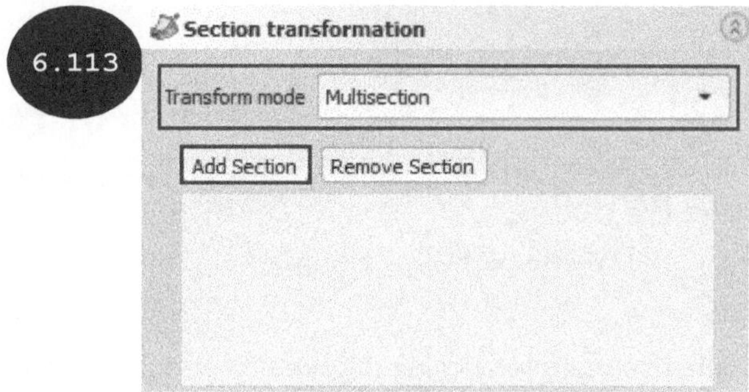

Now, you can select the second profile of the additive pipe feature.

14. Click on the **Add Section** button that appears below the **Transform mode** drop-down list, refer to Figure 6.113.

15. Select the second profile of the additive pipe feature in the 3D View area. The preview of the additive pipe feature gets modified in the 3D View area such that its cross-sectional shape gets transformed from one profile to another while following the path, see Figure 6.114.

16. Click on the **OK** button in the **Tasks Panel**. The additive pipe feature gets created, see Figure 6.115.

6.114 6.115

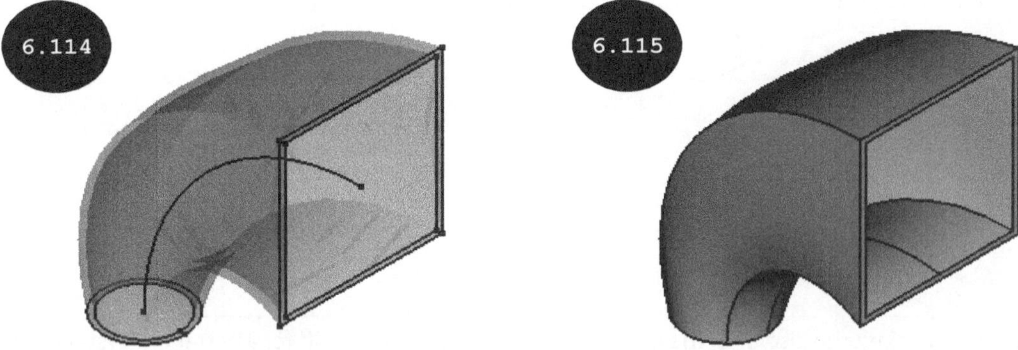

Section 3: Creating the Second Feature

Now, you can create the second feature of the model, which is a pad feature.

1. Invoke the **Sketcher** workbench by selecting the **XY_Plane** or the bottom planar face of the base feature as the sketching plane.

2. Select the **View section** tool in the **Sketcher** toolbar, see Figure 6.116. The section view of the model appears in the 3D View area by temporarily hiding the material that is in front of the sketching plane.

6.116

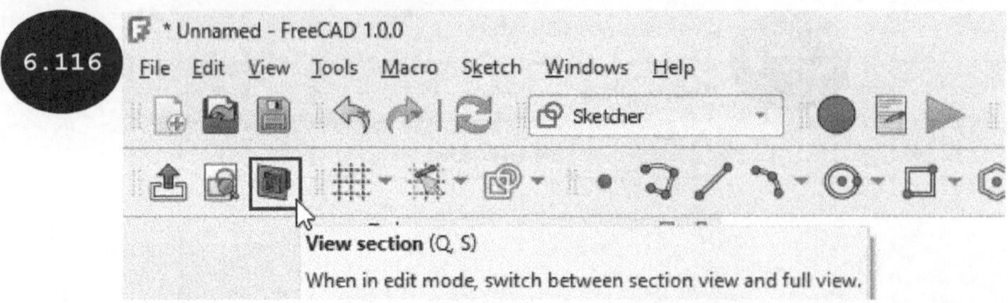

3. Create the sketch of the pad feature by using the sketching tools, see Figure 6.117. In this figure, the display of geometric constraints is turned off for a better understanding of the sketch.

6.117

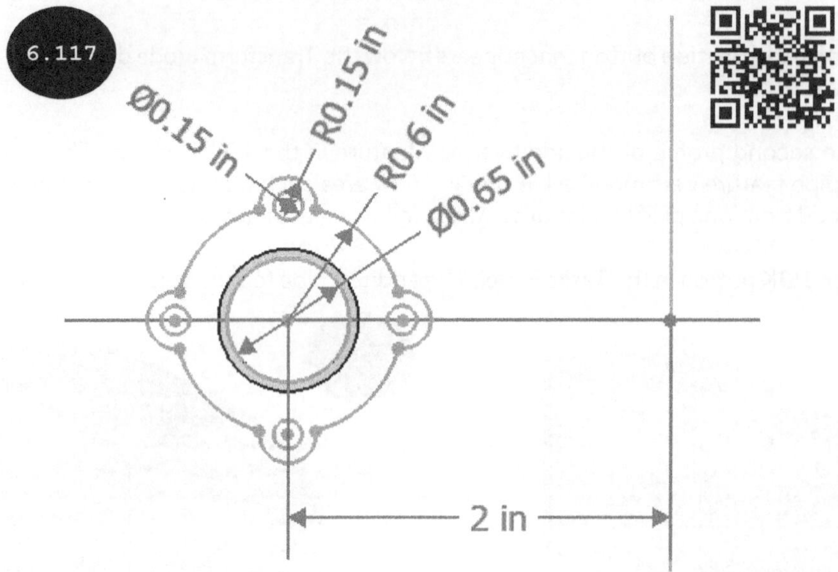

Note: In Figure 6.117, the display of the geometric constraints is turned off for a better understanding of the sketch. For doing so, ensure that the **Geometric** check box is selected in the **Filter** drop-down list of the **Constraints** sub-window in the **Task Panel** to display a list of applied geometric constraints of the sketch. Next, click on the **Hide Listed** button in the **Constraints** sub-window in the **Task Panel**. The display of geometric constraints gets turned off in the 3D View area. To turn on the display of geometric constraints, click on the **Show Listed** button in the **Constraints** sub-window of the **Task Panel**.

4. After creating the sketch, exit the **Sketcher** workbench to switch back to the **Part Design** workbench.

Now, you can extrude the sketch to create a pad feature.

5. Click on the **Pad** tool in the **Part Design Modeling** toolbar, see Figure 6.118. The preview of a pad feature appears in the 3D View area with default parameters. Also, the **Pad parameters** sub-window appears in the **Tasks Panel**.

6. Enter **0.1** inches in the **Length** field of the **Tasks Panel** and then press the TAB key to update the preview of the pad feature.

7. Select the **Reversed** check box in the **Pad parameters** sub-windows of the **Tasks Panel** to reverse the direction of extrusion downward.

8. Click on the **OK** button in the **Tasks Panel** to confirm the creation of the pad feature and exit the **Tasks Panel**. The second feature gets created, see Figure 6.119.

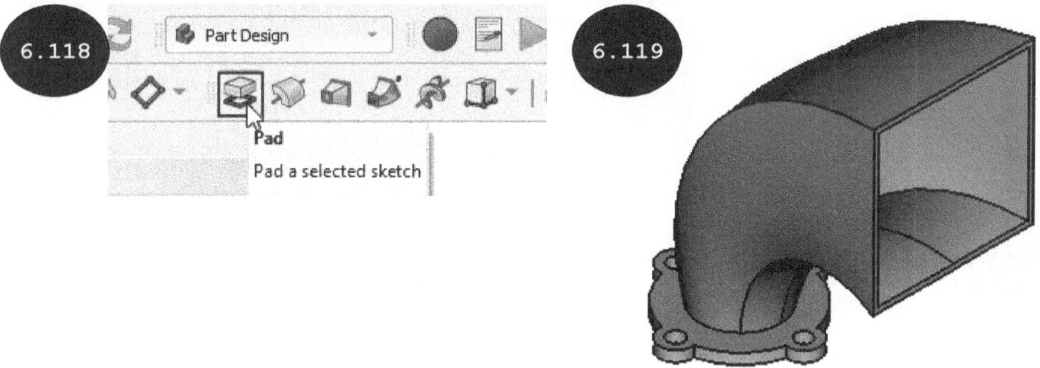

Section 4: Creating the Third Feature

Now, you can create the third feature of the model, which is also a pad feature.

1. Select the right planar face of the base feature (additive pipe) as the sketching plane (see Figure 6.120) and then click on the **Create sketch** tool in the **Part Design Helper** toolbar, see Figure 6.121. The **Sketcher** workbench gets invoked and the selected planar face gets oriented normal to the viewing direction.

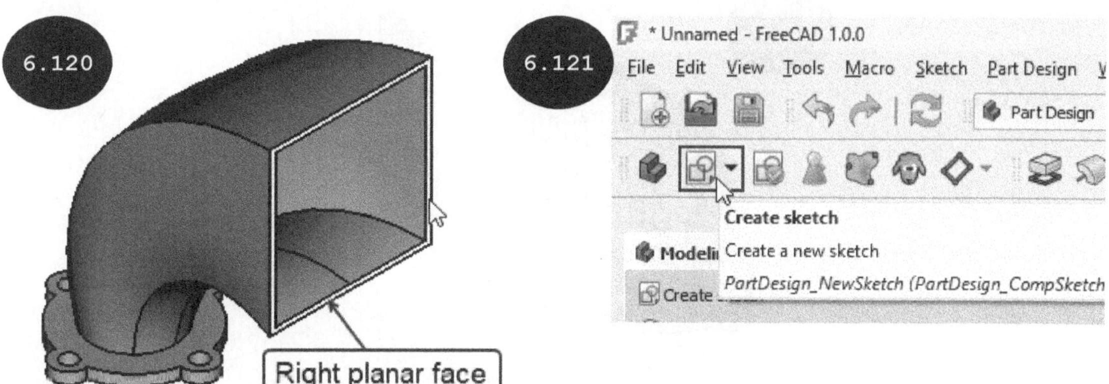

2. Create the sketch of the pad feature by using the sketching tools, see Figure 6.122.

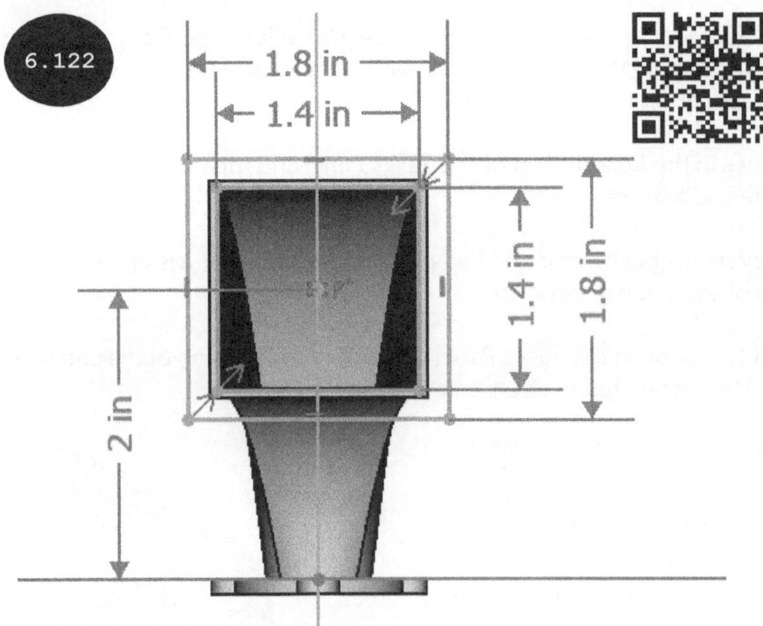

3. After creating the sketch, exit the **Sketcher** workbench to switch back to the **Part Design** workbench.

   Now, you can extrude the sketch to create a pad feature.

4. Click on the **Pad** tool in the **Part Design Modeling** toolbar and then enter **0.1** inches in the **Length** field of the **Tasks Panel** that appears. Next, press the TAB key to update the preview of the pad feature.

5. Click on the **OK** button in the **Tasks Panel** to confirm the creation of the pad feature and exit the **Tasks Panel**. The pad feature of specified length gets created, see Figure 6.123.

Section 5: Saving the Model

1. Click on the **Save** tool in the **File** toolbar (see Figure 6.124) or press the CTRL + S keys. The **Save FreeCAD Document** dialog box appears.

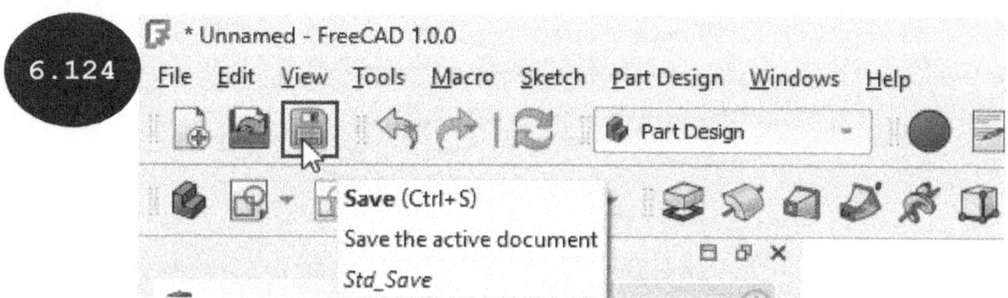

2. Browse to the required folder (:*FreeCAD > Chapter 06*) in the local drive of your system. Note that you need to create the Chapter 06 sub-folder inside the FreeCAD folder, if not created earlier.

3. Enter **Chapter 06-Tutorial 2** in the **File name** field of the dialog box. Next, click on the **Save** button in the dialog box. The model gets saved at the specified location (:*FreeCAD > Chapter 06*).

4. Click on the **File > Close** in the **Standard Menu** to close the current document, see Figure 6.125

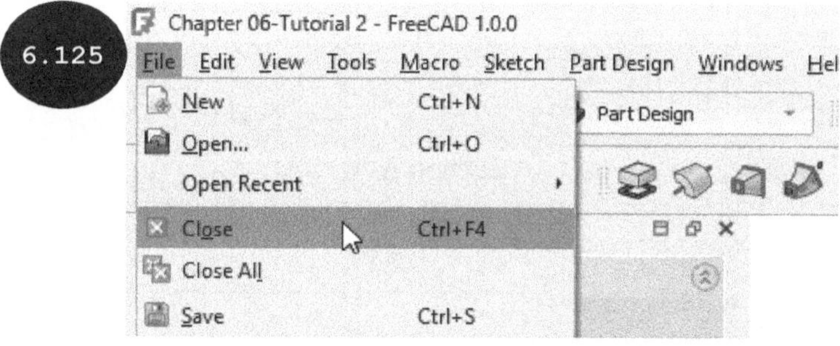

Hands-on Test Drive 1

Create the model shown in Figure 6.126. Different drawing views and dimensions of the model are given in Figure 6.127. All dimensions are in inches (in).

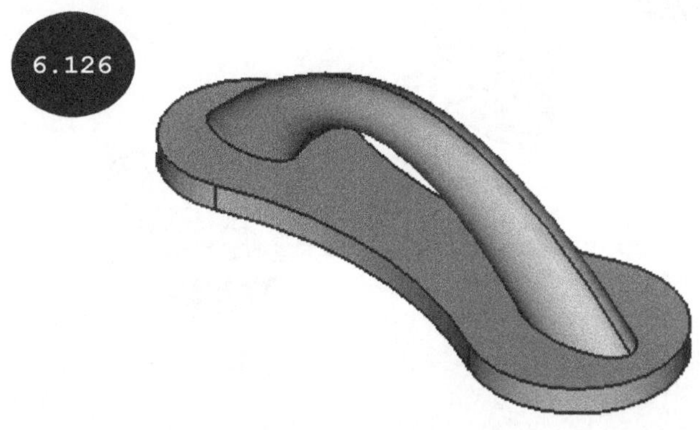

6.127

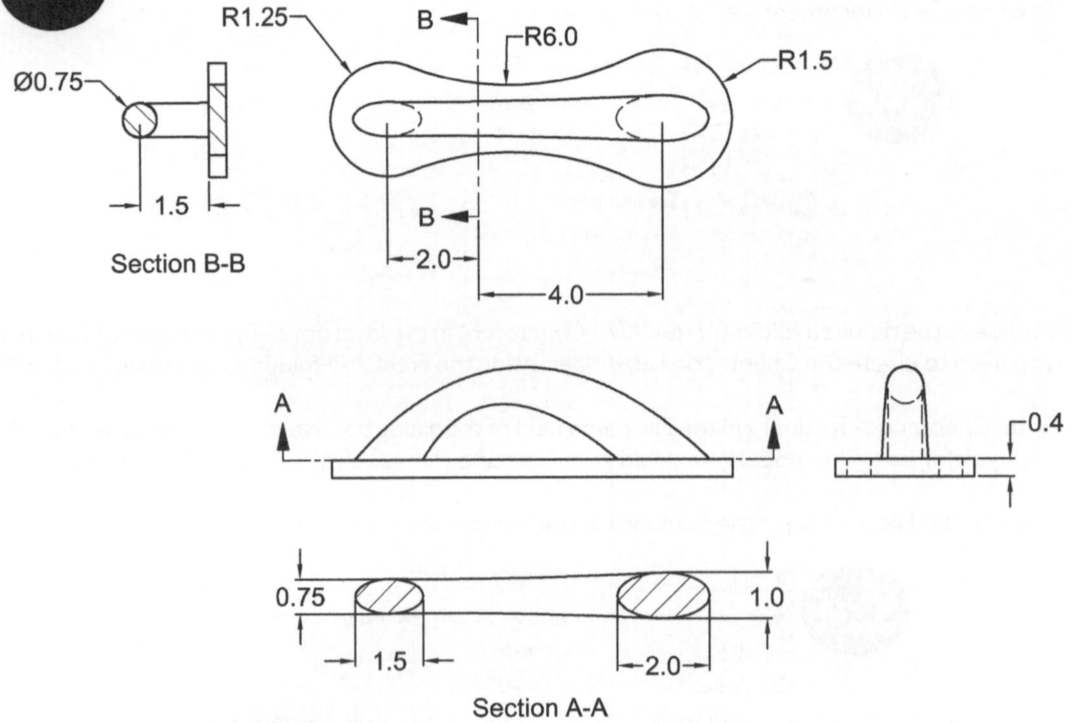

R1.25
R6.0
R1.5
Ø0.75
1.5
Section B-B
B
B
2.0
4.0
A
A
0.4
0.75
1.0
1.5
2.0
Section A-A

Hands-on Test Drive 2

Create the model shown in Figure 6.128. Different drawing views and dimensions of the model are given in Figure 6.129. All dimensions are in mm.

6.128

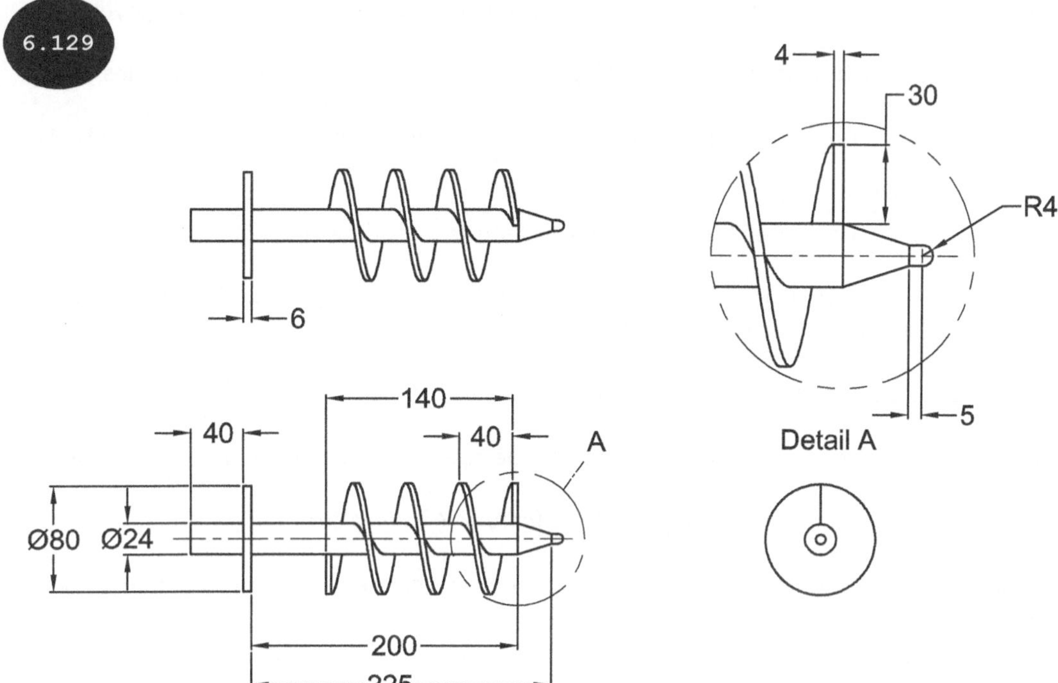

Summary

This chapter discussed how to create additive pipe features, multi-section additive pipe features, subtractive pipe features, additive loft features, and subtractive loft features, in addition to additive and subtractive helix features. The method for creating a helical curve in the **Part** workbench has also been discussed in this chapter.

Questions

Complete and verify the following sentences:

- The ________ tool is used for creating a pipe feature by adding material.
- While creating an additive pipe feature, the ________ option is selected in the **Orientation mode** drop-down list, by default. As a result, the profile follows the path such that the cross-section shape of the resultant feature is kept perpendicular throughout the path.
- The ________ option is used for creating an additive pipe feature with a single profile.

- The _________ option is used for creating an additive pipe feature with multiple profiles.
- An _________ feature is created by making a transition between two or more profiles.
- The _________ tool is used for creating a loft feature by removing the material from an existing body.
- The _________ tool is used for creating a helix feature by adding material.
- The _________ option is used for creating a helix by defining its total height, number of revolutions (turns), and incremental growth of the helical radius.
- The _________ option allows you to create a spiral coil.
- The profiles of an additive loft feature can either be opened or closed sketches. (True/False)
- In FreeCAD, you cannot create a tapered helix feature. (True/False)
- To create an additive loft feature, you first need to create all its profiles that define its cross-sectional shape. (True/False)

Mirroring and Patterning Features

This chapter discusses the following topics:

- Mirroring Features of a Model
- Patterning Features of a Model
- Create a Multi-transform Pattern

Mirroring and Patterning tools are used to transform existing features of a model. The methods for mirroring and patterning one or more features of a model are discussed next.

Mirroring Features of a Model

In FreeCAD, you can mirror one or more features of a model about a mirroring plane by using the **Mirrored** tool. Figure 7.1 shows a feature to be mirrored, a mirroring plane, and the resultant mirrored feature. The method for mirroring features of a model is discussed next.

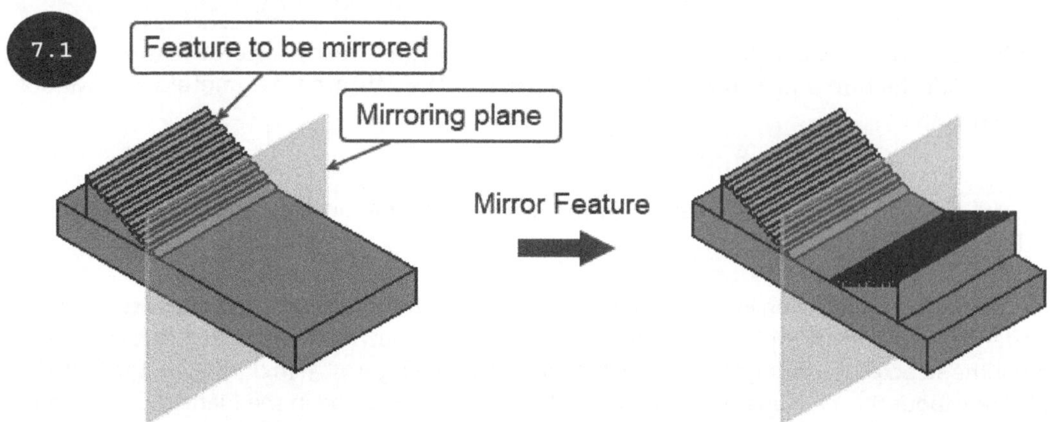

1. Click the **Mirrored** tool in the **Part Design Modeling** toolbar, see Figure 7.2. The **Mirrored Parameters** sub-window appears in the **Tasks Panel**, with the **Transform body** radio button selected by default. As a result, the entire body is selected for mirroring about the specified plane, and a preview of the mirrored geometry appears in the 3D View area.

Note: You can select features to be mirrored before or after invoking the **Mirrored** tool. If a feature is selected before invoking the **Mirrored** tool, a preview of its mirrored version automatically appears in the 3D View area about the vertical axis of its sketch.

2. Select the **Transform tool shapes** radio button in the **Mirrored Parameters** sub-window to choose an individual feature of a model for mirroring. After selecting the **Transform tool shapes** radio button, click the **Add Feature** button that becomes enabled below it. Then, select the feature to be mirrored in the 3D View area. A preview mirrored feature appears about the default mirroring plane.

   Alternatively, you can access the **Tree View** by clicking on the **Model** tab in the **Tasks Panel** and then selected feature to be mirrored, see Figure 7.3.

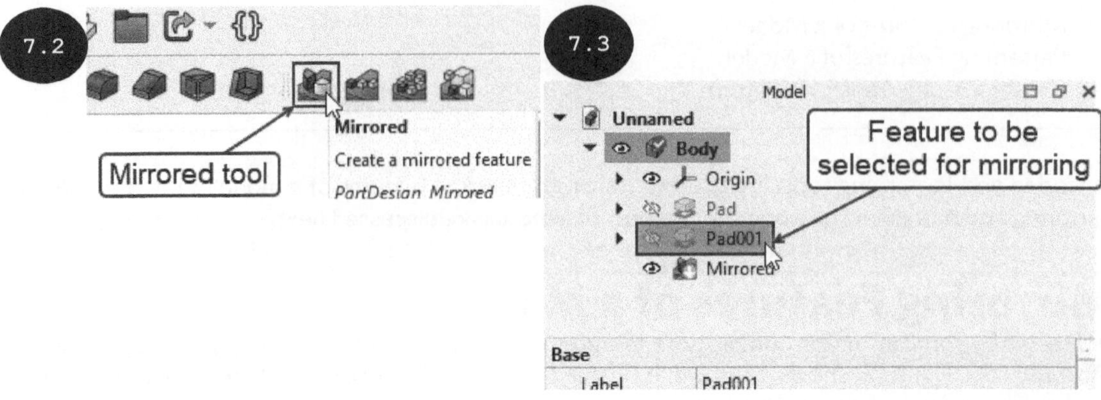

Tip: You can add additional features to be mirrored or remove already selected features by using the **Add feature** and **Remove feature** buttons of the **Mirrored parameters** sub-window, respectively.

3. Similarly, you can click the **Add Feature** button to select an additional feature in the 3D View area or **Tree View** for mirroring.

4. Specify the required option in the **Plane** drop-down list of the **Mirrored parameters** sub-window for defining the mirroring plane, refer to Figure 7.4. The preview of the mirrored feature appears about the selected mirroring plane in the 3D View area, see Figure 7.5. In this figure, the feature is mirrored about the YZ Plane by selecting the Base YZ plane option in the Plane drop-down list. The options in the Plane drop-down list are discussed next.

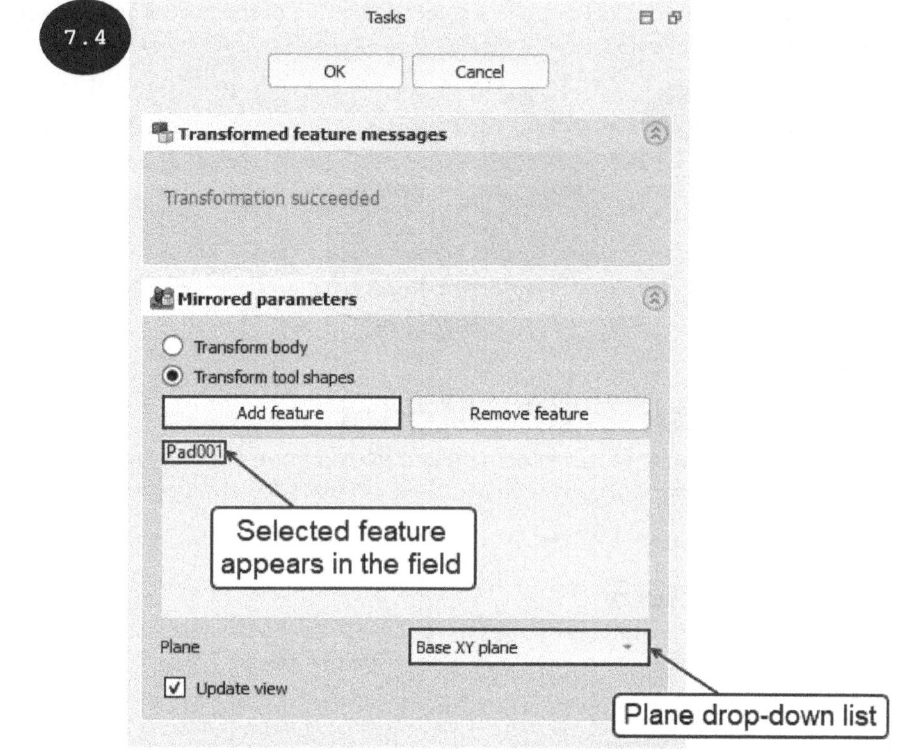

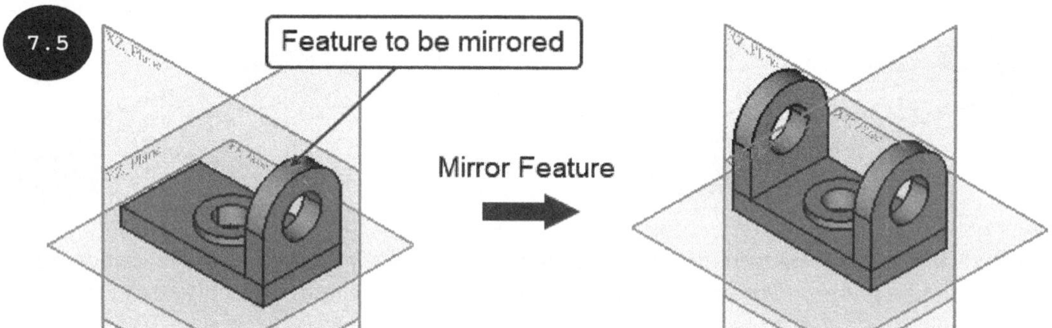

Base XY plane: The **Base XY plane** option is used for mirroring the selected feature of the model about the XY plane.

Base YZ plane: The **Base YZ plane** option is used for mirroring the selected feature of the model about the YZ plane.

Base XZ plane: The **Base XZ plane** option is used for mirroring the selected feature of the model about the XZ plane.

Select reference: The **Select reference** option is used for selecting a plane or a planar face of an existing feature as the mirroring plane for creating the mirrored feature.

5. Click on the **OK** button in the **Tasks Panel**. The selected feature of the model gets mirrored about the mirroring plane, see Figure 7.6.

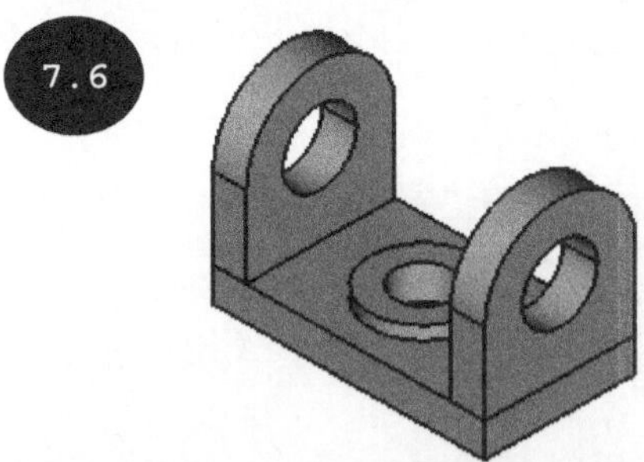

Patterning Features of a Model

In FreeCAD, you can create a linear pattern and a polar pattern of one or more features by using the **Linear Pattern** and **Polar Pattern** tools, respectively. The methods for creating both these types of patterns are discussed next.

Creating a Linear Pattern

A linear pattern creates multiple instances of one or more features of a model in a linear direction, see Figure 7.7. The method for creating a linear pattern is discussed below:

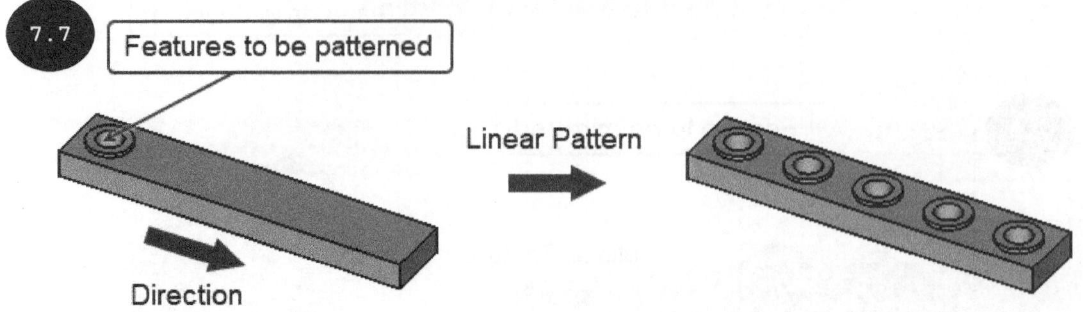

1. Select a feature to be patterned in the **Tree View** or the 3D View area. You can also select multiple features to be patterned by pressing the CTRL key in sequential order for better results.

2. After selecting a feature, click on the **LinearPattern** tool in the **Part Design Modeling** toolbar, see Figure 7.8. The **LinearPattern parameters** sub-window appears in the **Tasks Panel** and the name of the selected feature appears in its field, see Figure 7.9. Also, the preview of a linear pattern of the selected feature appears along the horizontal axis of its sketch with default parameters, since the **Horizontal sketch axis** option is selected in the **Direction** drop-down list of the **Tasks Panel**, by default.

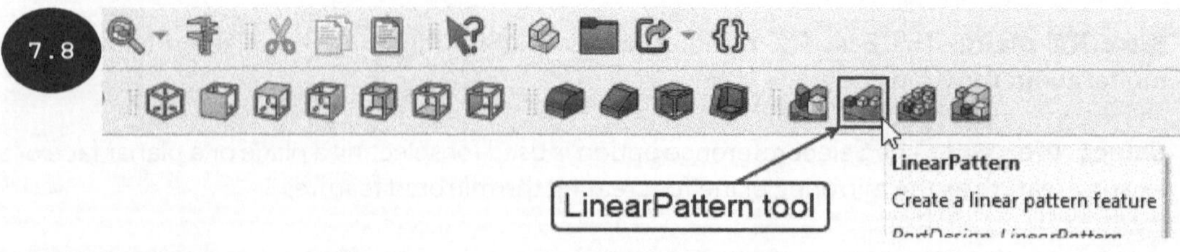

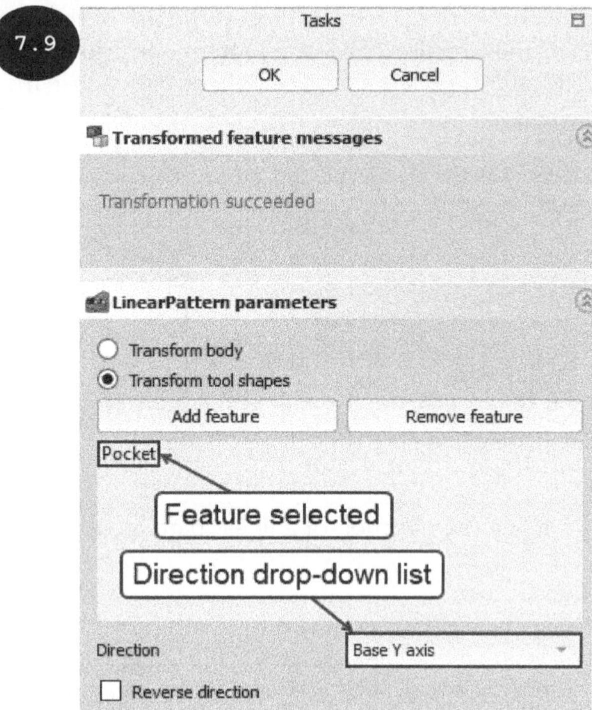

Note: You can select features to be patterned before or after invoking the **LinearPattern** tool.

If a feature to be patterned is not selected before invoking the **Linear Pattern** tool, first activate the **Transform tool shapes** radio button in the **Tasks Panel**. Then, click the **Add Feature** button and select the feature to be patterned from either the 3D View area or the **Tree View**.

Tip: You can add additional features to be patterned or remove already selected features by using the **Add feature** and **Remove feature** buttons of the **LinearPattern parameters** sub-window, respectively. You can also remove an already selected feature from the pattern list by right-clicking on its name in the **LinearPattern parameters** sub-window and then selecting the **Remove** option in the shortcut menu that appears.

3. Specify the required option in the **Direction** drop-down list of the **LinearPattern parameters** sub-window for defining the direction of a linear pattern, see Figure 7.10. The preview of a linear pattern of the selected feature appears along the defined direction in the 3D View area.

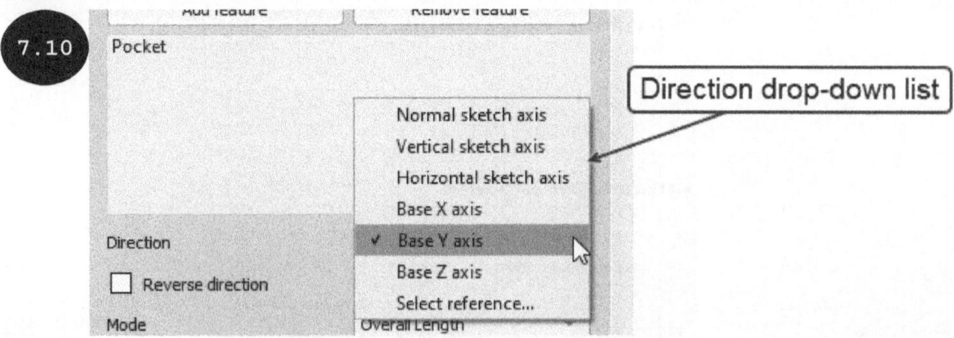

Note: The options to define the direction of a linear pattern work the same way as described earlier.

4. Enter the required total length of the linear pattern in the **Length** field of the **Tasks Panel** between which the specified number of pattern occurrences is to be created.

5. Enter the required number of pattern occurrences to be created in the **Occurrences** field of the Tasks Panel, see Figure 7.11. This figure shows the preview of a linear pattern after specifying **5** as the number of pattern occurrences to be created along the pattern direction.

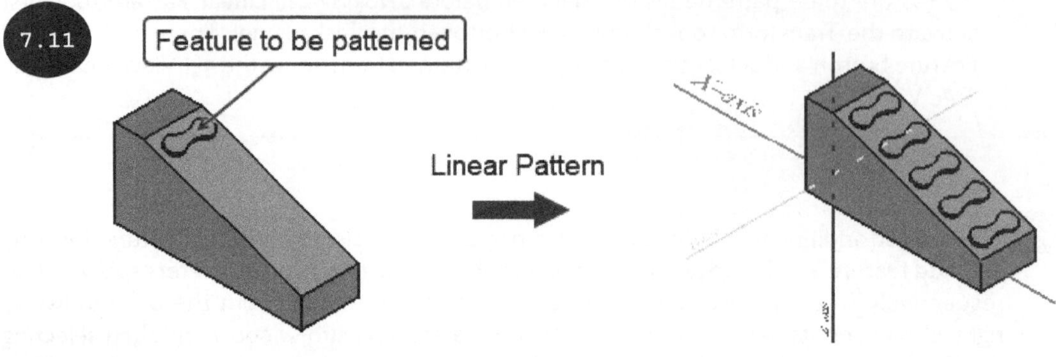

Note: The specified number of pattern occurrences is arranged equally between the total length specified in the **Length** field of the **Tasks Panel**.

Also, the number of pattern occurrences specified in the **Occurrences** field includes the source or parent feature.

6. Select the **Reverse direction** check box in the **LinearPattern parameters** sub-window to reverse the pattern direction if needed.

7. After specifying all the required parameters, click on the **OK** button in the **Tasks Panel**. The linear pattern of a specified number of pattern occurrences of the selected feature gets created, see Figure 7.12.

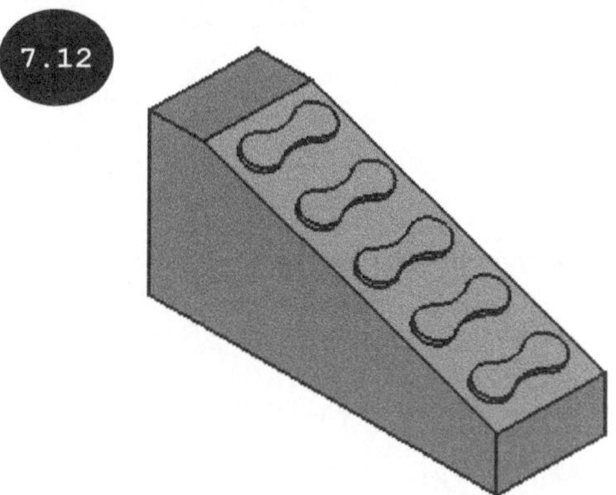

Creating a Polar Pattern

A polar pattern creates multiple instances of one or more features of a model around an axis of revolution, see Figure 7.13. The method for creating a polar pattern is discussed below:

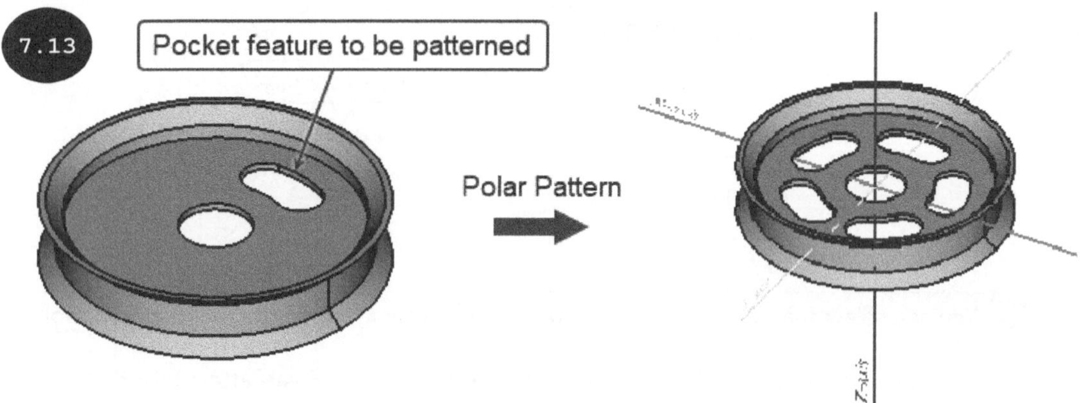

1. Select a feature to be patterned in the **Tree View** or the 3D View area. You can also select multiple features to be patterned by pressing the CTRL key.

2. After selecting a feature, click on the **PolarPattern** tool in the **Part Design Modeling** toolbar, see Figure 7.14. The preview of a polar pattern of the selected feature appears around the normal axis of its sketch in the 3D View area, since the **Normal sketch axis** option is selected in the **Axis** drop-down list of the **PolarPattern parameters** sub-window that appears in the **Tasks Panel**, see Figure 7.15.

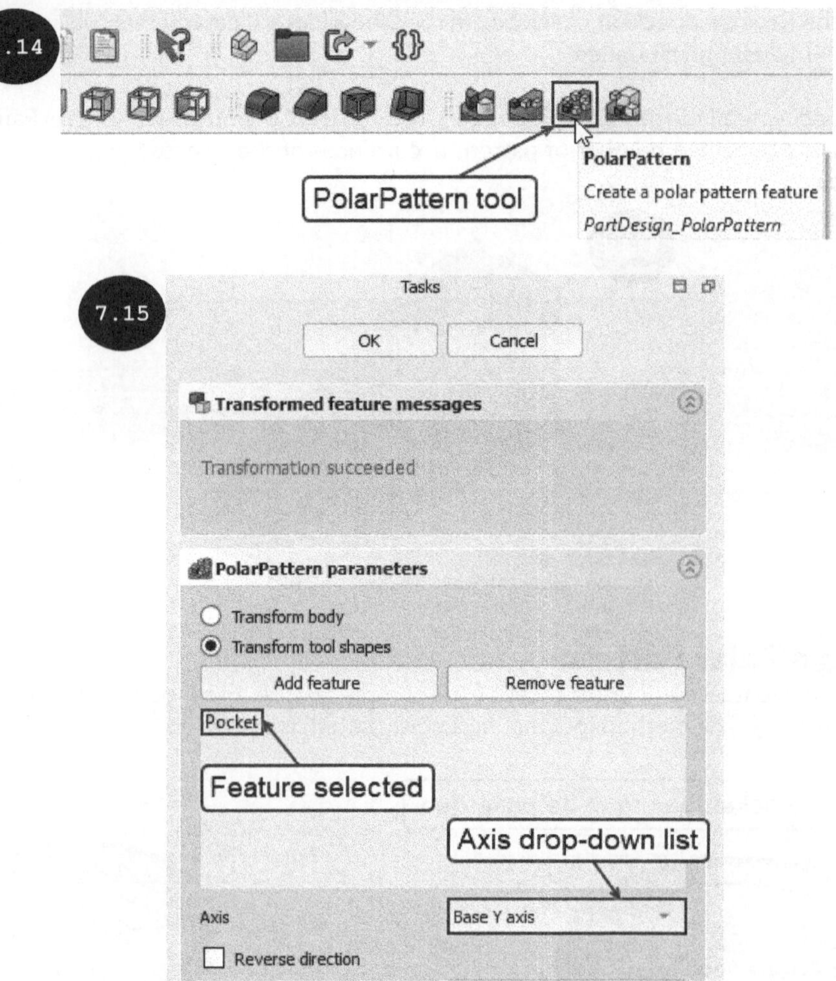

Note: You can select features to be patterned before or after invoking the **PolarPattern** tool.

If a feature to be patterned is not selected before invoking the **PolarPattern** tool, first activate the **Transform tool shapes** radio button in the **Tasks Panel**. Then, click the **Add Feature** button and select the feature to be patterned from either the 3D View area or the **Tree View**.

Tip: You can add additional features to be patterned or remove already selected features by using the **Add feature** and **Remove feature** buttons of the **PolarPattern parameters** sub-window of the **Tasks Panel**, respectively.

3. Specify the required option in the **Axis** drop-down list of the **PolarPattern parameters** sub-window for defining the axis of revolution of the polar pattern, see Figure 7.16. A preview of the polar pattern of the selected feature appears around the defined axis of revolution in the 3D View area.

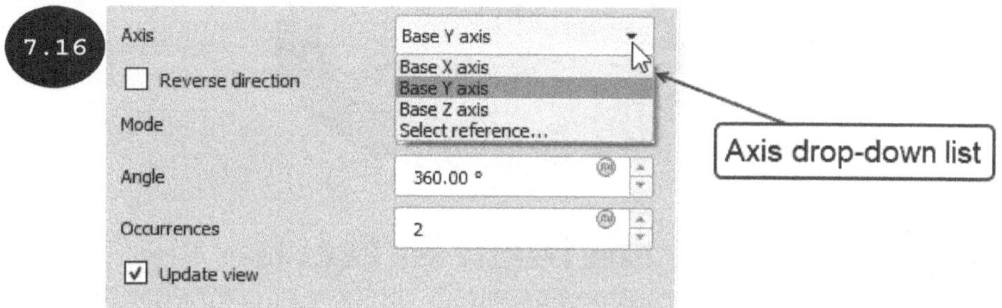

Tip: On selecting the **Select reference** option in the **Axis** drop-down list, you can select a circular edge, a cylindrical face, a linear edge, or an axis to define the axis of revolution.

4. Enter the required total angle value of the polar pattern in the **Angle** field of the **Tasks Panel** between which the specified number of pattern occurrences is to be arranged with equal angular spacing among all occurrences. By default, the 360-degree angle value is defined in this field.

5. Enter the required number of pattern occurrences to be created in the **Occurrences** field of the **Tasks Panel**, see Figure 7.17. This figure shows the preview of a polar pattern after specifying 3 as the number of pattern occurrences to be created between the specified angle value. Note that the number of pattern occurrences specified in the **Occurrences** field includes the parent feature.

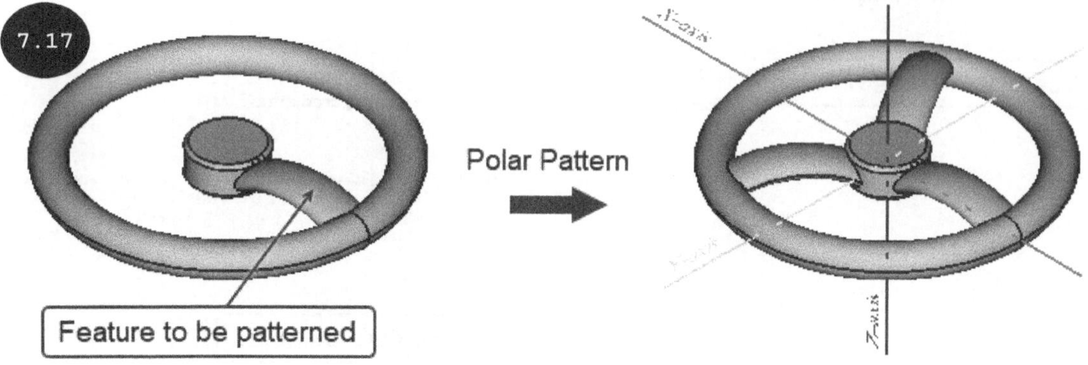

6. Select the **Reverse direction** check box in the **PolarPattern parameters** sub-window to reverse the pattern direction if needed. It works better if the angle value is specified less than 360 degrees.

7. After specifying all the required parameters, click on the **OK** button in the **Tasks Panel**. The polar pattern of a specified number of pattern occurrences gets created, see Figure 7.18.

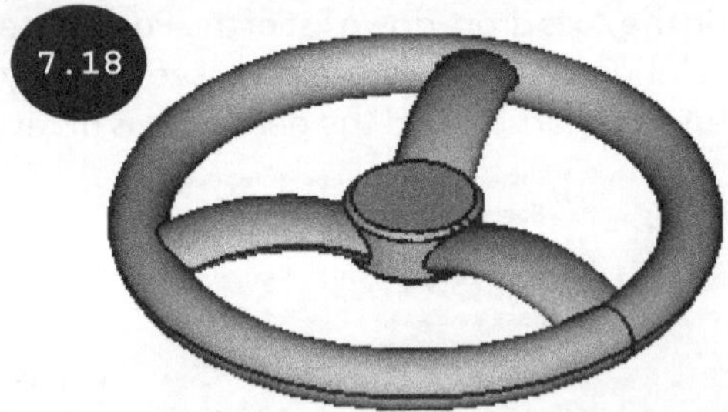

Creating a Multi-transform Pattern

In FreeCAD, you can create a multi-transform pattern by combining multiple transformations: Mirrored, Linear Pattern, Polar pattern, and/or Scaled by using the **MultiTransform** tool. The method for creating a multi-transform pattern is discussed below:

1. Select a feature to be patterned in the **Tree View** or the 3D View area. You can also select multiple features to be patterned by pressing the CTRL key.

2. After selecting a feature, click on the **Create MultiTransform** tool in the **Part Design Modeling** toolbar, see Figure 7.19. The **MultiTransform parameters** sub-window appears in the **Tasks Panel** and the name of the selected feature appears in its field, see Figure 7.20.

7.19

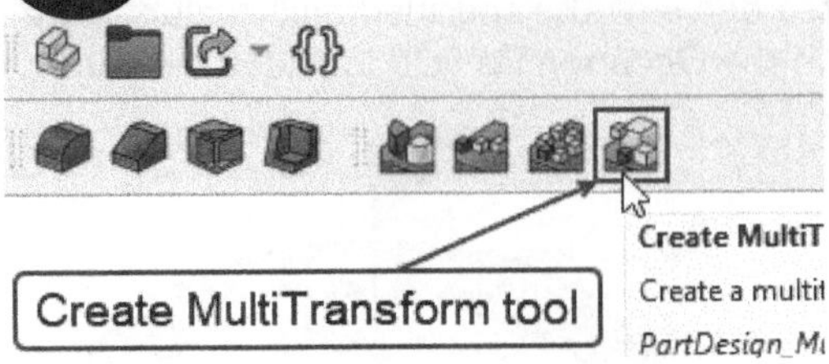

Create MultiTransform tool

7.20

Feature selected

Transformations field

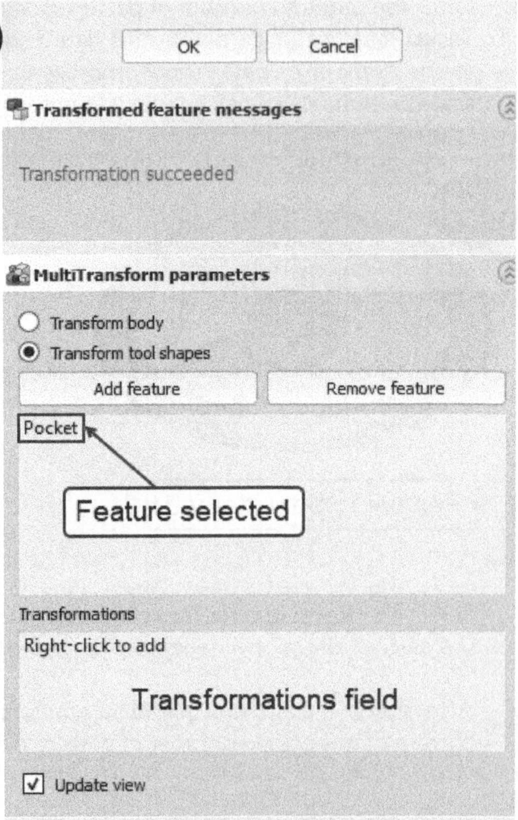

Now, you can define the first transformation (Mirrored, Linear Pattern, Polar pattern, or Scaled) to be applied to the selected feature.

3. Right-click on the **Transformations** field of the **Tasks Panel** and then select the required transformation (**Add mirrored transformation**, **Add linear pattern**, **Add polar pattern**, or **Add scaled transformation**) to be created in the shortcut menu that appears, see Figure 7.21. The transformation gets selected, and its name appears in the **Transformations** field of the **Tasks Panel**, see Figure 7.22. Also, the options to create the selected transformation appear at the bottom of the **Tasks Panel**. In Figure 7.22, the linear pattern transformation is selected. As a result, the options to create a linear pattern appear at the bottom of the **Tasks Panel**. These options are the same as discussed earlier.

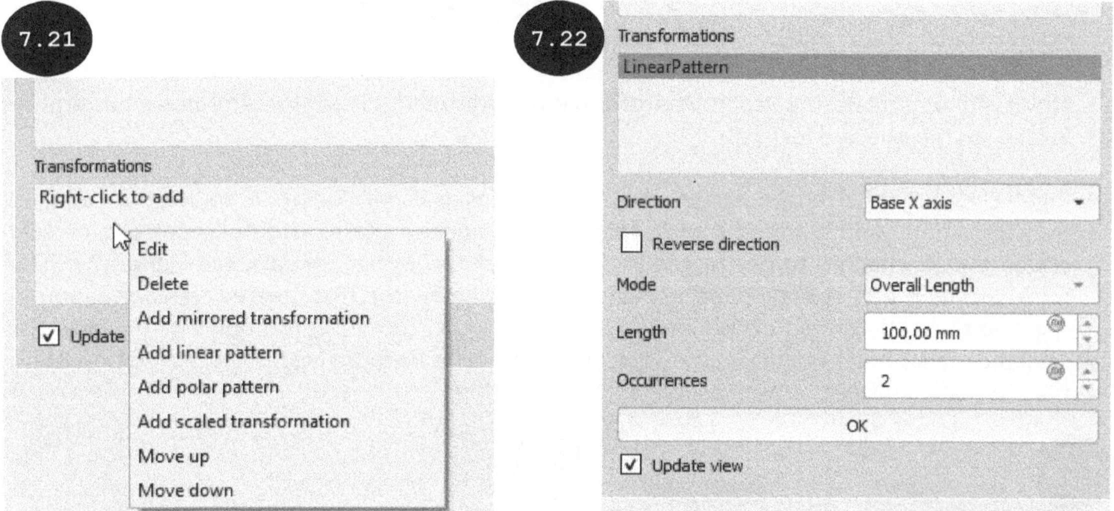

Transformation Options: The **Add mirrored transformation** option is used to add a mirrored transformation to the selected feature. The **Add linear pattern** option is used to add a linear pattern transformation to the selected feature. The **Add polar pattern** option is used to add a polar pattern transformation to the selected feature. The **Add scaled transformation** option is used to add a scaled transformation to the selected feature. All these transformations are discussed earlier and can be performed separately, except the scaled transformation.

4. Specify the required parameters for creating the selected transformation by using the respective options in the **Tasks Panel**. The preview of the transformation appears in the 3D View area, see Figure 7.23. This figure shows the preview of a linear pattern transformation of the hole feature.

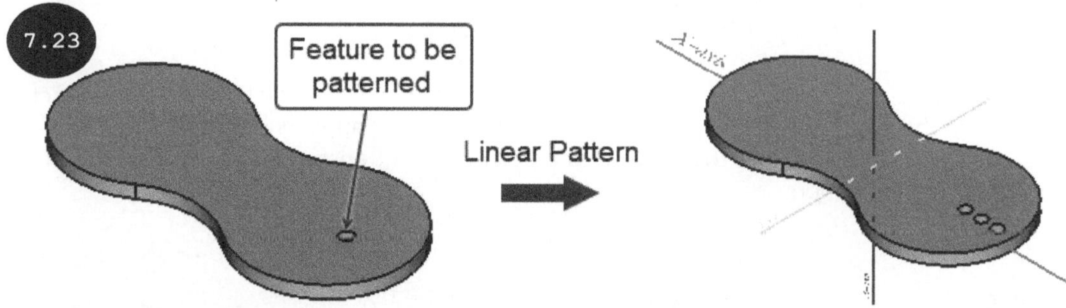

5. After specifying the required transformation parameters, click on the **OK** button at the bottom of the **Tasks Panel**. The selected transformation gets created, see Figure 7.24. In this figure, the linear pattern transformation of the hole feature is created by specifying 3 number of pattern occurrences.

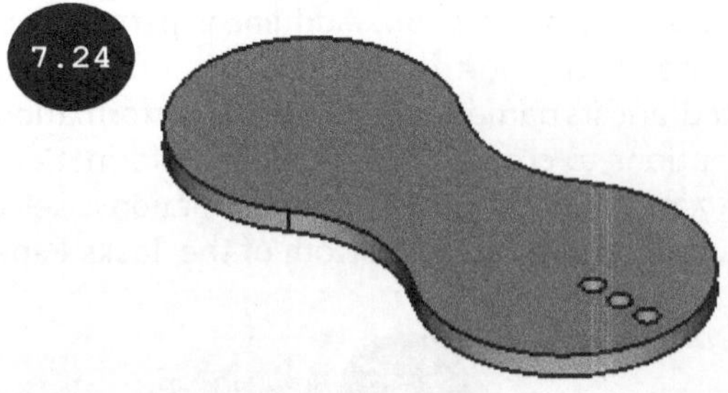

Now, you can create the second transformation (Mirrored, Linear Pattern, Polar pattern, or Scaled) to the selected feature.

6. Right-click on the **Transformations** field of the **Tasks Panel** and then select the required transformation (**Add mirrored transformation**, **Add linear pattern**, **Add polar pattern**, or **Add scaled transformation**) to be created in the shortcut menu that appears, see Figure 7.25. The transformation gets selected, and its name appears below the first created transformation in the **Transformations** field of the **Tasks Panel**, see Figure 7.26. Also, the options to create the selected transformation appear at the bottom of the **Tasks Panel**. In Figure 7.26, the polar pattern transformation is selected as the second transformation.

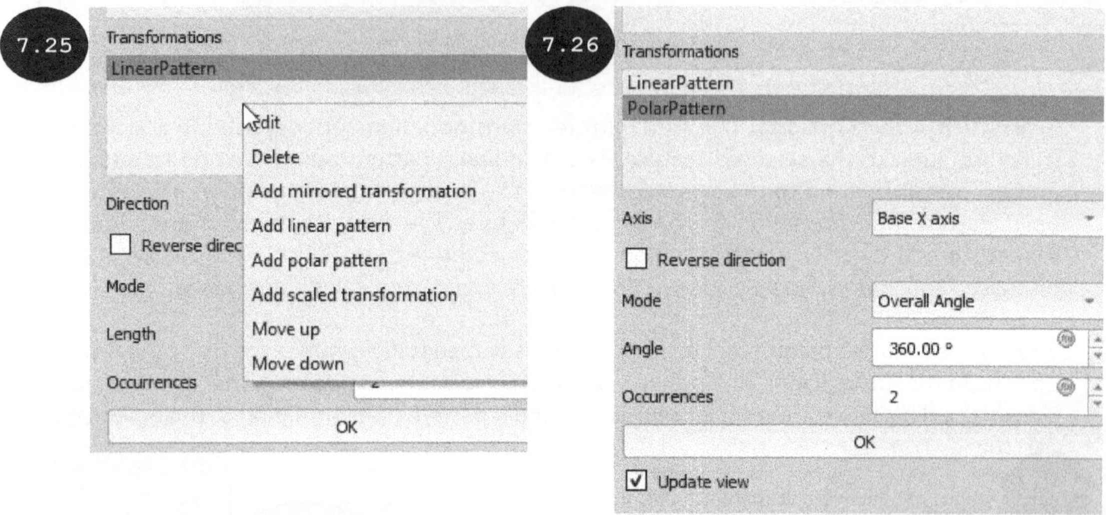

7. Specify the required parameters for creating the selected transformation by using the respective options in the **Tasks Panel**. The preview of the transformation appears in the 3D View area, see Figure 7.27. This figure shows the preview of a polar pattern transformation of the result of the previous transformation.

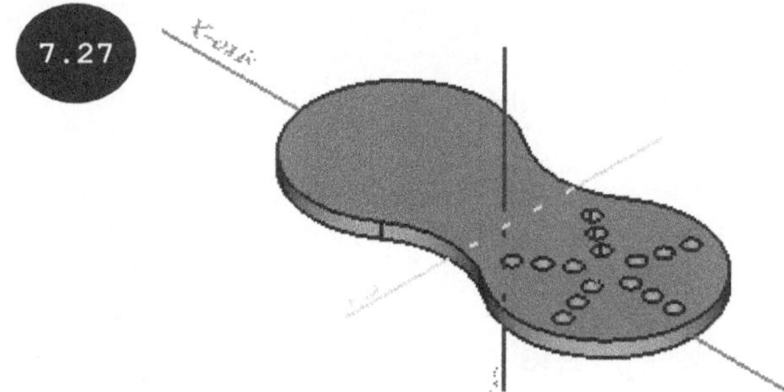

Note: Each subsequent transformation is applied to the result of the previous transformation.

8. Similarly, you can create the remaining transformations one after another. In Figure 7.28, the mirror transformation is created as the result of the previous transformation shown in Figure 7.27.

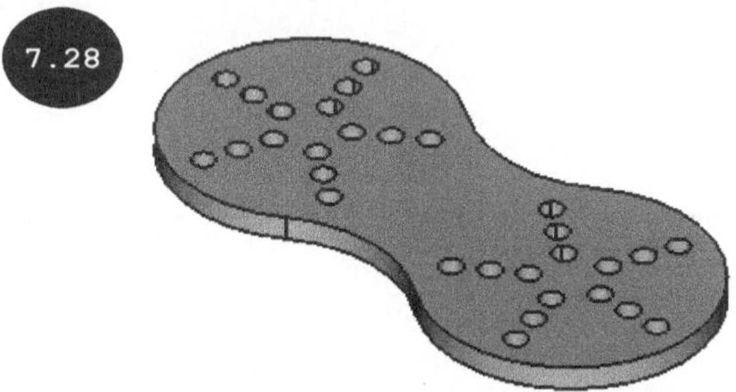

Note: As mentioned earlier, you can also perform a scaled transformation by using the **Add scaled transformation** option, see Figure 7.29. In this figure, first, a linear pattern transformation is performed for creating 5 occurrences of the pad feature, and then a scaled transformation is performed with a scale factor of 2 for 5 occurrences.

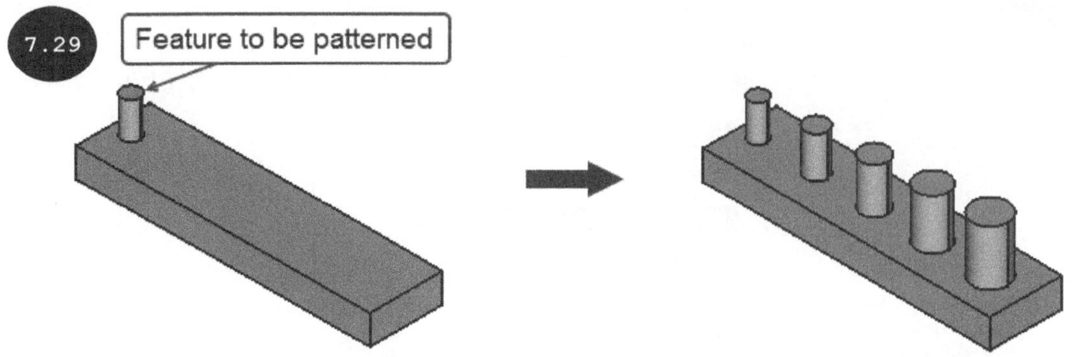

9. Click on the **OK** button to confirm the creation of a multi-transformation pattern and exit the Tasks Panel.

Tutorial 1

Create the model shown in Figure 7.30. All dimensions are in mm.

7.30

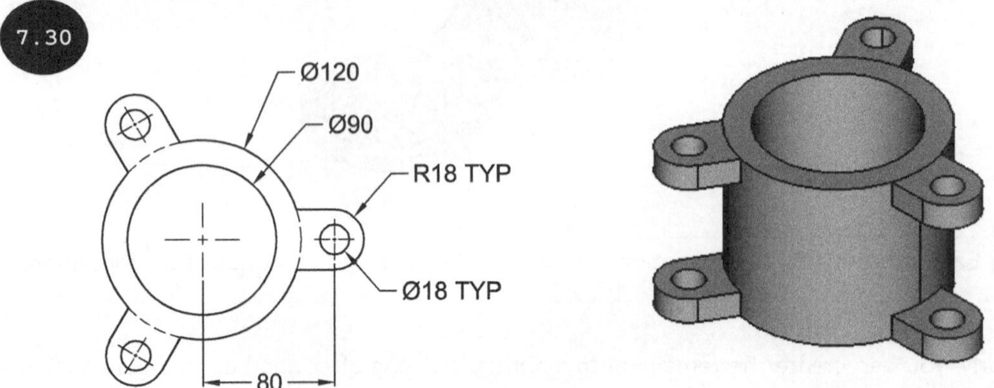

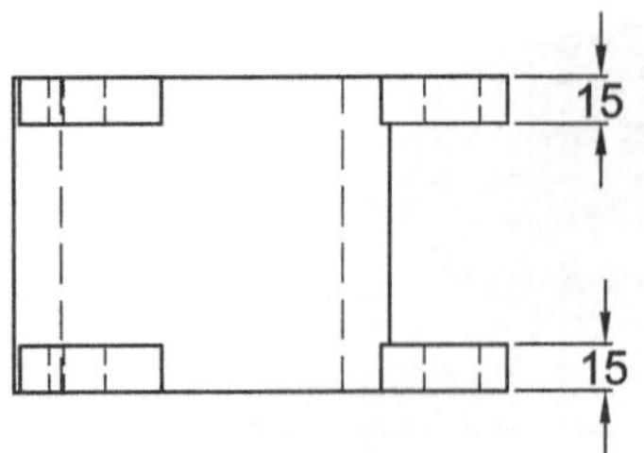

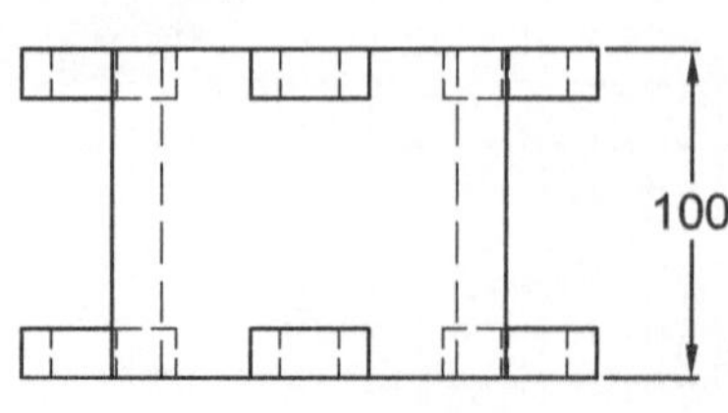

Section 1: Starting a New Part Document and Specifying Units

1. Start FreeCAD by double-clicking on the **FreeCAD 1.0** icon on your desktop. The startup user interface of FreeCAD appears, see Figure 7.31.

7.31

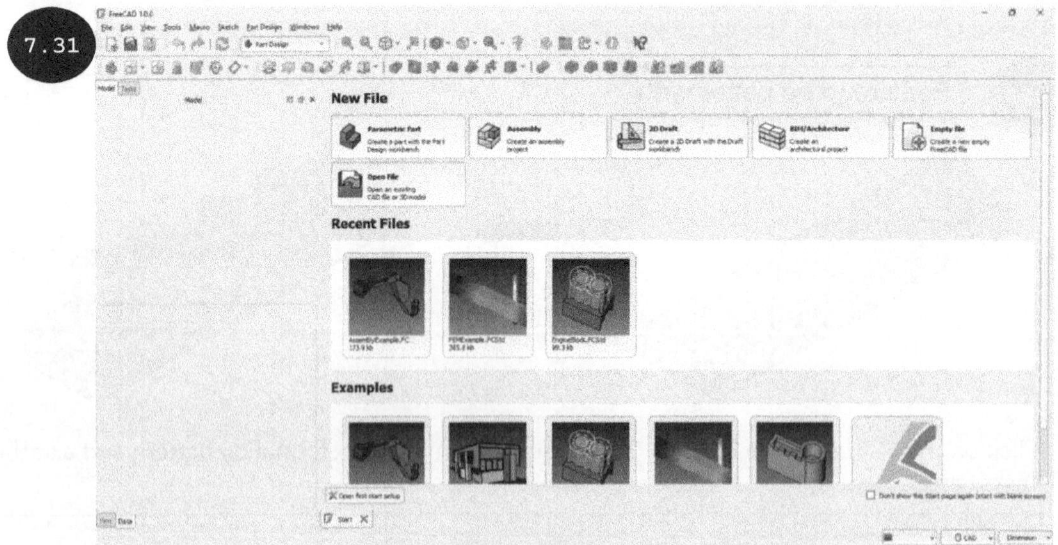

2. Click on the **Parametric Part** icon on the **Start** page (refer to Figure 7.31) or press the **CTRL + N** keys. A new part document gets invoked with the default name "**unnamed: 1**".

   Now, you need to specify millimeters (mm) as the measurement unit for the document.

3. Invoke the **Unit** flyout that appears at the lower right corner of the **Status Bar**, see Figure 7.32.

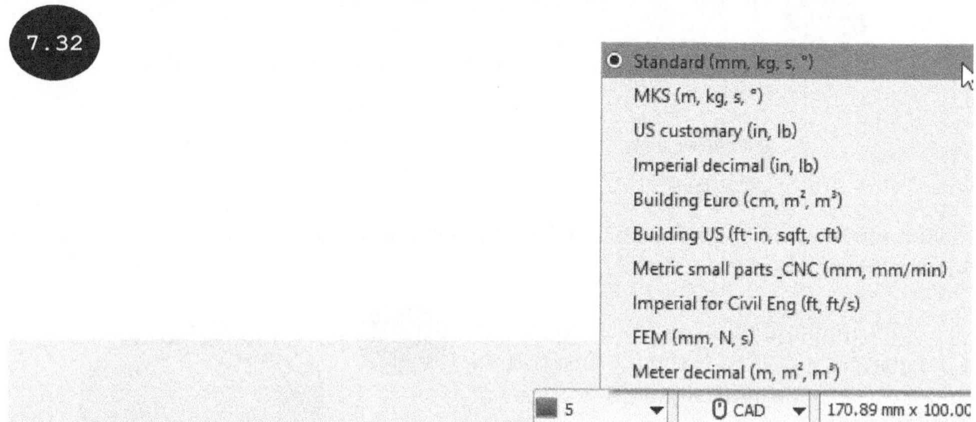

4. In this flyout, ensure that **Standard (mm, kg, s,*)** is selected as the unit system for the current design document.

Section 2: Creating the Base Feature

Now, you can create the base or first feature of the model, which is a pad feature.

1. Invoke the **Sketcher** workbench by selecting the **XY_Plane** as the sketching plane using the **Create sketch** tool and then create the sketch (two concentric circles) of the pad feature, see Figure 7.33. The center point of the circles is at the origin.

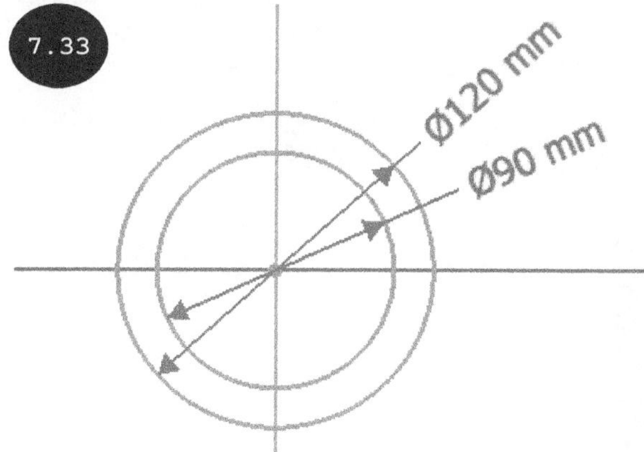

2. After creating the sketch, exit the **Sketcher** workbench to switch back to the **Part Design** workbench.

Now, you can extrude the sketch to create a pad feature.

3. Click on the **Pad** tool in the **Part Design Modeling** toolbar, see Figure 7.34. The preview of a pad feature appears in the 3D View area with default parameters. Also, the **Pad parameters** sub-window appears in the **Tasks Panel**.

4. Enter **100** mm in the **Length** field of the **Tasks Panel** and then press the TAB key to update the preview of the pad feature.

5. Select the **Symmetric to plane** check box in the **Pad parameters** sub-windows of the **Tasks Panel** to add material symmetrically on both sides of the sketching plane.

6. Click on the **OK** button in the **Tasks Panel** to confirm the creation of the pad feature and exit the **Tasks Panel**. The pad (base) feature of specified length gets created, see Figure 7.35.

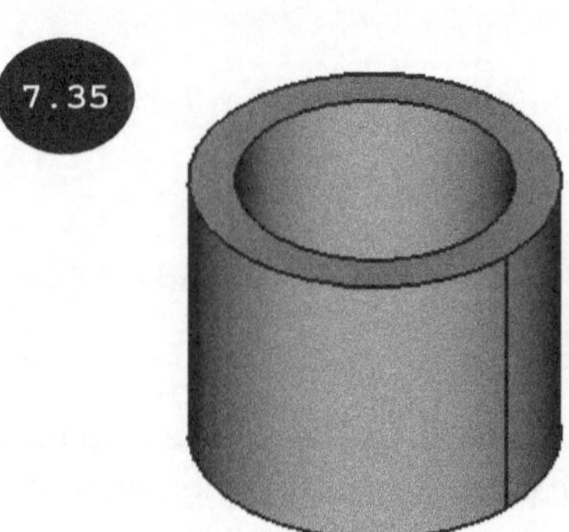

Section 3: Creating the Second Feature

Now, you can create the second feature of the model, which is also a pad feature.

1. Select the top planar face of the base feature (see Figure 7.36) and then click on the **Create sketch** tool in the **Part Design Helper** toolbar, see Figure 7.37. The **Sketcher** workbench gets invoked and the selected planar face gets oriented normal to the viewing direction.

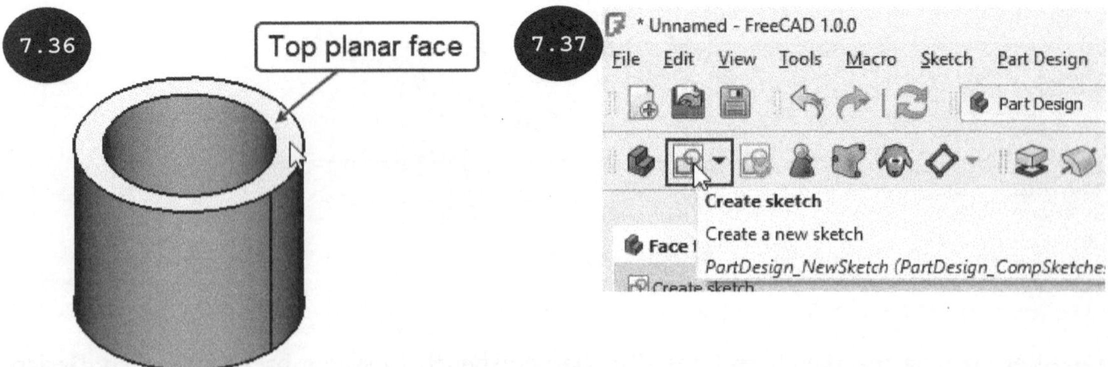

2. Create the sketch of the feature by using the sketching tools, see Figure 7.38.

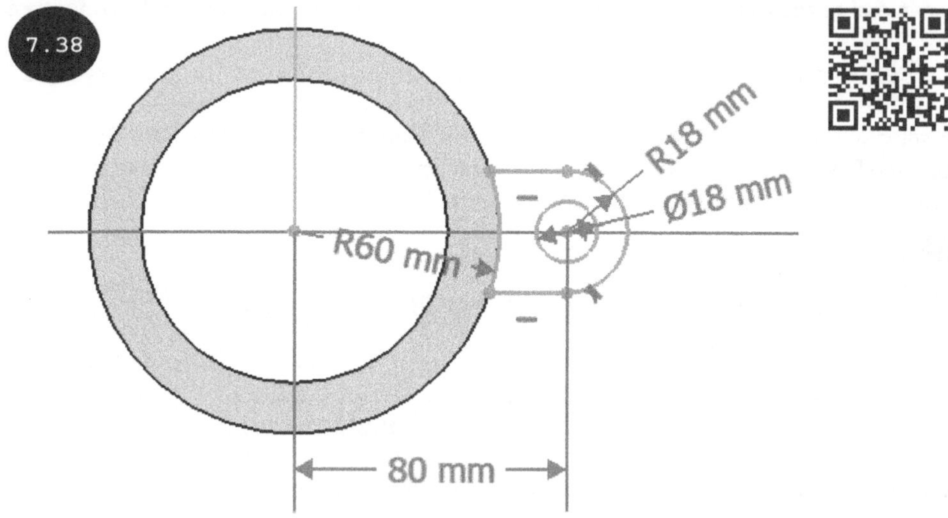

3. After creating the sketch, exit the **Sketcher** workbench to switch back to the **Part Design** workbench.

   Now, you can extrude the sketch to create a pad feature.

4. Click on the **Pad** tool in the **Part Design Modeling** toolbar, see Figure 7.39. The **Pad parameters** sub-window appears in the **Tasks Panel**. Ignore the error message that may appear in the **Report view** window at the bottom of the screen. You can close the **Report view** window by clicking on the cross mark × that appears in its top right corner.

5. Select the **Reversed** check box in the **Pad parameters** sub-windows of the **Tasks Panel** to reverse the direction of extrusion downward. The preview of the pad feature appears in the 3D View area.

6. Enter **15** mm in the **Length** field of the **Tasks Panel** and then press the TAB key to update the preview of the pad feature.

7. Click on the **OK** button in the **Tasks Panel** to confirm the creation of the pad feature and exit the **Tasks Panel**. The pad feature of specified length gets created, see Figure 7.40.

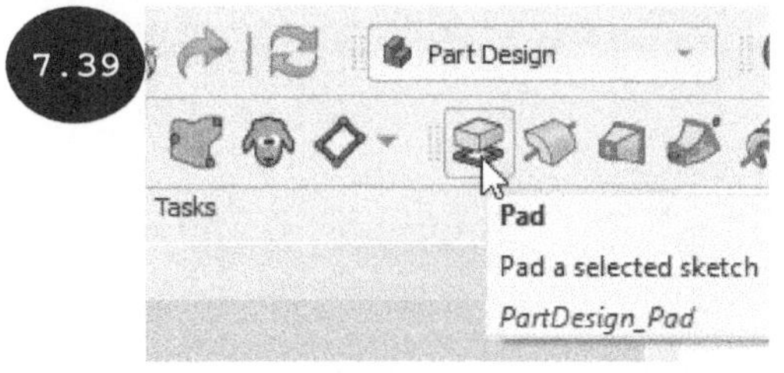

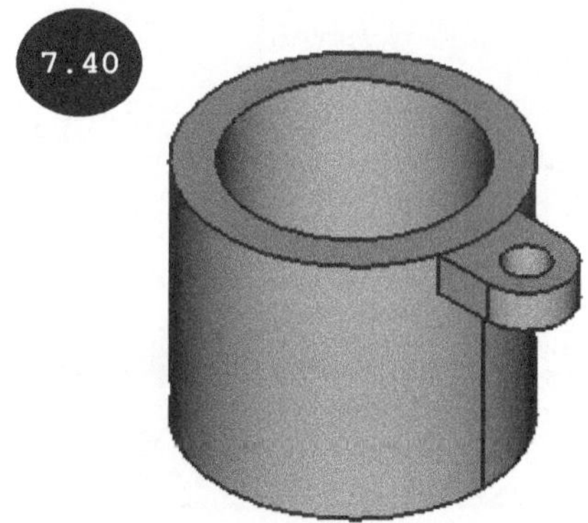

Section 4: Creating the Multi-transform Pattern Feature

Now, you can create the third feature of the model, which is a multi-transform pattern feature.

1. Select the previously created pad feature (second) in the **Tree View** or the 3D View area.

2. After selecting a feature, click on the **Create MultiTransform** tool in the **Part Design Modeling** toolbar, see Figure 7.41. The **MultiTransform parameters** sub-window appears in the **Tasks Panel** and the name of the selected feature appears in its field.

Now, you can define the first transformation to be applied to the selected feature.

3. Right-click on the **Transformations** field of the **Tasks Panel** and then select the **Add polar pattern** option in the shortcut menu that appears, see Figure 7.42. The polar pattern transformation gets selected and appears in the **Transformations** field of the **Tasks Panel**, see Figure 7.43. Also, the options to create a polar pattern appear at the bottom of the **Tasks Panel**.

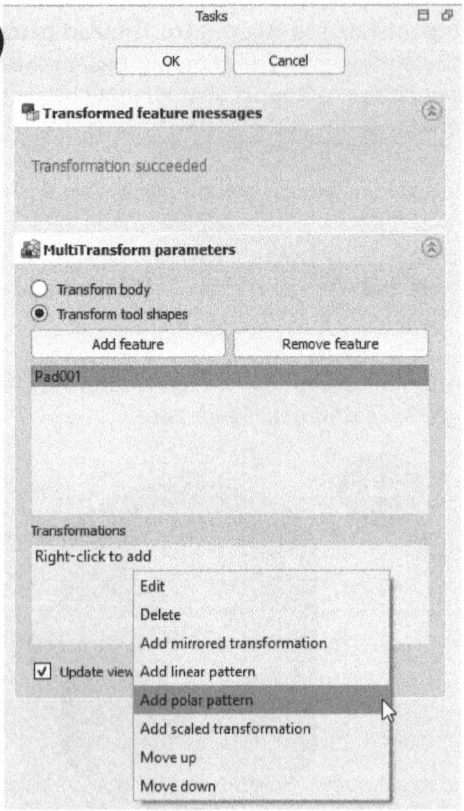

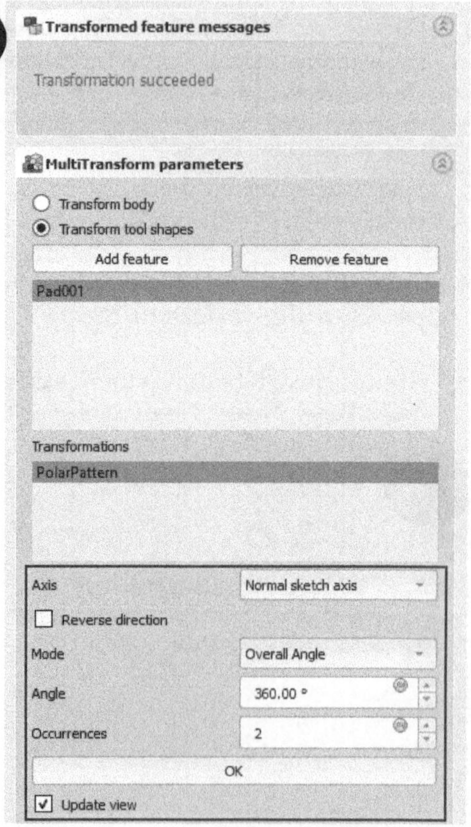

4. Ensure that the **Normal sketch axis** option is selected in the **Axis** drop-down list of the **Tasks Panel** to define the axis of revolution of the polar pattern, normal to the sketch of the selected feature.

5. Ensure that the **360**-degree angle value is defined in the **Angle** field of the **Tasks Panel**.

6. Enter **3** as the number of pattern occurrences to be created in the **Occurrences** field of the **Tasks Panel**.

7. Click on the **OK** button available at the bottom of the **Tasks Panel**. A polar pattern of specified parameters gets created, see Figure 7.44.

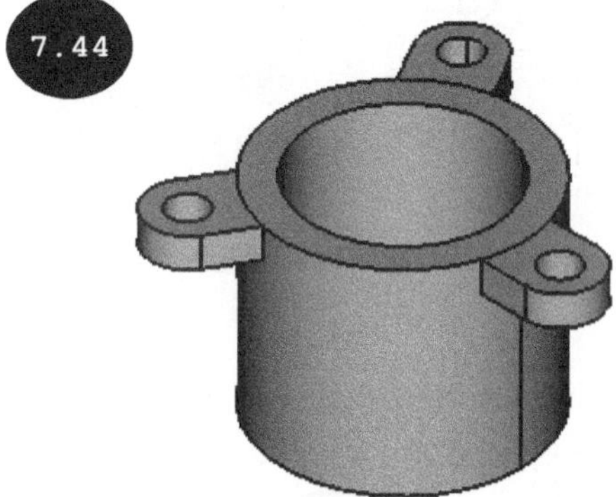

Now, you can create a mirrored transformation to mirror the result of the previously created polar pattern transformation.

8. Right-click on the **Transformations** field of the **Tasks Panel** and then select the **Add mirrored transformation** option in the shortcut menu that appears, see Figure 7.45. The options to mirror the result of the previously created polar pattern appear at the bottom of the **Tasks Panel**, see Figure 7.46.

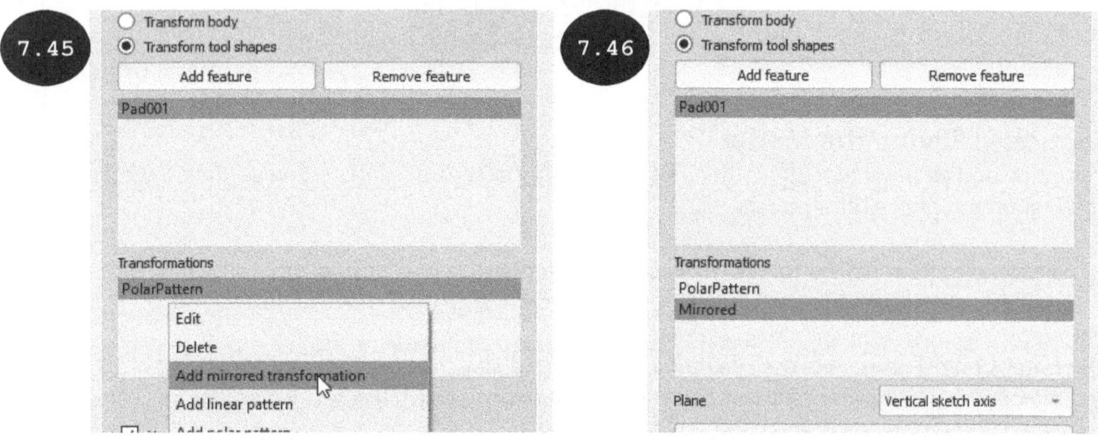

9. Select the **Base XY plane** option as the mirroring plane in the **Plane** drop-down list of the **Tasks Panel**. The preview of the mirrored transformation appears in the 3D View area, see Figure 7.47.

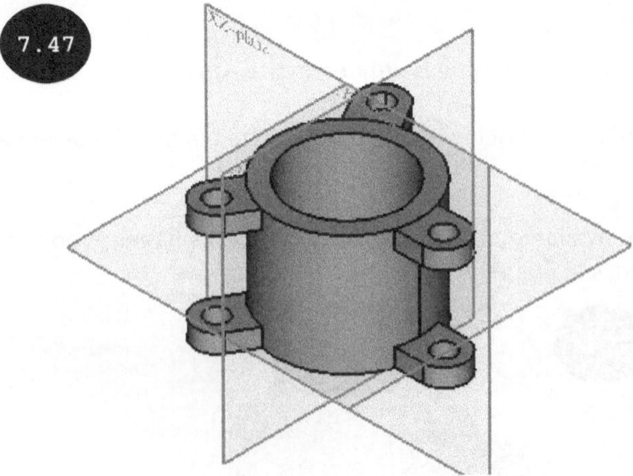

10. Click on the **OK** button available at the bottom of the **Tasks Panel**. The mirrored transformation gets created.

11. Select the **OK** button to exit the **Tasks Panel**. Figure 7.48 shows the final model.

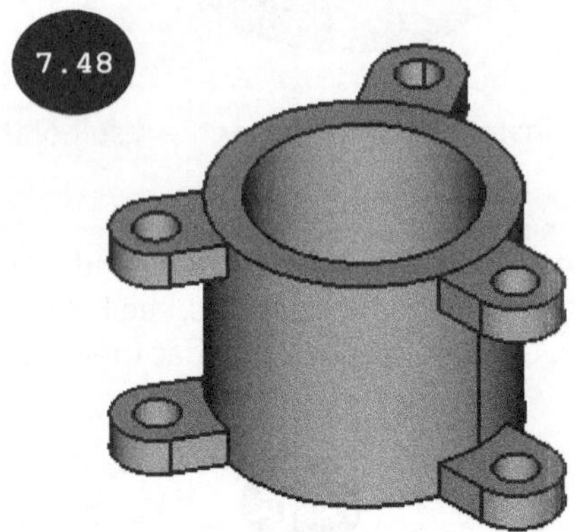

Section 5: Saving the Model

1. Click on the **Save** tool in the **File** toolbar or press the CTRL + S keys. The **Save FreeCAD Document** dialog box appears.

2. Browse to the required folder (:*FreeCAD > Chapter 07*) in the local drive of your system. Note that you need to create the Chapter 07 sub-folder inside the FreeCAD folder.

3. Enter **Ch07-Tutorial 1** in the **File name** field of the dialog box. Next, click on the **Save** button in the dialog box. The model gets saved at the specified location (:*FreeCAD > Chapter 07*).

4. Click on **File > Close** in the **Standard Menu** to close the current document.

Tutorial 2

Create a model, as shown in Figure 7.49. Different views and dimensions of the model are given in the same figure. All dimensions are in inches (in).

7.49

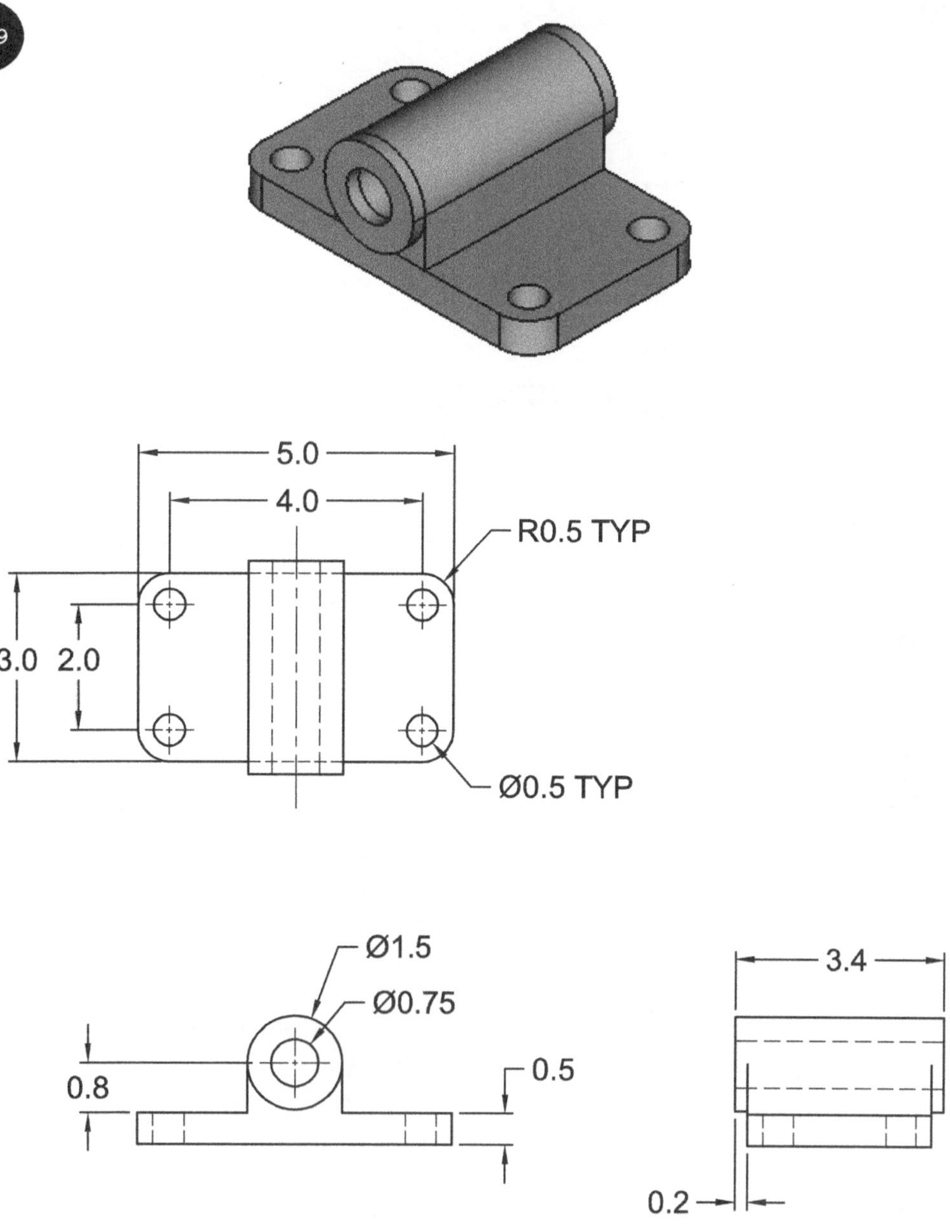

5.0
4.0
R0.5 TYP
3.0
2.0
Ø0.5 TYP

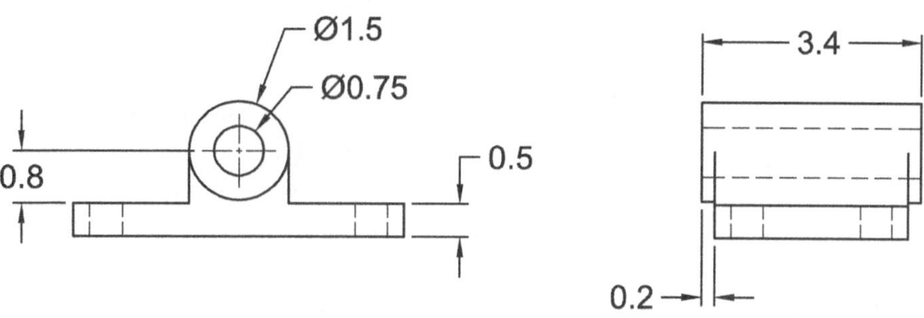

Section 1: Starting a New Part Document and Specifying Units

1. Start FreeCAD by double-clicking on the **FreeCAD 1.0** icon on your desktop. The startup user interface of FreeCAD appears, see Figure 7.50.

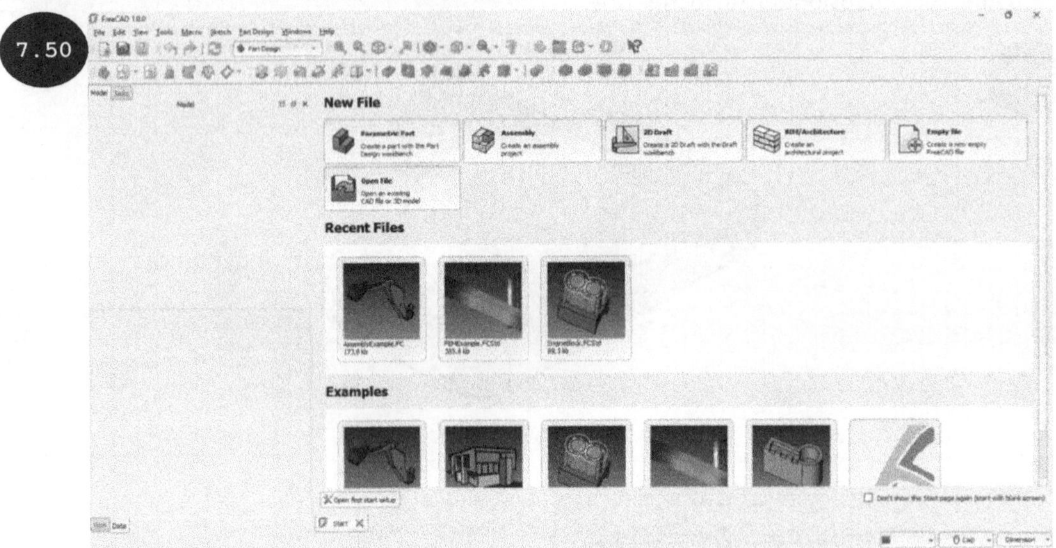

7.50

2. Click on the **Parametric Part** icon on the **Start** page (refer to Figure 7.50) or press the **CTRL + N** keys. A new part document gets invoked with the default name "**unnamed: 1**".

   Now, you can specify the required unit system.

3. Invoke the **Unit** flyout that appears at the lower right corner of the **Status Bar**, see Figure 7.51.

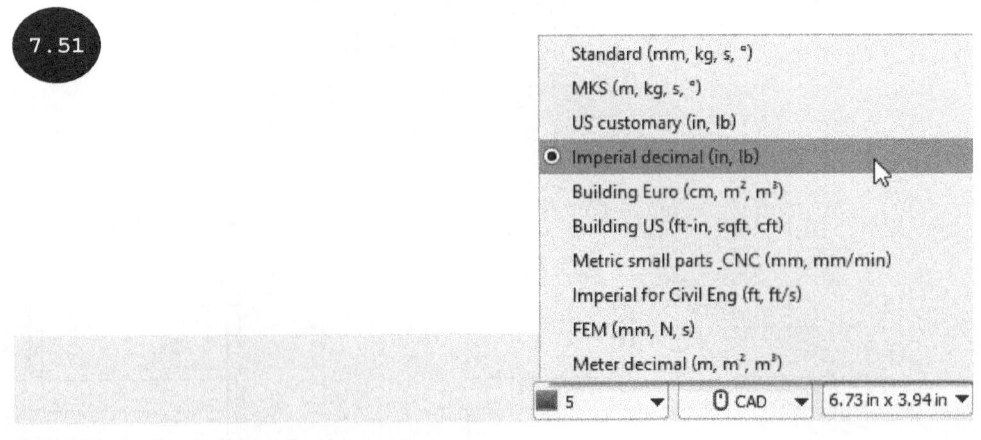

7.51

4. In this flyout, ensure that **Standard (mm, kg, s,*)** is selected as the unit system for the current design document.

Section 2: Creating the Base Feature

Now, you can create the base or first feature of the model, which is a pad feature.

1. Invoke the **Sketcher** workbench by selecting the **XY_Plane** as the sketching plane using the **Create sketch** tool and then create the sketch of the pad feature, see Figure 7.52.

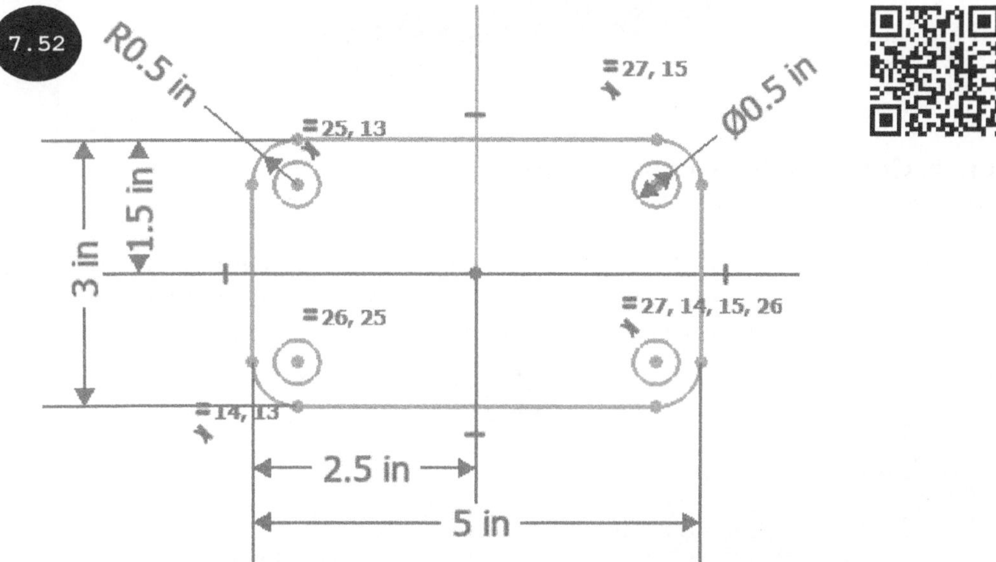

2. After creating the sketch, exit the **Sketcher** workbench to switch back to the **Part Design** workbench.

   Now, you can extrude the sketch to create a pad feature.

3. Click on the **Pad** tool in the **Part Design Modeling** toolbar, see Figure 7.53. The preview of a pad feature appears in the 3D View area with default parameters. Also, the **Pad parameters** sub-window appears in the **Tasks Panel**.

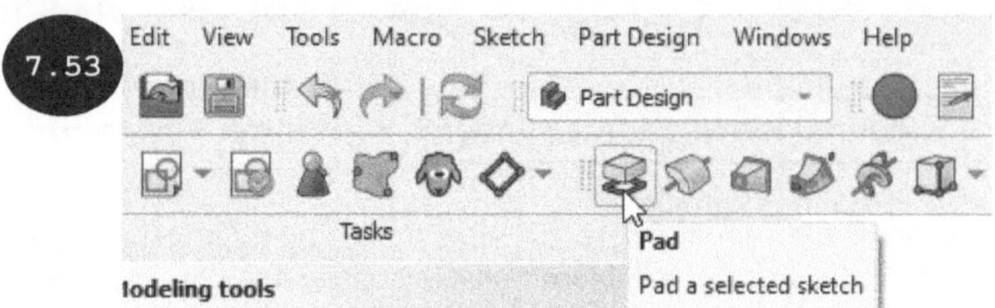

4. Enter **0.5** inches in the **Length** field of the **Tasks Panel** and then press the TAB key to update the preview of the pad feature.

5. Click on the **OK** button in the **Tasks Panel** to confirm the creation of the pad feature and exit the **Tasks Panel**. The pad (base) feature of specified length gets created, see Figure 7.54.

Section 3: Creating the Second Feature

Now, you can create the second feature of the model, which is also a pad feature.

1. Select the front planar face of the base feature (see Figure 7.55) and then click on the **Create sketch** tool in the **Part Design Helper** toolbar, see Figure 7.56. The **Sketcher** workbench gets invoked and the selected planar face gets oriented normal to the viewing direction.

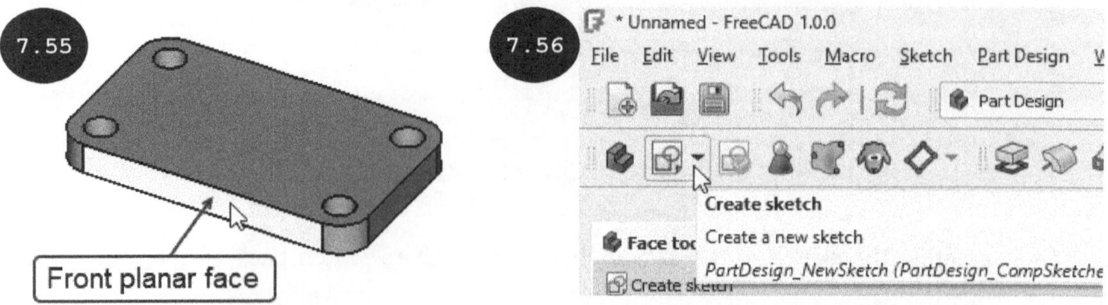

2. Click on the **Create external geometry** tool in the **Sketcher geometries** toolbar (see Figure 7.57) to project the top edge of the model as the linked construction entity onto the sketch.

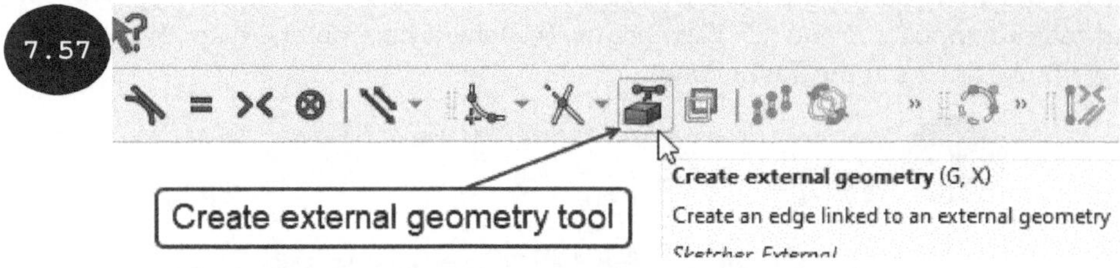

3. Select the top edge of the model in the 3D View area. The edge gets projected as the linked construction entity in the sketch, see Figure 7.58. Next, press the ESC key to exit the tool.

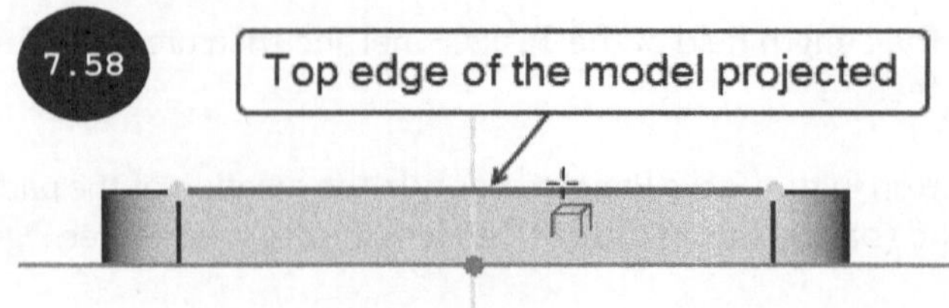

Now, you can create the sketch by taking reference to appear the linked construction entity.

4. Create the closed sketch of the feature by using the sketching tools, see Figure 7.59.

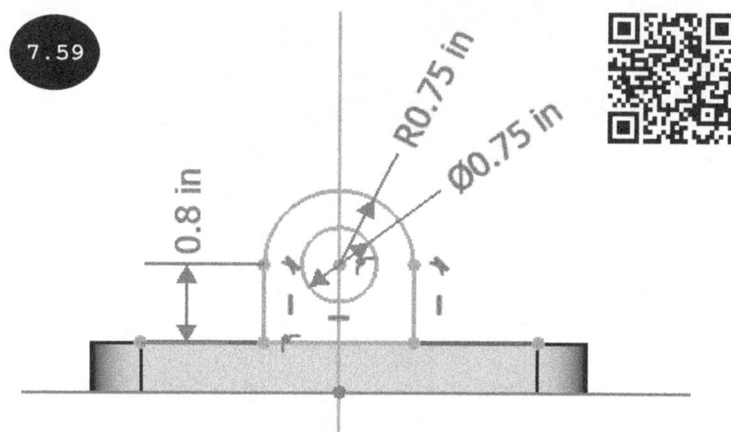

5. After creating the sketch, exit the **Sketcher** workbench to switch back to the **Part Design** workbench.

   Now, you can extrude the sketch to create a pad feature.

6. Click on the **Pad** tool in the **Part Design Modeling** toolbar, see Figure 7.60. The **Pad parameters** sub-window appears in the **Tasks Panel**. Ignore the error message that may appear in the **Report view** window at the bottom of the screen. You can close the **Report view** window by clicking on the cross mark × that appears in its top right corner.

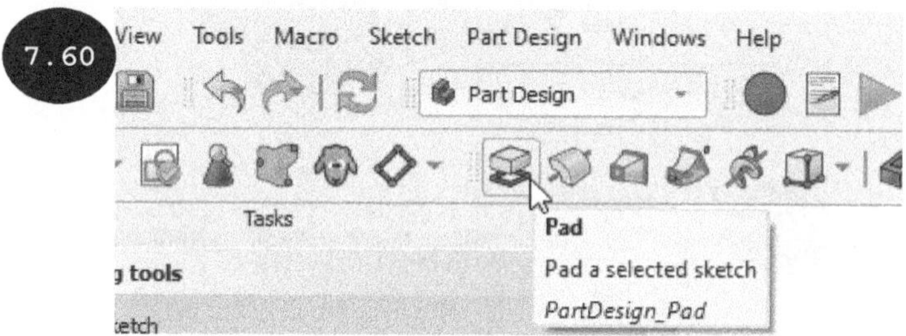

7. Select the **Reversed** check box in the **Pad parameters** sub-windows of the **Tasks Panel** to reverse the direction of extrusion towards the back. The preview of a pad feature appears in the 3D View area.

8. Enter **3** inches in the **Length** field of the **Tasks Panel** and then press the TAB key to update the preview of the pad feature.

9. Click on the **OK** button in the **Tasks Panel** to confirm the creation of the pad feature and exit the **Tasks Panel**. The pad feature of specified length gets created, see Figure 7.61.

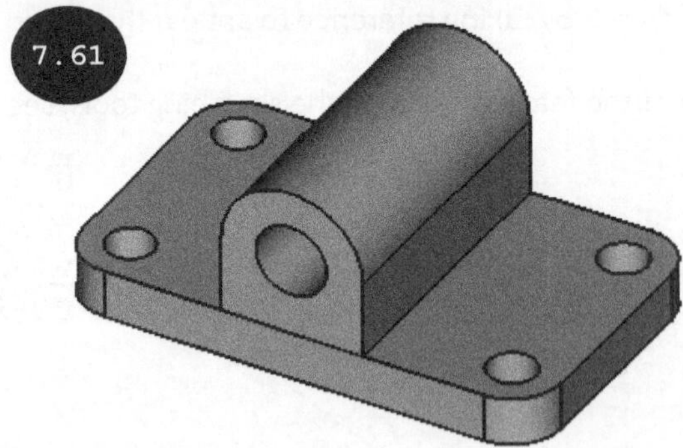

Section 4: Creating the Third Feature

Now, you can create the third feature of the model, which is also a pad feature.

1. Select the front planar face of the second feature (see Figure 7.62) and then click on the **Create sketch** tool in the **Part Design Helper** toolbar, see Figure 7.63. The **Sketcher** workbench gets invoked and the selected planar face gets oriented normal to the viewing direction.

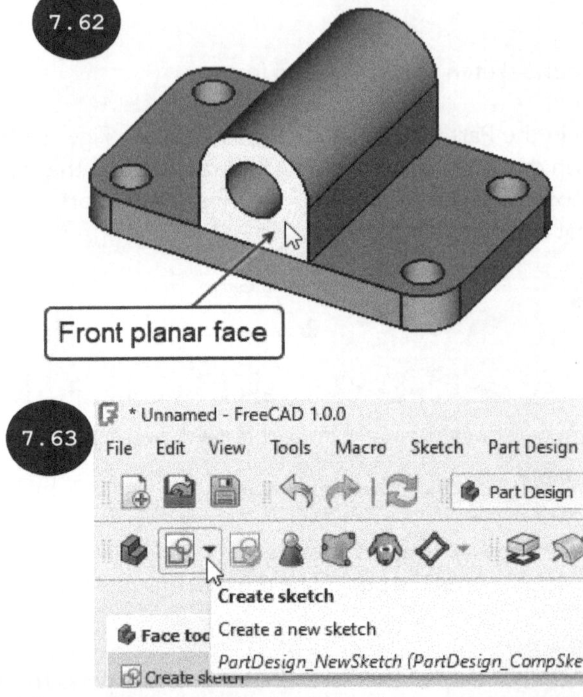

2. Create the sketch (two concentric circles) of the feature by using the sketching tools, see Figure 7.64.

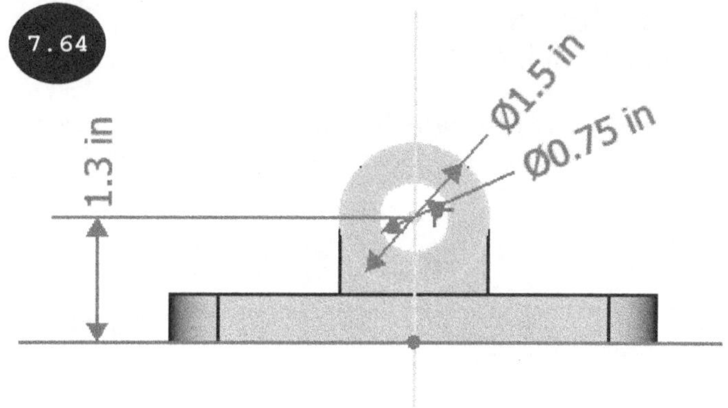

3. After creating the sketch, exit the **Sketcher** workbench to switch back to the **Part Design** workbench.

   Now, you can extrude the sketch to create a pad feature.

4. Click on the **Pad** tool in the **Part Design Modeling** toolbar, see Figure 7.65. The **Pad parameters** sub-window appears in the **Tasks Panel**. Also, the preview of the pad feature appears in the 3D View area.

5. Enter **0.2** inches in the **Length** field of the **Tasks Panel** and then press the TAB key to update the preview of the pad feature.

6. Click on the **OK** button in the **Tasks Panel** to confirm the creation of the pad feature and exit the **Tasks Panel**. The pad feature of specified length gets created, see Figure 7.66.

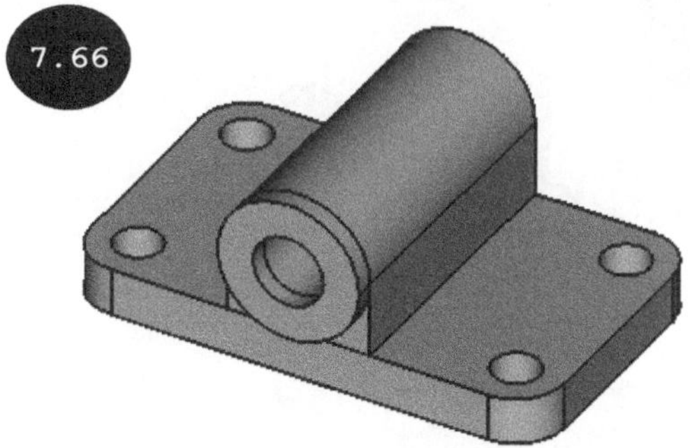

Section 5: Mirroring the Feature

Now, you need to mirror the previously created pad feature.

1. Select the previously created pad feature in the **Tree View** or the 3D View area and then click on the **Mirrored** tool in the **Part Design Helper** toolbar, see Figure 7.67. The **Mirrored parameters** sub-window appears in the **Tasks Panel**.

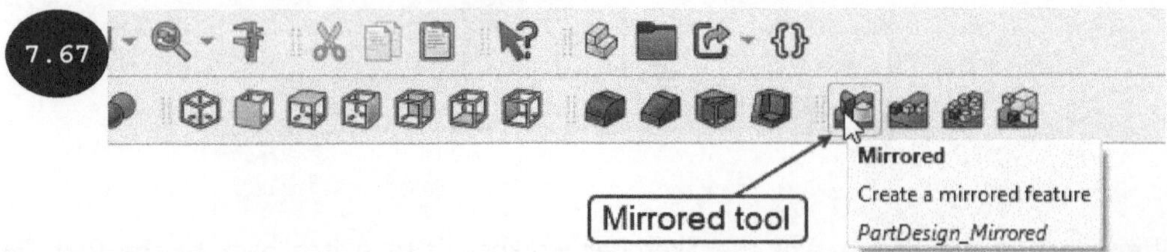

2. Select the **Base XZ plane** option as the mirroring plane in the Plane drop-down list of the Tasks Panel, see Figure 7.68. The preview of a mirror feature appears about the XZ plane of the model, see Figure 7.69.

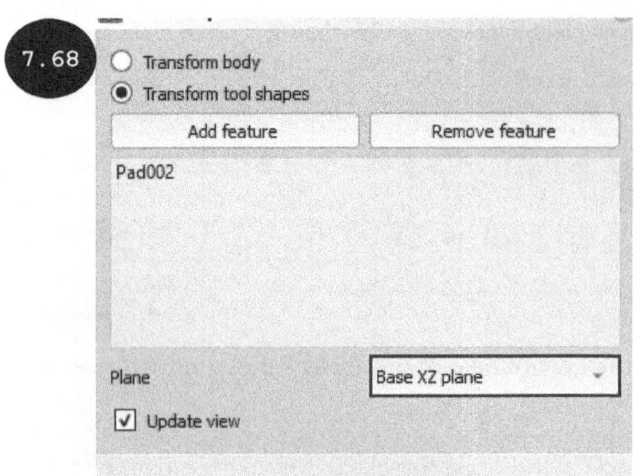

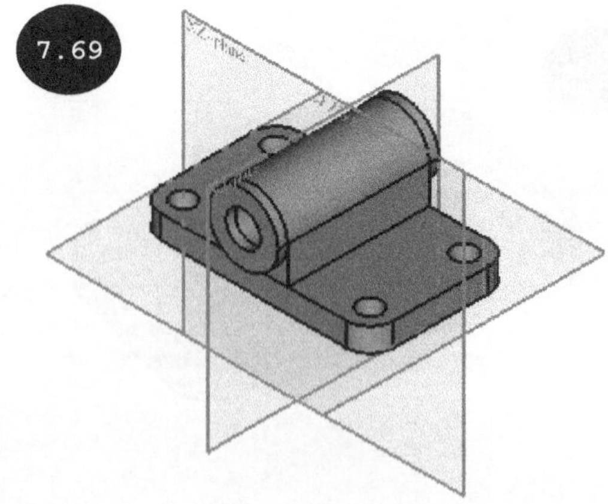

3. Click on the **OK** button in the **Tasks Panel** to confirm the creation of the mirrored feature and exit the **Tasks Panel**. The mirrored feature gets created. Figure 7.70 shows the final model.

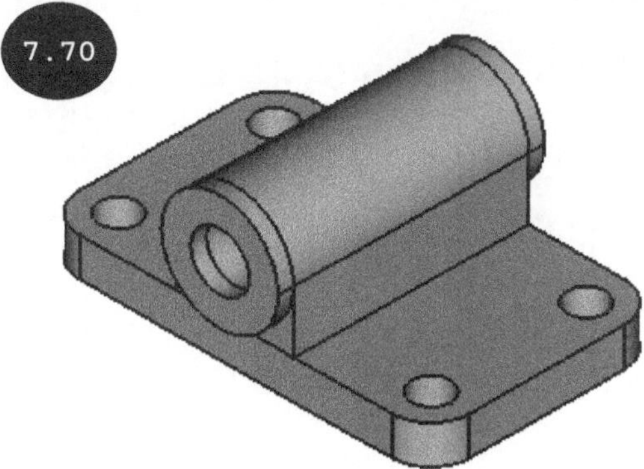

Section 6: Saving the Model

1. Click on the **Save** tool in the **File** toolbar or press the CTRL + S keys. The **Save FreeCAD Document** dialog box appears.

2. Browse to the required folder (*:\FreeCAD > Chapter 07*) in the local drive of your system. Note that you need to create the Chapter 07 sub-folder inside the FreeCAD folder, if not created earlier.

3. Enter **Ch07-Tutorial 2** in the **File name** field of the dialog box. Next, click on the **Save** button in the dialog box. The model gets saved at the specified location (*:\FreeCAD > Chapter 07*).

4. Click on **File > Close** in the **Standard Menu** to close the current document.

Hands-on Test Drive 1

Create a model shown in Figure 7.71. Different views and dimensions of the model are given in Figure 7.72. All dimensions are in inches (in).

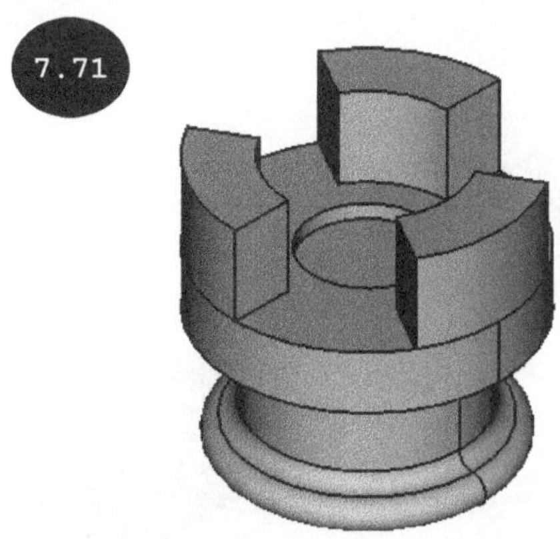

7.72

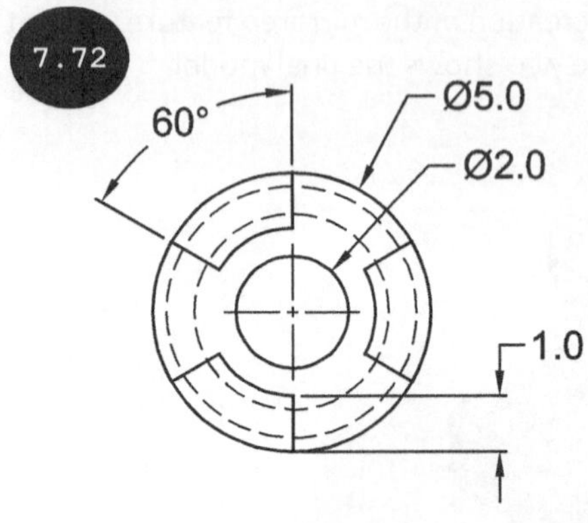

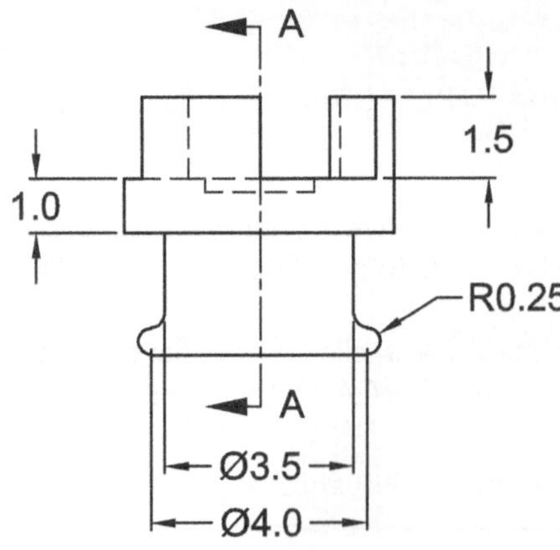

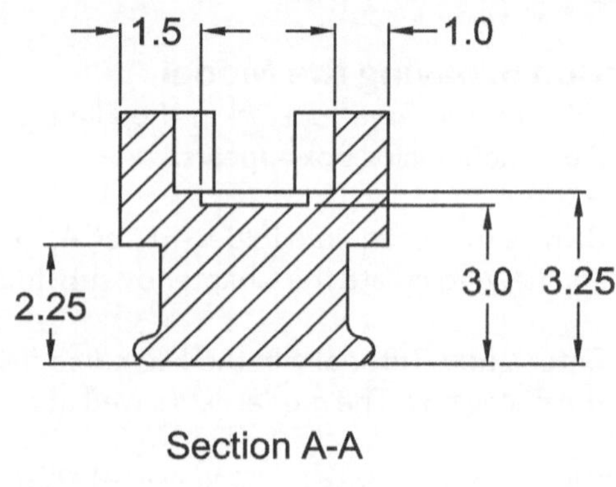

Hands-on Test Drive 2

Create a model shown in Figure 7.73. Different views and dimensions of the model are given in Figure 7.74. All dimensions are in mm.

7.73

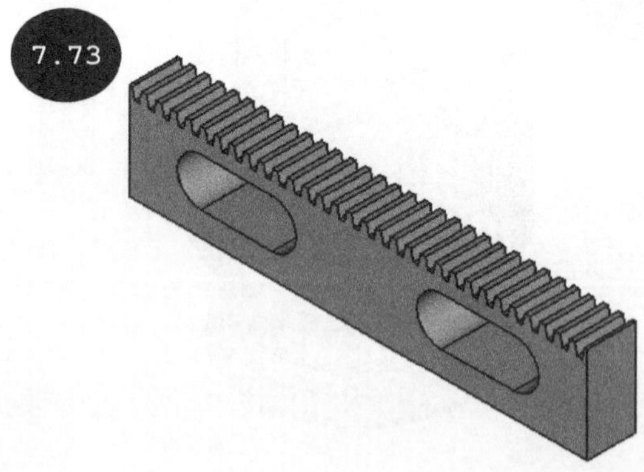

7.74

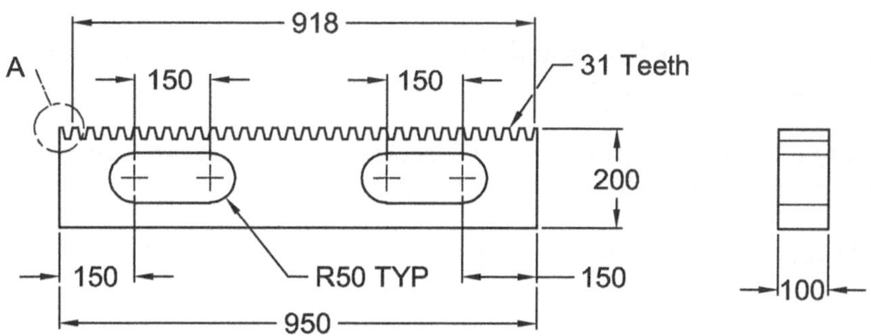

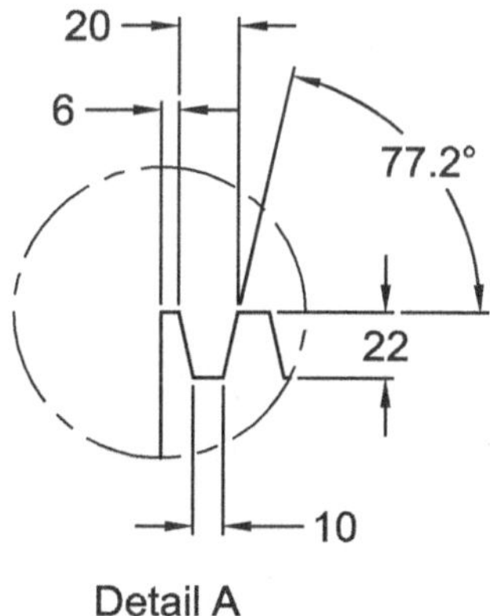

Summary

This chapter discussed how to mirror features of a model about a mirroring plane. It also discussed creating a linear pattern, a polar pattern, and a multi-transform pattern.

Questions

Complete and verify the following sentences:

- The _________ tool is used for creating multiple occurrences of one or more features along a linear direction.
- A _________ pattern creates multiple occurrences of one or more features of a model around an axis of revolution.
- The _________ tool is used for mirroring one or more features of a model about a mirroring plane.

- The _________ option allows you to select a plane or a planar face of an existing feature as the mirroring plane while creating a mirrored feature.
- The _________ tool is used for creating a multi-transform pattern by combining _________, linear pattern, _________, and/or _________ transformations.
- While creating a linear pattern, the number of occurrences specified in the **Occurrences** field also includes the parent or source feature. (True/False)
- In FreeCAD, you cannot select features to be patterned after invoking the tool. (True/False)
- In FreeCAD, the scaled transformation cannot be performed separately. (True/False)

Creating Holes and Dress-up Features

This chapter discusses the following topics:

- Creating Holes
- Creating Fillets
- Creating Chamfers
- Creating a Thick Shell Model
- Adding an Angular Draft

In this chapter, you will learn about creating standard or customized holes as per the standard specifications by using the **Hole** tool. You will also learn how to create dress-up features such as fillet, chamfer, and thickness (shell) for applying treatment to the existing edges and faces of a model.

Creating Holes

In FreeCAD, you can create standard or customized holes such as counterbore, countersink, and straight from a sketch containing one or more circles, see Figures 8.1 and 8.2. Figure 8.1 shows a counterbore hole created from a sketch containing one circle and Figure 8.2 shows two countersink holes created from a sketch containing two circles.

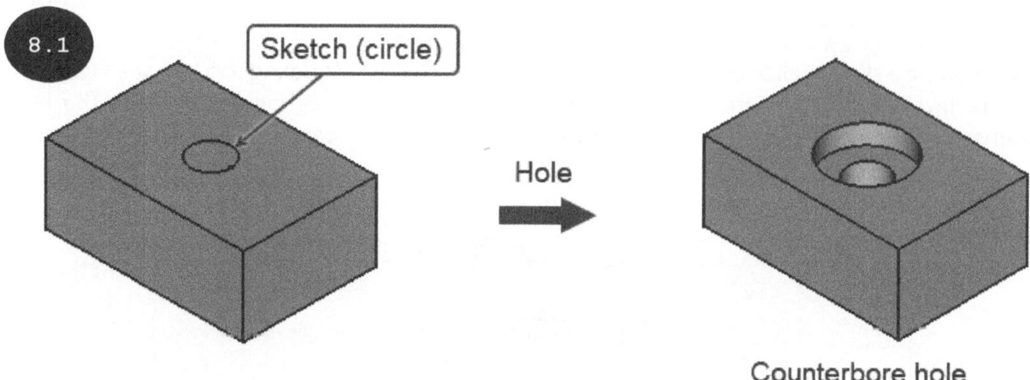

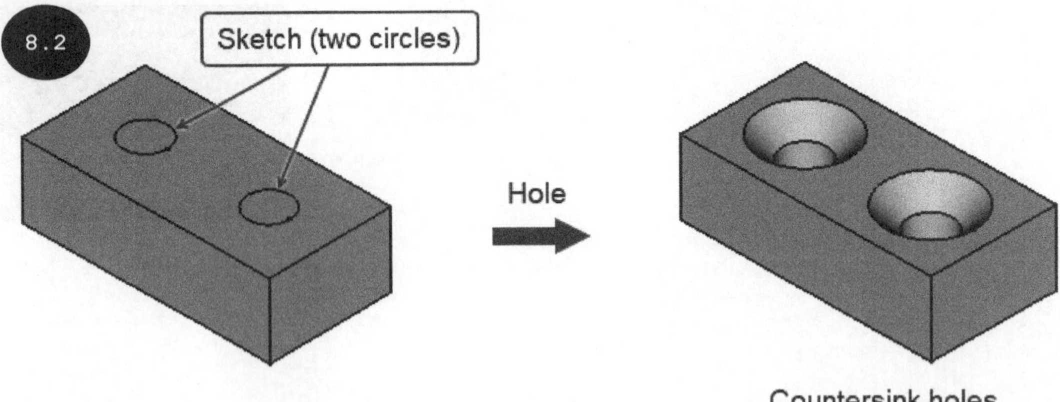

You can create different types of holes by using the **Hole** tool. The method for creating holes is discussed below:

1. Create a sketch containing one or more circles on a planar face of an existing model, see Figure 8.3. In this figure, a circle is created on the top planar face of the model to create a hole feature.

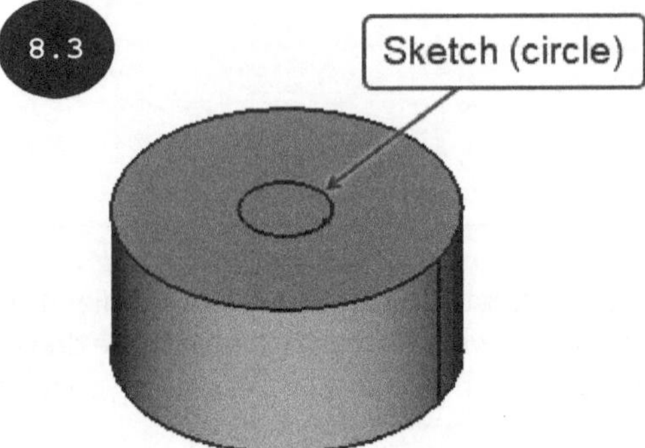

Note: A sketch of a hole feature may also contain arc entities. However, they must be a part of a closed contour/profile of the sketch.

The non-arc or non-circle entities of the sketch will be ignored, but they still must be a part of a closed contour/profile of the sketch.

2. After creating a sketch, click on the **Hole** tool in the **Part Design Modeling** toolbar, see Figure 8.4. The preview of a hole feature appears with default parameters, see Figure 8.5. Also, the **Hole parameters** sub-window appears in the **Tasks Panel** for defining hole parameters, see Figure 8.6.

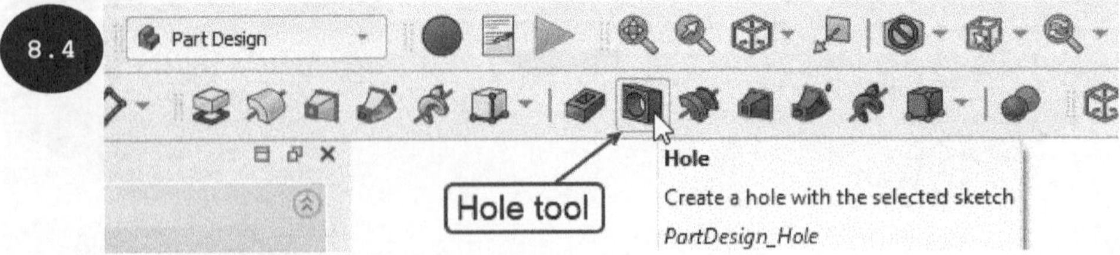

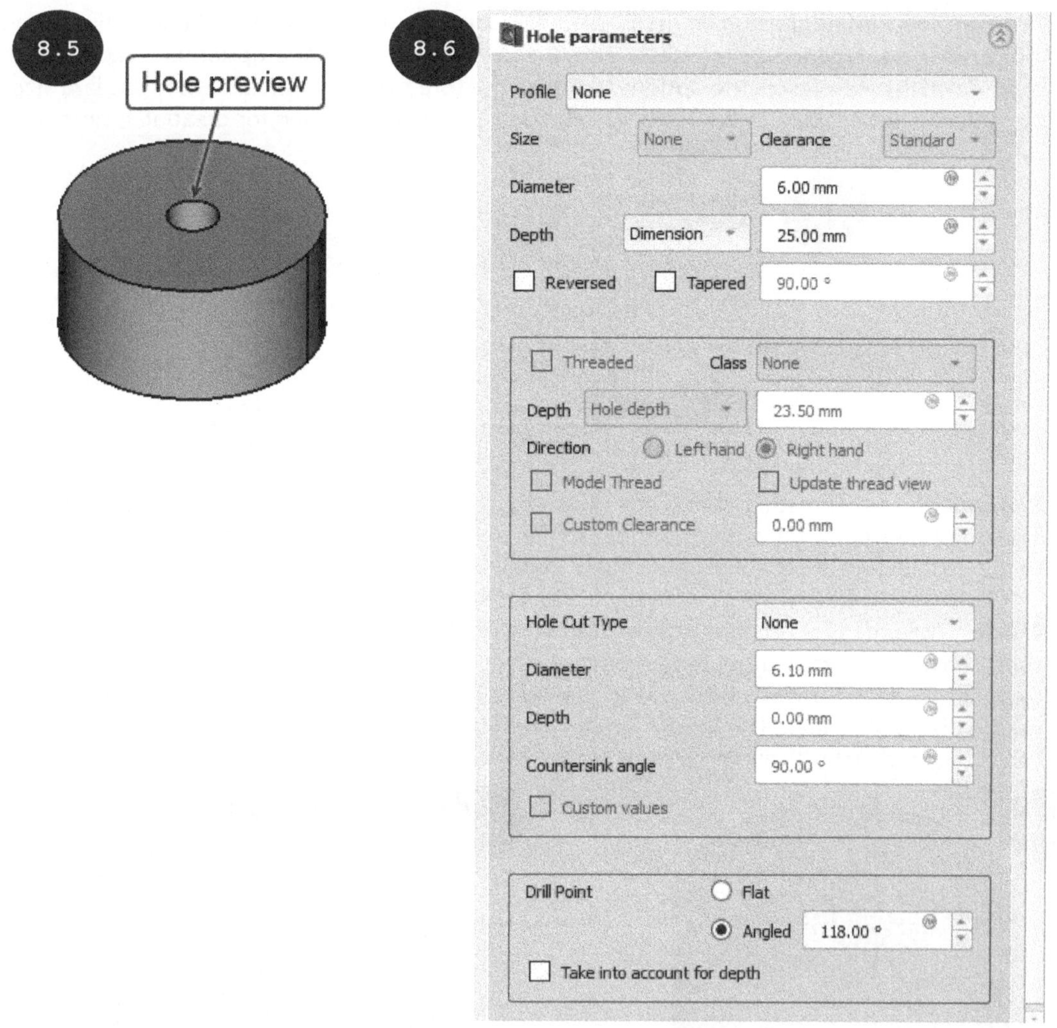

Note: The center of a circle or an arc entity of the sketch is used to define the center of the hole on the planar face of the model. However, its radius is not considered, and the diameter of the resultant hole is based on the defined parameters.

Tip: If only one sketch is available in the 3D View area, then on invoking the **Hole** tool, it will automatically be selected, and the preview of the hole appears in the 3D View area. However, if more than one sketch is available in the 3D View area, then the **Select feature** sub-window appears in the **Task Panel** for selecting a sketch of the hole feature.

The options in the **Hole parameters** sub-window are used for defining the required hole parameters and are discussed below:

Profile: The **Profile** drop-down list is used for selecting the type of standard profile such as ISO or UTS for creating a hole, see Figure 8.7. By default, the **None** option is selected in this drop-down list. As a result, the options to define the thread parameters and the standard size of the hole are not enabled in the **Tasks Panel**. The **None** option is used for creating a simple hole with a user-defined hole diameter.

8.7

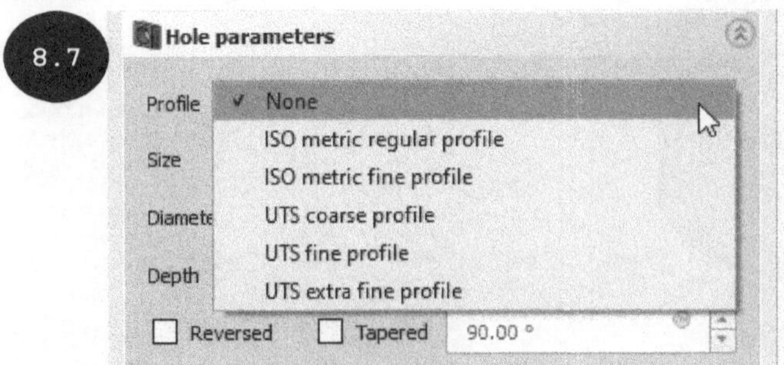

Threaded: The **Threaded** check box is used for creating a threaded hole. On selecting this **Threaded** check box, the options to define threaded data such as thread class and thread depth to the hole feature are enabled in the **Tasks Panel**.

Model Thread: On selecting the **Model Thread** check box, a real thread is modeled on a threaded hole by removing material from the model, see Figures 8.8 and 8.9. Note that you need to select the **Update view** check box in the **Tasks Panel** to update the preview of the threaded hole in the 3D View area. The **Model Thread** check box is enabled only when the **Threaded** check box is selected in the **Tasks Panel**.

8.8

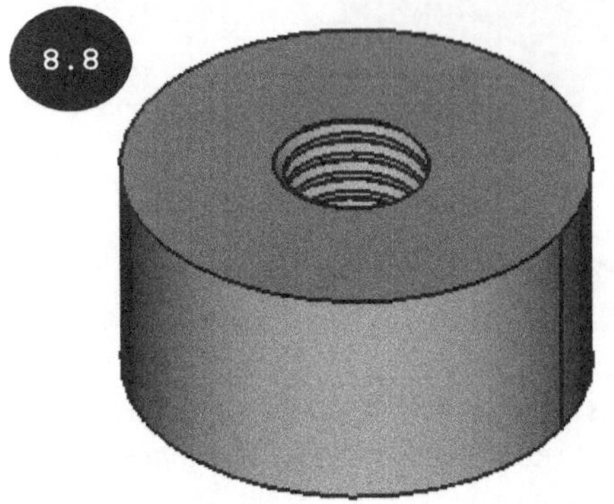

Threaded hole with Model Thread check box is selected

8.9

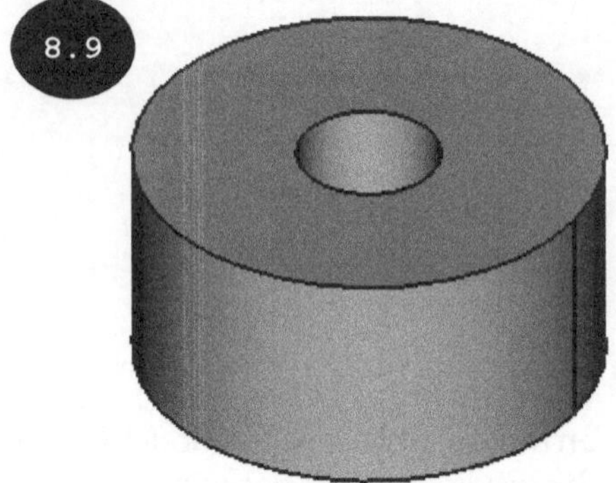

Threaded hole with Model Thread check box is cleared

Note: Creating a real thread by removing material from a model consumes more computing power. Therefore, it is recommended to create a threaded hole without removing the material to increase the overall system performance.

Custom Thread: On selecting the **Custom Thread** check box, a real thread is modeled on the threaded hole as per the custom clearance value specified in the **Clearance** field that is enabled in front of this check box in the **Tasks Panel**. Note that this check box is enabled only when the **Model Thread** check box is selected in the **Tasks Panel**.

Direction: The **Right hand** and the **Left hand** radio buttons in the **Direction** area of the **Tasks Panel** are used for defining the thread direction to the right hand or left hand, respectively. These radio buttons are enabled only when the **Threaded** check box is selected in the **Tasks Panel**.

Size: The **Size** drop-down list is used for selecting a standard size of the hole to insert a fastener, see Figure 8.10. Note that the availability of options in this drop-down list depends upon the option selected in the **Profile** drop-down list of the **Tasks Panel**.

8.10

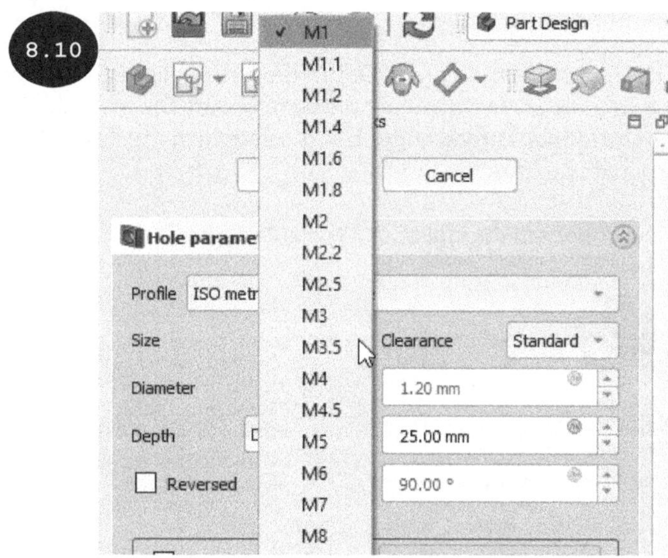

Clearance: The **Clearance** drop-down list is used for selecting the required option (**Standard**, **Close**, or **Wide**) to define the type of clearance/fit between the fastener and the hole. This drop-down list is enabled only while creating a non-threaded hole.

Class: The **Class** drop-down list is used for selecting the required tolerance class for the threaded hole.

Diameter: The **Diameter** field is used for specifying a user-defined hole diameter. Note that this field is enabled only when the **None** option is selected in the **Profile** drop-down list of the **Tasks Panel**.

Depth: The options in the **Depth** drop-down list are used for defining the depth of the hole from its placement plane. The **Dimension** option is used for specifying a depth value of the hole in the field that is enabled in front of the drop-down list, see Figure 8.11. The **Through all** option is used for creating a hole through the depth of the whole body, see Figure 8.12.

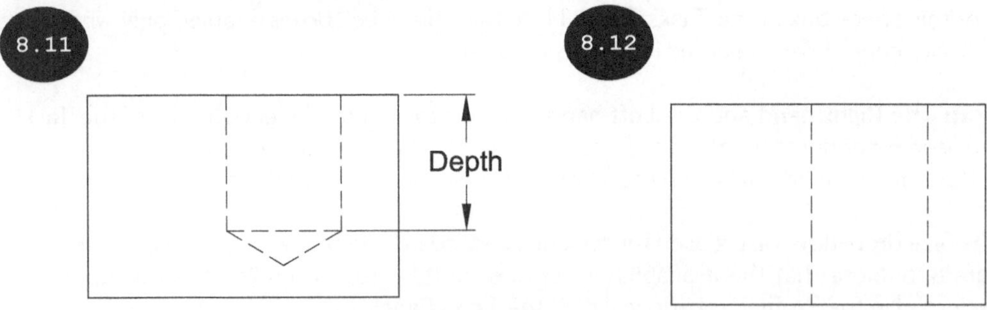

Thread Depth: The options in the **Thread Depth** drop-down list are used for defining the depth of the thread that is modeled on a threaded hole by removing the material. This drop-down list is enabled only when the **Model Thread** check box is selected in the **Tasks Panel** for creating a real thread by removing material from the model.

Hole Cut Type: The options in the **Hole Cut Type** area of the **Tasks Panel** are shown in Figure 8.13 and are discussed below:

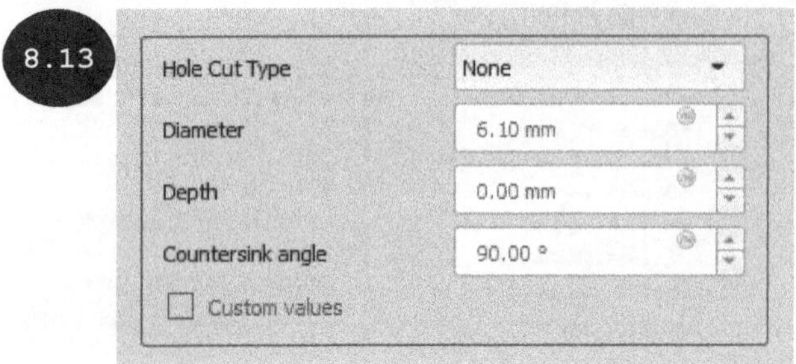

Hole Cut Type: The options in the **Hole Cut Type** drop-down list are used for defining the type of hole such as counterbore, countersink, or cap screw to be created, see Figure 8.14.

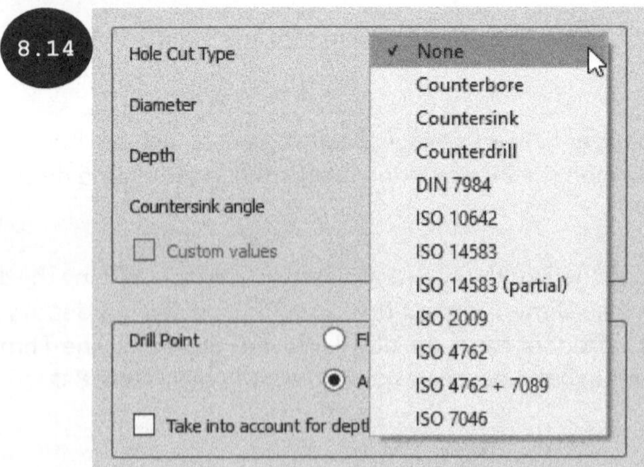

Diameter: The **Diameter** field is used for defining the upper diameter such as counterbore diameter or countersink diameter of the hole depending upon the type of hole selected in the **Type** drop-down list of the **Tasks Panel**, refer to Figure 8.15.

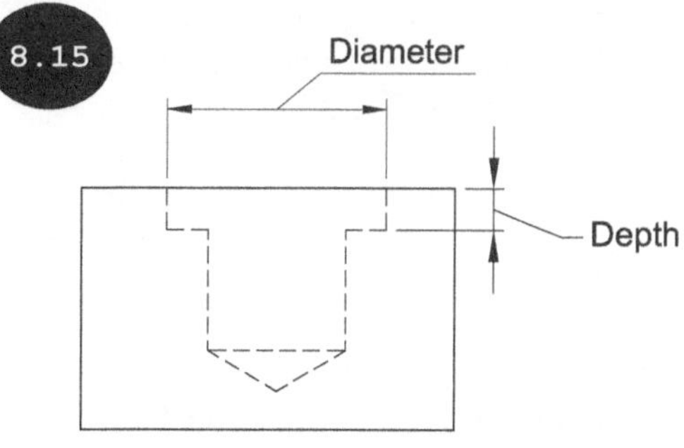

Depth: The **Depth** field is used for defining the depth of the upper hole such as counterbore depth or countersink depth depending upon the type of hole selected in the **Type** drop-down list, refer to Figure 8.15.

Countersink angle: The **Countersink angle** field is used for defining an angle value of the upper conical cut of the countersink hole, see Figure 8.16.

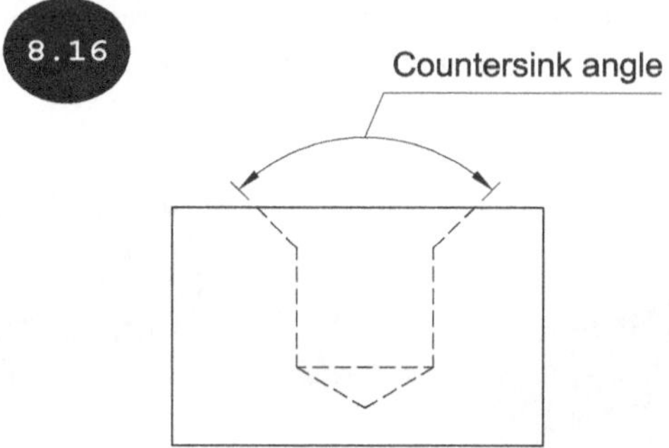

Drill point: The **Flat** radio button in the **Drill point** area of the **Tasks Panel** is used for creating a hole with a flat end, see Figure 8.17. The **Angled** radio button is used for creating a hole with a drilled/angled end, see Figure 8.18. You can also specify an angle value in the field that is enabled when the **Angled** radio button is selected in the **Tasks Panel**.

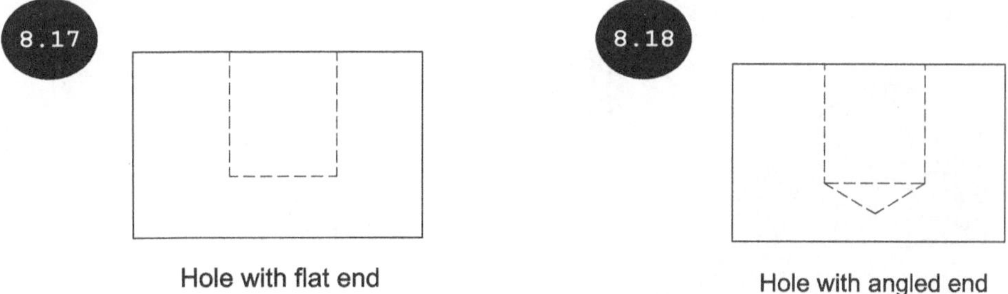

Misc: On selecting the **Tapered** check box in the **Misc** area of the **Tasks Panel**, you can create a hole with a taper angle specified in the field that appears in front of this check box. Note that the taper angle value specified in this field is calculated from the placement face of the hole. By default, 90 degrees is defined as the taper angle. As a result, a straight hole is created. A taper angle value less than 90 degrees creates a smaller hole radius at the bottom of the hole, whereas a taper angle value greater than 90 degrees creates an enlarged hole radius at the bottom of the hole. You can also reverse the hole extrusion direction by selecting the **Reversed** check box in the **Misc** area of the **Tasks Panel**.

3. Specify all the required hole parameters in the **Hole parameters** sub-window of the **Tasks Panel**, as discussed above.

4. After specifying all the hole parameters, click on the **OK** button in the **Tasks Panel**. A hole of specified parameters gets created, see Figure 8.19.

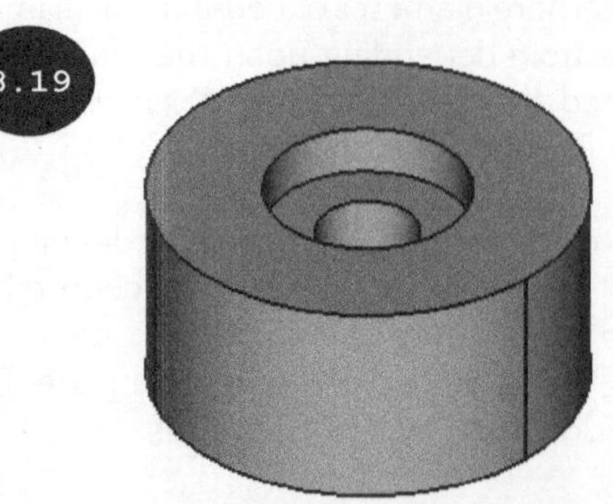

Creating Fillets

A fillet is a rounded face of a constant radius. It is used to remove the sharp edges of a model. Figure 8.20 shows a model before and after creating fillets on the edges of a model. In FreeCAD, you can create fillets by using the **Fillet** tool. The method for creating fillets is discussed below:

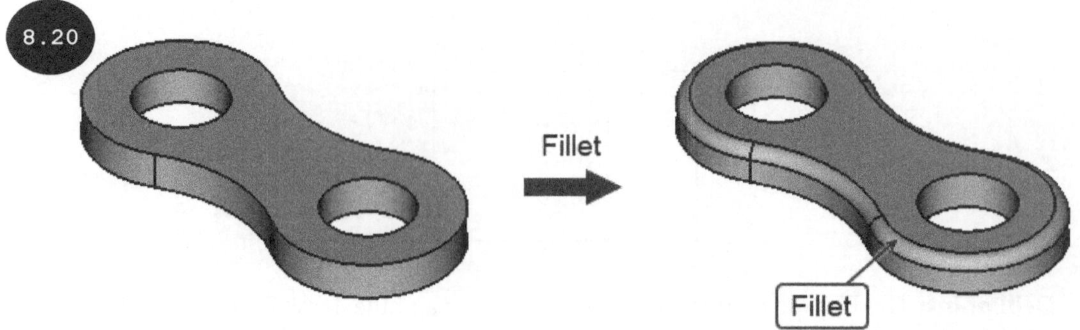

1. Select one or more edges, faces, or a feature of a model for creating a fillet in the 3D View area, see Figure 8.21. In this figure, an edge of a model is selected. To select multiple edges or faces of a model, you need to press the CTRL key.

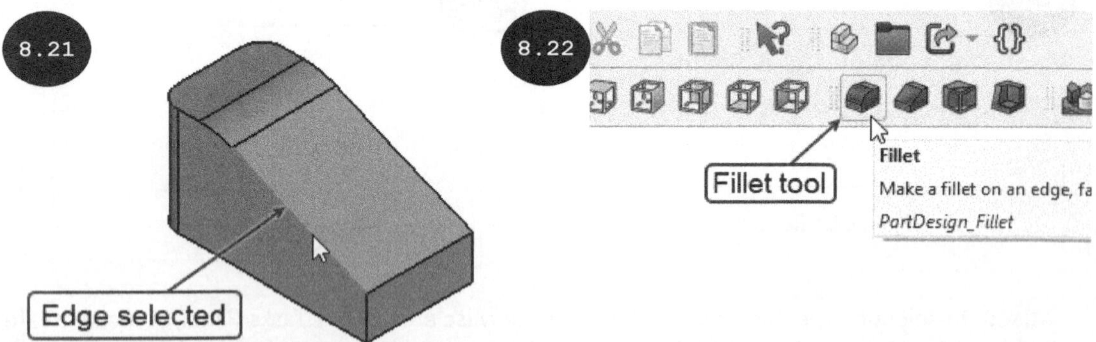

2. After selecting edges, faces, or a feature of a model, click on the **Fillet** tool in the **Part Design Modeling** toolbar, see Figure 8.22. The preview of a fillet appears on the selected edges of the

model with the default radius, see Figure 8.23. Also, the **Fillet parameters** sub-window appears in the **Tasks Panel**, see Figure 8.24.

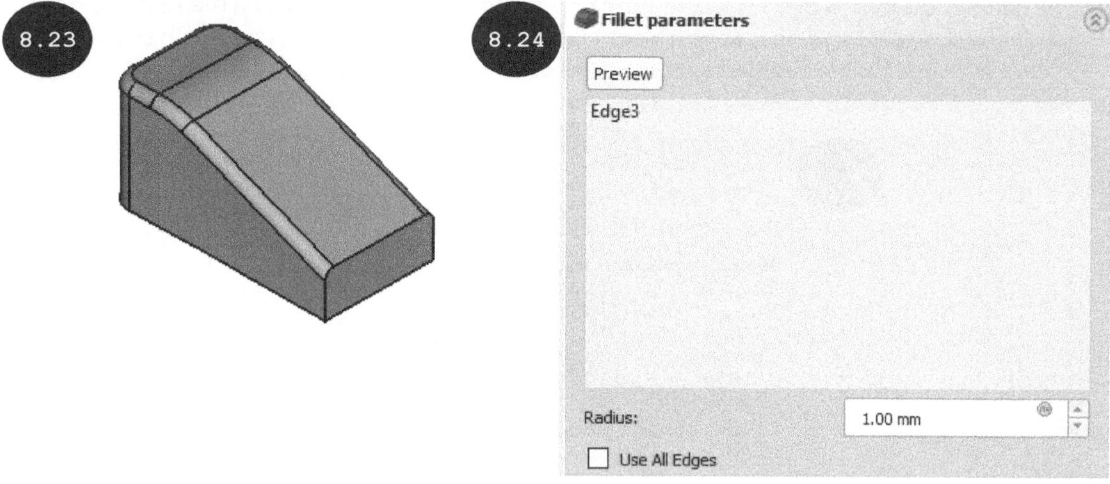

Note: You can select edges, faces, or a feature of a model for filleting either before or after activating the **Fillet** tool.

On selecting an edge of a model, all the edges that are connected tangentially to the selected edge of the model will also be filleted, refer to Figure 8.23.

If you select a face, all the edges of the selected face get filleted (see Figure 8.25) and if you select a feature, all the edges of the selected feature get filleted, see Figure 8.26. You can select a feature in the **Tree View** of the **Model** tab in the **Task Panel**.

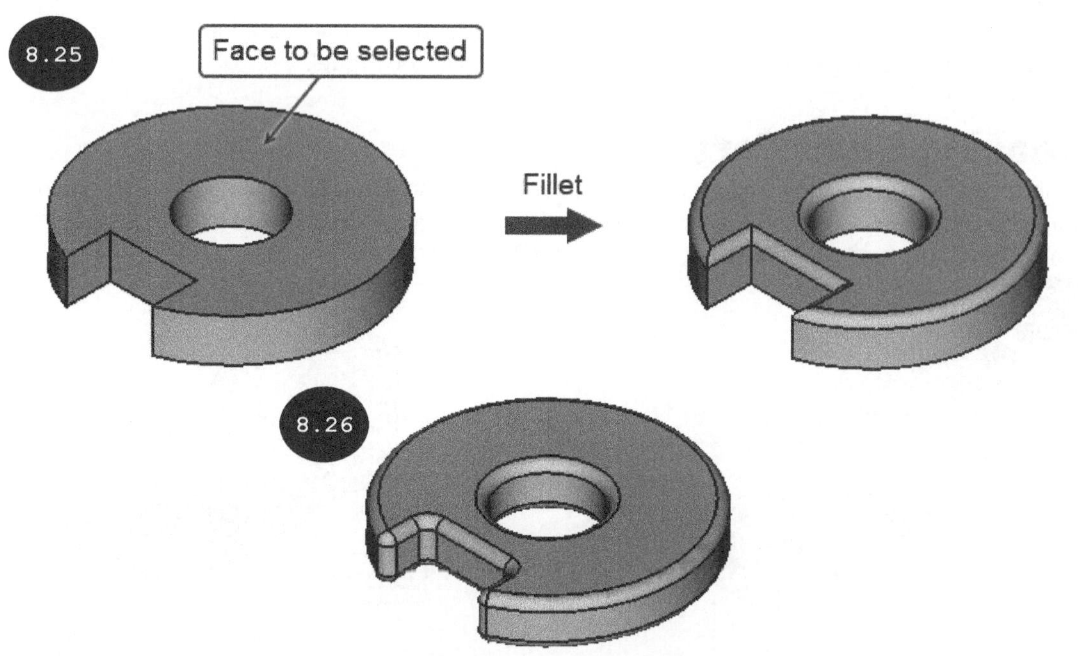

Tip: You can remove an already selected edge, face, or feature from the list by right-clicking on the name of the item (edge, face, or feature) to be removed and then click on the **Remove** option in the shortcut menu that appears, see Figure 8.27. The **Add all edges** option in this shortcut menu is used to include all edges of the model in the list to fillet.

8.27

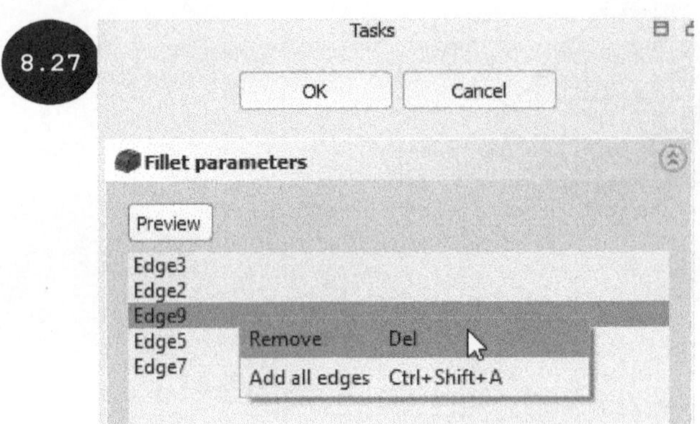

3. Enter the required radius value in the **Radius** field of the **Tasks Panel** and then press the TAB key. The preview of the fillet gets updated in the 3D View area.

   Use All Edges: On selecting the **Use All Edges** check box, all the edges of the model get filleted in the 3D View area.

   Preview/Select: The **Preview** or **Select** button in the **Fillet parameter** sub-window is used to switch between the preview of the fillet and the selection mode, respectively. In the selection mode, the selected edges of the model get highlighted in the graphics area.

4. After defining all the fillet parameters, click on the **OK** button in the **Tasks Panel**. A fillet feature of a specified radius gets created on the selected edges of the model.

Creating Chamfers

A chamfer is a beveled face that is not perpendicular to its adjacent faces. Figure 8.28 shows a model before and after creating a chamfer on its edge. In FreeCAD, you can create a chamfer by using the **Chamfer** tool. The method for creating a chamfer is discussed below:

8.28

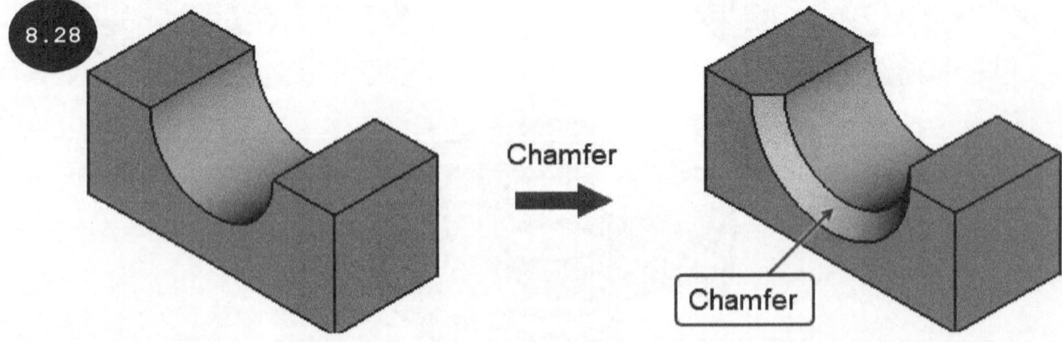

1. Select one or more edges, faces, or a feature of a model for creating a chamfer in the 3D View area, see Figure 8.29. In this figure, an edge of a model is selected. To select multiple edges or faces of a model, you need to press the CTRL key.

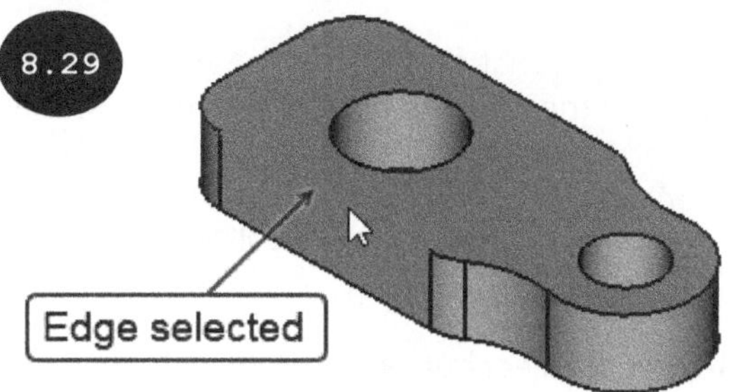

2. After selecting edges, faces, or a feature of a model, click on the **Chamfer** tool in the **Part Design Modeling** toolbar, see Figure 8.30. The preview of a chamfer appears on the selected edge or edges of the model with default parameters, see Figure 8.31. Also, the **Chamfer parameters** sub-window appears in the **Tasks Panel**, see Figure 8.32.

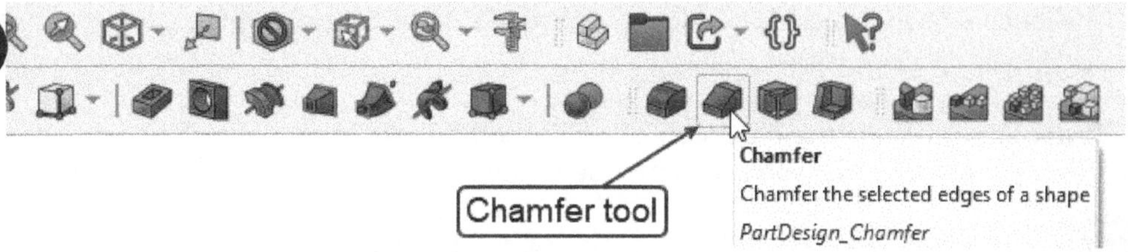

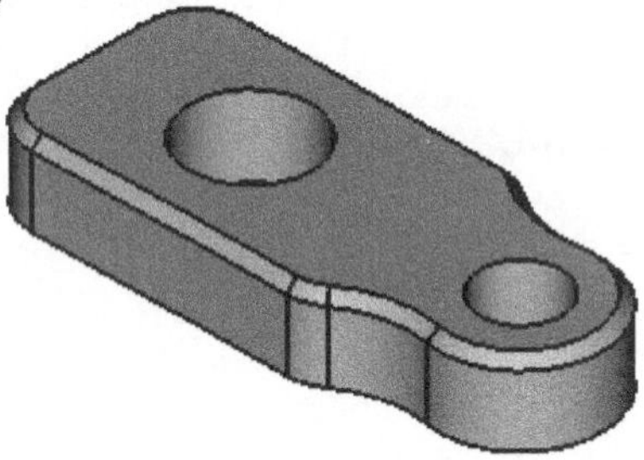

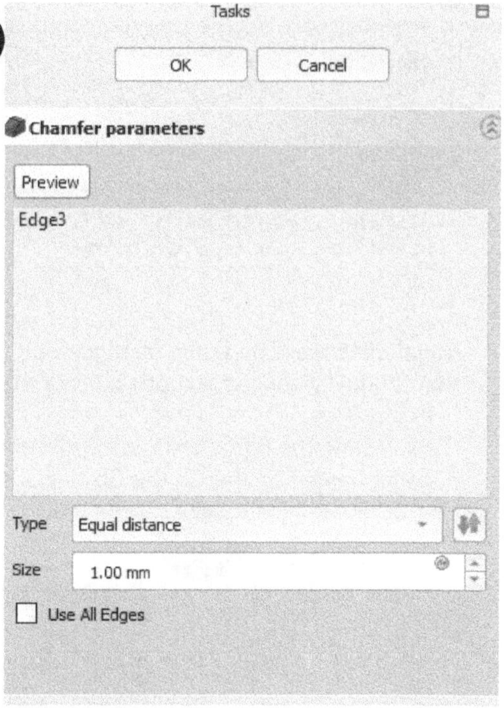

Note: You can select edges, faces, or a feature of a model for chamfering either before or after activating the **Chamfer** tool.

It is evident from Figure 8.31 that on selecting an edge of a model, all the edges that are connected tangentially to the selected edge of the model will also be chamfered.

Also, if you select a face, all the edges of the selected face will be chamfered and if you select a feature, all the edges of the selected feature will be chamfered.

Preview/Select: The **Preview** or **Select** button in the **Chamfer** parameter sub-window is used to switch between the preview of the chamfer and the selection mode, respectively. In the selection mode, the selected edges of the model get highlighted in the graphics area.

Tip: You can remove an already selected edge, face, or feature from the list by right-clicking on the name of the item (edge, face, or feature) to be removed and then click on the **Remove** option in the shortcut menu that appears, see Figure 8.33. The **Add all edges** option in this shortcut menu is used to include all edges of the model in the list to chamfer.

Type: The options in the **Type** drop-down list of the **Tasks Panel** are used to define a method for creating the respective type of chamfer, see Figure 8.34. These options are discussed next.

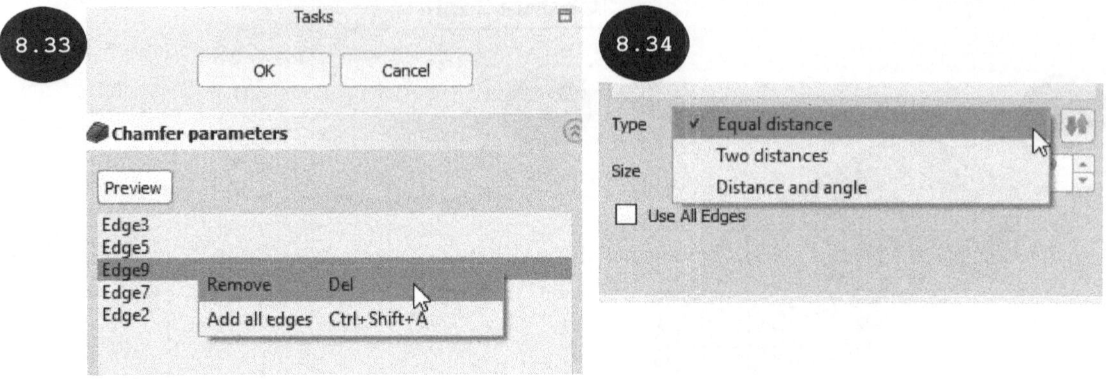

Equal distance: The **Equal distance** option creates a chamfer by specifying one distance value that is equally applied on both sides of the chamfered edge, see Figure 8.35.

On selecting the **Equal distance** option, the **Size** field appears in the **Tasks Panel**. Note that the distance value specified in this **Size** field is equally applied on both sides of the chamfer edge.

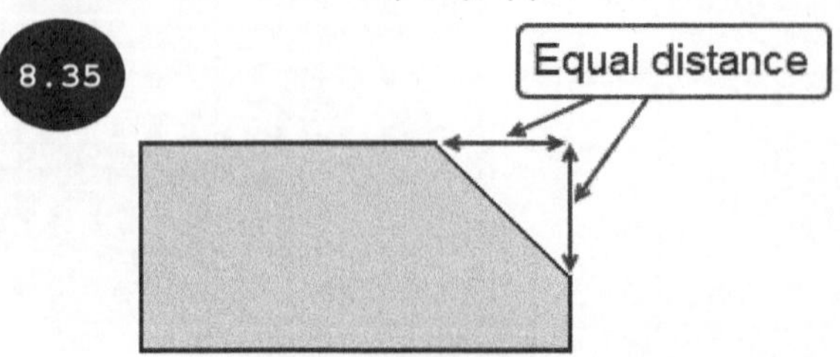

Two distances: The **Two distances** option creates a chamfer by specifying different distance values on both sides of the chamfered edge, see Figure 8.36.

On selecting the **Two distances** option, the **Size** and **Size 2** fields appear in the **Tasks Panel**. In the **Size** and **Size 2** fields, you can specify different distance values on both sides of the selected chamfered edge. You can also flip the sides of the chamfered edge by clicking on the **Flip direction** button available next to the **Type** drop-down list of the **Tasks Panel**.

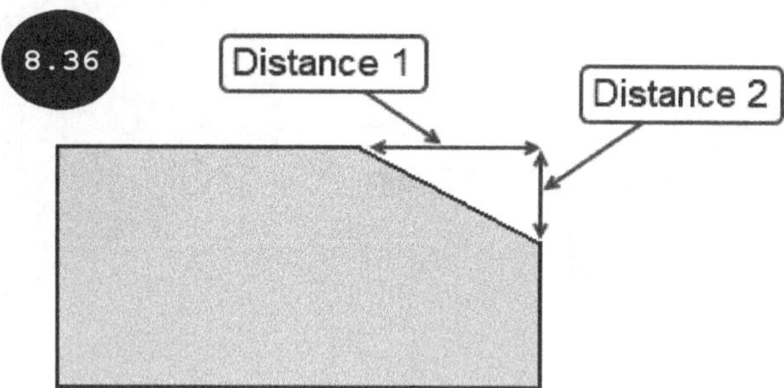

Distance and angle: The **Distance and angle** option creates a chamfer by specifying distance and angle values on the selected edge of the model, see Figure 8.37.

On selecting the **Distance and angle** option, the **Size** and **Angle** fields appear in the **Tasks Panel**. In these fields, you can specify the distance and angle values of the chamfer, respectively. You can also flip the sides of the chamfered edge by clicking on the **Flip direction** button available next to the **Type** drop-down list of the **Tasks Panel**.

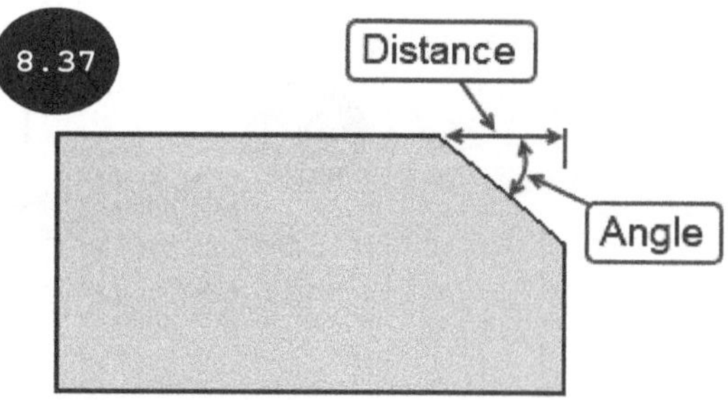

3. Select the required option (**Equal distance**, **Two distances**, or **Distance and angle**) in the **Type** drop-down list of the Tasks Panel for creating a chamfer, as discussed above.

4. Enter an equal distance, two distance values, or a distance and an angle value in the respective fields that appear depending upon the option selected in the **Type** drop-down list of the **Tasks Panel**.

   Use All Edges: On selecting the **Use All Edges** check box, all the edges of the model get chamfered in the 3D View area.

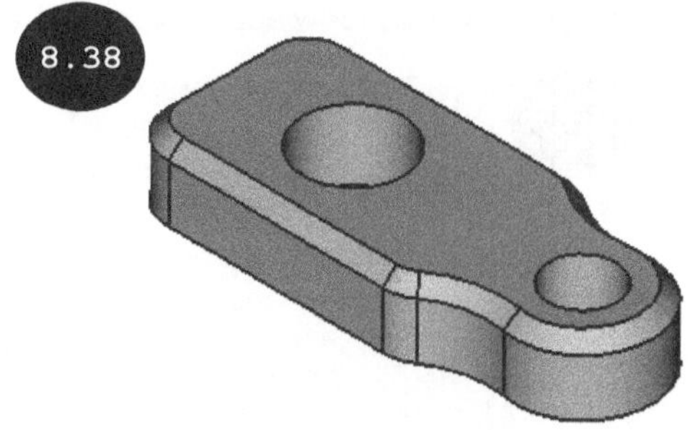

5. After defining all the required parameters, click on the **OK** button in the **Tasks Panel**. A chamfer feature of specified parameters gets created on the selected edge or edges of the model, see Figure 8.38.

Creating a Thick Shell Model

In FreeCAD, you can transform a 3D solid model into a thick shell model with a uniform wall thickness by removing at least one of its faces, see Figure 8.39. You can create a thick shell model by using the **Thickness** tool. The method for creating a thick shell model is discussed below:

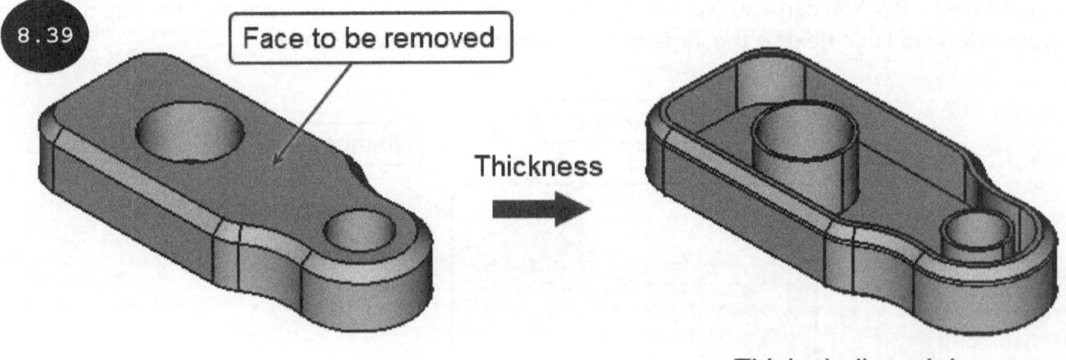

1. Select one or more faces of a model to be removed from the resultant shell model, see Figure 8.40. In this figure, the face of a model is selected to be removed. To select multiple faces of a model, you need to press the CTRL key.

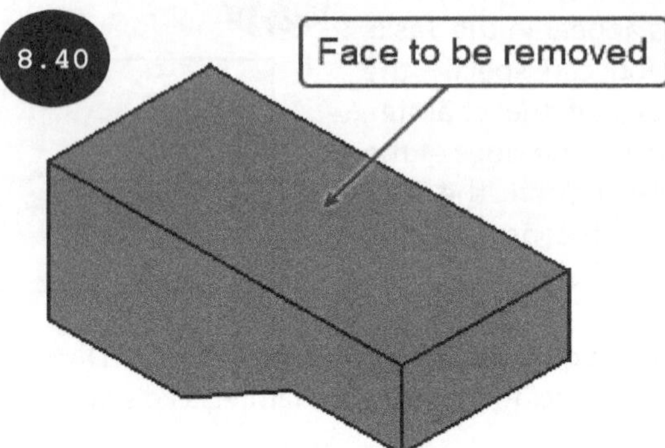

2. After selecting a face to be removed, click on the **Thickness** tool in the **Part Design Modeling** toolbar, see Figure 8.41. The preview of a thick shell model with default thickness appears in the 3D View area by removing the selected face of the model, see Figure 8.42. Also, the **Thickness parameters** sub-window appears in the **Tasks Panel**, see Figure 8.43.

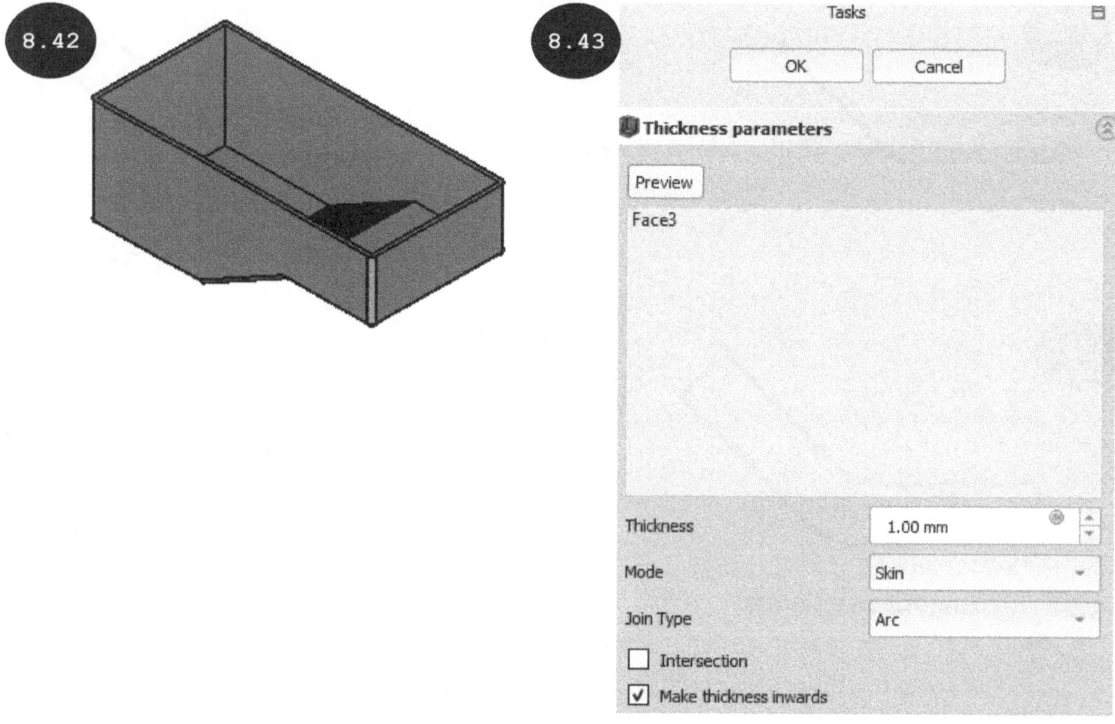

3. Enter the required wall thickness value in the **Thickness** field of the **Tasks Panel** and then press the TAB key. The thickness gets updated in the preview of the shell model, accordingly.

4. Select the required option (**Arc** or **Intersection**) in the **Join Type** drop-down list of the **Tasks Panel**, see Figures 8.44 and 8.45.

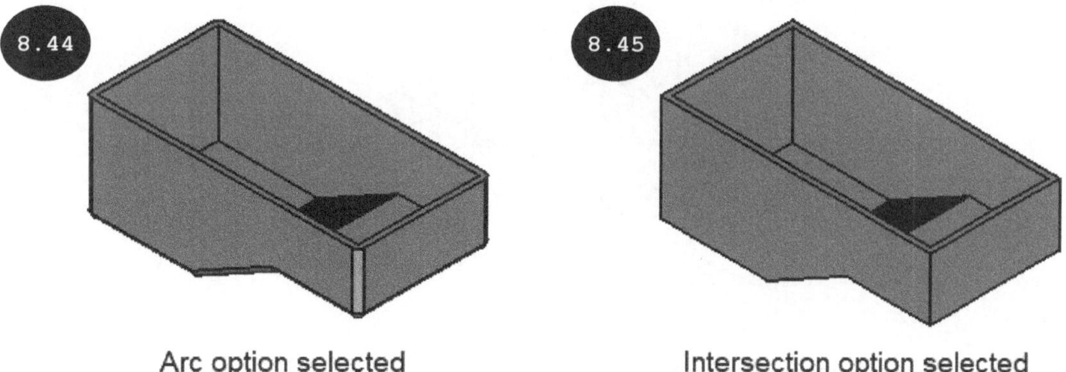

Arc option selected

Intersection option selected

Note: When the non-tangent faces of a model are offset to add thickness, a gap is created between them, refer to Figure 8.46. You can fill this gap by adding a fillet of the same radius as the defined thickness by using the **Arc** option, refer to Figure 8.47. You can also extend the offset faces at their virtual intersection to create a sharp corner by using the **Intersection** option, refer to Figure 8.48.

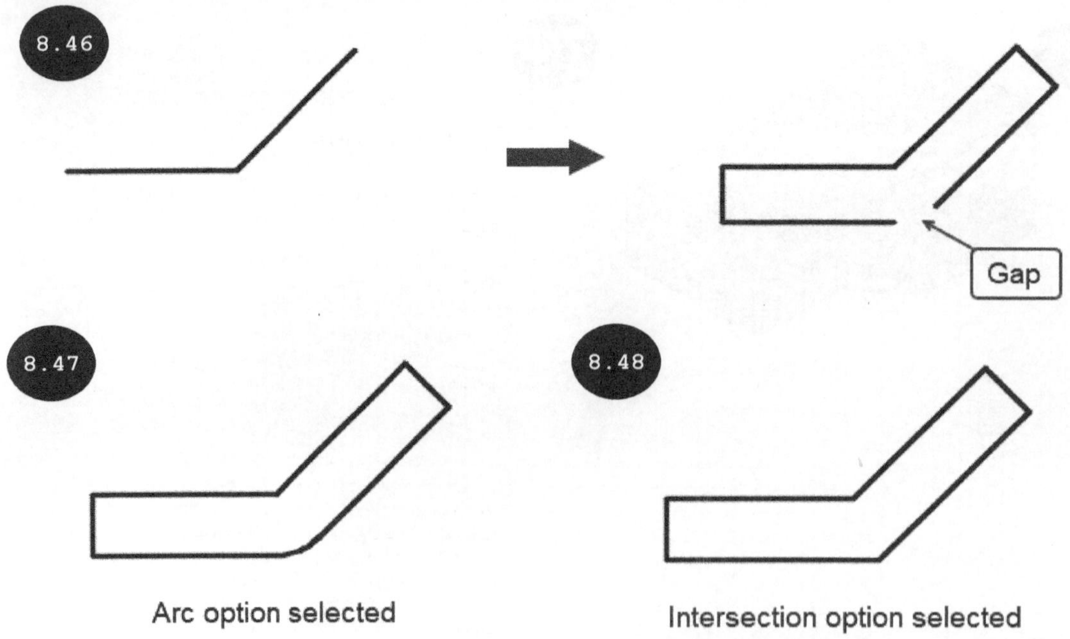

5. Select the **Make thickness inwards** check box if you want to add thickness inward to the model.

6. Click on the **OK** button in the **Tasks Panel**. A thick shell model of specified thickness gets created, see Figure 8.49.

Adding an Angular Draft

Adding an angular draft is a process of tapering one or more faces of a component so that it can easily separate from its cast while manufacturing. In FreeCAD, you can add an angular draft to selected faces of a model by using the **Draft** tool. The method for adding an angular draft is discussed below:

1. Select one or more faces of a model to add an angular draft to them in the 3D View area, see Figure 8.50. You can select multiple faces of a model by pressing the CTRL key.

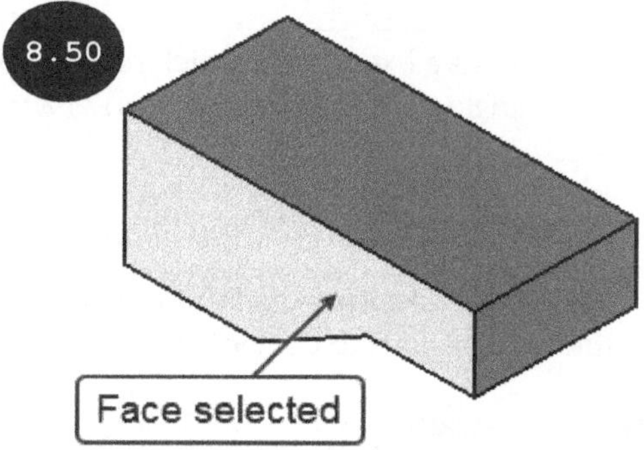

2. Click on the **Draft** tool in the **Part Design Modeling** toolbar, see Figure 8.51. The **Draft parameters** sub-window appears in the **Tasks Panel**, see Figure 8.52. Ignore the error message that may appear in the **Report view** window at the bottom of the screen. You can close the **Report view** window by clicking on the cross mark × that appears in its top right corner.

Now, you need to select a neutral plane for adding a draft.

3. Click on the **Neutral Plane** button in the Tasks Panel and then select a plane or a planar face as the neutral plane, see Figure 8.53.

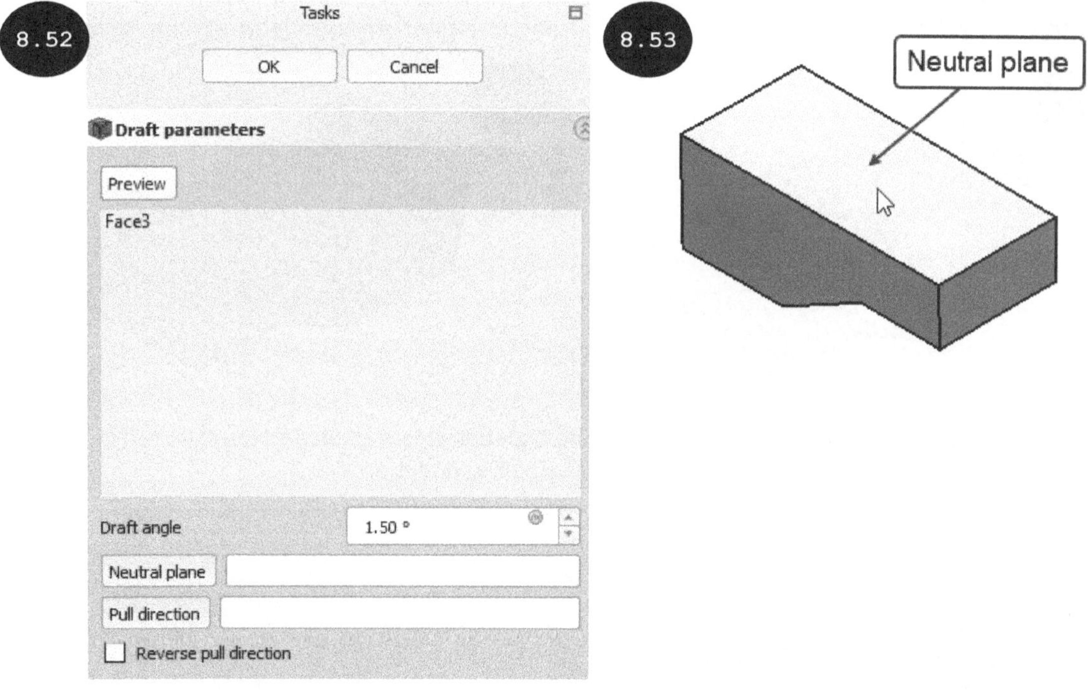

Note: The neutral plane is also known as a fixed plane which remains dimensionally unchanged while adding an angular draft angle to the selected face(s) of a model.

Now, you need to define the pulling direction for adding a draft.

4. Click on the **Pull direction** button in the **Tasks Panel** and then select a linear edge of the model to define the pulling direction of the angular draft to be applied, see Figure 8.54.

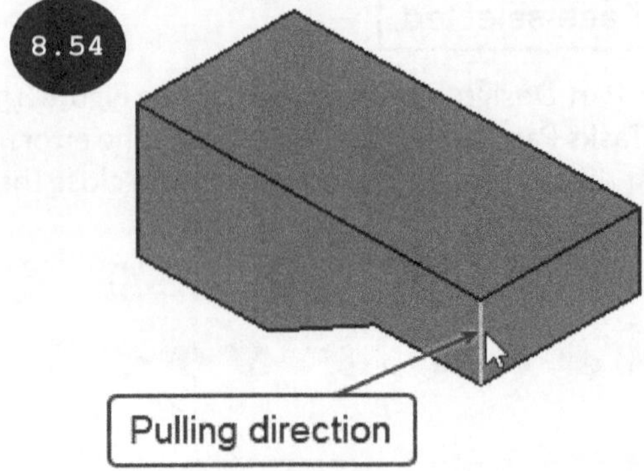

5. Enter the required draft angle value in the **Draft angle** field of the **Tasks Panel** and then press the TAB key. The preview appears such that the draft angle is applied to the selected face(s) of the model concerning the neutral plane and the pulling direction, see Figure 8.55.

6. Select the **Reverse pull direction** check box if you want to reverse the direction of the draft from outward to inward, see Figure 8.56.

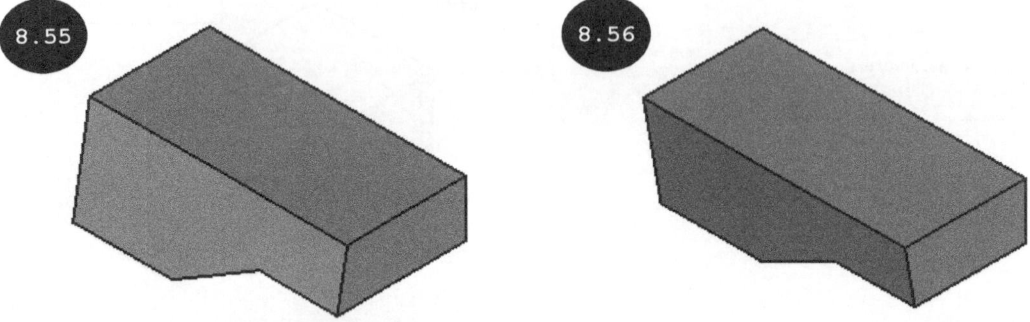

7. Click on the **OK** button in the **Tasks Panel**. The draft angle gets applied to the selected face(s) of the model concerning the neutral plane and the pulling direction.

Tutorial 1

Create the model shown in Figure 8.57. Different views and dimensions for creating the model are shown in Figure 8.58. All dimensions are in inches (in).

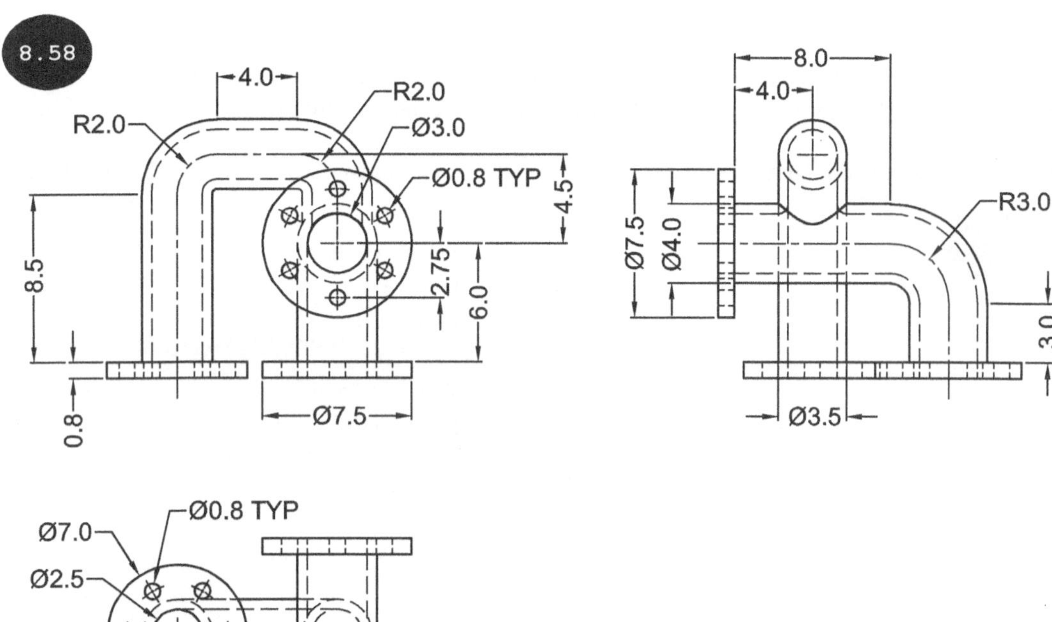

Section 1: Starting a New Part Document and Specifying Units

1. Start FreeCAD by double-clicking on the **FreeCAD 1.0** icon on your desktop. The startup user interface of FreeCAD appears, see Figure 8.59.

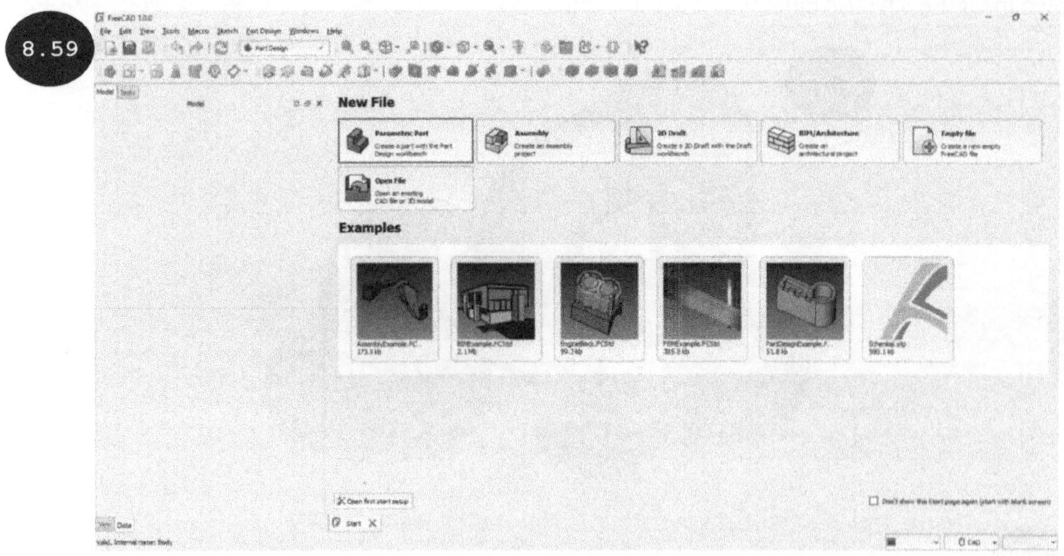

8.59

2. Click on the **Parametric Part** icon on the **Start page** (refer to Figure 8.59) or press the **CTRL + N** keys. A new part document gets invoked with the default name **"unnamed: 1"**.

3. Invoke the **Unit** flyout that appears at the lower right corner of the **Status Bar**, see Figure 8.60.

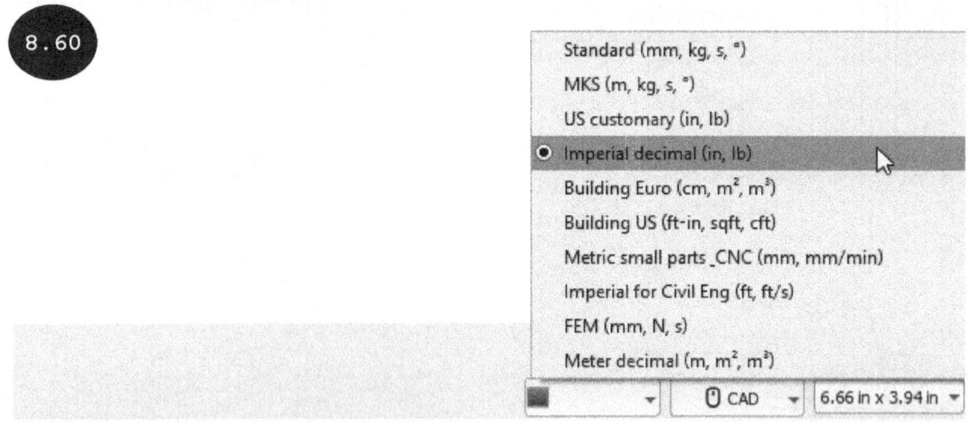

8.60

4. In this flyout, ensure that **Imperial decimal (in,lb)** is selected as the unit system for the current design document.

Section 2: Creating the Base Feature

Now, you can create the base or first feature of the model, which is an additive pipe feature.

1. Invoke the **Sketcher** workbench by selecting the **YZ_Plane** as the sketching plane using the **Create sketch** tool and then create the sketch (path) of the additive pipe feature, see Figure 8.61.

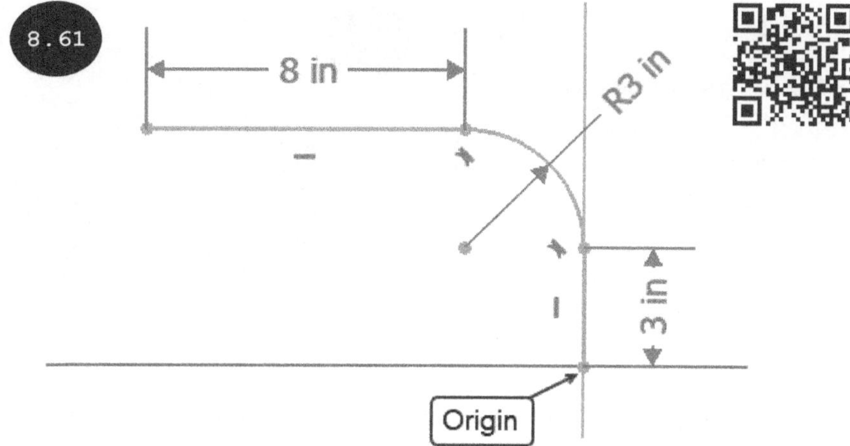

2. After creating the sketch, exit the **Sketcher** workbench to switch back to the **Part Design** workbench.

   Now, you can create the profile of the additive pipe feature.

3. Invoke the **Sketcher** workbench by selecting the **XY_Plane** as the sketching plane and then create a circle as the profile of the additive pipe feature, see Figure 8.62. Note that the center point of the circle is at the origin.

4. After creating the profile, exit the **Sketcher** workbench and then change the view orientation to isometric, see Figure 8.63. Click anywhere in the 3D View area to exit the current selection set.

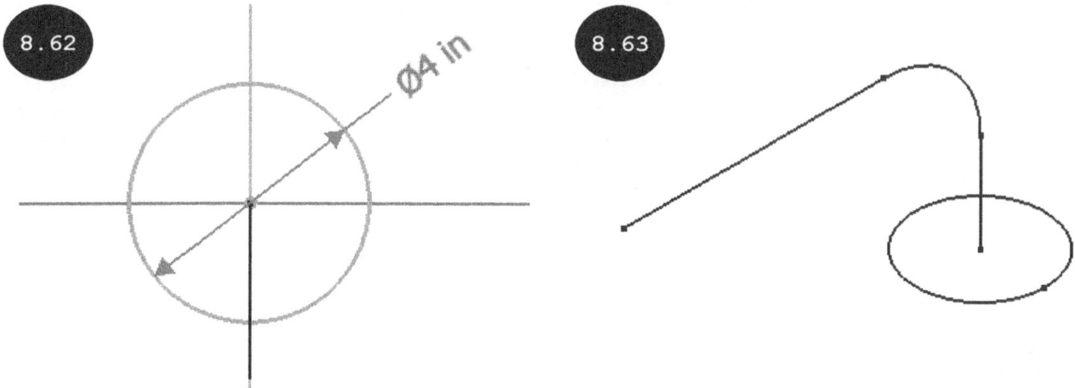

   Now, you can create the additive pipe feature.

5. Select the profile (**Sketch001**) and then the path (**Sketch**) in the **Tree View** of the **Model** tab in the **Tasks Panel** by pressing the CTRL key. Next, release the CTRL key.

6. After selecting the profile and the path in the **Tree View**, click on the **Additive pipe** tool in the **Part Design Modeling** toolbar, see Figure 8.64. The preview of the additive pipe feature appears in the 3D View area such that the profile follows the path, see Figure 8.65. Also, the **Pipe parameters** sub-window appears in the **Tasks Panel** with the options to create an additive pipe feature.

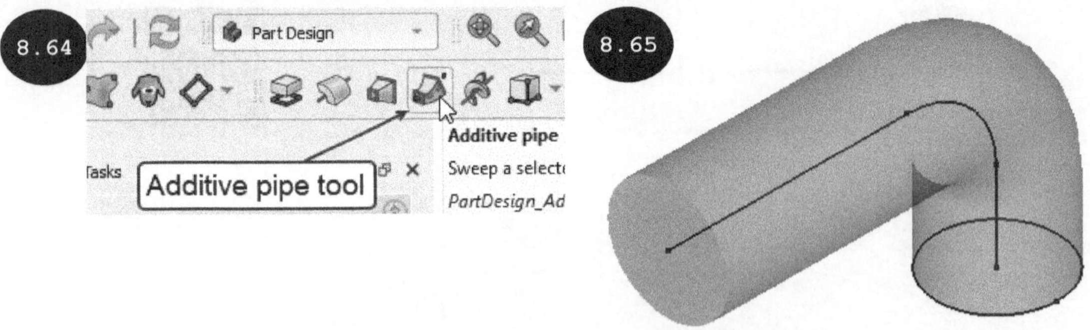

Tip: You can also select the profile and the path of the feature after invoking the **Additive pipe** tool.

7. Click on the **OK** button in the **Tasks Panel** and then click on the **OK** button. The additive pipe feature gets created, see Figure 8.66.

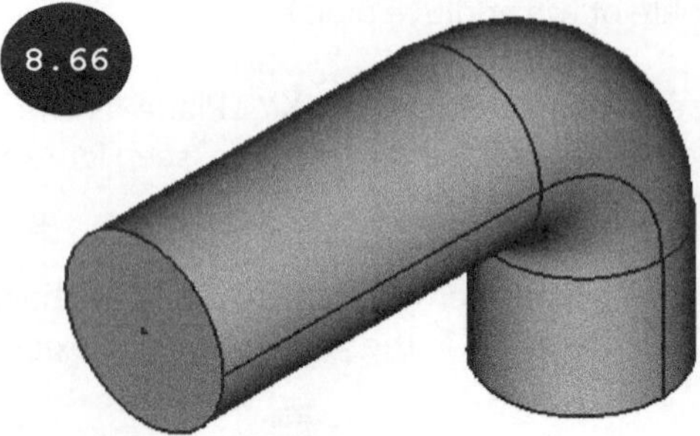

Section 3: Creating the Second Feature

Now, you can create the second feature of the model, which is also an additive pipe feature. To create this additive pipe feature, you need to first create a datum plane at an offset distance of 4 inches from the front planar face of the base feature.

1. Invoke the **Datum** menu in the **Part Design Helper** toolbar and then click on the **Create a datum plane** tool, see Figure 8.67. The **Datum Plane parameters** sub-window appears in the **Tasks Panel**. Also, you are prompted to select a first reference for creating a datum plane.

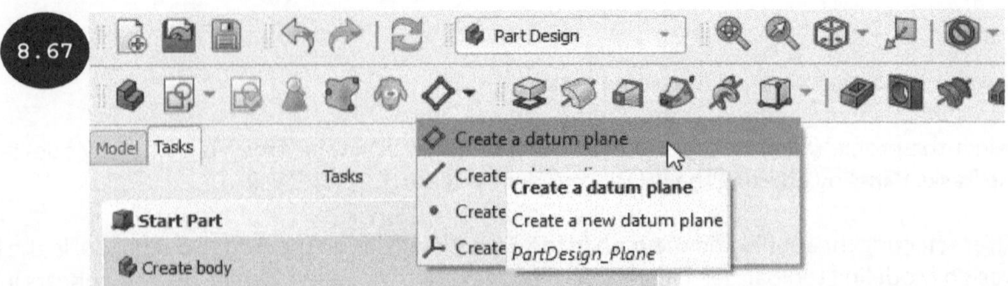

2. Select the front planar face of the base feature (additive pipe) as the first reference, see Figure 8.68. The preview of a datum plane appears in the 3D View area. Also, the Plane face mode gets activated automatically in the **Attachment mode** area of the **Tasks Panel**.

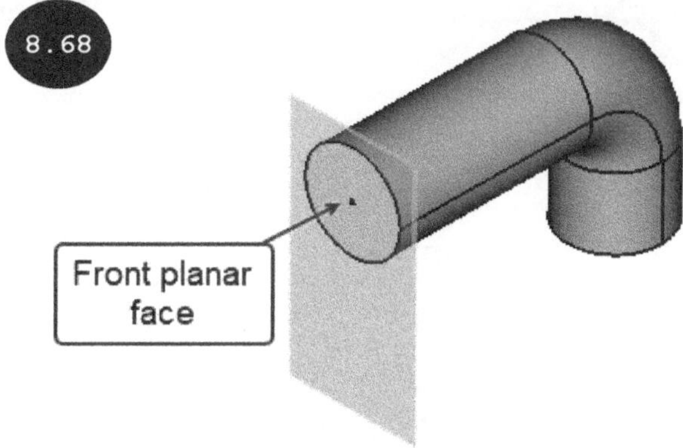

3. Enter -4 inches in the **In z-direction** field of the **Attachment Offset** area in the **Tasks Panel** as the offset distance between the selected planar face and the datum plane being created, see Figure 8.69. Next, press the TAB key. The preview of the datum plane gets updated in the 3D View area and appears like the one shown in Figure 8.70.

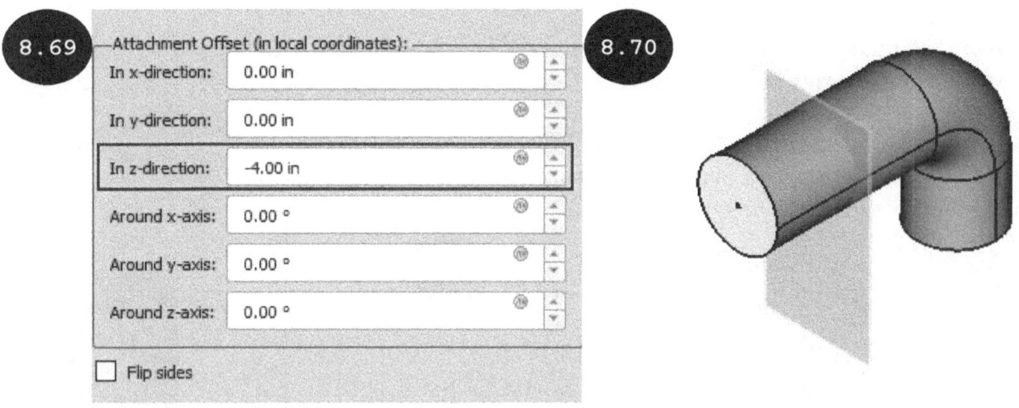

4. Click on the **OK** button in the **Tasks Panel** to confirm the creation of the datum plane and exit the **Tasks Panel**.

   Now, you can create the path of the additive pipe feature on the newly created datum plane.

5. Invoke the **Sketcher** workbench by selecting the newly created datum plane as the sketching plane using the **Create sketch** tool and then create the sketch (path) of the additive pipe feature, see Figure 8.71.

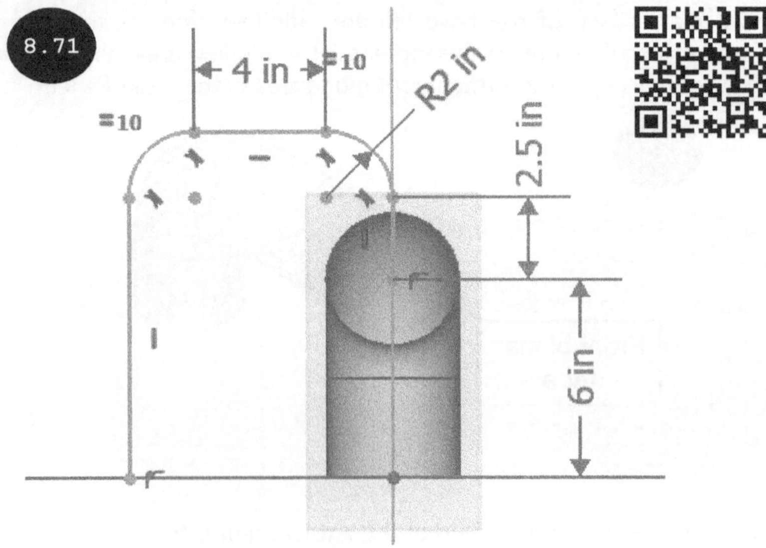

6. After creating the path, exit the **Sketcher** workbench to switch back to the **Part Design** workbench.

   Now, you can create the profile of the additive pipe feature.

7. Invoke the **Sketcher** workbench by selecting the **XY_Plane** as the sketching plane for creating the profile of the additive pipe feature.

8. Click on the **Create external geometry** tool in the **Sketcher geometries** toolbar (see Figure 8.72) and then click on the endpoint of the previously created sketch (path) as the entity to be projected onto the sketch, see Figure 6.73. Next, press the ESC key to exit the tool.

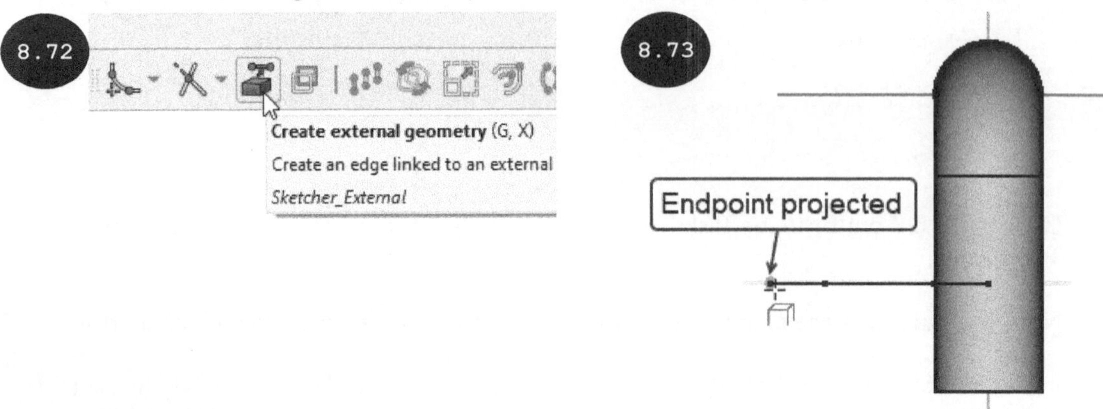

9. Create a circle as the profile of the additive pipe feature by taking reference of the projected construction endpoint, see Figure 8.74. Note that the center point of the circle is at the projected endpoint.

10. After creating the profile, exit the **Sketcher** workbench and then change the view orientation to isometric, see Figure 8.75. Click anywhere in the 3D View area to exit the current selection set.

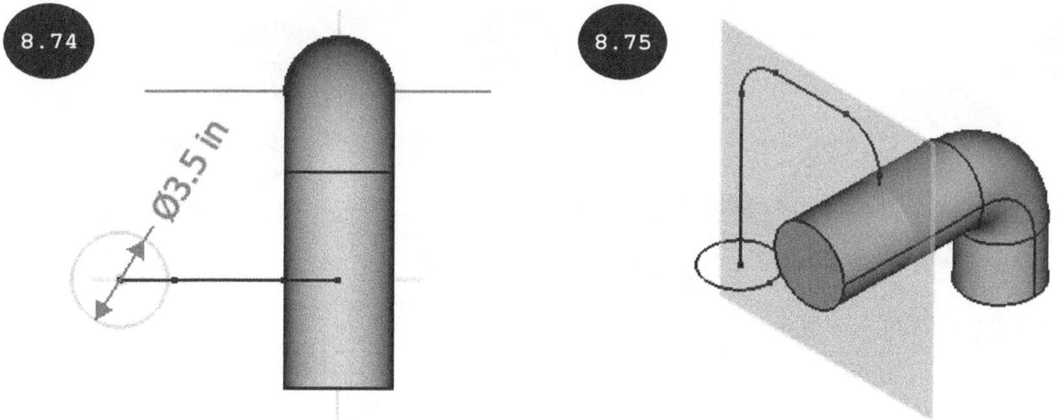

11. Select the datum plane in the 3D View area and then press SPACEBAR to hide the display of the datum plane in the 3D View area.

    Now, you can create the additive pipe feature.

12. Select the profile (**Sketch003**) and then the path (**Sketch002**) in the **Tree View** of the **Model** tab in the **Tasks Panel** by pressing the CTRL key. Next, release the CTRL key.

13. After selecting the profile and the path in the **Tree View**, click on the **Additive pipe** tool in the **Part Design Modeling** toolbar, see Figure 8.76. The preview of the additive pipe feature appears in the 3D View area such that the profile follows the path, see Figure 8.77. Also, the **Pipe parameters** sub-window appears in the **Tasks Panel** with the options to create an additive pipe feature.

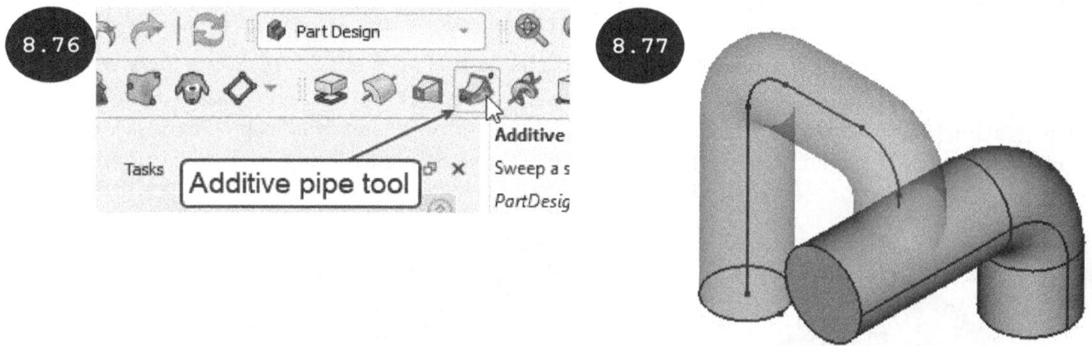

14. Click on the **OK** button in the **Tasks Panel** and then click on the **OK** button. The additive pipe feature gets created, see Figure 8.78.

Section 4: Creating the Third Feature

Now, you can create the third feature of the model, which is a thick shell feature.

1. Rotate the model and then select all the end planar faces (three) of the model in the 3D View area as the faces to be removed while creating the thick shell feature, see Figure 8.79.

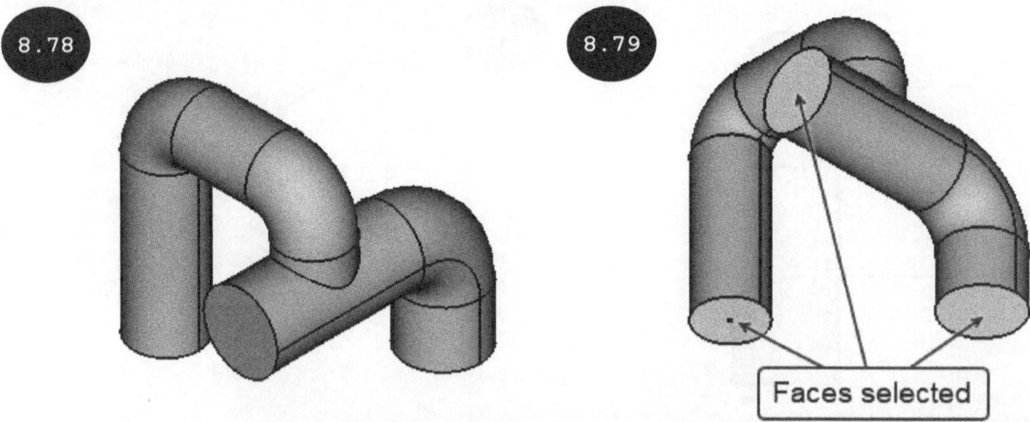

2. After selecting the faces, click on the **Thickness** tool in the **Part Design Modeling** toolbar, see Figure 8.80. The **Thickness parameters** sub-window appears in the **Tasks Panel**. Also, the preview of a thick shell model of default wall thickness appears in the 3D View area.

3. Enter **0.5** inches in the **Thickness** field of the **Tasks Panel** and then press the TAB key to update the preview in the 3D View area as per the specified wall thickness.

4. Select the **Make thickness inwards** check box in the **Tasks Panel** to add thickness inward.

5. Click on the **OK** button in the **Tasks Panel**. A thick shell model of specified wall thickness is created by removing the selected faces of the model, see Figure 8.81. Next, change the view orientation of the model to isometric, see Figure 8.82.

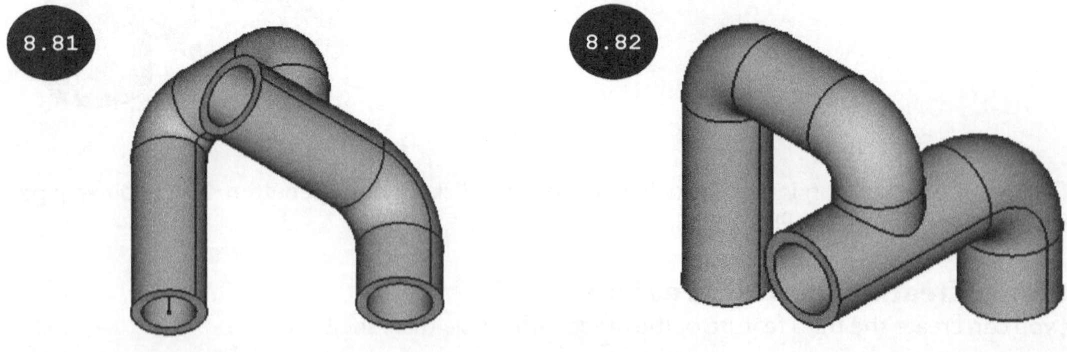

Section 5: Creating the Fourth Feature

Now, you can create the fourth feature of the model, which is a pad feature.

1. Select the front planar face of the model as the sketching plane (see Figure 8.83) and then click on the **Create sketch** tool to invoke the **Sketcher** workbench.

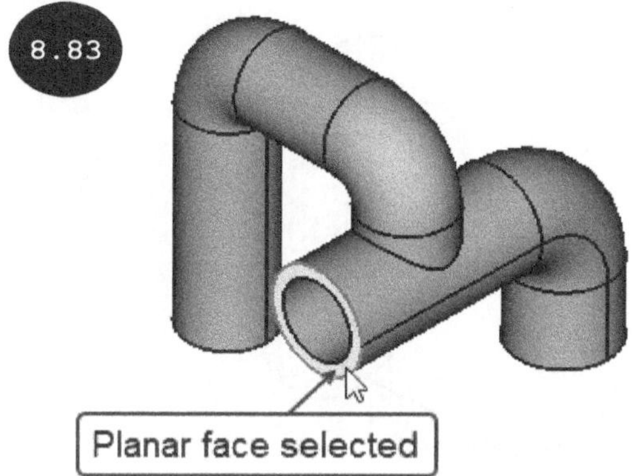

2. Create two concentric circles as the sketch of the pad feature, see Figure 8.84.

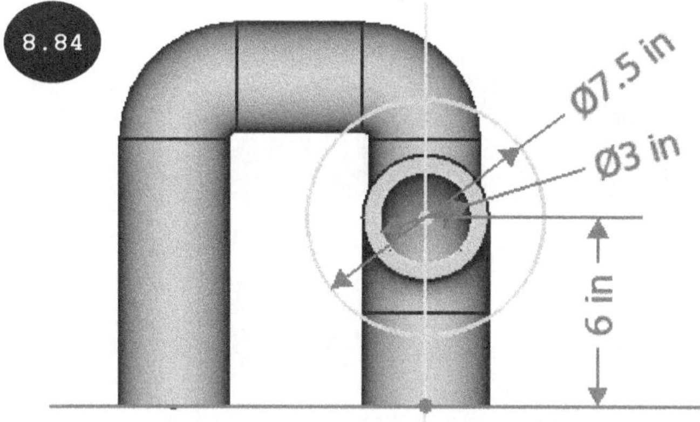

3. After creating the sketch, exit the **Sketcher** workbench and then extrude the sketch to **0.8** inches by using the **Pad** tool. Figure 8.85 shows the model after creating the pad feature.

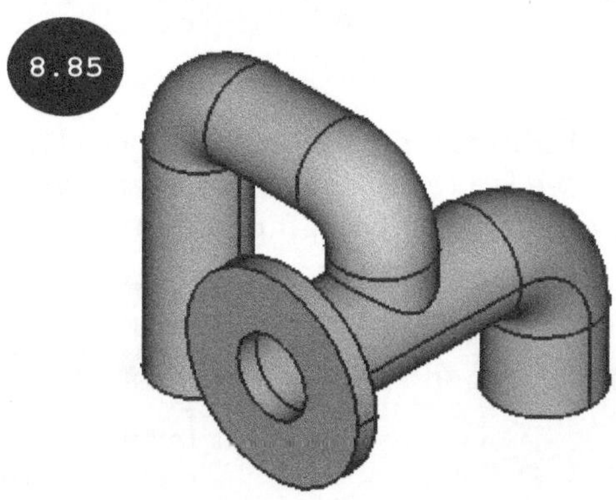

Section 6: Creating the Fifth Feature

Now, you can create the fifth feature of the model, which is a pocket feature.

1. Select the front planar face of the model as the sketching plane (see Figure 8.86) and then click on the **Create sketch** tool to invoke the **Sketcher** workbench.

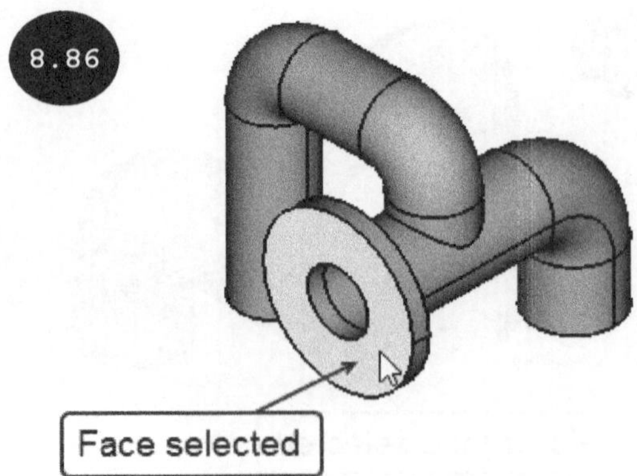

2. Create a circle of diameter **0.8** inches as the sketch of the pocket feature, see Figure 8.87.

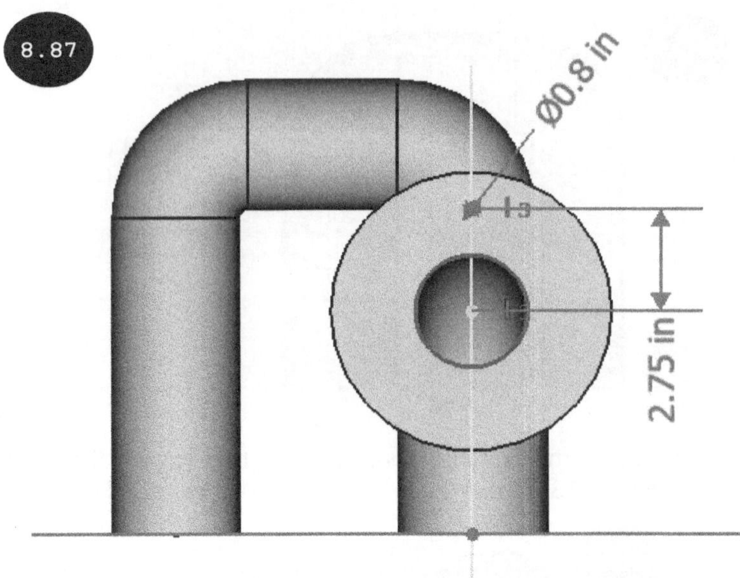

3. After creating the sketch, exit the **Sketcher** workbench and then click on the **Pocket** tool in the **Part Design Modeling** toolbar, see Figure 8.88. The **Pocket parameters** sub-window appears in the **Tasks Panel**. Also, the preview of the pocket feature appears in the 3D View area.

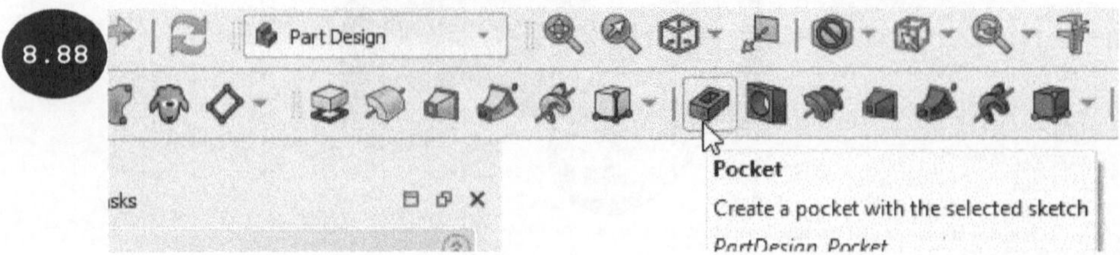

4. Select the **To first** option in the **Type** drop-down list of the **Pocket parameters** sub-window (see Figure 8.89) for creating a pocket feature by extruding the sketch up to its first or nearest intersecting face of the model.

5. Click on the **OK** button in the **Tasks Panel**. A pocket feature gets created, see Figure 8.90.

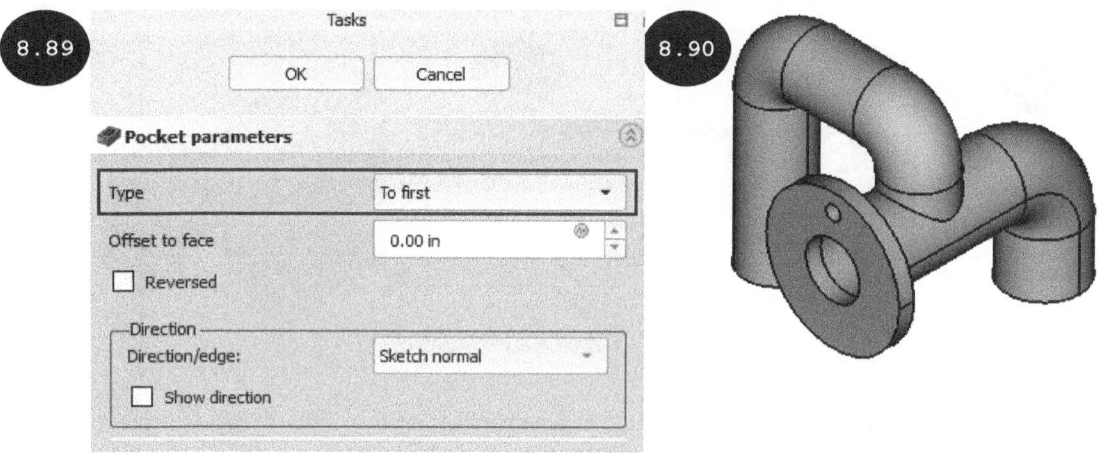

Section 7: Creating the Polar Pattern

Now, you can create the polar pattern of the previously created pocket feature for creating its remaining occurrences.

1. Select the previously created pocket feature in the **Tree View** of the **Model** tab in the **Tasks Panel** or the 3D View area.

2. After selecting the feature, click on the **PolarPattern** tool in the **Part Design Modeling** toolbar, see Figure 8.91. The **PolarPattern parameters** sub-window appears in the **Tasks Panel**.

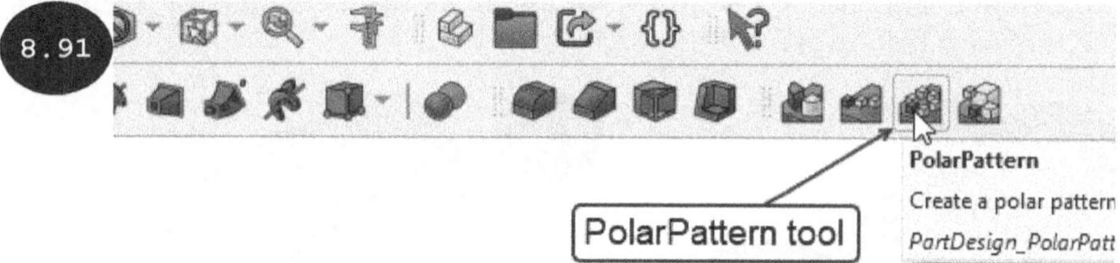

3. Select the **Select reference** option in the **Axis** drop-down list in the **Tasks Panel**, see Figure 8.92. You are prompted to select a reference entity to define the axis of revolution.

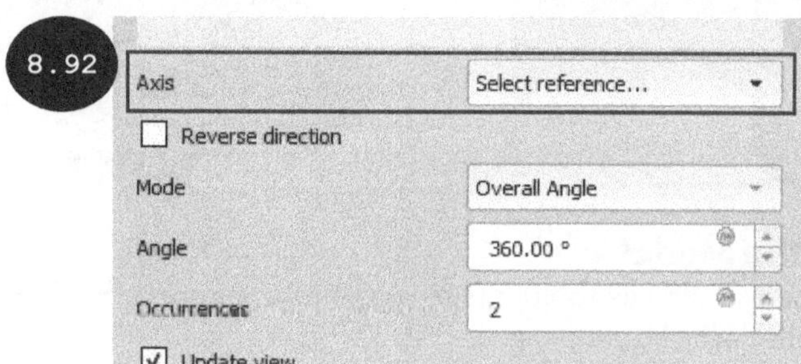

4. Select the front circular edge of the model to define the axis of revolution of the polar pattern, see Figure 8.93.

5. Enter **6** in the **Occurrences** field of the **Tasks Panel** as the number of occurrences to be created. The preview of the polar pattern of specified occurrences appears around the axis of revolution, see Figure 8.94.

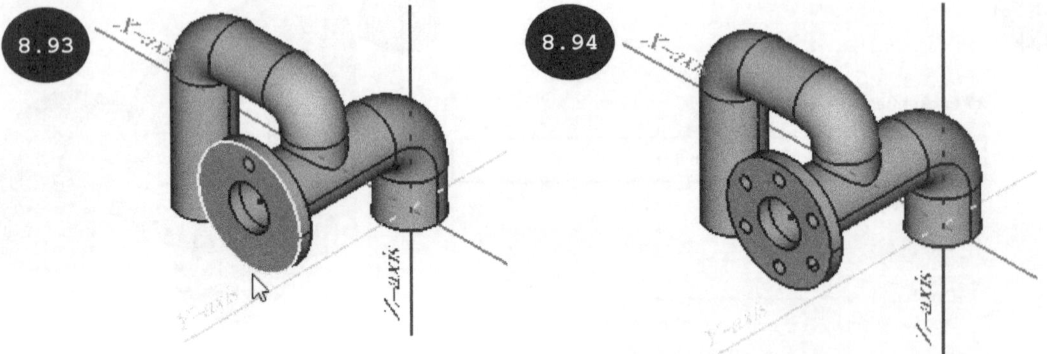

6. Ensure that the **360** degrees is specified in the **Angle** field of the **Tasks Panel** as the total angle between which the specified number of occurrences is to be arranged equally.

7. Click on the **OK** button in the **Tasks Panel**. A polar pattern of the specified number of occurrences of the selected pocket feature gets created, see Figure 8.95.

Section 8: Creating the Remaining Features

Now, you can create the remaining features of the model.

1. Create two more flanges on the other ends of the model one by one in a similar manner as described above. Note that each flange compresses a pad, a pocket, and a polar pattern feature. Figure 8.96 shows the final model after creating all its features. Refer to Figure 8.58 for the dimensions of each feature of the model.

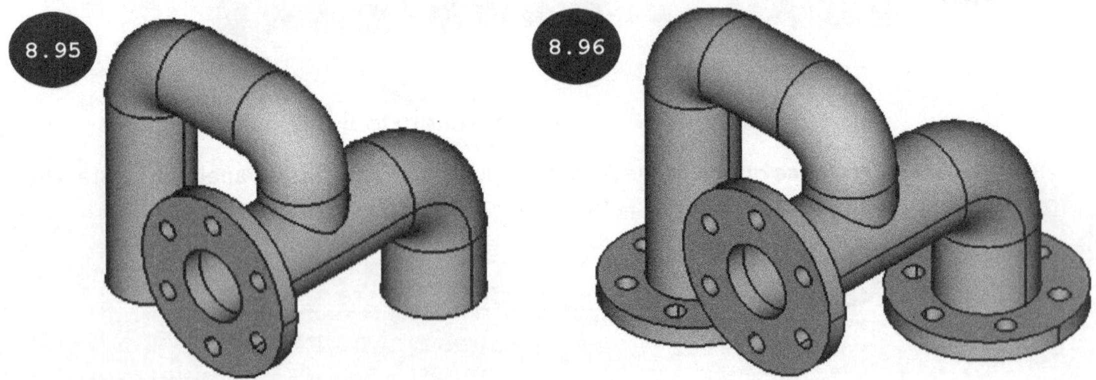

Section 9: Saving the Model

1. Click on the **Save** tool in the **File** toolbar (see Figure 8.97) or press the CTRL + S keys. The **Save FreeCAD Document** dialog box appears.

8.97

2. Browse to the required folder (:*FreeCAD > Chapter 08*) in the local drive of your system. Note that you need to create the Chapter 08 sub-folder inside the FreeCAD folder.

3. Enter **Ch08-Tutorial 1** in the **File name** field of the dialog box. Next, click on the **Save** button in the dialog box. The model gets saved at the specified location (:*FreeCAD > Chapter 08*).

4. Click on **File > Close** in the **Standard Menu** to close the current document.

Tutorial 2

Create the model shown in Figure 8.98. Different views and dimensions for creating the model are shown in the same figure. All dimensions are in mm.

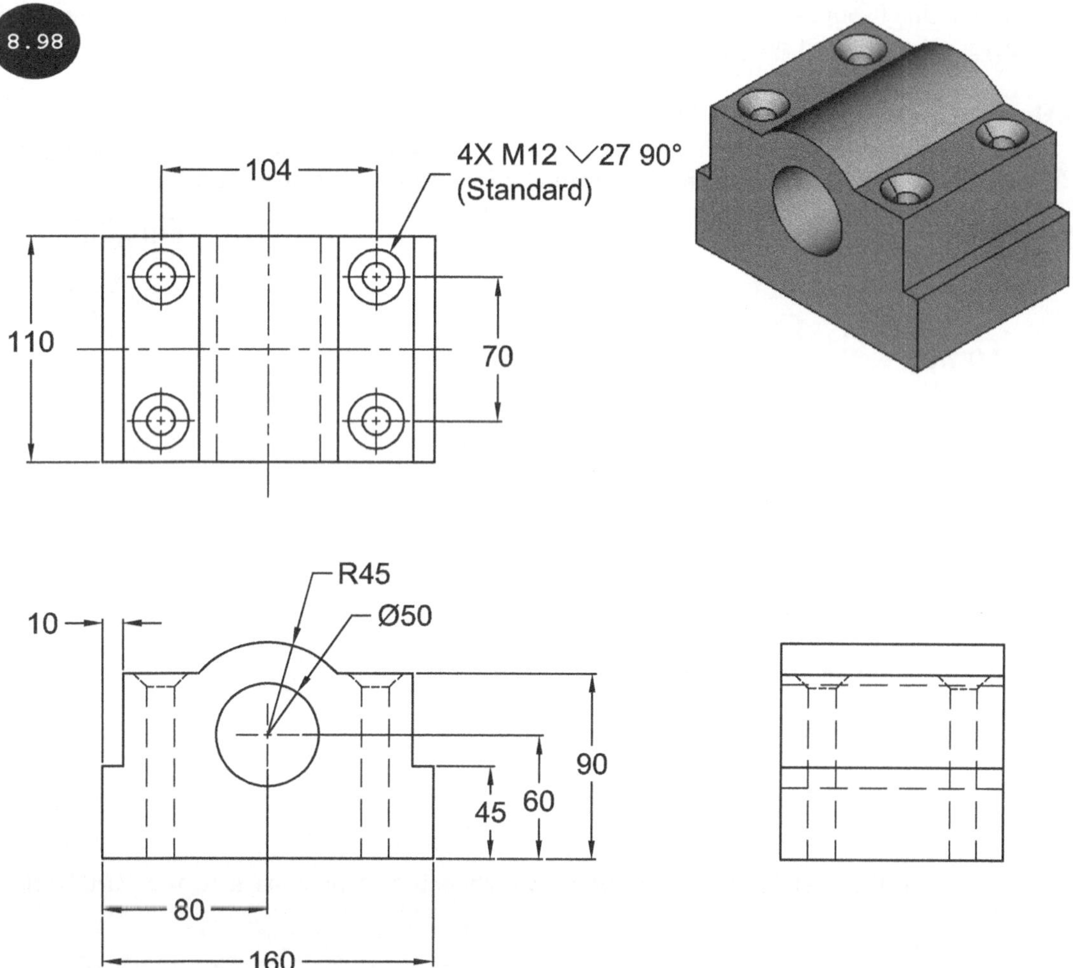

Section 1: Starting a New Part Document and Specifying Units

1. Start FreeCAD by double-clicking on the **FreeCAD 1.0** icon on your desktop, if not launched already.

2. Click on the **New** tool in the **File** toolbar, see Figure 8.99. A new empty document gets invoked with a default name.

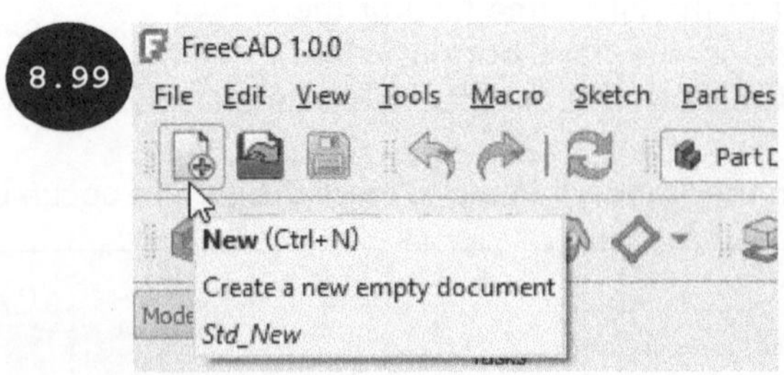

Now, you need to define the units of measurement for the current document.

3. Invoke the **Unit** flyout that appears at the lower right corner of the **Status Bar** and specify **Standard (mm, kg, s,*)** as the unit system for the current document.

Section 2: Creating the Base Feature

1. Invoke the **Sketcher** workbench by selecting the **XZ_Plane** as the sketching plane using the **Create sketch** tool and then create the sketch of the pad feature, see Figure 8.101.

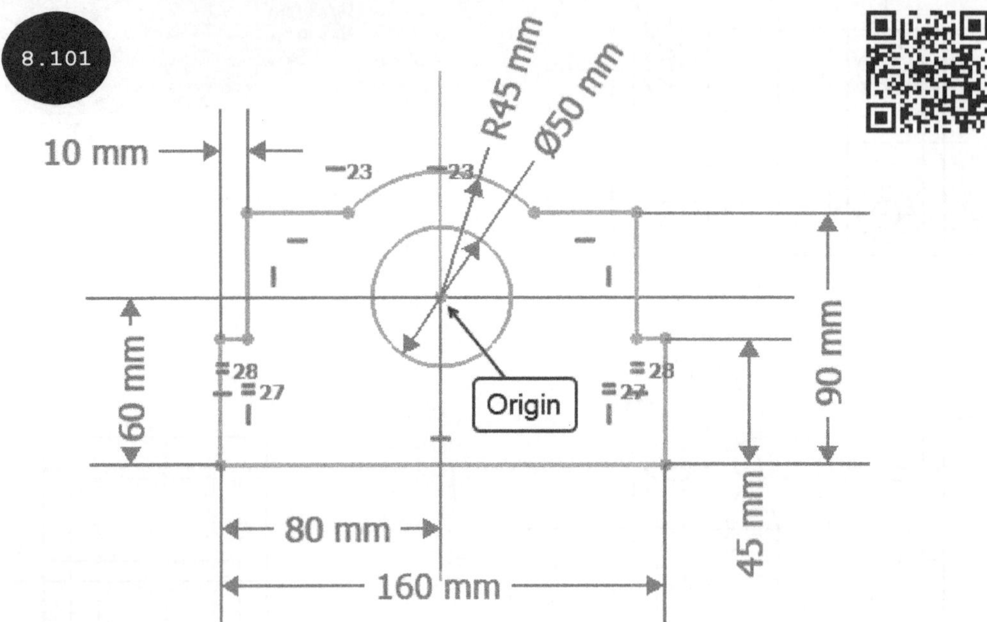

2. After creating the sketch, exit the **Sketcher** workbench to switch back to the **Part Design** workbench.

Now, you can extrude the sketch to create a pad feature.

3. Click on the **Pad** tool in the **Part Design Modeling** toolbar, see Figure 8.102. The preview of a pad feature appears in the 3D View area with default parameters. Also, the **Pad parameters** sub-window appears in the **Tasks Panel**.

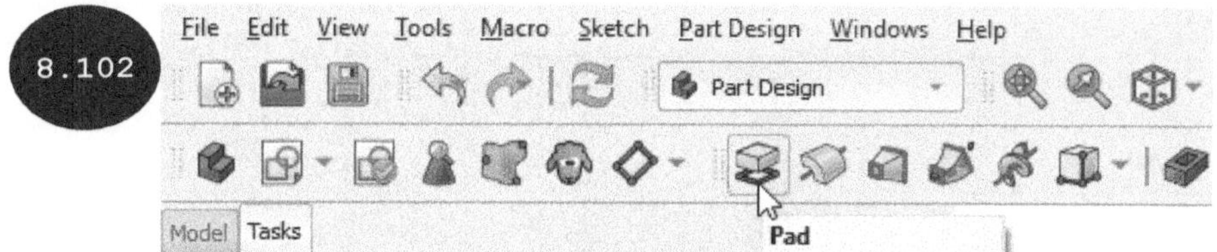

4. Enter **110** mm in the **Length** field of the **Tasks Panel** and then press the TAB key to update the preview of the pad feature in the 3D View area.

5. Select the **Symmetric to plane** check box in the **Tasks Panel** for adding material symmetrically on both sides of the sketching plane.

6. Click on the **OK** button in the **Tasks Panel** to confirm the creation of the pad feature and exit the **Tasks Panel**. The pad (base) feature of specified length gets created, see Figure 8.103.

Section 3: Creating the Holes

Now, you can create countersink holes in the model.

1. Select the top planar face of the model as the sketching plane (see Figure 8.104) and then click on the **Create sketch** tool . The **Sketcher** workbench gets invoked and the selected planar face gets oriented normal to the viewing direction.

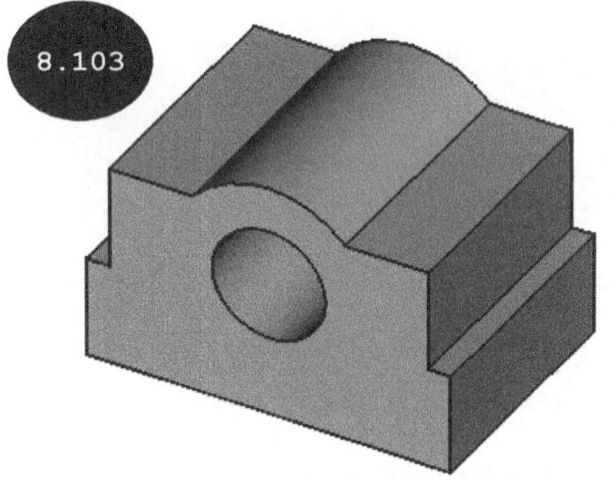

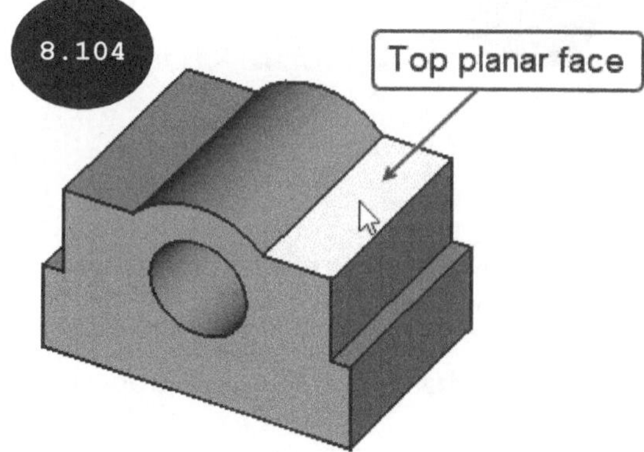

2. Select the **View section** tool in the **Sketcher** toolbar, see Figure 8.105. The section view of the model appears in the 3D View area by temporarily hiding the material that is in front of the sketching plane.

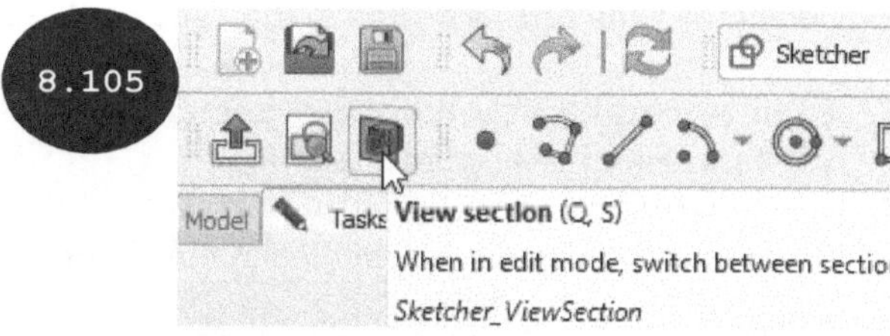

3. Create a circle to define the center of a hole concerning the origin, see Figure 8.106.

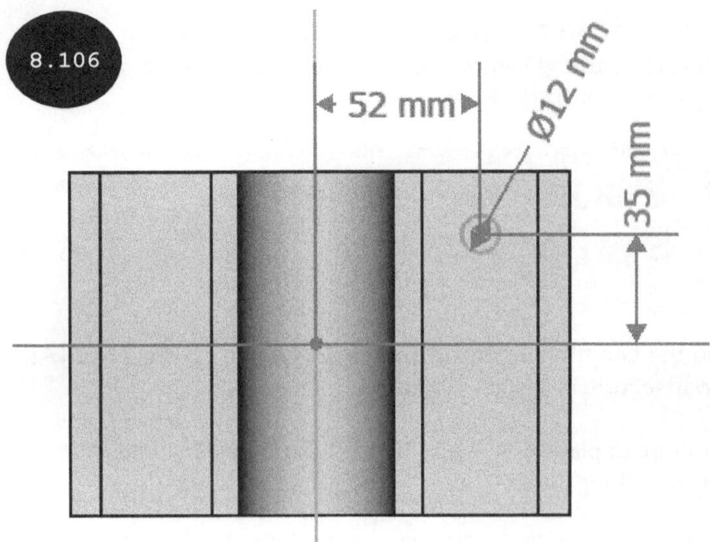

Note: The center of a circle defines the position of the hole center on the planar face of the model and its diameter will be ignored or not taken into account.

4. Exit the **Sketcher** workbench and then click on the **Hole** tool in the **Part Design Modeling** toolbar, see Figure 8.107. The preview of a hole appears in the 3D View area with default parameters. Also, the **Hole parameters** sub-window appears in the **Tasks Panel**.

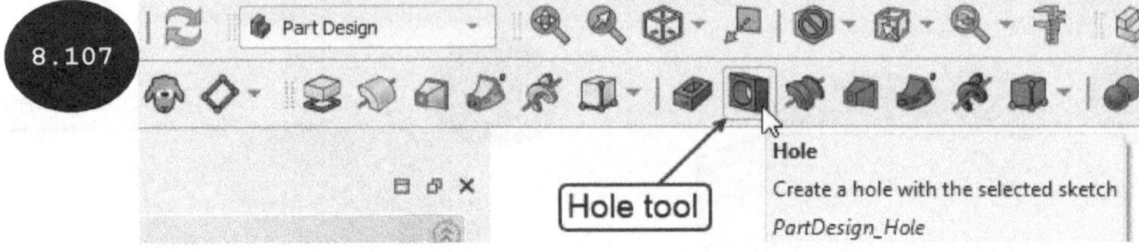

5. Select the **ISO metric regular profile** option in the **Profile** drop-down list of the **Tasks Panel**, see Figure 8.108.

6. Select the **M12** option in the **Size** drop-down list of the **Tasks Panel**, see Figure 8.108.

7. Select the **Through all** option in the **Depth** drop-down list of the **Tasks Panel**, see Figure 8.108.

8. Select the **Countersink** option in the **Type** drop-down list of the **Tasks Panel**, see Figure 8.108.

9. Enter **27** mm as the countersink diameter of the hole in the **Diameter** field of the **Hole cut** area in the **Tasks Panel**, see Figure 8.108.

10. Ensure that **90** degrees is specified in the **Countersink angle** field of the **Tasks Panel**.

8.108

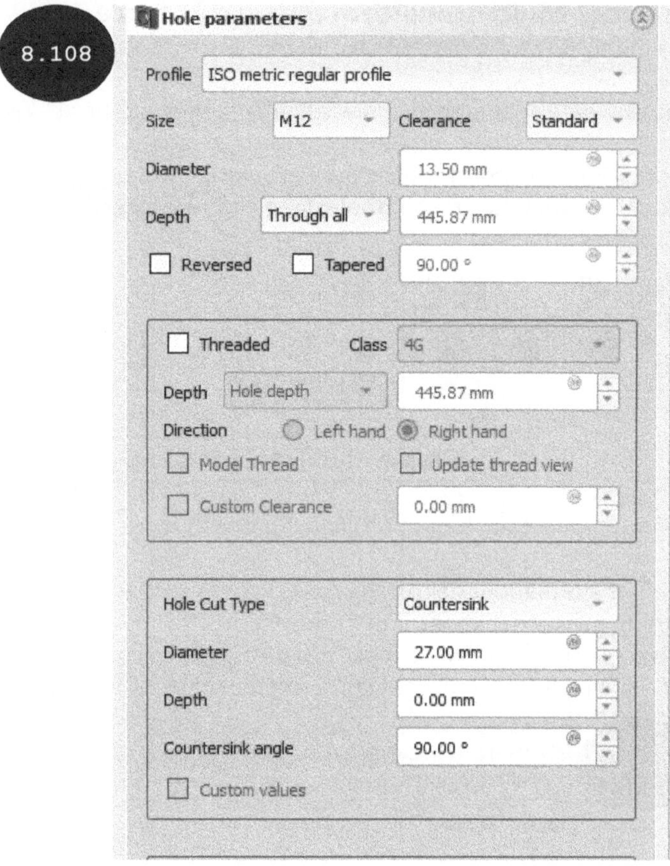

11. After specifying all the required parameters, click on the **OK** button in the **Tasks Panel**. The countersink hole of specified parameters gets created, see Figure 8.109.

8.109

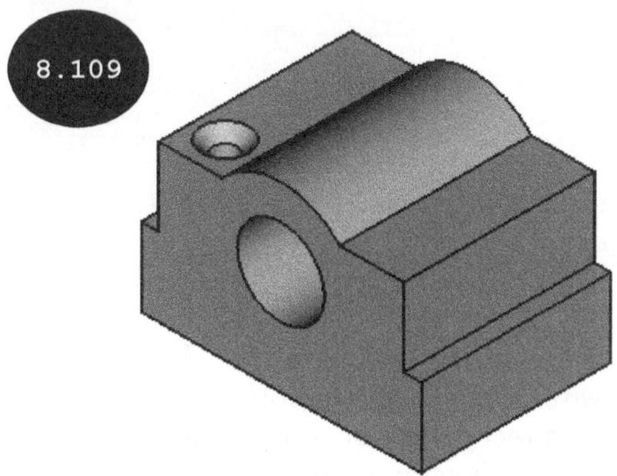

Section 4: Creating the Multi-transform Pattern Feature

Now, you can create a multi-transform pattern feature to create the remaining holes of the model.

1. Select the previously created countersink hole in the **Tree View** or the 3D View area.

2. Click on the **Create MultiTransform** tool in the **Part Design Modeling** toolbar, see Figure 8.110. The **MultiTransform parameters** sub-window appears in the **Tasks Panel** and the name of the selected feature appears in its field.

Now, you can define the first transformation (linear pattern) to be applied to the selected hole.

3. Right-click on the **Transformations** field of the **Tasks Panel** and then select the **Add linear pattern** option in the shortcut menu that appears, see Figure 8.111. The linear pattern transformation gets selected and appears in the **Transformations** field of the **Tasks Panel**, see Figure 8.112. Also, the options to create a linear pattern appeared at the bottom of the **Tasks Panel**.

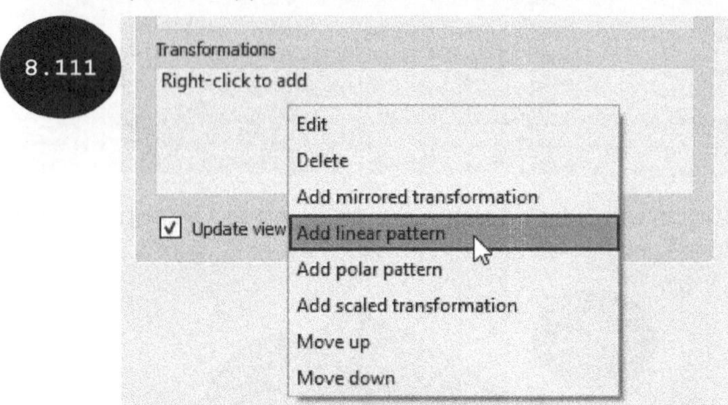

4. Enter **70** mm in the **Length** field of the **Tasks Panel** as the distance between two occurrences, see Figure 8.112.

5. Select the **Y axis** option in the **Direction** drop-down list of the **Tasks Panel** to define the pattern direction along the Y-axis of the model, see Figure 8.112. If the preview of the linear pattern does not appear like the one shown in Figure 8.113, then you can select any other option in this **Direction** drop-down list to define the correct pattern direction. If needed, you can also reverse the pattern direction by selecting the **Reverse direction** check box.

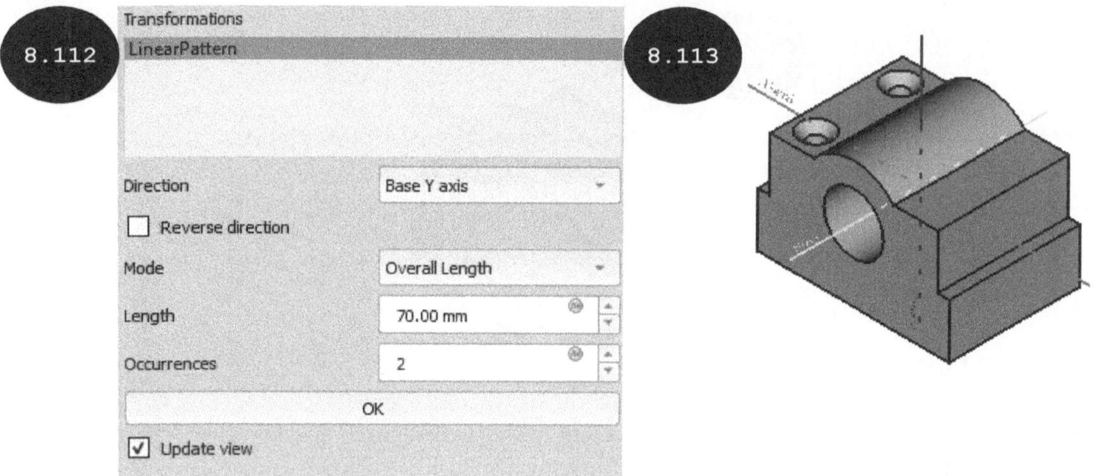

6. Ensure that **2** is specified in the **Occurrences** field of the **Tasks Panel** as the number of hole occurrences to be created along the defined pattern direction.

7. Click on the **OK** button available at the bottom of the **Tasks Panel**. A linear pattern of specified parameters gets created, see Figure 8.114.

   Now, you can create a mirrored transformation to mirror the result of the previously created linear pattern transformation.

8. Right-click on the **Transformations** field of the **Tasks Panel** and then select the **Add mirrored transformation** option in the shortcut menu that appears, see Figure 8.115. The options to mirror the result of the previously created linear pattern appear at the bottom of the **Tasks Panel**.

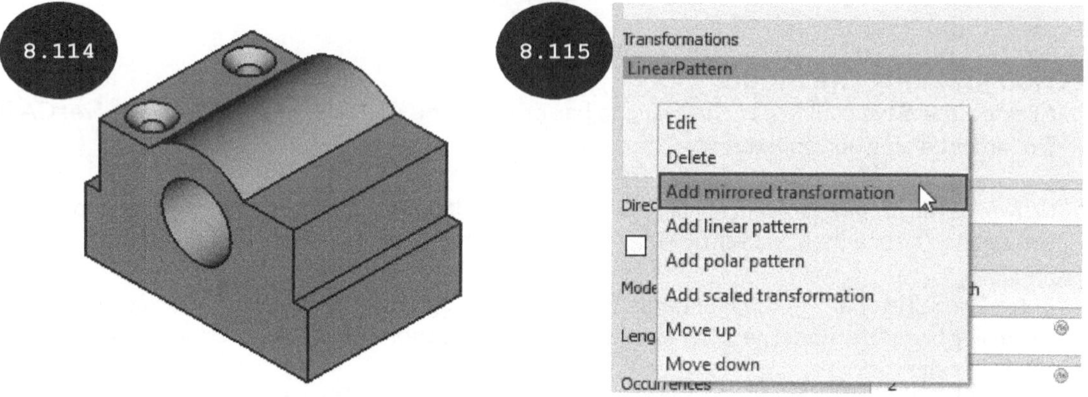

9. Ensure that the **Vertical sketch axis** is selected to define the mirroring plane in the **Plane** drop-down list of the **Tasks Panel**. If the preview of the resultant mirror feature does not appear like the one shown in Figure 8.116, then you need to select any other option in this **Plane** drop-down list to define the correct mirroring plane.

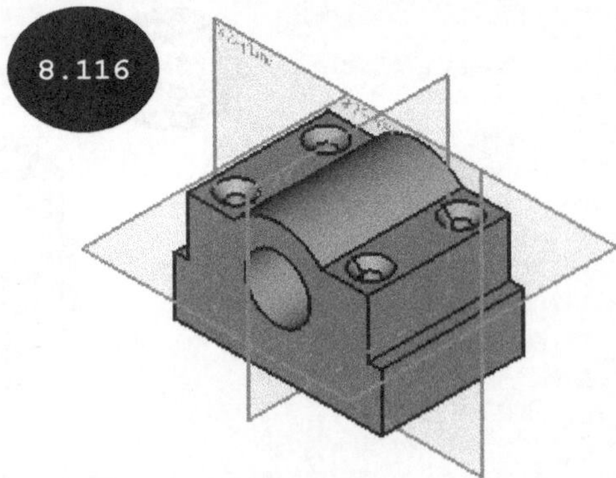

10. Click on the **OK** button available at the bottom of the **Tasks Panel**. The mirrored transformation gets created, see Figure 8.117.

11. Click on the **OK** button to exit the **Tasks Panel**. Figure 8.117 shows the final model.

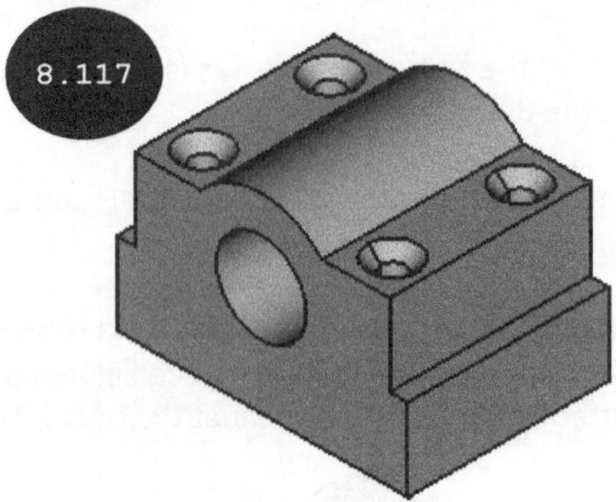

Section 5: Saving the Model

1. Click on the **Save** tool in the **File** toolbar or press the CTRL + S keys. The **Save FreeCAD Document** dialog box appears.

2. Browse to the required folder (:*FreeCAD > Chapter 08*) in the local drive of your system. Note that you need to create the Chapter 08 sub-folder inside the FreeCAD folder, if not created earlier.

3. Enter **Ch08-Tutorial 2** in the **File name** field of the dialog box. Next, click on the **Save** button in the dialog box. The model gets saved at the specified location (:*FreeCAD > Chapter 08*).

4. Click on **File > Close** in the **Standard Menu** to close the current document.

Hands-on Test Drive 1

Create the model shown in Figure 8.118. Different views and dimensions for creating the model are shown in the same figure. All dimensions are in mm.

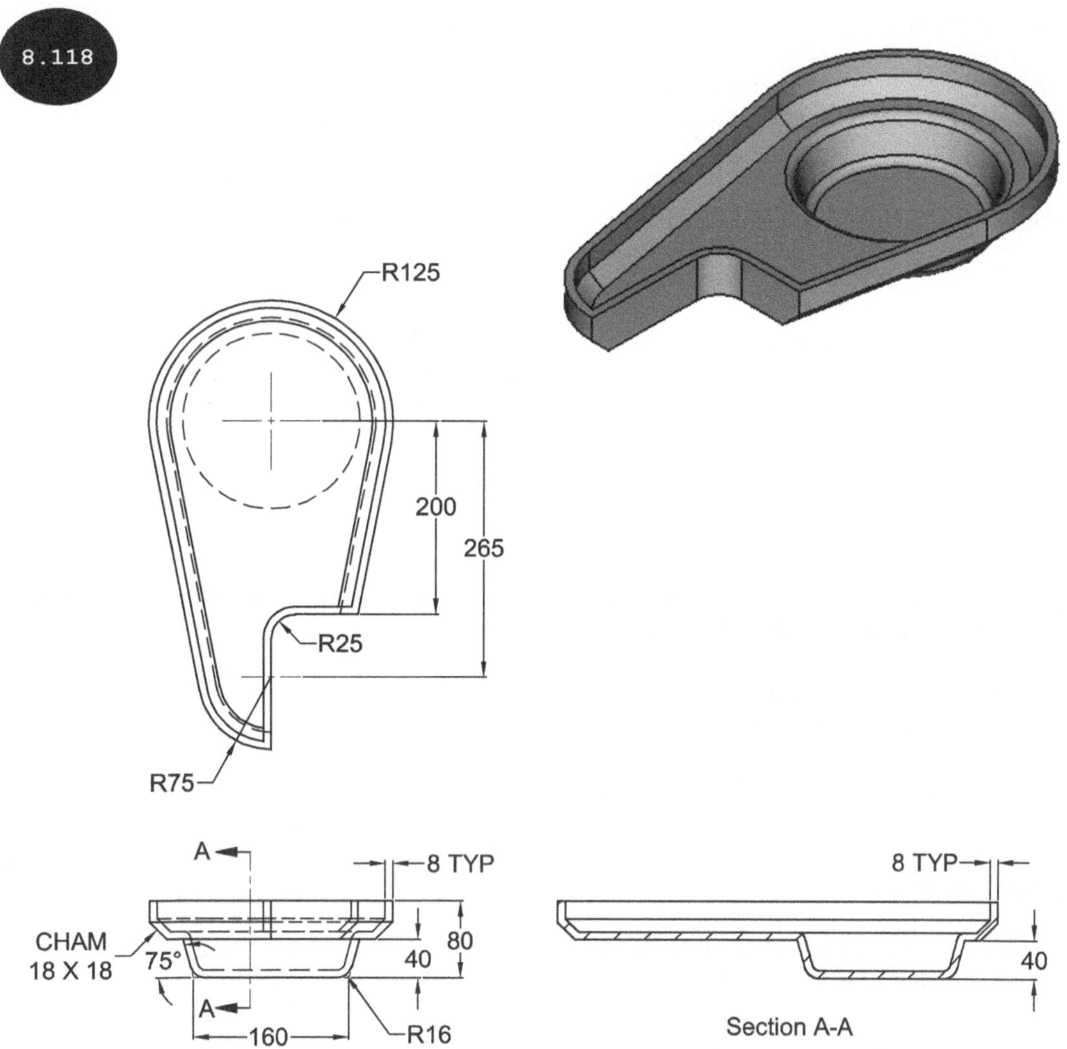

Summary

The chapter discussed how to create standard or customized holes such as counterbores and countersinks as per standard specifications. The chapter also described methods for creating different types of dress-up features: fillet, chamfer, thickness (shell), and angular draft for applying treatment to the existing edges and faces of a model.

Questions

Complete and verify the following sentences:

- The _________ tool is used for creating standard and customized holes such as counterbore and countersink.
- In FreeCAD, you can create dress-up features such as _________, _________, and _________ for applying treatment to the existing edges and faces of a model.
- On selecting the _________ check box in the **Hole parameters** sub-window, a real thread is modeled on a threaded hole by removing material from the model.
- A _________ is a rounded face of a constant radius.
- A _________ is a beveled face that is not perpendicular to its adjacent faces.
- The _________ tool is used for transforming a 3D solid model into a thick shell model of a uniform wall thickness by removing one or more faces.
- In FreeCAD, you add an angular draft to one or more selected faces of a model by using the _________ tool.
- The _________ plane is known as a fixed plane which remains dimensionally unchanged while adding an angular draft to the selected face(s) of a model.
- It is recommended to create a threaded hole without removing the material to increase the overall system performance. (True/False)
- You can create a thick shell model without removing any of its faces. (True/False)
- You can create a chamfer by specifying different distance values on both sides of the selected edge. (True/False)
- Adding an angular draft is a process of tapering one or more faces of a component so that it can easily separate from its cast while manufacturing. (True/False)

CHAPTER

9

Creating Assemblies

In this chapter, the following topics will be discussed:

- Creating an Assembly Using Top-down Approach
- Creating an Assembly Using Bottom-up Approach
- Invoking the Assembly Workbench
- Inserting Components in the Assembly Workbench
- Applying Joints

In the previous chapters, you have learned about various tools and techniques for creating real-world mechanical 3D solid parts. In this chapter, you will learn how to create mechanical assemblies. An assembly consists of two or more parts that are connected. Figure 9.1 shows an assembly in which multiple parts are connected.

9.1

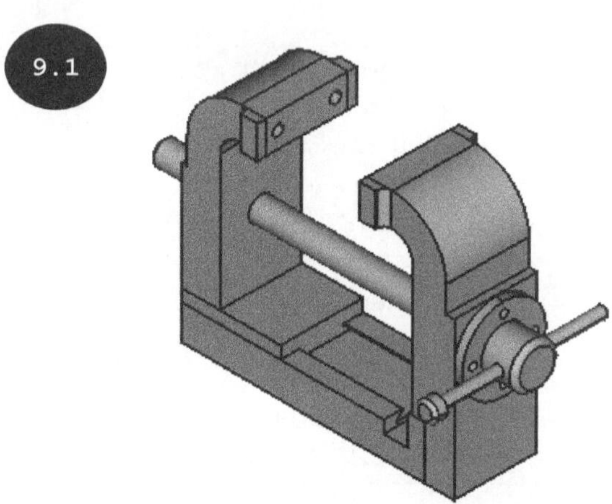

In FreeCAD, assemblies can be created using two primary approaches: **Top-down** and **Bottom-up**.

> **Top-down Assembly Approach:** All components of the assembly are designed as individual bodies within a single part document in the **Part Design** workbench.
>
> **Bottom-up Assembly Approach:** Pre-existing components are inserted one by one into the **Assembly** workbench and then assembled by applying the necessary joints to create the final assembly.

The **Assembly** workbench uses joints to precisely position and relate components to each other.

Creating an Assembly Using Top-down Approach

Creating all the components of an assembly as individual bodies within a single part document of the **Part Design** workbench is known as the Top-down assembly approach. The method of creating an assembly by using this approach is discussed below:

1. Start FreeCAD and then click on the **Parametric Part** button in the **Start page**, refer to Figure 9.2. A new part document gets invoked with the default name "**unnamed: 1**".

9.2

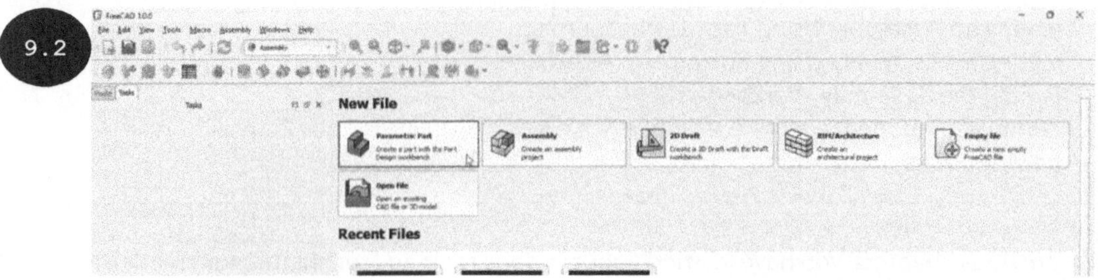

2. Invoke the **Unit** flyout available on the right corner of the **Status Bar** (see Figure 9.3), and ensure that the required measurement unit is selected for the current design document.

9.3

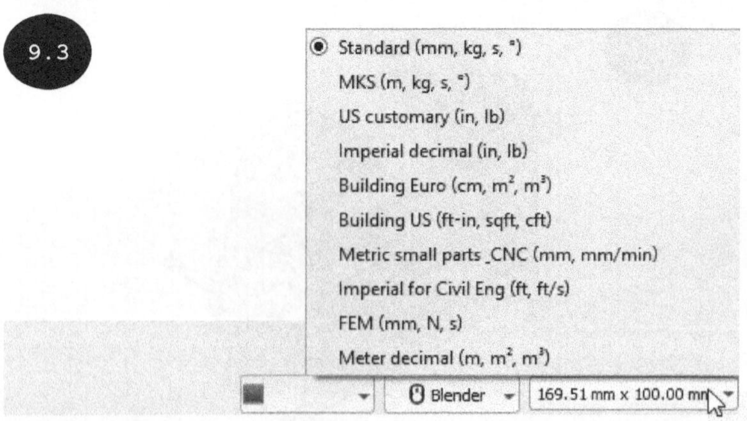

Now, you can create an assembly by creating its components as individual bodies.

Note: When you open a new part document, an empty part named "**Body**" is automatically added to the **Tree View** and activated. You can rename this default body as needed and start adding features.

3. Click on the **Model** tab of the **Combo View** to display the **Tree View** and then right-click on the default body to display a shortcut menu, see Figure 9.4.

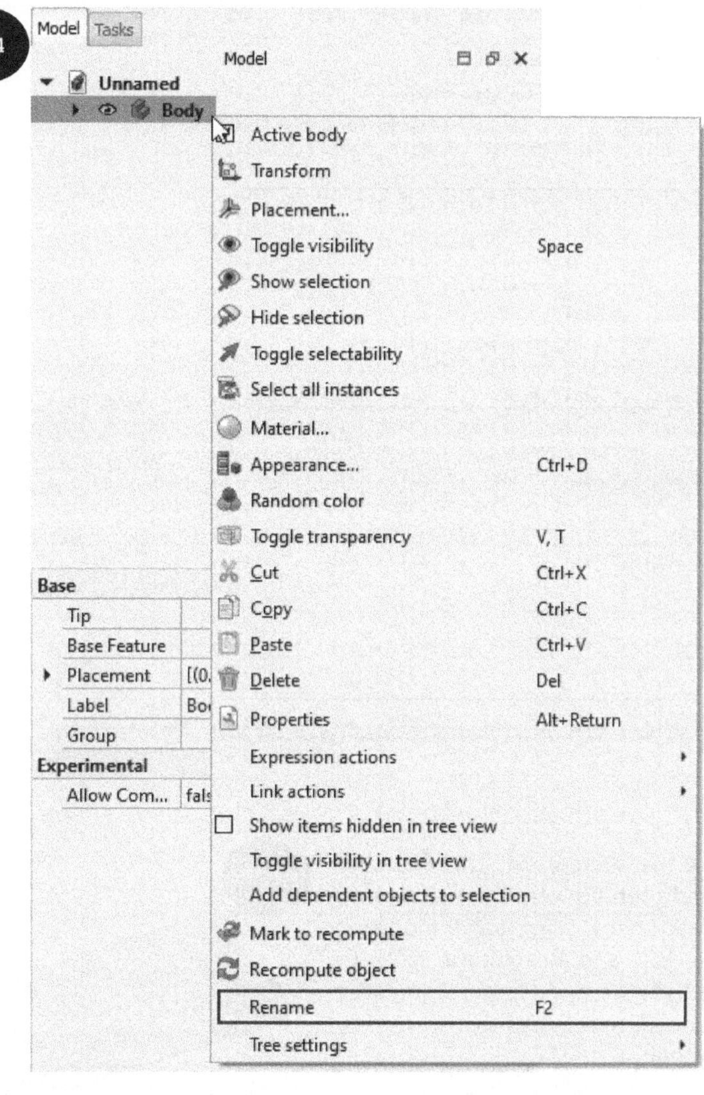

4. Click on the **Rename** option in the shortcut menu (refer to Figure 9.4) and then enter the name for the body/part in the edit field that appears in **Tree View**. Next, click anywhere in the 3D View area.

Now, you can create features of the active body/part similarly as discussed in earlier chapters.

5. Click on the **Create sketch** tool in the **Part Design Helper** toolbar (see Figure 9.5) and then select the desired plane for creating the sketch of the base feature. The **Sketcher** workbench gets invoked.

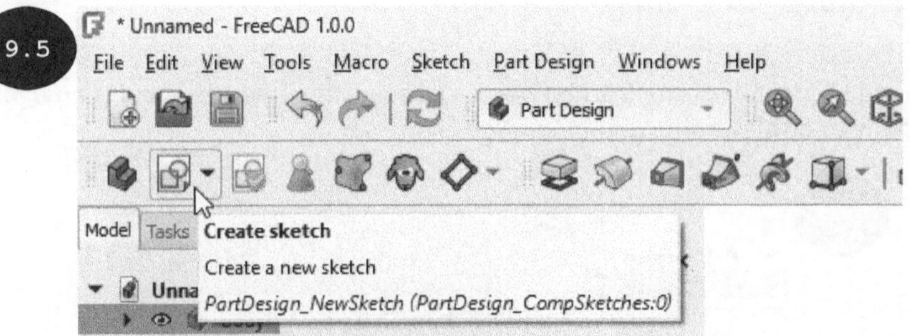

6. Create the sketch of the feature using the sketching tool, refer to Figure 9.6.

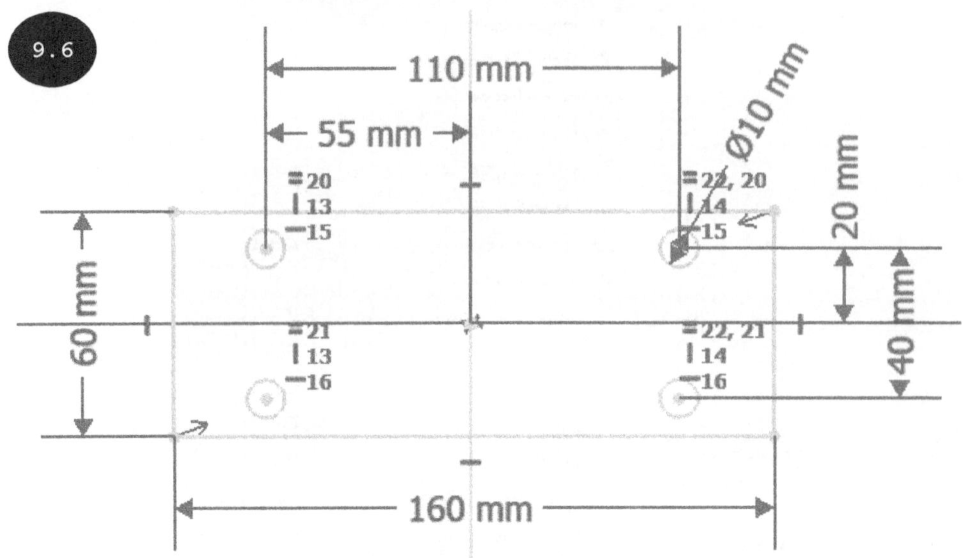

7. After creating the sketch, exit the **Sketcher** workbench and then convert the sketch into a 3D solid feature by using solid modeling tools such as **Pad** and **Revolution**, refer to Figure 9.7. In this figure, a pad feature is created by extruding the sketch to a depth of 10 mm by using the **Pad** tool.

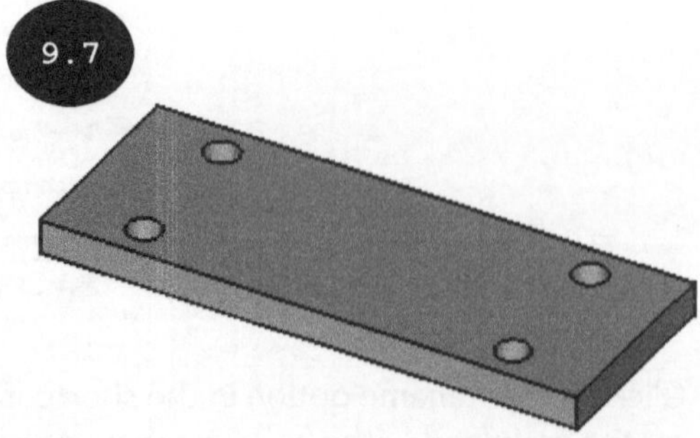

8. Similarly, you can create the remaining features of the body/part one by one.

After creating all the features of the first body/part, you can create the second part of the assembly.

9. Click on the **Create body** tool in the **Part Design Helper** toolbar, see Figure 9.8. A new empty body with the default name "**Body001**" gets created and appears in the **Tree View** of the **Model** tab, see Figure 9.9. Also, it becomes the active body of the current document to create its features.

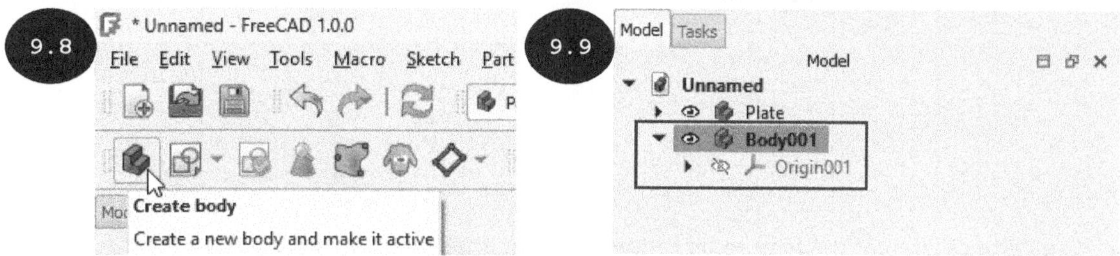

Now, you can rename the newly added body, as required.

10. Rename the newly added body/part in the **Tree View** of the **Model** tab, as discussed earlier.

    Now, you can create features of the second body/part of the assembly.

11. Ensure that the second body/part is activated in the **Tree View**.

Note: You can activate a body at any point in time by double-clicking on its name in the **Tree View**.

12. Click on the **Create sketch** tool in the **Part Design Helper** toolbar (see Figure 9.10) and then select the desired plane for creating the sketch of the base feature of the second body. The **Sketcher** workbench gets invoked.

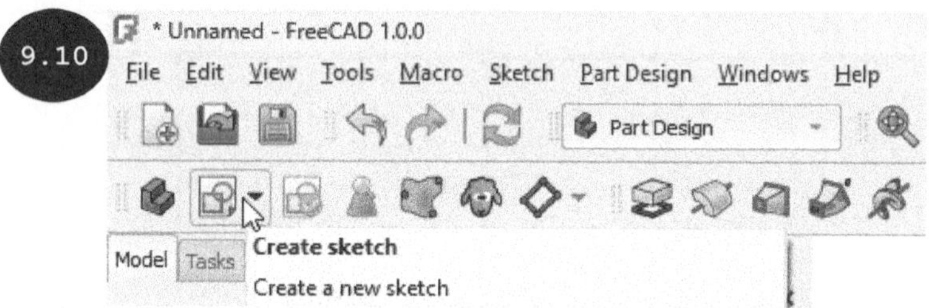

Note: You can also select a planar face of an existing body/part as the sketching plane for creating the base feature of the currently active body. To do this, select a planar face of an existing body in the 3D View area and then click on the **Create sketch** tool in the **Part Design Helper** toolbar. The **Reference** dialog box appears, see Figure 9.11. In this dialog box, select the **Make dependent copy** radio button for making the currently active body a dependent body of the existing selected body. Next, click on the **OK** button in the dialog box. The **Sketcher** workbench gets invoked. Ignore the error message that may appear in the **Report view** window at the bottom of the screen and close the **Report view** window by clicking on the cross mark that appears in its top right corner.

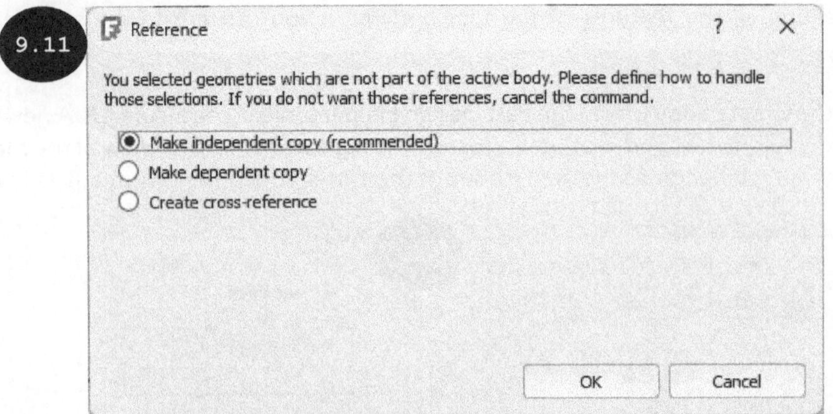

13. Create the sketch of the feature using the sketching tool, refer to Figure 9.12. In this figure, the sketch is created on the XZ Plane (Front Plane).

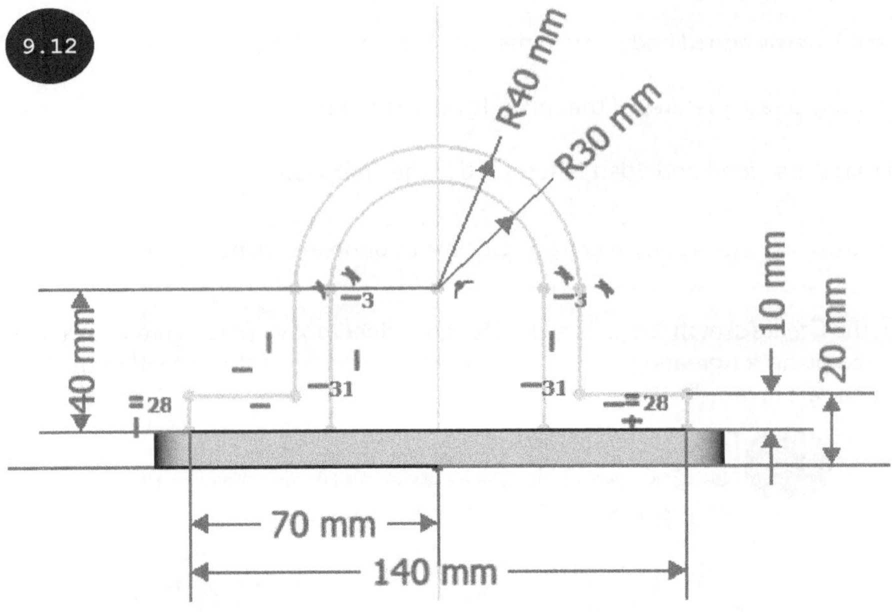

14. After creating the sketch, exit the **Sketcher** workbench and then convert the sketch into a 3D solid feature by using the solid modeling tool such as **Pad** and **Revolution**, refer to Figure 9.13. In this figure, a pad feature is created by extruding the sketch symmetrically to a depth of 60 mm using the **Pad** tool.

15. Create the remaining features of the second body/part one by one, refer to Figure 9.14.

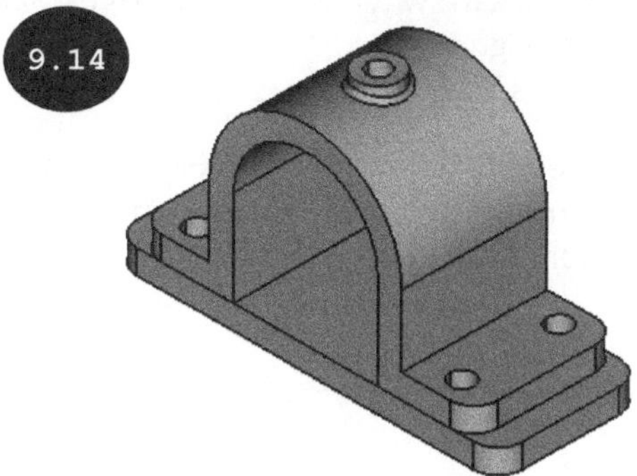

16. Similarly, you can create the other parts of the assembly one by one as separate bodies within the same part document.

17. After creating all the components of an assembly as individual bodies, you can save the document using the **Save** tool of the **File** toolbar.

Creating an Assembly Using Bottom-up Approach

Inserting already created components of an assembly one by one into the assembly workbench and then assembling them by applying joints is known as the Bottom-up assembly approach.

Invoking the Assembly Workbench

In FreeCAD, you can insert existing components into the **Assembly** workbench and assemble them by applying joints. The method for accessing the **Assembly** workbench is discussed below:

1. Start **FreeCAD** by double-clicking the **FreeCAD 1.0** icon on your desktop. The startup user interface of FreeCAD appears, displaying the **Start** page, see Figure 9.15.

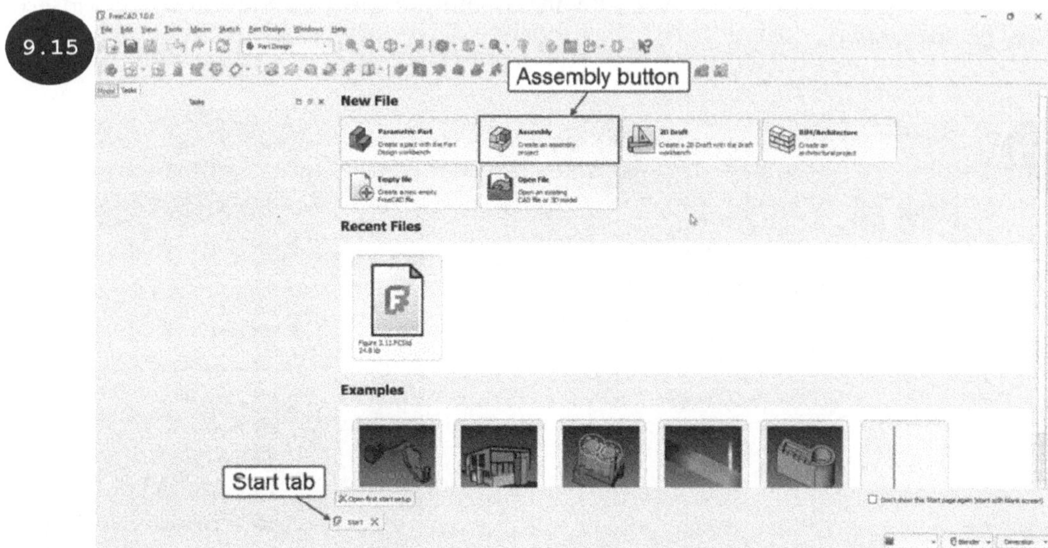

Note: If **FreeCAD** is already open, you can switch to the **Start** page by clicking the **Start** tab at the bottom of the screen, refer to Figure 9.15.

2. In the **Start page**, click on the **Assembly** button, refer to Figure 9.15. The **Assembly** workbench is invoked, and a new empty assembly document opens with the default name **"unnamed: 1"**, see Figure 9.16. Note that the **Assembly** workbench is automatically selected in the **Workbench Selector**.

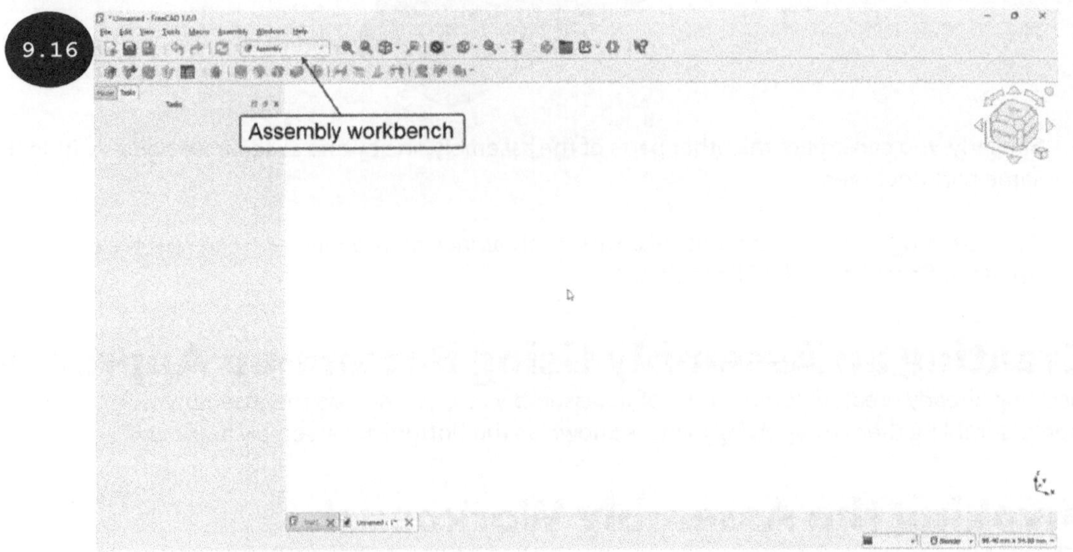

Tip: Alternatively, to access the **Assembly** workbench, click on the **New** tool in the **File** toolbar (see Figure 9.17) to start a new empty document, then select the **Assembly** workbench from the **Workbench Selector**, see Figure 9.18. Next, click the **Create Assembly** button in the **Assembly** toolbar or press **A** to add an assembly in the **Tree View** and begin inserting components.

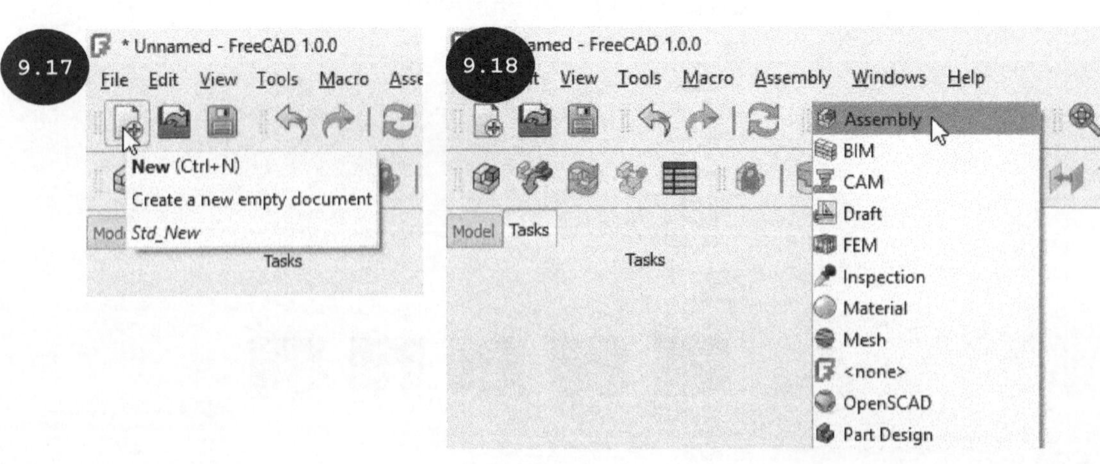

Inserting Components in the Assembly Workbench

After accessing the **Assembly** workbench, you can insert existing components and assemble them by applying joints. However, before inserting components, you must first save the document. The method for saving the document and inserting existing components is discussed below:

1. Save the assembly document to the desired location using the **Save** tool in the **File** toolbar, see Figure 9.19. It is recommended to save the assembly document with a unique name in the same location where all the components of the assembly are saved.

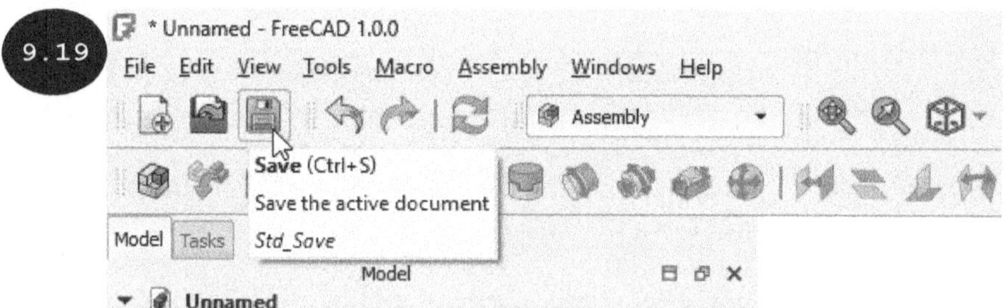

Now, you can insert the first component of the assembly in the **Assembly** workbench.

2. Click on the **Insert Component** tool in the **Assembly** toolbar, see Figure 9.20. The **Insert Component** sub-window appears in the **Tasks Panel**, see Figure 9.21.

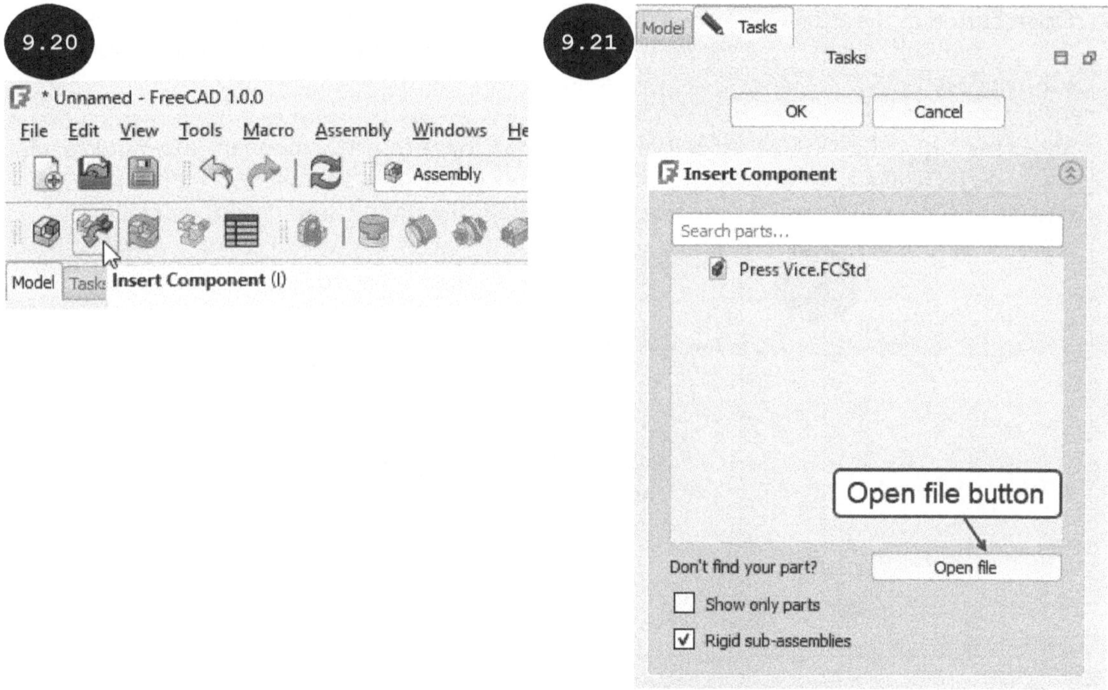

Note: The **Insert Component** sub-window displays a list of components that are open in the current **FreeCAD** session. If the desired component appears in this sub-window, you can select it to insert it into the **Assembly** document.

3. Click on the **Open file** button in the **Insert Component** sub-window, refer to Figure 9.21. The **Select FreeCAD documents to import parts from** dialog box appears, see Figure 9.22.

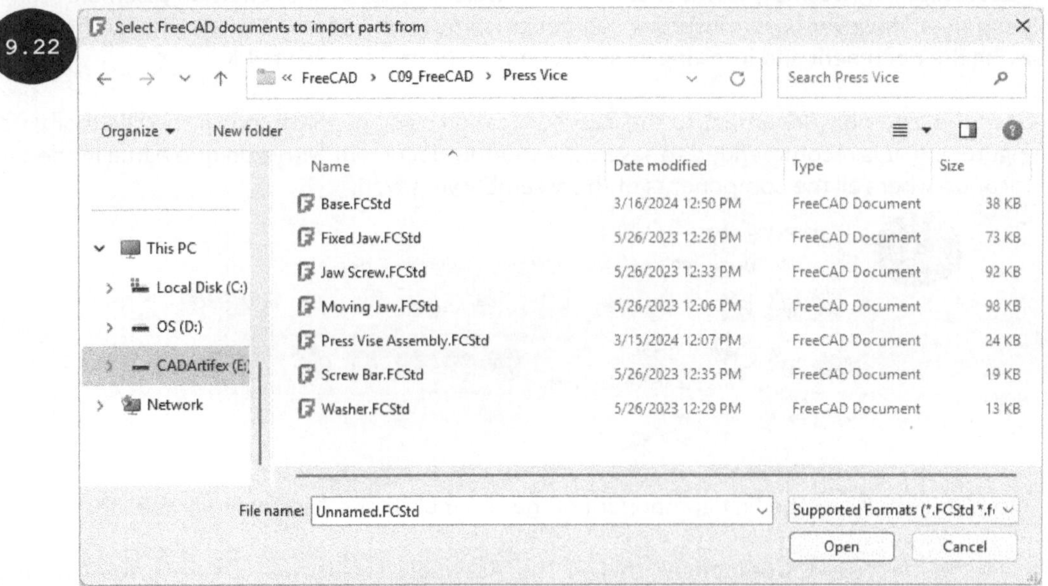

4. Browse to the required location and select the component to be inserted. Next, click on the **Open** button in the dialog box. The name of the selected component gets listed in the **Insert Component** sub-window, see Figure 9.23. In this figure, the **Base** component is listed in the sub-window.

5. Select the desired body of the newly listed component in the **Insert Component** sub-window, see Figure 9.23. **The Ground Part?** dialog box appears, see Figure 9.24. This dialog box prompts you to choose whether you want to fix the first part automatically in the **Assembly** document.

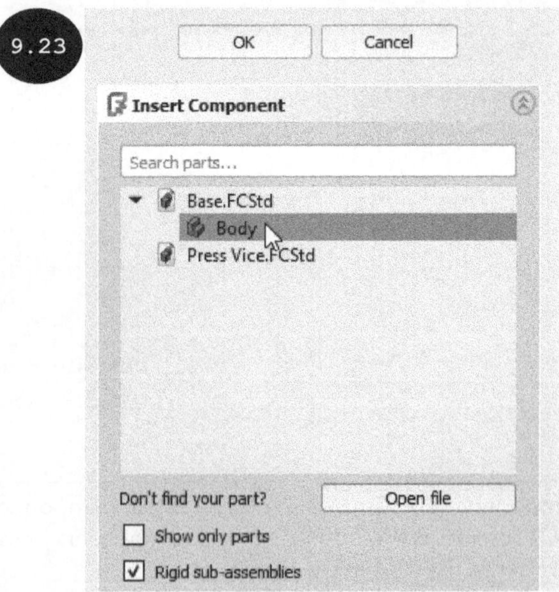

9.24

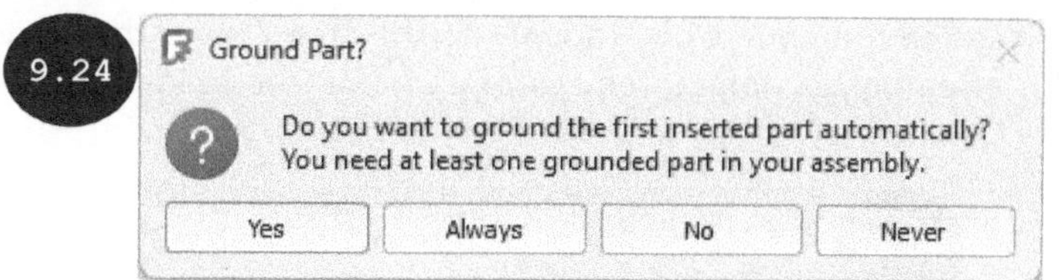

Note: Clicking the **Yes** button automatically fixes the first component in the current document. Selecting **Always** ensures that the first component is fixed by default in all future Assembly documents. Choosing **No** leaves the first component unfixed in the current document, while **Never** prevents the first component from being fixed in any future Assembly documents.

Tip: It is always recommended to fix the first component of the assembly in the **Assembly** workbench. A fixed component restricts all its degrees of freedom, preventing any translational or rotational movement.

6. Click the **Always button** in the **Ground Part?** dialog box to automatically fix the first component in **Assembly** document. The selected body of the component gets inserted and placed at the default location (origin) in the 3D View area of the workbench. Also, it becomes a fixed component. If needed, scroll the middle mouse button to adjust the view and fit the inserted component within the display area.

7. Click anywhere to exit the current selection set. The **Insert Component** sub-window remains displayed in the **Tasks Panel**. Figure 9.25 shows the Assembly document with the first component inserted and fixed at the origin.

9.25

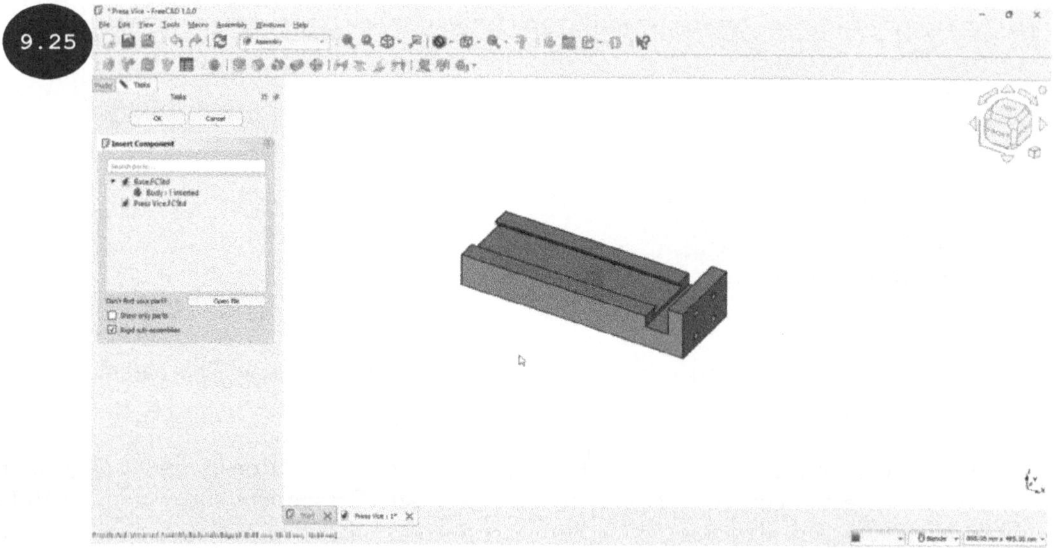

Notice that the inserted component body appears in the **Tree View** of the **Model** tab, listed under the name of the assembly document, see Figure 9.26. You can switch between the **Model** and **Tasks** tabs in the **Combo View** at any time during the design process.

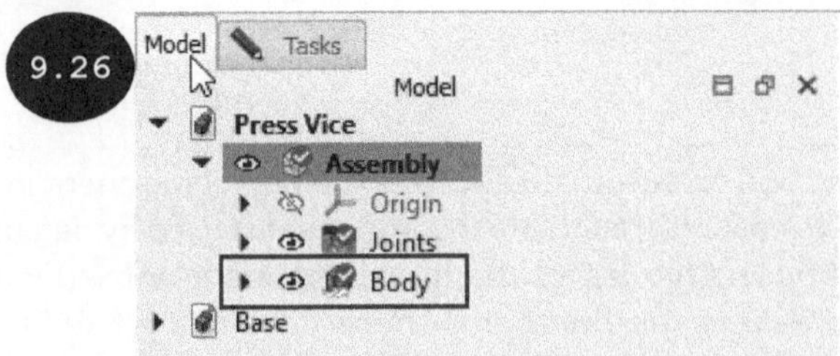

Now, you need to insert the second component of the assembly.

8. Ensure that the **Insert Component** sub-window is displayed in the **Tasks Panel**, see Figure 9.27. If this sub-window disappears, click on the **Insert Component** tool in the **Assembly** toolbar (see Figure 9.28) to reopen it for inserting components in the Assembly document.

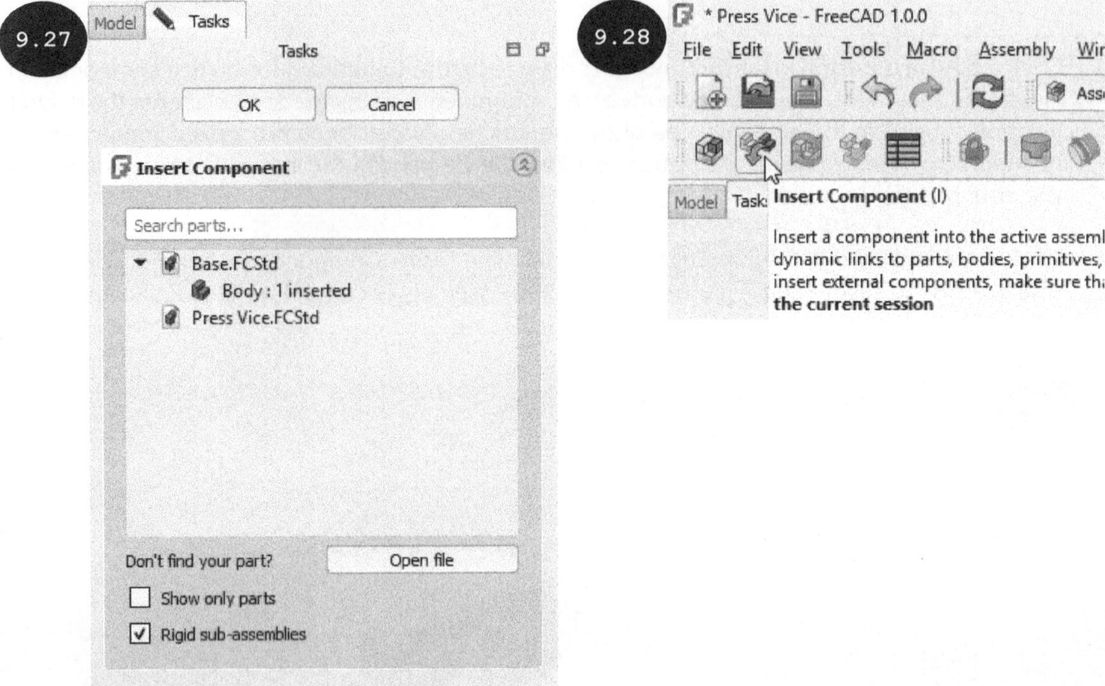

9. Click on the **Open file** button in the **Insert Component** sub-window. The **Select FreeCAD documents to import parts from** dialog box appears.

10. Select the component to be inserted and then click on the **Open** button in the dialog box. The name of the selected component gets listed in the **Insert Component** sub-window with the display of all its individual bodies.

11. Select the desired body of the newly listed component in the **Insert Component** sub-window, see Figure 9.29. The selected component is inserted at default location into the 3D View area, displaying translational and rotational handles, see Figure 9.30.

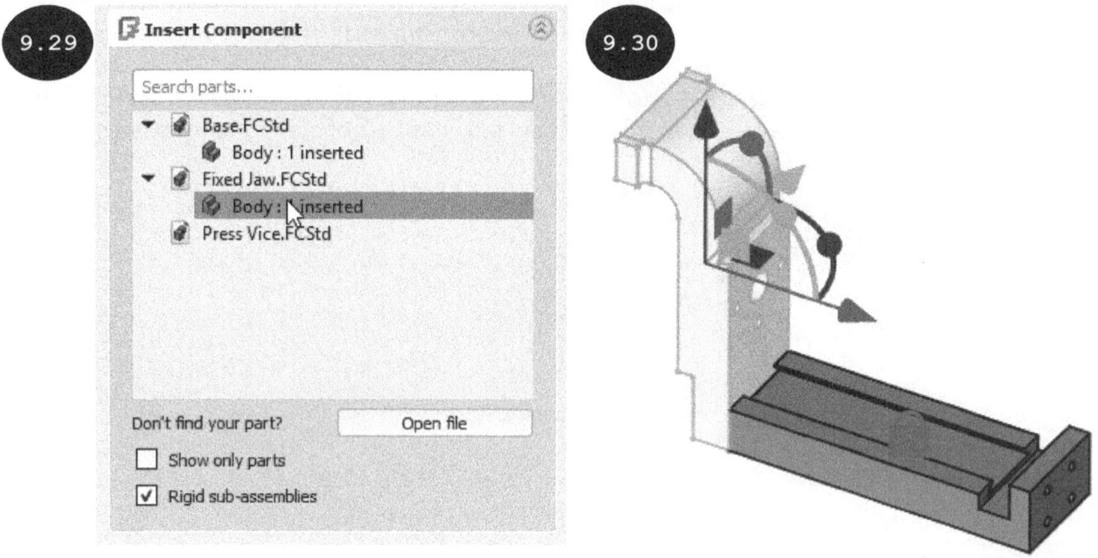

12. Define the placement of the newly inserted component in the 3D View area by dragging its translational and rotational handles, ensuring that it does not intersect with the first component.

Tip: It is recommended to define the position of the component in the **3D View** area such that it does not intersect with the existing components of the assembly.

13. After defining the position of the second component, click anywhere in the 3D View area to exit the current selection set. The second component is inserted at the defined position, see Figure 9.31. However, it remains free to translate and rotate in any direction, since all its degrees of freedom are unrestricted. You need to apply the required joints to constrain the necessary degrees of freedom of the second component.

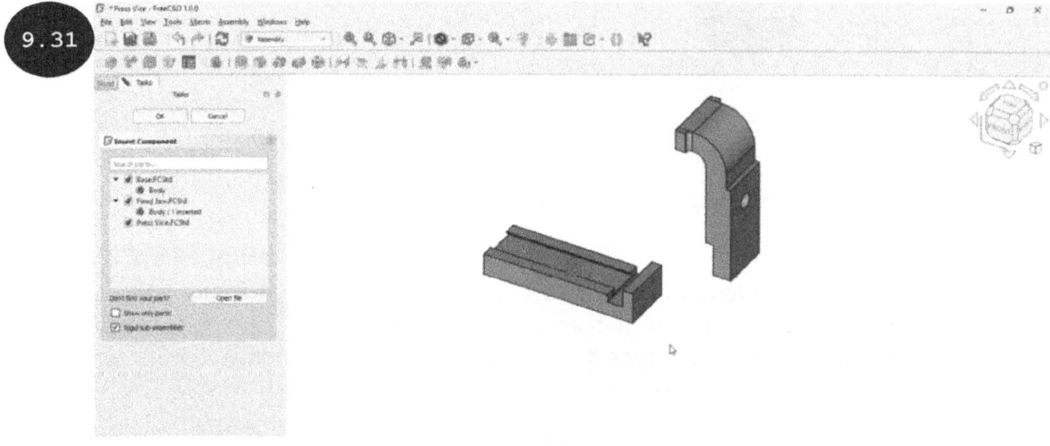

Note that the **Insert Component** sub-window remains displayed in the **Tasks Panel**, allowing you to continue inserting the remaining components of the assembly. However, it is recommended to first assemble the second component with the first component by applying the required joints before inserting the third or subsequent components using the **Insert Component** tool. This ensures that the components are properly aligned and constrained before adding more parts.

14. Click the **OK** button in the **Tasks Panel** to confirm the insertion of the components and close the panel. Figure 9.32 shows the **Tree View** in the **Model** tab with a list of components inserted in the current Assembly document.

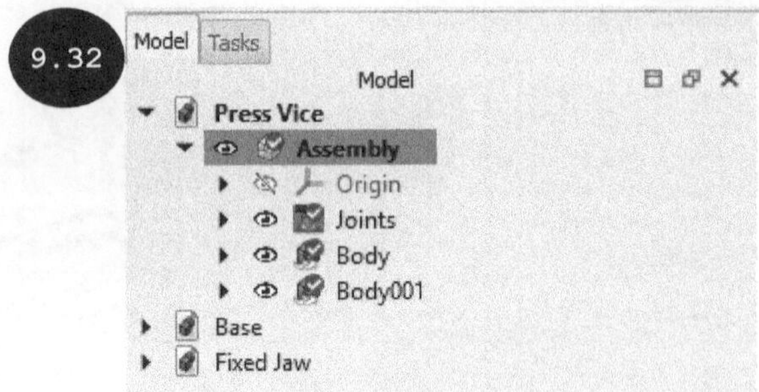

Applying Joints

Joints are used for positioning components of an assembly by restricting or reducing their degrees of freedom. In FreeCAD, you can apply various types of joints, such as Fixed, Revolute, Cylindrical, Slider, Ball, Distance, and Parallel, to define relationships between assembly components using the respective tools available in the **Assembly Joints** toolbar. The methods for applying these joints are discussed next.

Applying the Fixed Joint

The Fixed joint is used to lock or fix components together by removing all degrees of freedom, preventing any relative motion between the components, as illustrated in Figure 9.33. This joint is typically applied between components that are welded or bolted together, with no allowable motion between them. The method for applying the Fixed joint is discussed below:

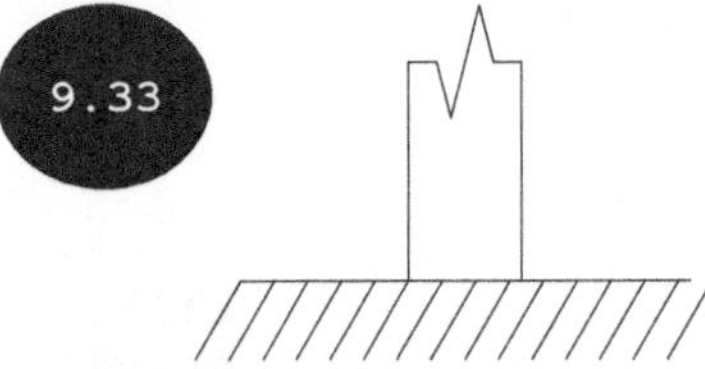

Rigid Joint

(No translation and rotational movements)

1. Click on the **Create a Fixed Joint** tool in the **Assembly Joints** toolbar (see Figure 9.34) or press the F key. The **Create Joint** sub-window appears in the **Tasks Panel**, see Figure 9.35. By default, the **Fixed** option is selected in the **Joint type** drop-down list in the sub-window, allowing you to apply the Fixed joint between two components.

Now, you need to define the joint connector on two different components to apply the selected joint type between them.

2. Move the cursor over a face, edge, or vertex of the first component to define the position of the joint connector. The respective geometry highlights, and a joint connector appears near the cursor, snapping to the nearest snap point on the highlighted geometry (see Figure 9.36). In this figure, the cursor is positioned over the face of a component, and the joint connector snaps to its center.

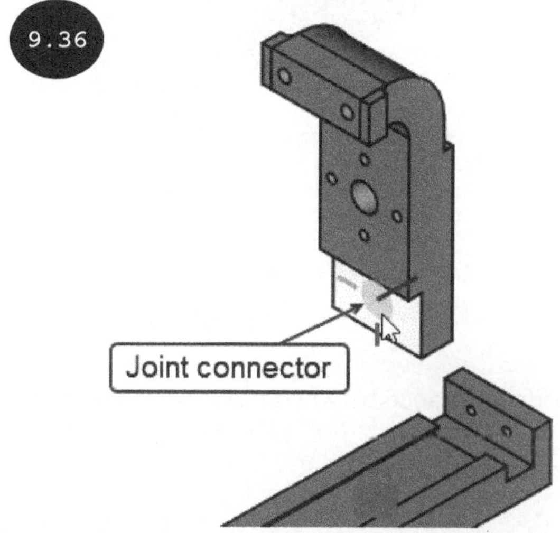

3. Click to specify the position of the joint connector on the highlighted geometry when the cursor snaps to the desired position.

   After defining the joint connector on the first component, proceed to define the joint connector on the second component.

4. Move the cursor over a face, edge, or vertex of the second component. The respective geometry highlights, and a joint connector appears near the cursor on the highlighted geometry, see Figure 9.37. In this figure, the cursor is positioned over a face of the second component, and the joint connector snaps to its center.

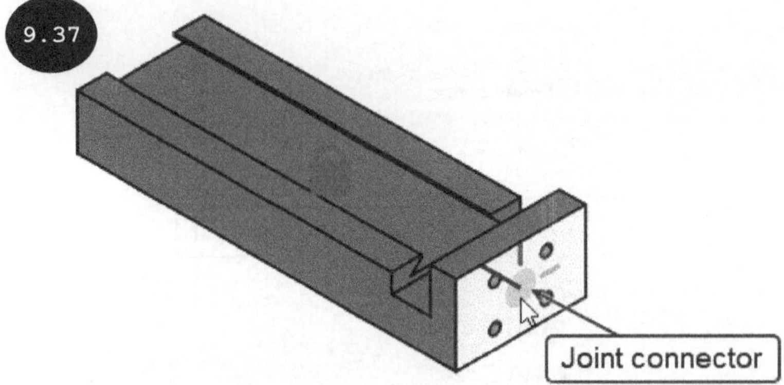

5. Click to define the position of the joint connector on the highlighted geometry of the second component. The second component moves toward the first component, or vice versa, depending on the available degrees of freedom, and the joint connectors of both components coincide in the 3D View area, see Figure 9.38.

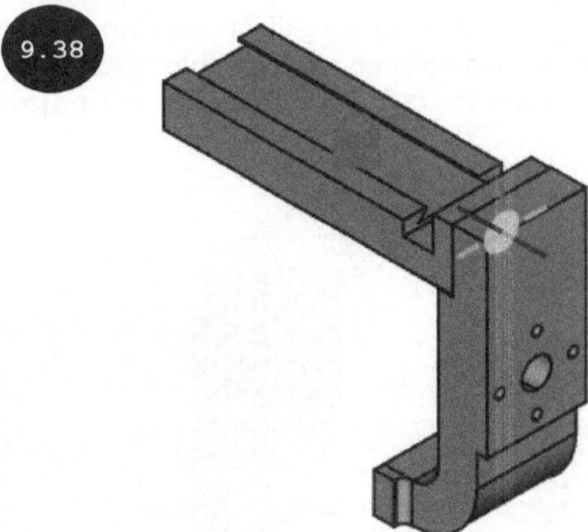

   Now, you can adjust the offset distance between the joint connectors and modify the angle of rotation, if needed.

Rotation: The **Rotation** field in the **Create Joint** sub-window allows you to enter the required angle of rotation. Figure 9.39 shows the components with an angle of rotation set to **0**, while Figure 9.40 shows the components with an angle of rotation set to 180 degrees.

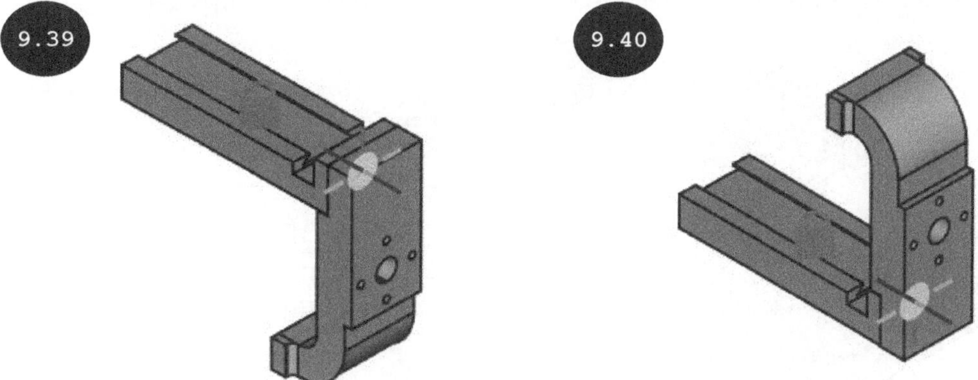

Offset: The **Offset** field in the **Create Joint** sub-window allows you to enter the required offset distance between the joint connectors of the components. By default, this field is set to **0**, making both joint connectors coincide with each other, see Figure 9.40, while Figure 9.41 shows an offset distance set between the joint connectors. You can also enter a negative value (-) in the **Offset** field to reverse the offset direction.

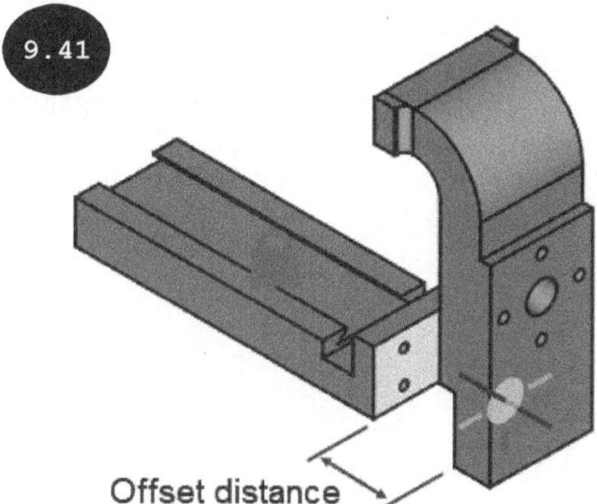

Show advanced offsets: Selecting the **Show advanced offsets** check box displays **Offset 1** and **Offset 2** fields, allowing you to define translational and rotational coordinates to position the joint connections of the components.

Reverse the direction of the joint: The **Reverse the direction of joint** button allows you to flip the alignment between the joint connectors of the components.

6. If needed, enter the offset distance and angle of rotation in their respective fields of the **Create Joint** sub-window, as discussed above.

7. After defining the joint connectors on two components and other required parameters, click on the **OK** button in the **Tasks Panel**. The Fixed joint is applied between the components, removing all degrees of freedom and locking the components together, refer to Figure 9.42. Also, the applied joint is listed under the **Joints** node in the **Tree View** of the **Model** tab, see Figure 9.43.

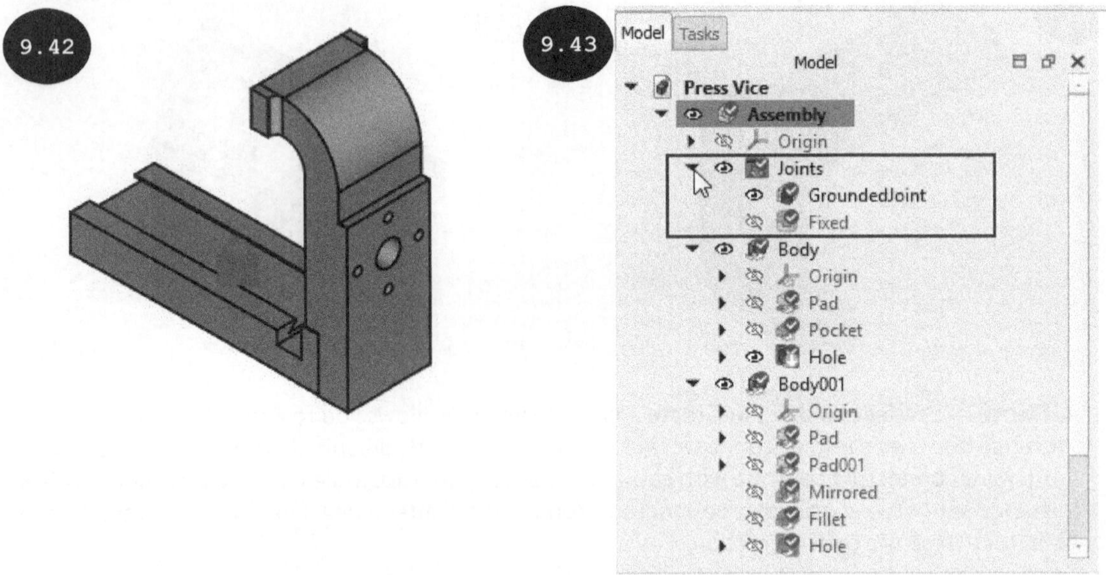

Applying the Revolute Joint

The Revolute joint allows a component to rotate about an axis by removing all degrees of freedom except one rotational degree of freedom, as illustrated in Figure 9.44. This joint type is used for rotating the component around an axis, which is defined by the joint connectors of the components. The method for applying the Revolute joint is discussed below:

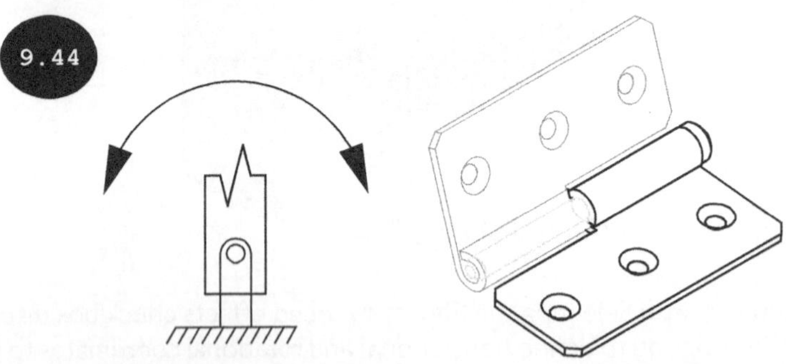

Revolute Joint
(No translational movement, only one rotational movement is allowed)

1. Click on the **Create Revolute Joint** tool in the **Assembly Joints** toolbar (see Figure 9.45) or press the **R** key. The **Create Joint** sub-window appears in the **Tasks Panel**, see Figure 9.46. By default, the **Revolute** option is selected in the **Joint type** drop-down list, allowing you to apply the Revolute joint between two components.

9.45

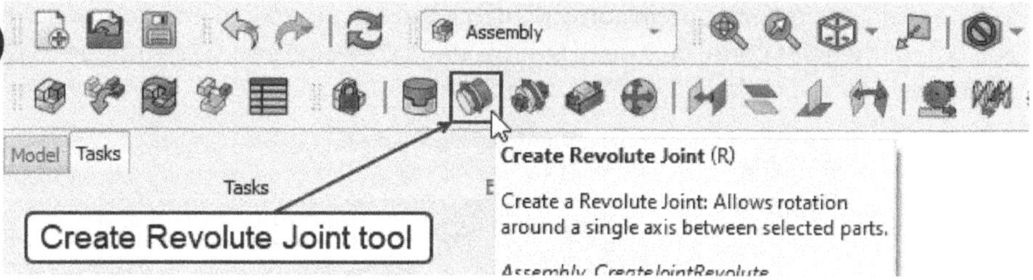

9.46

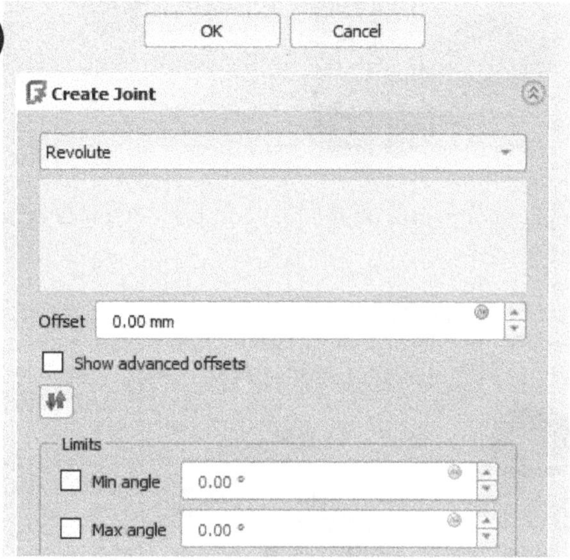

Now, you need to define the joint connector on two different components to apply the selected joint type between them.

2. Move the cursor over a face, edge, or vertex of the first component (rotational component) to define the joint connector on it. The respective geometry highlights, and the joint connector snaps to a snap point, see Figure 9.47. In this example, the cursor is positioned over the circular edge of the component, and the Joint connector snaps to its center.

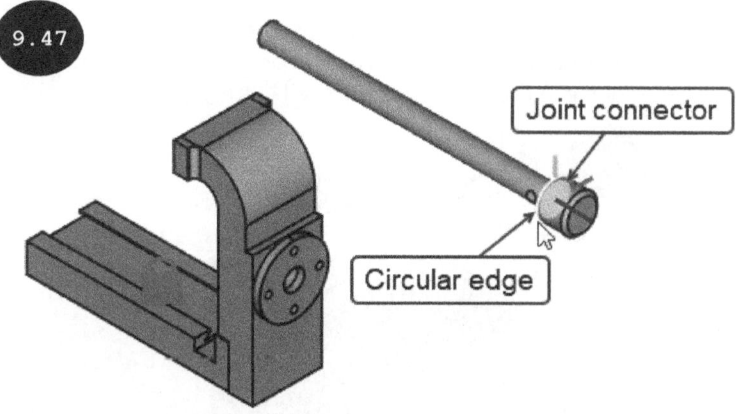

3. Click on the desired snap point on the highlighted geometry of the component to specify the position of the joint connector, see Figure 9.48. In this example, the joint connector is defined at the center of the circular edge of the component.

9.48

After defining the joint connector on the first component, proceed to define the joint connector on the second component.

4. Move the cursor over a face, edge, or vertex of the second component. The respective geometry highlights, and the joint connector snaps to it, see Figure 9.49. In this example, the joint connector is snapped to the center of the circular edge of the component.

9.49

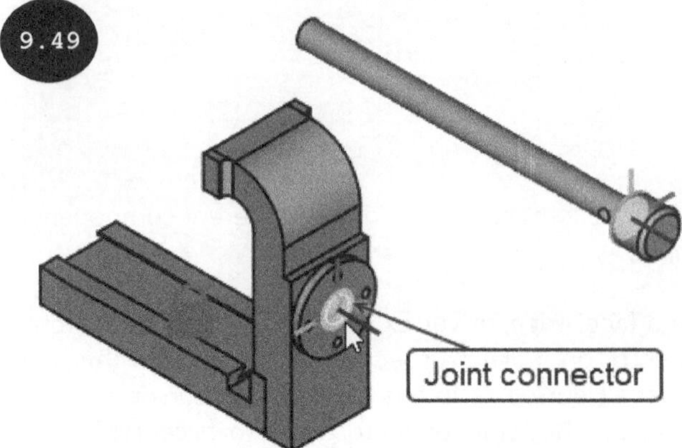

5. Click to define the position of the joint connector on the highlighted geometry of the second component. The first component moves toward the second component, and the joint connectors of both components coincide in the graphics area, see Figure 9.50.

9.50

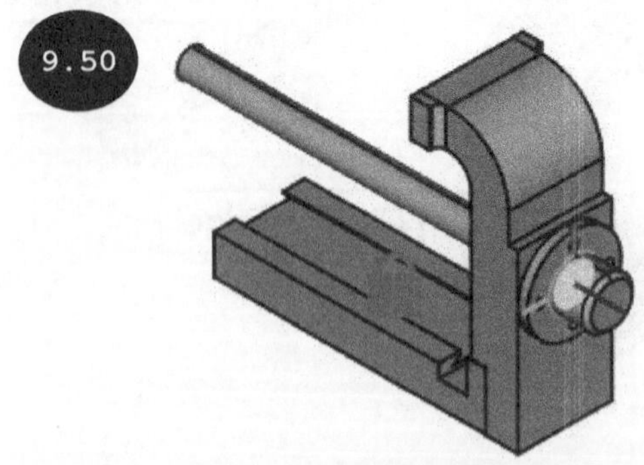

After defining the joint connectors on the components, you can specify additional parameters such as offset and angle limits in the **Create Joint** sub-window.

Offset: The **Offset** field in the **Create Joint** sub-window allows you to specify the offset distance between the components along the rotational axis, see Figure 9.51. To reverse the direction of the offset, you can enter a negative distance value in this field.

Limits: By default, in the Revolute joint, the rotational component can freely rotate 360 degrees about its axis without any restrictions. However, if needed, you can set minimum and maximum rotational limits to constrain the component's rotation within a specified range.

To set the rotational limits for the component, select the **Min angle** and **Max angle** check boxes in the **Create Joint** sub-window. This enables the **Minimum angle** and **Maximum angle** fields. In these fields, you can define the minimum and maximum rotational angles, respectively, refer to Figure 9.52. For instance, setting the minimum angle to **0** degrees and the maximum angle to **90** degrees will allow the component to rotate only within the **0** to **90** degrees range, refer to Figure 9.53. In this figure, the view orientation of the model is changed for better understanding.

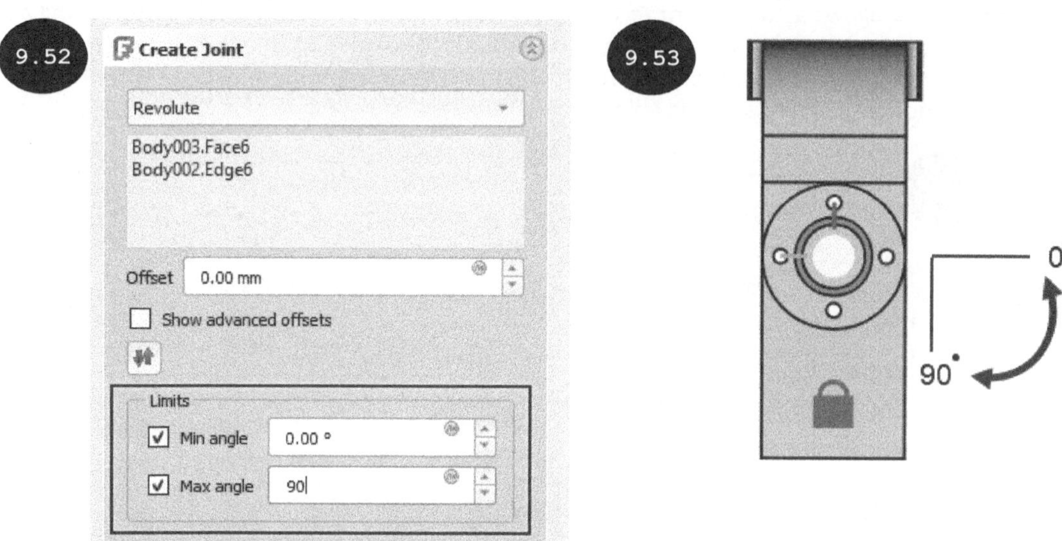

The remaining options, such as the **Show advanced offsets check box** and the **Reverse the direction of joint** button in the **Create Joint** sub-window, are the same as discussed earlier.

6. If needed, define the minimum and maximum limits for the rotational degree of freedom of the component by selecting the **Min angle** and **Max angle** check boxes, as discussed above.

Note: By default, the component can freely rotate about its rotational degree of freedom without any restrictions, as the minimum and maximum rotational limits are not set.

7. After defining the joint connectors on the two components and other parameters, click on the **OK** button in the **Tasks Panel**. The Revolute joint is applied between the components, removing all degrees of freedom except for one rotational degree of freedom, see Figure 9.54.

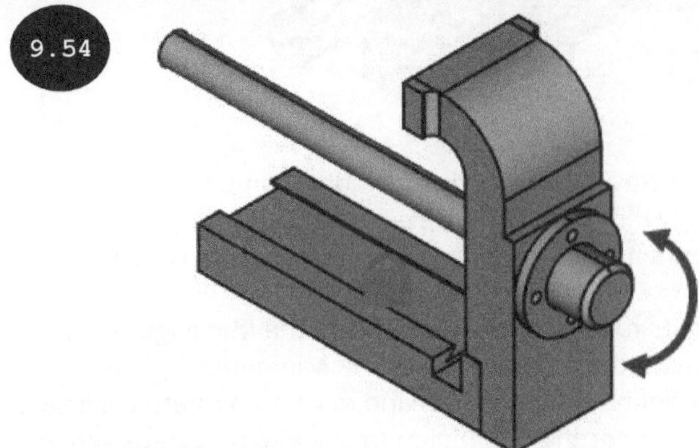

Applying the Cylindrical Joint

The Cylindrical joint allows a component to translate and rotate about a single axis by removing all degrees of freedom except one translational and one rotational degree of freedom, as illustrated in Figure 9.55. It is primarily used for forming a screw mechanism between components. The method for applying the Cylindrical joint is discussed below:

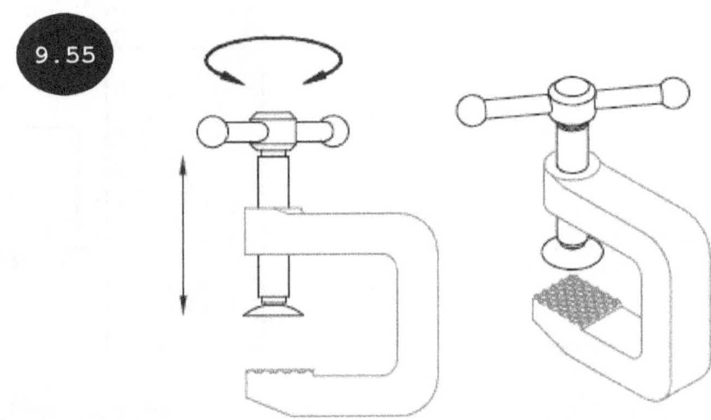

Cylindrical Joint
(One translational and one rotational movement are allowed along the same Z-axis)

1. Click on the **Create Cylindrical Joint** tool in the **Assembly Joints** toolbar (see Figure 9.56) or press the C key. The **Create Joint** sub-window appears in the **Tasks Panel** with the **Cylindrical** option selected in the **Joint type** drop-down list, by default, see Figure 9.57.

9.56

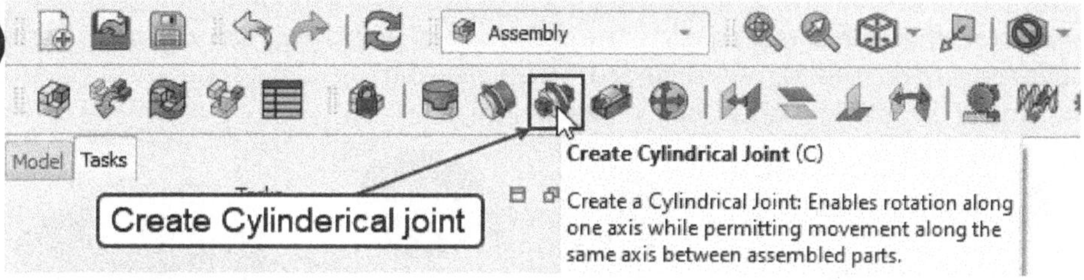

9.57

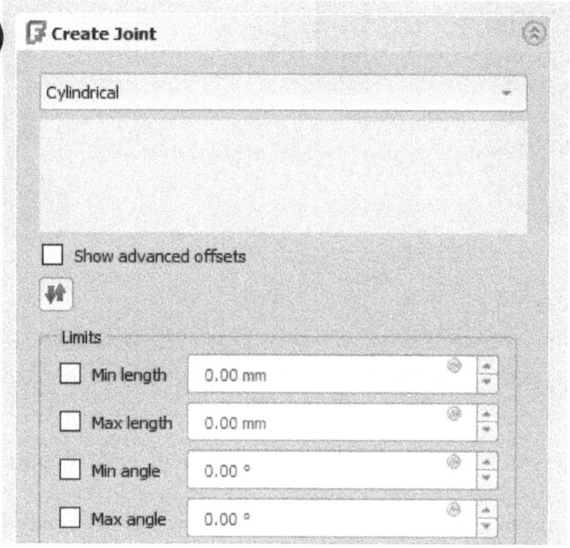

Now, you need to define the joint connector on two components to apply the selected joint type.

2. Move the cursor over a face, edge, or vertex of the first component and click to define the position of the joint connector when it snaps to correct snap point, see Figure 9.58. In this example, the joint connector is snapped to the center of the circular edge.

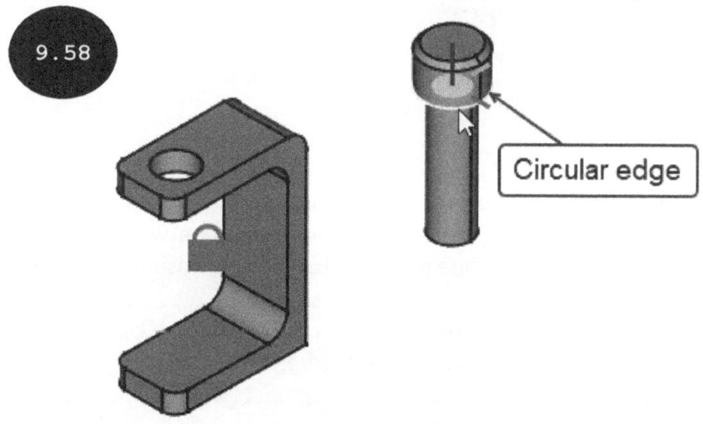

After defining the joint connector on the first component, proceed to define the joint connector on the second component.

3. Move the cursor over a face, edge, or vertex of the second component and click to define the joint connector when the cursor snaps to the desired snap point, see Figure 9.59. The first component moves toward the second component or vice-versa and the joint connectors of both components coincide in the graphics area, see Figure 9.60.

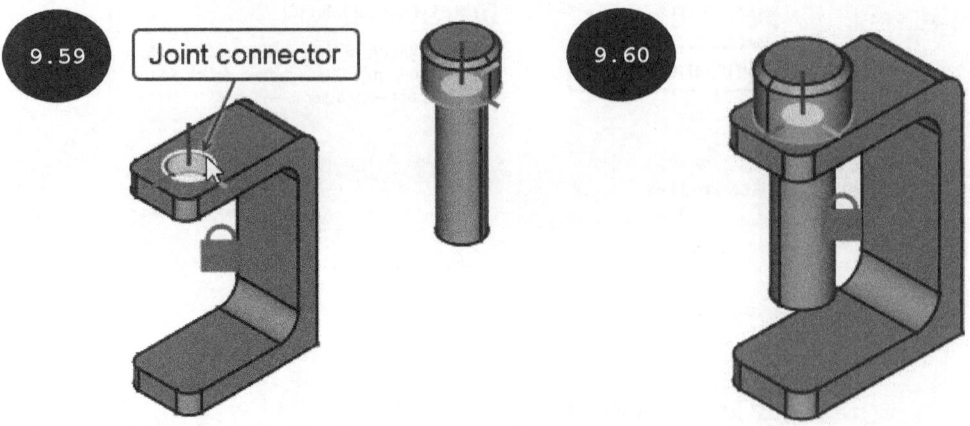

Note: By default, the component can freely rotate and translate along a single axis without any restrictions, as the minimum and maximum rotational and translational limits are not set.

4. If needed, set minimum and maximum translational and rotational limits by selecting their respective check boxes in the **Limits** area of the **Create Joint** sub-window, see Figure 9.61. This ensures that the component translates and rotates within the specified limits. In Figure 9.61, the translational limits are defined from 0 mm to 50 mm, while the rotational limits are left undefined, allowing the component to rotate freely through 360 degrees as it moves within the specified translational range.

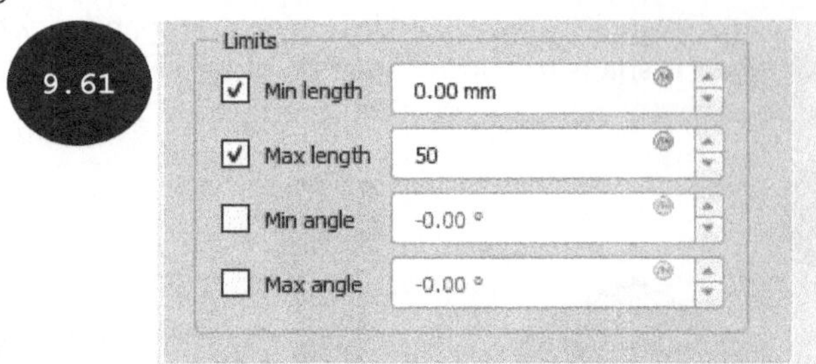

5. After defining the joint connectors on the two components and other parameters, click on the **OK** button in the **Tasks Panel**. The Cylindrical joint is applied between the components, removing all degrees of freedom except for one rotational and one translational degrees of freedom.

Note: After applying the joints, you can review the relative motion between the components by dragging them along or around their free degrees of freedom.

Applying the Slider Joint

The Slider joint allows a component to translate or slide along an axis by restricting all degrees of freedom except for one translational degree of freedom, as illustrated in Figure 9.62. The method for applying the Slider joint is discussed below:

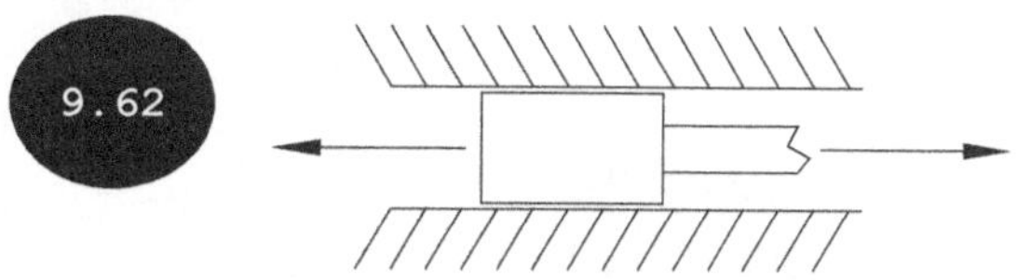

Slider Joint
(Moves freely along a single axis)

1. Click on the **Create Slider Joint** tool in the **Assembly Joints** toolbar (see Figure 9.63) or press the S key. The **Create Joint** sub-window appears in the **Tasks Panel** with the **Slider** option selected in the **Joint type** drop-down list, by default, see Figure 9.64.

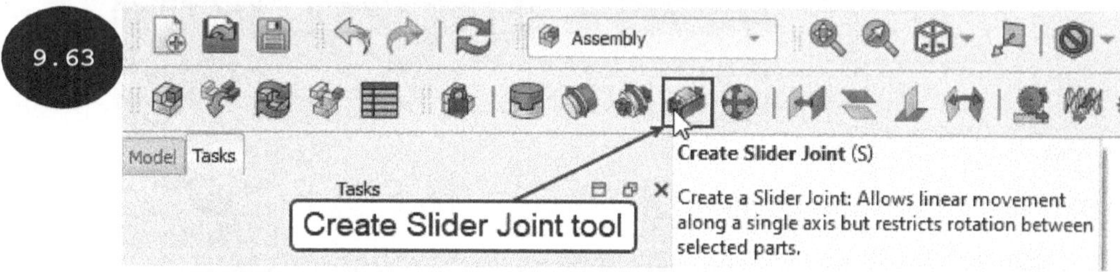

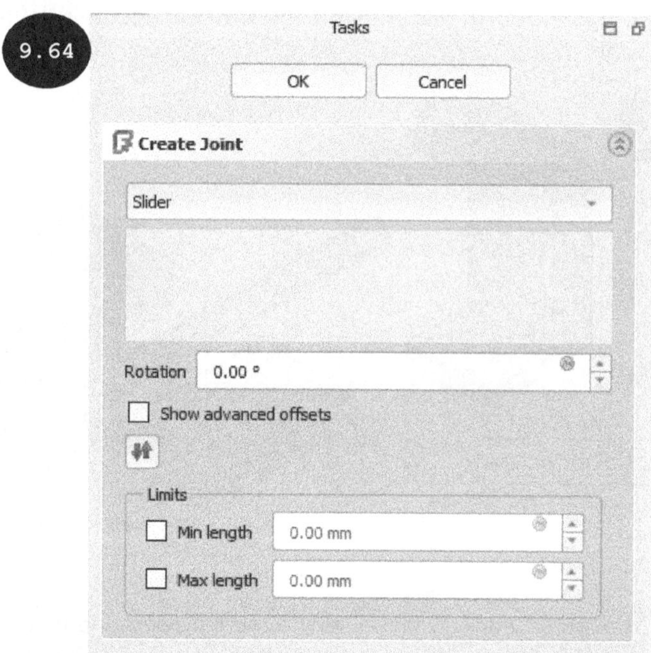

Now, you need to define the joint connector on two components to apply the selected joint type.

2. Move the cursor over a face, edge, or vertex of the first component to define the joint connector. The respective geometry highlights, and the joint connector snaps to its snap point, see Figure 9.65. In this example, the cursor is positioned over a linear edge of a component and the joint connector snaps to the center of the highlighted edge.

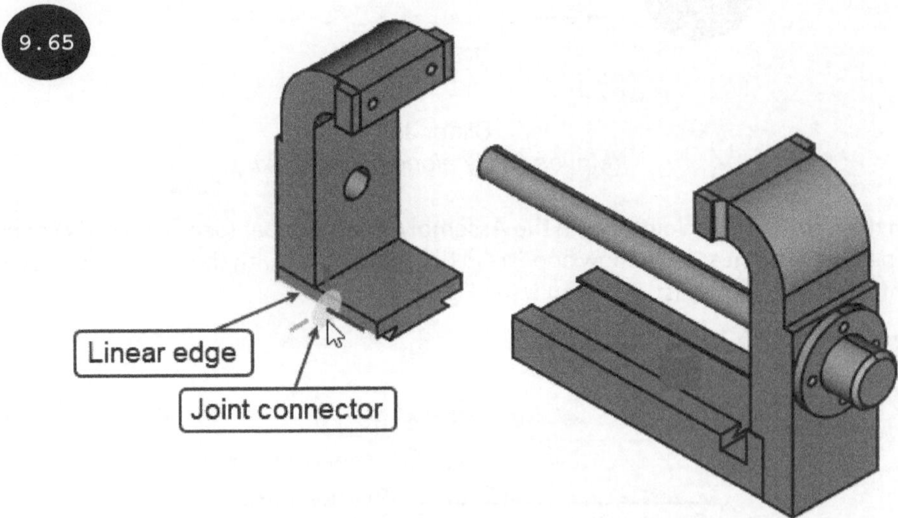

3. Click on the desired snap point on the highlighted geometry of the component to position of the joint connector, see Figure 9.66. In this example, the joint connector is defined on the center of the bottom linear edge.

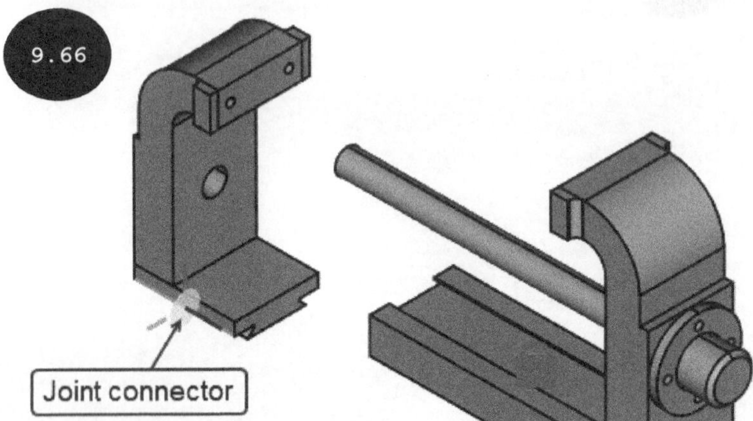

After defining the joint connector on the first component, proceed to define the joint connector on the second component.

4. Move the cursor over a face, edge, or vertex of the second component and then click to define the position of the joint connector on it, see Figure 9.67. The first component moves toward the second component, and the joint connectors of both components coincide in the graphics area, see Figure 9.68.

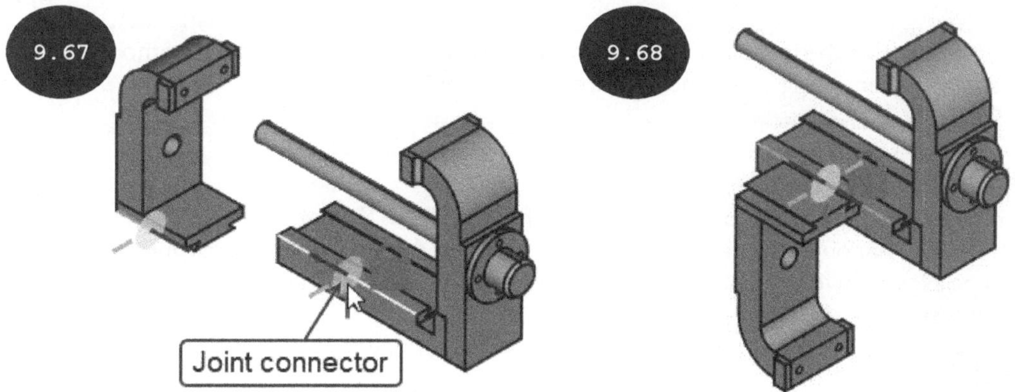

5. After defining the joint connectors on the components, you can specify additional parameters such as the rotational angle between them in the **Rotation** field, see Figure 9.69. In this figure, the 180-degree is defined as the rotational angle.

6. If needed, you can also reverse the alignment using the **Reverse the direction of joint** button.

7. If needed, set minimum and maximum translational limits by selecting the **Min length** and **Max length** check boxes in the **Create Joint** sub-window of the **Tasks Panel**. This ensures that the sliding component translates within the specified limits.

Note: Setting the minimum translation distance to **-60** and the maximum to **120** constrains the component's movement within this range, see Figure 9.70. Note that these distances are measured from the original position of the joint connectors.

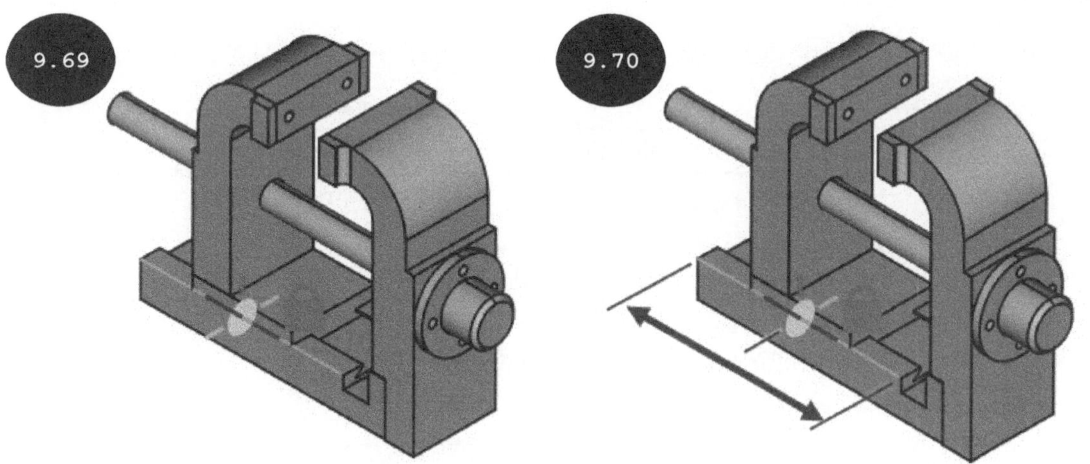

8. After defining the joint connectors on the two components and other parameters, click on the **OK** button in the **Tasks Panel**. The Slider joint is applied between the components, removing all degrees of freedom except for one translational degree of freedom.

Note: After applying the joints, you can review the relative motion between the components by dragging them along or around their free degrees of freedom.

Applying the Ball Joint

The Ball joint allows a component to rotate about all three X, Y, and Z rotational axes, see Figure 9.71. In this mate, all translational degrees of freedom are restricted, allowing the component to rotate about the three axes relative to a point defined by the joint connectors. The method for applying the Ball joint is discussed below:

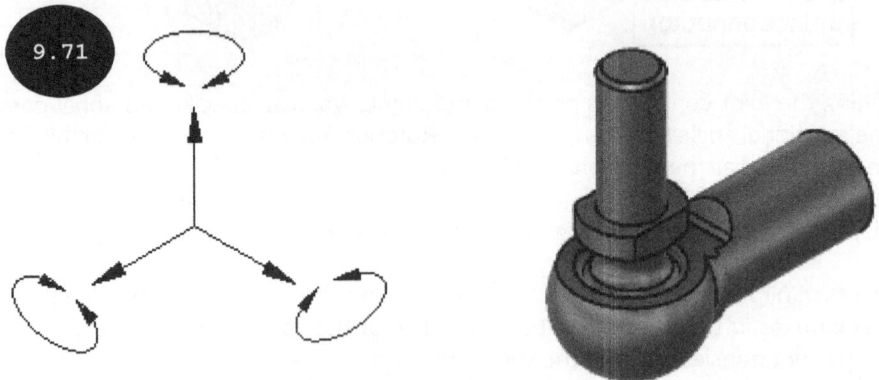

1. Click on the **Create Ball Joint** tool in the **Assembly Joints** toolbar (see Figure 9.72) or press the **B** key. The **Create Joint** sub-window appears in the **Tasks Panel** with the **Ball** option selected in the **Joint type** drop-down list, by default, see Figure 9.73.

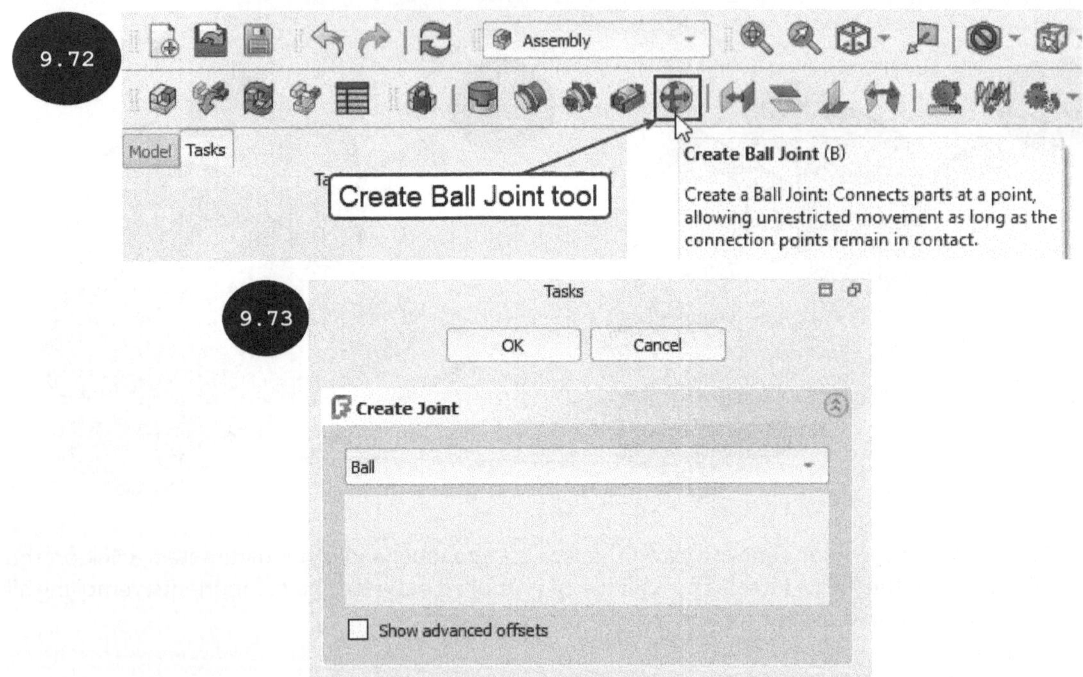

Now, you need to define the joint connector on two different components to apply the selected joint type.

2. Move the cursor over a face, edge, or vertex of the first component and click to define the position of the joint connector when it snaps to the desired point, see Figure 9.74. In this example, the joint connector is snapped to the center of a spherical face of the component.

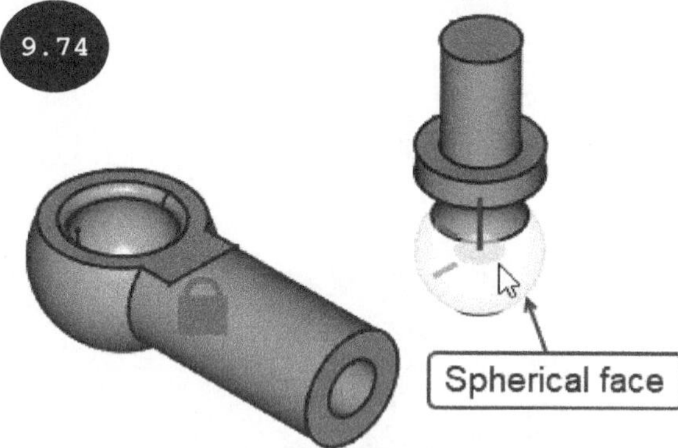

After defining the joint connector on the first component, proceed to define the joint connector on the second component.

3. Move the cursor over a face, edge, or vertex of the second component (see Figure 9.75) and click to define the joint connector when the cursor snaps to the desired snap point. The first component moves toward the second component or vice-versa and the joint connectors of both components coincide in the graphics area, see Figure 9.76.

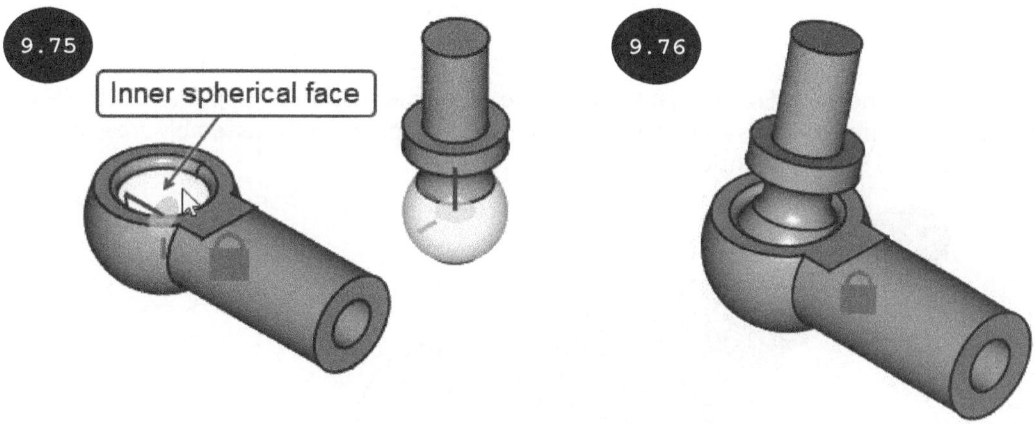

4. After defining the joint connectors on the two components, click on the **OK** button in the **Tasks Panel**. The Ball joint is applied between the components, removing all degrees of freedom except for three rotational degrees of freedom.

Note: After applying the joints, you can move or rotate a component to define its position, as required. To do this, double-click on the component to be moved or rotate in the 3D View area. The translational and rotational handles appear, see Figure 9.77. By using these handles, you can define the position of the component and then click anywhere to exit the tool. After defining the position of the component, press the F5 key to reset the model based on the applied joint type.

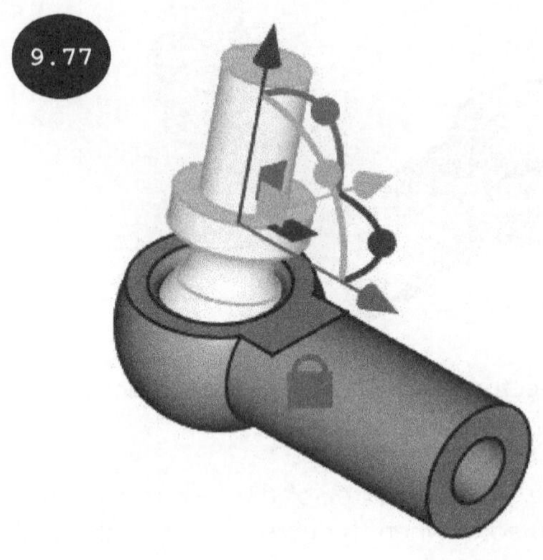
9.77

Tutorial 1

Create an assembly shown in Figure 9.78 by using the Top-down assembly approach in the **Part Design** workbench. Different views and dimensions of each component of the assembly are shown in Figures 9.79 through 9.82. All dimensions are in mm.

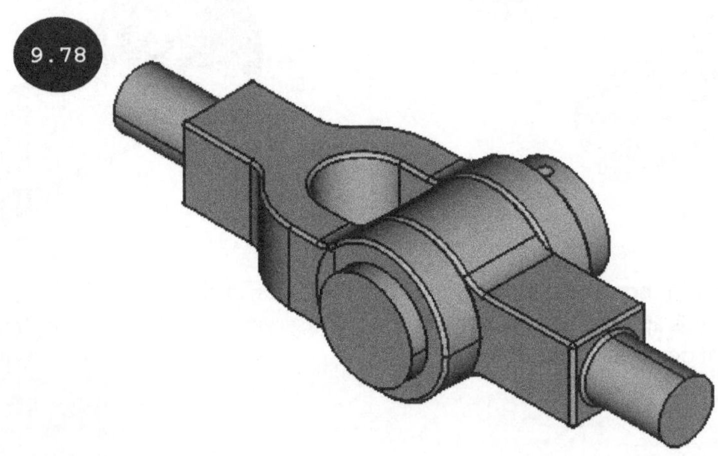
9.78

9.79

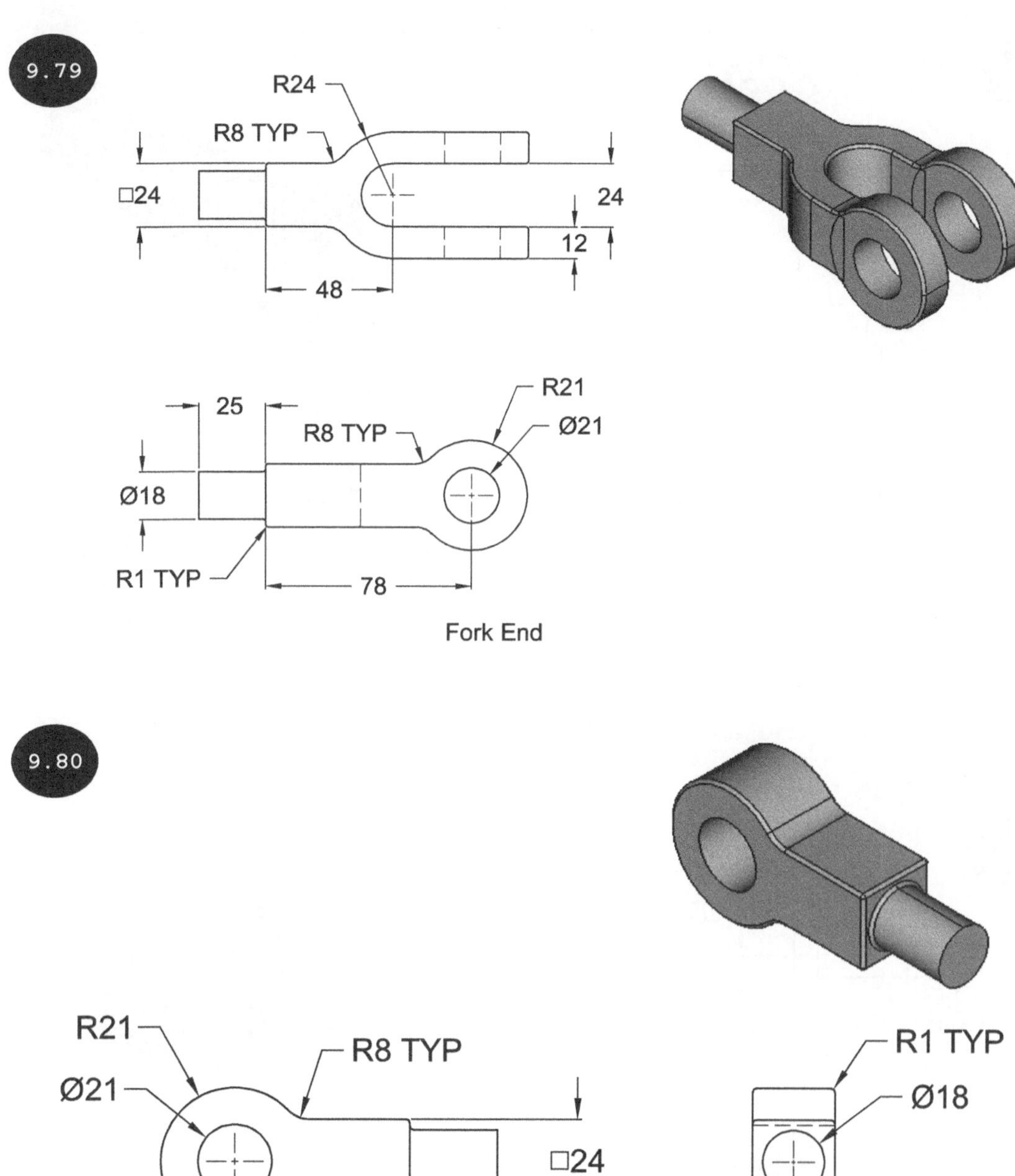

Fork End

9.80

Eye End

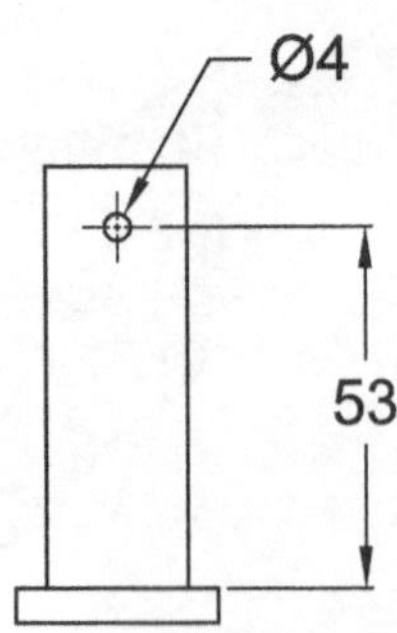

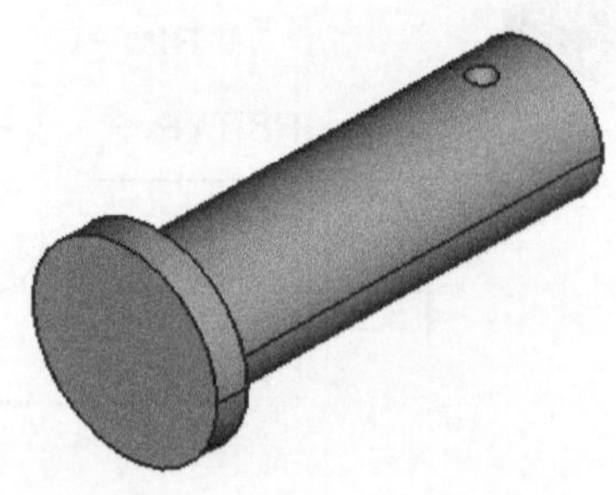

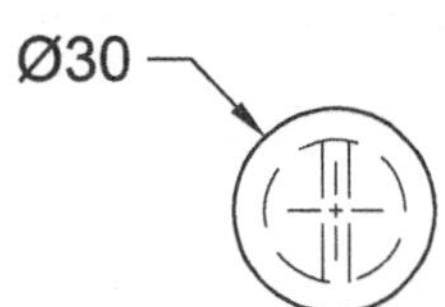

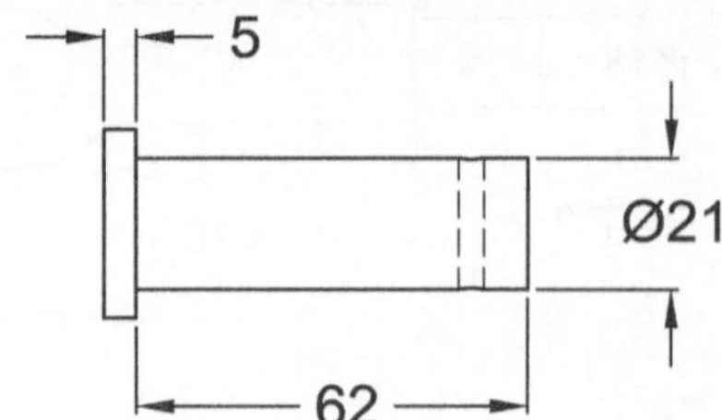

Pin

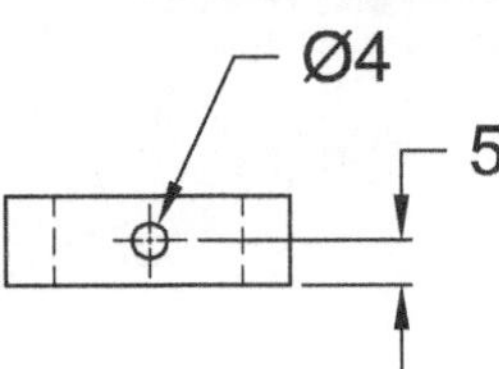

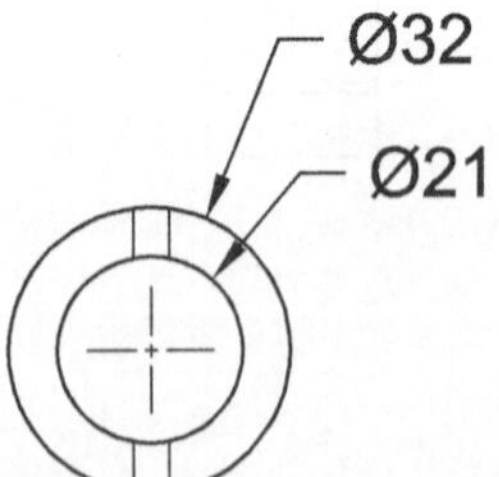

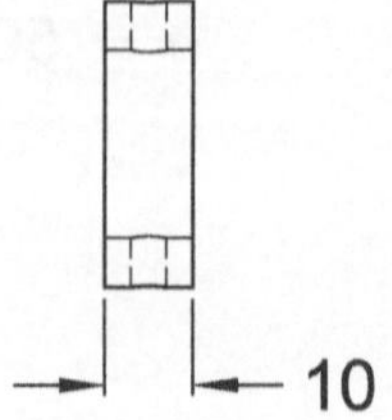

Collar

Section 1: Starting a New Part Document and Specifying the Units

1. Start FreeCAD by double-clicking on the **FreeCAD 1.0** icon on your desktop. The startup user interface of FreeCAD appears.

2. Click on the **New** tool in the **File** toolbar (see Figure 9.83) or press the **CTRL + N** keys. A new part document gets invoked with the default name "**unnamed: 1**".

3. Invoke the **Unit** flyout that appears at the lower right corner of the **Status Bar**, see Figure 9.84.

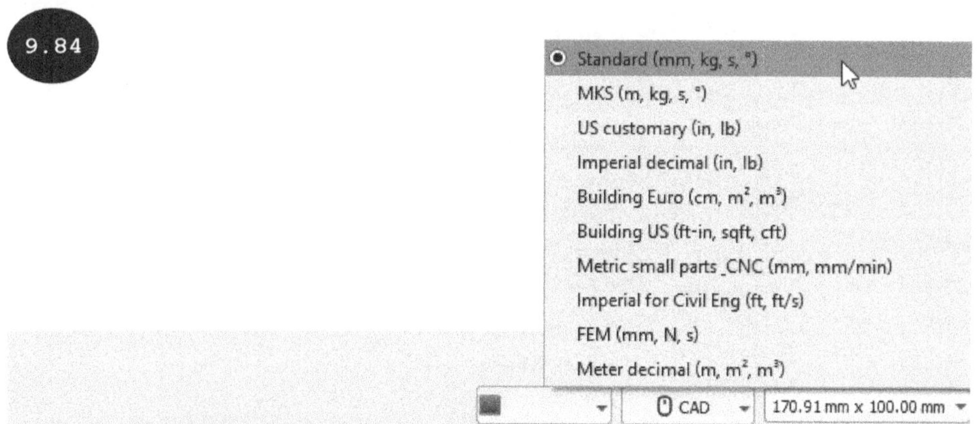

4. Ensure that the **Standard (mm, kg, s,*)** is selected as the unit system for the current design document in the **Unit** flyout, refer to Figure 9.84.

Section 2: Creating the First Component of the Assembly

Now, you can create the first component (Fork End) of the assembly as a body within the **Part Design** workbench.

1. Click on the **Create body** tool in the **Part Design Helper** toolbar, see Figure 9.85. A new empty body with the default name "**Body**" gets created and appears in the **Tree View** of the **Model** tab, see Figure 9.86. Also, it becomes the active body of the current document.

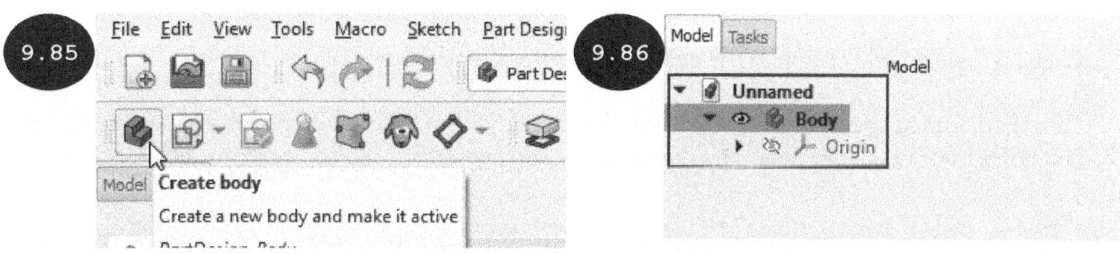

Now, you need to rename the newly added body.

2. Click on the **Model** tab of the **Combo View** to display the **Tree View** and then right-click on the newly created body to display a shortcut menu, see Figure 9.87.

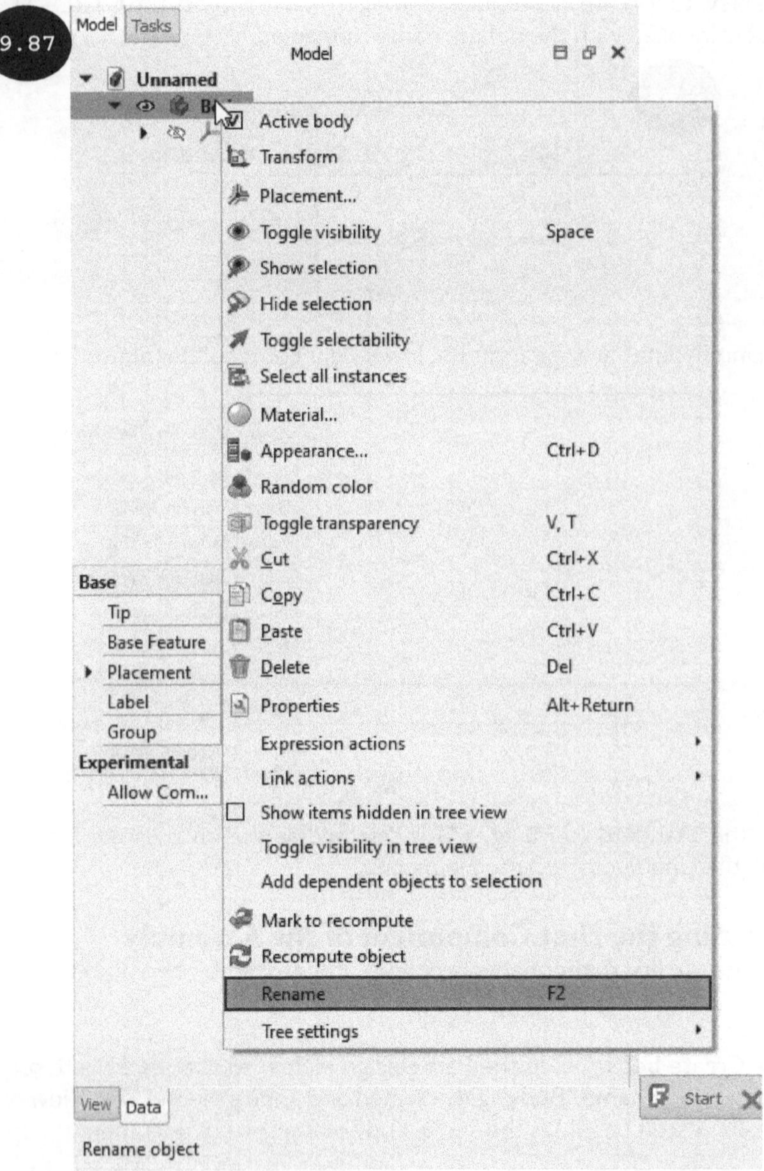

3. Click on the **Rename** option in the shortcut menu, refer to Figure 9.87.

4. Enter **Fork End** as the name of the body in the edit field that appears in the **Tree View**. Next, click anywhere in the 3D View area. The name of the body gets changed to Fork End, as specified.

Now, you can create features of the Fork End component of the assembly.

5. Click on the **Create sketch** tool in the **Part Design Helper** toolbar (see Figure 9.88) and then select the **XY_Plane** as the sketching plane. The **Sketcher** workbench gets invoked.

6. Create the sketch of the base feature by using the sketching tool, refer to Figure 9.89.

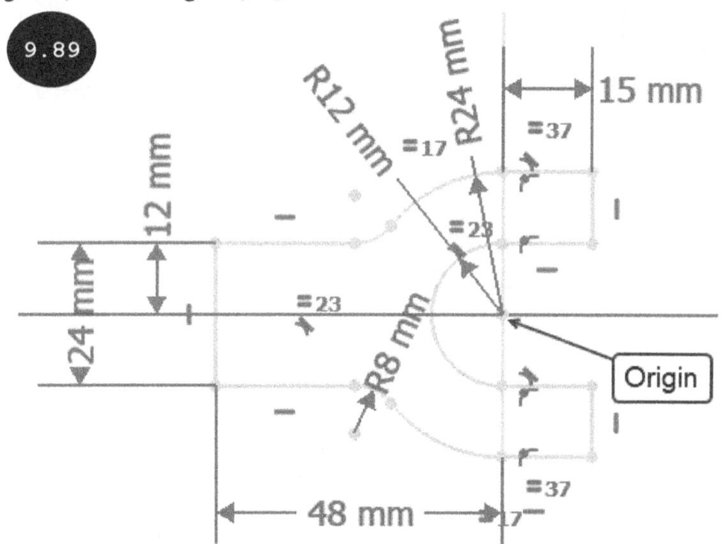

7. After creating the sketch, exit the **Sketcher** workbench and then extrude the sketch to a length of 24 mm, symmetrically on both sides of the sketching plane by using the **Pad** tool, see Figure 9.90.

Now, you need to create the second feature of the Fork End component.

8. Select the front planar face of the base feature (see Figure 9.91) and then click on the **Create sketch** tool in the **Part Design Helper** toolbar, see Figure 9.92. The **Sketcher** workbench gets invoked and the selected planar face gets oriented normal to the viewing direction.

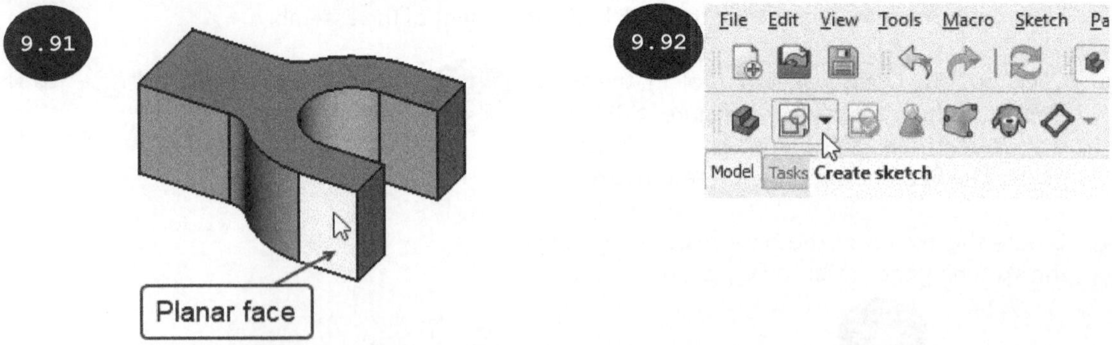

9. Create the sketch (two concentric circles) of the second feature, see Figure 9.93.

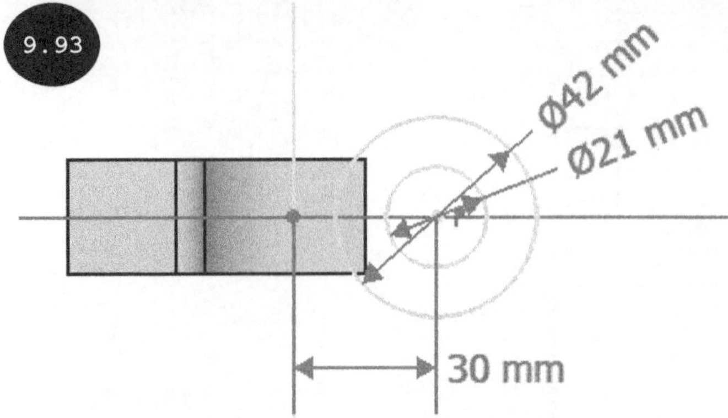

10. Exit the **Sketcher** workbench and then extrude the sketch to a length of 12 mm toward the back side of the sketching plane by using the **Pad** tool. Figure 9.94 shows the model after creating the second feature.

    Now, you need to create the third feature, which is a mirror feature.

11. Mirror the previously created feature by selecting the **XZ-Plane** as the mirroring plane using the **Mirrored** tool, see Figure 9.95.

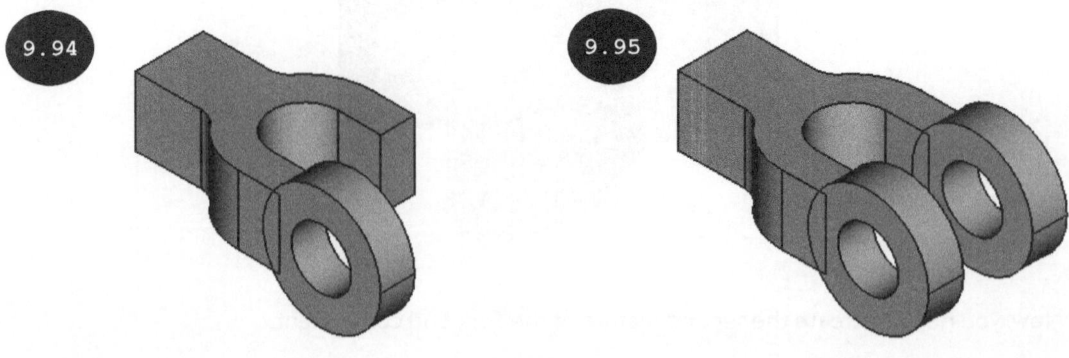

Now, you need to create the fourth feature.

12. Invoke the **Sketcher** workbench by selecting the back planar face of the model as the sketching plane using the **Create sketch** tool, see Figure 9.96. Note that you need to rotate the model to select the back planar face of the model.

13. Create a circle of diameter 18 mm as the sketch of the fourth feature (see Figure 9.97). After creating the sketch, exit the **Sketcher** workbench.

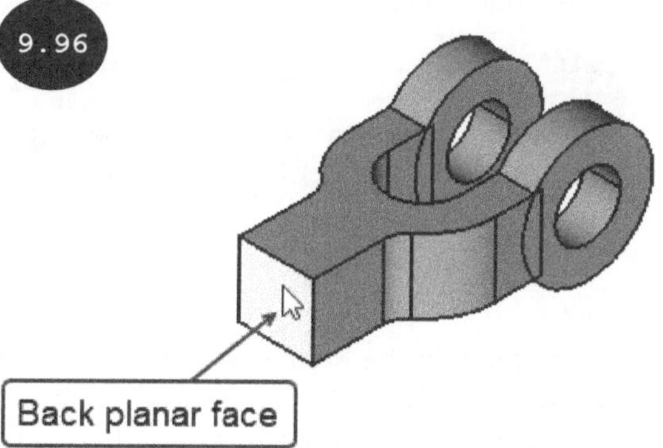

14. Create a pad feature by extruding the sketch to a depth of 25 mm using the **Pad** tool, see Figure 9.98. Next, change the view orientation of the model to isometric.

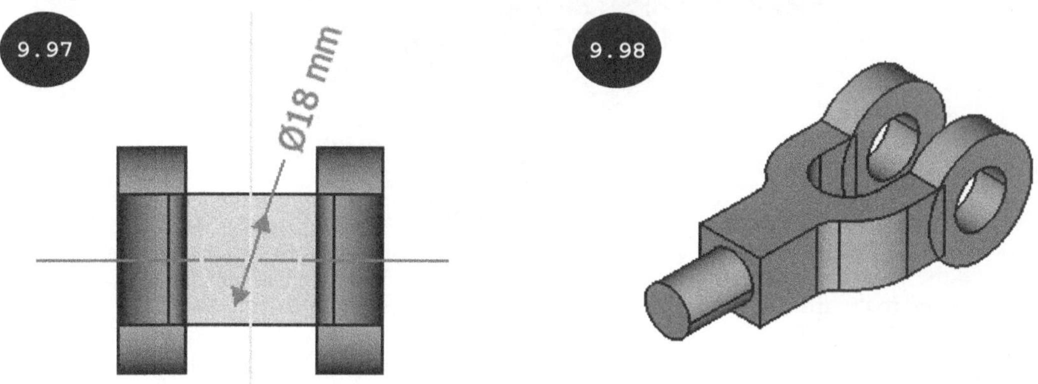

Now, you need to create fillets.

15. Select four edges of the model by pressing the CTRL key, see Figures 9.99 and 9.100. Note that you need to rotate the model to select these edges of the model.

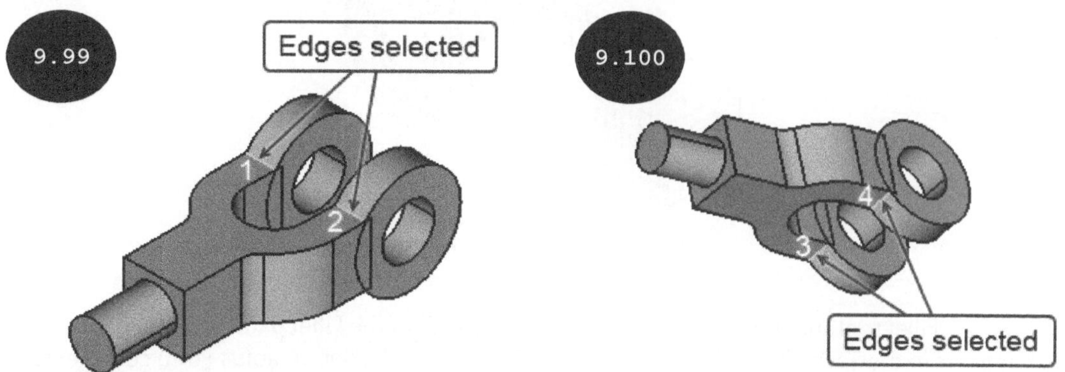

16. After selecting the edges, click on the **Fillet** tool, see Figure 9.101. The **Fillet parameters** sub-window appears in the **Tasks Panel**.

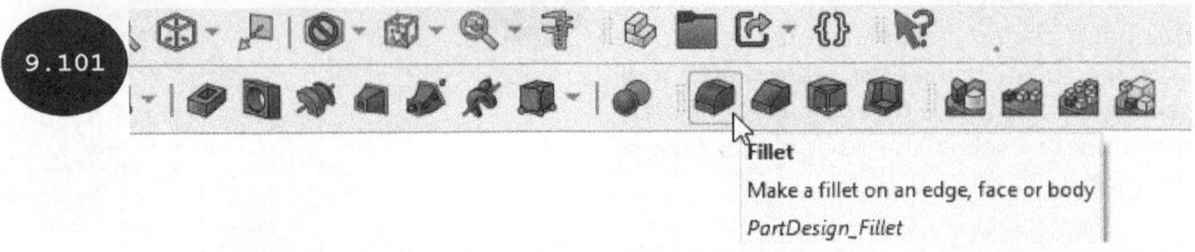

17. Enter **8** mm in the **Radius** field of the **Fillet parameters** sub-window and then click on the **OK** button in the **Tasks Panel**. A fillet of radius 8 mm gets created on the selected edges of the model, see Figure 9.102. Change the orientation of the model to isometric.

Now, you need to create fillets of radius 1 mm on the other edges of the model.

18. Rotate the model and then select the top and back planar faces of the model by pressing the CTRL key, see Figure 9.103.

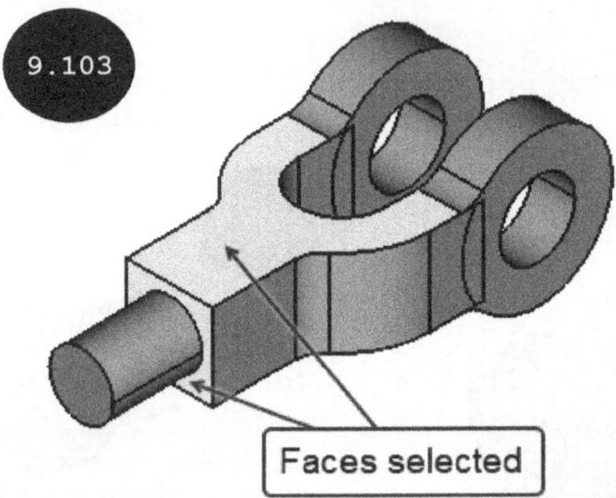

19. Click on the **Fillet** tool and then enter **1** mm in the **Radius** field of the **Fillet parameters** sub-window that appears in the **Tasks Panel**. Next, click on the **OK** button. A fillet of radius 1 mm gets created on all the edges of the selected faces of the model, see Figure 9.104.

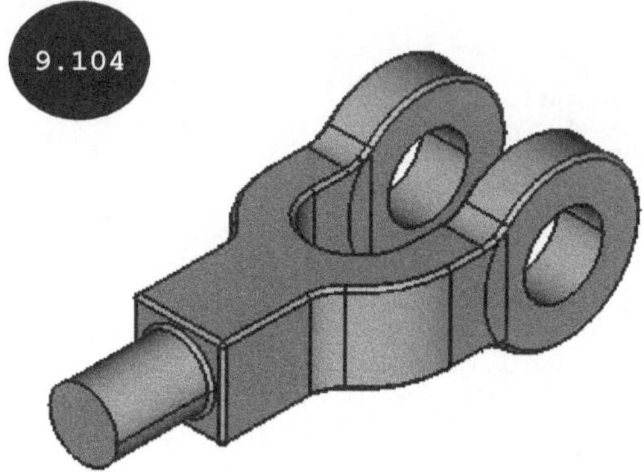
9.104

20. Change the orientation of the model to isometric, see Figure 9.105.

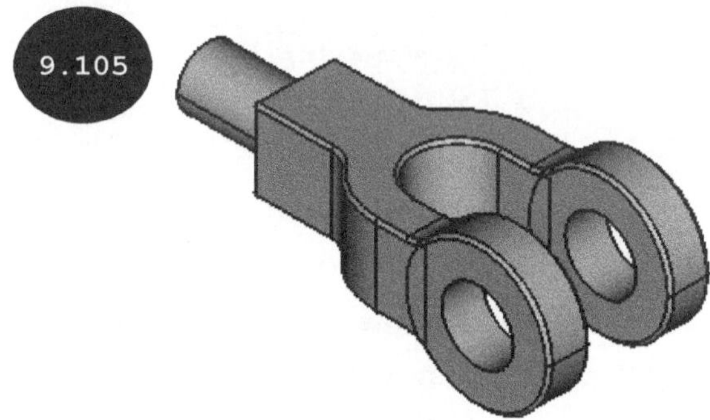
9.105

Section 3: Creating the Second Component

Now, you can create the second component (Eye End) of the assembly.

1. Click on the **Create body** tool in the **Part Design Helper** toolbar, see Figure 9.106. A new empty body with the default name "**Body**" gets created and appears below the first component (Fork End) in the **Tree View** of the **Model** tab, see Figure 9.107. Also, it becomes the active body of the current document.

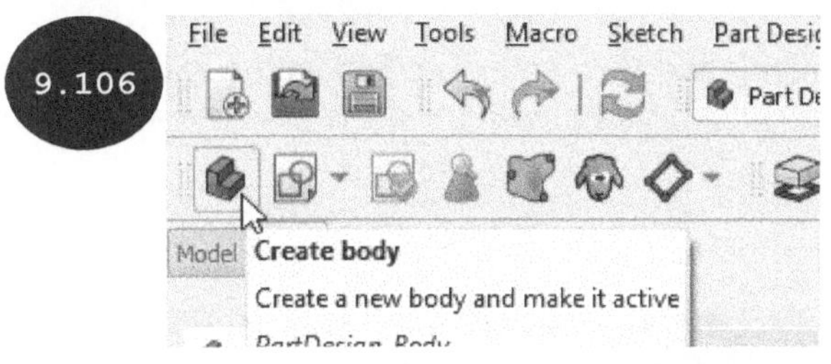

9.106

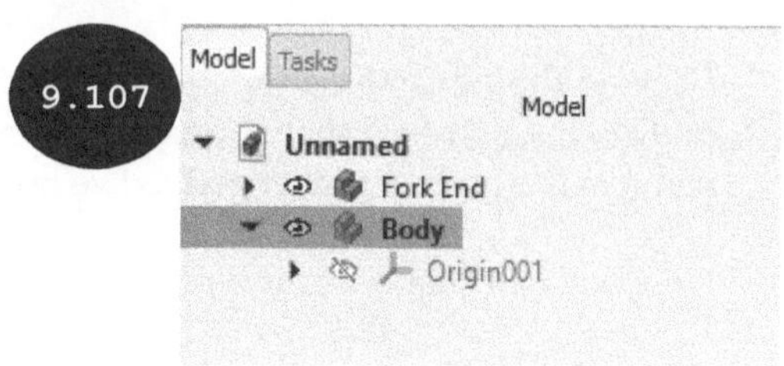

9.107

Now, you need to rename the newly added body.

2. Click on the **Model** tab of the **Combo View** to display the **Tree View** and then right-click on the newly created body "**Body**" to display a shortcut menu, see Figure 9.108.

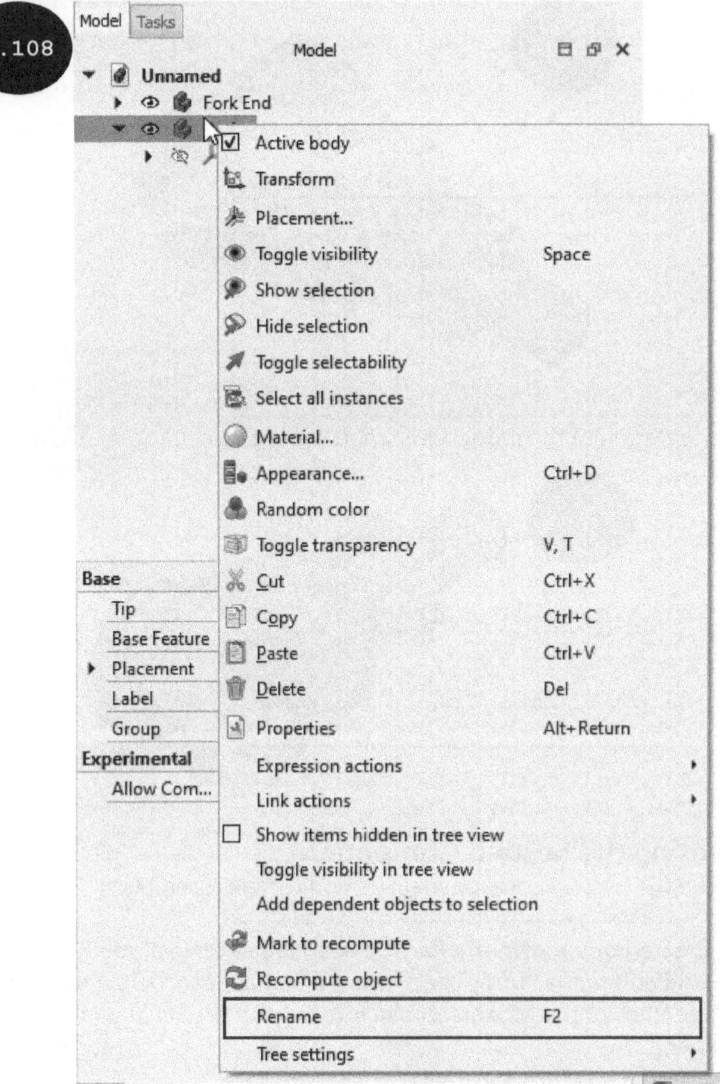

3. Click on the **Rename** option in the shortcut menu and then enter **Eye End** as the name of the body in the edit field that appears in **Tree View**. Next, click anywhere in the 3D View area. The name of the body gets changed to Eye End.

   Now, you can create features of the **Eye End** component of the assembly.

4. Click on the **Create sketch** tool in the **Part Design Helper** toolbar (see Figure 9.109) and then select the **XZ_Plane** as the sketching plane in the 3D View area. The **Sketcher** workbench gets invoked.

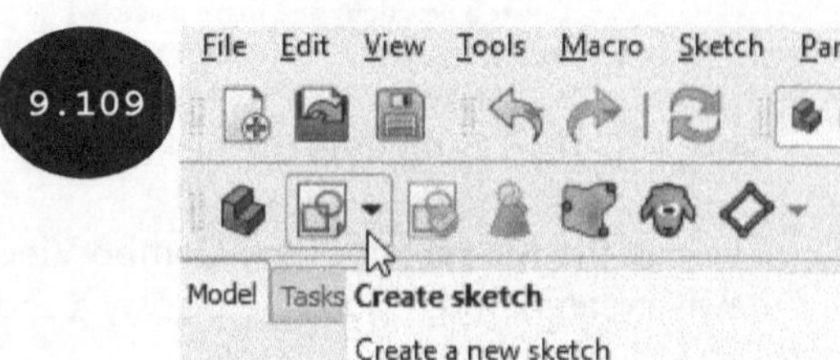

5. Click on the **View section** tool in the **Part Design Helper** toolbar to temporarily hide the material that is in front of the sketching plane, see Figure 9.110.

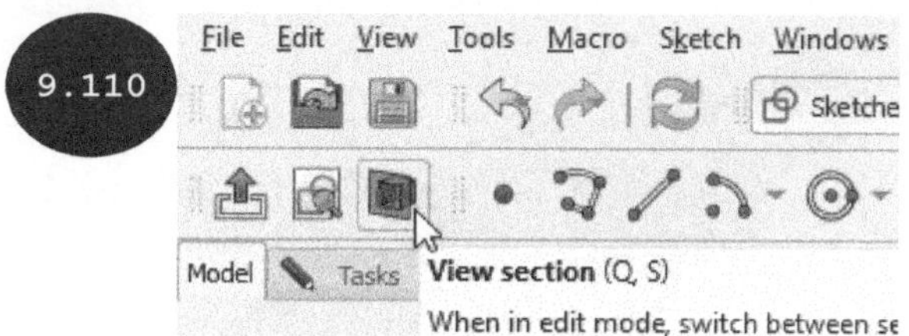

6. Create the sketch of the base feature of the component, refer to Figure 9.111.

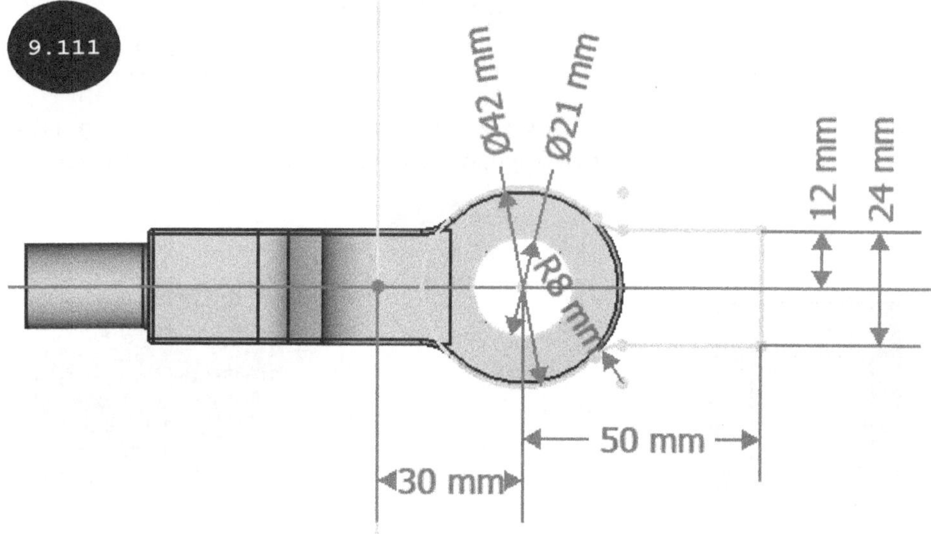

7. After creating the sketch, exit the **Sketcher** workbench and then extrude the sketch to a length of 24 mm, symmetrically on both sides of the sketching plane by using the **Pad** tool, see Figure 9.112.

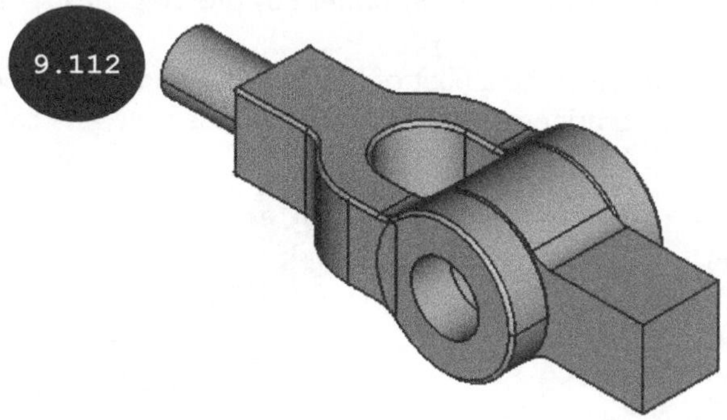

8. Invoke the Sketcher workbench by selecting the right planar face of the previously created base feature, see Figure 9.113.

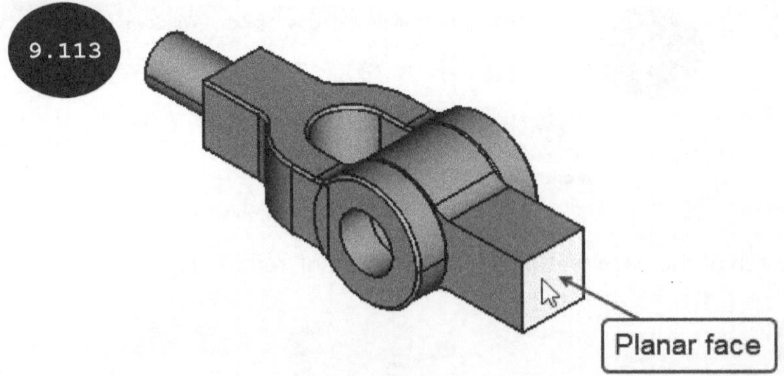

9. Create a circle of diameter 18 mm as the sketch of the second feature, (see Figure 9.114) and then create a pad feature by extruding it to a length of 25 mm using the **Pad** tool, see Figure 9.115.

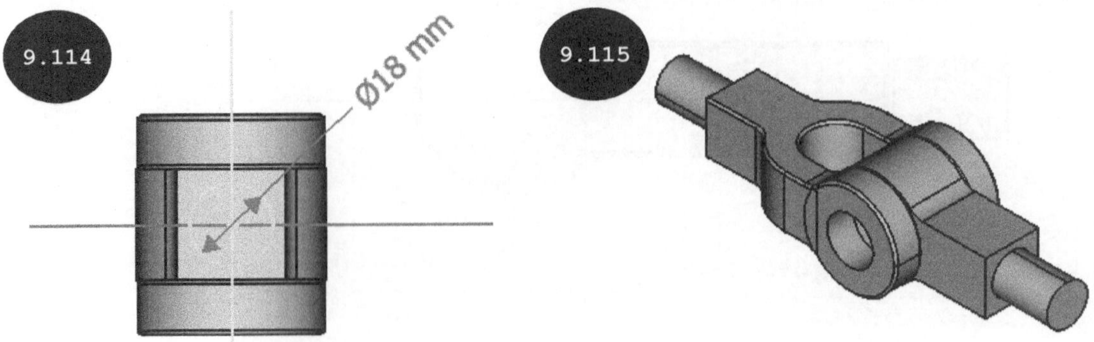

Now, you need to create the fillet on the edges of the Eye End component.

10. Select the top and right planar faces of the component by pressing the CTRL key, see Figure 9.116.

11. Click on the **Fillet** tool and then create a fillet of radius **1** mm on the edges of the selected faces, see Figure 9.117. The second component (Eye End) of the assembly gets created.

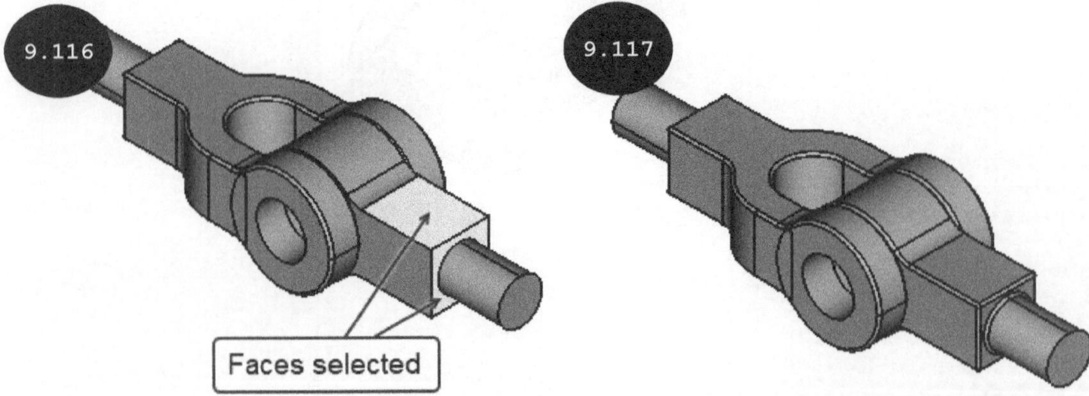

Section 4: Creating the Third Component

Now, you can create the third component (Pin) of the assembly.

1. Click on the **Create body** tool in the **Part Design Helper** toolbar, see Figure 9.118. A new empty body with the default name "**Body**" gets created and appears below the second component (Eye End) in the **Tree View** of the **Model** tab, see Figure 9.119. Also, it becomes the active body of the current document.

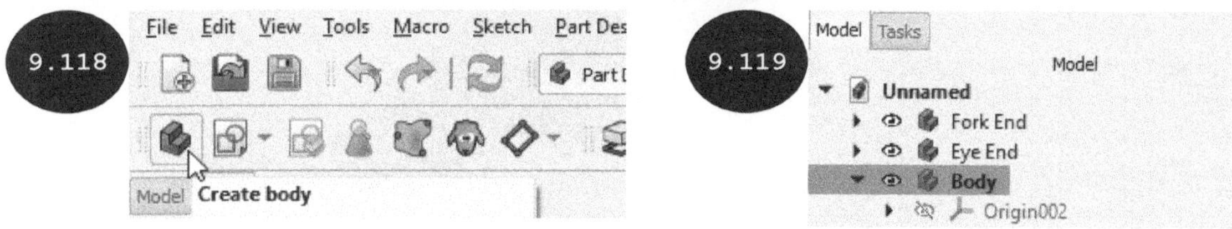

2. Rename the newly added body as **Pin** in the **Tree View**, as discussed earlier.

   Now, you can create features of the Pin component of the assembly.

3. Select the front planar face of the first component (see Figure 9.120) and then click on the **Create sketch** tool in the **Part Design Helper** toolbar, see Figure 9.121. The **Reference** dialog box appears.

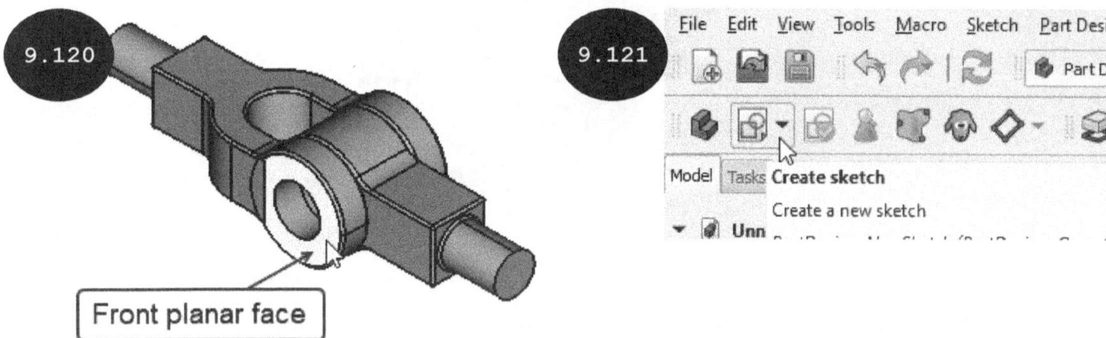

4. Select the **Make dependent copy** radio button in the **Reference** dialog box for creating a new body as the dependent copy of the first component. Next, click on the **OK** button in the dialog box. The **Sketcher** workbench gets invoked. Ignore the error message that may appear in the **Report view** window at the bottom of the screen. You can close the **Report view** window by clicking on the cross mark that appears in its top right corner.

5. Create a circle of diameter 21 mm as the sketch of the base feature of the Pin component, see Figure 9.122.

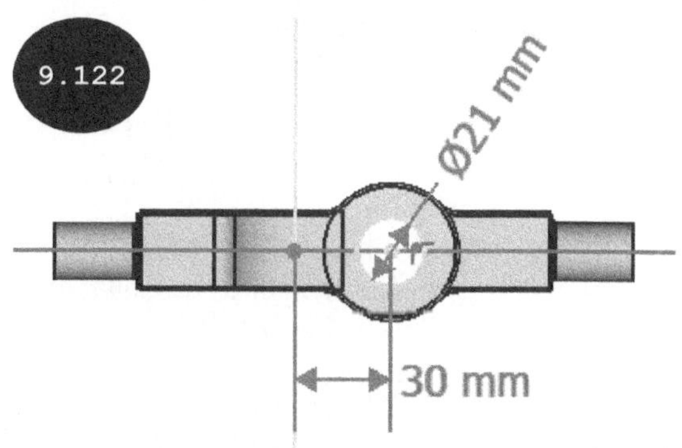

6. After creating the sketch, exit the **Sketcher** workbench and then extrude it to a length of 62 mm toward the back side of the sketching plane by using the **Pad** tool, see Figure 9.123.

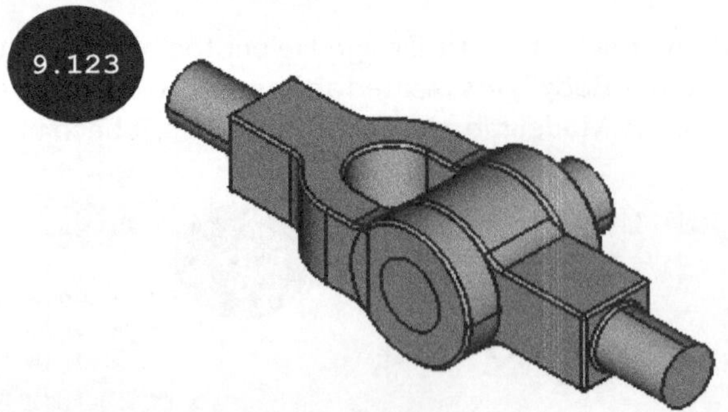

7. Similarly, create the remaining features (one pad and one pocket) of the Pin component one by one. Figure 9.124 shows the model after creating all its features. Refer to Figure 9.81 for dimensions to create these features of the Pin component.

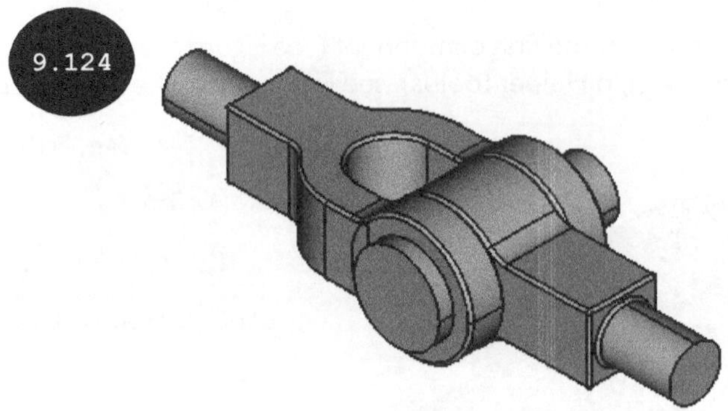

Section 5: Creating the Fourth Component

Now, you can create the fourth component (Collar) of the assembly.

1. Click on the **Create body** tool in the **Part Design Helper** toolbar, see Figure 9.125. A new empty body with the default name "**Body**" gets created and appears below the third component (Pin) in the **Tree View** of the **Model** tab. Also, it becomes the active body of the current document.

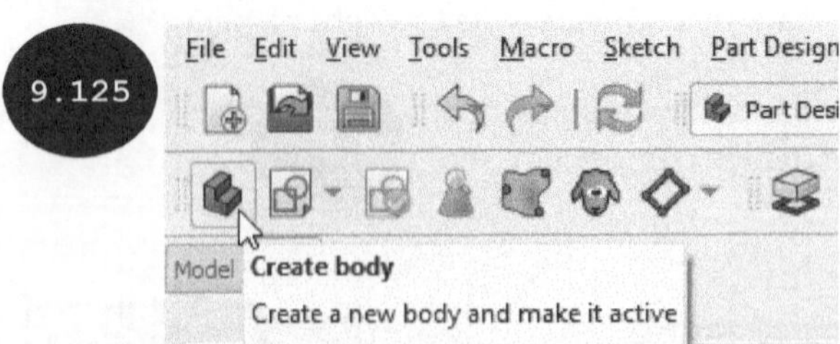

2. Rename the newly added body as **Collar** in the **Tree View**, as discussed earlier.

Now, you can create features of the Collar component of the assembly.

3. Rotate the assembly such that the back planar face of the first component can be visible, see Figure 9.126.

4. Select the back planar face of the first component (see Figure 9.126) and then click on the **Create sketch** tool in the **Part Design Helper** toolbar, see Figure 9.127. The **Reference** dialog box appears.

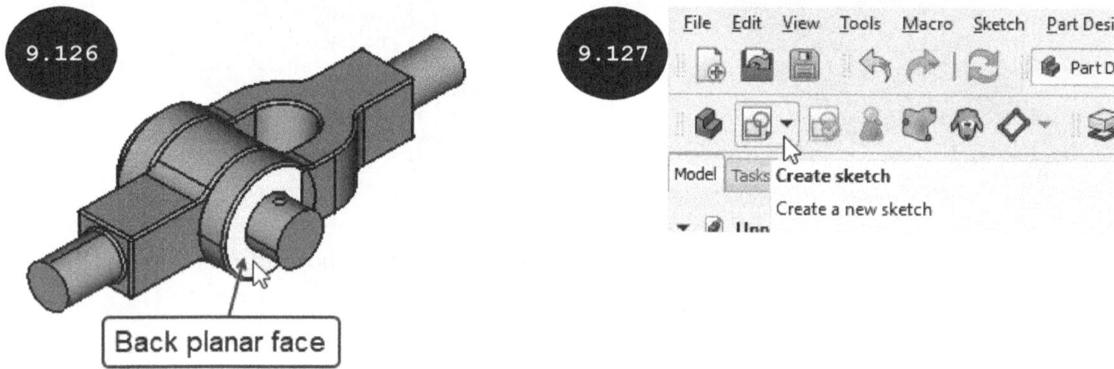

5. Select the **Make dependent copy** radio button in the **Reference** dialog box and then click on the **OK** button. The **Sketcher** workbench gets invoked. Ignore the error message that may appear in the **Report view** window at the bottom of the screen. You can close the **Report view** window by clicking on the cross mark that appears in its top right corner.

6. Click on the **View section** tool in the **Part Design Helper** toolbar to temporarily hide the material that is in front of the sketching plane, see Figure 9.128.

7. Create two concentric circles as the sketch of the base feature, see Figure 9.129.

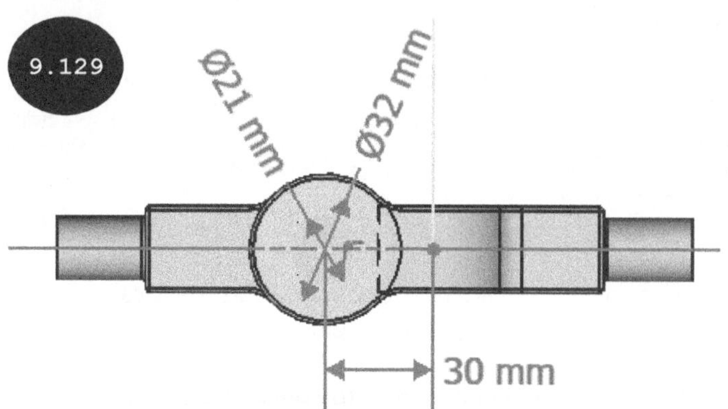

8. After creating the sketch, exit the **Sketcher** workbench and then extrude it to a length of 10 mm toward the back side of the sketching plane by using the **Pad** tool, see Figure 9.130.

9. Similarly, create a circular cut/hole of diameter 4 mm throughout the entire Collar component by using the **Pocket** tool, see Figure 9.131.

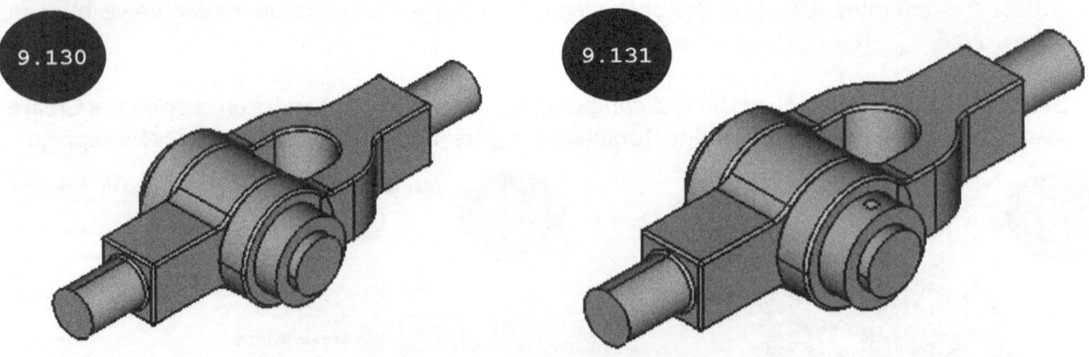

10. Change the view orientation of the model to isometric. Figure 9.132 shows the final assembly after creating all its components.

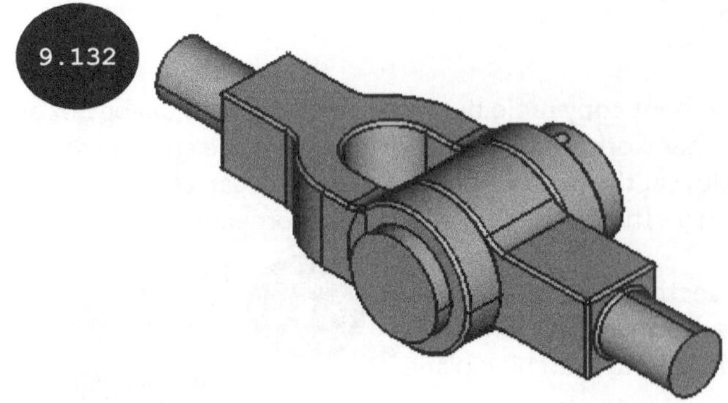

Section 6: Saving the Model

1. Click on the **Save** tool in the **File** toolbar (see Figure 9.133) or press the CTRL + S keys. The **Save FreeCAD Document** dialog box appears.

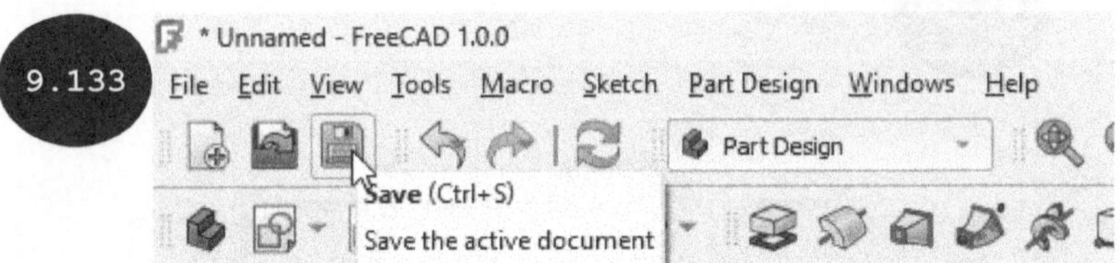

2. Browse to the required folder (:*FreeCAD > Chapter 09*) in the local drive of your system. Note that you need to create the Chapter 09 sub-folder inside the FreeCAD folder.

3. Enter **Ch09-Tutorial 1** in the **File name** field of the dialog box. Next, click on the **Save** button in the dialog box. The model gets saved at the specified location (:*FreeCAD > Chapter 09*).

4. Click on **File > Close** in the **Standard Menu** to close the current document.

Tutorial 2

Create an assembly, as shown in Figure 9.134 by applying the joints. Different views and dimensions of individual components of the assembly are shown in Figures 9.135 through 9.139. All dimensions are in mm.

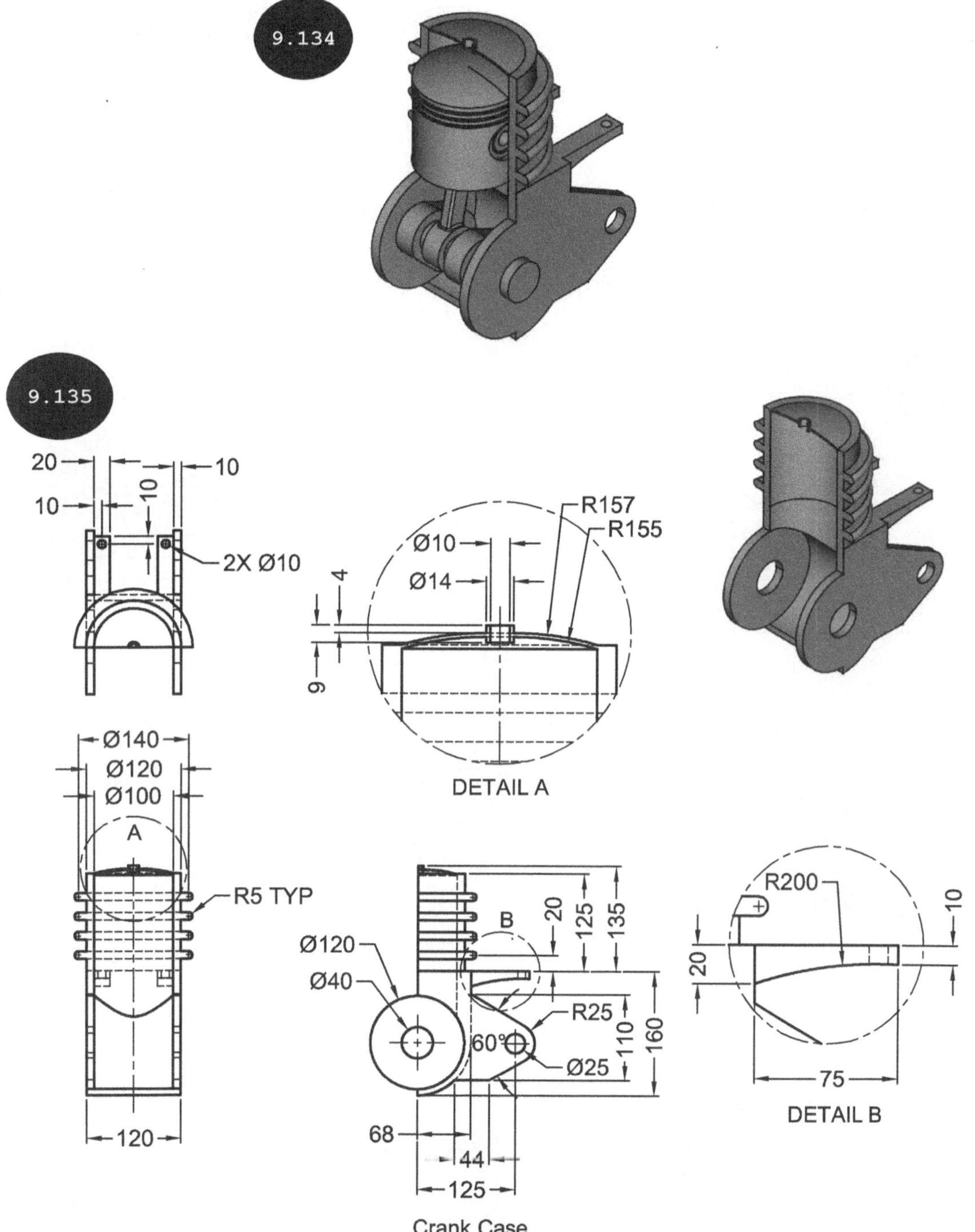

Crank Case

9.136

40
20
30
R30
Ø40
30
Ø30
R25

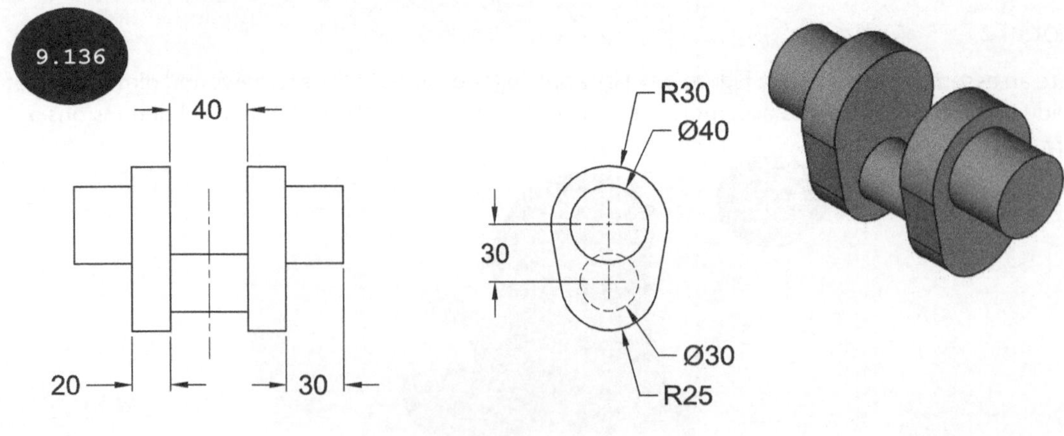

Crank Shaft

9.137

A
A
2
5
3 TYP
4 TYP
DETAIL B
90
B
16
100
20
40
Ø75
Ø86
Ø100
SECTION A-A
R135
Ø40
Ø30
45

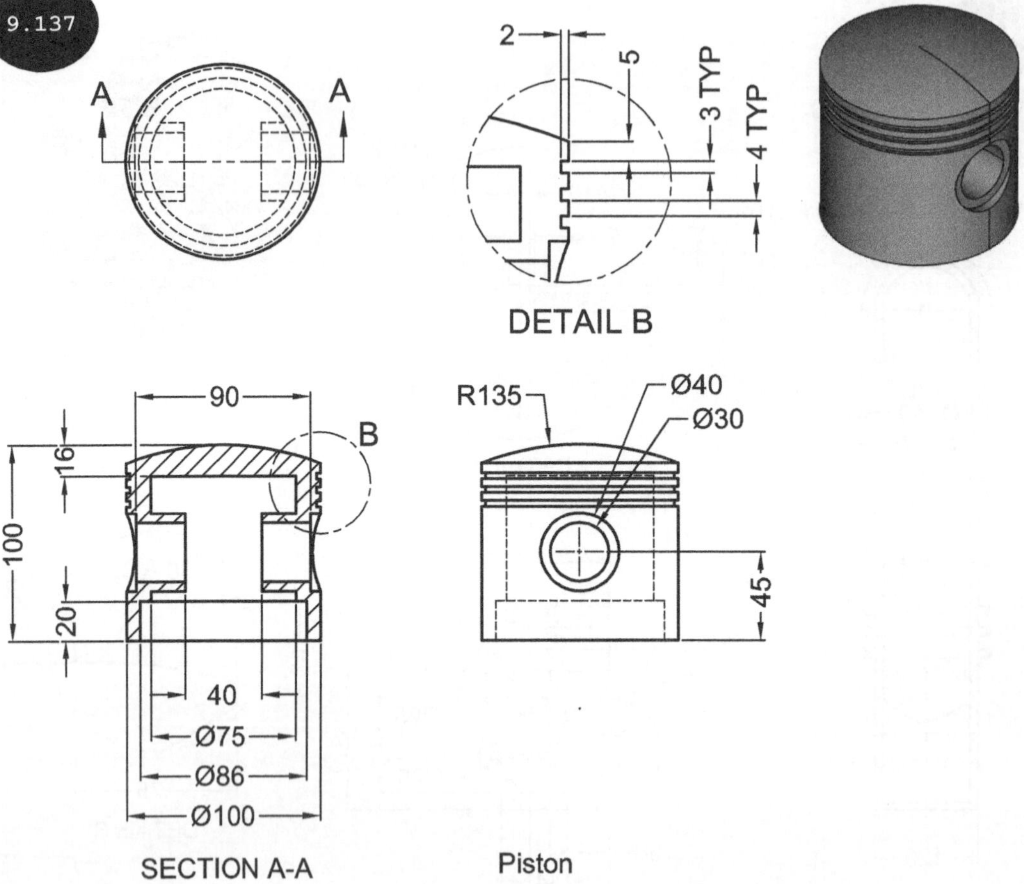

Piston

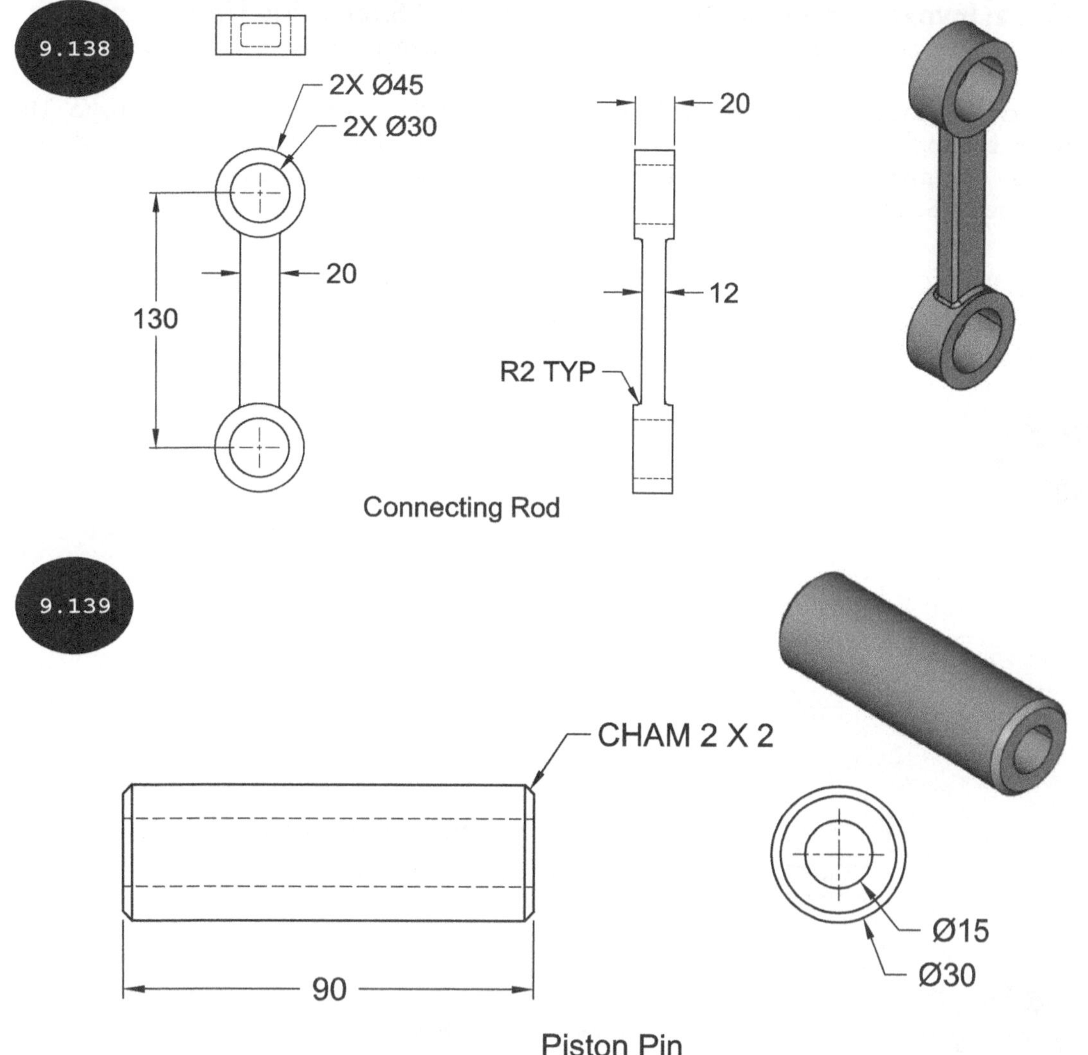

Section 1: Creating Assembly Components

In this section, you will create all the components of the assembly in the **Part Design** workbench one by one.

1. Start FreeCAD and create all components of the assembly one by one in the **Part Design** workbench. Refer to Figures 9.135 through 9.139 for the dimensions of each component. After creating each component, save it in the **Tutorial 2** folder within the **Chapter 09** directory. Note that you need to create these folders inside the main FreeCAD directory.

Note: You can also download all the components of the assembly by logging in to your account on CADArtifex website (***cadartifex.com/login***). If you are a new user, you need to first register yourself on the CADArtifex website (***cadartifex.com/register***) to access the online resources.

Section 2: Invoking the Assembly Workbench and Specifying Units

After creating all the components, you need to assemble them in the **Assembly** workbench.

1. Launch FreeCAD, then click on the **Assembly** button on the **Start** page, see Figure 9.140. The **Assembly** workbench is invoked, and a new empty assembly document opens with the default name "**unnamed: 1**". Note that the **Assembly** workbench is automatically selected in the **Workbench Selector**, see Figure 9.141.

Note: If FreeCAD is already open, you can switch to the **Start** page by clicking the **Start** tab at the bottom of the screen, refer to Figure 9.140.

9.140

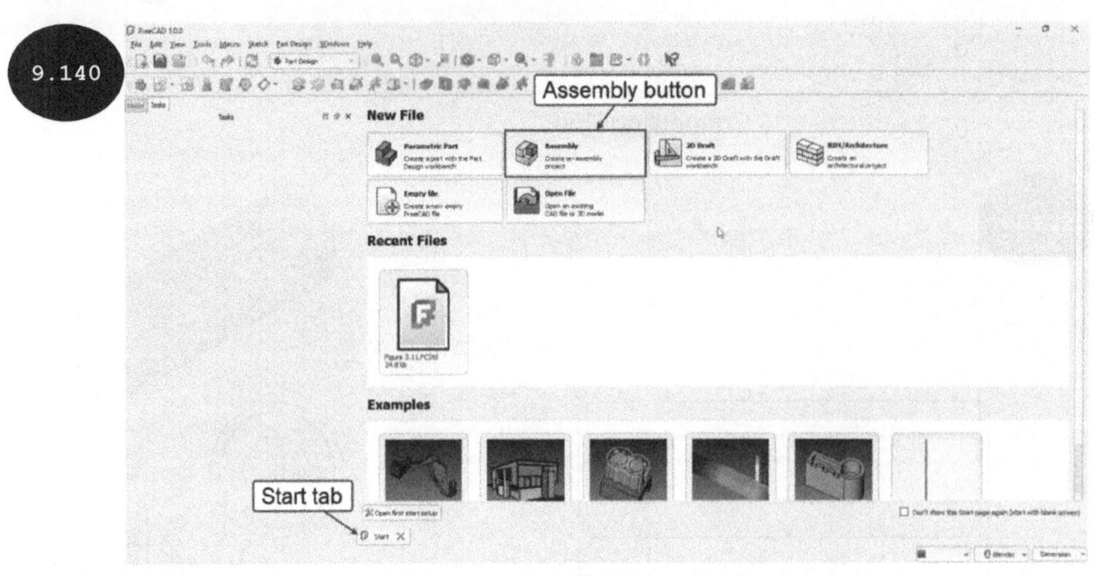

9.141

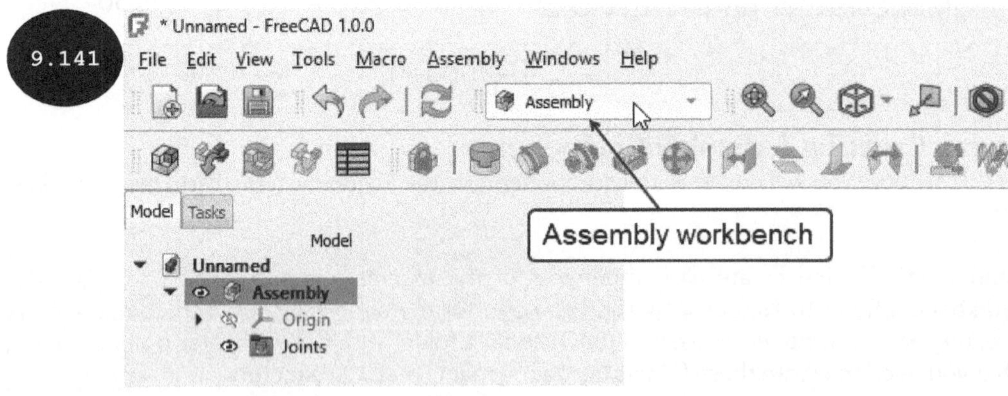

2. Invoke the **Unit** flyout that appears at the lower right corner of the **Status Bar**, see Figure 9.142.

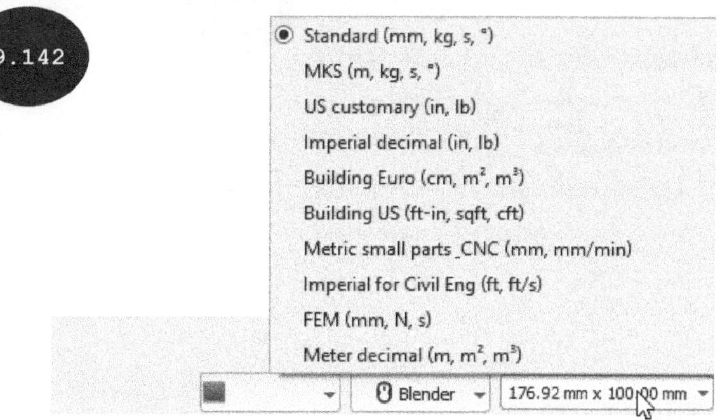

3. Ensure that the **Standard (mm, kg, s,*)** is selected as the unit system for the current design document in the **Unit** flyout, refer to Figure 9.142.

Section 3: Saving the Assembly Document

Before inserting the first component, it is recommended to save the Assembly document.

1. Click on the **Save** tool in the **File** toolbar (see Figure 9.143) or press the CTRL + S keys. The **Save FreeCAD Document** dialog box appears.

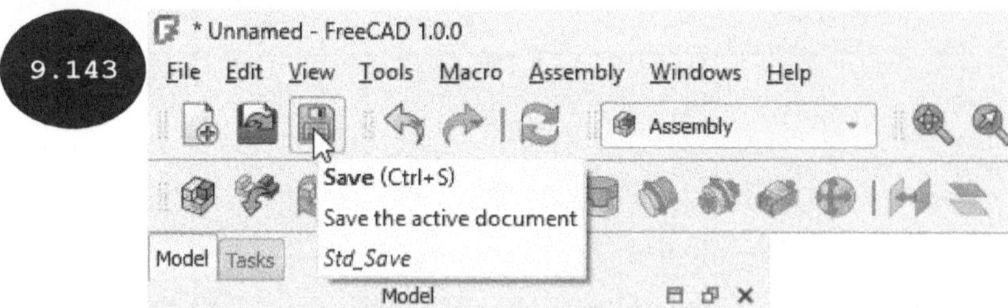

2. Browse to the required folder (:*FreeCAD* > *Chapter 09* > *Tutorial 2*) in the local drive of your system, where all components of the assembly are saved.

3. Enter **Ch09-Tutorial 2 (Single Cylinder Engine)** in the **File name** field of the dialog box. Next, click on the **Save** button in the dialog box. The Assembly document gets saved at the specified location (:*FreeCAD* > *Chapter 09* > *Tutorial 2*).

Section 4: Inserting the First and Second Components

Now, you can insert the first and second components (Crank Case and Crank Shaft) of the assembly.

1. Click on the **Insert Component** tool in the **Assembly** toolbar, see Figure 9.144. The **Insert Component** sub-window appears in the **Tasks Panel**, see Figure 9.145.

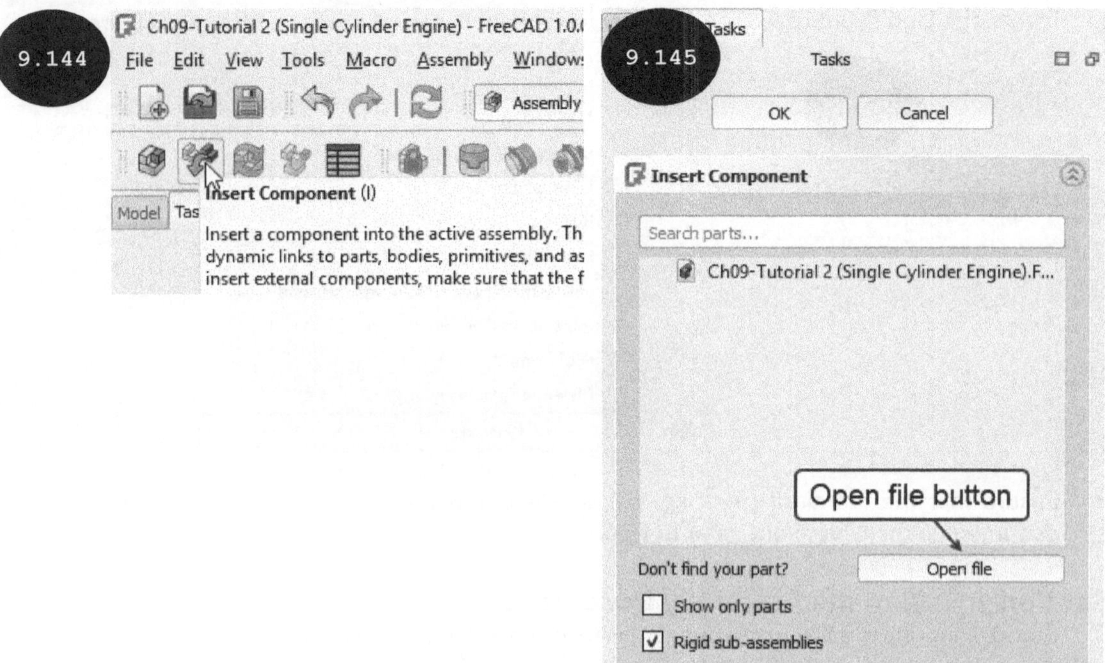

2. Click on the **Open file** button in the **Insert Component** sub-window, refer to Figure 9.145. The **Select FreeCAD documents to import parts from** dialog box appears, see Figure 9.146.

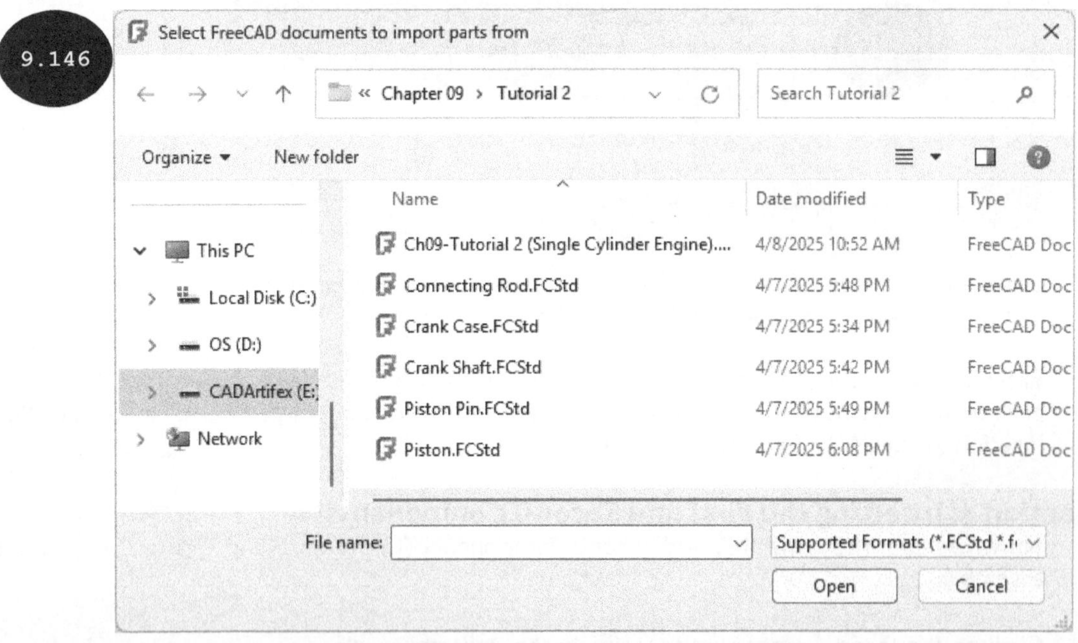

3. Browse to the required location *(:\FreeCAD > Chapter 09 > Tutorial 2)* and select the Crank Case component. Then, click the **Open** button in the dialog box. The Crank Case component now appears in the **Insert Component** sub-window, see Figure 9.147.

9.147

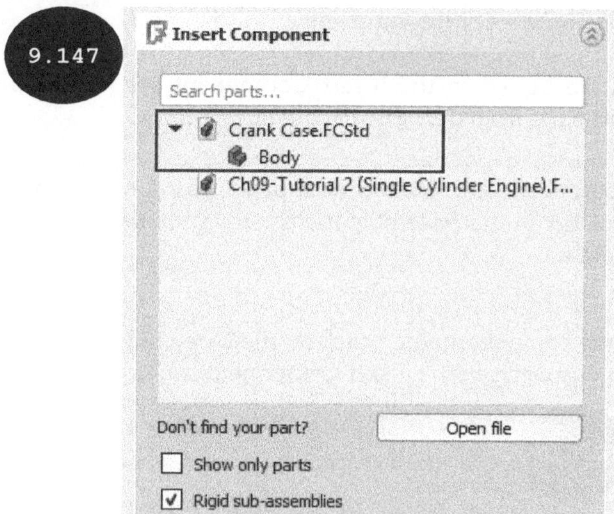

4. Select the **Body** of the Crank Case component in the **Insert Component** sub-window (refer to Figure 9.147). The selected body is inserted and placed at the default location (origin) in the 3D View area of the workbench. It also becomes a fixed component, by default. If needed, scroll the middle mouse button to adjust the view and fit the inserted component within the display area.

Note: If the **Ground Part?** dialog box appears on selecting the Crank Case Body, click on the **Yes** button to automatically fix the first component of the assembly in the current document.

5. Click anywhere in the workspace to exit the current selection set. The **Insert Component** sub-window remains visible in the **Tasks Panel**. Figure 9.148 shows the assembly document with the Crank Case component inserted and fixed at the origin.

9.148

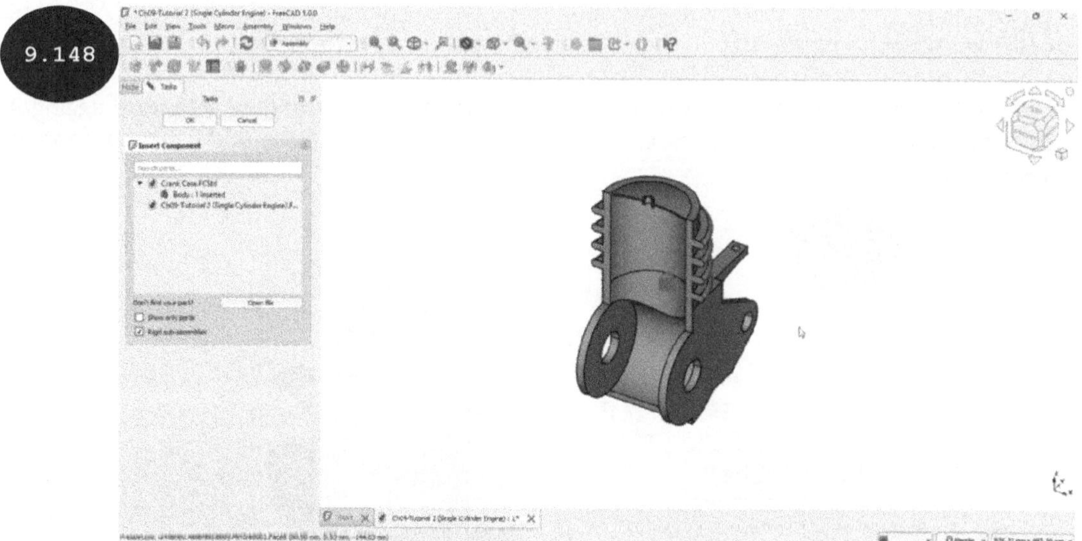

Now, you need to insert the second component of the assembly.

6. Click on the **Open file** button in the **Insert Component** sub-window. The **Select FreeCAD documents to import parts from** dialog box appears.

Tip: If the **Insert Component** sub-window disappears, you can reopen it by clicking the **Insert Component** tool in the **Assembly** toolbar to continue inserting components into the assembly document.

7. Select the Crank Shaft component, then click on the **Open** button in the dialog box. The Crank Shaft component now appears in the **Insert Component** sub-window, see Figure 9.149.

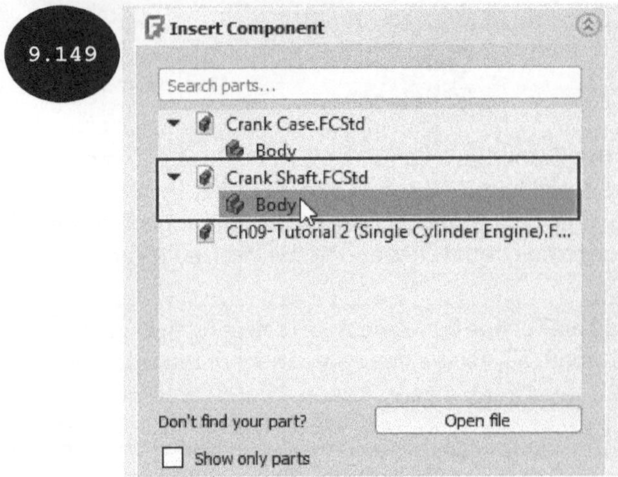

8. Select the **Body** of the Crank Shaft component in the **Insert Component** sub-window (refer to Figure 9.149). The Crank Shaft is inserted and placed at the default location in the 3D View area of the workbench with translational and rotational handles, refer to Figure 9.150.

9. Define the placement of the newly inserted component in the 3D View area by dragging its translational and rotational handles, ensuring that it does not intersect with the first component, see Figure 9.150.

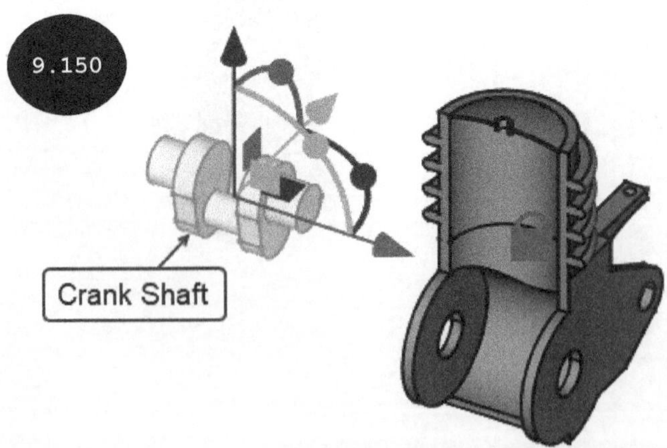

10. After defining the position of the Crank Shaft component, click anywhere in the 3D View area to exit the current selection set. The Crank Shaft is inserted at the defined position. However, it remains free to translate and rotate in any direction, since all its degrees of freedom are unrestricted.

11. Click the **OK** button in the **Tasks Panel** to confirm the insertion of the components and close the panel.

Section 5: Applying the Revolute Joint

Now, you need to apply a Revolute joint between the Crank Shaft and Crank Case components of the assembly to enable Crank Shaft to rotate about an axis.

1. Click the **Create Revolute Joint** tool in the **Assembly Joints** toolbar (see Figure 9.151), or press the **R** key. The **Create Joint** sub-window appears in the **Tasks Panel**, with the **Revolute** option selected by default in the **Joint type** drop-down list.

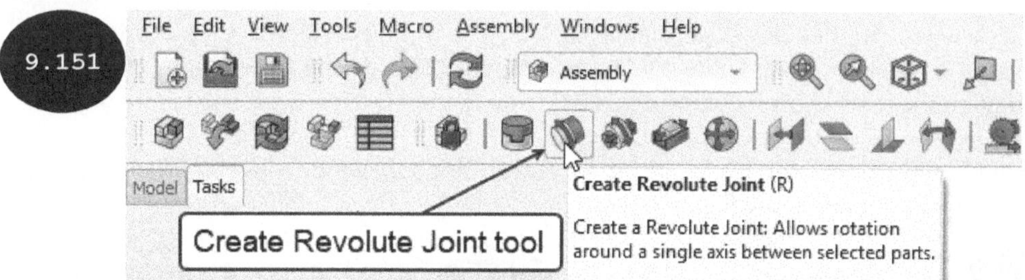

Now, you need to define the joint connector on the components.

2. Move the cursor over the rightmost circular edge of the Crank Shaft component, see Figure 9.152. The edge highlights, and the joint connector snaps to the center of the edge.

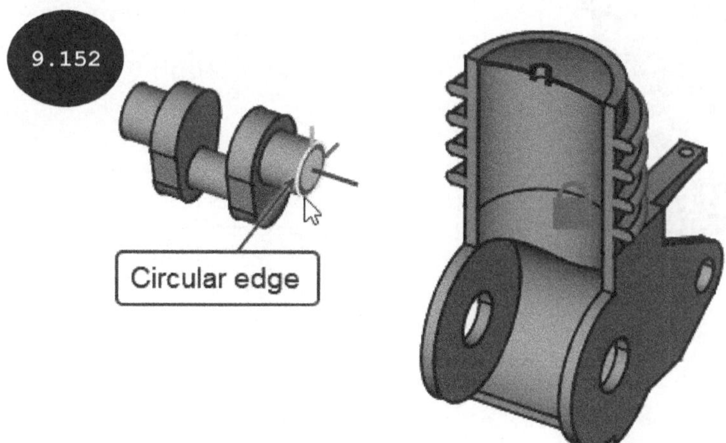

3. Click the left mouse button when the joint connector snaps to the center of the circular edge, refer to Figure 9.152. The position of the joint connector is defined at the center of the circular edge.

Now, you need to define the joint connector on the Crank Case component.

4. Move the cursor over the right circular edge of the Crank Case component, see Figure 9.153.

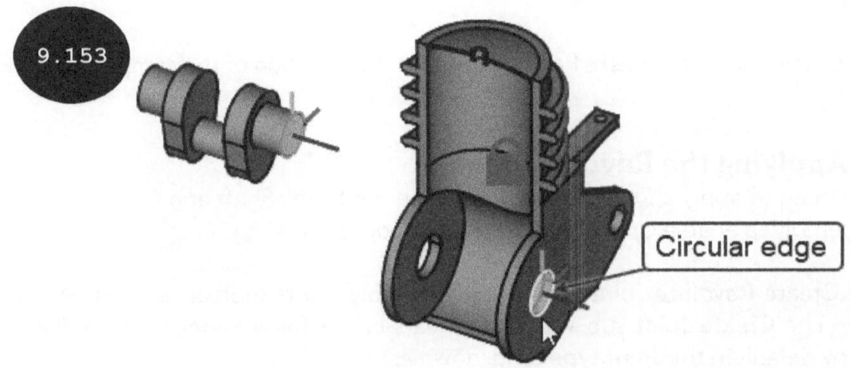

5. Click when the circular edge highlights, and the joint connector snaps to its center, refer to Figure 9.153. The Crank Shaft component moves towards the Crank Case component, and the joint connectors of both components coincide in the 3D View area, see Figure 9.154.

6. Enter **10** mm in the **Offset** field of the **Create Joint** sub-window as the offset distance between the joint connectors, see Figure 9.155.

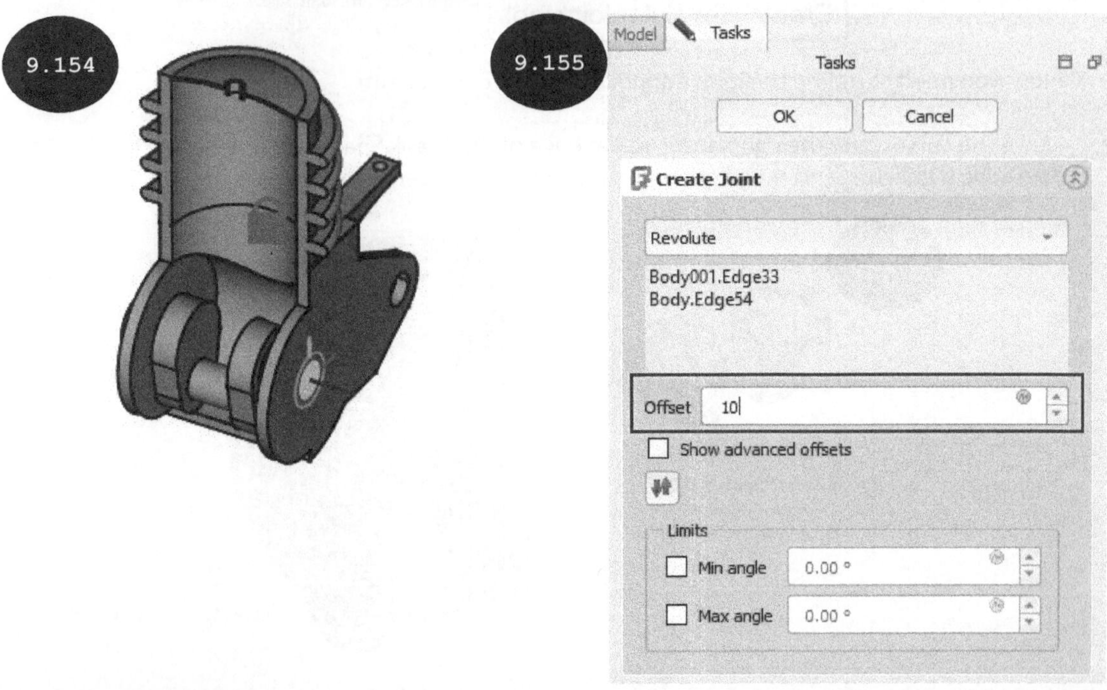

7. Click on the **OK** button the **Tasks Panel**. The Revolute joint is applied between the components, removing all degrees of freedom except for one rotational degree of freedom of the Crank Shaft component, see Figure 9.156.

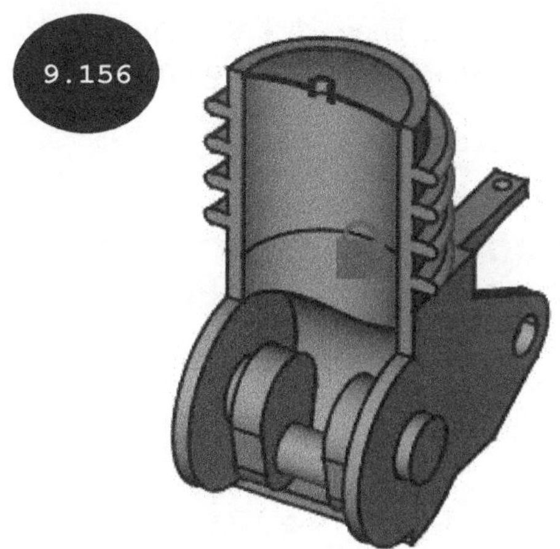

Section 6: Inserting and Assembling the Third Component

Now, you need to insert and assemble the Connecting Rod component of the assembly.

1. Click on the **Insert Component** tool in the **Assembly** toolbar, see Figure 9.157. The **Insert Component** sub-window appears in the **Tasks Panel**, see Figure 9.158.

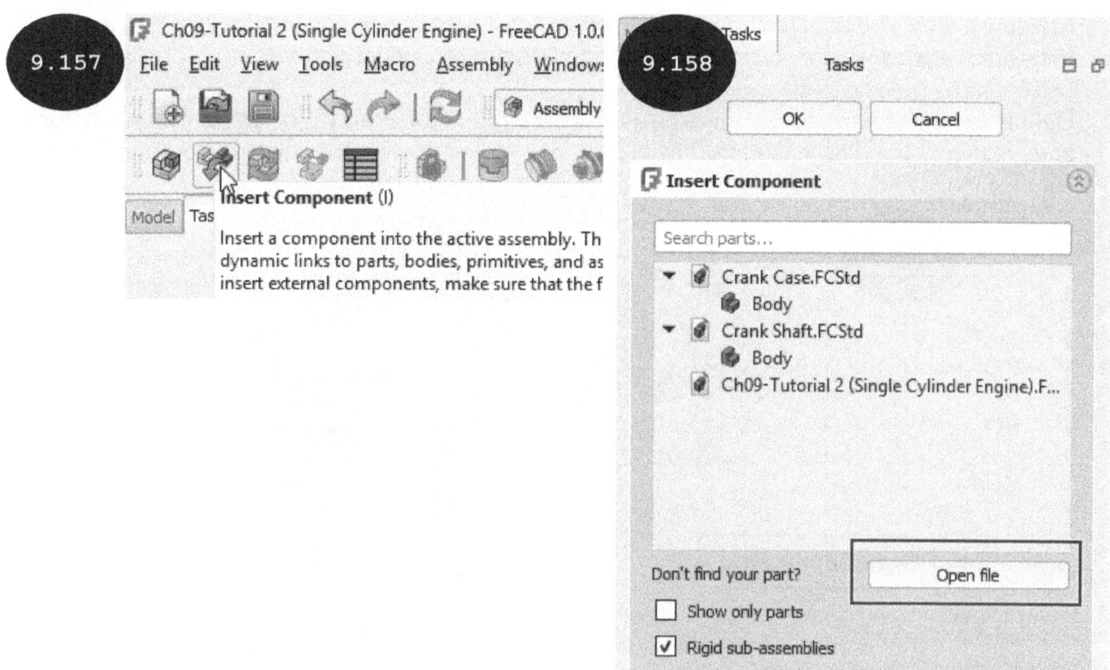

2. Click on the **Open file** button in the **Insert Component** sub-window, refer to Figure 9.158. The **Select FreeCAD documents to import parts from** dialog box appears.

3. Select the Connecting Rod component. Then, click the **Open** button in the dialog box. The Connecting Rod component now appears in the **Insert Component** sub-window, see Figure 9.159.

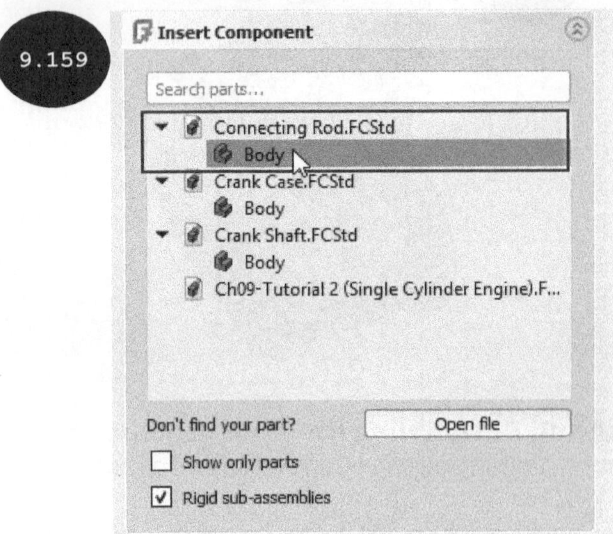

4. Select the **Body** of the Connecting Rod component in the **Insert Component** sub-window (refer to Figure 9.159). The selected body is inserted and placed at the default location (origin) in the 3D View area with translational and rotational handles, refer to Figure 9.160.

5. Define the placement of Connecting Rod in the 3D View area by dragging its translational and rotational handles, ensuring that it does not intersect with the existing components, see Figure 9.160.

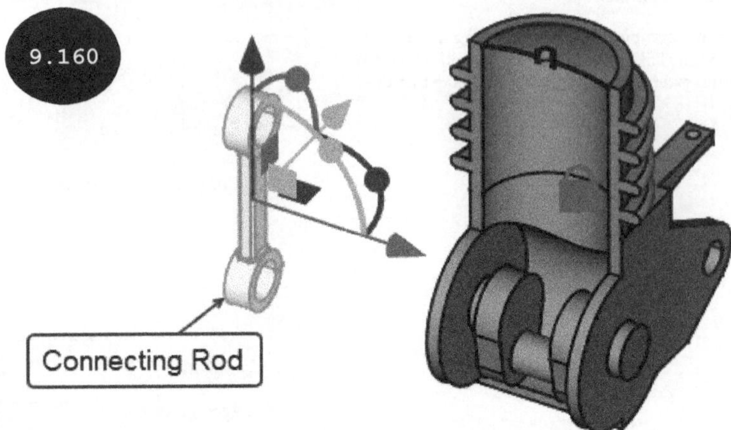

6. After defining the position of the Connecting Rod component, click anywhere in the 3D View area to exit the current selection set. The Connecting Rod is inserted at the defined position.

7. Click the **OK** button in the **Tasks Panel** to confirm the insertion of the component and close the panel.

Now, you need to assembly it by applying the Revolute joint.

8. Click the **Create Revolute Joint** tool in the **Assembly Joints** toolbar, see Figure 9.161. The **Create Joint** sub-window appears in the **Tasks Panel**, with the **Revolute** option selected by default in the **Joint type** drop-down list.

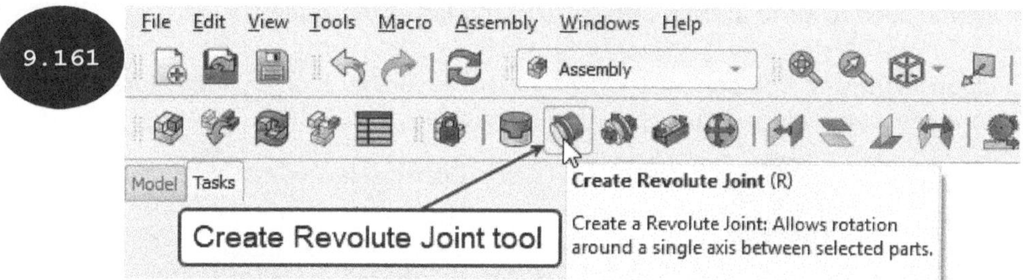

9. Move the cursor over the lower inner circular face of the Connecting Rod, then click the left mouse button to define the position of the joint connector at its center, see Figure 9.162.

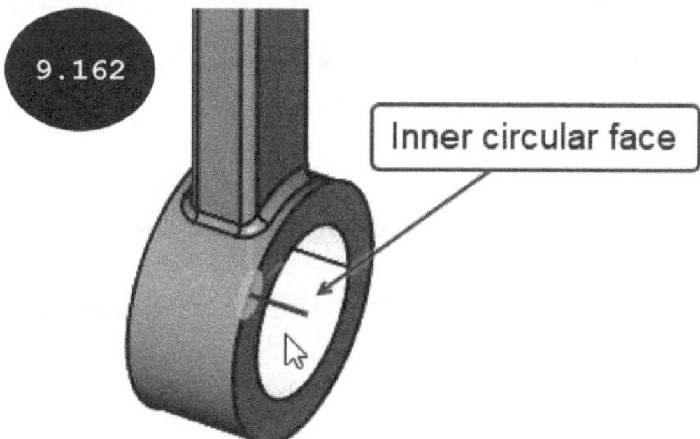

Now, you need to define the joint connector on the Crank Shaft component.

10. Move the cursor over the middle cylindrical face of the Crank Shaft component, then click the left mouse button to define the position of the joint connector at its center, see Figure 9.163. The Connecting Rod component moves towards the Crank Shaft, and the joint connectors of both components coincide in the 3D View area, see Figure 9.164.

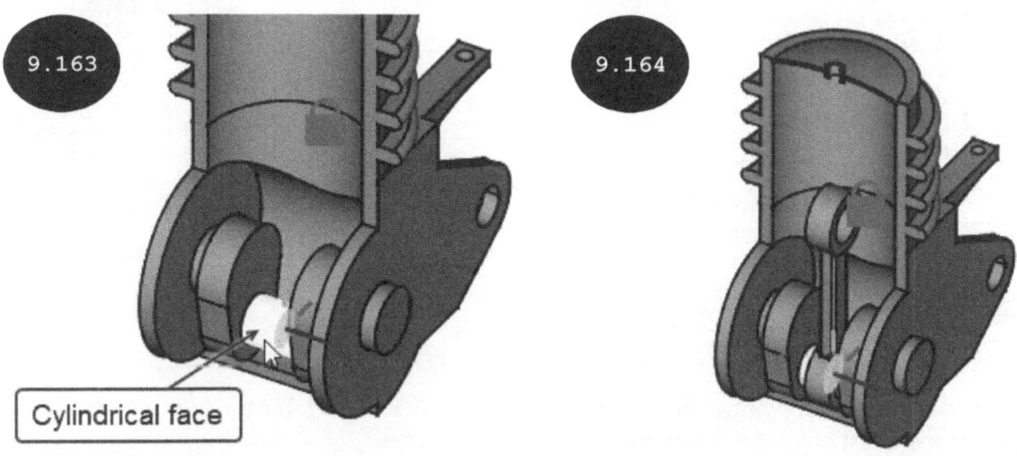

11. Click on the **OK** button the **Tasks Panel**. The Revolute joint is applied between the components, removing all degrees of freedom except for one rotational degree of freedom of the Connecting Rod component.

Section 7: Inserting and Assembling the Fourth Component

Now, you need to insert and assemble the Piston Pin of the assembly.

1. Click on the **Insert Component** tool in the **Assembly** toolbar, see Figure 9.165. The **Insert Component** sub-window appears in the **Tasks Panel**.

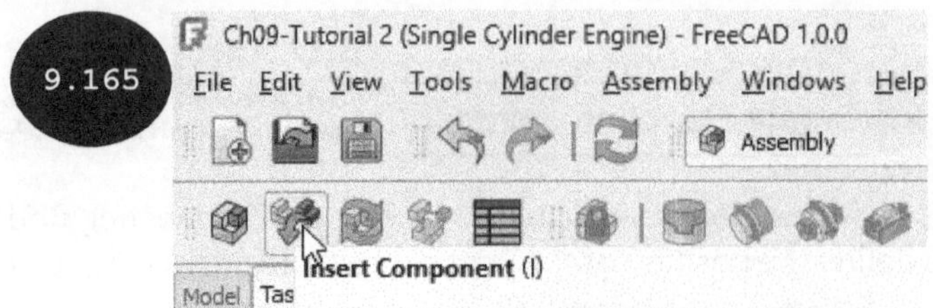

2. Click on the **Open file** button in the **Insert Component** sub-window. The **Select FreeCAD documents to import parts from** dialog box appears.

3. Select the Piston Pin component. Then, click the **Open** button in the dialog box. The Piston Pin component now appears in the **Insert Component** sub-window, see Figure 9.166.

4. Select the **Body** of the Piston Pin component in the **Insert Component** sub-window (refer to Figure 9.166). The selected body is inserted and placed at the default location in the 3D View area with translational and rotational handles, refer to Figure 9.167.

5. Define the placement of the Piston Pin in the 3D View area by dragging its translational and rotational handles, ensuring that it does not intersect with the existing components, see Figure 9.167.

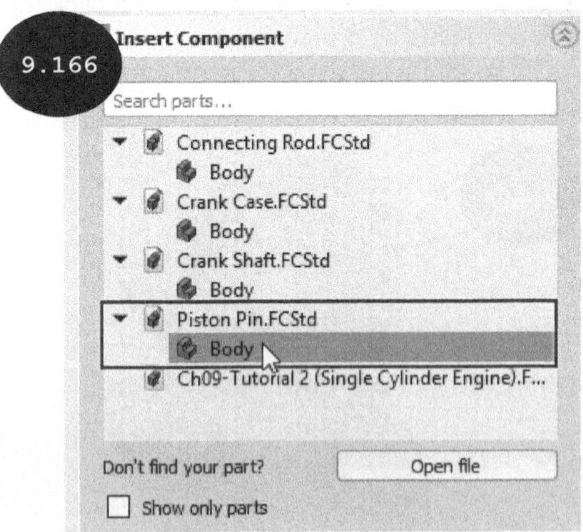

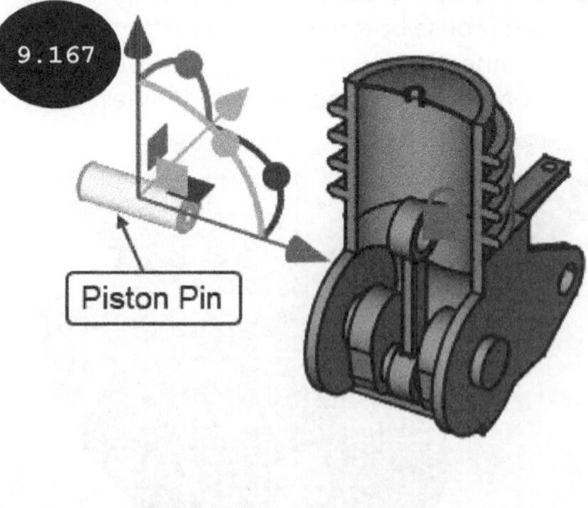

6. After defining the position of the Piston Pin component, click the **OK** button in the **Tasks Panel** to confirm the insertion of the component and close the panel.

Now, you need to assembly it by applying the Revolute joint.

7. Click the **Create Revolute Joint** tool in the **Assembly Joints** toolbar, see Figure 9.168. The **Create Joint** sub-window appears in the **Tasks Panel**, with the **Revolute** option selected by default.

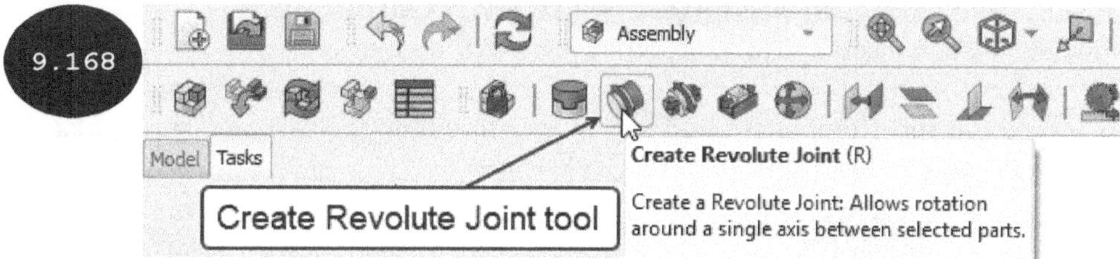

8. Move the cursor over the outer circular face of the Piston Pin, then click the left mouse button to define the position of the joint connector at its center, see Figure 9.169.

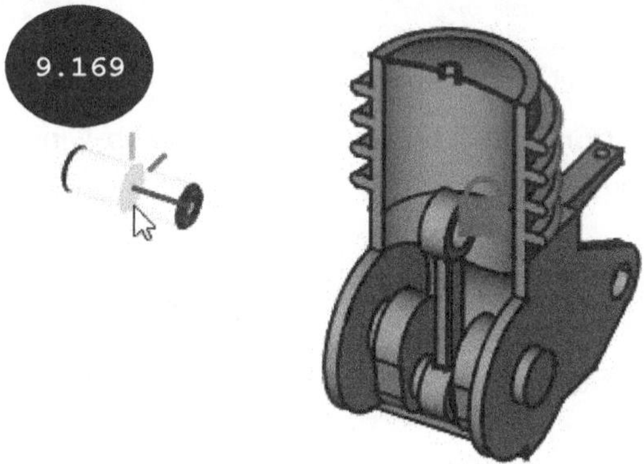

Now, you need to define the joint connector on the Connecting Rod component.

9. Move the cursor over the upper cylindrical face of the Connecting Rod component, then click the left mouse button to define the position of the joint connector at its center, see Figure 9.170. The Piston Pin component moves towards the Connecting Rod, and the joint connectors of both components coincide in the 3D View area, see Figure 9.171.

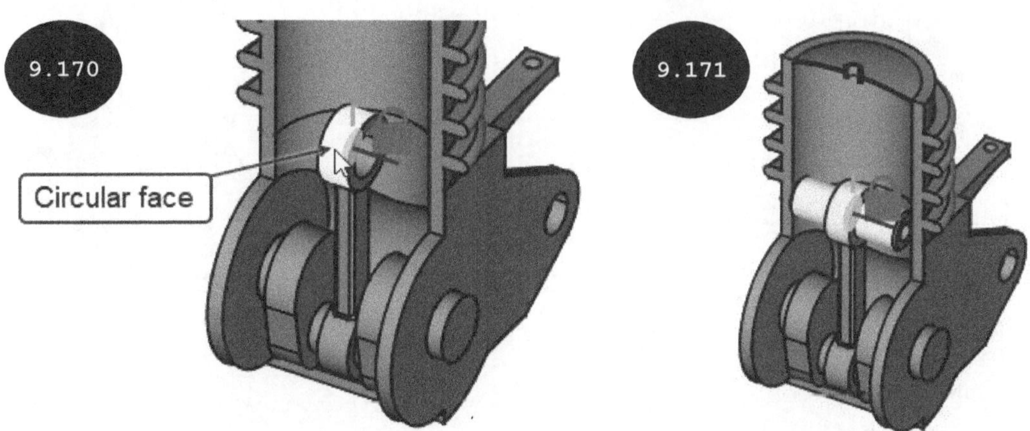

10. Click on the **OK** button the **Tasks Panel**. The Revolute joint is applied between the components, removing all degrees of freedom except for one rotational degree of freedom of the Piston Pin component.

Section 8: Inserting and Assembling the Fifth Component

Now, you need to insert and assemble the Piston of the assembly.

1. Click on the **Insert Component** tool in the **Assembly** toolbar, see Figure 9.172. The **Insert Component** sub-window appears in the **Tasks Panel**.

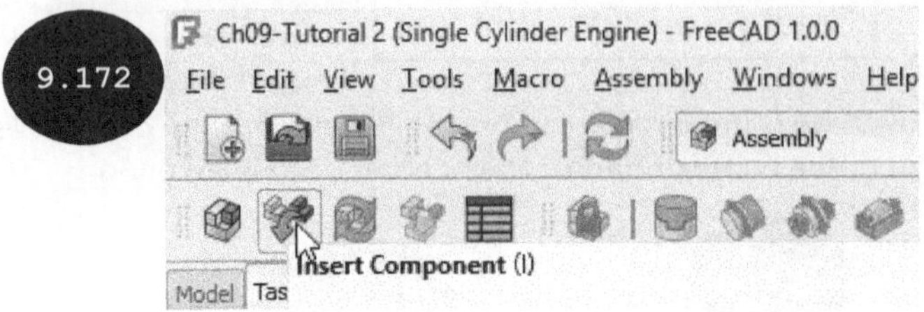

2. Click on the **Open file** button in the **Insert Component** sub-window. The **Select FreeCAD documents to import parts from** dialog box appears.

3. Select the Piston component. Then, click the **Open** button in the dialog box. The Piston component now appears in the **Insert Component** sub-window, see Figure 9.173.

4. Select the **Body** of the Piston component in the **Insert Component** sub-window (see Figure 9.173). The selected body is inserted and placed at the default location in the 3D View area with translational and rotational handles, refer to Figure 9.174.

5. Define the placement of the Piston in the 3D View area by dragging its translational and rotational handles, ensuring that it does not intersect with the existing components, see Figure 9.174.

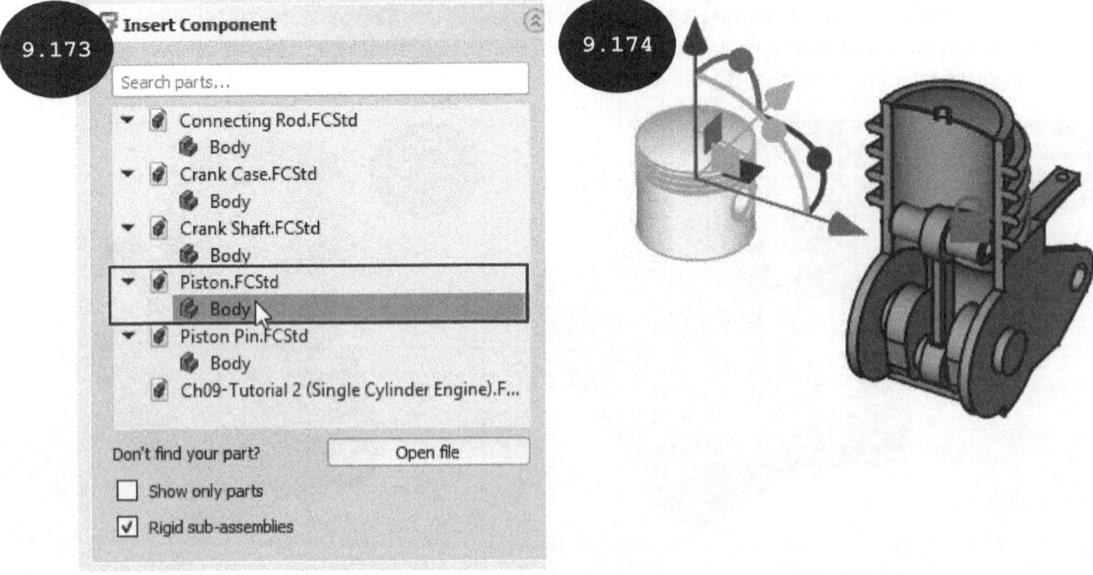

6. After defining the position of the Piston component, click the **OK** button in the **Tasks Panel** to confirm the insertion of the component and close the panel.

   Now, you need to assembly it by applying the Revolute and Slider joints.

7. Click the **Create Revolute Joint** tool in the **Assembly Joints** toolbar, see Figure 9.175. The **Create Joint** sub-window appears in the **Tasks Panel**, with the **Revolute** option selected by default.

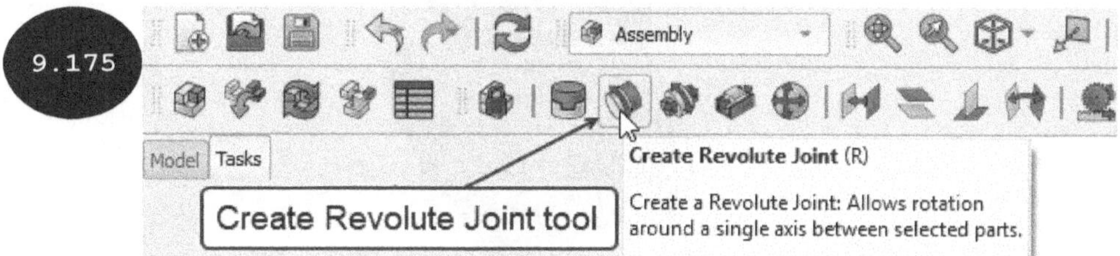

8. Move the cursor over the right inner circular edge of the Piston, then click the left mouse button to define the position of the joint connector at its center, see Figure 9.176.

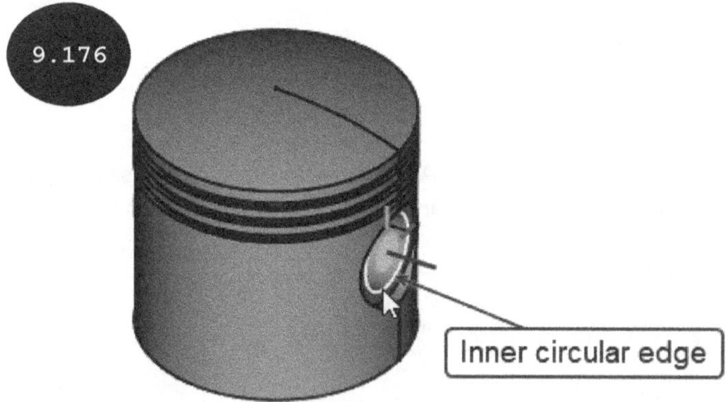

   Now, you need to define the joint connector on the Piston Pin component.

9. Move the cursor over the rightmost outer circular edge of the Piston Pin, see Figure 9.177.

10. Click the left mouse button to define the position of the joint connector at the center of the rightmost circular edge of the Piston Pin, refer to Figure 9.177. The Piston component moves

towards the Piston Pin, and the joint connectors of both components coincide in the 3D View area, see Figure 9.178.

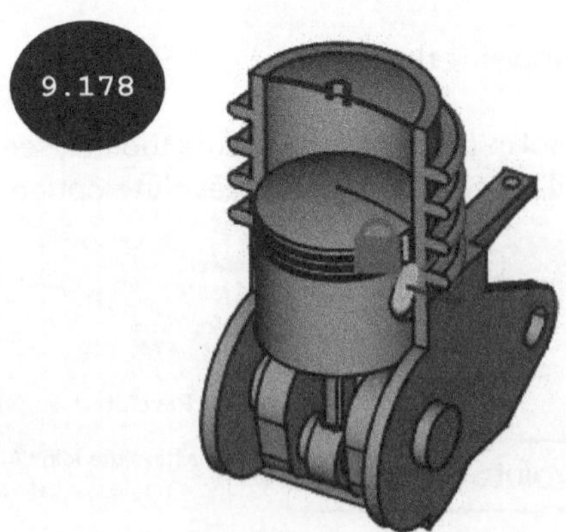

11. Click on the **OK** button the **Tasks Panel**. The Revolute joint is applied between the components.

Section 9: Applying the Slider Joint

Now, you need to apply the Slider joint between the Piston and Crank Case components to allow the Piston to slide along the axis of the Crank Case component.

1. Click the **Create Slider Joint** tool in the **Assembly Joints** toolbar, see Figure 9.179. The **Create Joint** sub-window appears in the **Tasks Panel**, with the **Slider** option selected by default.

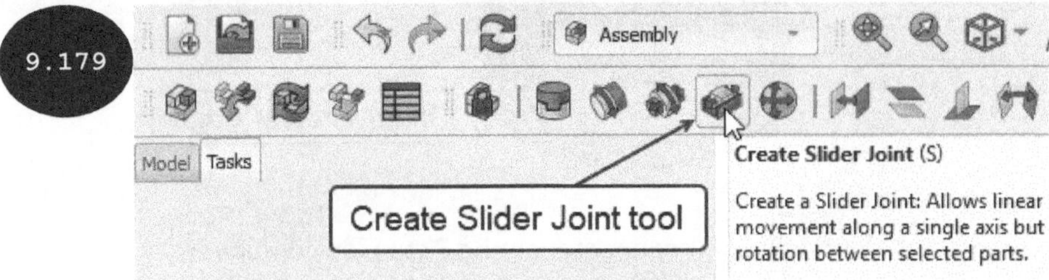

2. Move the cursor over the outer circular face of the Piston, then click the left mouse button to define the position of the joint connector at its center, see Figure 9.180.

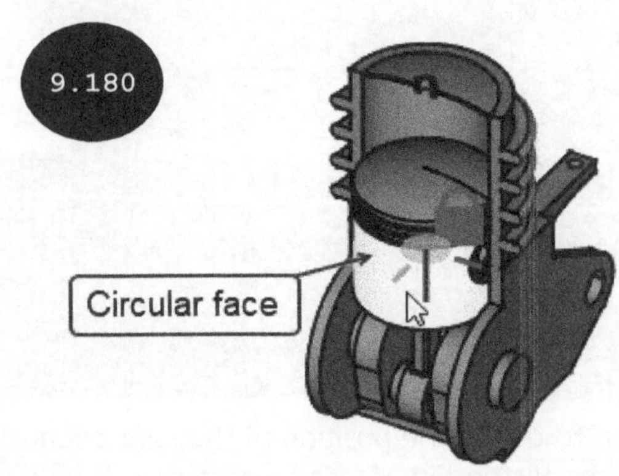

Now, you need to define the joint connector on the Crank Case component.

3. Move the cursor over the inner circular face of the Crank Case component (see Figure 9.181), then click the left mouse button to define the position of the joint connector.

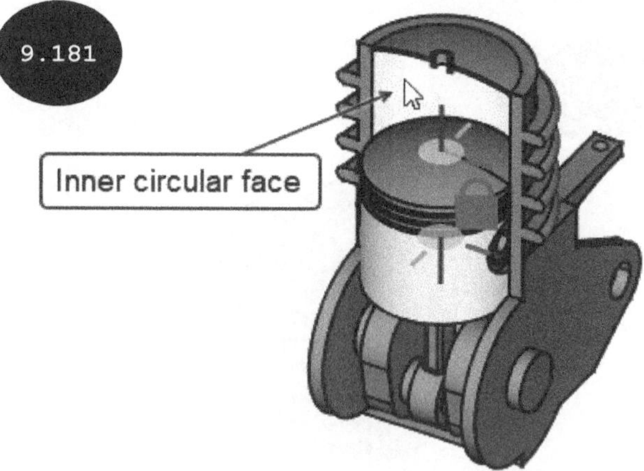

4. Click on the **OK** button the **Tasks Panel**. The Slider joint is applied between the components, allowing the Piston to slide up and down while the Crank Shaft rotates, see Figure 9.182.

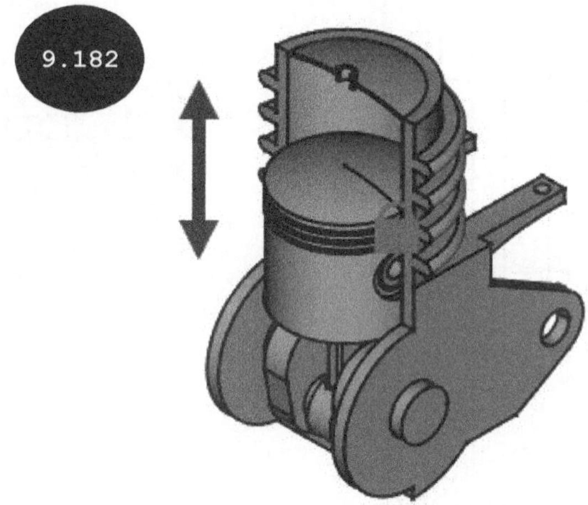

5. Rotate the Crank Shaft by dragging it to review the sliding motion of the Piston in the 3D View area.

   Now, you can save the assembly.

6. Press the CTRL + S keys to save the assembly.

Hands-on Test Drive 1

Create an assembly shown in Figure 9.183 by using the Top-down assembly approach in the **Part Design** workbench. Different views and dimensions of each component are shown in Figures 9.184 through 9.187. All dimensions are in inches.

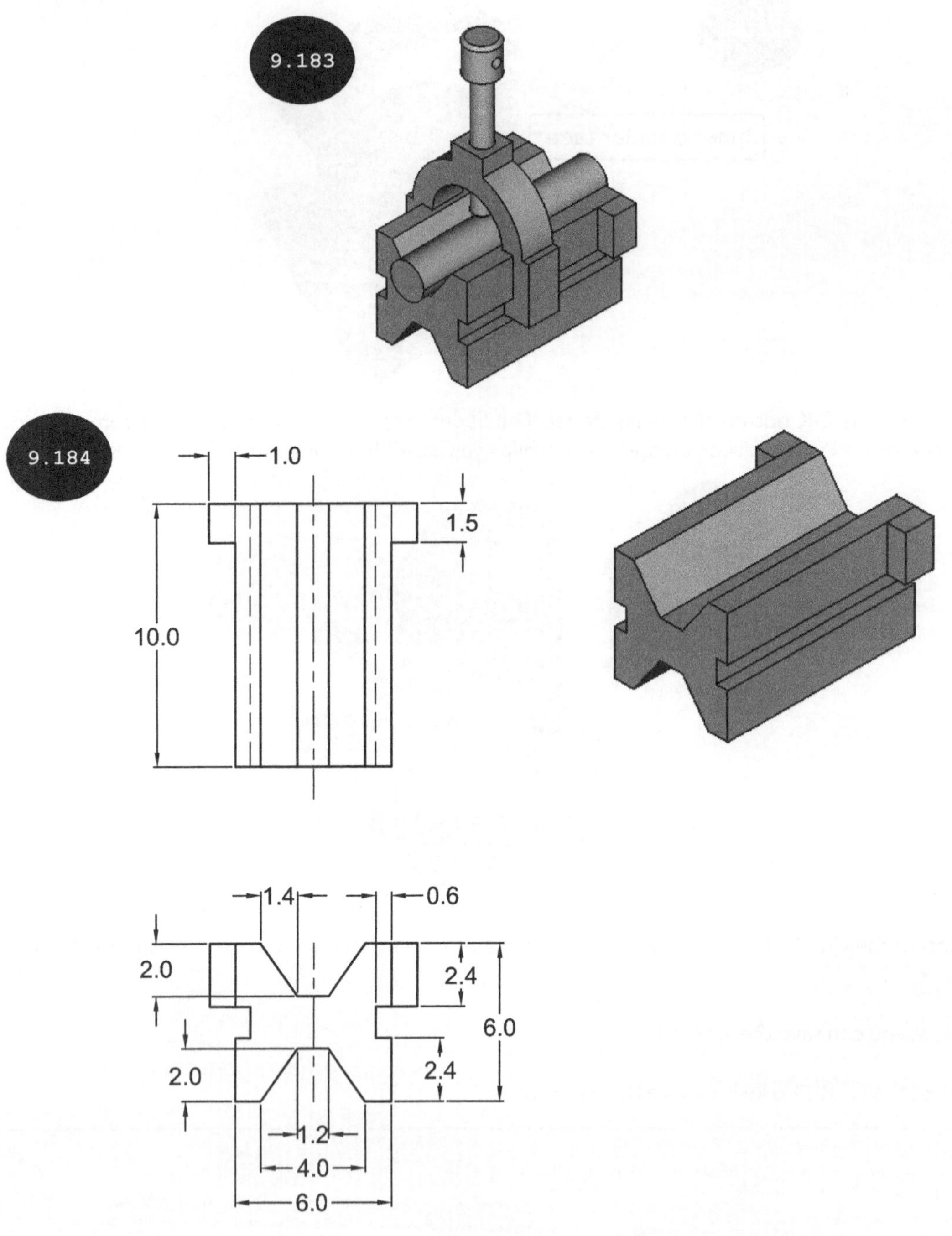

V-Block Body

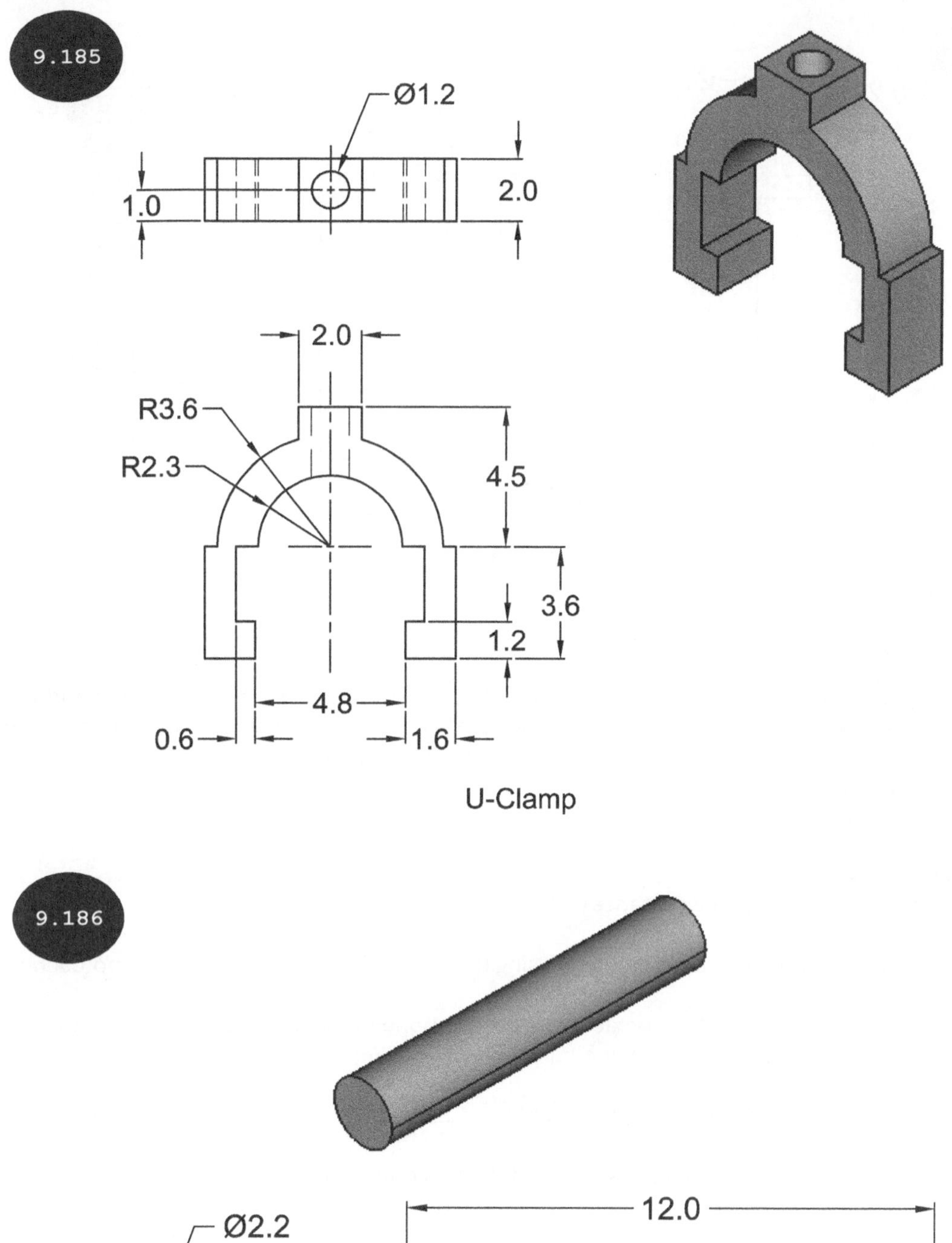

Ø2.2

12.0

Pipe

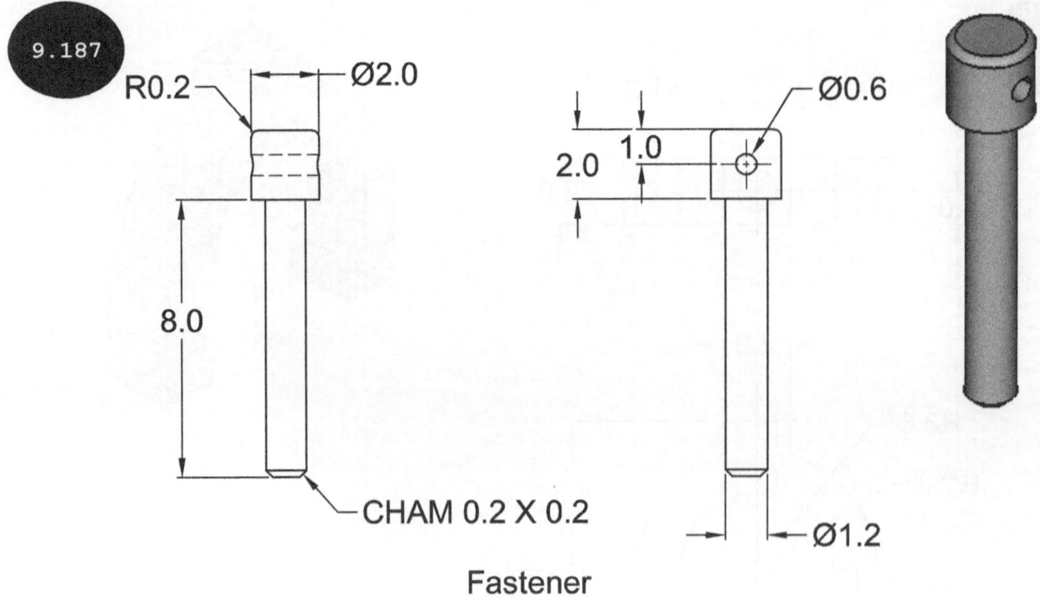

Fastener

Summary

The chapter discussed how to create assemblies using the Top-down assembly approach and the Bottom-up assembly approach. The methods for accessing the **Assembly** workbench, inserting components, and applying different various types of joints for assembling components were also discussed in this chapter.

Questions

Complete and verify the following sentences:

- In FreeCAD, you can create an assembly by using the _________ and _________ approaches.
- In the _________ assembly approach, all the components of an assembly are created as individual bodies within a single part document.
- You can activate the body of a part document by _________ on its name in the **Tree View**.
- In _________ workbench, you can assemble different components of an assembly.
- The _________ joint allows rotation around all three axes (X, Y, and Z), while restricting all translational degrees of freedom.
- After applying the joints, you can review the relative motion between components by dragging them along or around their free degrees of freedom. (True/False)
- In FreeCAD, you cannot create multiple bodies within a single part document. (True/False)

CHAPTER

10

Creating 2D Drawings

This chapter discusses the following topics:

- Invoking the TechDraw Workbench
- Inserting a Drawing Sheet
- Editing Title Block Text of a Sheet
- Creating Drawing Views
- Modifying the Scale of a 2D Projection View
- Displaying Hidden Lines on the Views
- Creating a Section View
- Creating a Detail View
- Applying Dimensions
- Exporting Drawing as a DXF File
- Exporting Drawing as an SVG File

After creating a 3D model, you can create a 2D drawing. A 2D drawing is a traditional drafting document, that contains all the required information such as drawing views, dimensions, annotations, notes, etc. about the product to be manufactured. In FreeCAD, you can create basic technical drawings of 3D models created with another workbench such as **Part, Part Design**, or **Assembly** in the **TechDraw** workspace. You can also create technical drawings of 3D models that are imported from other CAD applications in the **TechDraw** workspace.

Invoking the TechDraw Workbench

The method for invoking the **TechDraw** workbench for creating a 2D drawing of a 3D model is discussed below:

1. Start FreeCAD by double-clicking on the **FreeCAD 1.0** icon on your desktop. The startup user interface of FreeCAD appears.

Note: In FreeCAD, it is recommended to first open or create a 3D model before invoking the **TechDraw** workbench to create its 2D drawing views.

2. Start a new document and then create a 3D model in the **Part Design** workbench or open an existing 3D model to create its 2D drawing, see Figure 10.1. In this figure, Tutorial 2 of Chapter 8 is opened for creating its drawing views.

10.1

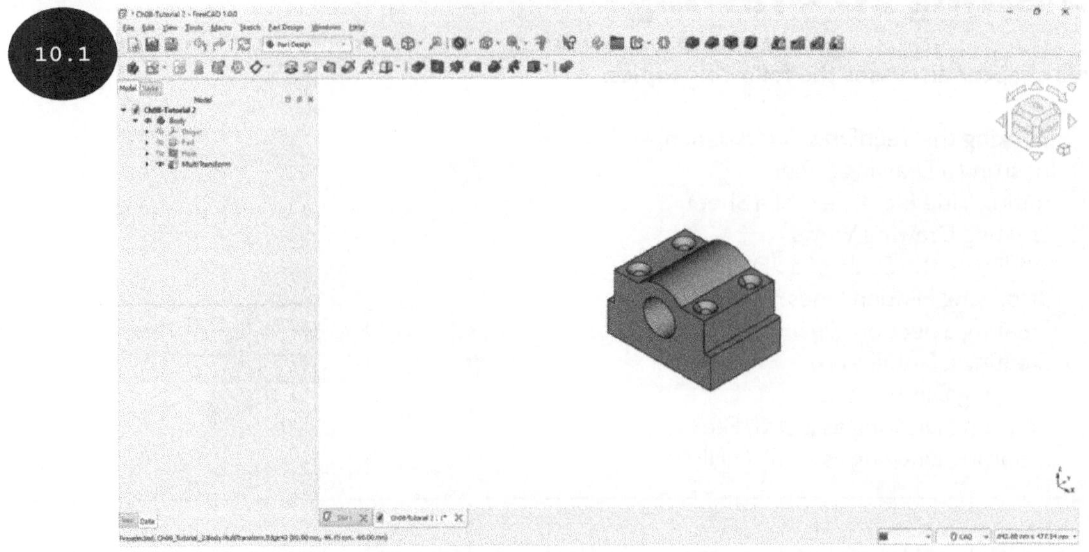

Tip: In FreeCAD, you can open an existing 3D model using the **Open** tool of the **File** toolbar. The method for opening a 3D model is discussed in Chapter 1.

Note: You can also open an assembly for creating its 2D drawing. In addition, you can import a 3D model that is created in another CAD application for creating its 2D drawing. The method for importing a 3D model is discussed in Chapter 1.

Now, you can invoke the **TechDraw** workbench to create a 2D drawing of the 3D model.

3. Invoke the **Workbench Selector** in the **Workbench** toolbar and then select the **TechDraw** workbench, see Figure 10.2. The **TechDraw** workbench gets invoked, see Figure 10.3.

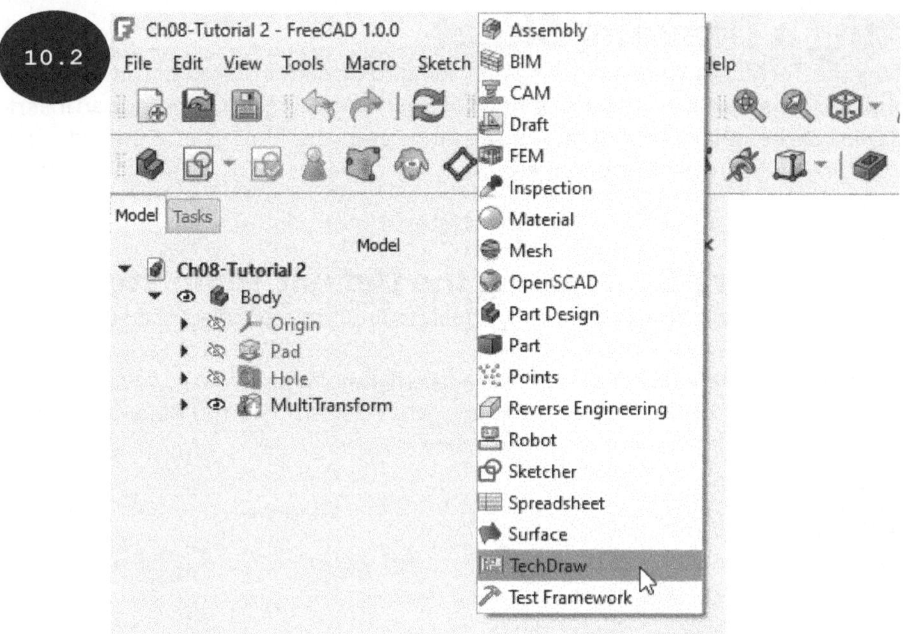

10.2

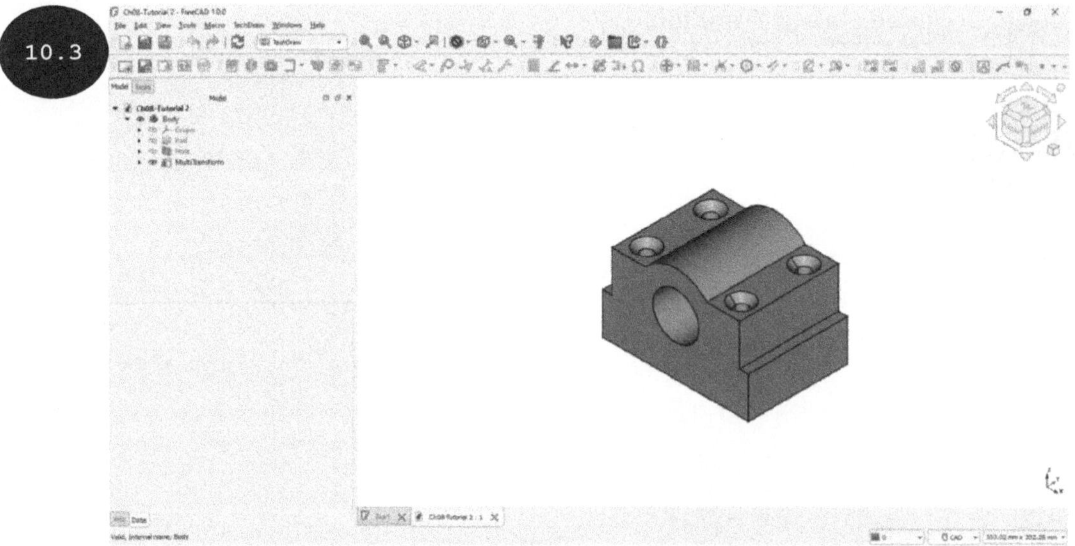

10.3

Note: Initially, most of the tools of the **TechDraw** workbench are not activated. Some of these tools get activated as soon as you insert a drawing sheet (page) of a specified template/size for creating different drawing views of the model and the remaining tools will be activated when you insert a drawing view on the sheet. The methods for inserting a sheet (page) and a drawing view of a 3D model are discussed next.

Inserting a Drawing Sheet

After invoking the **TechDraw** workbench, the first thing to do is to insert a drawing sheet (page) of a specific template to create different drawing views of a 3D model. In FreeCAD, you can insert a drawing sheet (page) using the default template or a selected template. Note that a template controls the sheet size, drafting standard, sheet border, etc. of a sheet. The methods for inserting a drawing sheet are discussed next.

Inserting a Drawing Sheet Using the Default Template

The method for inserting a drawing sheet using the default template is discussed below:

1. Click on the **Insert Default Page** tool in the **TechDraw Pages** toolbar, see Figure 10.4. A new drawing sheet (page) of the default template gets inserted with the default name "*Page*" in a separate tab and becomes active by default, see Figure 10.5.

10.4

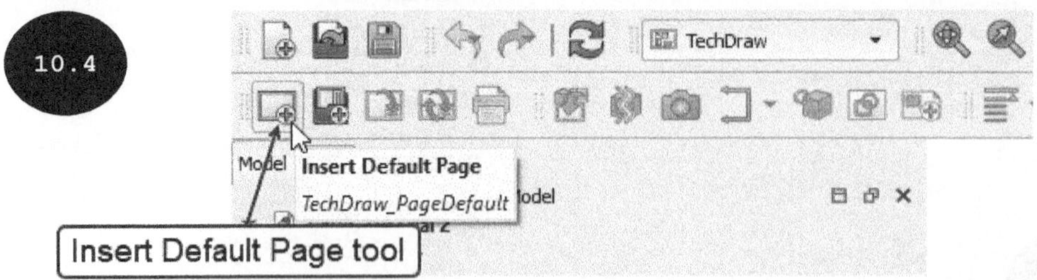

10.5

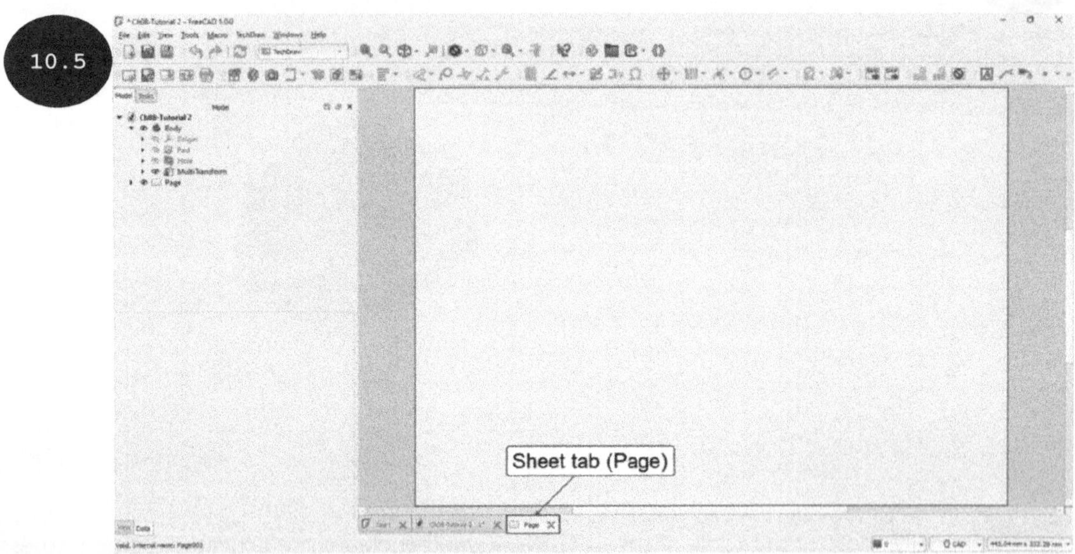

Tip: By default, the sheet gets inserted in a new separate tab. You may need to adjust or fit the sheet in the drawing display area by moving or zooming in or out it. You can move the sheet by pressing and holding the middle mouse button. You can zoom in or zoom out the sheet by scrolling the middle mouse button up or down on the sheet, respectively.

2. Similarly, you can insert multiple sheets (pages) using the default template for creating different drawing views of the 3D model, if needed.

Note: You can set the default template using the **Preferences** dialog box, as required. To do this, click on the **Edit > Preferences** in the **File** toolbar and then click on the **TechDraw** section in the left panel of the **Preferences** dialog box that appears, see Figure 10.6. The options to control the default template, drawing parameters, and other related settings appear on the right panel of the dialog box in the respective tabs. In the **General** tab of the dialog box, click on the **Browse** button next to the **Default Template** field in the **Files** area, see Figure 10.6. The **Select a file** window appears. In this window, browse to the **Templates** folder (>*\FreeCAD 0.21\data\Mod\TechDraw\Templates*) in the FreeCAD installation directory and then select the required template to be set as the default template for all new sheets/pages. Next, click on the **Open** button in the **Select a file** window and then click on the **Apply** button in the **Preferences** dialog box. The selected template gets set as the default template. Next, click on the **OK** button to exit the **Preferences** dialog box.

10.6

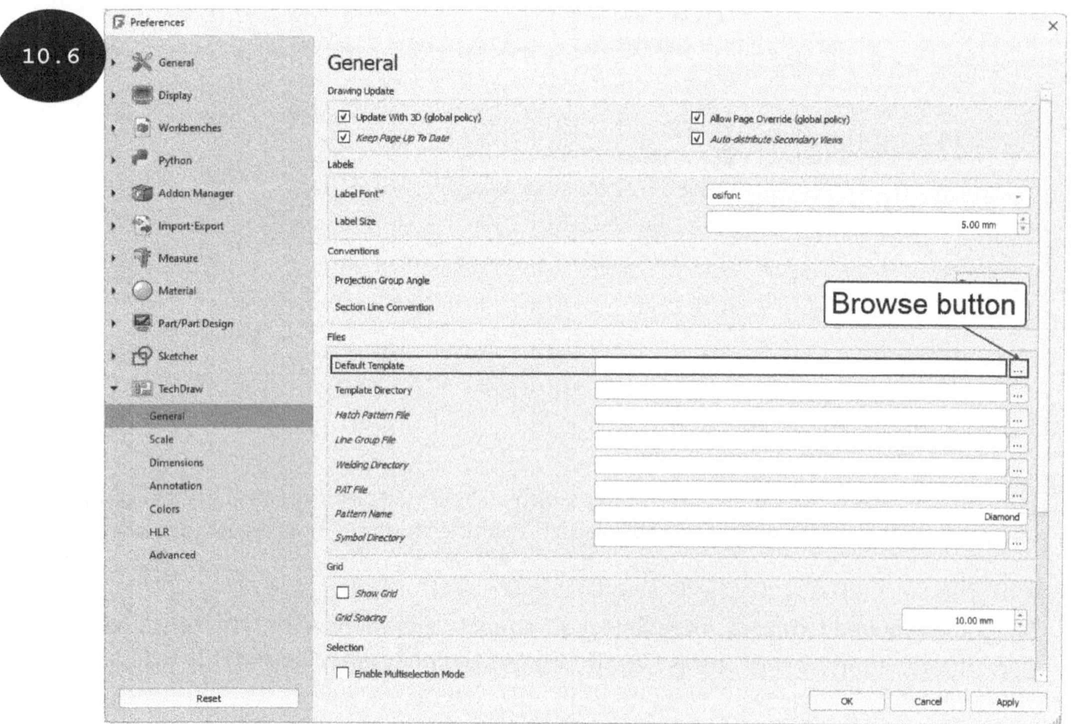

Inserting a Drawing Sheet Using a Selected Template

The method for inserting a drawing sheet using a selected template is discussed below:

1. Click on the **Insert Page using Template** tool in the **TechDraw Pages** toolbar, see Figure 10.7. The **Select a Template File** window appears with a list of available drawing templates, see Figure 10.8.

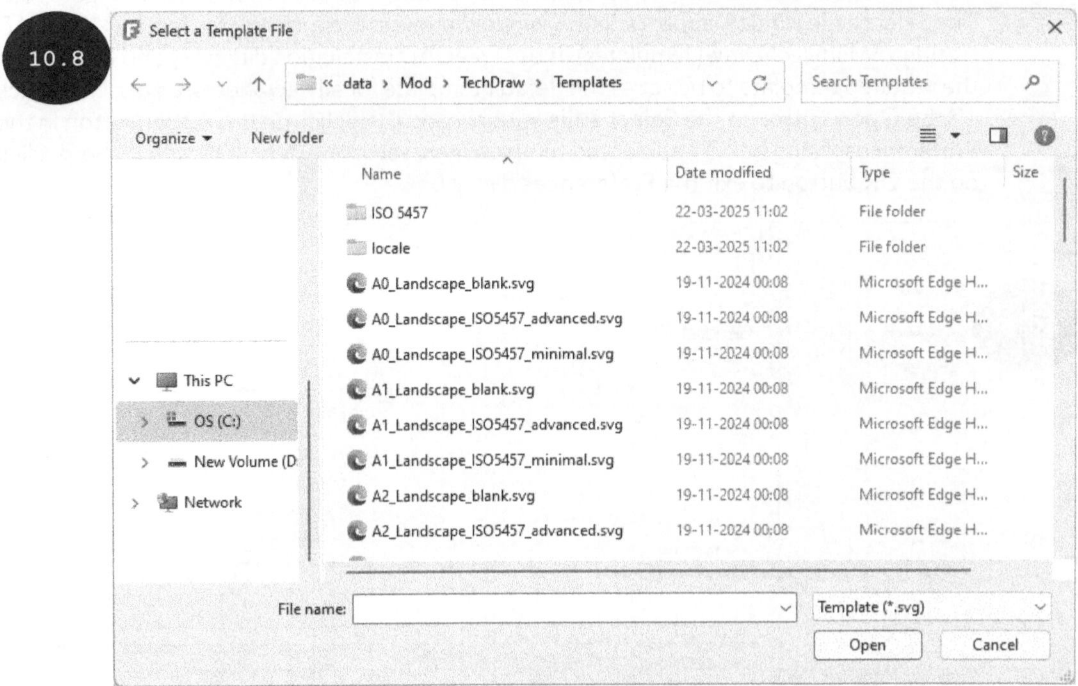

Tip: FreeCAD has various drawing templates with pre-defined drafting standards to create drawing views of a model. A template controls size, drafting standard, border, etc. of a sheet.

2. Select the required template in the **Select a Template File** window and then click on the **Open** button. A new drawing sheet (page) of the selected template gets inserted with a default name in a new separate tab and becomes active by default, see Figure 10.9.

Tip: In Figure 10.9, a drawing sheet of **A2_Landscape_ISO5457_advanced** template is inserted for creating drawing views.

Note: In FreeCAD, you can switch between different drawing sheets (pages) and the 3D model at any point in time by clicking on the respective tab available at the lower left corner of the drawing display area, see Figure 10.10.

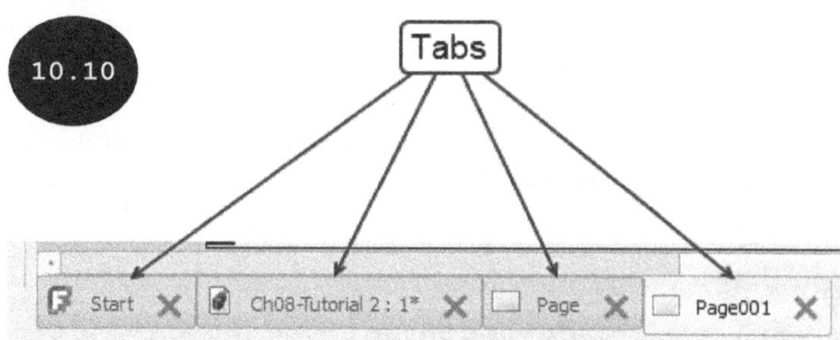

Editing Title Block Text of a Sheet

A drawing sheet/template contains the editable text for attributes such as Designed by Name, Date, Title, Subtitle, Scale, and Drawing number in its title block. These editable texts are highlighted in green color in the title block of the sheet. The method for editing an editable text of a sheet is discussed below:

1. Click on the highlighted portion of a text to be edited in the title block of the sheet, see Figure 10.11. The **Change Editable Field** dialog box appears, see Figure 10.12.

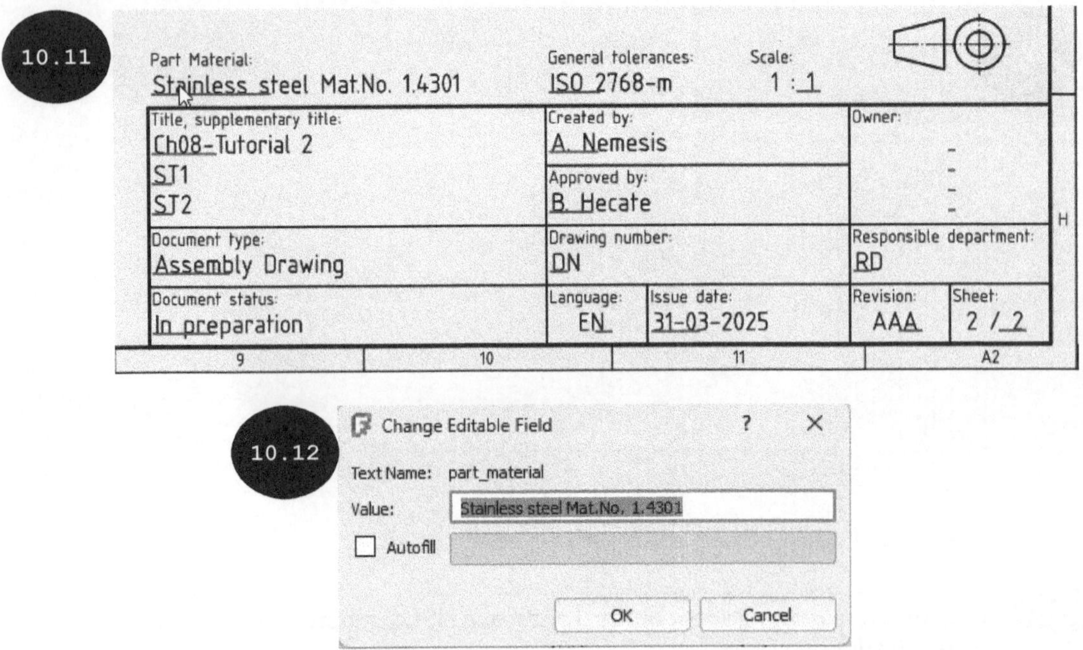

2. Enter a new text in the **Value** field of the dialog box, as required, and then click on the **OK** button. The text gets modified in the title block, as specified.

3. Similarly, you can edit the remaining editable texts of the sheet one by one by clicking on them.

Creating Drawing Views

After creating or opening a 3D model and inserting a drawing sheet of a specified template, you can start creating 2D drawing views of the model. The method for creating an independent 2D projection views of the 3D model is discussed below:

1. Switch to the 3D model by clicking on its tab at the lower left corner of the drawing display area whose drawing view is to be created, see Figure 10.13.

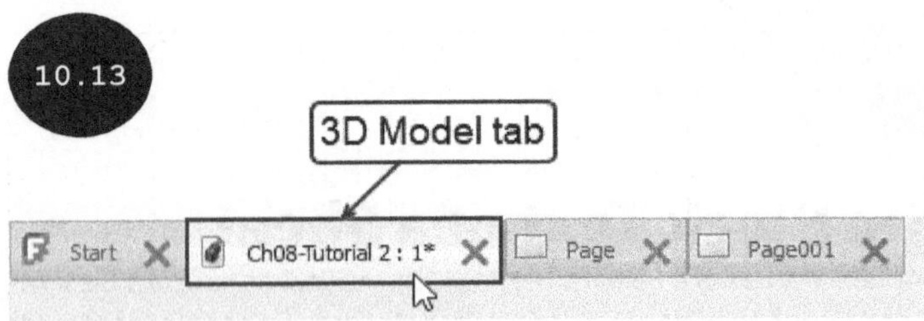

2. Click on the model "**Body**" in the **Tree View** to create its view on the sheet, see Figure 10.14. You can also select a face of the model in the 3D View area for creating its drawing views on the sheet.

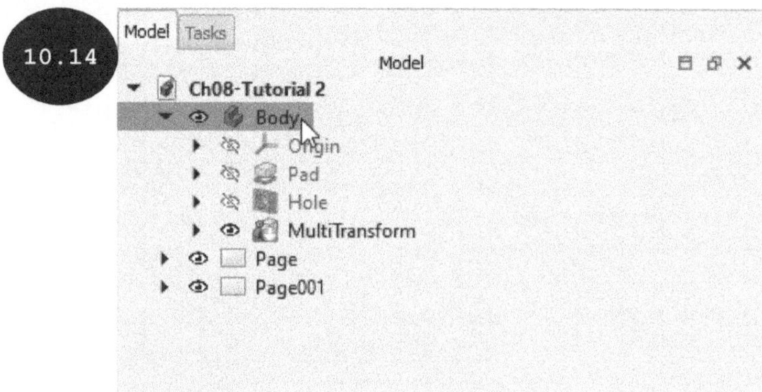

3. After selecting a body of the design in the 3D View area, switch to the drawing sheet (page) by clicking on its respective tab to create the drawing view of the selected model, see Figure 10.15.

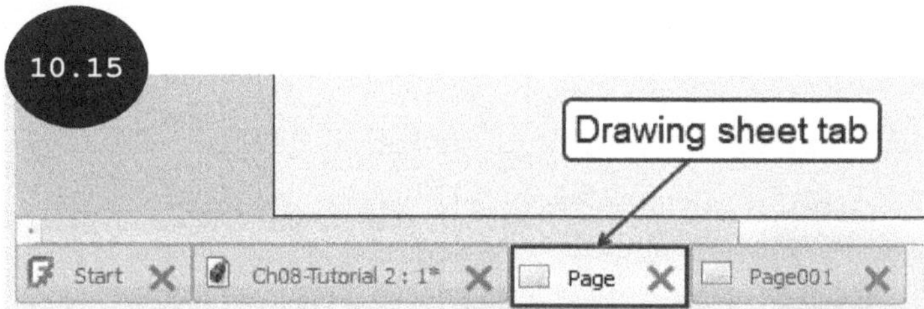

4. Click on the **Insert View** tool in the **TechDraw Views** toolbar, see Figure 10.16. The front view of the selected model gets created on the drawing sheet (page) with default settings, see Figure 10.17. Additionally, the **Part View** sub-window appears in the **Tasks Panel**, allowing you to control the current view orientation of the model and create secondary projection views, see Figure 10.18.

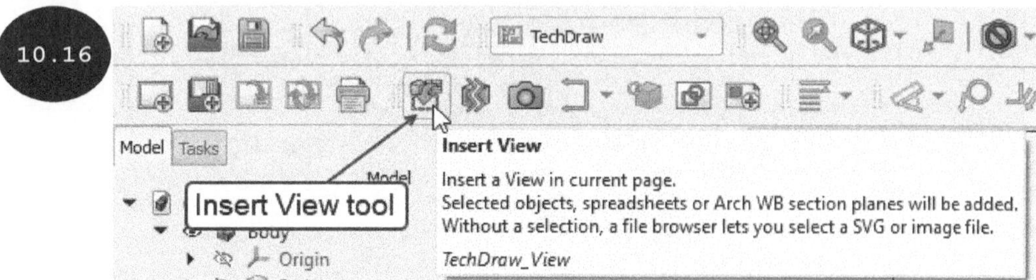

Insert View: The **Insert View** tool is used for creating an independent 2D projection view of the selected model on the drawing sheet (page).

Note: If the model whose views are to be created is not selected before invoking the **Insert View** tool, the **FreeCAD** message window will appear, informing you that an existing object must be selected before using this tool. However, if no object is selected, a file browser will open instead, allowing you to insert an **SVG** or **image** file to represent the model view.

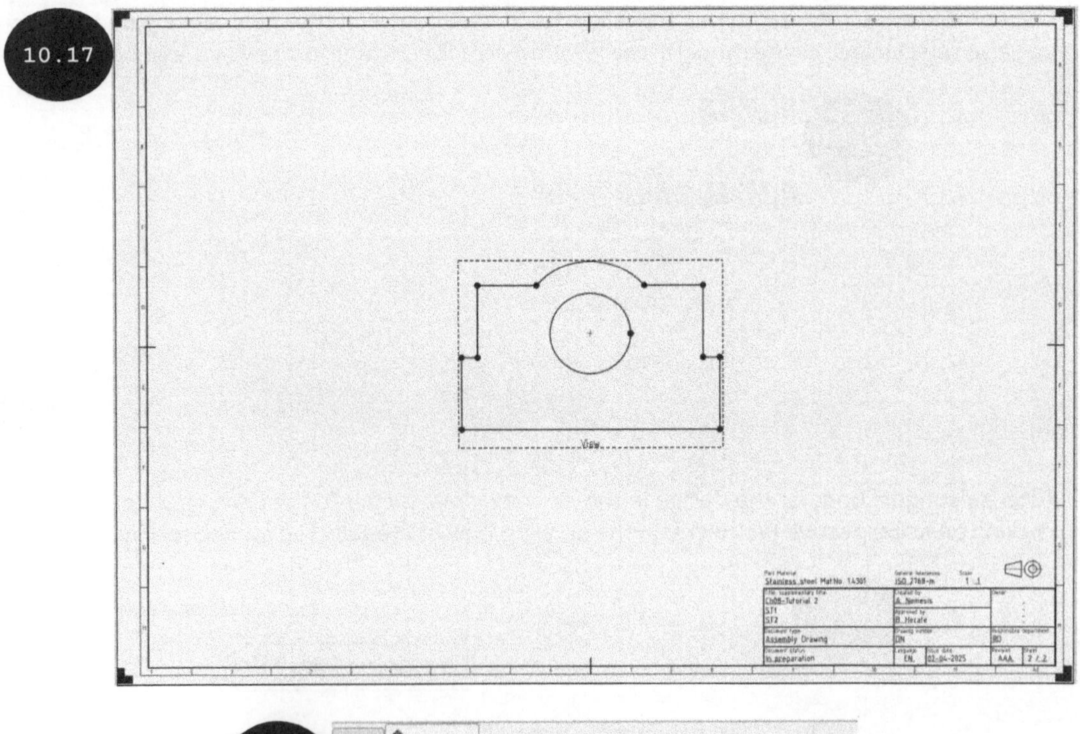

10.17

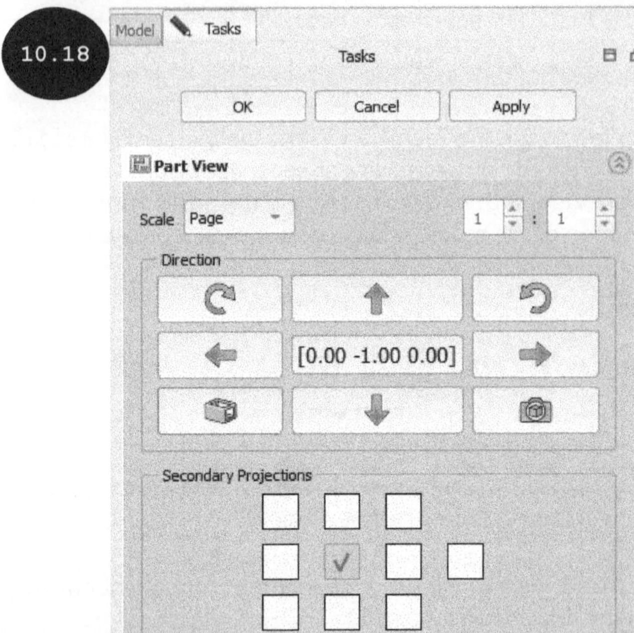

10.18

The options in the **Part View** sub-window of the **Tasks Panel** are discussed below:

Scale: The options (**Page**, **Automatic**, and **Custom**) in the **Scale** drop-down list are used for defining a scale factor for the views. The options to define a scale are discussed below:

Direction: The **Page** option is used to set the view scale as per the default specified scale of the sheet (page). This option is selected, by default. As a result, when you create a view, it displays on the sheet as per the default sheet (page) scale.

Automatic: The **Automatic** option is used to set the view scale automatically, to fit it on the sheet (page).

Custom: The **Custom** option is used to set a custom scale for the selected view. On selecting this option, the **Scale** field gets enabled below the **Scale Type** drop-down list in the **Property Editor**, refer to Figure 10.18. In this field, you can specify a custom scale value for the selected view, as required, and then press ENTER. Note that a scale factor like 1:2 can be written as 0.5 (1/2).

5. Select the required option (**Page**, **Automatic**, or **Custom**) to define the scale of the drawing view, as discussed above.

   Direction: The four arrows in the **Direction** area of the **Tasks Panel** are used for adjusting the orientation of the primary view of the model. Note that each time you click on an arrow in this area, the primary view of the model rotates at an incremental angle of 90 degrees along the direction of the corresponding arrow.

6. If needed, change the current view orientation of the model using the direction arrows in the **Direction** section of the **Part View** sub-window.

   Secondary Projections: The check boxes in the **Secondary Projections** area of the **Tasks Panel** are used for creating the respective projection views such as the **Top**, **Right**, **Left**, and **Isometric** of the primary view. Note that the creation of projection views, by selecting the check boxes, depends on the angle of projection selected in the **Projection** drop-down list of the **Tasks Panel**.

7. Once the desired base view is set, you can create additional secondary projection views by selecting the corresponding check boxes in the **Secondary Projections** section of the **Tasks Panel**, refer to Figure 10.19. In this figure, Top and Side views check boxes are selected to create the correcponding secondary projection views of the Front view.

8. Select the required angle of projection for creating the projection views in the **Projection** drop-down list that enabled in the **Secondary Projections** section of the **Tasks Panel**, see Figure 10.19.

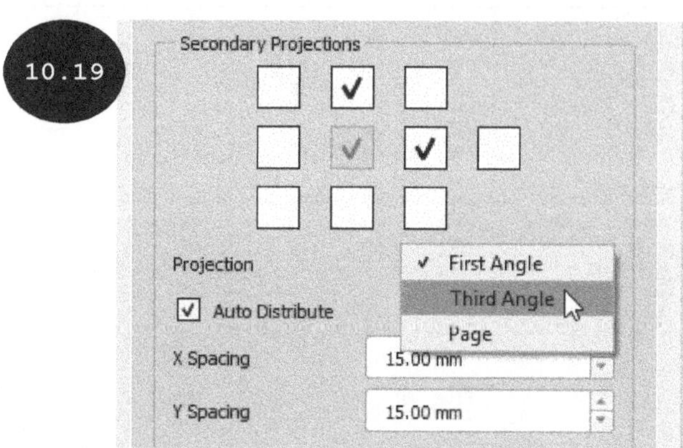

Tip: If needed, you can move the primary view of the model to a new location on the sheet, as required. To do this, move the cursor over the outer frame of the primary view on the sheet and then drag it to a new location by pressing and holding the left mouse button. Notice that when you move the primary view, all its linked projection views will also be moved, accordingly. You can also move an individual projected view of a model by dragging its frame.

9. If needed, you can also control the spacing between the projection views and the base view using the **X Spacing** and **Y Spacing** fields in the **Tasks Panel**. After entering the desired values, click the **Apply** button to confirm the changes.

10. After defining the required settings, click on the **OK** button in the **Tasks Panel**. The drawing view of specified settings gets created on the sheet, see Figure 10.20.

10.20

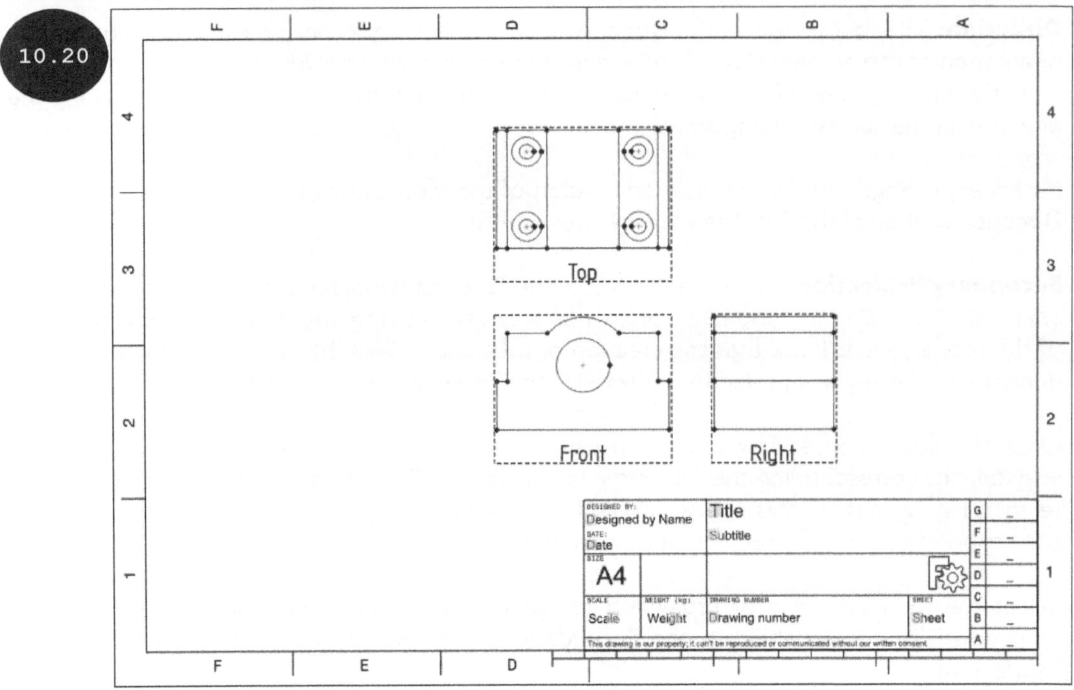

Modifying the Scale of a 2D Projection View

After creating a 2D projection view, you may need to further modify its scale value to adjust its display on the sheet (page), as required. The method for modifying the scale of a view is discussed below:

1. Select a drawing view in the sheet (page) whose scale value is to be modified. The **Property Editor** appears at the lower section of the **Model** tab in the **Combo View** with **View** and **Data** tabs at its bottom, see Figure 10.21.

2. Click on the **Data** tab at the bottom of the **Property Editor** to display the properties of the selected view, see Figure 10.21.

10.21

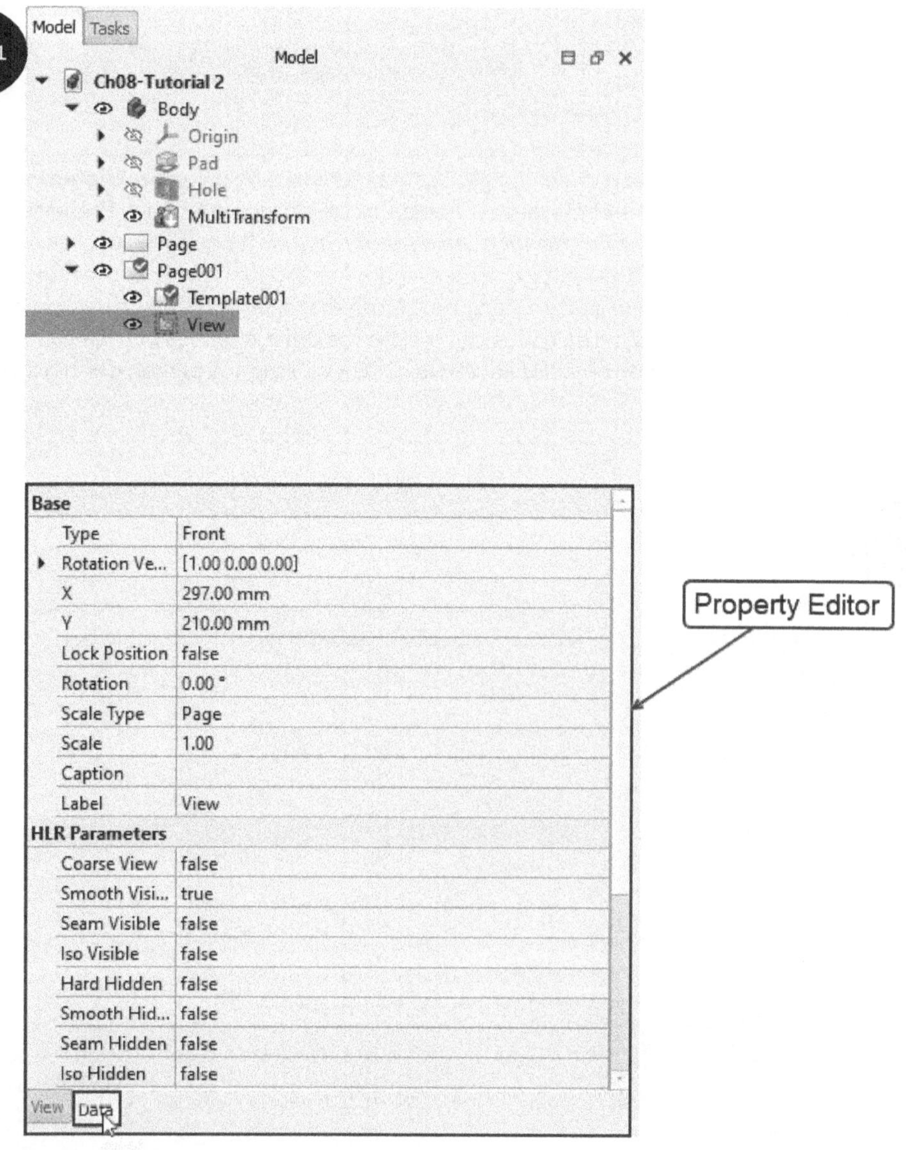

3. Click twice on the **Scale Type** field in the **Property Editor** and then select the **Custom** option in the drop-down list that appears, see Figure 10.22. The options in this drop-down list are discussed earlier.

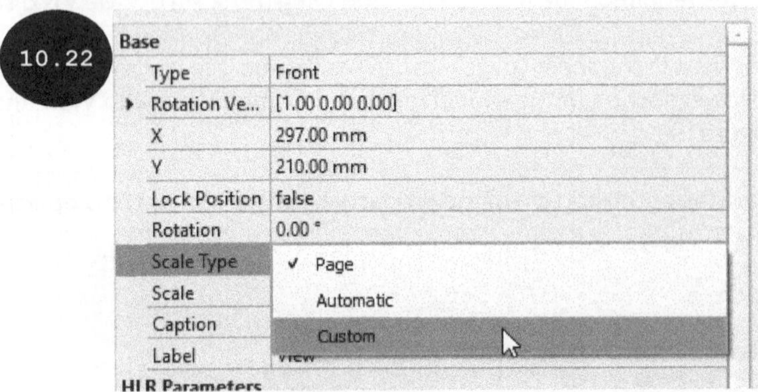

Note: You can set the default sheet (page) scale as required by using the **Preferences** dialog box. To do this, invoke the **Preferences** dialog box by clicking on **Edit > Preferences** in the **File** toolbar and then click on the **TechDraw** section in its left panel. Next, click on the **Scale** tab on the right panel of the dialog box (see Figure 10.23) and then enter the required scale valve in the **Page Scale** field of the dialog box. Note that the modified values of the items/fields that appear in *italics* in the dialog box will be the default values of the new objects and will not affect the existing objects/views. Next, click on **Apply** and then **OK** button in the dialog box.

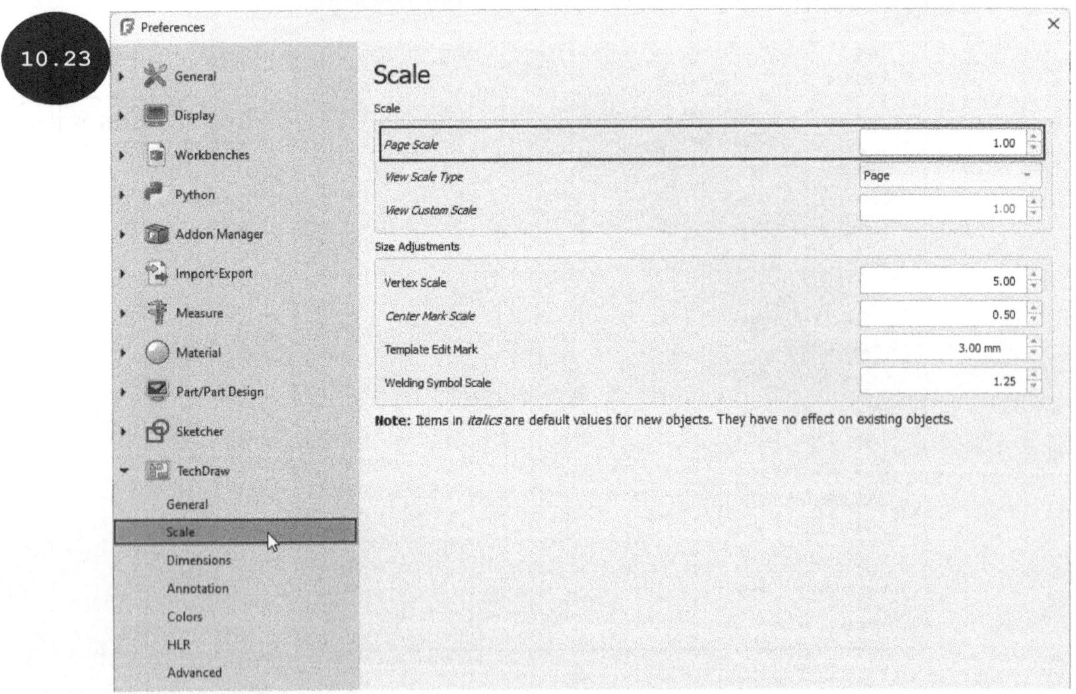

4. After selecting the **Custom** option in the **Scale Type** drop-down list of the **Property Editor**, enter the required scale value for the selected view in the **Scale** field, see Figure 10.24. Next, press ENTER.

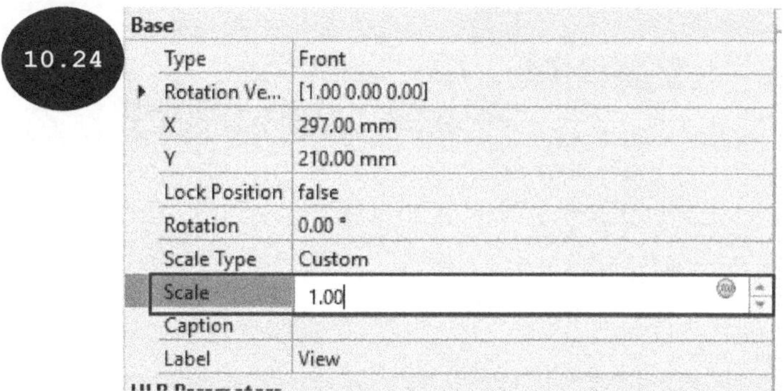

5. Click on the **Redraw Page** in the **TechDraw Pages** toolbar, see Figure 10.25. The drawing view gets updated on the sheet as per the newly defined scale value.

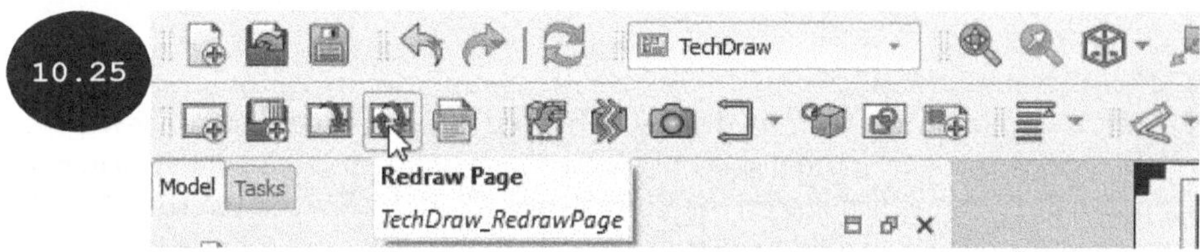

Note: To delete an existing drawing view of a model, select the view to be deleted on the sheet (page) and then press the DELETE key.

Displaying Hidden Lines on the Views

In FreeCAD, you can toggle the display of hidden lines/edges of the model on the 2D projection views. The method for displaying the hidden lines/edges of the model on the views is discussed below.

1. Select one or more 2D projection views on the sheet (page) by clicking the left mouse button on the respective outer frame/boundary to display the hidden lines. Note that you need to press and hold the CTRL key to select multiple views in **Tree View**. The **Property Editor** appears at the lower section of the **Model** tab in the **Combo View** with **View** and **Data** tabs, refer to Figure 10.26.

2. Click on the **Data** tab at the bottom of the **Property Editor** to display the properties of the selected views, refer to Figure 10.26.

3. Click twice on the **Hard Hidden** field in the **Property Editor** and then select the **true** option in the drop-down list that appears, see Figure 10.26.

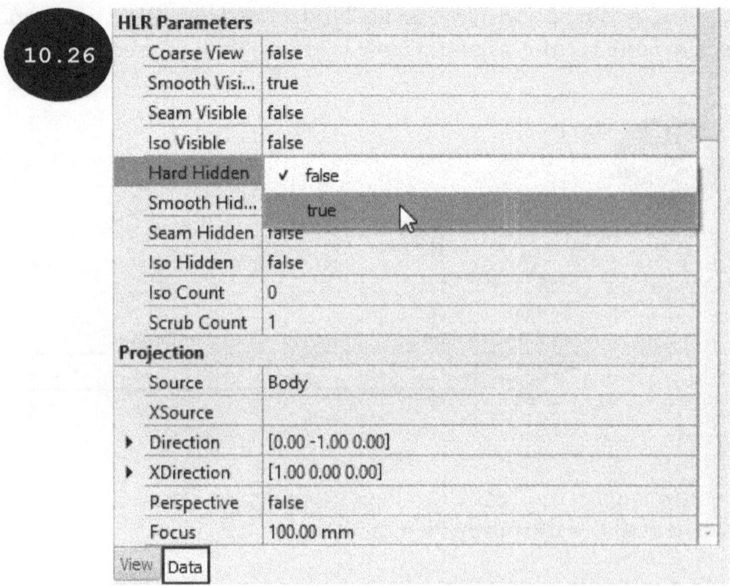

Note: The **true** option turns ON the display of hidden lines on the selected views, whereas the **false** option turns OFF the display of hidden lines on the selected views. You may need to update the views by clicking on the **Refresh** tool in the **File** toolbar to reflect the change made in the display of hidden lines.

4. Click anywhere on the sheet. The display of hidden lines gets turned ON in the selected views with the default hidden line style, see Figure 10.27.

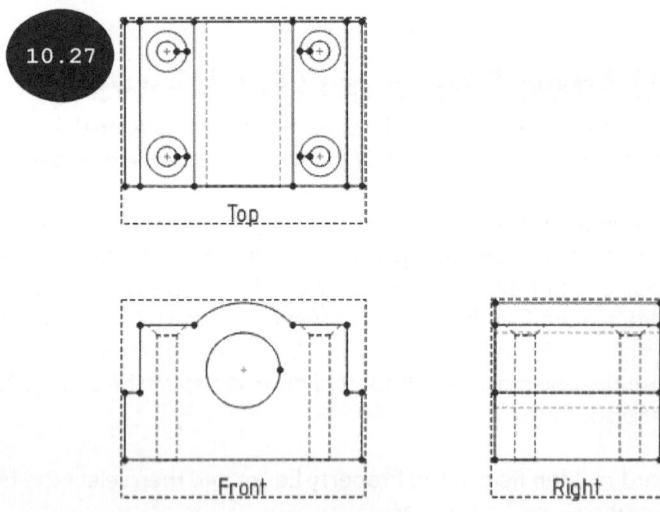

Note: In FreeCAD, you can set the default hidden line style to control the display of hidden lines of views using the **Preferences** dialog box. To do this, invoke the **Preferences** dialog box by clicking on **Edit > Preferences** in the **File** toolbar and then click on the **TechDraw** section in its left panel. Next, select the **Annotation** option and then select the required line type in the **Hidden Line Style** drop-down list of the **Lines** area as the default hidden line style, see Figure 10.28. Next, click on the **Apply** button and then the **OK** button in the dialog box to confirm the change made and exit the dialog box.

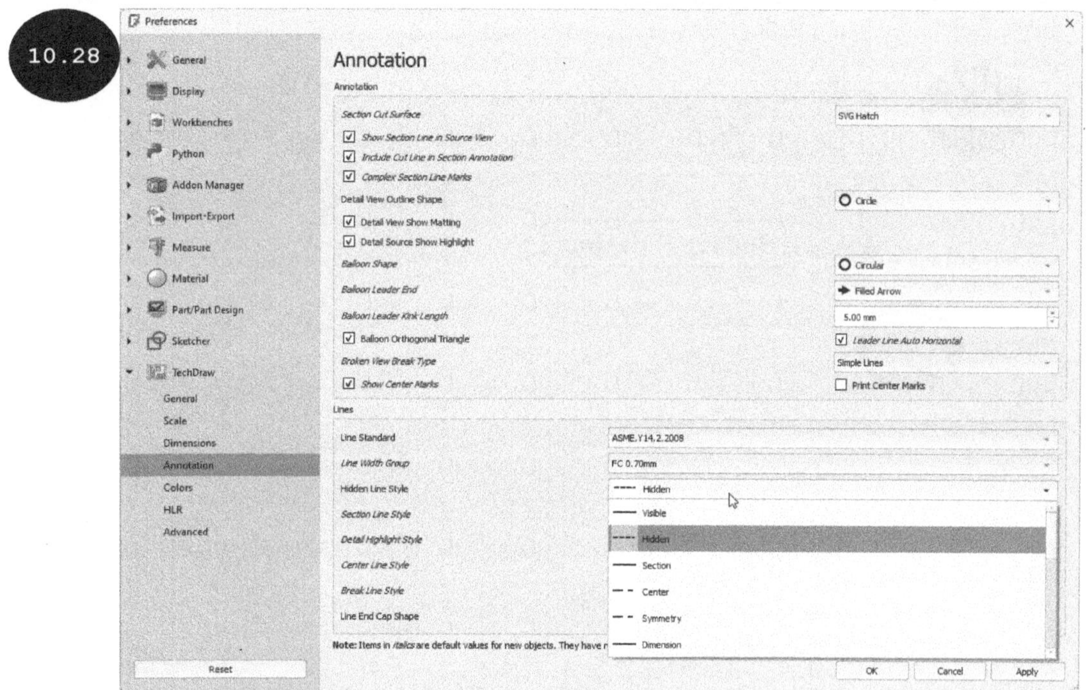

Creating a Section View

A section view is created by cutting a model using a section line and then viewing it from the direction normal to the section line. A section view represents a cross-section of a model to illustrate its internal details. In FreeCAD, you can create a section view by using the **Section View** tool and **Complex Section** tool.

The **Section View** tool is used for creating a simple section view with the help of a predefined section line, whereas the **Complex Section** tool is used for creating a complex section view with the help of a user-defined sketched section line. The method for creating a section view by using these tools is discussed next.

Creating a Simple Section View

The method for creating a simple section view of an existing drawing view using a predefined section line is discussed below:

1. Select an existing view as the parent view in the 3D View area or in the Tree View for creating the section view.

2. After selecting an existing drawing view, click on the **Section View** tool in the **Section** flyout of the **TechDraw Views** toolbar, see Figure 10.29. The **Create Section View** sub-window appears in the **Tasks Panel**, see Figure 10.30.

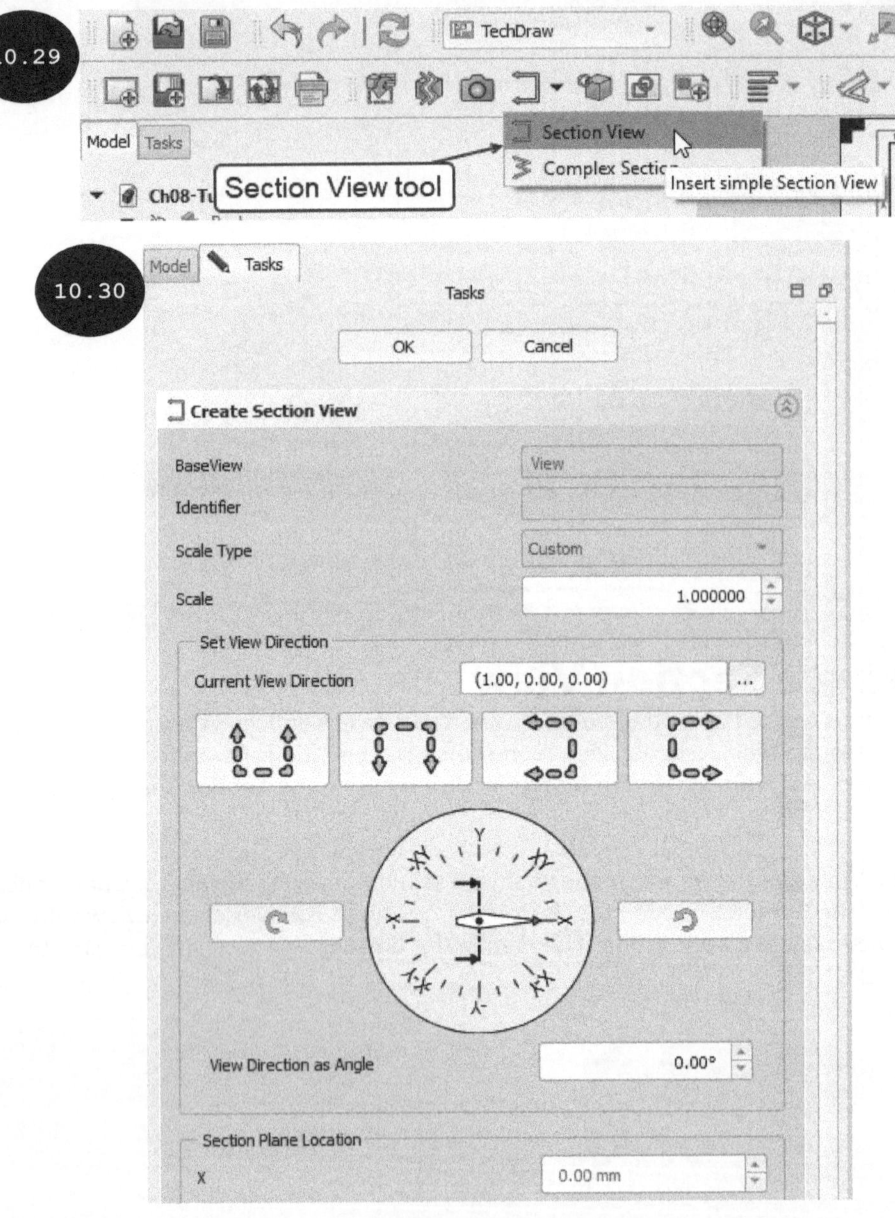

3. Select the required section line button (**Looking up**, **Looking down**, **Looking left**, or **Looking right**) in the **Set View Direction** area of the **Tasks Panel**, see Figure 10.31.

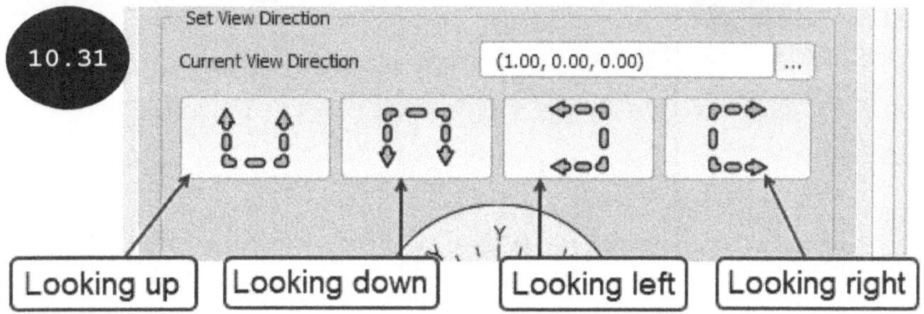

4. Scroll down to the **Preview** area in the **Tasks Panel** and then select the **Live Update** check box. A preview of the respective section view of the model appears on the sheet, see Figure 10.32. You can move the section view to a required location on the sheet by dragging it.

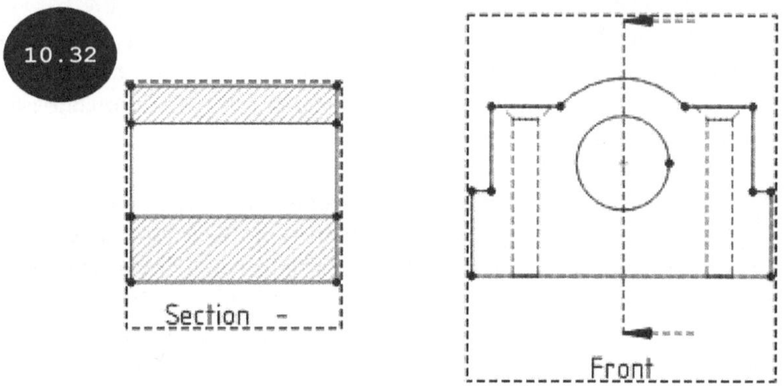

Note: A section view is created by cutting the model using the selected section line and then viewing it from the direction normal to the section line.

The direction of the arrows of the section line represents the viewing direction.

5. Enter the required name for the section line like A, B, C, or D in the **Identifier** field of the **Tasks Panel** and then click anywhere on the sheet. The specified identifier name gets assigned to the section line and section view on the sheet, see Figure 10.33. In this figure, A is specified as the identifier name.

Note: When the **Live Update** check box is selected, the preview of the section view being created updates dynamically on the drawing sheet after every change made in its properties.

The **Update Now** button in the **Preview** area of the **Task Panel** is used to manually update the preview of the section view being created.

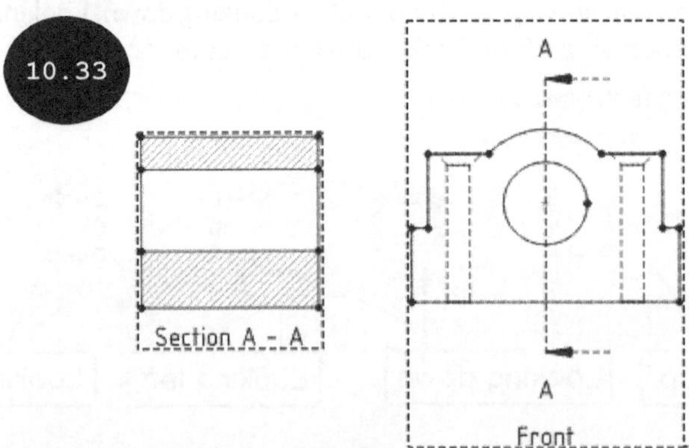

6. Specify the scale of the section view by selecting the required option in the **Scale Type** drop-down list of the **Tasks Panel**.

7. Enter the required X, Y, and Z distance values in the respective fields of the **Section Plane Location** area to define the location of the section line concerning the center of the view. By default, 0 distance is specified in the **X**, **Y**, and **Z** fields. As a result, the section line is created such that it passes through the center of the selected view.

Note: You can also enter an angle value in the **View Direction as Angle** field of the **Task Panel** to rotate the section line concerning the center of the view, see Figure 10.34. You can also use the rotational arrows available in the **Set View Direction** area of the **Task Panel** to define the rotation angle of the section line, see Figure 10.34. By default, the orientation (angle) of the section line is defined based on the button (**Looking up**, **Looking down**, **Looking left**, or **Looking right**) activated in the **Set View Direction** area of the **Task Panel**.

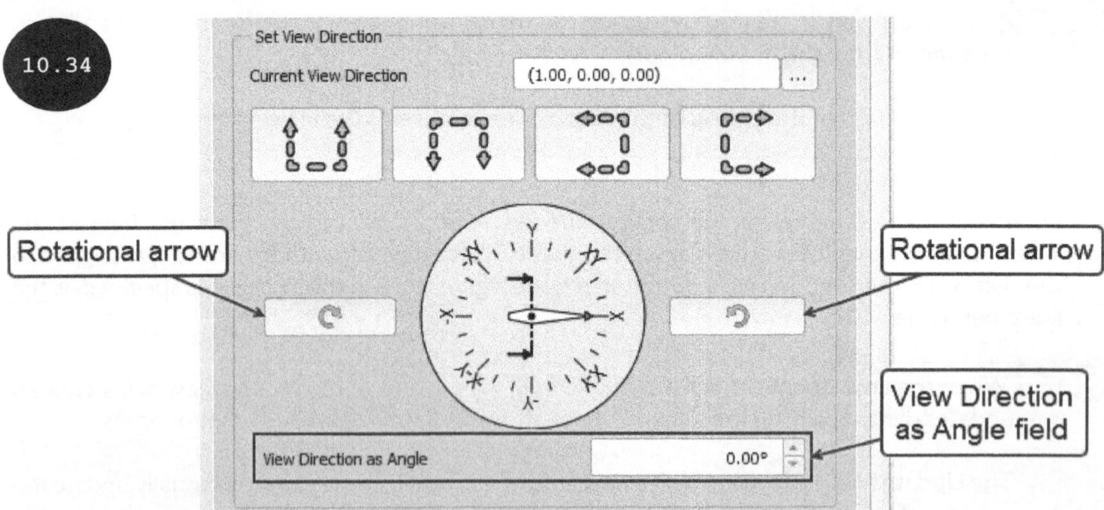

8. Click on the **OK** button in the **Tasks Panel** to confirm the creation of the section view. A section view of the specified section line and parameters gets created. You can move the section view to the required location on the sheet by dragging it after pressing and holding the left mouse button.

Note: If needed, you can control or edit the scale of the hatching lines of the section view. To do this, select the section view by clicking the left mouse button. The **Property Editor** appears at the lower section of the **Model** tab in the **Combo View** with **View** and **Data** tabs, refer to Figure 10.26. Ensure that the **Data** tab is activated in the **Property Editor** and then scroll down to display the **Hatch Scale** field, see Figure 10.35. Next, enter the required scale value in the **Hatch Scale** field of the **Property Editor** and click anywhere on the sheet. Figure 10.36 shows a section view with its hatch scale modified from 1 to 3.

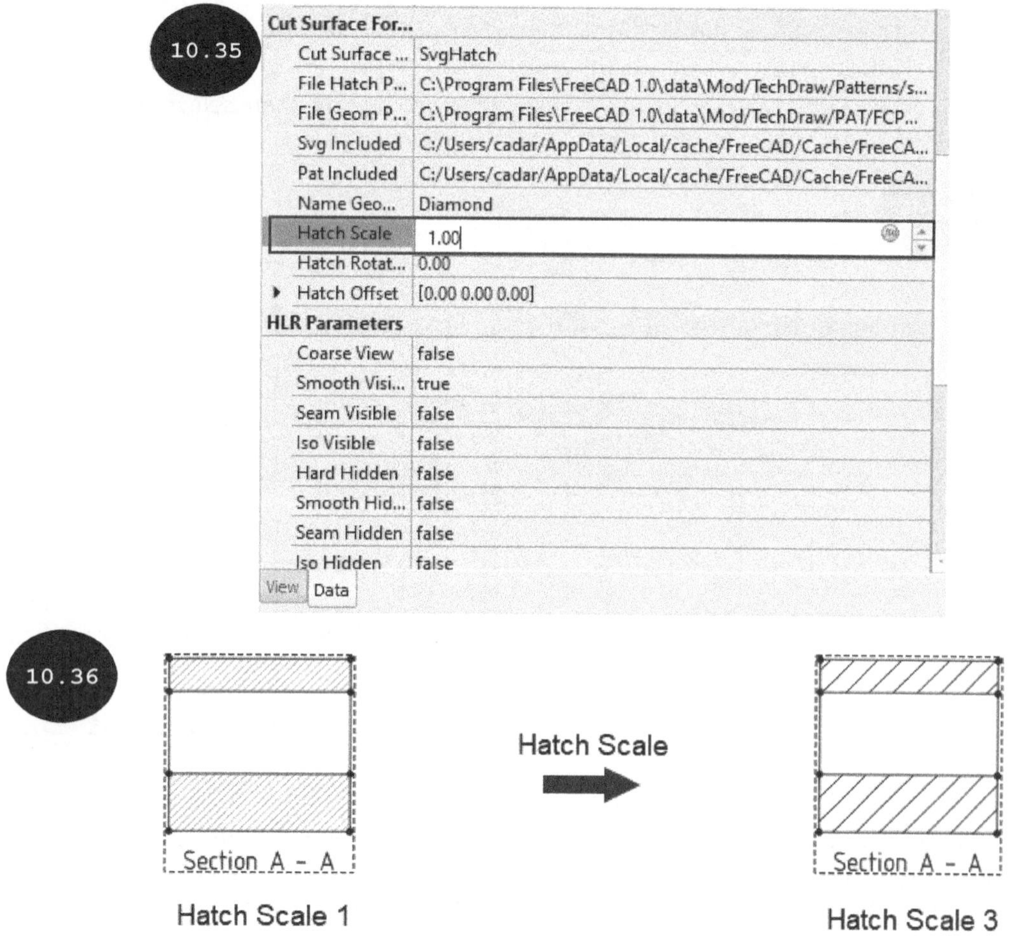

Creating a Complex Section View

The method for creating a complex section view of an existing drawing view using a user-defined sketched section line is discussed below:

1. Switch to the 3D model by clicking on its tab at the lower left corner of the drawing display area whose drawing view is created, see Figure 10.37.

Note: To create a complex section view, you need to first create an open sketch as the section line on the model in the 3D View area.

10.37

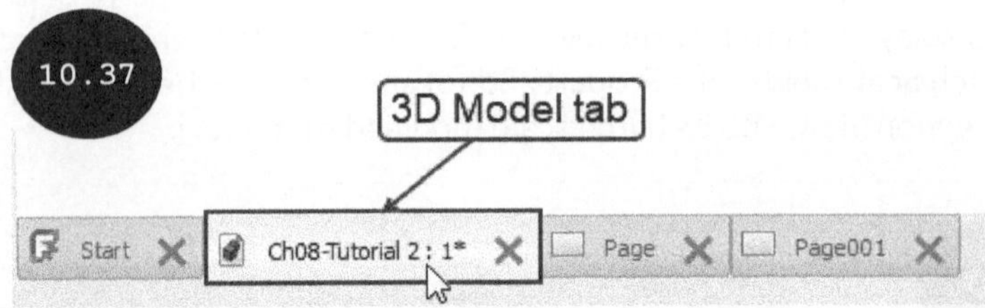

2. Invoke the **Workbench Selector** in the **Workbench** toolbar and then select the **Sketcher** workbench, see Figure 10.38. The **Sketcher** workbench gets invoked.

10.38

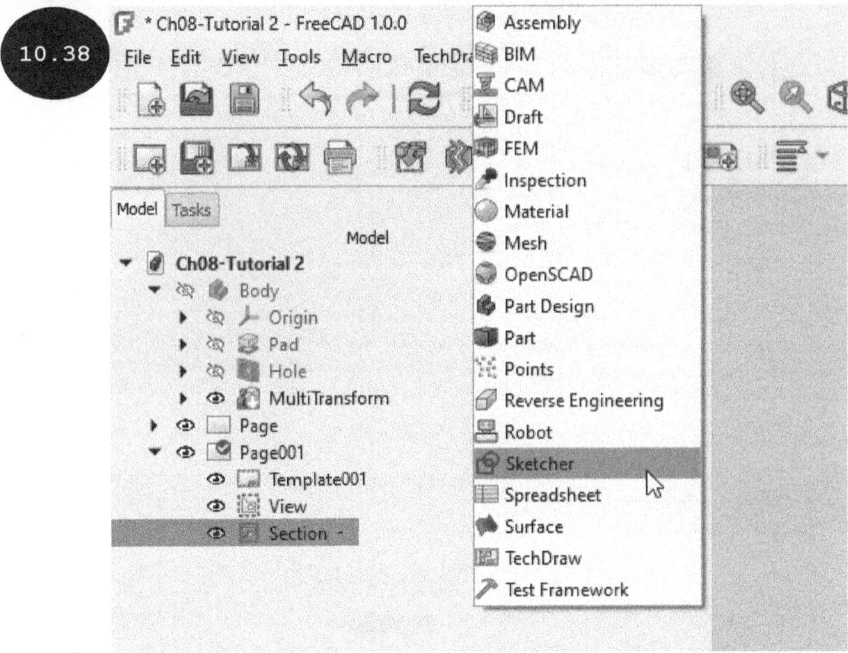

3. After invoking the **Sketcher** workbench, click on the **Create sketch** tool in the **Sketcher** toolbar, see Figure 10.39. The **Choose orientation** dialog box appears in the 3D View area, see Figure 10.40. In this dialog box, select the required radio button (**XY-Plane**, **XZ-Plane**, or **YZ-Plane**) as the sketching plane for creating a section line. If needed, you can also define an offset distance from the selected sketching plane in the **Offset** field of the dialog box to create a section line at an offset distance from the selected sketching plane. Next, click on the **OK** button. The Sketch editing mode of the **Sketcher** workbench gets invoked for creating a sketch.

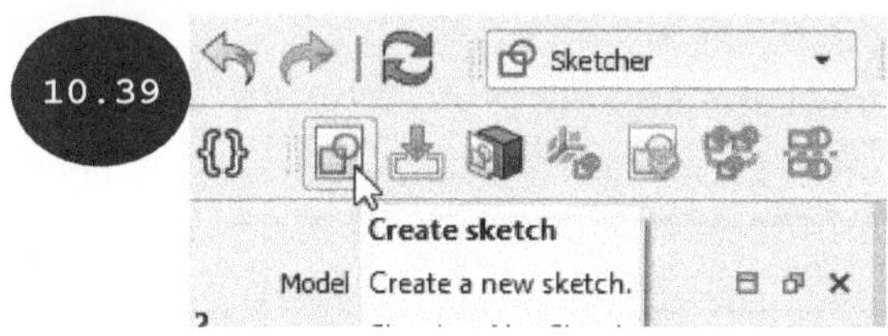

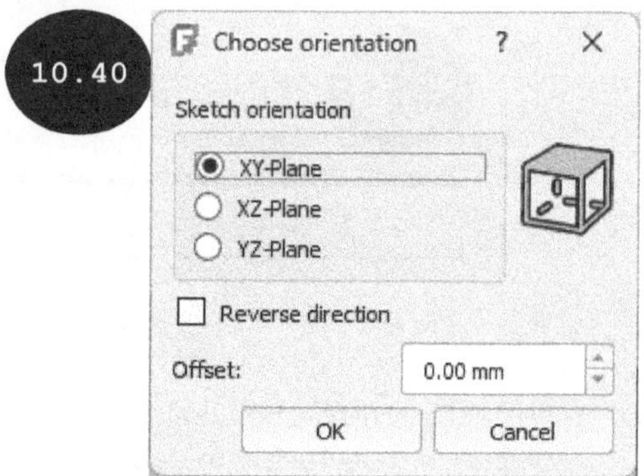

4. Create an open sketch as the section line by using the sketching tools in the **Sketcher** workbench, see Figure 10.41. Note that you can create a section view of the model by activating the **View section** tool to temporarily hide the material that is in front of the sketching plane. This enables easy creation of a section line.

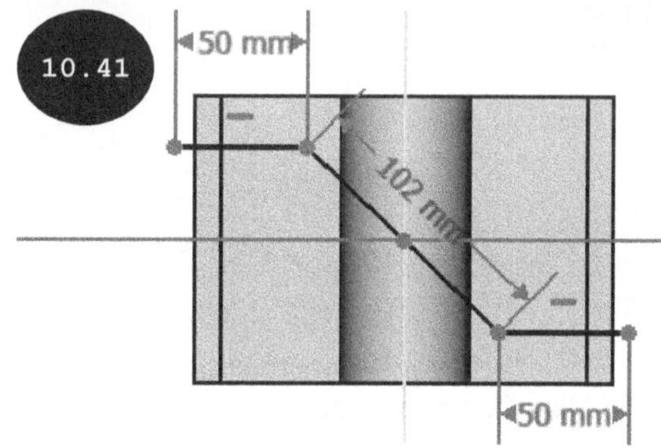

5. After creating an open sketch, exit the **Sketcher** Workbench by clicking on the **Leave sketch** tool in the **Sketcher edit mode** toolbar, see Figure 10.42.

Now, you need to switch to the drawing sheet (page)

6 Switch to the drawing sheet (page) by clicking on its respective tab to create a section view, see Figure 10.43.

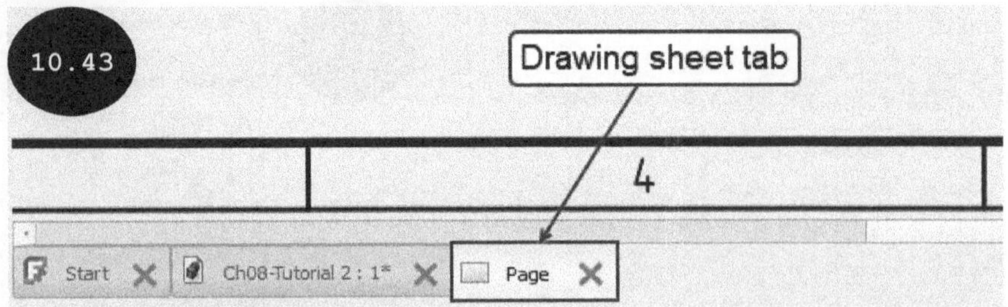

7. Invoke the **Workbench Selector** in the **Workbench** toolbar and then select the **TechDraw** workbench. The **TechDraw** workbench gets invoked.

8. Select a profile of an existing view in the drawing sheet for creating its section view, see Figure 10.44.

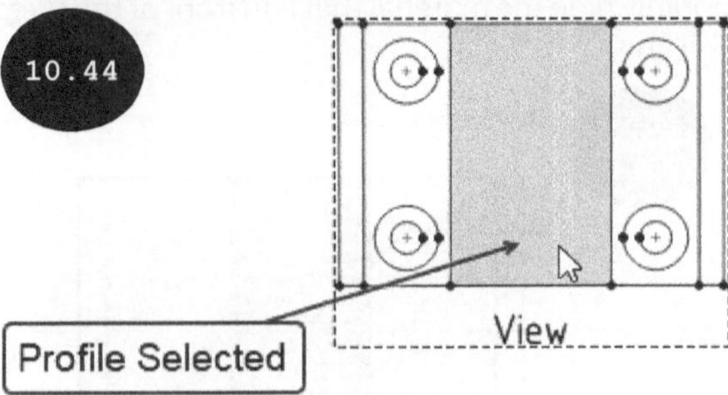

9. Invoke the **Section** flyout in the **TechDraw Views** toolbar and then click on the **Complex Section** tool, see Figure 10.45. The **New Complex Section** sub-window appears in the **Tasks Panel**, see Figure 10.46.

10.46

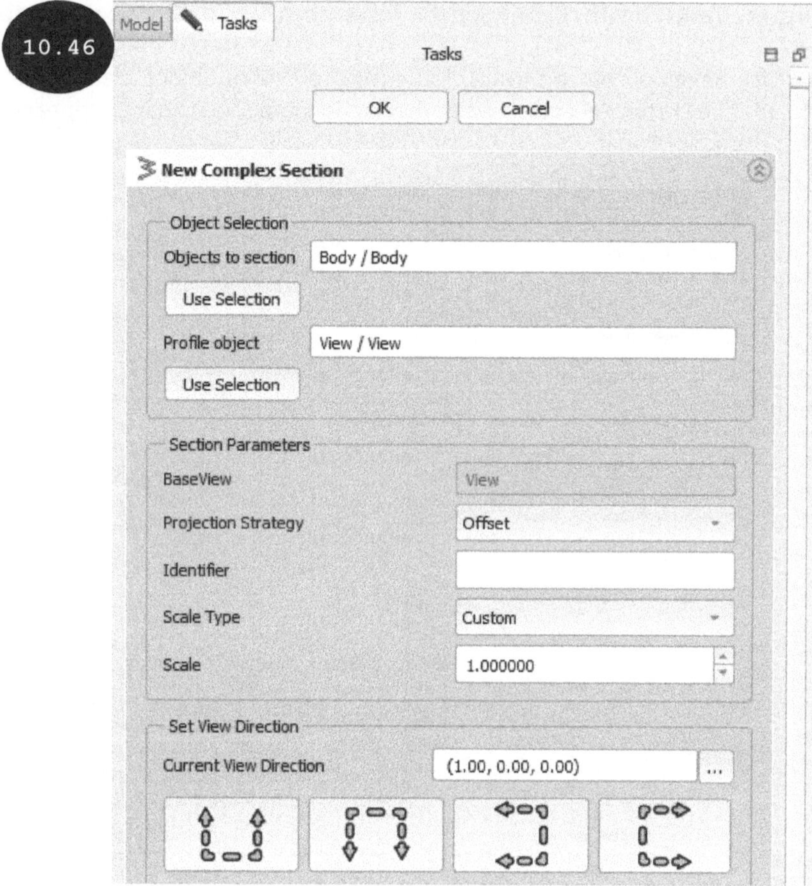

Now, you need to select a section line.

10. Click on the **Model** tab in the **Combo View** to display the **Tree View** of the model, see Figure 10.47.
11. Select an open sketch as the section line in the **Tree View**, see Figure 10.47.

10.47

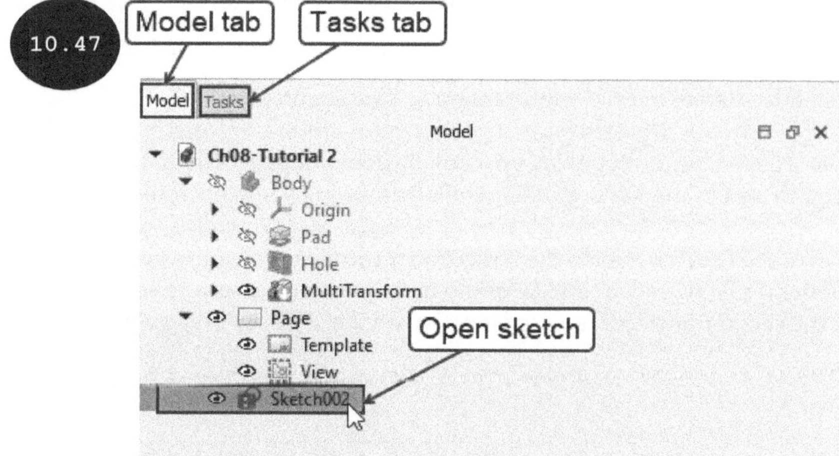

12. Switch back to the **Tasks Panel** by clicking on the **Tasks** tab in the **Combo View**, refer to Figure 10.47.

13. Click on the **Use Selection** button available below the **Profile object** area in the **Tasks Panel**, see Figure 10.48. The sketch gets selected as the section line and its name appears in the **Profile object** field of the **Tasks Panel**.

10.48

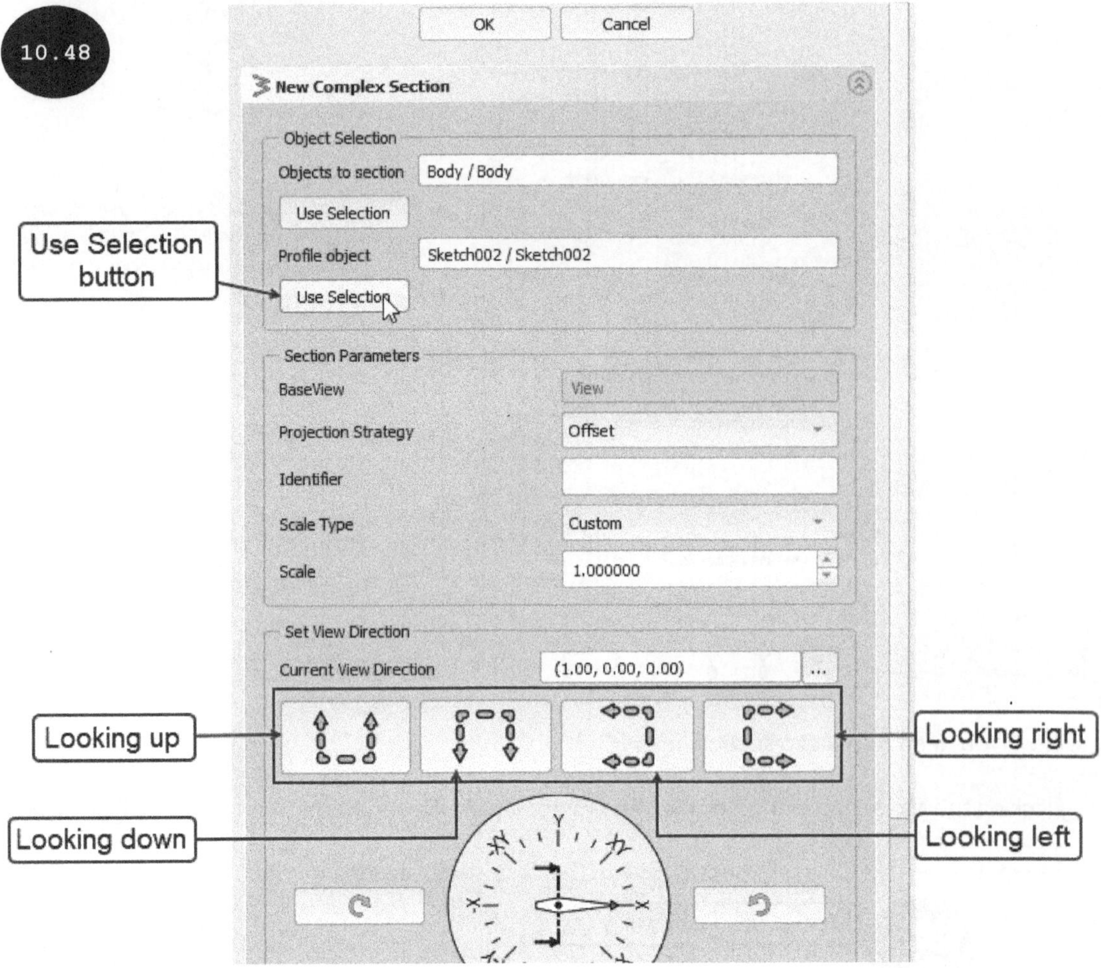

Now, you need to define the viewing direction of the section view.

14. Click on the required button (**Looking up**, **Looking down**, **Looking left**, or **Looking right**) in the **Set View Direction** area of the **Tasks Panel** to define a viewing direction, refer to Figure 10.48.

15. Scroll down to the **Preview** area in the **Tasks Panel** and then select the **Live Update** check box. A preview of the respective section view of the model appears on the sheet, see Figure 10.49. You can move the section view to a required location on the sheet by dragging it.

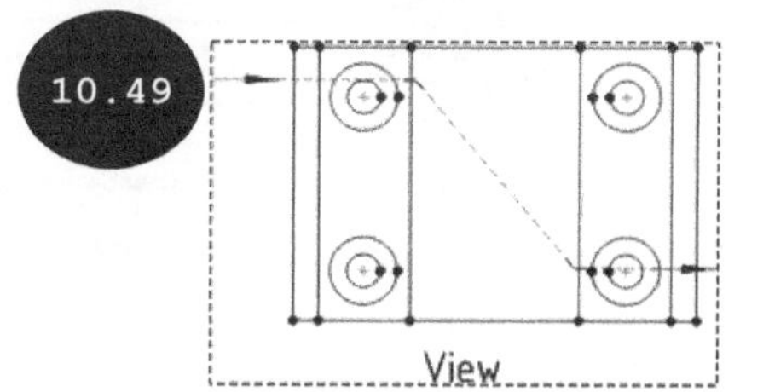

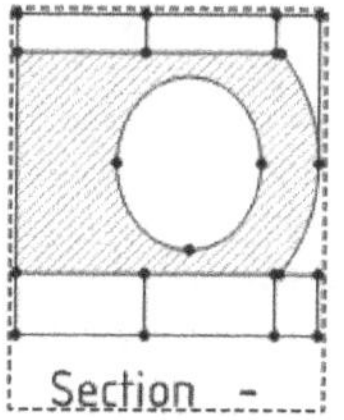

16. Enter the required name for the section line like A, B, C, or D in the **Identifier** field of the **Tasks Panel.**

17. After specifying the required options in the **Tasks Panel,** click on the **OK** button. A section view concerning the section line and the specified parameters gets created, see Figure 10.50. You can move the section view to the required location on the sheet by dragging it after pressing and holding the left mouse button.

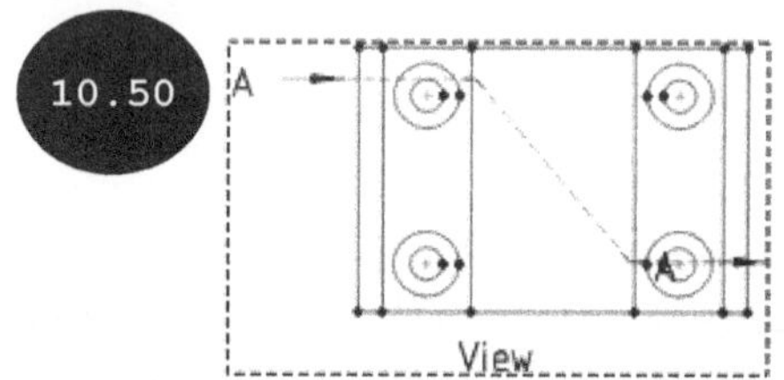

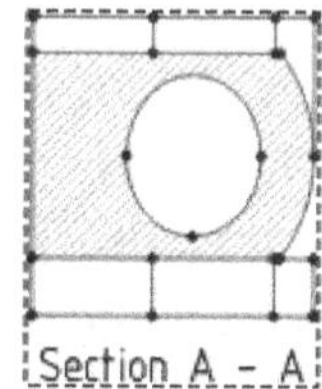

Creating a Detail View

A detail view is used for showing a portion of an existing drawing view on an enlarged scale. The method for creating a detail view is discussed below:

1. Select an existing view as the parent view in the 3D View area or in the **Tree View** to create a detail view.

2. After selecting an existing view, click on the **Insert Detail View** tool in the **TechDraw Views** toolbar, see Figure 10.51. The **New Detail View** sub-window appears in the **Tasks Panel** with default parameters that define a circular portion of the selected view to be detailed, see Figure 10.52. Also, the preview of the detail view that is enclosed inside the circular portion appears on the sheet, see Figure 10.53.

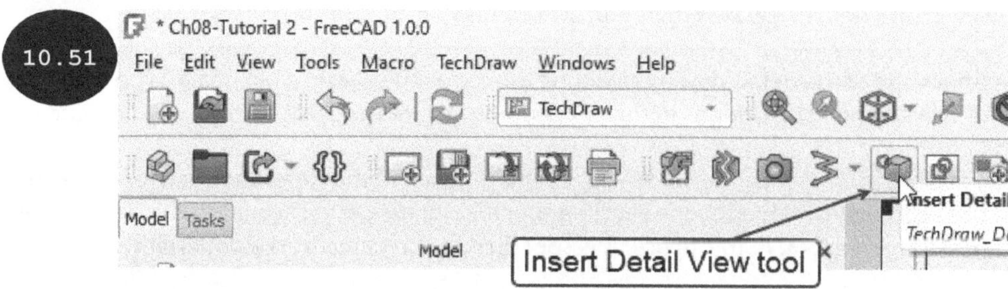

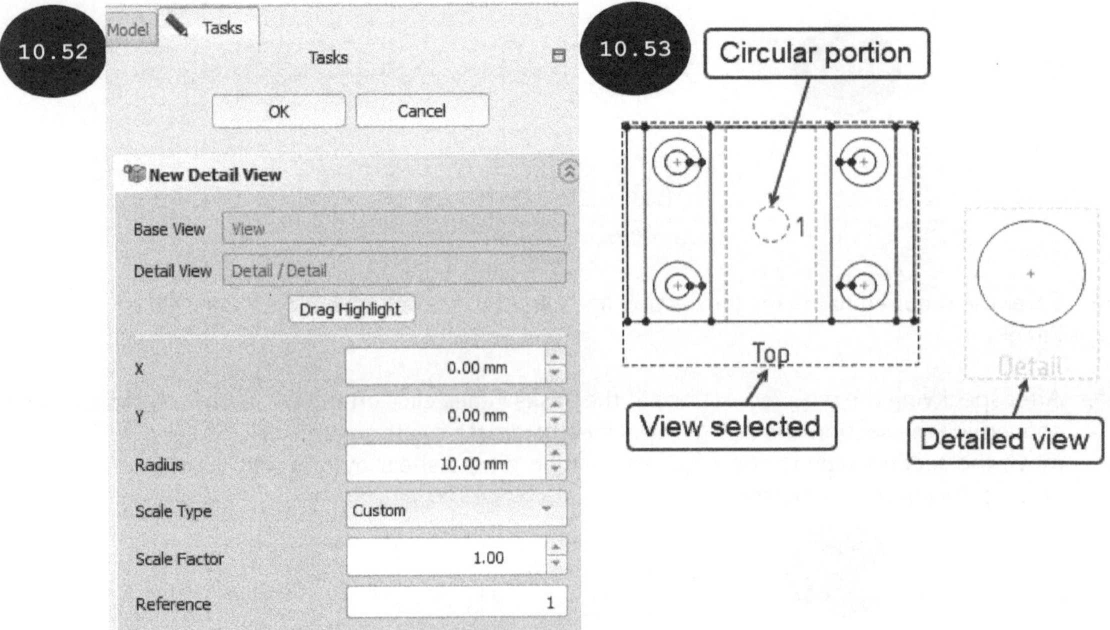

3. Define a new position for the circular portion on the selected view (see Figure 10.53) by entering X and Y distance values in the respective fields of the **Tasks Panel**. The preview of the detail view gets updated accordingly on the sheet. Note that the X and Y distance values measure from the center of the selected view.

Tip: By default, the circular portion is defined at the center of the selected view, since the X and Y distance values are specified as **0** in the respective fields of the **Task Panel**, refer to Figure 10.52.

Note: You can also define the position of the circular portion of the selected view by dragging it. To do this, click on the **Drag Highlight** button in the **Task Panel**. The circular portion gets highlighted on the view. Next, drag and drop the circular portion to the required location on the view to be detailed by pressing and holding the left mouse button.

4. Enter the radius of the circular portion to be detailed in the **Radius** field of the **Tasks Panel**. The preview of the detail view gets updated, accordingly.

5. Specify a scale of the detail view by selecting the required option in the **Scale Type** drop-down list of the **Tasks Panel**. The options in this drop-down list are the same as discussed earlier.

6. Enter a name for the detail view like A, B, C, D, 1, 2, 3, or 4 in the **Reference** field of the **Tasks Panel** and then click anywhere on the sheet. The specified name gets assigned to the detail view on the sheet, see Figure 10.54. In this figure, A is specified as the name of the detail view.

7. Click on the **OK** button in the **Tasks Panel**. A detail view gets created such that a portion of the selected view that is enclosed inside the circular portion gets enlarged, see Figure 10.54. You can move the detail view to the required location on the sheet by dragging it after pressing and holding the left mouse button.

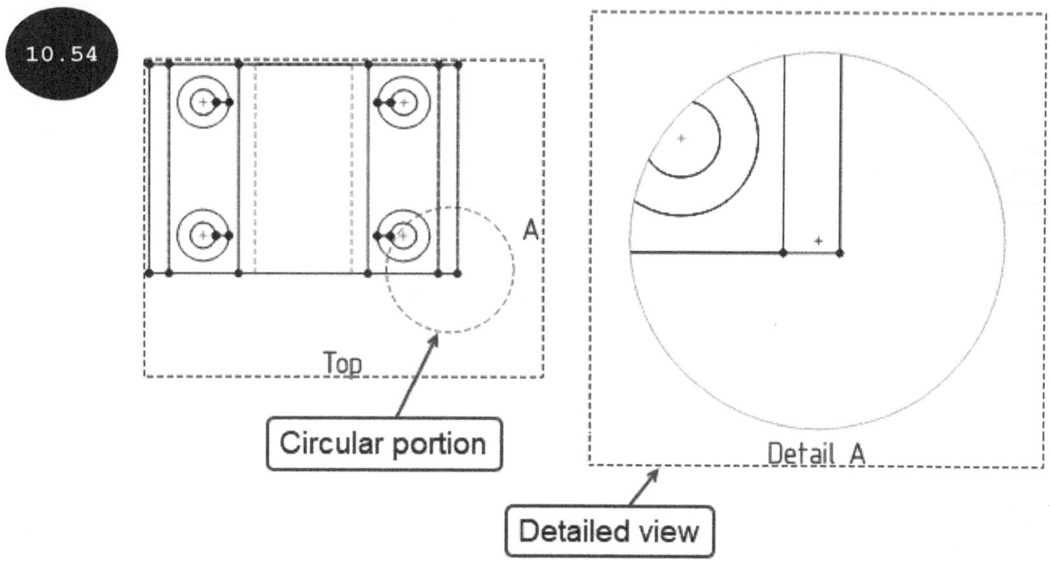

Applying Dimensions

After creating various drawing views of a part or an assembly on a sheet (page), you need to apply dimensions to them. In FreeCAD, you can apply dimensions by using the dimension tools such as **Insert Dimension**, **Insert Length Dimension**, **Insert Horizontal Dimension**, **Insert Radius Dimension**, and **Insert Diameter Dimension** available in the **Dimension** menu of the **TechDraw Dimensions** toolbar, see Figure 10.55.

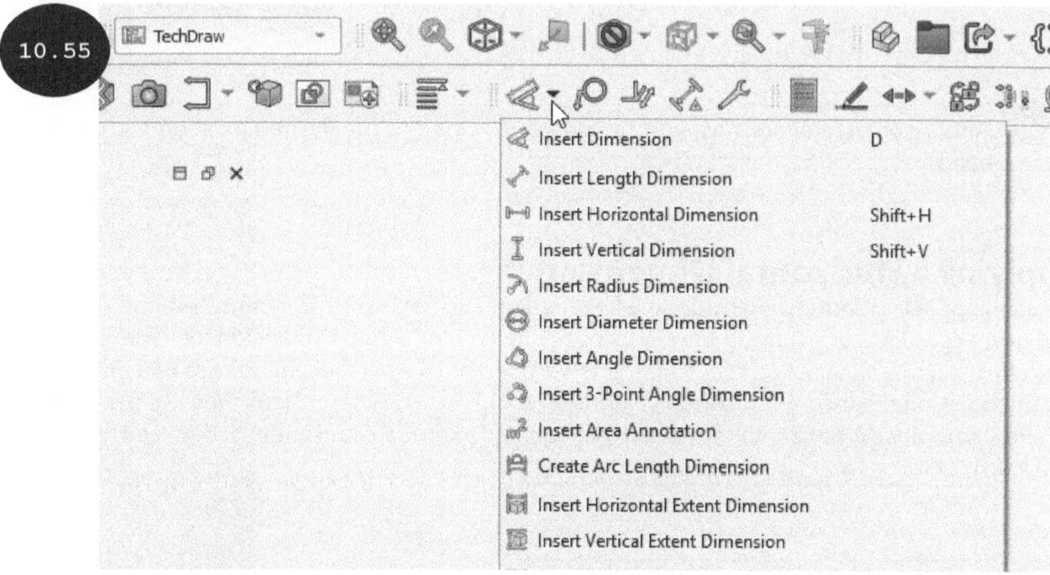

Applying a Length Dimension

You can apply a length dimension to a linear edge/line, between two points/vertices, or between two linear edges/lines of a drawing view by using the **Insert Length Dimension** tool, see Figure 10.56. To do this, select a linear edge/line, two points/vertices, or two parallel edges/lines of a drawing view. Note that you need to press and hold the CTRL key to select two entities for applying a dimension. Next, click on the **Insert Length Dimension** tool in the **Dimensions** menu of the **TechDraw Dimensions** toolbar, refer to Figure 10.55. A length dimension gets applied to the selected entity or between the selected entities.

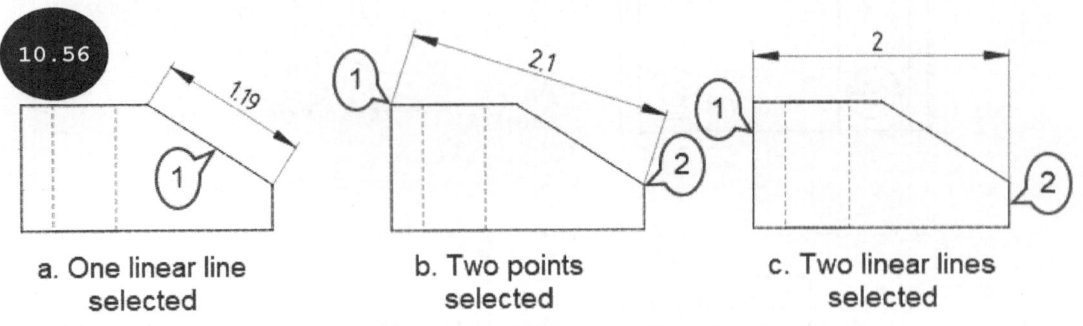

Note: In Figure 10.61, the display of outer frames/boundaries and labels of the views is turned OFF. You can toggle the display of outer frames and labels of views by clicking on the **Turn View Frames On/Off** tool in the **TechDraw Decoration** toolbar, see Figure 10.57.

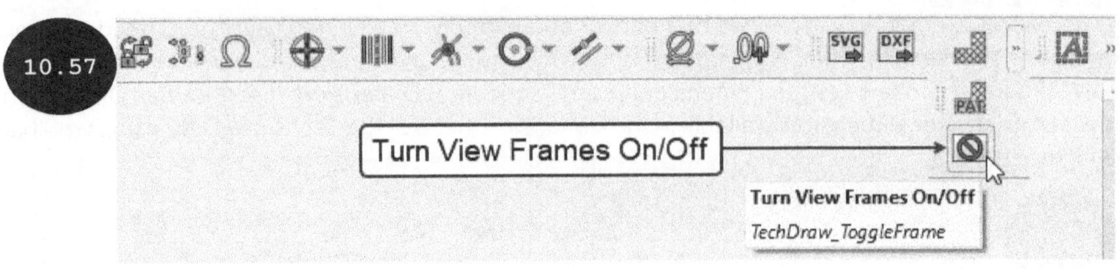

Tip: After applying a dimension, you can drag and drop it to the desired location on the sheet, if needed.

Applying a Horizontal Dimension

You can apply a horizontal dimension to a linear edge/line, between two points/vertices, or between two linear edges/lines of a drawing view by using the **Insert Horizontal Dimension** tool, see Figure 10.58. To do this, select a linear edge/line, two points/vertices, or two parallel edges/lines of a drawing view and then click on the **Insert Horizontal Dimension** tool in the **Dimensions** menu of the **TechDraw Dimensions** toolbar. A horizontal dimension gets applied to the selected entity or between the selected entities.

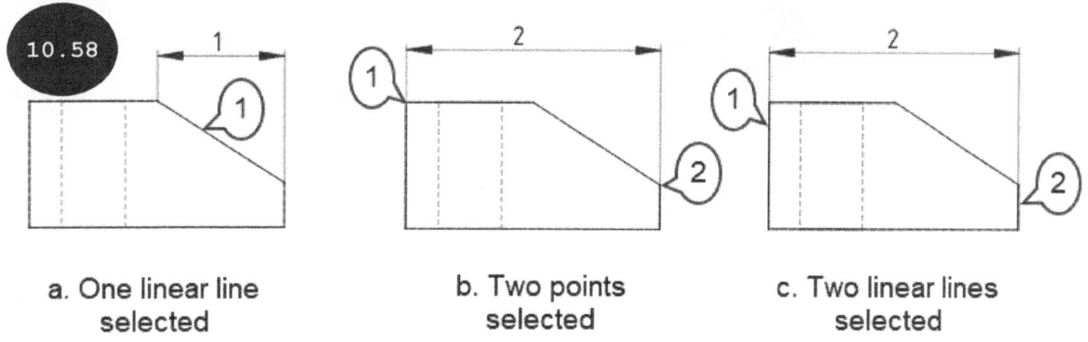

Applying a Vertical Dimension

You can apply a vertical dimension to a linear edge/line, between two points/vertices, or between two linear edges/lines of a drawing view by using the **Insert Vertical Dimension** tool, same as to applying a horizontal dimension.

Applying a Radius Dimension

You can apply a radius dimension to a circular edge (circle or arc) of a drawing view by using the **Insert Radius Dimension** tool. To do this, select a circular edge (circle or arc) of a drawing view and then click on the **Insert Radius Dimension** tool in the **Dimensions** menu of the **TechDraw Dimensions** toolbar. A radius dimension is applied to the selected circular entity of the view, see Figure 10.59.

Applying a Diameter Dimension

You can apply a diameter dimension to a circular edge (circle or arc) of a drawing view by using the **Insert Diameter Dimension** tool, in a manner similar to applying a radius dimension, see Figure 10.60.

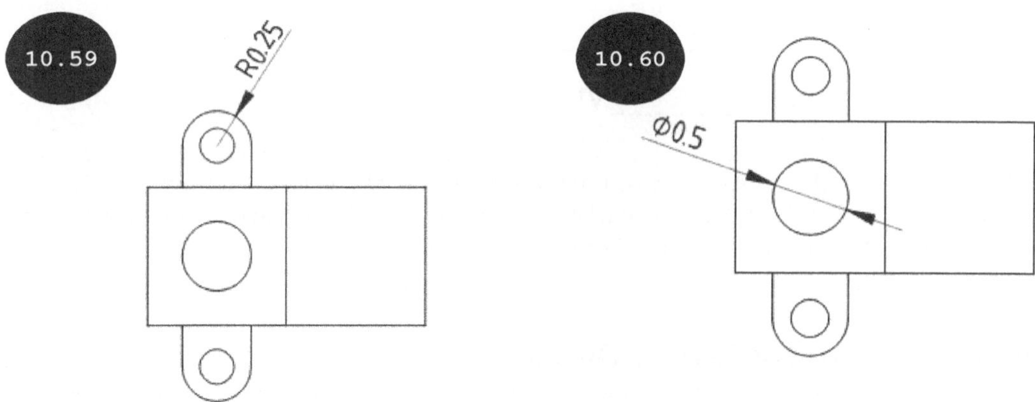

Applying an Angle Dimension

You can apply an angular dimension between two linear edges/lines of a drawing view by using the **Insert Angle Dimension** tool. To do this, select two linear edges/lines of a drawing view and then click on the **Insert Angle Dimension** tool in the **Dimensions** menu of the **TechDraw Dimensions** toolbar. An angular dimension is applied between the selected entities, see Figure 10.61.

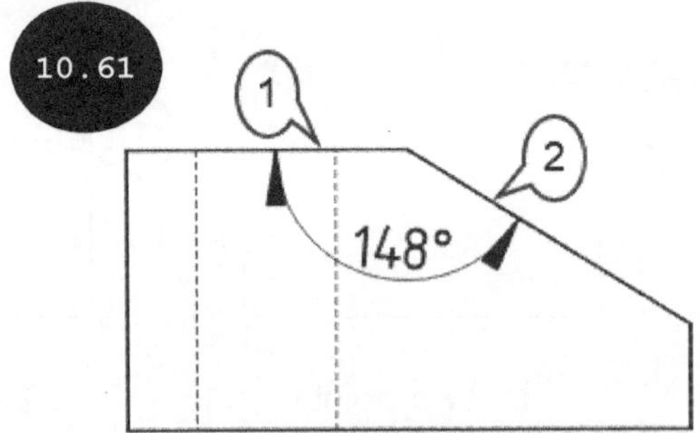

Applying a 3-Point Angle Dimension

You can apply a 3-point angular dimension by selecting three vertices or points of a drawing view by using the **Insert 3-Point Angle Dimension** tool. To do this, select three vertices or points of a drawing view by pressing the CTRL key. Note that the second selected vertex or point should be the apex of the angle. After selecting three vertices or points, click on the **Insert 3-Point Angle Dimension** tool in the **Dimensions** menu of the **TechDraw Dimensions** toolbar. An angular dimension is applied by selecting three vertices, see Figure 10.62.

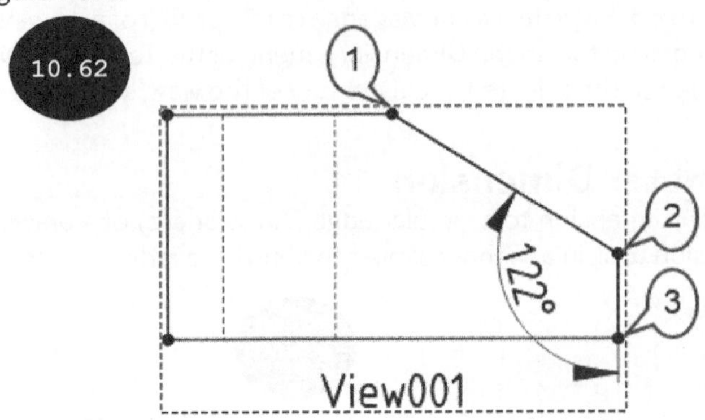

Note: In Figure 10.62, the display of the outer frame and label of the view is turned ON. You can toggle the display of outer frames and labels of the views by clicking on the **Turn View Frames On/Off** tool in the **TechDraw Decoration** toolbar.

Applying a Horizontal Extent Dimension

You can apply a horizontal extent dimension between the leftmost and rightmost points of a selected edge by using the **Insert Horizontal Extent Dimension** tool, see Figure 10.63. To do this, select an edge (linear, curve, or circular) of a drawing view and then click on the **Insert Horizontal Extent Dimension** in the **Dimensions** menu tool of the **TechDraw Dimensions** toolbar, see Figure 10.64 A horizontal extent dimension is applied between the leftmost and rightmost points of the selected edge.

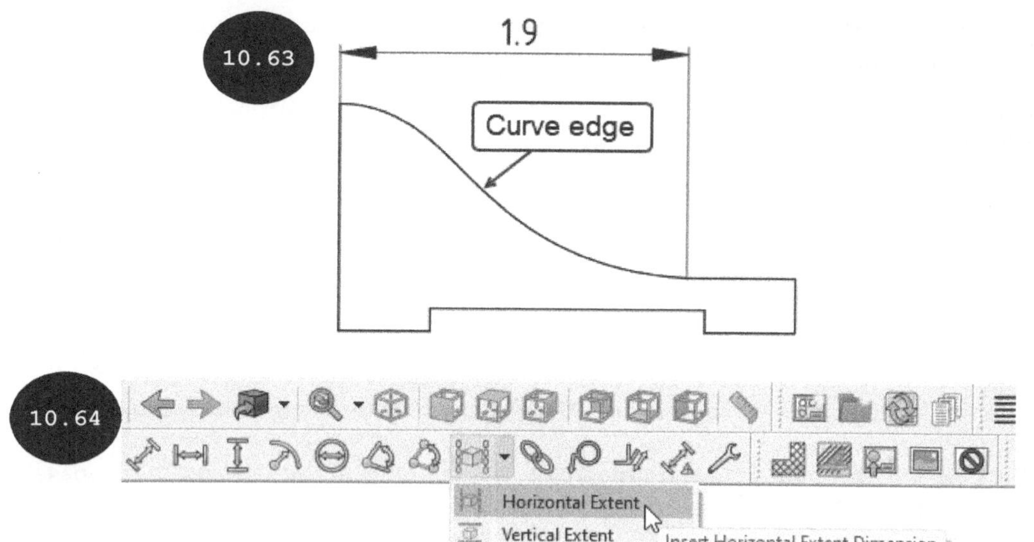

Applying a Vertical Extent Dimension

You can apply a vertical extent dimension between the bottommost and topmost points of a selected edge by using the **Insert Vertical Extent Dimension** tool, similar to applying a horizontal extent dimension, see Figure 10.65.

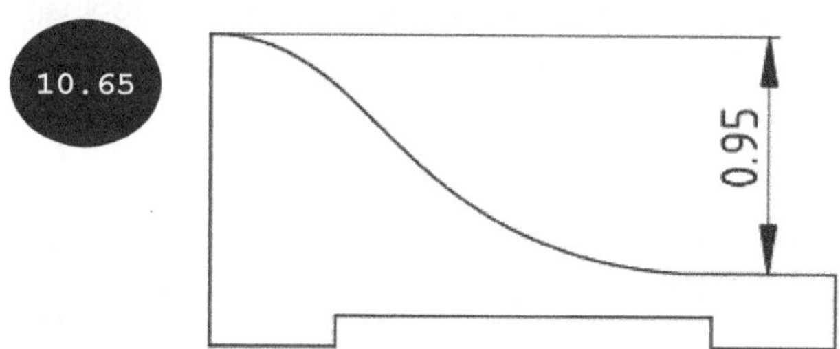

Note: In FreeCAD 1.0, instead of using separate tools for each type of dimension, you can apply various dimensions using the single **Insert Dimension** tool of the **Dimension** menu. This tool intelligently detects the selected entity and automatically assigns the appropriate dimension type. For example, selecting a circular edge applies a diameter dimension, while selecting a linear edge applies a linear dimension.

Exporting Drawing as a DXF File

After creating drawing views of a model and applying the required dimensions, you can export the drawing sheet (page) as a DXF file. The method for exporting the current sheet (page) as a DXF file is discussed below:

1. Click on the **Export Page as DXF** tool in the **TechDraw File Access** toolbar, see Figure 10.66. The **Save DXF file** dialog box appears.

2. In this dialog box, browse to the required location where you want to save the DXF file.

3. Enter the required name of the file in the **File name** field of the dialog box, as required.

4. Click on the **Save** button in the dialog box. The currently active drawing sheet (page) gets exported to the DXF file and saved at the specified location.

Exporting Drawing as an SVG File

You can also export the currently active drawing sheet (page) as an SVG file. The method for exporting the current sheet (page) as an SVG file is discussed below:

1. Click on the **Export Page as SVG** tool in the **TechDraw File Access** toolbar, see Figure 10.67. The **Save DXF file** dialog box appears.

2. In this dialog box, browse to the required location where you want to save the SVG file and then enter the required name of the file in the **File name** field.

3. Click on the **Save** button in the dialog box. The currently active drawing sheet (page) gets exported to the SVG file and saved at the specified location.

Tutorial 1

Open the model created in Tutorial 1 of Chapter 5 and then create different drawing views: front, top, right, isometric, and section, as shown in Figure 10.68 in the A4_LandscapeTD sheet template. Also, you also need to apply dimensions. Note that the third angle of projection needs to be used for creating drawing views. All dimensions are in mm.

10.68

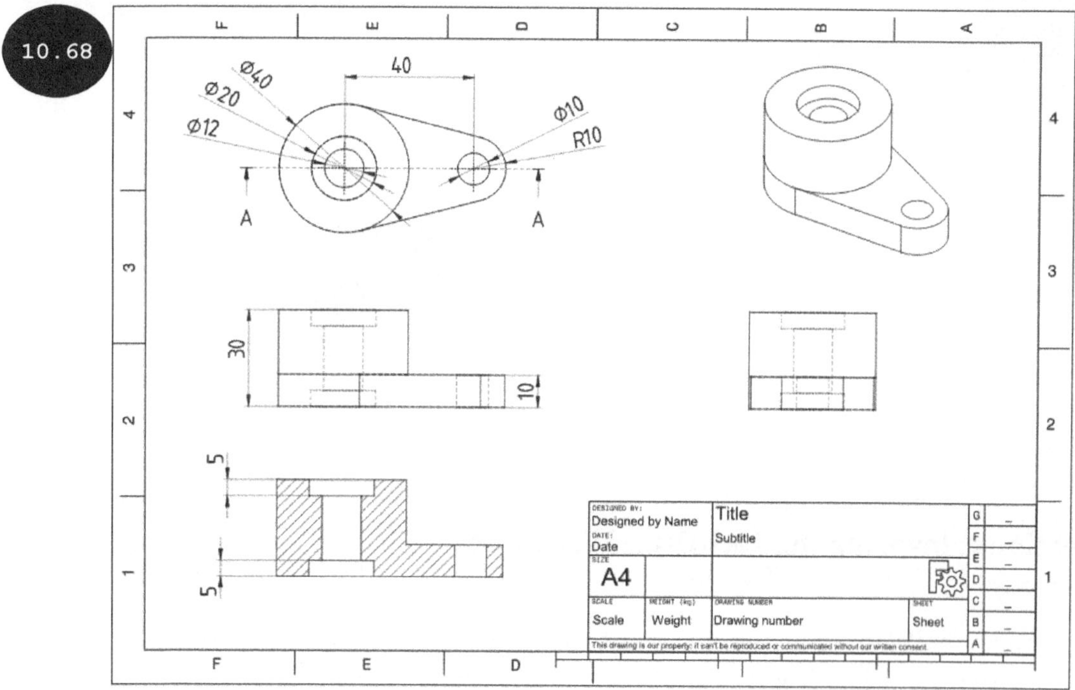

Section 1: Opening Tutorial 1 of Chapter 5

1. Start FreeCAD by double-clicking on the **FreeCAD 0.21** icon on your desktop, if not started already. The startup user interface of FreeCAD appears.

   Now, you need to open the model created in Tutorial 1 of Chapter 5 to create its drawing.

2. Click on the **Open** button in the **File** toolbar, see Figure 10.69. The **Open document** dialog box appears. Alternatively, press the CTRL + O keys to invoke this dialog box.

10.69

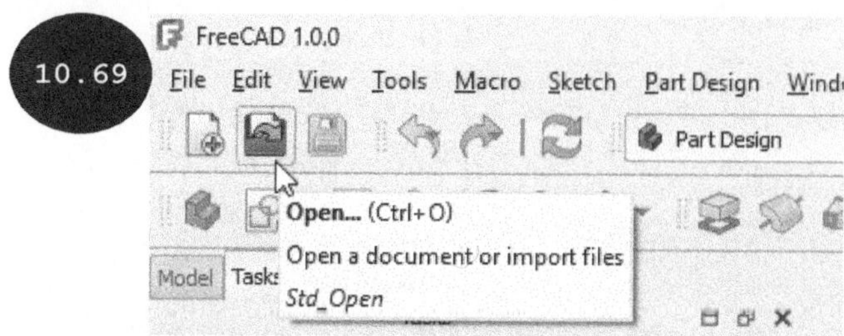

3. In the **Open document** dialog box, browse to the **Chapter 5** folder and then select the **Ch05-Tutorial 1** model. Note that you need to create this model, if not created in Chapter 5.

4. After selecting the model, click on the **Open** button in the dialog box. The model created in Tutorial 1 of Chapter 5 gets opened in a separate tab and is active, by default, see Figure 10.70.

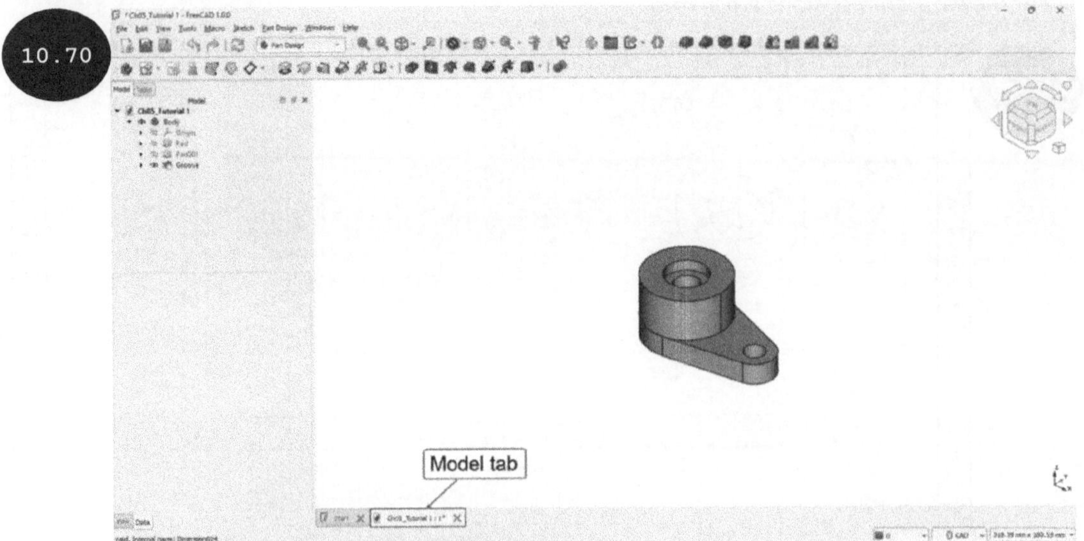

Section 2: Invoking the TechDraw Workspace

Now, you need to invoke the **TechDraw** workspace to create a 2D drawing of the opened model.

1. Invoke the **Workbench Selector** in the **Workbench** toolbar and then select the **TechDraw** workbench, see Figure 10.71. The **TechDraw** workbench gets invoked.

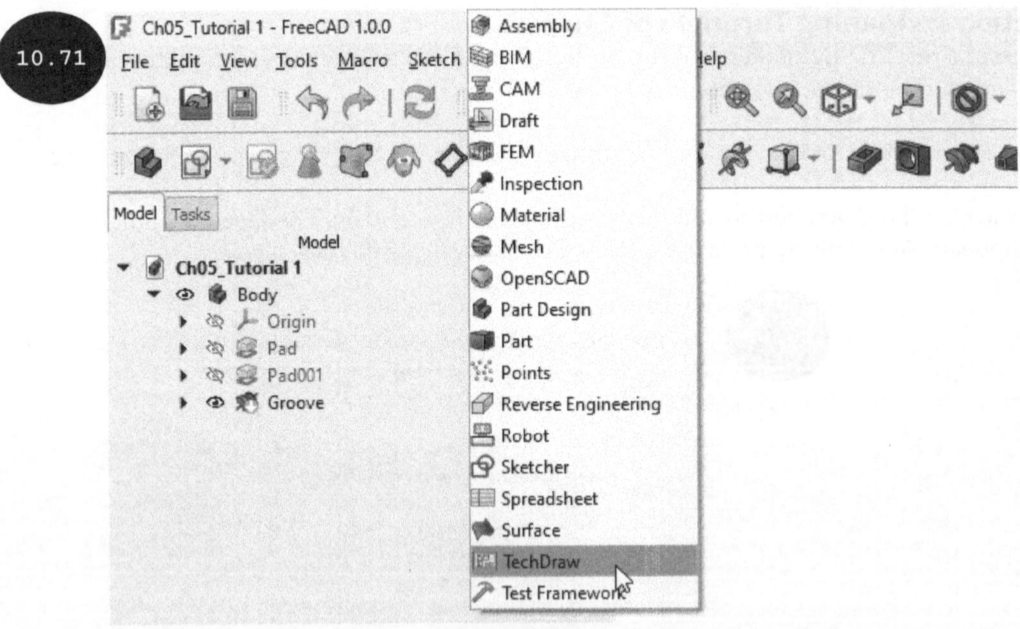

Section 3: Inserting a Drawing Sheet (Page)

Now, you need to insert a drawing sheet (page) in the A4_LandscapeTD sheet template for creating different drawing views of the 3D model.

1. Click on the **Insert Page using Template** tool in the **TechDraw Pages** toolbar, see Figure 10.72. The **Select a Template File** window appears with a list of available drawing templates, see Figure 10.73.

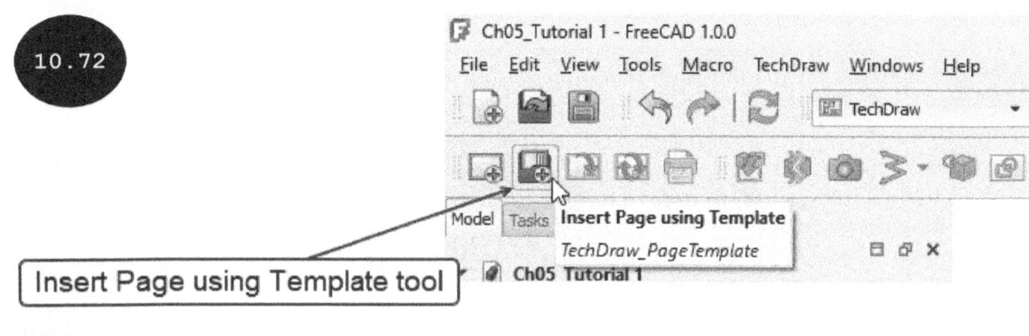

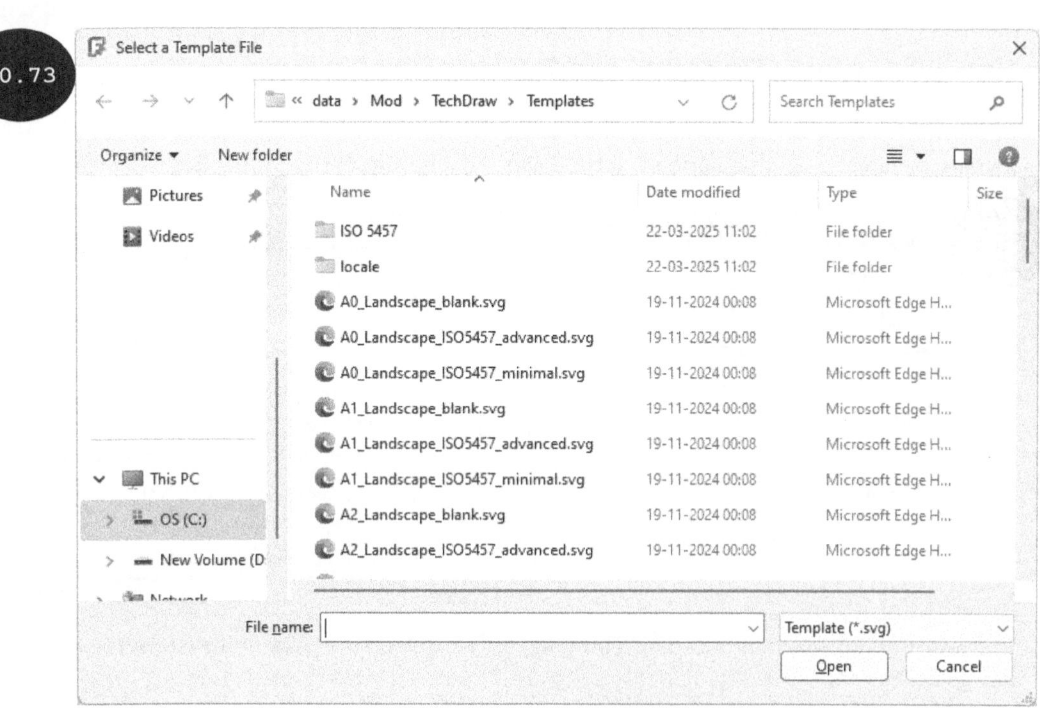

2. In this dialog box, scroll down and select the **A4_LandscapeTD** template. Next, click on the **Open** button. A new drawing sheet (page) with the selected template gets inserted with a default name "***Page***" in a new separate tab and becomes active by default, see Figure 10.74.

10.74

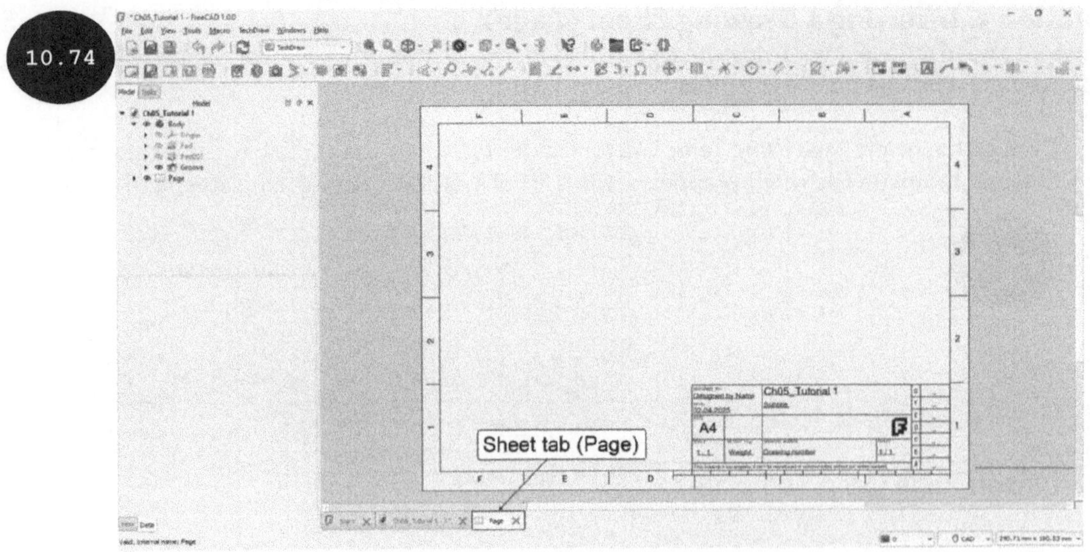

Section 4: Specifying Units and Hidden Line Display Style

Now, you need to specify millimeters (mm) as the measurement unit for the document.

1. Invoke the **Unit** flyout that appears at the lower right corner of the **Status Bar**, see Figure 10.75.

10.75

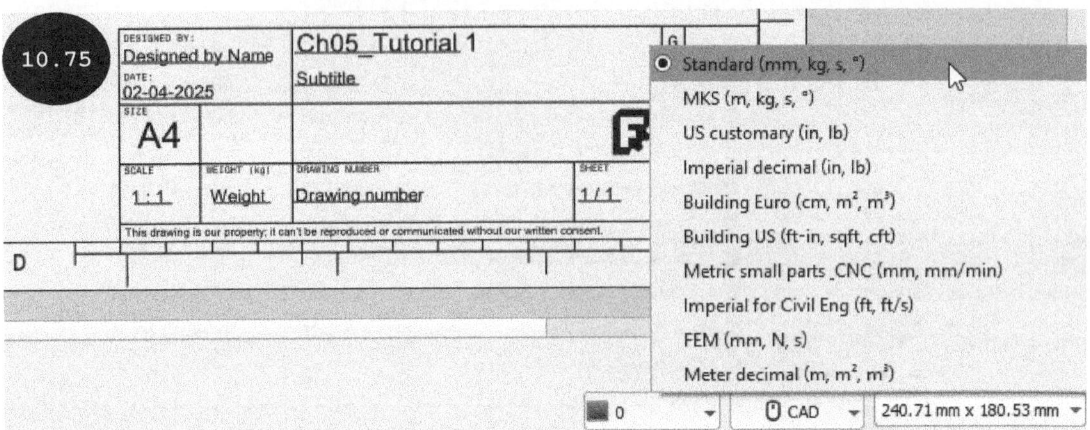

2. In this flyout, ensure that **Standard (mm, kg, s, *)** is selected as the unit system for the current design document.

   Now, you can define the hidden line display style as dashed.

3. Click on **Edit > Preferences** in the **Standard Menu**. The **Preferences** dialog box appears.

4. In the **Preferences** dialog box, click on the **TechDraw** section and then click on **Annotations** displayed under the **TechDraw** section in the left panel. Next, select the **Hidden** option in the **Hidden Line Style** drop-down list as the hidden line style, see Figure 10.76.

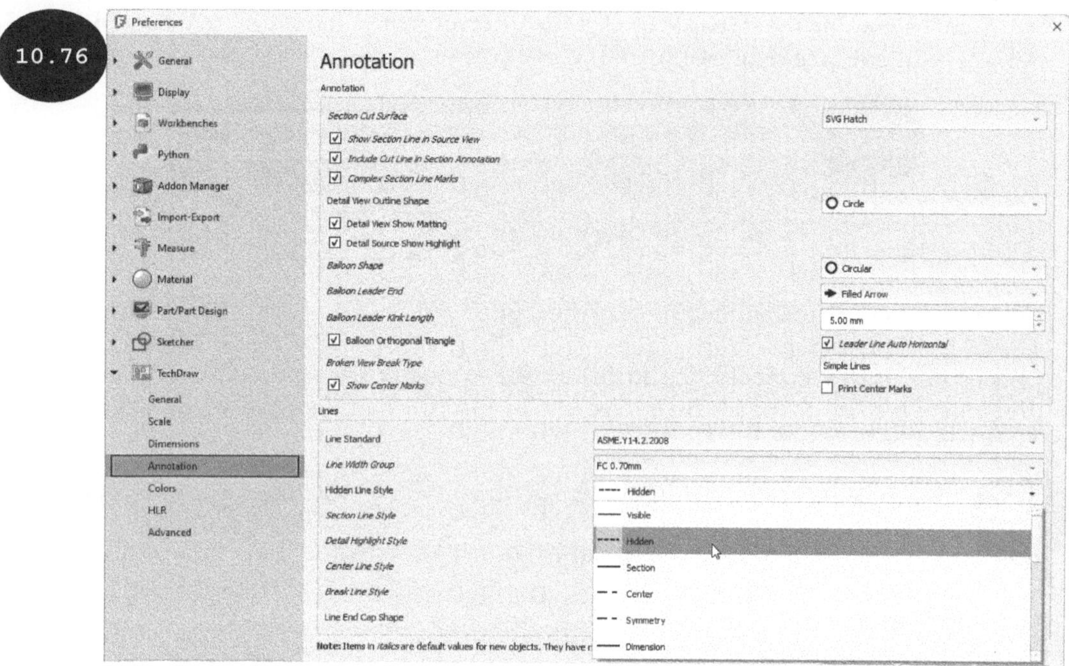

5. Click on the **Apply** button and then the **OK** button in the **Preferences** dialog box. The selected unit system and the hidden line style are defined, and the dialog box is closed.

Section 5: Creating Drawing Views

Now, you need to create multiple linked 2D projection drawing views.

1. Switch to the 3D model by clicking on its tab at the lower left corner of the drawing display area whose drawing views are to be created, see Figure 10.77.

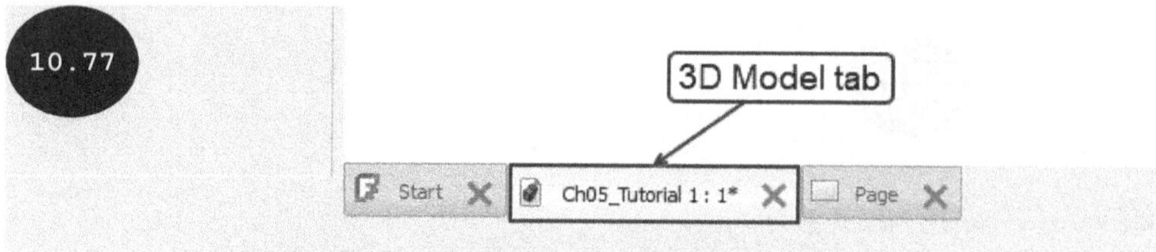

2. Click on the model "**Body**" in the **Tree View** to create its views, see Figure 10.78.

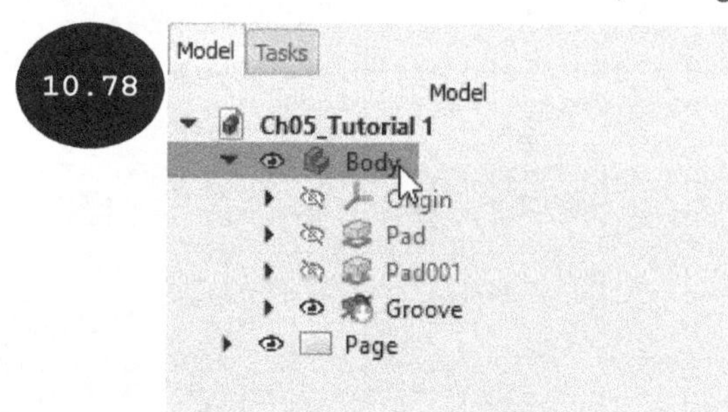

3. Switch to the drawing sheet (page) by clicking on its respective tab "***Page***" to create the drawing views of the model, see Figure 10.79.

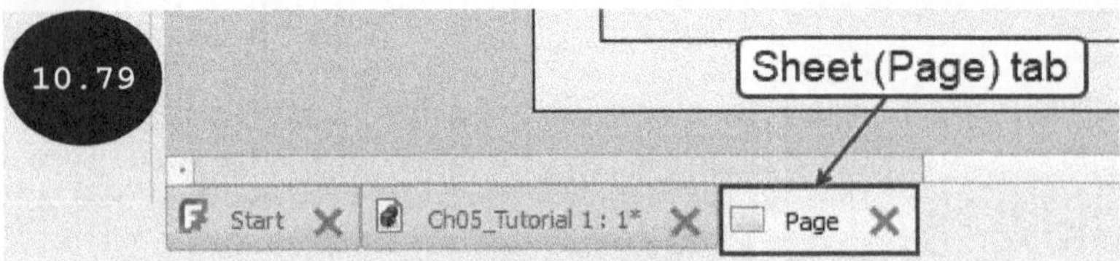

Now, you can create the drawing views of the model.

4. Click on the **Insert View** tool in the **TechDraw Views** toolbar, see Figure 10.80. The Front view of the model is created on the sheet, see Figure 10.81. Also, the **Part View** sub-window appears in the **Tasks Panel**, see Figure 10.82.

10.80

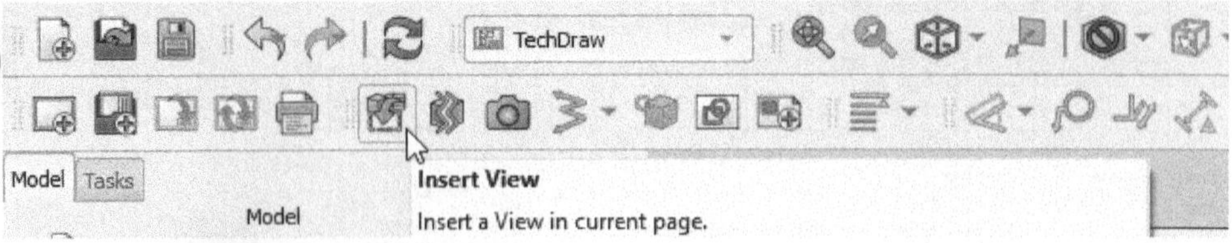

10.81

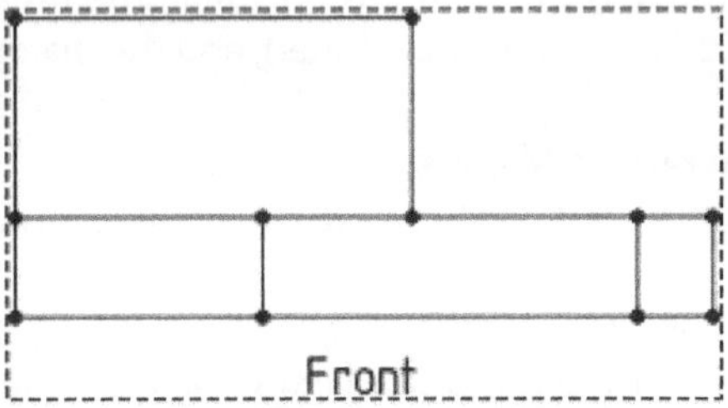

10.82

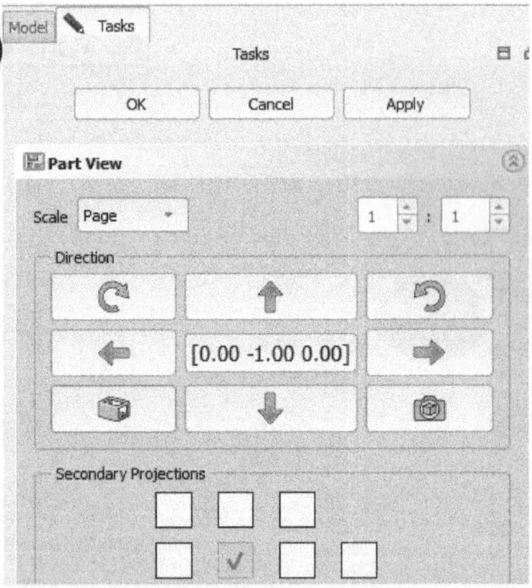

5. Select the **Top**, **Right**, and **FrontTopRight** check boxes in the **Secondary Projections** area of the **Tasks Panel**, see Figure 10.83. The respective drawing views get created on the sheet as per default selected angle of projection, see Figure 10.84.

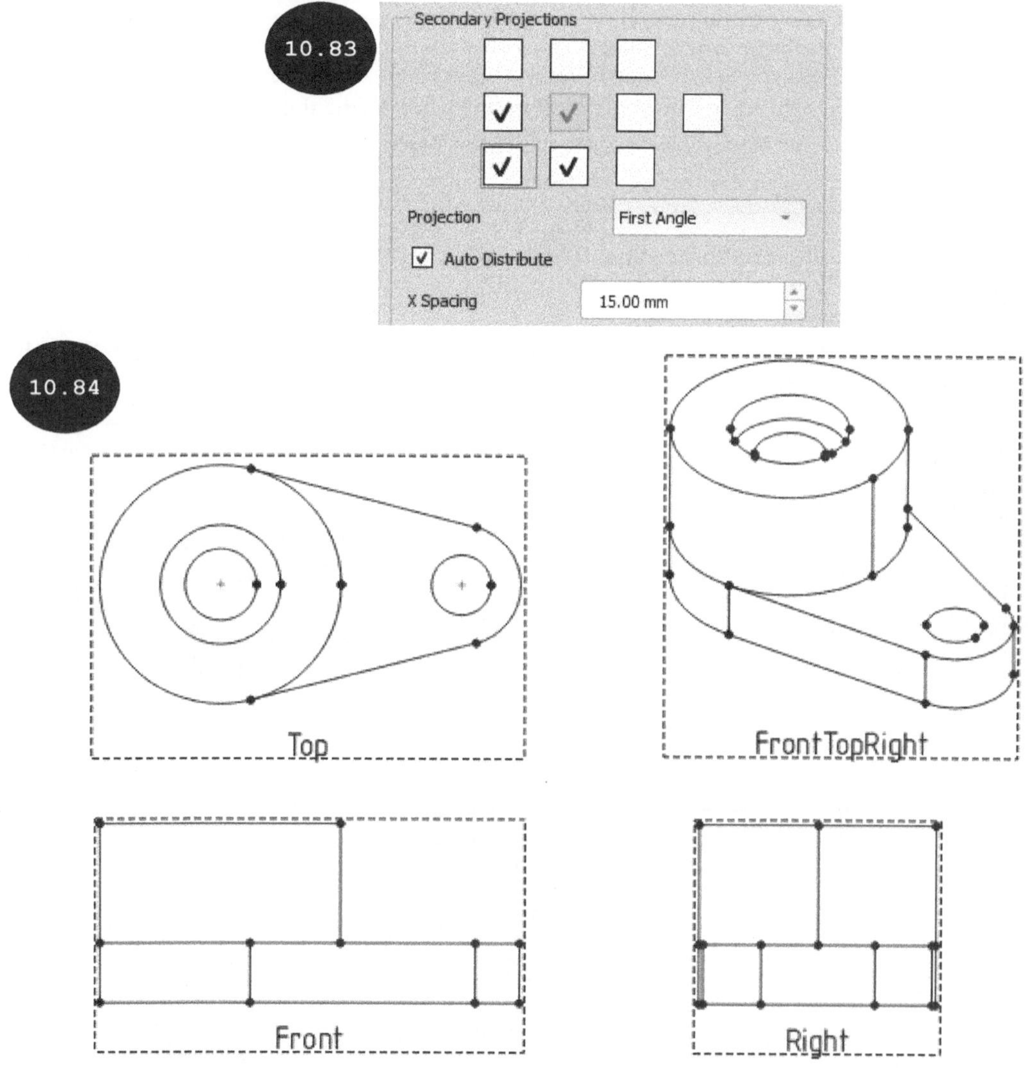

6. Select the **Third angle** option in the **Projection** drop-down list of the **Tasks Panel** to define the third angle of projection for creating the drawing views.

Note: After changing the angle of projection, the position of the view on the sheet may shift. If needed, you can manually drag the views to re-position them on the sheet similar to the one shown in Figure 10.85. To do this, move the cursor over the outer frame of the view to be moved and then drag it to a new location on the sheet by pressing and holding the left mouse button. Note that when you move the primary view, all its linked projection views will also be moved, accordingly.

7. Select the **Custom** option in the **Scale** drop-down list and then set the scale factor to **1:1** in the respective **Custom Scale** fields of the **Tasks Panel**. Next, press the TAB key and then the F5 key to update the view on the sheet as per the specified scale factor.

Note: You may need to move the drawing views of the model to position them on the sheet, as required. To do this, move the cursor over the outer frame of the view to be moved and then drag it to a new location on the sheet by pressing and holding the left mouse button. Note that when you move the primary view, all its linked projection views will also be moved, accordingly.

8. Click on the **OK** button in the **Tasks Panel**. The multiple linked 2D projection views get created on the sheet.

9. Define the position of the drawing views like the one shown in Figure 10.85. You can drag the views to define their position on the sheet, as required.

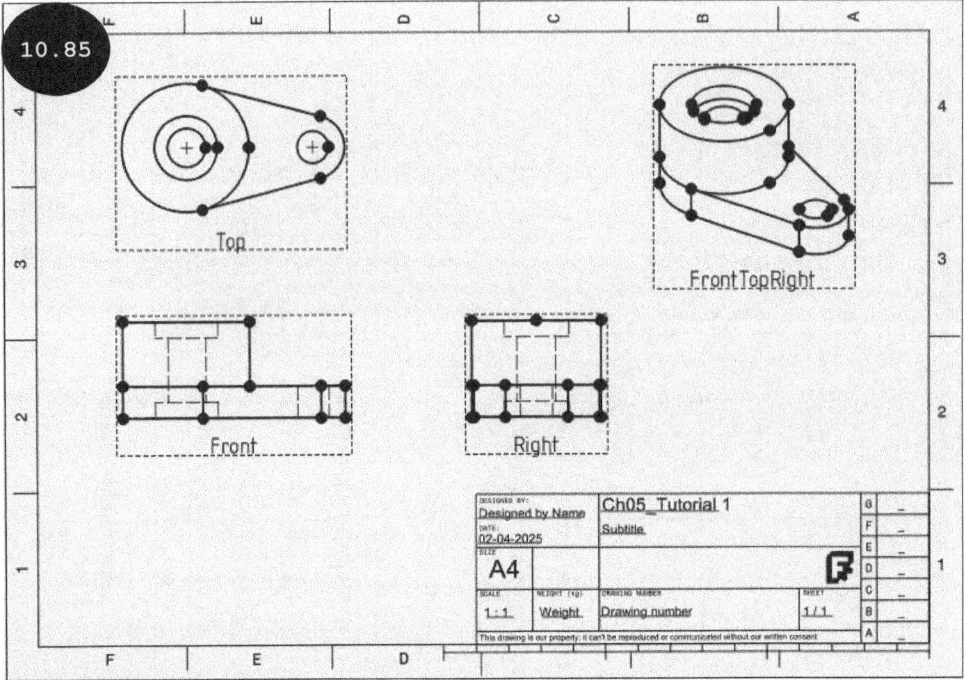

Section 6: Displaying Hidden Edges

Now, you need to turn on the display of hidden edges of the model on the drawing views.

1. Select the Front, Top, and Right views by clicking the left mouse button in **Tree View**. You need to press the CTRL key to select multiple views. The **Property Editor** appears at the lower section of the **Model** tab in the **Combo View** with **View** and **Data** tabs, refer to Figure 10.86.

2. Ensure that the **Data** tab is activated at the bottom of the **Property Editor**, refer to Figure 10.86.

3. Click twice on the **Hard Hidden** field in the **Property Editor** and then select the **true** option in the drop-down list that appears, see Figure 10.86.

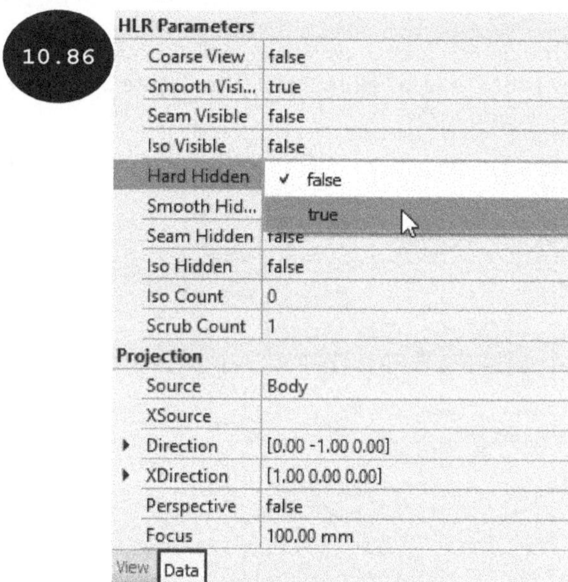

4. Click anywhere on the sheet. The display of hidden lines gets turned ON in the selected views with the default hidden line style, see Figure 10.87. Note that you may need to update the views by clicking on the **Refresh** tool in the **File** toolbar to display the hidden lines.

10.87

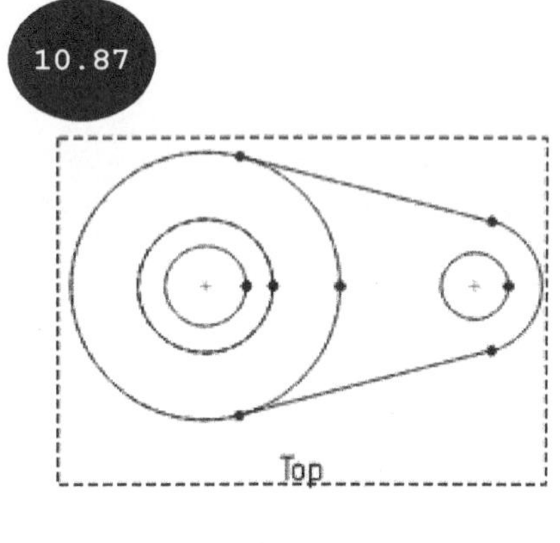

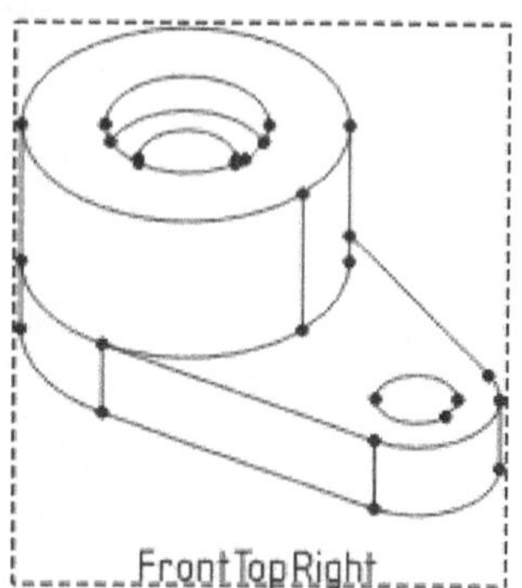

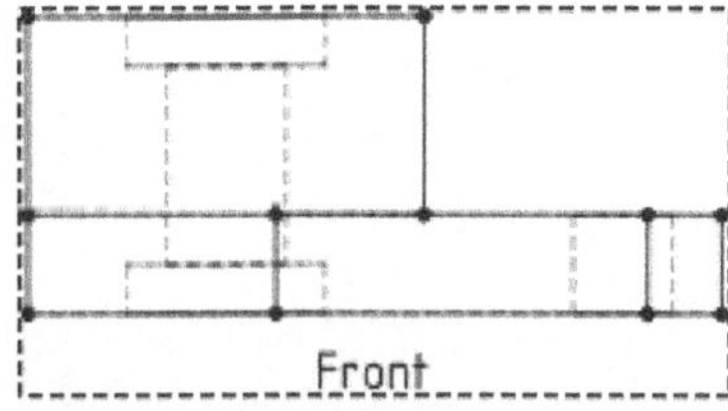

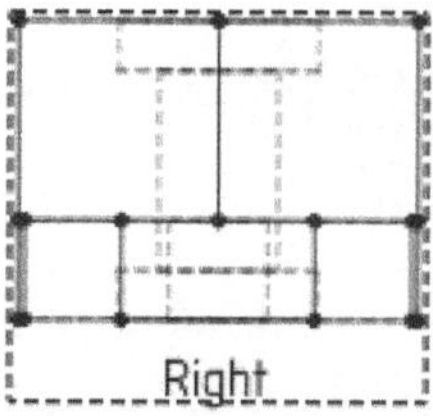

Section 7: Creating the Section View

Now, you need to create a section view.

1. Select the Top view as the parent view for creating the section view.

2. Invoke the **Section** flyout in the **TechDraw Views** toolbar and then click on the **Section View** tool in the **TechDraw Views** toolbar, see Figure 10.88. The **Create Section View** sub-window appears in the **Tasks Panel**, see Figure 10.89.

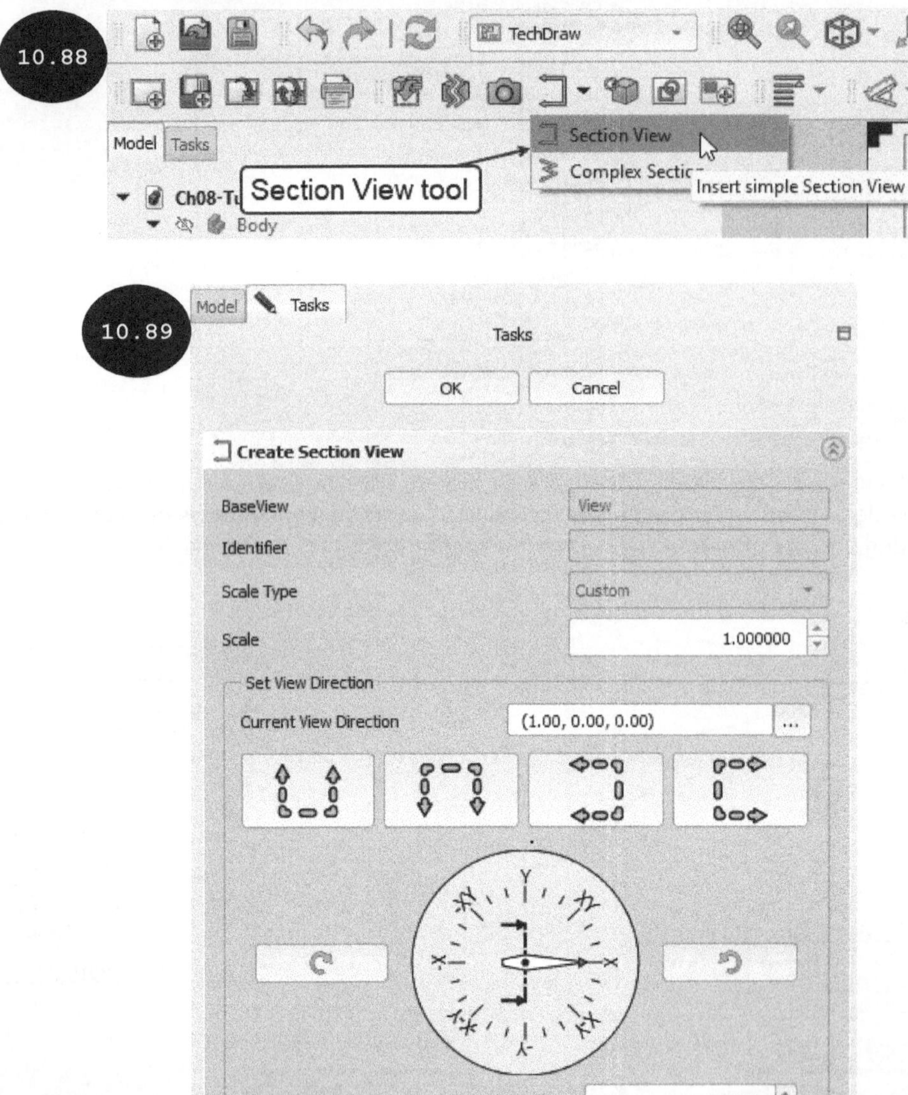

3. Select the **Looking up** section line button in the **Set View Direction** area of the **Tasks Panel** and scroll down to the **Preview** area in the **Tasks Panel** and then select the **Live Update** check box. A preview of the respective section view of the model appears on the sheet, refer to Figure 10.90.

4. Move the section view to below the Front view on the sheet by dragging it, refer to Figure 10.90.

5. Enter **A** as the name for the section view in the **Identifier** field of the **Tasks Panel** and click anywhere on the sheet. The specified identifier name gets assigned to the section line and section view on the sheet, refer to Figure 10.90.

6. Click on the **OK** button in the **Tasks Panel** to confirm the creation of the section view. The section view gets created, refer to Figure 10.90.

7. Move the section view as well as the other drawing views to the required locations on the sheet by dragging them after pressing and holding the left mouse button one by one, see Figure 10.90.

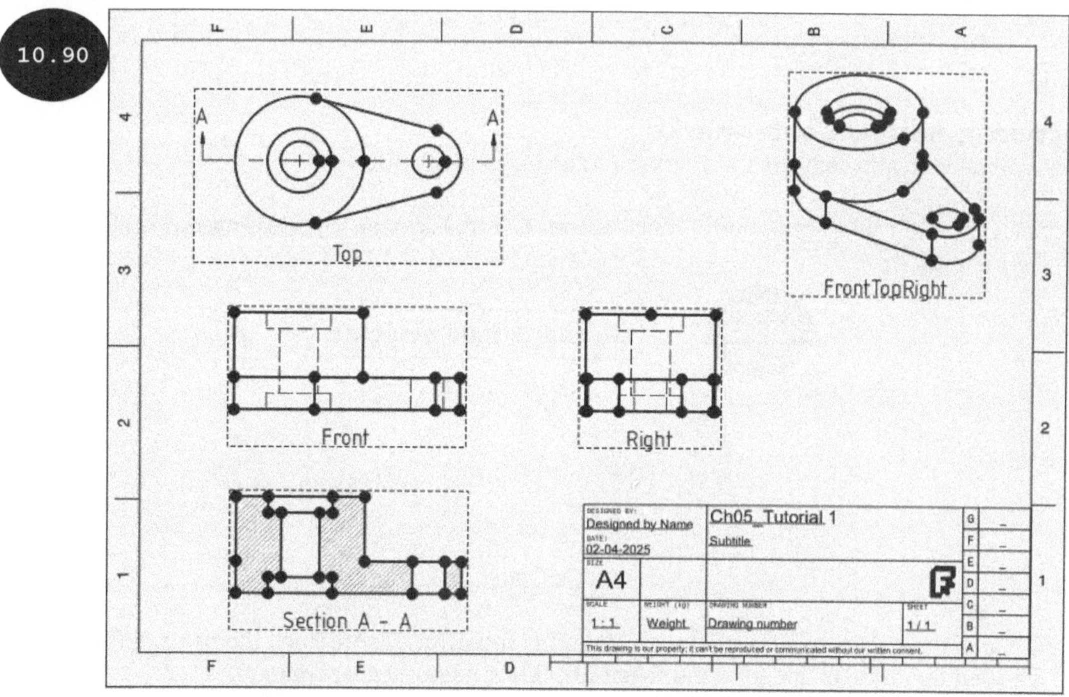

Section 8: Changing the Scale of Hatch Lines

Now, you can change the scale of the hatch lines of the section view.

1. Select the section view by clicking the left mouse button. The **Property Editor** appears at the lower section of the **Model** tab in the **Combo View** with **View** and **Data** tabs, see Figure 10.91.

2. Ensure that the **Data** tab is activated in the **Property Editor** and then scroll down to display the **Hatch Scale** field, see Figure 10.91.

3. Enter the **2** in the **Hatch Scale** field of the **Property Editor** (see Figure 10.91) and click anywhere on the sheet. Figure 10.92 shows a section view with its hatch scale set to 2.

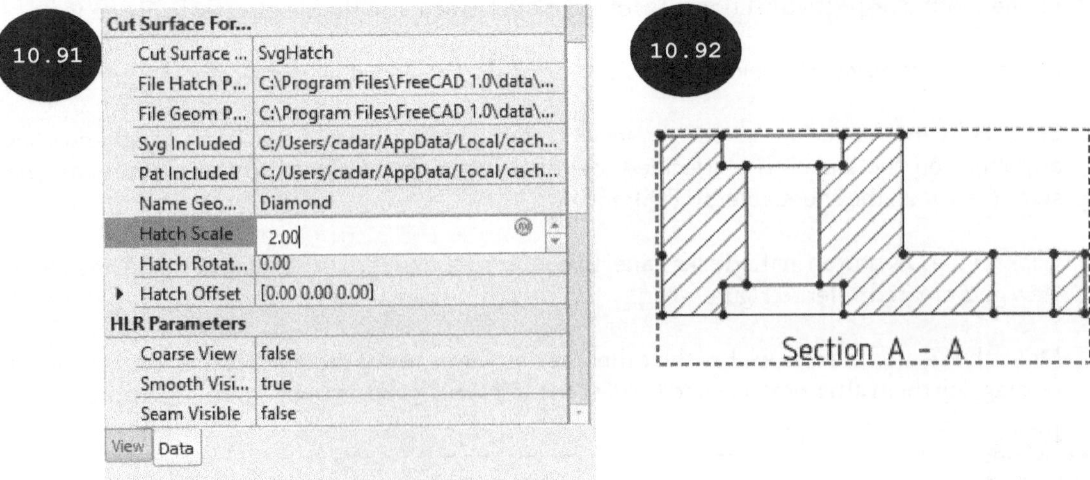

Section 9: Adding CenterMarks

Now, you need to add centermarks to the circular edges of the Top view.

1. Select the left and right inner circular edges of the Top view by pressing the CTRL key, see Figure 10.93.

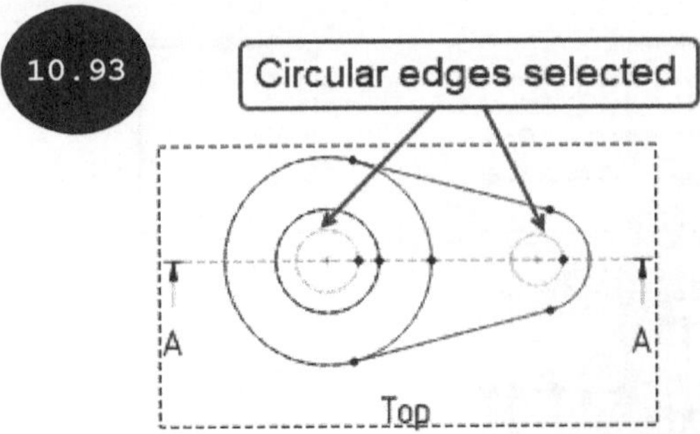

2. Click on the **Add Circle Centerlines** tool in the **TechDraw Centerlines** toolbar, see Figure 10.94. The centermarks get added to the selected circular edges, see Figure 10.95.

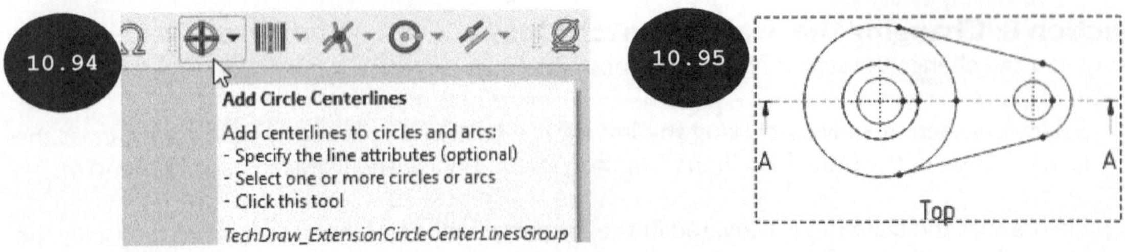

Section 10: Applying Dimensions

Now, you need to apply the required dimensions to the drawing views.

1. Select the vertical centerlines of the centermarks created on the Top view by pressing the CTRL key and then click on the **Insert Horizontal Dimension** tool in the **Dimension** menu, see Figure 10.96. A horizontal dimension is applied between the selected centerlines, see Figure 10.97.

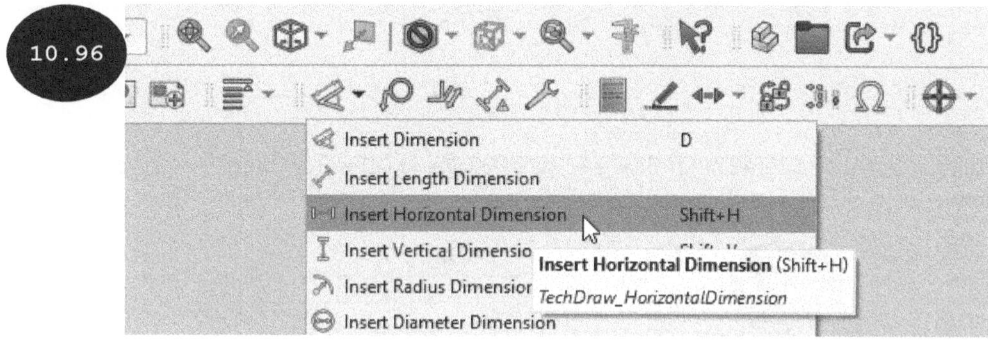

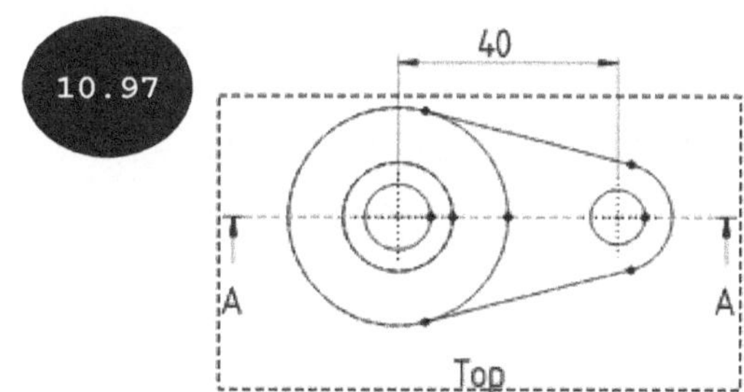

2. Move the dimension vertically upward and place it like the one shown in Figure 10.97. You can move a dimension by dragging it by pressing and holding the left mouse button.

3. Select the left outer circular edge of the Top view and then click on the **Insert Diameter Dimension** tool, see Figure 10.98. A diameter dimension is applied to the selected circular edge of the Top view, see Figure 10.99. Note that after applying a dimension, you need to define its position on the sheet by dragging it.

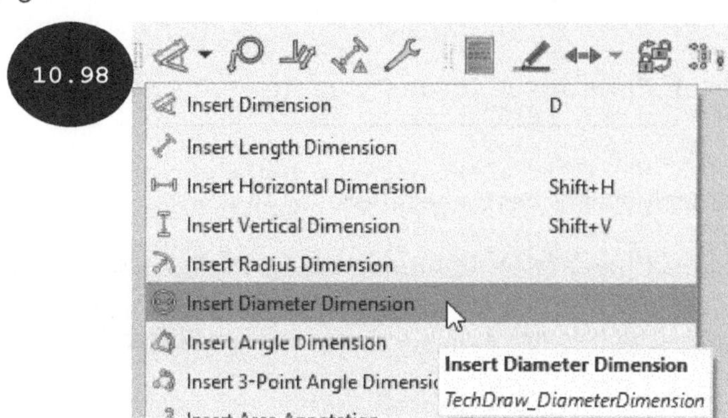

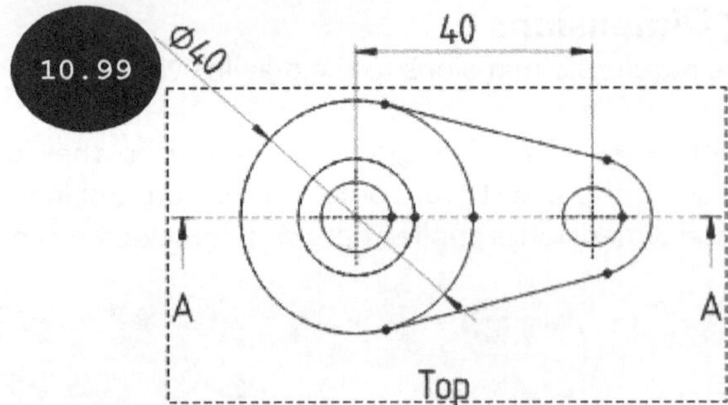

4. Similarly, apply the remaining diameter dimensions on the Top view by using the **Diameter Dimension** tool, see Figure 10.100.

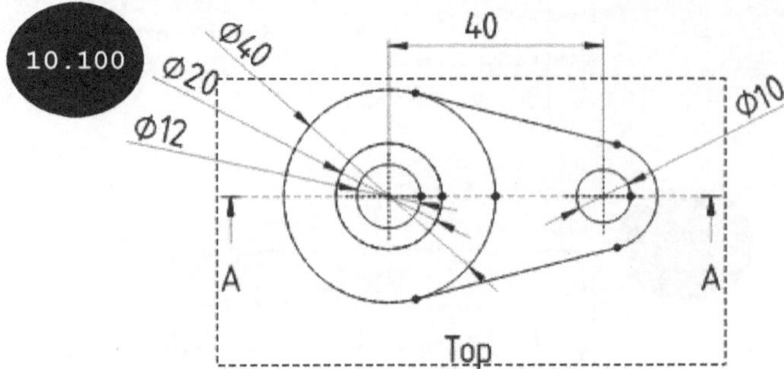

5. Select the right semi-circular (arc) edge of the Top view and then click on the **Insert Radius Dimension** tool. A radius dimension gets applied on the selected edge, see Figure 10.101. After applying a dimension, you need to define its position.

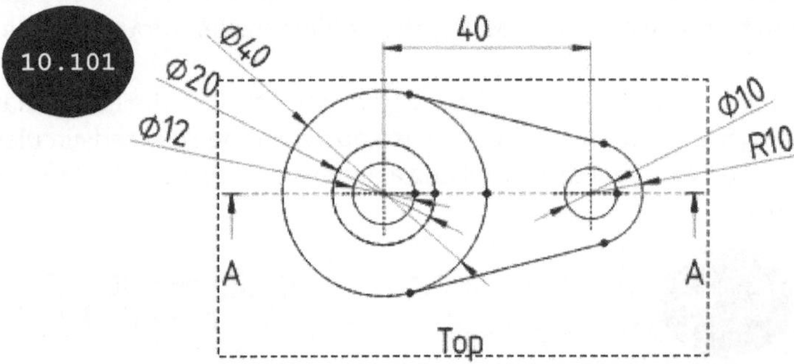

Now, you need to apply dimensions to the other drawing views.

6. Select the topmost and bottommost horizontal edges of the Front view by pressing the CTRL key and then click on the **Insert Vertical Dimension** tool in the **Dimension** menu, see Figure 10.102. A vertical dimension of length 30 mm is applied between the selected edges, see Figure 10.103.

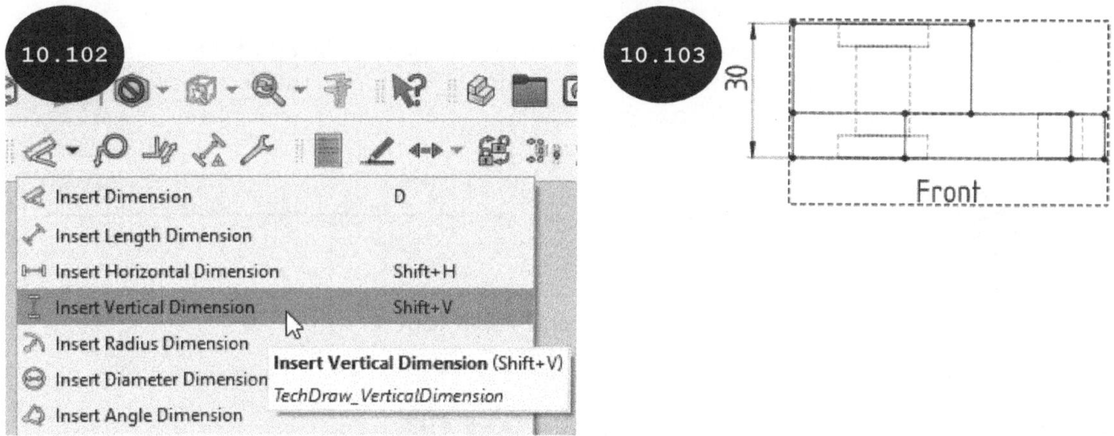

7. Select the rightmost vertical edge of the Front view and then click on the **Insert Vertical Dimension** tool. A vertical dimension of length 10 mm is applied to the selected edge, see Figure 10.104.

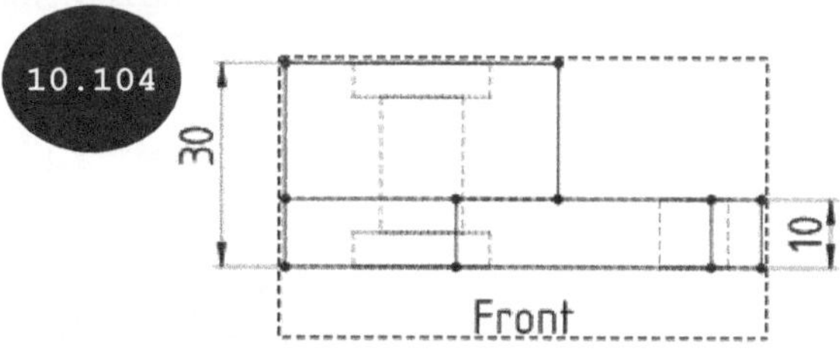

8. Similarly, apply the vertical dimensions to the Section view. Figure 10.105 shows the drawing views after applying all the required dimensions.

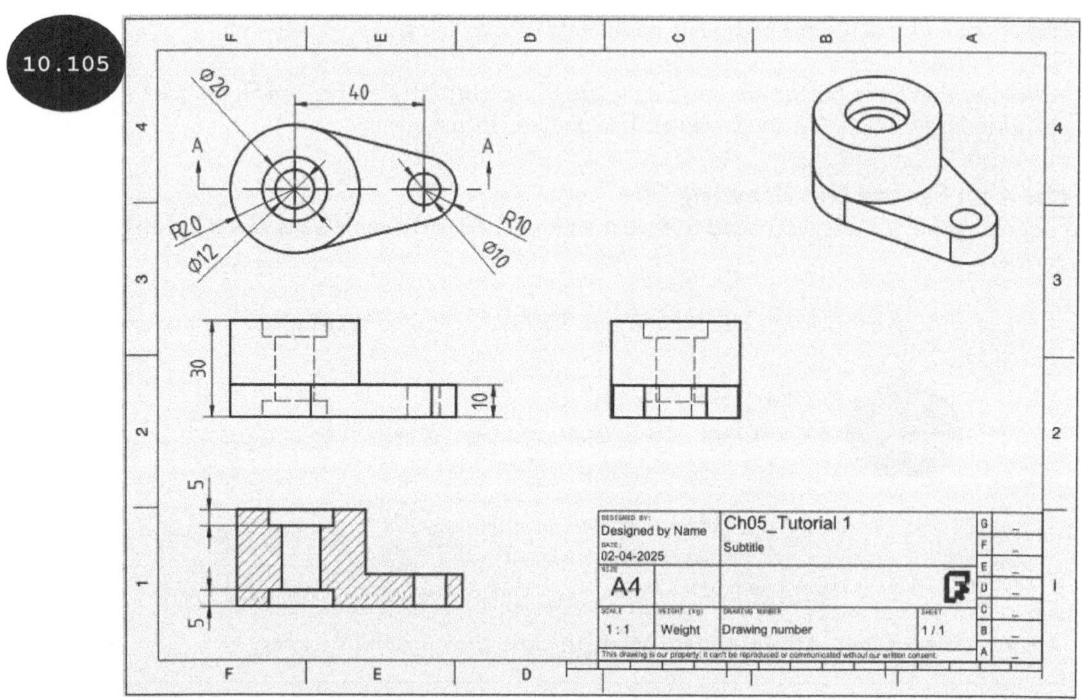

Note: In Figure 10.105, the display of outer frames/boundaries and labels of the views is turned OFF. To do this, click on the **Turn View Frames On/Off** tool in the **TechDraw Decoration** toolbar, see Figure 10.106. It's a toggle tool.

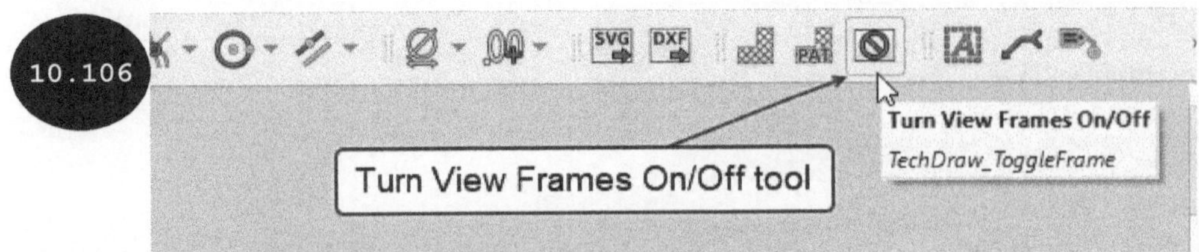

Section 11: Exporting the Drawing File as a DXF File

Now, you can export the currently active drawing sheet (page) as a DXF file.

1. Click on the **Export Page as DXF** tool in the **TechDraw File Access** toolbar, see Figure 10.107. The **Save DXF file** dialog box appears.

2. Browse to the required location where you want to save the DXF file.

3. Enter the name of the file in the **File name** field of the dialog box, as required.

4. Click on the **Save** button in the dialog box. The currently active drawing sheet (page) gets exported to the DXF file and saved at the specified location.

Section 12: Saving the Drawing File

After creating the drawing, you need to save it. In FreeCAD, a drawing file is saved internally in its 3D model file.

1. Click on the **Save** tool in the **File** toolbar, see Figure 10.108. The drawing file is saved as an internal file to its 3D model.

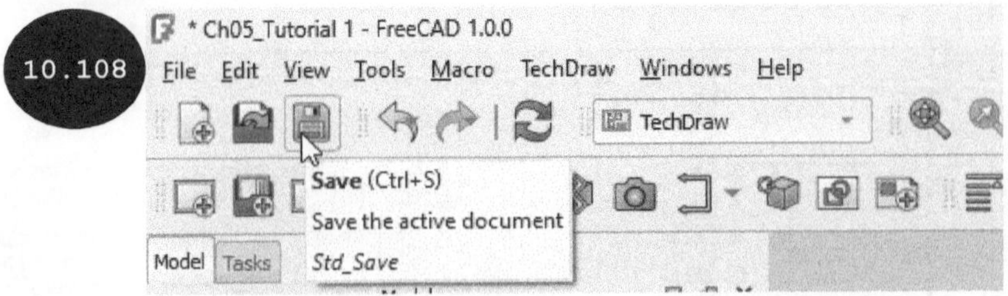

2. Click on **File > Close** in the **Standard Menu** to close the current document.

Hands-on Test Drive 1

Open the model created in Tutorial 2 of Chapter 4 and then create different drawing views: front, top, right, and section, as shown in Figure 10.109, in the A4_Landscape_ISO7200_Pep sheet template. Also, you also need to apply dimensions. Note that the third angle of projection needs to be used for creating drawing views. All dimensions are in inches (in).

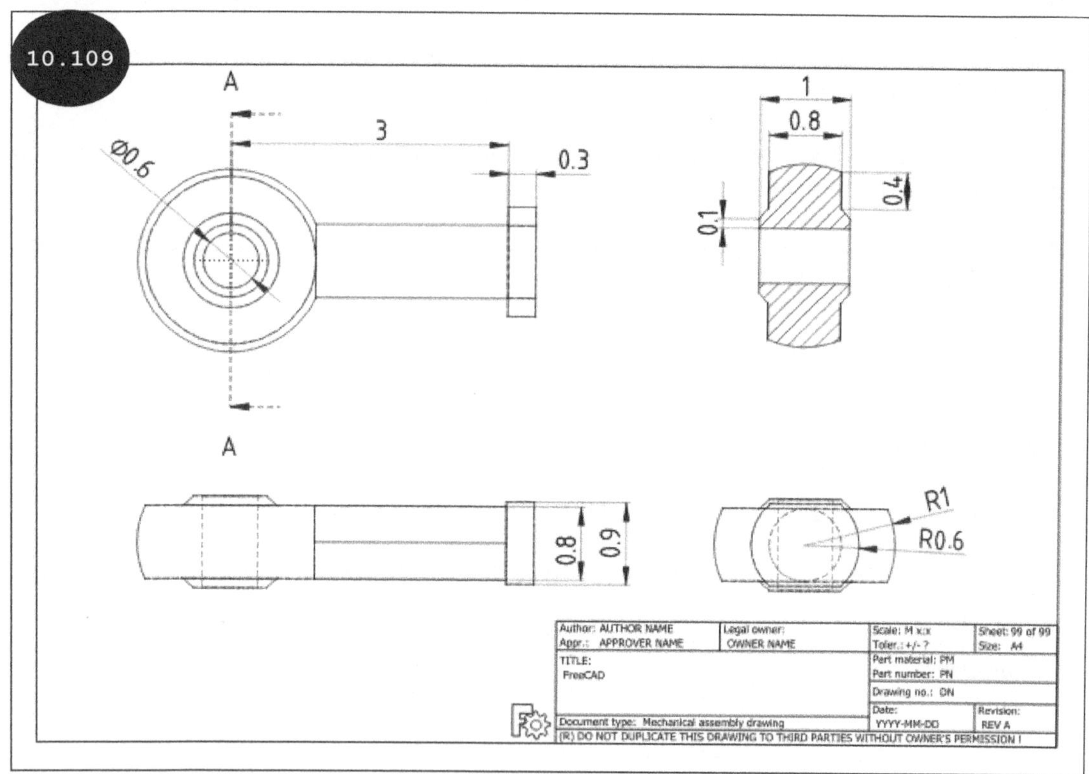

Summary

The chapter discussed how to invoke the **TechDraw** workspace to create a 2D drawing of a part or an assembly. It explained how to insert a drawing sheet, edit the title block text of a sheet, create an independent 2D projection view, modify the scale of a view, create multiple linked 2D projection views of a model, and display hidden lines on the views. It also discussed creating a section view and a detail view. The methods for applying dimensions and exporting a drawing as DXF and SVG files have also been discussed in this chapter.

Questions

Complete and verify the following sentences:

- In the _________ workbench of FreeCAD, you can create a basic 2D drawing of a 3D model.
- A _________ controls the sheet size, drafting standard, sheet border, etc. of a sheet.
- The _________ tool is used for inserting a new drawing sheet (page) with a default template for creating drawing views.
- The _________ tool is used for creating an independent 2D projection view of a selected model on the drawing sheet (page).
- The _________ option is used for setting the scale of a drawing view as per the default specified scale of the sheet (page).
- The _________ tool is used for creating multiple linked 2D projection views such as the Front, Top, Left, and Right of a 3D model simultaneously on a sheet.
- FreeCAD supports _________ and _________ projection methods for creating drawing views.
- A _________ view represents a cross-section of a model for illustrating its internal details.
- A _________ view is used for showing a portion of an existing drawing view on an enlarged scale.
- The _________ tool is used for applying a radius dimension to a circular edge (circle or arc) of a drawing view.
- The _________ tool is used for applying an angular dimension between two linear edges/lines of a drawing view.
- The _________ tool is used for exporting the currently active drawing sheet (page) as a DXF file.
- A drawing sheet contains the editable text for attributes such as Designed by Name, Date, Title, Subtitle, Scale, and Drawing number in its title block. (True/False)
- After creating a drawing view, you cannot change its scale. (True/False)
- The direction of the arrows of the section line represents the viewing direction of a section view. (True/False)

INDEX

C

Other Publications by CADArtifex

Some of the other Publications by CADArtifex are given below:

AutoCAD Textbooks

AutoCAD 2025: A Power Guide for Beginners and Intermediate Users
AutoCAD 2024: A Power Guide for Beginners and Intermediate Users
AutoCAD 2023: A Power Guide for Beginners and Intermediate Users
and more

AutoCAD For Architectural Design Textbooks

AutoCAD 2023 for Architectural Design: A Power Guide for Beginners and Intermediate Users
AutoCAD 2022 for Architectural Design: A Power Guide for Beginners and Intermediate Users
AutoCAD 2021 for Architectural Design: A Power Guide for Beginners and Intermediate Users
and more

Autodesk Fusion 360 Textbooks

Autodesk Fusion 360: A Power Guide for Beginners and Intermediate Users (7th Edition)
Autodesk Fusion 360: A Power Guide for Beginners and Intermediate Users (6th Edition)
Autodesk Fusion 360: A Power Guide for Beginners and Intermediate Users (5th Edition)
and more

Autodesk Fusion 360 Surface and T-Spline Textbooks

Autodesk Fusion 360 Surface Design and Sculpting with T-Spline Surfaces (7th Edition)
Autodesk Fusion 360 Surface Design and Sculpting with T-Spline Surfaces (6th Edition)
and more

Autodesk Inventor Textbooks

Autodesk Inventor 2025: A Power Guide for Beginners and Intermediate Users
Autodesk Inventor 2024: A Power Guide for Beginners and Intermediate Users
Autodesk Inventor 2023: A Power Guide for Beginners and Intermediate Users
and more

FreeCAD Textbooks

FreeCAD 1.0: A Power Guide for Beginners and Intermediate Users
FreeCAD 0.21: A Power Guide for Beginners and Intermediate Users
FreeCAD 0.20: A Power Guide for Beginners and Intermediate Users

Onshape Textbooks
Onshape 2025: A Power Guide for Beginners and Intermediate Users

PTC Creo Parametric Textbooks
Creo Parametric 11.0: A Power Guide for Beginners and Intermediate Users
Creo Parametric 10.0: A Power Guide for Beginners and Intermediate Users
Creo Parametric 9.0: A Power Guide for Beginners and Intermediate Users
and more

SOLIDWORKS Textbooks
SOLIDWORKS 2025: A Power Guide for Beginners and Intermediate User
SOLIDWORKS 2024: A Power Guide for Beginners and Intermediate User
SOLIDWORKS 2023: A Power Guide for Beginners and Intermediate User
SOLIDWORKS 2021: A Power Guide for Beginners and Intermediate User
and more

SOLIDWORKS Sheet Metal and Surface Design Textbooks
SOLIDWORKS Sheet Metal and Surface Design 2025 for Beginners and Intermediate Users
SOLIDWORKS Sheet Metal and Surface Design 2024 for Beginners and Intermediate Users
and more

SOLIDWORKS Simulation Textbooks
SOLIDWORKS Simulation 2025: A Power Guide for Beginners and Intermediate User
SOLIDWORKS Simulation 2024: A Power Guide for Beginners and Intermediate User
SOLIDWORKS Simulation 2023: A Power Guide for Beginners and Intermediate User
SOLIDWORKS Simulation 2022: A Power Guide for Beginners and Intermediate User
and more

Exercises Books
Some of the exercises books are given below:

100 AutoCAD Exercises - Learn by Practicing (2 Edition)
Autodesk Inventor Exercises - Learn by Practicing
Autodesk Fusion 360 Exercises Learn by Practicing (2023-24)
SOLIDWORKS Exercises - Learn by Practicing (3 Edition)

Project-Based Video Courses*

- Autodesk Fusion 360 Project-Based eBook/ Video Courses Bundle
- SOLIDWORKS Project-Based eBook/Video Courses Bundle

For more information about eBook courses, visit: **cadartifex.com*